Forensic Interviews Regarding Child Sexual Abuse

William T. O'Donohue • Matthew Fanetti
Editors

Forensic Interviews Regarding Child Sexual Abuse

A Guide to Evidence-Based Practice

Springer

Editors
William T. O'Donohue
Department of Psychology
University of Nevada
Reno, NV, USA

Matthew Fanetti
Department of Psychology
Missouri State University
Springfield, MO, USA

ISBN 978-3-319-21096-4 ISBN 978-3-319-21097-1 (eBook)
DOI 10.1007/978-3-319-21097-1

Library of Congress Control Number: 2015951953

Springer Cham Heidelberg New York Dordrecht London

Printed on acid-free paper

Springer International Publishing AG Switzerland is part of Springer Science+Business Media (www.springer.com)

Preface

During the decades of the 1980s and 1990s, a significant problem arose. General concern regarding child sexual abuse dramatically increased because of aggressive media coverage of cases of alleged abuse at several child daycare centers potentially involving hundreds of children (e.g., McMartin, Fells Acres, and Kelly Michaels). Fears of the widespread abuse of children seemed to overpower the limited scope of professional's abilities to accurately understand children's ability to make accurate report about such matters. The public and many professionals become polarized. The arguments of one side took positions such as "children never lie about sexual abuse," or, on the other hand, "children are just too unreliable to serve as accurate witnesses." Of course, both of these positions are overly simplistic, but a lack of relevant research—or a lack of research integration—had failed to resolve these questions in the minds of the public or in the minds of many professionals.

But fortunately this is a problem where the need for scientific knowledge seems to have been at least partly answered. Well-known researchers such as Professors Elizabeth Loftus, Steven Ceci, Gail Goodman, Maggie Bruck, David Finkelhor, and James Wood as well as others drove a push for knowledge so strongly that the field has begun to coalesce around principles of memory, suggestibility, and sound forensic interviewing practices that answer the question, "How did these reports of abuse happen?"

If there is a set of problems that the field of psychology can be credited with improving, both dramatically and quickly, then this must be foremost among them. As the field figures out how to apply relevant scientific principles to very difficult assessment problems like child sexual abuse, specific recommendations emerge as "best-practices" or "guidelines" to reduce errors and mistakes. This does not mean that the assessment of sexual abuse will no longer improve or develop. Quite the contrary: The scientific push to understand forensic interviewing and event memory will likely encourage ever more study and refinement. But the field has come a long way from the interviewing practices used in the McMartin case, for example.

The purpose of this book is to gather some of the most notable results in the scientific pursuit of knowledge related to child sexual abuse assessment, and to allow the working professional to better understand the problems, demands, and practices that will comprise an effective method of assessing these children. We hope that this encourages the use of good practices which can only strengthen the pursuit of justice for all concerned.

Acknowledgements

We would like to thank our editor Janice Stern for all her expertise, good will, and support. I would also like to thank my family, Jane, Katie, and Anna for all the ways they make my life wonderful.

—Bill

I want to thank my children, Alex and Lauren, for making me so proud and showing me what life is supposed to be about. I enjoy watching you grow and look forward to seeing you find ever more love and happiness in your lives. I would also like to thank my wife, Svetla, for her love and devotion through the years. Without you, I am lost.

—Matthew

Contents

Contributors

Natalie Bennett, B.S. Department of Psychology, University of Nevada, Reno, Reno, NV, USA

Lorraine T. Benuto, Ph.D. Department of Psychology, University of Nevada, Reno, Reno, NV, USA

Marian E. Berryhill, Ph.D. Memory & Brain Laboratory, Program in Cognitive and Brain Sciences, Department of Psychology, University of Nevada, Reno, NV, USA

April R. Bradley, Ph.D. Psychology, University of North Dakota, Grand Forks, ND, USA

Stephen Ceci Department of Human Development, Cornell University, Ithaca, NY, USA

Olga Cirlugea, B.A. Department of Psychology, University of Nevada, Reno, Reno, NV, USA

Kresta Daly Barth Daly LLP, Sacramento, CA, USA

Misty C. Duke Intelligence and National Security Studies, National Security Studies Institute, University of Texas at El Paso, El Paso, TX, USA

Becky Earhart Department of Psychology, Wilfrid Laurier University, Waterloo, ON, Canada

Kathleen Coulborn Faller University of Michigan School of Social Work, Ann Arbor, MI, USA

Matthew Fanetti Department of Psychology, Missouri State University, Springfield, MO, USA

Jena Garrick, B.A. Department of Psychology, University of Nevada, Reno, Reno, NV, USA

Gail S. Goodman Department of Psychology, University of California, Davis, CA, USA

Filiz Gözenman, M.S. Memory & Brain Laboratory, Program in Cognitive and Brain Sciences, Department of Psychology, University of Nevada, Reno, NV, USA

Ashley K. Hall Department of Psychology, University of Southern Indiana, Evansville, IN, USA

Rachel Fondren Happel, M.S., L.P.C. Department of Psychology, Missouri State University, Springfield, MO, USA

Amelia Hritz Department of Human Development, Cornell University, Ithaca, NY, USA

Jonni L. Johnson Department of Psychology, University of California, Davis, CA, USA

Kevin T. Jones, M.A., Ph.D. Cognitive Neuropsychology Lab, Center for Aphasia Research and Rehabilitation, Georgetown University Medical Center, Washington, DC, USA

Mark Krueger Carson City District Attorney's Office and Lyon County District Attorney's Office, Carson City, NV, USA

Michael Lamb Department of Psychology, University of Cambridge, Cambridge, UK

David La Rooy University of Abertay, Dundee, UK

School of Law, Royal Holloway, University of London, Egham, UK

Cara Laney Psychology, The College of Idaho, Caldwell, ID, USA

John-Paul Legerski, Ph.D. Psychology, University of North Dakota, Grand Forks, ND, USA

Scott O. Lilienfeld, Ph.D. Department of Psychology, Emory University, Atlanta, GA, USA

Elizabeth F. Loftus Psychology & Social Behavior, Criminology, Law & Society, Cognitive Sciences, School of Law, University of California, Irvine, Irvine, CA, USA

Kamala London Department of Psychology, University of Toledo, Toledo, OH, USA

Kristen J. MacLeod, M.D. Washoe County Child Abuse Response and Evaluation Team, Reno, NV, USA

Kristin E. Matson, M.S. University of North Dakota, Portland, OR, USA

Kelly McWilliams Gould School of Law, University of Southern California, Los Angeles, CA, USA

William T. O'Donohue, Ph.D. Department of Psychology, University of Nevada, Reno, Reno, NV, USA

Dwight J. Peterson, M.A., Ph.D. Memory and Cognitive Aging Laboratory, Department of Psychological Sciences, University of Missouri, Columbia, MO, USA

Brianna Piper Department of Psychology, University of California, Davis, CA, USA

Heather Price Department of Psychology, University of Regina, Regina, SK, Canada

Monica Rohrabaugh Department of Psychology, University of Toledo, Toledo, OH, USA

Caisa Royer Department of Human Development, Cornell University, Ithaca, NY, USA

Alexandra E. Shelley Department of Psychology, University of California, Davis, CA, USA

Jaclyn A. Stephens, M.S.O.T., Ph.D. Memory & Brain Laboratory, Program in Cognitive and Brain Sciences, Department of Psychology, University of Nevada, Reno, NV, USA

Katie Thomas, M.A. University of North Dakota, Portland, OR, USA

Elizabeth R. Uhl Georgia Southwestern State University, Americus, GA, USA

James M. Wood Department of Psychology, University of Texas at El Paso, El Paso, TX, USA

Chapter 1
History of Forensic Interviewing

Cara Laney and Elizabeth F. Loftus

When a person, whether a child or an adult, makes an accusation of sexualabuse (or is suspected of being a victim in the absence of a specific accusation), forensic interviews are used to explore what really happened. The history of interviews of abuse victims (and purported victims) is complicated, and this history has led directly to many of the specific practices used in forensic interviewing today. Human memory is a central player in this complexity and its tendency to err is central to the need for precise techniques. In this chapter, we discuss some of the key events of recent decades that have helped shape the modern forensic interview. We also describe some of the research that is relevant to the practice.

Events and accusations from the decades of the 1980s and 1990s were particularly relevant to the evolution of the modern forensic interview. The early 1980s saw a raft of highly public accusations of sex abuse by preschool teachers, including accusations of satanic ritual abuse. Later in the 1980s and well into the 1990s, accusations of satanic ritual abuse spread, and others made more mundane allegations of sex abuse and other crimes on the basis of purported "repressed" and "recovered" memories (controversial constructs).

What are the possible explanations for these reports, made by children and adults? There are three basic possibilities. First, it is possible that some of these accusations are true—that these children and adults really did experience atrocities at the hands of their family members and others, and then remembered them accurately, sometimes shortly thereafter and sometimes decades later. Second, it is pos-

C. Laney (✉)
Psychology, The College of Idaho, 2112 Cleveland Blvd, Caldwell, ID 83605, USA
e-mail: claney@collegeofidaho.edu

E.F. Loftus
Psychology & Social Behavior, Criminology, Law & Society, Cognitive Sciences, School of Law, University of California, Irvine, 2393 Social Ecology II, Irvine, CA 92697, USA
e-mail: eloftus@uci.edu

W.T. O'Donohue, M. Fanetti (eds.), *Forensic Interviews Regarding Child Sexual Abuse*, DOI 10.1007/978-3-319-21097-1_1

sible that the accusers are lying, to benefit themselves or others. Finally, and perhaps most intriguingly, it is possible that these children and adults genuinely believe that they were sexually abused, but these memories are false.

For each of these possibilities, human memory is a central issue. If the events really happened, then we need to ask how accurate children's memory for events is, and whether memory repression and recovery is a reasonable explanation for the changing stories of the adults. If the purported victims are lying, we need to consider how they (especially if they are children) can maintain two inconsistent versions of events in their memory. And finally, if the memories are false, we need to consider where these false memories come from, and how they are maintained. Before we discuss each of these issues, we outline some of the accusations.

Daycare Accusations

Although accusations made by children have been taken seriously enough to cause serious repercussions for centuries—consider the Salem Witch Trials of the 1690s—the 1980s brought a new raft of accusations and a new moral panic. This time, the accusations were not of witchcraft, but of child sexual abuse. The cultural context was also different. Rather than deep and all-consuming religion, the new context involved a decade of more and more mothers going off to work, and leaving their young children with daycare providers, and also a new broad realization that child sexual abuse was a common occurrence. This realization was fuelled by research conducted in the 1960s (e.g., De Francis, 1969; Kempe, Silverman, Steele, Droegemueller, & Silver, 1962) and later work by Judith Herman (1981) and others working with adults who had long hidden their victimization. An early outcry by feminists that children were being unfairly blamed for their own victimization transitioned into arguments that we must always "believe the children," unless of course the children deny that they have been victimized (Clancy, 2009; Nathan & Snedeker, 1995; Talbot, 2001; Tavris & Aronson, 2007; Zirpolo & Nathan, 2005).

A few key cases led the way, and the memories of the children were key (for discussion, see Nathan & Snedeker, 1995). At the McMartin preschool in Southern California, a mother came forward to say that her child had been sexually assaulted (Nathan & Snedeker, 1995; Talbot, 2001). Subsequent interviews of hundreds of children who had attended the school produced a set of horrible and often bizarre allegations of ritualized sexual abuse, though no physical evidence (despite meticulous searches of dozens of buildings and vehicles). Eventually six teachers in the school were charged with 208 counts of child abuse (Timnick, 1985). The trial process went on for more than 5 years and was the most expensive criminal case in American history (Talbot, 2001). But in the end most charges led to acquittals and others were dropped.

Other cases produced convictions and long prison terms. In Kern County, California, more than 30 people were convicted of abusing their own and other children after interviews produced allegations of eight separate satanic ritual abuse sex rings, in an area with just 130,000 people (Nathan & Snedeker, 1995). The sentences ranged up to 405 years in prison per person. Kelly Michaels was convicted after children from the Wee Care preschool in New Jersey testified that she had repeatedly raped them with various objects, made them eat feces, and threatened them into silence. She was sentenced to 47 years in prison, but was released on appeal after 5 years (Faison, 1993). These vivid accusations are of course just a (biased) sample of the accusations of the time period (Schreiber et al., 2006). There were also many more accusations (and denials) of more mundane abuse made in more ordinary contexts, without media attention or high-powered legal teams. The vivid cases are useful because they clearly illustrate how forensic interviewing can contribute to false accusations, and because they led to research that has produced better forensic inteview techniques. The goal of these improved techniques is to maximize signal over noise.

Adult Accusations

Allegations of childsexualabuse are not made exclusively by children. Many people (likely a large majority of those abused as children) do not report that abuse at the time (Goodman, 2006; Hanson, Resnick, Saunders, Kilpatrick, & Best, 1999; London, Bruck, Ceci, & Shuman, 2005). Thus sometimes adults make accusations about abuse that happened years or decades before. Research suggests that these delays occur for three primary reasons. Some reports are delayed because the perpetrator is a close family member (or teacher, or babysitter, or priest) and the victim doesn't even realize at the time that abuse is occurring, often because he or she does not have sufficient understanding of sex or victimization (Clancy, 2009). Other reports are delayed because children are afraid of the consequences of reporting the abuse—that they won't be believed, or that they will be blamed, or that it is simply hard to accuse trusted and respected adults, even when their behavior is horrible (Clancy, 2009). Finally, some individuals claim that their victimization was so traumatic at the time that their memories of their own victimization were repressed and they only remembered years or decades later that they were in fact victims (e.g., Briere & Conte, 1993; Freyd, 1996; Herman & Schatzow, 1987).

As in the history of child accusations, the history of delayed reports of child abuse is at times scandalous, and often legally complicated. In one particularly well-publicized case, Eileen Franklin–Lipster reported, after a delay of 20 years, that her father had raped and murdered her childhood friend Susan Nason (Loftus, 1993; Pennebaker & Memon, 1996). Franklin–Lipster claimed that she suddenly remembered the horrible events of 1969 all at once when her own young daughter looked at her a particular way (though later evidence suggested that techniques used in her therapy sessions at the time may have been causal in producing the memories). George Franklin was prosecuted and convicted on the basis of this "recovered memory" evidence, and in the absence of any physical or other evidence. His conviction was subsequently overturned when additional facts came to light, but this was not the end of recovered memories being used as evidence in court.

Holly Ramona accused her father of repeatedly raping her when she was between the ages of five and 16, though she had no memories of these events until she was a 19-year-old college student (Johnston, 1997; Tavris & Aronson, 2007). The memories appeared in her mind in a scattershot fashion while she was being treated by a local therapist for an eating disorder. The therapist told her that 80 % of victims of bulimia, like her, were sexually abused as children (though there is no evidence for this claim; Pope & Hudson, 1992). The memories coalesced into a full, horrible picture when she was interviewed under the influence of sodium amytal. Gary Ramona lost his high-paying job, his house, his marriage, and contact with all three of his daughters (Johnston, 1997).

Additional accusations based on recovered memories followed in the 1990s and beyond. In 1991, Roseanne Barr Arnold was on the cover of *People* magazine, claiming that she had recovered memories of being sexually and emotionally abused by her parents (Arnold, 1991). Also in 1991, former Miss America Marilyn Van Derbur went public with her recovered memories of being raped by her father (Van Derbur, 2003). In 1997, Corwin and Olafson published reports of a teenager called Jane Doe. Corwin had interviewed Doe at the age of six, making accusations of abuse against her mother. When interviewed a decade later, Doe first denied abuse, then watched the tape of the interview of her younger self, and then apparently recovered her memories of that abuse. Thousands of people have been sent to prison or lost their families on the basis of recovered memories like these (False Memory Syndrome, 2009).

Sexual abuse accusations based on recovered memories have become less frequent in recent years, but they have certainly not disappeared. While most of the accusations in the ongoing Catholic Church sex abuse scandal have been cases of delayed reporting where the victims continuously remembered the abuse but were afraid or ashamed to accuse, there have also been a few cases of purported repressed and recovered memories. For example, Paul Shanley, a priest in Boston, was accused by a man in his 20s of sexual abuse years earlier (Rauch, 2005). The man claimed that he had repressed memories of the abuse for decades, and only remembered after the scandal broke in the media. Shanley was convicted in 2005 and sentenced to 12–15 years in prison, and denied a retrial in 2010 (Wolfe & Guyer, 2010).

Other recent accusations of abuse that have developed in therapeutic situations have tended to be about alien abduction and exploitation (Clancy, 2005; Clancy, McNally, Schacter, Lenzenweger, & Pitman, 2002), but these, while certainly interesting to memory experts, are less relevant to forensic interviewing practices.

Possible Explanations

As mentioned above, there are several possible explanations for the variety of child and adult (delayed) accusations described here. The first of these possibilities is that these accusations reflect the truth. Extensive evidence demonstrates that sexual exploitation and abuse of children is common (Freyd et al., 2005; Vogeltanz et al., 1999).

Perhaps the cases described so far are merely a few particularly extreme examples. To address this possibility, we need to consider the accuracy and suggestibility of children's memory as well as the plausibility of memory repression and later recovery.

Accuracy of Children's Memory

The general consensus on whether children's memories can be trusted has had its own rocky history. In some eras, people have refused to believe any information provided by children because they were seen as lesser humans. Later, children were seen as incorruptible vessels of the truth—how could they possibly lie, especially about things (like sex) that they know nothing about (Nathan & Snedeker, 1995)? In the last few years, the research community has settled on a more nuanced view: children can usually report accurately on events they have experienced, but their memories are often corruptible in some predictable situations (Ceci & Bruck, 1995; Goodman, 2006; Malloy & Quas, 2009). In general they are somewhat more susceptible to leading questions and other forms of misinformation than adults are (Ceci & Bruck, 1993), perhaps especially when they are asked closed questions (Dickinson, Poole, & Laimon, 2005) and when they are sad (Levine, Burgess, & Laney, 2008). Children's memory and likelihood of reporting victimization also vary somewhat with age and perhaps social status (London et al., 2005).

So what were the interviews like that apparently produced the bizarre allegations of satanic ritual abuse by preschoolers in the 1980s? The social workers who interviewed the McMartin children used several specific techniques to get them to make accusations: asking highly suggestive questions, claiming that others (including older kids) had already made accusations, rewarding accusations, expressing disappointment at non-accusations, repeating questions to imply that a prior answer was inadequate, and asking children to speculate on what might have happened (Garven, Wood, Malpass, & Shaw, 1998; Schreiber et al., 2006). Anatomically detailed dolls, hand puppets, and active engagement in fantasy play were also used extensively in these and other interviews with young children (Nathan & Snedeker, 1995; Zirpolo & Nathan, 2005).

Subsequent research has shown that each of these techniques can dramatically increase the likelihood of false allegations (Bruck & Ceci, 2009; Bruck, Ceci, Francouer, & Resnick, 1995; Garven et al., 1998.) Some of the accusations arising in the daycare scandals of the 1980s may be truthful allegations. But there are good, scientific reasons to believe that many of them are not. In particular, subsequent research has demonstrated that the forensic interviews used in these cases, rather than uncovering the truth, may have perpetuated and even fostered false allegations. As Nathan and Snedeker (1995) argue, "what came from the mouths of babes were juvenile renderings of grownups' anxieties," (p. 3) rather than truthful accounts of their own suffering.

Specifically, in the 1990s, researchers copied some of the techniques used in these interviews (though with much stronger ethical constraints). They found that they could easily get young children to make accusations that the researchers knew were false, or remember events that researchers were sure had not actually happened (Ceci, Huffman, Smith, & Loftus, 1994; Garven et al., 1998; Garven, Wood, & Malpass, 2000; Leichtman & Ceci, 1995; Poole & Lindsay, 1995, 2001; Schreiber & Parker, 2004; Thompson, Clarke-Stewart, & Lepore, 1997).

For example, Garven et al. (1998) interviewed 3–6-year-old children a week after a class visitor had told them a story and handed out cupcakes. They found that children who were interviewed using social influence ("Well, I already talked to the big kids and they said that Manny did some bad things. I want to see if you have a good memory like they did. Are you smart enough to remember?"; p. 351) and reinforcement (praise for assenting to inappropriate behavior on the part of the visitor) made significantly more accusations (58 %) against the innocent class visitor than did children merely asked suggestive questions (17 %).

The techniques used by Ceci et al. (1994) were milder. They interviewed 122 3–6-year-olds and gave them lists of events (that had been elicited from the children's parents). Children were told (truthfully) that some events happened to them and some did not (information not normally given to children in the daycare cases). The children were asked to think about these events between seven and ten times, over a total of 10 weeks. Overall, 34 % of the children assented to one or both of the false events.

Thompson et al. (1997) had 5- and 6-year-olds watch a "janitor" either clean toys or play with toys. Each child was then interviewed by two different interviewers in either a neutral way, or a leading way (suggesting that he had either cleaned or played). Children were then interviewed in a neutral way by their parents. The researchers found that the directions of the initial interviews predicted children's ultimate reports. If they were interviewed in a neutral way, their reports were accurate. When the interviews were leading, the reports matched the direction of the interviews, such that children remembered that the janitor had played (or cleaned) with the toys, whether they had seen him cleaning (or playing).

When real cases of abuse were analyzed, it became clear that highly suggestive techniques, like the ones used in the studies just described, had been employed. Sometimes these techniques led to reports of satanic ritual abuse and other extreme brutalization. Yet, in the end, no evidence was ever found that any satanic ritual abuse had actually happened, despite accusations in more than 100 localities in the United States and beyond (Goodman, Qin, & Bottoms, 1994; Nathan & Snedeker, 1995). Other research suggests that the interviews in these media-drenched cases were not in fact typical of the time (Goodman, 2006; Malloy & Quas, 2009; Schreiber et al., 2006; but see Nathan & Snedeker, 1995). Nonetheless, we can learn (and have learned) from what went wrong in these interviews to improve interviewing practices (e.g., Lamb, Hershkowitz, Orbach, & Esplin, 2008). It is also worth noting that the forensic interviewers are not the only people with access to children between the suspected abuse and trial. Nathan and Snedeker (1995) highlight several cases of parents and other relatives beating children who failed to accuse, and denying them food and sleep until they accused. Some accusations are also apparently the product of custody battles. Forensic interviewers need to be aware that although their actions can certainly have a negative effect on the accuracy of children's memory, they are not the only source of false accusations, and indeed children's memories may have been corrupted even before they arrive for an interview.

Repression and Memory Recovery

Sigmund Freud is still a hugely powerful figure in Psychology. The modern idea of memoryrepression is largely derived from his theories of development and defense mechanisms. And yet, Freud himself rejected important aspects of his own theory. In 1933, he wrote "I was driven to recognize in the end that these reports were untrue and so came to understand that the hysterical symptoms are derived from phantasies and not from real occurrences," (Freud, 1933/1999, p. 120). Many modern clinicians and some memory researchers prefer to take Freud at his original word, and argue that research has validated Freud's early claims. (For more thorough analyses of this research, see Davis & Loftus, 2009; Goodman et al., 2003; Laney & Loftus, 2005; Laney & Loftus, 2013; Porter & Peace, 2006.)

The modern explanation of memoryrepression and recovery, revived in the 1970s by feminists and others (Nathan & Snedeker, 1995) suggests that the common response to a traumatic event like childsexualabuse (though see Clancy, 2009) is to bury all awareness and thus memory of that event deep in the subconscious, or perhaps in a separate or dissociated personality. The victim thus becomes entirely oblivious to her (or perhaps his, but not usually) own experience and suffering. This repressed memory does present problems for the victim's future mental health, however, leading eventually to depression or eating disorders or sexual dysfunction. When the victim seeks help for these surface problems, the therapist helps her to recover her memories for the original trauma. Now that she is a capable adult with support from the therapist, she is able to deal with the original trauma in a more useful way, and thus eliminate the resulting problems.

On the surface, this theory provides a nice explanation for what happens when a person must cope with a traumatic situation. The problem is that the theory does not tally with a long history of scientific evidence regarding how human memory works. First, there is copious evidence that the normal response to trauma is a more vivid memory, or even too much memory, not a lack of memory (McNally, 2003; Peace, Porter, & ten Brinke, 2008; Porter & Peace, 2006). Second, there is evidence that no one—not even highly trained therapists—can really tell whether specific memories are true, without some sort of independent corroboration (Campbell & Porter, 2002; Leichtman & Ceci, 1995). And some therapists even argue against seeking any sort of independent corroboration. They argue that to do so is to mistrust the victim of abuse, which is damaging.

In fact it is now clear that certain therapeutic practices are actually causal in producing false memories of victimization, rather than uncovering true memories.

Techniques like guided imagination, dream interpretation, group therapy, hypnosis (and even drugs like sodium amytal) have been modeled in the laboratory to produce false memories (see the section on false memories below). These techniques were widely used in the 1990s (Poole et al., 1995) and the beliefs that underlie their use are still widespread in some circles today (Patihis, Ho, Tingen, Lilienfeld, & Loftus, 2014). These research data provide a better explanation of the existence of non-continuous memories (including memories of victimization) than does the theory of repression and recovery (though the theory is sufficiently unscientific that it cannot actually be disproved; Clifasefi, Garry, & Loftus, 2007).

Before delving into the false memory literature, though, we will reassess a few of the delayed accusations described above. First, the case of Holly Ramona. Some 4 years after her initial accusations, Gary Ramona sued Holly's therapist for malpractice, on the grounds that they had implanted false memories in his daughter. The jury agreed with him that the therapists' actions had led to the collapse of his family and awarded a $500,000 settlement (Johnston, 1997; Tavris & Aronson, 2007). Holly Ramona (as well as her mother, grandmother, and sisters) did not accept the verdict and repudiate her memories. Instead, she went to graduate school to become a therapist herself, helping her own clients to recover their buried memories of abuse (Tavris & Aronson, 2007).

The case of Jane Doe has received extensive attention from the research community. Skeptical of the evidence provided by Corwin and Olafson (1997), one of us (Loftus) and fellow psychologist/lawyer, Mel Guyer, dug into the case to discover more (Loftus & Guyer, 2002). We searched public records to find the identities of those involved and then interviewed several of them. We found that Corwin and Olafson had been biased in their reporting of events, and that there were good reasons to consider the possibility that Jane's initial allegations of abuse had been false, produced in aide of a bitter custody dispute. Thus, rather than triggering a recovery of true abuse memories, the emotionality of her younger self in the videotape had merely persuaded the older Jane (falsely) that she had been abused. (See also Geis, Loftus, & Taus, 2009, for details of the aftermath of this publication.)

Although Holly Ramona and Jane Doe held fast to their recovered memories in the face of substantial contradictory information, others have retracted their recovered memories (Maran, 2010; Ost, Costall, & Bull, 2002). This (small) literature suggests that retracting recovered memories is a long and difficult process of detecting and working through logical inconsistencies in memories that is very different from the process of recovering memories.

What does this discussion of supposedly repressed and recovered (and perhaps even retracted) memory have to do with the practice of forensic interviews? The point of a forensic interview is to uncover the truth of what really happened, not merely what the interviewee remembers happening. As such, the source of the memories matters. This issue will be addressed further in the section on false memories below. For the cases where the truth doesn't seem to be a good explanation of the accusations of sexualabuse made by children or adults, there remain two additional possibilities: intentional lying and false memory.

Intentional Lies

There is evidence that some children and adults knowingly make false accusations of sexualabuse. For example, at least one of the McMartin accusers has since come forward to say that he was never abused, and intentionally lied to investigators in order to be helpful (Zirpolo & Nathan, 2005). Several of the accusers in the Kern County cases also retracted their allegations in their 20s, saying that they had never been abused (Jones, 2004).

Apart from isolated examples, there is an extensive psychological literature on deception and its detection (e.g., C.F. Bond & DePaulo, 2006; Ekman, 2001; Granhag & Vrij, 2005; Vrij, 2008; Wolpe, Foster, & Langleben, 2005). Lying is an intensely human activity that we all engage in—deeply intertwined with emotion and social relationships. Complicated lies can be hard to maintain, and professional lie detectors (police officers and other investigators) attempt to use this against liars, seeking out inconsistencies and using their experience and beliefs about lying to call out liars. Despite this, the evidence suggests that even young children can and do lie, and even highly trained adults are generally poor at detecting lies. Tools for lie detection, including the polygraph, also have a poor track record in scientific analysis (National Research Council, 2003).

Forensic interviewers need to know that lies are possible, even from children making accusations of sexualabuse, and that they are probably not as good as they think they are at detecting lies. The research indicates that most people perform no better than chance at detecting the lies of others (C.F. Bond & DePaulo, 2006; G.D. Bond, Thompson, & Malloy, 2005; Vrij, 2008), with most people demonstrating a tendency to label statements as truthful unless they have a good reason to suspect otherwise. Of particular relevance to forensic interviewing, this "truth bias" has been shown to be particularly strong when statements are presented in audio-visual format rather than in transcript form (Bond & DePaulo, 2006; Burgoon, Blair, & Strom, 2008). Additional research suggests that people tend to use the wrong cues, especially visual cues, to detect lying (Akehurst, Köhnken, Vrij, & Bull, 1996), though they are more likely to use content information when they have more content-relevant knowledge (Reinhard, Sporer, Scharmach, & Marksteiner, 2011).

One potential solution to the problem of detecting deception is specific training on this skillset—what are the most indicative cues to lying, and how are these best detected? Unfortunately, research demonstrates that even good quality (scientifically based) training can fail to improve detection deception skill (Akehurst, Bull, & Vrij, 2006), and training based on common (but inaccurate) interrogation manuals (especially that of Inbau, Reid, Buckley, & Jayne, 2001) is likely to make trainees' skills even worse (Kassin & Fong, 1999; Mann, Vrij, & Bull, 2004).

False Memory

We have already alluded above to the possibility that many of the more outlandish accusations made by children and adults claiming recovered memories of abuse may in fact be false memories. That is, these individuals genuinely believe that they have experienced satanic ritual abuse or other horrors that they have not actually experienced. Human memory does not work like a video recorder (see Clifasefi et al., 2007). Instead memory is reconstructive and malleable. New information, new assumptions, existing knowledge, stereotypes, and other experiences are blended together with accurate memory information, so that memory changes over time. Leading questions and other forms of misinformation have been shown to alter the memories of adults (Davis & Loftus, 2007; Loftus, 2005) and children (as discussed above).

Researchers have also been able to create false memories out of whole cloth in the minds of their subjects (Hyman, Husband, & Billings, 1995; Loftus & Pickrell, 1995; Porter, Yuille, & Lehman, 1999). Early false memory research specifically modeled traumatic childhood events (but in an ethically acceptable way), and used procedures that mimicked the therapist techniques that researchers feared were causing false memories in the real world. Loftus and Pickrell (1995) gave college students false memories for being lost in a shopping mall for an extended period of time and then rescued by an older adult, using a diary and brief repeated interview procedure. Hyman et al. (1995) used a similar procedure to get college student subjects to believe that they had been hospitalized overnight as children. Porter et al. (1999) got subjects to believe that they had been attacked by a small animal or suffered a serious indoor or outdoor accident.

Researchers also modeled other therapeutic techniques, including dream interpretation (Mazzoni, Loftus, Seitz, & Lynn, 1999), guided imagination (Garry, Manning, Loftus, & Sherman, 1996; Heaps & Nash, 1999), hypnosis (Scoboria, Mazzoni, Kirsch, & Milling, 2002), using (genuine) childhood pictures to cue memories (Lindsay, Hagen, Read, Wade, & Garry, 2004), and social modeling (Peterson, Kaasa, & Loftus, 2009). Mazzoni et al. (1999), for example, had undergraduate subjects participate in what they believed were two different studies. In the first study, they were asked how confident they were that they had experienced certain events in childhood, including having been harassed by a bully, twice, about four weeks apart. In the second study, which took place between the two parts of the first study, subjects met a clinical psychologist (actually one of the study's authors) who interpreted a recent dream. No matter the content of the dream, the psychologist always interpreted it as being "the overt manifestation of repressed memories of events that happened before the age of 3," (Mazzoni et al., 1999, p. 129), specifically the event of having been bullied. After this strong and personalized suggestion, fully half of the experimental subjects (those whose dreams had been interpreted) became more confident that they had been bullied, compared to just 11 % of the control subjects.

A frequent retort to these studies from the recovered memory community was that researchers were merely recovering genuine memories rather than implanting false ones (e.g., Freyd, 1998). In response to this critique, false memory researchers began implanting impossible false memories, including meeting Bugs Bunny at Disneyland (impossible because Bugs is a Warner Brothers character; Braun, Ellis, & Loftus, 2002) and leading subjects to misremember events as having happened in the laboratory when they had not (Goff & Roediger, 1998; Thomas & Loftus, 2002).

Other false memory implantation techniques are simpler, designed to give large numbers of subjects false memories quickly (Berkowitz, Laney, Morris, Garry, & Loftus, 2008; Bernstein, Laney, Morris, & Loftus, 2005; Laney & Loftus, 2008; Laney, Morris, Bernstein, Wakefield, & Loftus, 2008). An important goal of this research is to root out differences between true and false memories that could be useful to forensic interviewers and other actors in the legal system. In the false feedback technique, subjects (normally undergraduates) attend the lab on two occasions, about a week apart. On the first occasion they are given sets of questionnaires on a particular theme (childhood experiences with food, childhood experiences at Disneyland, etc.) and are told that their data will be entered into a special computer system for analysis. When they return to the lab, they are given a short set of supposedly computer generated feedback that is actually the manipulation of the study. Subjects are told that they had a certain experience as child. The extent to which the subject accepts the feedback, as well as several other characteristics of their memories, are then assessed.

In these false feedback studies the typical sample size is over 200, and approximately a third of experimental subjects form false beliefs or memories (with this proportion exceeding half for some items; Laney & Takarangi, 2013). These numbers allow researchers to compare the false memories of some subjects to the true (that is, consistently held from before any manipulation) memories of other subjects. If consistent differences could be found between true and false memories, this would be a boon to forensic interviewing and the legal system generally. So far, researchers have looked for differences in confidence, detail, brain activity, consequentiality, longevity, language use, and emotional content (Bernstein, Laney, Morris, & Loftus, 2005; Lampinen, Meier, Arnal, & Leding, 2005; Laney, Bowman Fowler, Nelson, Bernstein, & Loftus, 2008; Laney & Loftus, 2008; Laney & Takarangi, 2013; Sederberg et al., 2007; Vrij, 2005). So far, none of these analyses have produced useful (consistent, substantial) differences between true and false memories. That is, although some studies produce significant differences between mean levels of confidence or detail between true and false memories, these differences are never sufficient to categorically distinguish whether a particular memory is true or false (Bernstein & Loftus, 2009; Laney & Loftus, 2008; Vrij, 2005). For example, Laney and Loftus (2008) found that false memories of emotional childhood events (being hospitalized overnight, catching one's parents having sex, or witnessing a physically violent fight between one's parents) could be just as emotional and just as confidently held as true memories for the same events, such that neither confidence nor emotionality was sufficient to identify a particular memory as true. Further research is needed to identify other potential differences between true and false memories that could be used to determine whether a particular memory arising in a legal context is true or false.

To address this problem from a different angle, a small number of studies have asked whether individuals can differentiate between true and false memories when given transcripts or videos of people telling the truth or describing false memories (Campbell & Porter, 2002; Heiss, Laney, Kaasa, & Loftus, 2013; Leichtman & Ceci, 1995). Although this literature is much smaller than that comparing true statements to lies (as discussed above), the broad conclusions are the same: third parties are not very good at differentiating between true and false memories once they have been established. The implications of this for the practice of forensic interviewing are clear, if not optimistic. Interviewers need to be aware the false memory is a realistic explanation of a particular report, and that there is no magic bullet (besides corroborating evidence) to determine whether a particular memory is true or false.

Conclusions and Implications for Forensic Interviewing Practices

Forensic interviews with suspected abuse victims are walks through well-charted but still dangerous territory. These interviews delve into human memory, a deep and rich source of information, but also a home for misinformation. Interviews can produce true and accurate reports of events—even traumatic and uncomfortable to discuss events. But they can also fail to detect—or even produce—highly corrupted false reports. Children's memories can be tainted by leading questions and biased interviews. Adults are also susceptible, and interviewers should be especially suspicious of reports of non-continuous memories. Children and adults do lie, and these lies can be difficult to detect. Children and adults can produce memories that are entirely false, and these memories can be emotional, detailed, confidently held, and consequential in their lives.

The solution to this difficult situation is to arm oneself with the latest research and best practices for conducting scientifically sound forensic interviews. This book is designed to help in that goal.

References

Akehurst, L., Bull, R., & Vrij, A. (2006). The effects of training professional groups and lay persons to use criteria-based content analysis to detect deception. *Applied Cognitive Psychology, 18*, 877–891.

Akehurst, L., Köhnken, G., Vrij, A., & Bull, R. (1996). Lay persons' and police officers' beliefs regarding deceptive behaviour. *Applied Cognitive Psychology, 10*, 461–471.

Arnold, R. (1991, October 7). A star cries incest. *People Magazine*. Retrieved from http://www.people.com.

Berkowitz, S. R., Laney, C., Morris, E. K., Garry, M., & Loftus, E. F. (2008). Pluto behaving badly: False beliefs and their consequences. *American Journal of Psychology, 121*, 643–660.

Bernstein, D. M., Laney, C., Morris, E. K., & Loftus, E. F. (2005). False beliefs about fattening foods can have healthy consequences. *Proceedings of the National Academy of Sciences, 102*, 13724–13731.

Bernstein, D. M., & Loftus, E. F. (2009). How to tell if a particular memory is true or false. *Perspectives on Psychological Science, 4*, 370–374.

Bond, C. F., & DePaulo, B. M. (2006). Accuracy of deception judgments. *Personality and Social Psychology Review, 10*, 214–234.

Bond, G. D., Thompson, L. A., & Malloy, D. M. (2005). Vulnerability of older adults to deception in prison and nonprison contexts. *Psychology and Aging, 20*, 60–70.

Braun, K. A., Ellis, R., & Loftus, E. F. (2002). Make my memory: How advertising can change our memories of the past. *Psychology & Marketing, 19*, 1–23.

Bricrc, J., & Conte, J. (1993). Self-reported amnesia for abuse in adults molested as children. *Journal of Traumatic Stress, 6*, 21–31.

Bruck, M., & Ceci, S. J. (2009). Reliability of child witnesses' reports. In J. L. Skeem, K. S. Douglas, & S. O. Lilienfeld (Eds.), *Psychological science in the courtroom: Consensus and controversy* (pp. 149–171). New York, NY: Guilford.

Bruck, M., Ceci, S. J., Francouer, E., & Resnick, A. (1995). Anatomically detailed dolls do not facilitate preschoolers' reports of a pediatric examination involving genital touching. *Journal of Experimental Psychology. Applied, 1*, 95–109.

Burgoon, J. K., Blair, J., & Strom, R. E. (2008). Cognitive biases and nonverbal cue availability in detecting deception. *Human Communication Research, 34*, 572–599.

Campbell, M. A., & Porter, S. (2002). Pinpointing reality: How well can people judge true and mistaken emotional childhood memories? *Canadian Journal of Behavioural Sciences, 34*, 217–229.

Ceci, S. J., & Bruck, M. (1993). The suggestibility of the child witness: A historical review and synthesis. *Psychological Bulletin, 113*, 403–439.

Ceci, S. J., & Bruck, M. (1995). *Jeopardy in the courtroom: A scientific analysis of children's testimony*. Washington, DC: American Psychological Association.

Ceci, S. J., Huffman, M. L. C., Smith, E., & Loftus, E. F. (1994). Repeatedly thinking about a non-event: Source misattributions among preschoolers. *Consciousness and Cognition, 3*, 388–407.

Clancy, S. A. (2005). *Abducted: How people come to believe they were kidnapped by aliens*. Cambridge, MA: Harvard University Press.

Clancy, S. A. (2009). *The trauma myth: The truth about the sexual abuse of children—and its aftermath*. New York, NY: Basic Books.

Clancy, S. A., McNally, R. J., Schacter, D. L., Lenzenweger, M. F., & Pitman, R. K. (2002). Memory distortion in people reporting abduction by aliens. *Journal of Abnormal Psychology, 111*, 455–461.

Clifasefi, S. L., Garry, M., & Loftus, E. F. (2007). Setting the record (or video camera) straight on memory: The video camera model and other memory myths. In S. Della Sala (Ed.), *Tall tales about the mind and brain: Separating fact from fiction* (pp. 60–75). Oxford, England: Oxford University Press.

Corwin, D. L., & Olafson, E. (1997). Videotaped discovery of a reportedly unrecallable memory of child sexual abuse: Comparison with a childhood interview videotaped 11 years before. *Child Maltreatment, 2*, 91–112.

Council, N. R. (2003). *The polygraph and lie detection*. Washington, DC: National Academy Press.

Davis, D., & Loftus, E. F. (2007). Internal and external sources of misinformation in adult witness memory. In M. P. Toglia, J. D. Read, D. F. Ross, & R. C. L. Lindsay (Eds.), *The handbook of eyewitness psychology* (Memory for events, Vol. 1, pp. 195–237). Mahwah, NJ: Lawrence Erlbaum.

Davis, D., & Loftus, E. F. (2009). The scientific status of "repressed" and "recovered" memories of sexual abuse. In J. L. Skeem, K. S. Douglas, & S. O. Lilienfeld (Eds.), *Psychological science in the courtroom: Consensus and controversy* (pp. 55–79). New York, NY: Guilford.

De Francis, V. (1969). *Protecting the child victim of sex crimes committed by adults*. Denver: American Humane Association.

Dickinson, J. D., Poole, D. A., & Laimon, R. L. (2005). Children's recall and testimony. In N. Brewer & K. D. Williams (Eds.), *Psychology and law: An empirical perspective* (pp. 151–176). New York, NY: Guilford.

Ekman, P. (2001). *Telling lies: Clues to deceit in the marketplace, politics, and marriage*. New York, NY: Norton.

Faison, S. (1993, March 27). Child-abuse conviction of woman is overturned. *The New York Times*. Retrieved from http://www.nytimes.com.

False Memory Syndrome Foundation (2009, Summer). *Newsletter*. Retrieved from http://www.fmsfonline.org.

Freud, S. (1999). *The standard edition of the complete psychological works of Sigmund Freud*. New York, NY: Vintage. Original work published 1933.

Freyd, J. J. (1996). *Betrayal trauma: The logic of forgetting childhood abuse*. Cambridge, MA: Harvard University Press.

Freyd, J. J. (1998). Science in the memory debate. *Ethics & Behavior, 8*, 101–113.

Freyd, J. J., Putnam, F. W., Lyon, T. D., Becker-Blease, K. A., Cheit, R. E., Siegel, N. B., & Pezdek, K. (2005). The science of child sexual abuse. *Science, 308*, 501.

Garry, M., Manning, C. G., Loftus, E. F., & Sherman, S. J. (1996). Imagination inflation: Imagining a childhood event inflates confidence that it occurred. *Psychonomic Bulletin and Review, 3*, 208–214.

Garven, S., Wood, J. M., Malpass, R. S., & Shaw, J. S., III. (1998). More than suggestion: The effect of interviewing techniques from the McMartin Preschool case. *Journal of Applied Psychology, 83*, 347–359.

Garven, S., Wood, J. M., & Malpass, R. S. (2000). Allegations of wrongdoing: The effects of reinforcement on children's mundane and fantastic claims. *Journal of Applied Psychology, 85*, 38–49.

Geis, G., Loftus, E. F., & Taus, V. (2009). Loftus: Determining the legal ground rules for scholarly inquiry. *Journal of Forensic Psychology Practice, 9*, 147–162.

Goff, L. M., & Roediger, H. L., III. (1998). Imagination inflation for action events: Repeated imaginings lead to illusory recollections. *Memory & Cognition, 26*, 20–33.

Goodman, G. S. (2006). Children's eyewitness memory: A modern history and contemporary commentary. *Journal of Social Issues, 62*, 811–832.

Goodman, G. S., Ghetti, S., Quas, J. A., Edelstein, R. S. Alexander, K. W., Redlich, A. D., & Cordon, I. M. (2003). A prospective study of memory for child sexual abuse: New findings relevant to the repressed-memory controversy. *Psychological Science, 14*, 113–118.

Goodman, G. S., Qin, J., & Bottoms, B. L. (1994). *Characteristics and sources of allegations of ritualistic child abuse*. Washington, DC: National Center on Child Abuse and Neglect.

Granhag, P. A., & Vrij, A. (2005). Deception detection. In N. Brewer & K. D. Williams (Eds.), *Psychology and law: An empirical perspective* (pp. 43–92). New York, NY: Guilford.

Hanson, R. F., Resnick, H. S., Saunders, B. E., Kilpatrick, D. G., & Best, C. (1999). Factors related to the reporting of childhood rape. *Child Abuse and Neglect, 23*, 559–569.

Heaps, C., & Nash, M. (1999). Individual differences in imagination inflation. *Psychonomic Bulletin and Review, 6*, 313–338.

Heiss, M.S., Laney, C., Kaasa, S.O., & Loftus, E.F. (2013). *Judging Memory: How people differentiate between true witness statements, false witness statements, and outright lies*. Manuscript in preparation.

Herman, J. (1981). *Father-daughter incest*. Cambridge, MA: Harvard University Press.

Herman, J. L., & Schatzow, E. (1987). Recovery and verification of memories of childhood sexual trauma. *Psychoanalytic Psychology, 4*, 1–14.

Hyman, I. E., Jr., Husband, T. H., & Billings, F. J. (1995). False memories of childhood experiences. *Applied Cognitive Psychology, 9*, 181–197.

Inbau, F. E., Reid, J. E., Buckley, J. P., & Jayne, B. C. (2001). *Criminal interrogation and confessions* (4th ed.). Gaithersburg, MD: Aspen.

Johnston, M. (1997). *Spectral evidence: The Ramona case—Incest, memory, and the truth on trial in Napa Valley*. Boulder, CO: Westview Press.

Jones, M. (2004, September 19). Who was abused? *The New York Times*. Retrieved from http://www.nytimes.com.

Kassin, S. M., & Fong, C. T. (1999). "I'm innocent!": Effects of training on judgments of truth and deception in the interrogation room. *Law and Human Behavior, 23*, 499–516.

Kempe, C. H., Silverman, F. N., Steele, B. F., Droegemueller, W., & Silver, H. K. (1962). The battered-child syndrome. *The Journal of the American Medical Association, 181*, 17–24.

Lamb, M., Hershkowitz, I., Orbach, Y., & Esplin, P. W. (2008). *Tell me what happened: Structured investigative interviewing of child victims and witnesses*. Chichester, UK: Wiley.
Lampinen, J. M., Meier, C. R., Arnal, J. D., & Leding, J. K. (2005). Compelling untruths: Content borrowing and vivid false memories. *Journal of Experimental Psychology. Learning, Memory, and Cognition, 31*, 954–963.
Laney, C., Bowman Fowler, N., Nelson, K. J., Bernstein, D. B., & Loftus, E. F. (2008). The persistence of false beliefs. *Acta Psychologica, 129*, 190–197.
Laney, C., & Loftus, E. F. (2005). Traumatic memories are not necessarily accurate memories. *Canadian Journal of Psychiatry, 50*, 823–828.
Laney, C., & Loftus, E. F. (2008). Emotional content of true and false memories. *Memory, 16*, 500–516.
Laney, C., & Loftus, E. F. (2013). Recent advances in false memory research. *South African Journal of Psychology, 43*, 137–146.
Laney, C., Morris, E. K., Bernstein, D. M., Wakefield, B. M., & Loftus, E. F. (2008). Asparagus, a love story: Healthier eating could be just a false memory away. *Experimental Psychology, 55*, 291–300.
Laney, C., & Takarangi, M. K. T. (2013). False memories for aggressive acts. *Acta Psychologica, 143*, 227–234.
Leichtman, M. D., & Ceci, S. J. (1995). The effects of stereotypes and suggestions on preschoolers' reports. *Developmental Psychology, 31*, 568–578.
Levine, L. J., Burgess, S. L., & Laney, C. (2008). Effects of discrete emotions on young children's suggestibility. *Developmental Psychology, 44*, 681–694.
Lindsay, D. S., Hagen, L., Read, J. D., Wade, K. A., & Garry, M. (2004). True photographs and false memories. *Psychological Science, 15*, 149–154.
Loftus, E. F. (1993). The reality of repressed memories. *American Psychologist, 48*, 518–537.
Loftus, E. F. (2005). Planting misinformation in the human mind: A 30-year investigation of the malleability of memory. *Learning and Memory, 12*, 361–366.
Loftus, E. F., & Guyer, M. J. (2002). Who abused Jane Doe? The hazards of the single case study. *Skeptical Inquirer 26* (May–June), 24–32; (July–August), 37–40, 44.
Loftus, E. F., & Pickrell, J. E. (1995). The formation of false memories. *Psychiatric Annals, 25*, 720–725.
London, K., Bruck, M., Ceci, S. J., & Shuman, D. W. (2005). Disclosure of child sexual abuse: What does the research tell us about the ways that children tell? *Psychology, Public Policy, and Law, 11*, 194–226.
Malloy, L. C., & Quas, J. A. (2009). Children's suggestibility: Areas of consensus and controversy. In K. Kuehnle & M. Connell (Eds.), *The evaluation of child sexual abuse allegations: A comprehensive guide to assessment and testimony* (pp. 267–297). Hoboken, NJ: Wiley.
Mann, S., Vrij, A., & Bull, R. (2004). Detecting true lies: Police officers ability to detect suspects' lies. *Journal of Applied Psychology, 89*, 137–149.
Maran, M. (2010). *My lie: A true story of false memory*. San Francisco, CA: Jossey-Bass.
Mazzoni, G. A. L., Loftus, E. F., Seitz, A., & Lynn, S. J. (1999). Changing beliefs and memories through dream interpretation. *Applied Cognitive Psychology, 13*, 125–144.
McNally, R. J. (2003). *Remembering trauma*. Cambridge, MA: Harvard University Press.
Nathan, D., & Snedeker, M. (1995). *Satan's silence: Ritual abuse and the making of a modern American witch hunt*. New York, NY: Basic Books.
Ost, J., Costall, A., & Bull, R. (2002). A perfect symmetry? A study of retractors' experiences of making and then repudiating claims of early sexual abuse. *Psychology, Crime & Law, 8*, 155–181.
Patihis, L., Ho, L. Y., Tingen, I. W., Lilienfeld, S. O., & Loftus, E. F. (2014). Are the "memory wars" over? A scientist-practitioner gap in beliefs about repressed memory. *Psychological Science, 25*, 519–530.
Peace, K., Porter, S., & ten Brinke, L. (2008). Are memories for sexually traumatic events "special"? A within-subjects investigation of trauma and memory in a clinical sample. *Memory, 16*, 10–21.

Pennebaker, J. W., & Memon, A. (1996). Recovered memories in context: Thoughts and elaborations on Bowers and Farvolden (1996). *Psychological Bulletin, 119*, 381–385.

Peterson, T., Kaasa, S. O., & Loftus, E. F. (2009). Me too!: Social modeling influences on early autobiographical memories. *Applied Cognitive Psychology, 23*, 267–277.

Poole, D. A., & Lindsay, D. S. (1995). Interviewing preschoolers: Effects of nonsuggestive techniques, parental coaching and leading questions on reports of nonexperienced events. *Journal of Experimental Child Psychology, 60*, 129–154.

Poole, D. A., & Lindsay, D. S. (2001). Children's eyewitness reports after exposure to misinformation from parents. *Journal of Experimental Psychology. Applied, 7*, 27–50.

Poole, D. A., Lindsay, D. S., Memon, A., & Bull, R. (1995). Psychotherapy and the recovery of memories of childhood sexual abuse: U.S. and British practitioners' beliefs, practices, and experiences. *Journal of Consulting and Clinical Psychology, 6*, 426–437.

Pope, H. G., & Hudson, J. I. (1992). Is childhood sexual abuse a risk factor for bulimia nervosa? *American Journal of Psychiatry, 149*, 455–463.

Porter, S., & Peace, K. (2006). The scars of memory: A prospective, longitudinal investigation of the consistency of traumatic and positive emotional memories in adulthood. *Psychological Science, 18*, 435–441.

Porter, S., Yuille, J. C., & Lehman, D. R. (1999). The nature of real, implanted, and fabricated memories for emotional childhood events: Implications for the recovered memory debate. *Law and Human Behavior, 23*, 517–537.

Rauch, J. (2005, March 14). Is Paul Shanley guilty? If Paul Shanley is a monster, the state didn't prove it. *Reason Magazine*. Retrieved from reason.com/archives.

Reinhard, M.-A., Sporer, S. L., Scharmach, M., & Marksteiner, T. (2011). Listening not watching: Situational familiarity and the ability to detect deception. *Journal of Personality and Social Psychology, 101*, 467–484.

Schreiber, N., Bellah, L. D., Martinez, Y., McLaurin, K. A., Strok, R., Garven, S., & Wood, J. M. (2006). Suggestive interviewing in the McMartin Preschool and Kelly Michaels daycare abuses cases: A case study. *Social Influence 1*, 16–47.

Schreiber, N., & Parker, J. F. (2004). Inviting witnesses to speculate: Effects of age and interaction on children's recall. *Journal of Experimental Child Psychology, 89*, 31–52.

Scoboria, A., Mazzoni, G. A. L., Kirsch, I., & Milling, L. S. (2002). Immediate and persisting effects of misleading questions and hypnosis on memory reports. *Journal of Experimental Psychology. Applied, 8*, 26–32.

Sederberg, P. B., Schulze-Bonhage, A., Madsen, J. R., Bromfield, E. B., Litt, B., Brandt, A., et al. (2007). Gamma oscillations distinguish true from false memories. *Psychological Science, 18*, 927–932.

Talbot, M. (2001, January 7). The lives they lived: 01-07-01: Peggy McMartin Buckey, b. 1926: The devil in the nursery. *New York Times*. Retrieved from http://www.nytimes.com.

Tavris, C., & Aronson, E. (2007). *Mistakes were made (but not by me): Why we justify foolish beliefs, bad decisions, and hurtful acts*. Orlando, FL: Harcourt.

Thomas, A. K., & Loftus, E. F. (2002). Creating bizarre false memories through imagination. *Memory & Cognition, 30*, 423–431.

Thompson, W. C., Clarke-Stewart, K. A., & Lepore, S. J. (1997). What did the janitor do? Suggestive interviewing and the accuracy of children's accounts. *Law and Human Behavior, 21*, 405–426.

Timnick, L. (1985, January 25). McMartin student appears to recant earlier testimony. *Los Angeles Times*. Retrieved from http://articles.latimes.com.

Van Derbur, M. (2003). *Miss America by day: Lessons learned from ultimate betrayals and unconditional love*. Denver, CO: Oak Hill Ridge Press.

Vogeltanz, N. D., Wilsnack, S. C., Harris, T. R., Wilsnack, R. W., Wonderlich, S. A., & Kristjanson, A. F. (1999). Prevalence and risk factors for childhood sexual abuse in women: National survey findings. *Child Abuse and Neglect, 23*, 579–592.

Vrij, A. (2005). Criteria-based content analysis: A qualitative review of the first 37 studies. *Psychology, Public Policy, and Law, 11*, 3–41.

Vrij, A. (2008). *Detecting lies and deceit: Pitfalls and opportunities* (2nd ed.). Chichester, England: Wiley.
Wolfe, A. J., & Guyer, M. J. (2010). Repressed memories in a controversial conviction. *Journal of the American Academy of Psychiatry and the Law, 38*, 607–609.
Wolpe, P. R., Foster, K. R., & Langleben, D. D. (2005). Emerging nanotechnologies for lie-detection: Promises and perils. *The American Journal of Bioethics, 5*, 39–49.
Zirpolo, K., & Nathan, D. (2005, October 30). McMartin pre-schooler: 'I lied': A long-delayed apology from one of the accusers in the notorious McMartin Pre-School molestation case. *The Los Angeles Times*. Retrieved from http://web.archive.org/.

Chapter 2
The Purpose of the Forensic Interview: A Lawyer's Perspective

Kresta Daly

From the legal perspective the forensic interview of a child who may be the victim of a sexual assault serves numerous important purposes. In order for a prosecutor to file charges the prosecutor has to know where to file the charges, who to file the charges against, how many charges to file, and many other things.

Jurisdiction

The first issue in a legal matter is whether or not the court has jurisdiction to hear the case. The modern concept of jurisdiction has its roots in the American Revolution. Prior to the American Revolution and the subsequent adoption of the constitution there were few limits on the power of the court in this country. Historically a court was nothing more than an extension of the crown and the court was expected to do the crown's bidding. The American revolutionaries and in particular the Federalists sought to impose limitations on the government's power over people and their lives. It was from this desire that modern jurisdiction evolved.

There are many kinds of jurisdiction. The two most fundamental and which you are most likely to hear about are jurisdiction over the person and jurisdiction over the subject matter. Lawyers and judges more often refer to these two kinds of jurisdiction as *in personam* [jurisdiction over the person] and *in rem* jurisdiction [jurisdiction over the subject matter].

In a case where a person is suspected of molesting a child, personal jurisdiction asks whether or not the court has jurisdiction over the suspect. If the suspect lives in the state in which the case arose or traveled to that state the court has personal jurisdiction. If a person is accused of committing a crime within the boundaries of

K. Daly (✉)
Barth Daly LLP, 431 I Street, Suite 201, Sacramento, CA 95814, USA
e-mail: kdaly@barth-daly.com

W.T. O'Donohue, M. Fanetti (eds.), *Forensic Interviews Regarding Child Sexual Abuse*, DOI 10.1007/978-3-319-21097-1_2

a state or federal district the court will have personal jurisdiction over the suspect. It doesn't matter whether or not the suspect is legally in the state. In other words if someone is an undocumented immigrant and their right to be present in any given state is unclear, a court still has personal jurisdiction over them so long as they are or were physically present in the state. Issues involving personal jurisdiction are rare in criminal cases but they can arise when a suspect has diplomatic immunity and is beyond the reach of the court.

Subject matter jurisdiction addresses whether or not the court has the authority to decide the issue. In all legal cases the case begins when the plaintiff, or in a criminal case, the prosecutor, files a legal document alleging some legal wrong. In a civil case it could be that a person's civil rights were violated or a contract was breached. In a criminal case it is always that the defendant allegedly violated a specific law. Subject matter jurisdiction is whether or not the court may hear and decide the issue in controversy. This is an area where the principles of Federalism had a major impact on the operation of the American legal system.

Federalists wanted the states to retain the power to govern themselves with as little interference from the federal government as possible. Therefore state courts are courts of general jurisdiction, meaning they have subject matter jurisdiction over everything that occurs in that state except for controversies the state itself decides it does not want to hear or for issues which are exclusively the province of federal court. Federal courts are courts of limited jurisdiction and can only hear cases which fall in the scope of Article III, Section 2 of the constitution and congressional statutes. It is possible for state and federal courts to have concurrent subject matter jurisdiction and, in fact, that is frequently the case when criminal allegations are made.

During the course of a forensic interview of a child among the things, the prosecutor is listening for who allegedly committed the crime? What is the alleged crime? If a state court prosecutor thinks there is concurrent federal jurisdiction that prosecutor may decide to include a federal prosecutor in the investigation.

Venue

The next thing a prosecutor is listening for during a forensic interview in information about where the alleged crime occurred. Location is important because location determines venue. A case is normally venued in the county in which the criminal acts allegedly occurred. In other words if a crime was committed in Teton County, Wyoming it cannot be prosecuted in Park County. There are occasions in which venue is proper in multiple counties or even multiple states.

When the Crime Allegedly Occurred

Prior to beginning a forensic interview prosecutors often remind the mental health professional conducting the interview to ask the child about when the conduct occurred. Prosecutors often urge interviewers to obtain as much date specific information as possible. When the conduct occurred is especially important. When a prosecutor files criminal accusations, the law requires the prosecutor include the date the conduct allegedly occurred. The law allows the prosecutor plead a range of time and not just a specific day. In other words the prosecutor could plead something like "on or about and between January 1, 2010 and December 31, 2010." The law requires dates be plead for several reasons.

A defendant in a criminal case has a constitutional right to know with what he or she is being charged. That constitutional right includes being on notice of when the conduct allegedly occurred. If the crime was alleged to have occurred during 2010 and the defendant was traveling overseas for some or all of that year the defendant would have an alibi defense. It would be almost impossible for a defendant in a criminal case to build a defense if the defendant and the defendant's lawyers didn't know when the conduct was alleged to have occurred.

Another reason the dates the conduct allegedly occurred is important has to do with sentencing and punishment. The law changes, sometimes rapidly. When a defendant is convicted and sentenced the defendant has to be sentenced under the laws as they existed when the conduct occurred. Consider the following: a defendant committed a crime in 2010. At that time the crime carried a maximum sentence of 5 years. In 2011 the law changed and made the punishment for the defendant's conduct much more severe and the maximum sentence became 15 years. In 2012 the defendant went to trial, was convicted and sentenced. If the defendant was sentenced consistent with the change in the law that occurred after the conduct occurred and given 15 years that sentence would violate the *ex post facto* clause of the constitution. The *ex post facto* clause prohibits the government from making criminal laws apply retroactively, in other words criminalizing conduct that was legal when it was originally performed. The *ex post facto* clause also prohibits retroactively applying a greater punishment for a crime.

A final reason it is important to know when criminal conduct occurred has to do with the statute of limitations. The government has a specific period of time after the commission of a crime during which criminal charges must be brought. The statute of limitations is best thought of as a clock. If charges are not brought during that period of time and the clock expires the charges are forever barred. The statute of limitations defines what the time period is for any given crime. Some crimes have very short statutes of limitations, other crimes have no statute of limitations meaning charges could be brought for as long as the defendant is alive.

The specific statute of limitations for crimes such as child molest vary greatly from state to state. In 2007 the federal government abolished the statute of limitations for most sex crimes. Many, if not all states, have some form of tolling or revival of the statute of limitations. If a statute of limitations is tolled that means there is certain conduct which essentially pauses the clock. Revival statutes apply when the clock runs out and certain conduct adds more time to the clock. Applying the statute of limitations can be very complicated, often times determining when the statute started running and when it expired can be difficult. For purposes of a forensic interview of a child it's important to get as much detailed information about when the alleged conduct occurred.

Exactly What Happened

Perhaps the most important part of a forensic interview of a child is finding out exactly what happened in as much detail as possible. First and foremost the prosecutor needs this information to figure out what crimes to charge. The statute criminalizing consensual sex with a minor is very different than the statute criminalizing forcible sex with the same minor. In some circumstances it can be difficult for prosecutors to change the charges if the prosecutor obtains more detail about the alleged conduct and wants to allege a violation of a different statute.

Prosecutors also have to decide how many counts to charge. In order to do so they need to know how many separate times specific conduct allegedly occurred. Conduct that occurred over a period of time can also give rise to different crimes in some states. For example in California if a child was sexually abused on two occasions a prosecutor would charge those two occasions, perhaps under Penal Code section 288, lewd act upon a child. If the same child was sexually assaulted on three or more occasions over several months by someone who lived in the home the prosecutor might charge Penal Code section 288.5, continuous sexual abuse of a child. The criminal penalties for these two code sections are very different. The maximum sentence for each violation of Penal Code section 288 is 8 years. The maximum sentence for a violation of Penal Code section 288.5 is 16 years.

Both prosecutors and defense lawyers want to hear a child describe the conduct in detail in part as a test of whether or not they believe the child is telling the truth or has been coached about their testimony. While children, particularly young children, are not expected to be able to relate the same kind of collateral details an adult might be expected to relate the complete inability to relate any collateral details can be an indicator that the allegations may not be truthful. Collateral details can be almost anything such as which room of a house the conduct occurred in, what colors the walls were, some detail about the furniture or other verifiable information that tends to prove the child was present.

Identify the Defendant

It sounds obvious that the forensic interview would have to identify the alleged perpetrator but it's important to mention. If a prosecutor is going to file charges based on the information gained from a forensic interview they have to know who to file charges against. Ideally children provide the name of the person who assaulted them, such as John Doe. If a child can identify their assailant from a photograph this can be sufficient identification. Problems can arise when a child can only provide a nickname and cannot identify their assailant. For example a child said they were walking home in the dark when they were grabbed by a person and assaulted. Because it was dark the child didn't get a look at their attacker so the child cannot identify the person. The child said some other people shouted at the attacker and called him TJ. Because TJ is a nickname even if law enforcement thinks they know which TJ was the attacker this is generally not a sufficient identification on which to support a prosecution. In most situations children know their assailant so these issues don't arise.

Although rare, there are cases in which more than one person may be criminally liable. For example often times in cases involving the production of child pornography two or more adults are involved in the abuse. In this kind of case it is important not only for the child to identify all the perpetrators of abuse but, to the extent possible, distinguish which individual engaged in what conduct.

Competence to Testify

Among the goals of a forensic interview of a child is to establish whether or not the child has the ability or the capacity to testify. Interviewers question children about their ability to distinguish between the truth and a lie, they ask about the consequences of a lie. Particularly in the case of young children it's important to establish the child knows the difference between real and make-believe. Competency-oriented questions during a forensic interview are legally significant. Fortunately the bar to establish the competency of child witnesses has been lowered.

The competence of children to testify is a concept that has evolved consistent with the evolution of how children are viewed and treated in society. In order to testify in court every witness has to be competent. Each state has its own statute defining competence but generally those statutes say a person is competent to testify as a witness if they can perceive, remember, communicate, and believe they are legally or morally obligated to tell the truth. In most circumstances adults are presumed competent to testify. The rules are different when dealing with children, particularly young children.

Historically most children were considered incompetent to testify. *R. v. Brasier*, 1 Leach 199, 168 E.R. 202 is a case decided in England in 1779. In *Brasier* the defendant was accused of assault with intent to commit rape of a 7-year-old girl. The girl did not testify at trial but her mother and another woman who lived with the child testified. The defendant was initially convicted but his conviction was overturned. The court overturned the conviction because the child did not testify. The court also wrote that while it is possible for children to take the oath to testify in a criminal case the child must prove they possess sufficient knowledge of the nature and consequences of taking an oath. The court wrote:

> …[T]here is no precise or fixed rule as to the time when infants are excluded from giving evidence; but their admissibility depends upon the sense and reason they entertain of the danger and impiety of falsehood, which is to be collected from their answers to questions propounded to them by the Court; but if they are found incompetent to take an oath their testimony cannot be received.

American courts took the same view of child witnesses at the time. Children's testimony was viewed with even greater suspicion when the child was to testify about their own victimization.

More than 100 years after the decision in *Braiser* the United States Supreme Court formally adopted a similar standard in *Wheeler v. U.S.*, (1895), 159 U.S. 523, 524–525:

> While no one should think of calling as a witness an infant only 2 or 3 years old, there is no precise age which determines the question of competency. This depends on the capacity and intelligence of the child, his appreciation of the difference between truth and falsehood, as well as of his duty to tell the former. The decision of this question rests primarily with the trial judge, who sees the proposed witness, notices his manner, his apparent possession or lack of intelligence, and may resort to any examination which will tend to disclose his capacity and intelligence, as well as his understanding of the obligations of an oath.

The effect of this standard was that children under the age of 14 were presumed incompetent to testify. This presumption was rebuttable. Normally a child would be placed on the witness stand outside the presence of the jury and questioned. The judge typically asked the questions and made the final decision as to whether or not the child was competent to testify. The result was predictable, children frequently were not allowed to testify.

In recent years there have been significant changes in how the testimony of children is treated. There is no modern definition of competence that applies to all states. The Federal Rule of Evidence is contained in Rule 601 which states "[e]very person is competent to be a witness except as otherwise provided in these rules." A significant number of states including Mississippi, Minnesota, Iowa, Florida, Michigan, New Jersey, Pennsylvania, Wisconsin, Alaska, Montana, Nebraska, North Carolina, Ohio, Texas, Utah, and Wyoming have modeled their statute on the federal statute.

Some states still require a hearing be held to determine whether or not a child is competent to testify but the presumption has shifted toward permitting children to testify. Other states reach the same presumption as the federal rule but state it somewhat differently in that they presume all people, children included, are competent to testify unless the contrary is proven. Even though different states approach the issue differently the frequency with which children have been permitted to testify has greatly increased in recent decades.

Courts have held that most testimonial competency issues affect the weight not the admissibility of evidence. In other words the presumption has shifted to the point where courts err on the side of allowing a child witness to testify and issues which previously led to the exclusion of the child's testimony are now a basis for cross examination and impeachment.

Consider the case of *Halloway v. State*, 312 Ark. 306, 849 S.W.2d 473 (1993). In *Halloway* the defendant and his wife ran a day care center. A number of children accused the defendant of molesting them. On appeal the defendant argued that two children, identified as L.S. and Je.Ca., ages four and six respectively, were not competent to testify. The defendant claimed L.S. was not competent because she could not demonstrate that she knew the difference between the truth and a lie. She also lacked good recall of events, she could not remember anything that happened while she was at the day care center other than the defendant forced her to perform oral sex on him. L.S. could not remember how the sexual contact occurred and, if she remembered the circumstances she refused to describe them.

The defendant argued Je.Ca. was not competent because she could not give an example of a lie to demonstrate that she knew the difference between the truth and a lie. Je.Ca. also changed the location of where the defendant sexually molested her, she could not remember what the defendant was wearing or many other details.

Under the historical rule such as the one from *Wheeler* neither of these children would have been permitted to testify. The Arkansas court that heard this case allowed both of these children to testify. On appeal the Supreme Court of Arkansas found that while there was imprecision in the children's testimony and an inability to define concepts such as truth these issues did not warrant a finding of testimonial incompetence but rather were issues for the jury to resolve. The court also wrote that children are competent to testify even when their testimony is not the "model of lucidity." (*Halloway v. State*, 312 Ark. 306, 317.)

Even very young children have been found competent to testify. In *Escamilla v. State*, 334 S.W.3d 263 (Tex. App. San Antonio, 2010) the defendant was convicted of molesting his daughter when she was two. The daughter, identified as D.A.E., made the accusations against her father close in time to when the conduct occurred and was interviewed at the Children's Advocacy Center. On one occasion the interviewers at the center were unable to interview D.A.E. because she was not verbal enough. D.A.E. took medication for attention deficit hyperactivity disorder and there was a history of mental illness in the family although no direct evidence that D.A.E. herself suffered from any mental illness. The trial occurred when D.A.E. was 3 years and 9 months old. The trial court found D.A.E. competent to testify and the appellate court affirmed that ruling. In this case, just as in *Halloway*, the court wrote that confusing and inconsistent responses from a child are not a basis on which to determine the child is incompetent to testify, rather those responses go the credibility of the testimony and the weight the jury should give the testimony.

If, during the course of a forensic interview, a child starts giving nonsensical, fantastic or nonresponsive answers it's important to delve into these areas. Sometimes nonresponsive answers are nothing more than evidence that a child is bored with an interview or doesn't want to talk about what happened to them. In other instances fantastic details can be indicative of children not telling the truth. The classic example of this is the McMartin Preschool abuse case.

In the McMartin case children claimed that in addition to having been sexually abused they saw witches fly, traveled in hot air balloons and were taken through underground tunnels. There were also claims that orgies occurred at car washes and airports and children were flushed down toilets to secret rooms. Ideally the forensic interview is the only time a child has to recount the entire story of their abuse prior to trial. In many ways the forensic examiner serves a sort of gate keeper function—just as it is important to establish what happened it's equally as important to establish if something didn't happen. It's the role of the forensic examiner to question things that don't make sense. Fortunately with the modernization of competency standards, forensic examiners can ask these questions without fearing it may lead to the child ultimately being barred from the witness stand.

Anatomy of a Trial

Forensic mental health professionals are frequently called as witnesses in criminal trials. Because of the frequency with which mental health professionals are called to court it's important to have an understanding of how the jury trial process works and what happens both before and after the mental health professional testifies.

Jury Selection

Jury selection is often referred to as voir dire. The term voir dire can refer to two very different events in a trial. When the term voir dire is being used to describe jury selection is refer to process whereby community members are summoned to court and questioned about their suitability to serve as jurors. The process of questioning the perspective jurors is formally known voir dire. (We will discuss the other meaning of voir dire later in the sections about competency hearings and qualifying experts.) The group of perspective jurors called in a case are collectively referred to as the venire.

During voir dire there are strict rules about what questions can be asked and who can ask the questions. In some states only judges are allowed to voir dire prospective jurors. In other states the prosecutor and the defense attorney conduct voir dire. In other states and many federal jurisdictions it's a combination—both the judge and the lawyers voir dire jurors.

The purpose of voir dire is to select jurors who are not already familiar with the case and who are open minded and willing to listen to all the evidence before making up their minds. What is appropriate to ask on voir dire changes based on the specific circumstances of the case. In a child molest case it's appropriate to ask jurors if they or anyone close to them has been the victim of molest. Most, if not all, courts will allow jurors to answer these kinds of questions out of the hearing of other prospective jurors. It is appropriate to question jurors about any biases they may have. For example if the defendant is a member of a racial minority questions about stereotypes of that racial minority are generally appropriate.

It's generally impermissible to ask jurors about their religion, political views, age, or sexual orientation. At the conclusion of voir dire both the prosecutor and the defense are allowed to excuse or challenge jurors. There are two kinds of challenges, for cause and peremptory. A challenge for cause means the lawyer making the challenge believes there is a specific legal reason why a prospective juror cannot sit on the jury. It could be because the prospective juror already knows about the case or has said or done something that indicates a bias against one side or the other. When a challenge for cause is made typically the arguments about whether or not the legal standard has been met are held outside the presence of all prospective jurors. The court rules on the challenge for cause after hearing each party's reasons why a certain prospective juror should be excused or should remain. If the challenge is granted the prospective juror is excused from service on that particular jury. If the challenge is denied the prospective juror remains as part of the venire. The side that lost the challenge for cause is allowed to use a peremptory challenge to excuse the perspective juror. The parties, the prosecutor, and the defense have an unlimited number of challenges for cause.

A peremptory challenge is a challenge whereby a prospective juror can be excused and the party excusing that juror does not have to give a reason. The number of peremptory challenges is limited and varies depending on the rules in each state as well as the nature of the changes. Generally the parties will have a greater number of peremptory challenges the more serious the potential penalty. While the lawyer using the peremptory challenge does not have to state a reason for excusing a particular juror, there are strict rules about why prospective jurors can be excused. Prospective jurors cannot be excused because of their race, religion, age, sexual orientation, or political affiliation. If one party, say the defense, believes the prosecutor improperly used a peremptory challenge the defense can raise that issue to the trial judge. The remaining venire is excused and the prosecutor can be required to explain why certain jurors were excused. The trial court then rules on whether or not the peremptory challenges were used properly. If they were used properly jury selection continues. If the peremptory challenges were used improperly the entire venire is dismissed and the process starts over. In addition in some states the improper use of peremptory challenges must be reported to the state bar and can be the basis for discipline against the lawyer.

Competency Hearings

Competency hearings are formal hearings held outside the presence of the jury to determine whether or not a witness is competent to testify. Courtrooms are intimidating places to many adults—they are much more so to children. Many courts allow child witnesses to come into the courtroom when court is not in session and get familiar with the courtroom. The child can sit in the witness box, look at and even sit on the bench (the bench is where the judge sits), go in the jury box, sit at counsel table, etc.

Under the constitution the defendant in a criminal case has the right to be present at all phases of the proceedings against him or her. A defendant also has a right to confront the witnesses and evidence against them. Both of these rights stem from the right to due process of law and to be allowed to assist in their own defense. There are many exceptions to a defendant's right to be present. For example if a jury goes out to view a crime scene a defendant does not have the right to go with the jury.

During competency hearings and indeed during trial many children do not wish to face the person who assaulted them. It can make it much more difficult for the child to qualify as a competent witness. There is some evidence that suggests the child is traumatized all over again if forced to see their abuser and recount the abuse in front of that person.

For years the law has grappled with the tension between a defendant's right to be present and a child's desire not to face the defendant. Some jurisdictions have addressed this issue by allowing competency hearings to be conducted via closed circuit camera. The defendant can see and hear the child's testimony but the child cannot see or hear the defendant. Other jurisdictions exclude the defendant although under the somewhat questionable theory that the right of confrontation is a trial right and competency is not formally part of the trial.

When the child is on the witness stand in a competency hearing the child is voir dired. In this context it means the judge or the lawyers are asking the child questions to establish the child's competency to testify as a witness.

Qualifying as an Expert

When mental health professionals are called to the witness stand, either due a forensic interview or to render an opinion, the lawyer calling them to the witness stand will likely qualify the mental health professional as an expert. Most witnesses who take the stand are fact witnesses; they are permitted to testify about what they saw or what they heard. Expert witnesses are different because they are allowed to render an opinion. When a witness is qualified as an expert it means the court accepts the witness's educational and professional credentials as sufficient to allow the expert witness to give opinion testimony.

The parties often disagree about potential expert testimony. Either one party does not believe the individual has the necessary qualifications to make that person an expert witness or one party does not believe the opinion the perspective expert would like to render is appropriate. If there is a dispute over whether or not a witness can or should qualify as an expert a hearing is held outside of the presence of the jury. The prospective expert is voir dired; questioned on their training and experience and the court ultimately rules whether or not the witness can testify as an expert.

The United States Supreme Court has decided two different cases which provide the framework for resolving disputes about proposed expert testimony. Those cases are *Daubert v. Merrell Dow Pharmaceuticals, Inc.*, 509 U.S. 579 (1993) and *Kumho Tire Co., Ltd. v. Carmichael*, 526 U.S. 137 (1999). Both *Daubert* and *Kumho Tire* are case names frequently discussed in courtrooms across the country. An understanding of these cases is helpful for mental health professionals likely to testify.

In *Daubert* two minor children and their parents' alleged prenatal ingestion of Merrell Dow's prescription drug, Bendectin, caused serious birth defects. Each side had multiple expert opinions to support their position. At the trial court level the trial court refused to admit the testimony of the children's experts because the methodology employed by their experts was "not sufficiently established to have general acceptance in the field to which it belongs." (*Daubert* at 583.) Prior to the decision in *Daubert* "general acceptance" was the test for all proposed scientific expert testimony. In *Daubert* the court rejected the "general acceptance" test. The Supreme Court ruled that expert testimony is admissible only if the opinion rests on a reliable foundation and is relevant to the case at hand. In order to determine whether or not the opinion "rests on a reliable foundation" the high court stated that specific things like testing, peer review, error rates, and acceptability in the scientific community were all things that would help determine the reliability of a particular theory or technique. (*Daubert*, at 593–594.) In *Daubert* the court stated that trial courts are the gatekeepers tasked with the duty to ensure pertinent evidence based on scientifically valid principles is admitted into evidence.

The decision in *Daubert* initially only applied to scientific expert testimony. *Kuhmo Tire* extended the reach of the *Daubert* decision. In *Kuhmo Tire* a tire on a vehicle driven by Patrick Carmichael blew out causing the vehicle to overturn. One passenger died and others were injured. The survivors brought a lawsuit against Kuhmo Tire, the distributor of the tire, claiming that tire was defective. The survivors sought to introduce the testimony of a tire failure analyst. A dispute arose among the parties regarding whether or not *Daubert* would apply to nonscientific testimony.

The United States Supreme Court held that the rule in *Daubert*, that all expert-testimony is admissible so long as the opinion rests on a reliable foundation and is relevant, extends to all expert testimony and is not limited to scientific experts. These two rulings, *Daubert* and *Kuhmo Tire*, opened the door to many more types of expert testimony that were previously inadmissible.

Mental health professionals have always been allowed to testify about a forensic interview but now they can also testify about a much wider array of topics. It is unlikely a mental health professional would be called to testify about a forensic interview and render an expert opinion in the same case. A more likely scenario is that a forensic interview is conducted. A different forensic mental health professional is retained by the lawyers for the defense to review the video of the forensic interview. This mental health professional is asked to consider the factors that have been identified in empirical research related to potential bias in forensic interviews of children. (Fanetti, M. & Boles, R. (2004). Forensic interviewing and assessment issues with children.) In W. O'Donohue and E. Levensky, *Handbook of Forensic Psychology: Resource for Mental Health and Legal Professionals*. Elsevier Academic Press: New York. Those factors are:

1. The child, due to rapport problems, may not have been comfortable and therefore may not have answered in a complete and accurate manner.
2. The child did not know that she could say, "I don't know" when she did not know the truth.
3. The child did not understand what it means to tell the truth.
4. The child did not know the importance of telling the truth.
5. The child did not understand her role in the interview or the purpose of the interview and therefore her answers may have been distorted.
6. The child might have felt uncomfortable discussing certain topics with the interviewer, therefore may not have answered in a complete and accurate manner.
7. The child had experienced some sort of externally derived threatening experience, which may have served to distort answers (e.g., fear of threats to self, loved ones, or property).

8. The child did not feel as though she had a choice in the type of responses she provided.
9. The child answered in a certain way in an attempt to please an authority figure.
10. There were leading questions.
11. The child's verbalizations at times were disconfirmed.
12. The interviewer inappropriately reinforced certain types of answers.
13. There were repetitive and perhaps coercive questions.
14. There were aspects of the child's total response (e.g., body posture, facial expressions, etc.) that gave a different interpretation to the child's answer.
15. The interviewer encouraged the child to speculate about important details, after the child had indicated that she was not sure about an answer or did not have the information.
16. The interviewer referenced the fact that other individuals (e.g., peers) had been interviewed regarding the interview topic and/or indicated what the other individuals' responses were.
17. The interviewer focused or redirected the child toward information about a specific detail or individual.
18. The child's report has been contaminated by some outside source, such as experience with another professional (e.g., retroactive interference from some other interviews).

After reviewing the forensic interview for these factors the expert is often asked to write a report and testify about their opinions. What experts should expect when they testify is discussed in more detail later in this chapter.

There are no set rules for when a court has to conduct hearings regarding witness competency and/or admissibility of expert testimony. In most cases the court will make any necessary rulings about the admissibility of expert testimony and the competency of witnesses prior to the parties selecting a jury or giving their opening statements. The reason for this is that the lawyers need to know what to voir dire the jury on and what to say in their opening statements. The lawyers therefore need to know how the court is going to rule on these issues in advance.

Opening Statements

An opening statement is the first time the jury really gets to hear from the lawyers about the case. While the lawyers for each side may have spoken with the jurors during voir dire, the lawyers are not allowed to preview the facts of the case or their theory of the case during voir dire. Opening statements are when each side gets to outline what evidence they expect the jury to hear and the lawyers' theories for why the jury should decide the case one way or another.

Opening statements serve as road maps for the jury. This is important for a couple of reasons. Jurors are not supposed to have any advance knowledge of what a case is about. This is next to impossible to accomplish in high profile trials or in small communities; in those instances the judge instructs the jury prior to opening statements that they are not to consider information from any outside source or preconceived notions about the case. The opening statement is intended to be the jury's first introduction to the facts of the case.

Trials rarely proceed with a chronological recitation of the facts. The realities of witness availability and the court's schedule means the order in which witnesses are called is often random. The opening statement provides a framework for the jury so they can understand how the different pieces of evidence fit, or don't fit, together.

Opening statements can be dramatic, they can be very vivid. They cannot be argumentative. Opening statements are not supposed to suggest the inferences the lawyers want the jury to draw from the evidence. In reality the line between a "statement" and an "argument" can be difficult to draw. Most experienced lawyers know how to state their "arguments" in a manner that makes them into statements. For example depending on the situation the phrase "John Smith is a liar" could be considered argumentative. Most lawyers would restate this as "the evidence will show John Smith is a liar." This change has removed any objectionable qualities from the statement.

In a criminal case the prosecution gives their opening statement first because they bear the burden of proof. The defense gives their opening statement second. The defense has the option of giving their opening statement after the close of the prosecution's case and before the defense starts putting on its case. Few defense lawyers elect this option because the jury goes for so long without hearing the defense's version of events. Neither side is technically required to give an opening statement however opening statements are rarely, if ever, waived.

The Taking of Evidence

The bulk of the trial is spent taking evidence. "Taking evidence" means the process where witnesses are called to the witness stand, questioned, cross-examined and physical or demonstrative evidence is admitted. Physical or demonstrative evidence cannot just be presented to the jury—it has to be admitted by the court.

In order to admit evidence, say a copy of a forensic interview, the party seeking to introduce the interview first has to lay a foundation. In order to lay a foundation the prosecutor might call the forensic mental health professional who conducted the interview to the stand. The witness would then be asked questions such as where do they work, how many years have they worked in this profession, are they acquainted with the alleged victim, does the room the interview occur in contain video recording equipment, etc. Laying a foundation means introducing sufficient preliminary evidence regarding the authenticity and relevance of the evidence sought to be admitted.

Different courts handle formal rulings on the admissibility of evidence differently. Normally after the lawyer for one side has asked what they believe to be enough questions in order to admit evidence they will say something like "the prosecution moves to admit [name of item]" and the court will rule on whether or not the item is admitted into evidence. The formal rule is that the lawyers may not show any item of evidence to a jury, even those that have been admitted into evidence, without the court's permission. If a lawyer wants to show the item to the jury they ask something like "permission to publish." If the court grants permission the item is then shown to the jury. This formal rule is not followed in many courtrooms for several reasons. One, because once evidence is admitted it is assumed the jury can see it. Two, because asking this question after every item of evidence has been admitted is tedious and redundant for the jury.

Witness testimony is rarely the dramatic, flashy experience depicted on television. Examining witnesses can go on for hours, sometimes days. The side calling the witness gets to question that witness first on direct examination. When the direct is done, the lawyer for the side gets to cross-examine the witness. When cross is done the first lawyer is entitled to redirect, then there is recross. During the course of witness testimony the side not questioning the witness can object both to the questions being asked and the answers being given. The list of possible objections is far too lengthy to cover here. Most objections are ruled on instantly by the trial judge. For more complicated issues the lawyers for both sides are called to the judge's bench and the issue is discussed outside the presence of the jury and the witness. In some instances the objection is so important or the issue so complex that the judge will order the jury and the witness into the hall way while the lawyers and the judge hash the issue out. Once the issue is resolved and the court has ruled, the judge calls the jury and the witness back into the courtroom.

Closing Arguments

Once the prosecution has called all of its witnesses, the prosecution rests. This is a formal announcement and goes something like this:

Judge: Madame prosecutor, please call your next witness.
Prosecutor: Your honor, the prosecution rests.

Once the prosecution has rested the defense is allowed to start calling their witnesses. A defendant in a criminal case is not required to present evidence and in fact, frequently defendants do not present their own evidence.

Once both sides have rested closing arguments are heard. Closing arguments are truly arguments. Lawyers try to sway the jurors to agreeing with their side. In a criminal case the prosecution always bears the burden of proof; the law requires the prosecutor prove the accused is guilty beyond a reasonable doubt. Often times large parts of both the prosecution and defense closing arguments are devoted to discussions about whether or not the prosecution has met its burden. There are few rules governing arguments other than the lawyers must accurately restate the evidence presented in court and must accurately state the law.

Many courts set time limits for how long the parties can argue during their closing arguments. Typically the longer and more complex a case, the longer time the parties will be allotted. Years ago lawyers would argue their closing arguments for hours, sometimes even several days. Courts rarely permit such lengthy arguments except in the rarest of instances.

Jury Deliberations and Verdict

Either before the closing arguments or after them, the court will instruct the jury on the law. The court is required to actually read the law aloud to the jury. Once the jury has heard the arguments and the law, they retire to the jury room for deliberations. Jury deliberations are secret. No one other than the jurors is allowed to be present. Except for some very limited exceptions, no one is allowed to ask the jury about their deliberations. The secrecy of jury deliberations is necessary to preserve the integrity of the jury process. No one other than the 12 people who heard all the evidence, heard the arguments of counsel, and who heard the law as announced by the judge should be able to influence the jury's verdict. Jury tampering is extremely rare. More common is the situation in which jurors decide to look something up on their phones or computers or attempt to visit a crime scene on their own. This is juror misconduct and while it is often done with the best of intentions, it can and frequently does result in a mistrial being declared. When a mistrial is declared the jurors are dismissed without rendering a verdict and the entire trial process, starting with selecting a jury, has to start over.

There is no limit to how long a jury can deliberate or what form their deliberations must take. Jurors are allowed to ask questions of the court during deliberations. If the jury wants to ask a question they write the question down on paper and the question is sent to the judge. The judge's clerk contacts the lawyers and tells them to come to court. The question as well as the proposed answer is discussed before being provided to the jury. If the parties cannot agree on the answer the court decides the answer.

Once the jury reaches their decision they send a note to the court announcing that they have a verdict. The parties are contacted and summoned to court. The verdict is then read aloud in open court. Once the verdict has been read the jury is dismissed. If the defendant has been acquitted the defendant is free to leave and the case is over. If the defendant is convicted a date and time for sentencing is set.

Sentencing

Sentencing is the formal process whereby the defendant is ordered to serve a specific amount of time in jail or in prison for their conduct. Forensic mental health professionals often serve a role in the sentencing process. Defense lawyers frequently hire psychologists to conduct forensic evaluations of their clients. Those evaluations are often used by the defense in court as part of an argument for a lesser sentence and/or for treatment for their client.

Sentencing is perhaps the one time when a judge's true opinion of a case becomes relevant. Prior to sentencing judges try very hard to be unbiased and to not be swayed either way by the evidence. At sentencing, after they have heard a forensic interview and they have heard a child witness testify, some judges are free with their opinions about the case and the defendant.

In cases where there are child victims of sex crimes, sentencing can be complicated and frustrating for everyone involved. There has been a push over the past several decades for longer and longer sentences in these cases. Judges have largely been stripped of their discretion to fashion appropriate sentences for defendants in these cases—instead the courts are forced to issue mandatory sentences because of legislative agendas. There are instances where justice dictates an individual receive a lesser or different sentence because of some factor specific to that individual but in many cases judges are prohibited from issuing the sentences they believe just.

What to Expect on The Witness Stand

Mental health professionals conducting forensic interviews of children will almost always be called to the witness stand by the prosecution. Often the prosecutors arrange meetings with their witnesses a week or so prior to trial. The purpose of these meetings is to discuss the questions the prosecutor anticipates asking the witness at trial. To the extent the prosecutor knows, the prosecutor will often inform the witness of the defense's theory or of any potential weaknesses in the prosecution's case that the prosecutor expects the defense to exploit.

On direct examination, when the prosecutor is questioning their witnesses, the questioning is straight forward and the tempo of the questions is about the speed of a normal conversation. Most lawyers do not write out individual questions in advance, they work from outlines that go through the subject areas they want to cover with each witness. This means the lawyers are formulating the precise questions as they go. Trials, particularly long or extremely contentious ones are exhausting for the lawyers involved. Asking consistently intelligent questions under these circumstances can be challenging even for the most seasoned of trial lawyers. If a lawyer asks a question, on cross or on direct, that doesn't make sense say so. It's perfectly acceptable to ask a lawyer on either side to rephrase their question.

Cross examination is very different than direct. On direct examination the questions have to be open-ended—they cannot be leading. On cross examination lawyers are allowed to use leading questions. In fact most lawyers will only ask leading questions on cross examination. Lawyers often try to change the tempo on cross. They will rapid fire questions at a witness as fast as they can and then they will slow down and take a very long time between each answer and the next question. Direct examination is normally chronological or follows some other internal order than makes sense under the circumstances. Cross is rarely chronological. Lawyers ask questions out of order intentionally. Lawyers are allowed to be pretty aggressive on cross examination—they cannot ask questions that are argumentative, but they can be intense and intimidating. The purpose of all of this is to test the veracity and reliability of the witness. A witness who is lying or hiding something is likely to slip up under these circumstances. Mental health professionals testifying about a forensic interview that was properly conducted have little to worry about on cross. The best lawyer in the world cannot impeach or undermine the testimony of a witness who is unbiased, did their job properly and is telling the truth.

Legal Issues

There are a number of legal decisions over the years that affect the forensic interviews of children. An exhaustive list would be nearly impossible to prepare but a summary of some of the major ones are presented below.

Taint Hearings

A taint hearing is typically a pretrial hearing used to determine whether or not the statements from alleged child abuse victims should be excluded. The argument is that the child's testimony is tainted because of improper law enforcement interview techniques, improper forensic interviews, and/or bias or influence from another source that has significantly affected the child's testimony.

Among the best known cases discussing a taint hearing is *State v. Michaels*, 136 N.J. 299, (1994). In September 1984, Margaret Kelly Michaels was hired by Wee Care Day Nursery as a teacher's aide for preschoolers. Michaels had no prior experience as a teacher at any level.

During the 7-month period that Michaels worked at Wee Care, she performed satisfactorily. Wee Care never received a complaint about her from staff, children, or parents. On April 26, 1985, the mother of M.P., a 4-year-old in Michaels's nap class, noticed he was covered with spots. She took the child to his pediatrician and had him examined. During the examination, a pediatric nurse took M.P.'s temperature rectally. In the presence of the nurse and his mother, M.P. stated, "this is what my teacher does to me at nap time at school." M.P. indicated to the nurse that his teacher, Kelly (the name by which Michaels was known to the children), was the one who took his temperature. M.P. added that Kelly undressed him and took his temperature daily.

M.P. was questioned by his mom some more and eventually told his mom that Kelly did the same to S.R. M.P.'s mother contacted the New Jersey Division of Youth and Family Services to inform them of her son's disclosures. The Prosecutor's office ultimately assumed investigation of the complaint.

The Prosecutor's office interviewed several Wee Care children and their parents. During that period of investigation, Michaels was submitted to approximately nine hours of questioning. Additionally, Michaels consented to taking a lie detector test, which she passed. Extensive additional interviews and examinations of the Wee Care children by the prosecutor's office followed. By the time the trial concluded Michaels was charged with 131 counts of child molest. The majority of the state's evidence was the testimony of children. Limited physical evidence supported the contention that the children had been molested. Michaels was convicted on numerous counts and sentenced to 47 years in prison.

On appeal the issue before the court was the interview techniques employed in both law enforcement and forensic interviews of the children involved. The court wrote:

> That an investigatory interview of a young child can be coercive or suggestive and thus shape the child's responses is generally accepted. If a child's recollection of events has been molded by an interrogation, that influence undermines the reliability of the child's responses as an accurate recollection of actual events.
>
> A variety of factors bear on the kinds of interrogation that can affect the reliability of a child's statements concerning sexual abuse. We note that a fairly wide consensus exists among experts, scholars, and practitioners concerning improper interrogation techniques. They argue that among the factors that can undermine the neutrality of an interview and create undue suggestiveness are a lack of investigatory independence, the pursuit by the interviewer of a preconceived notion of what has happened to the child, the use of leading questions, and a lack of control for outside influences on the child's statements, such as previous conversations with parents or peers. [Citation omitted].
>
> The use of incessantly repeated questions also adds a manipulative element to an interview. When a child is asked a question and gives an answer, and the question is immediately asked again, the child's normal reaction is to assume that the first answer was wrong or displeasing to the adult questioner. (*See* Debra A. Poole and Lawrence T. White, *Effects of Question Repetition on Eyewitness Testimony of Children and Adults*, 27 *Developmental Psychology*, November (1991) at 975.) The insidious effects of repeated questioning are even more pronounced when the questions themselves over time suggest information to the children. [Citation omitted].
>
> The explicit vilification or criticism of the person charged with wrongdoing is another factor that can induce a child to believe abuse has occurred. (*Ibid.*) Similarly, an interviewer's bias with respect to a suspected person's guilt or innocence can have a marked effect on the accuracy of a child's statements. [Citation omitted]. The transmission of suggestion can also be subtly communicated to children through more obvious factors such as the interviewer's tone of voice, mild threats, praise, cajoling, bribes and rewards, as well as peer pressure.
>
> The Appellate Division recognized the considerable authority supporting the deleterious impact improper interrogation can have on a child's memory. [Citation omitted]. Other courts have recognized that once tainted the distortion of the child's memory is irremediable. (*See* State v. Wright, 116 Idaho 382, 775 P.2d 1224, 1228 (1989) ("Once this **tainting** of memory has occurred, the problem is irredeemable. That memory is, from then on, as real to the child as any other.")) The debilitating impact of improper interrogation has even more pronounced effect among young children. (Maryann King and John C. Yuille, *Suggestibilityand the Child Witness*, in *Children's Eyewitness Memory*, 29 (Stephen J. Ceci et al. eds., 1987) and Stephen J. Ceci, *Age Differences in Suggestibility*, in *Children's Eyewitness Memory* 82 (Stephen J. Ceci, et al. ed., 1987).)
>
> The critical influence that can be exerted by interview techniques is also supported by the literature that generally addresses the reliability of children's memories. Those studies stress the importance of *proper* interview techniques as a predicate for eliciting accurate and consistent recollection. (*See*, Gail S. Goodman, et al., *Optimizing Children's Testimony*: *Research and Social Policy Issues Concerning Allegations of Child Sexual Abuse* in *Child Abuse, Child Development, and Social Policy* 1992, Dante Cicchetti & Sheree L. Toth (Eds.).)

> The conclusion that improper interrogations generate a significant risk of corrupting the memories of young children is confirmed by government and law enforcement agencies, which have adopted standards for conducting interviews designed to overcome the dangers stemming from the improper interrogation of young children.
>
> (*State v. Michaels* 136 N.J. at 309–311.)

The *Michaels* court issued a resounding criticism of the interviews conducted in the case. The court characterized them as cajoling, biased, and improper among other things. The court's criticism of the interview techniques went on for several pages and concluded a taint hearing must be held.

Given the training that modern forensic interviewers receive as well as the training received by many law enforcement officers, fewer taint hearings are held. More recently taint hearings tend to occur mainly because of prejudice and influence exerted on a child witness because of family members. Defense lawyers have no small burden persuading a court to hold a taint hearing—the defense has to produce evidence, not just speculation, that the child witness' memory has been improperly and unduly influenced before the court will hold a taint hearing.

A Little Less Hearsay

Until 2004 the law in many states permitted the introduction of the entire forensic interview of a child in many circumstances. Defense lawyers objected to this practice because it violated the rules prohibiting the introduction of hearsay and it violated the Confrontation Clause in the United States Constitution. Hearsay is any statement made outside of court, repeated in court and is offered for the truth of the matter asserted. In a forensic interview the interview [the statements] was done at a child safety center [outside of a courtroom] and the contents of the interview would be offered in court for proof of what the child alleged to have occurred. There are numerous exceptions to the hearsay rule. Forensic interviews were admissible under the exception which allowed in statements that have a "sufficient indicia of reliability." The Confrontation Clause is contained in the Sixth Amendment to the constitution and states a defendant in a criminal trial has the right to confront and cross-examine the witnesses against him or her. If a forensic interview is introduced into evidence, the defendant cannot interject and ask questions, the interview already occurred, and it occurred when neither he nor his lawyer was present. The Confrontation Clause also encompasses the notion that the jury is entitled to see how a witness reacts to a question. Again something that cannot occur when a taped interview is involved. There have always been recognized exceptions to the Confrontation Clause.

In 2004 the United States Supreme Court issued a ruling in a case called *Crawford v. Washington*, 541 U.S. 36 (2004). In that case the high court held that hearsay statements generally cannot be used in court if the person who made the statement is unavailable to be cross-examined. While there are exceptions to this rule the net effect of the rule has been to require more children to testify in cases where previously they may not have been required to testify. Fewer forensic interviews can be admitted into evidence at trial.

Consider the Michigan case *People v. Douglas*, 496 Mich. 557 (2014). In that case the defendant was accused of making his daughter, KD, perform fellatio on him and touch his penis. The allegations arose approximately 1 year after KD's parents split up. KD made the allegations first to her mother. In response her mother moved up KD's preexisting appointment with a therapist. The therapist contacted CPS after speaking with KD. KD participated in a forensic interview at Care House and during the interview discussed the alleged fellatio and touching. KD was 3½ years old at the time the alleged abuse occurred, four when she reported it and five by the time she actually testified. (*People v. Douglas*, 496 Mich. At 561–562.)

At trial KD testified. The prosecutor introduced testimony from forensic interviewer Jennifer Wheeler who testified about the contents of the forensic interview. The jury was shown a video recording of the interview. The defendant was convicted. On appeal the Michigan Supreme Court ruled that the hearsay statements introduced by the forensic interviewer as well as the playing of the forensic interview were in error and the defendant was entitled to a new trial because of the error. (*People v. Douglas*, 496 Mich. at 600–601.) The ruling in this case was highly influenced by the United States Supreme Court's decision in *Crawford* and is indicative of how forensic interviews have been handled in the wake of that decision.

Failure to Protect

All states have laws that require parents or other adults with the care and custody of a child to protect that child. These laws require one parent to protect the child from another parent if the other parent is abusive or neglectful.

Some years ago there was a case in California in which a couple had three children; a 3-year-old and infant twins. The parents were both developmentally disabled and numerous county agencies were involved with the family. The parents were probably not capable of caring for three young children on their own. The infants suffered from severe diaper rash and were malnourished. Both the father and the mother very much wanted to keep their children and, probably because they wanted their children, social services continued to work with the family instead of attempting to remove the children from the home. There were notations in the CPS worker's file that she told the father they were doing a good job of caring for the twins but needed to work harder at resolving their diaper rash and generally keeping the twins cleaner.

Unrelated to the care of the children, the father was convicted of a misdemeanor for taking money from an employer and sentenced to perform community service. It was summertime and very hot. One day while the father was performing his court ordered community service the mother left the infant twins in the upstairs of an apartment that had no air conditioning. That afternoon a CPS worker stopped to check in on the twins. The mother refused to allow the CPS worker in the house. The CPS worker became concerned and contacted local police and fire. When the fireman gained entry into the home they found the twin girls had died from heat exposure.

The mother was prosecuted and convicted for the murder of her children. The father was prosecuted and convicted for failing to protect the children from their mother.

Compare that case to the following: A husband and wife had two biological children. They were asked by family members to take in a 4-year-old niece whose mother was unable to care for her. The niece had developmental and emotional disabilities. The husband was a construction worker who left before the children got out of bed in the morning and frequently returned after they had gone to bed at night.

The wife physically abused the niece. The young girl was ultimately brought to the hospital when a glass shower door allegedly fell off of its hinges hitting the girl in the head. Medical workers found severe burns on the palms of her hands and bruising that appeared unrelated to the incident involving the shower door. Because of her disabilities the niece was unable to communicate to medical workers or law enforcement how she had received her injuries. The husband and wife were prosecuted and convicted; the wife for the abuse and the husband for failing to protect the child from the wife.

The men in both scenarios were sentenced to fairly similar prison terms, each received about 2 years in prison. In both cases there was little direct evidence that the men were aware of the dangers to the children. Certainly the father in the first example was aware the twins had diaper rash and social services was concerned with the children's failure to gain weight. The husband in the second scenario brought the child to hospital but it was unclear whether or not he knew or should have known about the abuse prior to that night.

While the legal standard in both of these cases demanded proof beyond a reasonable doubt that these men had failed to protect the children involved the reality is that each jury required relatively little evidence in order to return convictions. People who have the care and custody of children are legally required to protect them—the law is willing to place a high burden on those in the best position to uncover and address child abuse.

Conclusion

The modern forensic interview of a child bears on an entire criminal prosecution. Because of that the role of the forensic interviewer has become increasingly important—they are the one person who talks with the child pretrial. The forensic interviewer has to be at least minimally familiar with the basics of the criminal process and with developments that may affect the scope of their testimony.

Chapter 3
Working with the Multidisciplinary Team

Kristen J. MacLeod

Vignette

R is a 10-year-old boy who has disclosed sexualabuse by his father. His father has been arrested and is currently in jail. R is seen for a sexual assault exam, referred by local police. The victim advocate comes to the exam to support R's mother and make sure she has access to the resources necessary to access help for her and her family. Neither Child Protective Services (CPS) nor law enforcement is present for the exam. The clinician does not have access to the forensic interview and does not even know that it has occurred. The clinician performing the exam recommends mental health services for the child as soon as possible and social services for the mother, as the child has indicated that there is often nothing in their refrigerator. The mother requests a cab voucher to get home from the exam. The results of the exam are faxed to the law enforcement and local child protective services. Two days later, the clinician receives a call from the pediatric hospitalist, requesting a consult for an 8-year-old girl who was admitted to the hospital 7 days ago for psychiatric reasons. She has been making inappropriate sexual gestures, using profane sexual language and propositioning aides. She has been placed in the pediatric Intensive Care Unit because she requires 1:1 nursing for safety. Psychiatry has been consulted, but won't see her for 2 more days, because it is a weekend. The Child Abuse clinician arrives at the hospital and the nurse caring for the child says that CPS has been involved with the case for several weeks. She believes this child's sibling, R, was recently seen for a sexual assault exam at the sexual assault facility. The clinician is upset that she had not been made aware that R's sibling was inpatient at the hospital with concerns of sexualized behavior, sexual abuse, and other mental health issues.

K.J. MacLeod, M.D. (✉)
Washoe County Child Abuse Response and Evaluation Team, Reno, NV 89519, USA
e-mail: kj_macleod@sbcglobal.net

W.T. O'Donohue, M. Fanetti (eds.), *Forensic Interviews Regarding Child Sexual Abuse*, DOI 10.1007/978-3-319-21097-1_3

The nurse practitioner at CPS is upset that she was not made aware that R had made a disclosure and had been referred for a sexual assault exam. No report was made to law enforcement about the sibling in the hospital.

This case vignette illustrates several of the negative consequences that occur when the multidisciplinary approach to these cases of suspected childabuse fails. Not only do the professionals involved experience frustration in delivery care, but more importantly, a family and children are failing to receive essential services in a timely, coordinated manner. Evidence can be lost and investigations impeded without full involvement from the members of a multidisciplinary team. This exposes the children and non-offending caregiver to repeated trauma and prevents the child victim from receiving the highest quality of care available to him or her in the community.

Introduction

At its core, the care of abused children has always been a multidisciplinary field. The universal need for close collaboration between multiple professional disciplines in caring for suspected victims of child abuse makes the field of child abuse unique. Kempe's landmark article in 1962, "The Battered Child Syndrome" published in The Journal of the American Medical Association was the first in medical field to clearly state the need for the physician to have liaisons to professionals in social work, law enforcement, and mental health (Kempe, Silverman, Steele, Droegemueller, & Silver, 1962). The article recognized the reticence of some medical professionals to become involved in the legal aspects of such cases. However, the protection of abused and neglect children in our communities evolved neither out of the clinical fields of medicine or mental health nor even the field of law enforcement. Almost unbelievably, Kaplan points out in his 2011 textbook, it arose out of the entirely unrelated Society for the Prevention of Cruelty to Animals and the plight of Mary Ellen Wilson, a horribly physically abused 9-year-old (American Humane Association, 2013; Kaplan, Adams, Starling, & Giardino, 2011). In 1874 in New York City, Henry Bergh, the founder of the American Society for the Prevention of Cruelty to Animals (ASPCA) acted through the urging of concerned private citizens and used his connections to send a NYSPCA investigator to Mary Ellen's home. An ASPCA attorney provided the petition for her removal from the abusive home, initially making her a ward of the court. Mr. Bergh's willingness to act on his principles of humane treatment for all living things, likely saved Mary Ellen's life and provided a ground swell for the establishment of our modern day child protective services, as well as the need for legal involvement in these cases (Watkins, 1990).

This concept of using a multidisciplinary approach in the complex care of children who may have been abused has become well accepted over the last 25 years (Hochstadt & Harwicke, 1985; Jones, Cross, Walsh, & Simone, 2005; Kempe et al., 1962; Lashley, 2002; U.S. Department of Justice & Office of Juvenile Justice and Delinquency Prevention, 2000; Watkins, 1990). All 50 states and the federal government mandate various versions of multidisciplinary collaboration in child protection investigation (Child Welfare Information Gateway, 2013; U.S. Department of Health et al., 2002). The main goals of the multidisciplinary team are to facilitate timely, thorough, and successful investigations, while improving the welfare of the children and non-offending caretakers (Fontana & Robison, 1976; U.S. Department of Justice & Office of Juvenile Justice and Delinquency Prevention, 2000). Two critical pieces to improving this welfare involve the reduction of stress and trauma for the child victim and increasing the reliability of child disclosures through reducing the number of child interviews (Bruck, Ceci, & Hembrooke, 1998; Jaudes & Martone, 1992). Multiple barriers, such as competing professional mandates and the unpopularity of child abuse cases must be overcome in each professional discipline involved in order to achieve these goals. Cases of child sexual assault are considered difficult, unpopular, and anxiety-provoking. Physicians, who might routinely perform below-the-knee amputations or care for dying cancer patients, shrink away at the thought of child sexual assault evaluations. Law enforcement professionals who deal routinely with gang warfare can find cases of child sexual assault less desirable to investigate than other crimes (Newman, Dannenfelser, & Pendleton, 2005). By virtue of such challenges, this field has advanced the concept of multidisciplinary care to a level which surpasses most other case collaborations (Kaplan et al., 2011). The composition of the team, approach to collaboration, measures of effectives and development of best practice standards remain in progress. This chapter will take a look at the development of the multidisciplinary Team (MDT), the roles of the various members, the variations in approach to its implementation across the nation and the development of best practice standards for MDT's. The rising presence of Children's Advocacy Centers (now more than 800 operating), as the means by which to provide multidisciplinary care has reemphasized a child-focused approach to these difficult cases (National Children's Advocacy Center, 2014a).

Roles of the MDT Members

Perhaps one of the greatest and most unique challenges to smooth functioning of the multidisciplinary team is the need for each professional to completely fulfill both his individual professional mandate and the collaborative goals set out by the MDT. Core members of the MDT include professionals from law enforcement, child protective services, the prosecutor's office, mental health, medicine and victim advocate programs (often through law enforcement agencies). Additional contributing members include those from the juvenile justice program, public health, domestic violence programs, and the school truancy board. A thorough understanding of the professional parameters and mandates of each member of the team is critical to effective collaboration between the members and has been shown to be directly related to the effectiveness of the team (Lashley, 2002; Lalayants, Epstein, & Adamy, 2011).

Child Protective Services

Over the century and a half following the case of Mary Ellen and the birth of the New York Society for the Prevention of Cruelty to Children, our present day Child Protective Services (CPS) has grown into the primary agency responsible for investigating and intervening in cases of suspected childabuse and neglect where the perpetrator is a caregiver. CPS serves both an investigative and therapeutic role, as the professionals charged with securing the safety and welfare of children within the families in which they live. CPS has primary responsibility for determining the residency or placement of the child in a safe environment. They are the only agency that remains intimately involved with the child and family from the initial investigative phase through the court system and into the therapeutic phase. CPS procures the family services necessary to improve the functional well-being of the family and the environment in which the child lives. The concept of the child-centered social worker may even include providing direct clinical therapy to the child (Anderson, Weston, Doueck, & Krause, 2002). CPS must function within the family court on the civil side of the law to ensure safe residence for the child. This residence may be in the home with support provided by external services or it may require removal from the home for out of home placement. They must work within the constraints of the family court system, while remaining accountable to federal, state, and county guidelines. In their investigative role, CPS may conduct minimal fact interviews, forensic interviews, and scene investigations. The collection of collaborative reports and documents such as school, childcare, and healthcare records routinely falls to the child protective service worker in assessing the safety of the child's environments. CPS routinely refers their cases to the jurisdictionally appropriate law enforcement agency. Law enforcement, not CPS, will then determine the need for criminal investigations and charges.

Law Enforcement

As the agency responsible for investigating crimes and securing the safety of citizens in its community, law enforcement's role in cases of childabuse and neglect is closely related to both the prosecutor's office and Child Protective Services (CPS). In fact many states require co-investigation with CPS and law enforcement (LE) in suspected cases of abuse and neglect (Cross, Finkelhor, & Ormrod, 2005; Cross, Walsh, Simone, & Jones, 2003). Their primary responsibility in cases of CAN is to gather evidence and determine if a crime has been committed against a child, with subsequent arrest of the suspect and preparation of charges for the criminal court. As the first responders, they often have exclusive access to the initial scene. The responsibility for collecting evidence at the scene of the suspected abuse falls primarily to LE. Each law enforcement agency has its own professional and legal framework within which it must operate. LE must ultimately answer to the office of the district attorney or the attorney general, for agencies such as, the Bureau of

Indian Affairs and the Department of Public Safety. In each of these agencies, successful criminal prosecution depends on LE's approach to investigation and knowledge of the legal intricacies of their jurisdiction. This can at times put them at odds with the other members of the MDT whose professional obligations are centered solely on the needs of the child and family. This includes demands from professionals such as medical and mental health providers and child protective service workers. It bears remembering that LE often physically assists CPS in the removal of children from an imminently dangerous situation and may even perform the removal without CPS present if necessary. Given the variety of roles, both investigatory and protective that LE plays in these cases, there will be a large variability in training and experience with child abuse cases (Portwood, Grady, & Dutton, 2000). A patrol officer will generally have far more limited knowledge of the intricacies of CPS investigations than will a detective in the child crimes unit. The LE personnel in a rural district will have less opportunity for specific training in CAN cases given the great distance they have to cover and the small budgets. By virtue of their rural designation they will have a lower volume of cases and may be working with prosecutors who have little experience in bringing these cases before the court. Despite disparate settings and variations in agency training and investigatory practice, the ability to recognize child maltreatment and a basic knowledge of child development have been cited as key common areas for improvement in law enforcement training (Portwood et al., 2000). The multidisciplinary team and the emergence of CAC provide routine contact with multiple child abuse professionals who can provide knowledge in these areas (Newman et al., 2005).

Much has been written and studied about the often successful, though at times contentious collaboration between law enforcement agencies and child protective services. (Cross et al., 2005; Faller & Henry, 2000; Jordan, Yampolskaya, Gustafson, & Armstrong, 2011; Newman et al., 2005; Pence & Wilson, 1994; Tjaden & Anhalt, 1994). Child sexualabuse cases in particular require interaction between the two agencies, as these charges rise to the level of criminal rather than civil prosecution in most cases. The two systems collide most frequently due to different professional mandates and different timeline requirements in investigation (Newman et al., 2005). CPS workers have a strict timeframe in which they must meet requirements for removal of a child. Law enforcement does not have the same constraints. Law enforcement may want to wait and gather more evidence before interviewing potential suspects and victims, so as not to jeopardize the criminal charges. CPS needs to perform interviews to gather their information and determine imminent risk often within just a few days. The early investigations by CPS workers can interfere with evidence collection from the point of view of criminal prosecution. These early interviews can tip off perpetrators the quality of law enforcement investigations (Newman et al., 2005).

The 1974 federal Child Abuse Prevention and Treatment Act and subsequent mandated reporting laws led to a massive increase in reports and enormous investigatory burden on CPS over the next decade (Reece & Jenny, 2005). In the late 1990s concerns arose that the investigatory burden on CPS was becoming too great and hindered their ability to provide services to these high risk families (Center for the

Study of Social Policy, 2000). Inadequate investigation and inadequate services can have deadly consequences. Two states, FL and AK therefore experimented with moving the investigatory responsibility for childabuse cases under the jurisdiction of law enforcement agencies, essentially creating a separate unit within LE to conduct the investigative aspect of these cases (Kinnevy, Huang, Dichter, & Gelles, 2003, 2005). There is limited data demonstrating the effect of this shift in roles. The follow-up study by Jordan and colleagues in 2011 looking at the consequences of this change in Florida shows higher rates of substantiated cases in areas where law enforcement was responsible for child protection investigation compared to the areas where the child welfare agency assumed this responsibility (Jordan et al., 2011). Unfortunately, the results also show an increase in the odds of experiencing recurrent maltreatment, especially for younger children, in areas where law enforcement assumed the role of child protection investigations (Jordan et al., 2011). The explosion of Children's Advocacy Centers (CACs) seems to have replaced models such as those in AK and FL in an attempt to improve outcomes in terms of both substantiation and recurrence of maltreatment.

Court System

The criminal courts and civil child protection or family courts both play a large role in cases of child abuse and neglect. Understanding the major differences between these two courts and the constraints they place upon agencies involved in the investigation of these cases greatly enhances the understanding of the often problematic differences in various MDT members' approaches to the investigation. Law enforcement is guided by the legal standards and statutes of the criminal court. CPS answers to the statutes and timetables of the civil family court. Criminal prosecutor's offices spearheaded several early multidisciplinary teams across the country. The model for our current CACs grew out of such a team. Efforts by former district attorney and Congressman Robert E. "Bud" Cramer of Alabama led to the formation of the first CAC in 1985, now a national model and training center (National Children's Advocacy Center, 2014a). The participation of the court system is critical to the success of the multidisciplinary team.

The criminal court and civil court vary in their impacts on the child and family, their processes for hearing evidence and the burden of evidence required for judgments in these cases. The family court most often directly impacts the child's life by determining abuse or neglect by caregiver or guardians (Kaplan et al., 2011), while the higher profile criminal court seeks justice in those child abuse offenses that have reached the level of a major crime. The civil side of the court system works closely with child protection and child welfare agencies in every case to determine residency, or placement of the child. Two important factors further distinguish it from the criminal court. In the civil court evidentiary proceedings are most often heard in front of a judge instead of a jury. This may make it easier for experts such as medical or mental health professionals to give evidence, as they can directly address the judge who presumably has a higher level of education than the average juror and a significant amount of experience in these cases (Kaplan et al., 2011). Experts giving testimony in criminal court must be able to explain complicated scientific concepts to the jury. With the gravity of the charges and the severity of the potential sentences experts may find it difficult to testify due to interruptions from lawyers on both sides. Perhaps the most significant difference between the civil child protection court and the criminal court, however, concerns the burden of proof required to win a case. The civil courts hold to a standard called "preponderance of evidence," while the criminal court must meet the standard for evidence "beyond a reasonable doubt" in order to make a conviction. This means that in cases of child abuse and neglect, safe placement of a child, including removal from his or her family can be achieved without meeting the hefty criminal court burden of "beyond a reasonable doubt." Members of the multidisciplinary team may be able to affect safe placement of the child in many cases where the prosecutor's office is unable to seek justice in the criminal courts.

Victim Advocates

Victim Advocates play a critical role in linking the victim, the MDT process and community services together to minimize trauma to the victim and facilitate healing (Campbell, 2006). Victim services and the role of the advocate has been strengthened greatly by the federal Violence Against Women's Act of 1994 (Violence Against Women's Act. Title IV & sec. 40001–40703 of the Violent Crime Control and Law Enforcement Act of 1994) which initially granted 1.6 billion dollars over 5 years to improve services to victims, increase criminal penalties, and broaden resources for investigators in the field.

Financial analyses of net social costs of the program indicate that the services provided through VAWA funding have saved almost $15 billion dollars in averted social costs (Clark, Biddle, & Martin, 2002). Victim advocates act as a liaison to community services for the victims and families (Long, Willkinson, & Kays, 2011). They help the families access funding and guide them through the investigatory and courtroom process. Victim advocate support becomes critical as the child and family prepare for criminal trial. Some advocates work out of grant funded community programs. Others are provided by local law enforcement agencies or the prosecutor's office.

As a truly victim-centered member of the MDT, advocates are ethically and legally bound by rules of confidentiality. Communications between victim and advocate are considered confidential and fall under the protection of VAWA's RCW 5.60.060 (U.S. Department of Justice & Office of Juvenile Justice and Delinquency Prevention, 2000) *Privileged Communications* requirement. Advocates may not disclose any information or conversation with the victim without consent from the victim. They cannot be subject to questioning by police as to information provided to them in privileged conversations with the victim. This requirement, while crucial to fulfilling their role, may limit the information they can contribute in multidisciplinary settings. Even when the advocates cannot disclose specific information about a victim, they may guide the team in addressing system-based concerns that can improve the overall outcome of the case (Micheel, 2011).

Mental Health Providers

The mental health providers involved in childabuse cases assist the members of the MDT in both investigation and substantiation. Their role encompasses evaluation of disclosures and behavioral concerns. They are also called upon to provide therapeutic assessment and intervention for the child and often even family members (American Psychological Association [APA], 2013; Kaplan et al., 2011). Given this broad range of roles, there may be more than one mental health provider participating in the MDT. In accordance with current American Psychological Association Guidelines and Ethics Code, a clinician directly treating the child or family member involved in the allegations should not be primarily responsible for assessing the validity of allegations (American Psychological Association, 2013). Therefore there may be psychologists, as well as clinical social workers assisting in child protection cases. All cases require the mental health provider to employ evidence-based standards in decision making and treatment whenever possible (American Psychological Association, 2013; Cohen, Deblinger, Mannarino, & Steer, 2004; Cohen, Mannarino, & Knudsen, 2005; Herman, 2005).

Mental health providers routinely provide guidance to the team when the child in the case exhibits concerning behavior. Quite commonly this behavior is sexualized in nature. These cases are particularly challenging for the investigative members of the team, as over 90 % of child sexualabuse cases will have normal physical exams and no retrievable DNA evidence (Adams, Harper, Knudson, & Revilla, 1994; Heger, Ticson, Velasquez, & Bernier, 2002; Kellogg, Menard, & Santos, 2004; Thackeray, Hornor, Benziger, & Scribano, 2011). The mental health provider must have the relevant skills and knowledge to help the team interpret these behaviors as developmentally appropriate or concerning, given the child's age and cultural milieu. This may include use of tools such as the Child Sexual Behavior Inventory, developed by Dr. Friedrich and colleagues (Friedrich et al., 2001; Friedrich, Fisher, Broughton, Houston, & Shafran, 1998), as well as specific cultural knowledge and understanding of any disabilities the child may have.

Traditionally, mental health professionals have been asked to interpret not only concerning behaviors, but also the validity of disclosures or even lack of disclosure. In communities where the MDT does not utilize a dedicated, trained forensic interviewer, mental health providers may be asked to review interviews from various team members, traditionally LE and CPS, to determine credibility of the disclosures or reasons for lack of disclosure. Guidelines for conducting such an evaluation delineate special competencies required by the APA Ethics code, such as use of evidence-based knowledge, experience and training in cases of childabuse and declination of cases in which the provider has a preestablished therapeutic role with the child, suspect or family member which will threaten objectivity and impartiality (American Psychological Association, 2013; Herman, 2005). This presents particular challenges for many geographic areas, in particular rural areas with a shortage of mental health providers.

Finally, the mental health providers engaged in an MDT are uniquely poised to guide the team in securing mental health treatment for both the victim and non-offending family members. In this role the providers must be equally insistent on procuring evidence-based therapy whenever possible and when necessary, referring to medical providers for medication. In this sense mental health providers are responsible for both the efficacy and the timeliness of therapy in these cases. Trauma Focused Cognitive Behavioral Therapy has emerged as a promising evidence-based form of therapy for victims of childabuse who are suffering from symptoms of post-traumatic stress (Cohen et al., 2004, 2005). The mental health provider can educate MDT members, such as social workers and medical providers on how these symptoms may manifest in children, as well as adult family members. In the course of therapy more disclosures may occur and issues regarding validity of disclosure may become apparent to the therapist. This again underscores the necessity of avoiding crossover between the therapeutic role of treatment provider and the role of consultant regarding validity of disclosures.

Medical Providers

Caffey's, 1946 landmark article on long bone fractures and subdural hematomas in infants was the first published peer-reviewed article declaring the medical community's responsibility to recognize childabuse as a distinct medical disorder (Caffey, 1946). Kempe's 1962 article was the first to call for collaboration between medical providers and professionals in the community to ensure the proper care and safety of these young victims (Kempe et al., 1962). The presence and active participation of specialty trained child abuse clinicians provides both clinical and educational expertise to members of the MDT. Participants often include forensically trained nurses, both RNs and APNs, and pediatricians or emergency room physicians with training in child abuse and neglect. Each of these providers must comply with mandates from the state board governing his or her practice, such as the state medical board and the state nursing board. Above all else, they must adhere to their code of healthcare ethics in delivering compassionate and competent expert medical care to the child victim. Highly trained clinician members of the MDT ultimately deliver top quality forensically defensible healthcare.

There is a longstanding tradition of specialty trained sexual assault nurses performing evidence collection in adult cases. For many decades they have worked closely with law enforcement agencies. Nursing participation has grown rapidly in the field of child and adolescent sexual assault with the introduction of the SANE-P certification through the International Association of Forensic Nurses (IAFN).

The IAFN is the most well recognized and clinically advanced subspecialty accrediting body for forensic nurses, setting forth specific requirements for obtaining Sexual Assault Nurse Examiner certification for both adult and pediatric victims. Forensic nurses are now recognized as extremely valuable and technically competent in collecting forensic evidence and guiding initial care in acute cases of child and adolescent sexual assault (Bechtel, Ryan, & Gallagher, 2008; Hornor, Scribano, & Hayes, 2006; Hornor, Thackeray, Scribano, Curran, & Benzinger, 2012). Nurse practitioners, considered mid-level providers, can provide diagnoses and may be involved in more ongoing treatment of a child and referral to other medical or mental health specialists. As with all clinicians in this field, training must include a thorough understanding of court room proceedings and communication, as well as guidance in assessing current scientific literature.

The role of physicians in cases of childabuse and neglect is even more wide-ranging than that of their nursing colleagues. The American Board of Pediatrics, subspecialty board certification in Child Abuse and Neglect represents the most comprehensive medical child abuse certification available. It requires more than 2 years of additional subspecialty training above and beyond general pediatric residency training.

Pediatricians with subspecialty board certification in childabuse and neglect are uniquely poised to provide both education to their child abuse colleagues in other professions and clinical intervention for the child abuse victim. They must have a comprehensive understanding of the psychosocial dynamics of the family (Reece & Jenny, 2005), competency in identifying and documenting injuries or medical conditions related to child abuse or neglect and up to date knowledge of factors involved in transmission, treatment, and diagnosis of sexually transmitted infection. Child Abuse Pediatricians are required to have training in courtroom communication and experience with complex scientific testimony (Kaplan et al., 2011). Pediatricians are often called upon to educate law enforcement or CPS colleagues on normal child development and how this may reflect on the plausibility of a given injury mechanism for a child of a given age (Reece & Jenny, 2005).

Developmentally normal childsexual behaviors often raise questions in suspected cases of child sexual assault. Both the pediatric and mental health providers may be asked to interpret the developmental appropriateness of such behaviors (Friedrich et al., 1998, 2001; Kellogg, Committee on Child Abuse and Neglect, & American Academy of Pediatrics, 2009). In cases of child sexual abuse DNA evidence and physical evidence of injury are rare (Adams et al., 1994; Heger et al., 2002; Kellogg et al., 2004; Thackeray et al., 2011). The clinician will be asked to educate the judge or jury as to how a lack of physical evidence does *not* mean that the child was *not* assaulted. In children who do suffer injuries from inflicted sexual trauma, pediatricians may be asked to estimate the impacts of such injuries and the risk for future disability, as this will impact both social welfare decisions and decisions surrounding criminal charges.

One important current issue facing the medical providers in cases of childabuse and neglect is the impact of the Supreme Court decision in *Crawford v Washington* (2004). The precedent set by the decision in this case has challenged the medical provider's exception to hearsay in cases of child abuse and neglect. In the past, medical testimony regarding conversations with the patient in a therapeutic setting qualified for exception to hearsay. *Crawford v. Washington* challenged that exception, asserting that aside from excited utterance, testimony from medical providers in cases of child abuse and neglect may be considered testimonial unless the information was being gathered for the purposes of medical diagnosis and treatment. *Crawford v Washington* asserts that the medical provider places himself in a potentially investigatory role when asking detailed historical questions that stray beyond those necessary for medical diagnosis and treatment. In this sense, that history would become "testimonial" and would count as hearsay testimony against the defendant. Additionally, there is no current scientific evidence base to instruct child abuse professionals on how the medical history taking may impact the case if the medical history differs from the information obtained in the forensic interview. For these reasons, medical clinicians providing initial care and evaluation to potential victims of child abuse and neglect must conduct their history solely for the purposes of medical diagnosis and treatment. The clinician must document that historical details being gathered are meant to specifically guide diagnosis and treatment. Additional details will be obtained in investigatory and forensic interviews. The active participation of the medical provider in the MDT will ensure that he or she receives access to more extensive information surrounding the case as it becomes available.

Assessing Effectives and Developing Best Practices

Despite the now accepted MDT model as the standard for handling suspected cases of childabuse and neglect, the evidence base for effectiveness and best practices in implementation remains incomplete. One of the barriers to adequate research is what Reece calls the "patchwork quilt of services" developed to address the needs of agencies and communities in child protection cases (Reece & Jenny, 2005). The variations in MDT implementation, composition, provision of services and measures of accountability remain enormous. Some teams are very well-coordinated, with routine case review, a physical location that allows daily contact between members and easy access to medical and mental health services. In other communities, the collaboration is less formal and contains no structured method for quality assurance. Without consistent, universally accepted definitions and standardized approaches, outcomes are difficult to measure and high quality, prospective research is difficult to perform. Interestingly, this is the same issue that impedes large-scale meaningful studies in other areas of Child Abuse and Neglect.

The relevant research available to date indicates preliminary success in attaining a few important goals. An MDT can assist in the avoidance of repetitive child victim interviews (Jaudes & Martone, 1992; Jones et al., 2005) and thereby reduction in stress for the child, as well as reduction in the risk for inaccurate recall or false memories (Bruck et al., 1998). Improvement in case outcomes may include higher substantiation rates and higher rates of successful prosecution (Faller & Henry, 2000;

Jaudes & Martone, 1992; Tjaden & Anhalt, 1994). A functional team allows for better collaboration between agencies to avoid interference in case investigation (Hammond, Lanning, Promisel, Shepherd, & Walsh, 2001; Pence & Wilson, 1994). Complete and timely access to services for the victim and family can also be facilitated by the MDT approach (Walsh, Jones, & Cross, 2003). Identified areas of continued weakness in multidisciplinary team functioning may include cross agency case tracking (Sedlak et al., 2006) and access to mental health services. Two studies (Lalayant et al., 2011; Lashley, 2002) have looked at the approach to implementation of MDT's and identified common themes to healthy functioning. Elements such as communication in day-to-day tasks outside the MDT meetings and a thorough understanding of the roles and cultures of collaborating agencies can be attained through the commitment of the individuals participating in the team. Other factors such as adequate resources and structural supports depend on the systems in which the agencies function and may be harder to achieve. It is exactly this type of barrier to implementation of desirable MDT quality indicators that makes it so difficult to study outcomes. Ultimately, a well-functioning MDT needs to support members of the team in fulfilling their individual professional mandates while contributing to the future health and safety of the victim and other vulnerable populations within the community.

Two of the most controversial areas surrounding the forensic interview of the child include identifying which professionals should interview the child and what the optimal timing is for the interview. Can the medical exam take place before the interview? What happens to the accuracy and validity of the subsequent forensic interview when CPS or LE has already conducted minimal facts interviews to determine the safety and disposition of the child?[1] Unfortunately, there is no good evidence base to answer either of these questions. They remain a source of much debate on many multidisciplinary teams. It is generally accepted that interviewers should be trained in a protocol for forensic interviewing, but there is little consensus and no good evidence base for which protocol(s) is most valid and effective. It is generally accepted that the interview should be conducted in a neutral, child-friendly facility and as soon as possible, but there is no evidence base to indicate exactly how the time frame will affect accuracy and validity of the interview. As soon as the child discloses, he or she begins to see the consequences of that disclosure. How does this influence the accuracy and validity of the forensic interview? The vast majority of child sexualabuse cases involve a delayed disclosure, obviating the need for emergent medical examination and forensic evidence collection. In these cases, the forensic interview should be scheduled prior to the exam. If DNA or injury evidence needs to be obtained, or if there is a suspected medical condition that needs treatment, the medical exam can precede the forensic interview. In these cases the clinician will be especially rigorous in obtaining his or her history for the purposes

[1] Minimal facts interviews are often conducted by LE or CPS when they need information to determine the placement of the child, the safety of the child and the potential need for forensic evidence collection. These often have to take place at the scene or prior to the scheduled forensic interview.

of medical diagnosis and treatment only. As is the case with minimal facts interviews, there is no good evidence base to inform our practice as to the influence of the medical history taking on the subsequent forensic interview.

Fortunately, the rising popularity of Child Advocacy Centers (CACs) as the child-friendly centralized location for MDTs and the services they provide (Walsh et al., 2003) has the potential to create a forum for standardizing approaches to collaborative child-centered care and core outcome measures in cases of suspected child abuse. Data from the National Children's Alliance indicates that 286,457 children were served through CAC in 2012 (National Children's Advocacy Center [NCA], 2014a). The NCA delineates ten core components for accreditation (NCA, 2014b). Although many CACs function without accreditation, these core components serve as a common frame around which communities can build their programs. The single MDTforensic interview in a child-friendly setting is one of these core components. The research is not yet clear on whether or not CACs are consistently effective at achieving this goal (Cross et al., 2008). Preliminary research seems to indicate that suspected child abuse cases handled in a CAC setting more often include collaboration with law enforcement (Cross et al., 2008; Smith, Witte, & Fricker-Elhai, 2006) and are more likely to receive medical examinations and mental health referrals (Cross et al., 2008; Smith et al., 2006; Walsh, Cross, Jones, Simone, & Kolko, 2007). These CAC cases may also lead to higher rates of substantiation and more frequent referral for prosecution (Smith et al., 2006; Wolfteich & Loggins, 2007; Miller & Rubin 2009). There is a clear trend among researchers in the field toward larger scale studies to examine the efficacy of the MDT model within the CAC setting in order to guide more concrete best practice guidelines for the future.

Acknowledgements I would like to acknowledge the late Rich Kaplan, MSW, MD in the writing of this chapter. May his role as an educational pioneer, collaborator extraordinaire and selfless mentor continue on in those who were fortunate enough to learn from him.

References

Adams, J. A., Harper, K., Knudson, S., & Revilla, J. (1994). Examination findings in legally confirmed child sexual abuse. It's normal to be normal. *Pediatrics, 94*, 310–317.

American Humane Association. (2013). *Mary Ellen Wilson: How one girl's plight started the child-protection movement.*

American Psychological Association. (2013). Guidelines for psychological evaluations in child protection matters. *American Psychologist, 68*(1), 20–31.

Anderson, L. E., Weston, E. A., Doueck, H. J., & Krause, D. J. (2002). The child-centered social worker and the sexually abused child: Pathway to healing. *Social Work, 47*(4), 368–378.

Bechtel, K., Ryan, E., & Gallagher, D. (2008). Impact of sexual assault nurse examiners on the evaluation of sexual assault in a pediatric emergency department. *Pediatric Emergency Care, 24*(7), 442–447.

Bruck, M., Ceci, S. J., & Hembrooke, H. (1998). Reliability and credibility of young children's reports: From research to policy and practice. *American Psychologist, 53*(2), 136–151.

Caffey, J. (1946). Multiple fractures in long bones of infants suffering from chronic subdural hematoma. *American Journal of Roentography, 56*, 164–173.

Campbell, R. (2006). Rape survivors' experiences with the legal and medical systems: Do rape victim advocates make a difference? *Violence Against Women, 12*(1), 30–45.

Center for the Study of Social Policy. (2000). *An assessment of the transfer of responsibility for the child abuse and neglect hotline and for investigation of abuse to the Arkansas state police.* Washington, DC: Center for the Study of Social Policy.

Child Welfare Information Gateway. (2013). *Cross-reporting among responders to child abuse and neglect.* U.S. Department of Health and Human Services/Children's Bureau. Retrieved from http://www.childwelfare.gov.

Clark, K., Biddle, A., & Martin, S. (2002). A cost-benefit analysis of the violence against women act of 1994. *Violence Against Women, 4*(8), 417–428.

Cohen, J., Deblinger, E., Mannarino, A., & Steer, R. (2004). A multi-site, randomized controlled trial for children with abuse-related PTSD symptoms. *Journal of the American Academy of Child and Adolescent Psychiatry, 43*(4), 393–402.

Cohen, J., Mannarino, A., & Knudsen, K. (2005). Treating sexually abused children: 1 year follow-up of a randomized controlled trial. *Child Abuse & Neglect, 29*, 135–145.

Crawford v. Washington, 541 US 36(2004).

Cross, T., Finkelhor, D., & Ormrod, R. (2005). Police involvement in Child Protective Services investigations: Literature review and secondary data analysis. *Child Maltreatment, 10*(3), 224–244.

Cross, T., Jones, L., Walsh, W., Simone M., Kolko, D., Cryns, A., …Magnuson, S. (2008) Evaluating Children's Advocacy Centers response to child sexual abuse. *OJJDP Juvenile Justice Bulletin.* Retrieved from https://www.ncjrs.gov/pdffiles1/ojjdp/218530.pdf.

Cross, T., Walsh, W., Simone, M., & Jones, L. (2003). Prosecution of child abuse: A meta-analysis of rates of criminal justice decisions. *Trauma Violence, 4*, 323–340.

Faller, K. C., & Henry, J. (2000). Child sexual abuse: A case study in community collaboration. *Child Abuse & Neglect, 24*(9), 1215–1225.

Fontana, V., & Robison, E. A. (1976). Multidisciplinary approach to the treatment of child abuse. *Pediatrics, 57*, 760.

Friedrich, W. N., Fisher, J. L., Broughton, D., Houston, M., & Shafran, C. (1998). Normative sexual behavior in children: A contemporary sample. *Pediatrics, 101*(4), 1–10. doi:10.1542/peds.101.4.e9.

Friedrich, W. N., Fisher, J. L., Dittner, C. A., Acton, R., Berliner, L., Butler J.,…Wright, J. (2001). Child Sexual Behavior Inventory: normative, psychiatric and sexual abuse comparisons. *Child Maltreat, 6(1)*, 37–39.

Hammond, C. B., Lanning, K. V., Promisel, W., Shepherd, J. R., & Walsh, B. (2001).*Law enforcement response to child abuse series: Portable guide.* Retrieved March 31, 2004, from http://www.ncjrs.org/txtfiles/162425.txt.

Heger, A., Ticson, L., Velasquez, O., & Bernier, R. (2002). Children referred for possible sexual abuse: Medical findings in 2384 children. *Child Abuse & Neglect, 26*, 645–659.

Herman, S. (2005). Improving decision making in forensic child sexual abuse evaluations. *Law and Human Behavior, 29*(1), 87–120.

Hochstadt, N. J., & Harwicke, N. J. (1985). How effective is the multidisciplinary approach? A follow-up study. *Child Abuse & Neglect, 9*, 365–372.

Hornor, G., Scribano, P., & Hayes, J. (2006). Child sexual assault findings: A knowledge assessment of sexual assault nurse examiners. *American Journal of Nurse Practitioners, 10*, 10–20.

Hornor, G., Thackeray, J., Scribano, P., Curran, S., & Benzinger, E. (2012). Pediatric sexual assault nurse examiner care: Trace forensic evidence, ano-genital injury, and judicial outcomes. *Journal of Forensic Nursing, 8*(3), 105–111.

Jaudes, P. K., & Martone, M. (1992). Interdisciplinary evaluations of alleged sexual abuse cases. *Pediatrics, 89*(6), 1164–1168.

Jones, L., Cross, T., Walsh, W., & Simone, M. (2005). Criminal investigations of child abuse. The research behind "Best Practices". *Trauma, Violence & Abuse, 6*(3), 254–268.

Jordan, N., Yampolskaya, S., Gustafson, M., & Armstrong, M. (2011). Comparing child protective investigation performance between law enforcement agencies and child welfare agencies. *Child Welfare, 90*(2).

Kaplan, R., Adams, J., Starling, S., & Giardino, A. (2011). *A medical response to child sexual abuse; a resource for professionals working with children and families*. St. Louis, MO: STM Learning.

Kellogg, N. D., Committee on Child Abuse and Neglect, & American Academy of Pediatrics. (2009). Clinical report—The evaluation of sexual behaviors in children. *Pediatrics, 124*(3), 992–998.

Kellogg, N. D., Menard, S. W., & Santos, A. (2004). Genital anatomy in pregnant adolescents: "normal" does not mean "nothing happened". *Pediatrics, 113*(1 Pt 1), 67–69.

Kempe, C. H., Silverman, F., Steele, B., Droegemueller, W., & Silver, H. (1962). The battered child syndrome. *Journal of the American Medical Association, 181*, 17–24.

Kinnevy, S., Huang, V., Dichter, M., & Gelles, R. (2003). *Evaluation of the transfer of responsibility for child protective investigations to Law enforcement in Florida: An analysis of manatee, Pasco, and Pinellas counties 1990–2003*. Philadelphia, PA: Center for Research on Youth and Social Policy\University of Pennsylvania.

Kinnevy, S., Huang, V., Dichter, M., & Gelles, R. (2005). *The Transfer of Responsibility for Child Protective Investigations to Law Enforcement in Florida: Supplemental Study. Final Report.* NCJ 210489, Philadelphia, PA: Center for Research on Youth and Social Policy\University of Pennsylvania.

Lalayant, M., Epstein, I., & Adamy, D. (2011). Multidisciplinary consultation in child protection: A clinical data-mining evaluation. *International Journal of Social Work, 20*, 156–166.

Lashley J. (2002). Multidisciplinary review and team facilitator handbook. Children's Advocacy centers of Georgia, Retrieved from www.cacga.org.

Long, J., Willkinson, J., & Kays, J. (2011). Ten strategies for prosecuting child sexual abuse at the hands of a family member. *Strategies: The Prosecutor's Newsletter on Violence Against Women, 5*, 1–8.

Micheel, L., (2011). *Multidisciplinary teams*, Washington Coalition of Sexual Assault Programs. Retrieved from http://www.wcsap.org/sites/wcsap.huang.radicaldesigns.org/files/uploads/documents/MDT2011.pdf

Miller, A., & Rubin, D. (2009). The contribution of children's advocacy centers to felony prosecutions to felony prosecutions of child sexual abuse. *Child Abuse & Neglect, 1*(33), 12–18.

National Children's Advocacy Center. (2014a). Retrieved from http://www.nationalcac.org/history/history.html.

National Children's Alliance. (2014b). Retrieved from http://www.nationalchildrensalliance.org/cacstatistics.

Newman, B. S., Dannenfelser, P. L., & Pendleton, D. (2005). Child abuse investigations: Reasons for using Child Advocacy Centers and suggestions for improvement. *Child and Adolescent Social Work Journal, 22*, 165–181.

Pence, D. M., & Wilson, C. A. (1994). Reporting and investigating child sexual abuse. *Future of Children, 4*(2), 70–83.

Portwood, S., Grady, M., & Dutton, S. (2000). Enhancing law enforcement identification and investigation of child maltreatment. *Child Abuse & Neglect, 24*(2), 195–207.

Reece, R., & Jenny, C. (2005). Medical training in child maltreatment. *American Journal of Preventive Medicine, 29*(582), 266–271.

Sedlak, A., Schultz, D., Wells, S., Lyons, P., Doueck, H., & Gragg, F. (2006). Child protection and justice systems processing of serious child abuse and neglect cases. *Child Abuse & Neglect, 30*, 657–677.

Smith, D. W., Witte, T. H., & Fricker-Elhai, A. E. (2006). Service outcomes in physical and sexual abuse cases: A comparison of child advocacy center-based and standard services. *Child Maltreatment, 11*(4), 354–360.

Thackeray, J., Hornor, G., Benziger, E., & Scribano, P. (2011). Forensic evidence collection and DNA identification in acute child sexual assault. *Pediatrics, 28*(2), 227–232.

Tjaden, P. G., & Anhalt, J. (1994). *The impact of joint law enforcement-child protective services investigations in child maltreatment cases.* Denver, CO: Center of Policy Research.

U.S. Department of Health and Human Services; Administration for Children and Families; Administration on Children, Youth, and Families; Children's Bureau. (2001). *Child abuse and neglect state statute series: Reporting laws—Cross-reporting among systems.* Washington, DC: National Clearinghouse on Child Abuse and Neglect Information. Retrieved from http://aspe.hhs.gov/hsp/cps-status03/state-policy03/index.htm.

U.S. Department of Justice, Office of Juvenile Justice and Delinquency Prevention. (2000). *Forming a multidisciplinary team to investigate child abuse* by Mark Ells. Retrieved from https://www.ncjrs.gov/pdffiles1/ojjdp/170020.pdf. doi: 10.13140/2.1.2809.4400. OJJDP

Violence Against Women's Act. Title IV, sec. 40001–40703 of the Violent Crime Control and Law Enforcement Act of 1994, H.R. 3355.

Walsh, W., Cross, T., Jones, L., Simone, M., & Kolko, D. (2007). Which sexual abuse victims receive a forensic medical examination? The impact of children's advocacy centers. *Child Abuse & Neglect, 31*, 1053–1068.

Walsh, W., Jones, L., & Cross, T. (2003). Children's advocacy centers: One model, many programs. *APSAC Advisor, 16*(2).

Watkins, S. A. (1990). The Mary Ellen myth: Correcting child welfare history. *Social Work, 35*(6), 500–503.

Wolfteich, P., & Loggins, B. (2007). Evaluation of the children's advocacy center model: Efficiency, legal and revictimization outcomes. *Child and Adolescent Social Work Journal, 24*(4), 333–352.

Chapter 4
Forensic Interviewing and Charging: A Prosecutor's Perspective

Mark Krueger

A report of child sexual abuse may occur at any time and may be made in a variety of ways. A child may report sexual abuse at the time of the abuse, shortly following the abuse, days, weeks, months, or even years later. Or, the child may never report the abuse. When a child delays in reporting sexual abuse, it is referred to as "delayed reporting." If a child reports sexual abuse, the report may be made in a variety of ways and under nearly any circumstance imaginable. The report could be spontaneous, blurted out, reasoned, made in response to a question, totally unrelated to an incident or conversation, or simply as a result of a stimuli or trigger. It can be made orally, in writing, by way of a drawing, or through action. There is simply no gauge or label that can be placed upon the manner, time, place, or event in which a report is made.

All reports of child sexual abuse, whether immediate or delayed, should be treated by law enforcement, social workers, persons conducting a forensic interview with the child, and all persons who interact with the child, as the report being a truthful report. The function of the forensic interview is to objectively gather evidence in the forms of statements by the victim, to arrange a forensic examination if appropriate to determine the existence or absence of any physical evidence, and to provide information to the victim about treatment programs and funding sources for victims of violent crimes. Available treatment programs include counseling which is often available and beneficial to the child and immediate household members or relatives.

The person conducting a forensic interview should remain neutral and unbiased throughout the interview and investigation. The person conducting the forensic interview should not judge the child or reporting party or make any conclusions or inferences simply because a child has reported sexual abuse. The report of child sexual abuse is a serious matter for everyone involved, the child, the perpetrator, household members, relatives, friends, volunteers, the community, law enforce-

M. Krueger (✉)
Former Assistant District Attorney, Carson City District Attorney's Office and Lyon County District Attorney's Office, 2329 Kingsview Way, Carson City, NV 89703, USA
e-mail: mkrueger.esq@gmail.com

W.T. O'Donohue, M. Fanetti (eds.), *Forensic Interviews Regarding Child Sexual Abuse*, DOI 10.1007/978-3-319-21097-1_4

ment, social services, medical providers, counselors, schools, etc. Accordingly, every report of child sexual abuse should be handled and investigated seriously, even if it turns out the report is a false report.

Often times the person conducting a forensic interview of the child reporting sexual abuse is not the initial responder in the case. It is important that only persons trained in forensic interviewing in cases of child sexual abuse actually conduct an interview with the child or children who report sexual abuse. In most instances, persons trained in forensic interviewing of children reporting child sexual abuse are local investigating law enforcement officers, usually detectives. However, some social services case workers, nurses, or other specialists are trained in forensic interviewing of children reporting child sexual abuse. It is recommended that local agencies work with law enforcement to develop a plan, education, and training, to establish and coordinate who or which agency will be responsible for conducting the forensic interview when there is a report of child sexual abuse.

Irrespective of who conducts the forensic interview, it is very important that the person conducting a forensic interview remains objective in gathering information and evidence about the report of child sexual abuse. Interviewers, especially law enforcement, that do not approach the cases objectively, will undermine their own investigation and ultimately circumvent the search for the truth about what, if anything, happened. In addition, persons who conduct forensic interviews who do not remain objective lose credibility when testifying; not only for the current case but also for all other cases they investigate.

Crimes of sexual abuse against a child are generally referred to as crimes of secrecy. What this means is that sexual abuse against children are generally committed by a perpetrator when there are no witnesses to see the abuse. This does not mean that persons who could potentially be persons who could potentially be witnesses are not in the immediate vicinity where the abuse occurred. Often, the abuse occurs any time the perpetrator gets an opportunity; for example, a stepfather lies down with a stepdaughter for purposes of putting the child to bed and takes that opportunity to commit sexual abuse against the stepdaughter while in the bed. The mother of the child may be only a few feet away in the very next room. As will be explored later, it is a misnomer to think that a child will respond by calling for help or even voicing an objection when the sexual abuse occurs even if the help is nearby, such as in the next room.

The fact that a crime of sexual abuse occurs in secret is the reason why it is critical that the forensic interview and law enforcement's investigation are conducted in a manner that collects the most reliable evidence. At the conclusion of a trial, but before closing arguments, a jury is read specific instructions about the law they must apply in the case. One of the legal instructions in a child sexual abuse case informs the jury that they may convict the defendant based solely on the testimony of the victim alone. In short, that means that if the jury believes the child victim's testimony that the sexual abuse occurred by the defendant, the jury can find the defendant guilty of child sexual abuse without considering any other evidence. As will be discussed later in this chapter and throughout this book, in the majority of cases of sexual abuse against a child, the only evidence of sexual abuse is the statements by the victim describing the abuse that occurred.

In this chapter, we will explore the prosecutor's role in making charging decisions in cases of child sexual abuse. We will discuss the importance of the forensic interview in investigating reports of child sexual abuse, and law enforcement's investigation for purposes of a prosecutor's charging decision. We will also examine charging considerations, and issues concerning the prosecution of a case through a jury trial.

Charging Decision

Prosecutors take an oath to uphold the Constitution and laws of the USA as well as the laws of the State and jurisdiction in which they prosecute. The American Bar Association has promulgated standards by which a prosecutor should adhere to in conducting the prosecutorial function. Those standards include:

Standard 3- 1.1 The Function of the Standards

These standards are intended to be used as a guide to professional conduct and performance. They are not intended to be used as criteria for the judicial evaluation of alleged misconduct of the prosecutor to determine the validity of a conviction. They may or may not be relevant in such judicial evaluation, depending upon all the circumstances.

Standard 3- 1.2 The Function of the Prosecutor

(a) The office of prosecutor is charged with responsibility for prosecutions in its jurisdiction.
(b) The prosecutor is an administrator of justice, an advocate, and an officer of the court; the prosecutor must exercise sound discretion in the performance of his or her functions.
(c) ***The duty of the prosecutor is to seek justice, not merely to convict.***
(d) It is an important function of the prosecutor to seek to reform and improve the administration of criminal justice. When inadequacies or injustices in the substantive or procedural law come to the prosecutor's attention, he or she should stimulate efforts for remedial action.
(e) It is the duty of the prosecutor to know and be guided by the standards of professional conduct as defined by applicable professional traditions, ethical codes, and law in the prosecutor's jurisdiction....

ABA Standards for Criminal Justice: Prosecution and Defense Function, 3d ed., ©1993 American Bar Association, emphasis added. In short, a prosecutor has a duty to seek justice. As will be examined more fully, that duty begins at the time the prosecutor reviews a report of investigation of allegations of child sexual abuse.

A prosecutor generally relies on various agencies, usually law enforcement agencies, to investigate cases. A prosecutor generally becomes involved at the time the prosecutor receives a report of investigation from a law enforcement agency. It is important to note that on occasion, a law enforcement official may seek legal guidance or assistance from the prosecutor on a case they are investigating to ensure they are following lawful procedures and protecting the rights of all the parties involved. An example of this is when a law enforcement officer contacts a prosecutor for assistance in obtaining a search warrant during the investigation of a case. That interaction may, and often does, occur before the prosecutor receives the full report of investigation from law enforcement.

When a prosecutor receives a report of investigation, a prosecutor begins with a review of the report, including supporting materials which may be in the form of recordings, photographs, statements, admissions, test results, etc. In reports of investigation containing allegations of child sexual abuse, a prosecutor in most instances, will likely have very little additional evidence supporting the allegations that a child sexual abuse has occurred other than the statements of the victim. It cannot be stressed enough that during the process of reviewing the report, a prosecutor must remember and adhere to the ABA standard: the prosecutor has a duty to seek justice.

That duty has a heavy emotional burden for the prosecutor. On one hand, child sexual abuse is a horrific crime and justice and the law dictate that the victim must be protected and the perpetrator be held accountable. On the other hand, filing charges that accuse an innocent person of the crime of child sexual abuse can have a lasting impact on a person which can affect that person's ability to live life peacefully in the pursuit of happiness without peer scrutiny and societal deprivation or scorn.

An overzealous prosecutor may be inclined to file charges immediately. An overly cautious prosecutor may be reluctant to file charges at all, or may delay in filing charges. In many instances, before making a decision to charge a crime, prosecutors will request that additional investigation, generally referred to as "follow-up" be conducted by law enforcement. The follow-up may include a request that law enforcement conduct additional interviews with witnesses or the victim, gather addition evidence, or obtain and provide the results of testing or examinations. The prosecutor may even discuss the case with experts, such as medical doctors, nurses, or other forensic experts, for opinions regarding the evidence in the case. However, at some point, the prosecutor must make a decision to either charge a crime of child sexual abuse, a different crime, or decline to charge any crime at all.

Forensic Investigation

A person who interviews a child that reports sexual abuse should be trained in the proper method of conducting a forensic interview before attempting to interview a child victim, or any victim, of sexual abuse. There is a vast body of literature and trainings on what is considered to be the appropriate technique for conducting forensic interviews of children that report sexual abuse. The techniques for conducting forensic interviews of children reporting sexual abuse used in the past are different from those used today, so it is important that persons conducting these interviews have current training.

The shift in the way forensic interviews of children are conducted today take into account skepticism, case law, criticism, challenges, and developments that professionals and persons conducting forensic interviews of children have encountered throughout time in interviewing and investigating reports of child sexual abuse. However, the goal of a forensic interview has remained the same: to objectively obtain factual statements from the child victim about the sexual abuse that occurred. Objective factual statements are unbiased and strive to be in the words of the child victim without fear, anticipation of reward, coaching or suggestibility. Today, experts generally agree that persons conducting forensic interviews of child victims of sexual abuse, referred to as forensic interviewers, should use a phased interview approach.

Forensic Phased Interview

In simple terms, a phased interview approach is an interview that is broken into several phases the forensic interviewer moves through in conducting the forensic interview with the child victim. There are multiple resources that address the number and types of phases that are recommended to be used for forensic interviewing of children, but there is no consistency in exactly which of these phased interview approaches is the best or most reliable one to use. Perhaps this is because the phases by themselves must be utilized on a case-by-case basis, most often depending on the development of the child and the facts in the case. As the interviewer moves through the interview with the child victim, certain phases may be skipped, addressed quickly, addressed out of order, or may take additional time.

Prior to beginning a forensic interview using a phased interview approach, the forensic interviewer should address certain pre-interview considerations. As is the case with the varying opinions as to the phases of the forensic interview itself, there are multiple resources that address pre-interview considerations. However, generally children that report being victims of sexual abuse fall into approximately four categories to be considered. The importance of understanding these categories provides guidance for the considerations and decisions an interviewer must make prior to conducting the forensic interview and during the forensic interview itself. We will discuss these categories and several of these considerations keeping in mind that this is simply a general discussion and not an exhaustive list of considerations.

The first category is children of approximately 1–2½ years of age. Most experts agree that children at this age are too young to be interviewed. While it is highly unlikely a forensic interview would elicit any statements from children of this age, experts generally agree that a child of this age would not be competent to testify. Moreover, most prosecutors or judges would not allow a child of this age to testify in any court proceeding. Accordingly, it is recommended that a forensic interviewer not attempt to interview a child in this category unless the development of the child is such that the child fits more properly into a different category.

The second category is children of approximately 2½–7 years of age. In this category, children can generally describe concepts of whom, what, and where. However, they have difficulty describing concepts of time or the ability to describe past tense events. This is particularly important to understanding how a child in this category may, during the interview, be able to describe the sexual acts themselves but have difficulty describing how many times the acts occurred or even how much time passed between the occurrence of multiple acts. Sex is a learned behavior. The child in this category would not likely have knowledge of sexual acts unless they occurred. Moreover, the reliability of the child's report increases if the child relates details about the acts that are perpetrated upon them, the child describes who perpetrated those acts upon them, and relates generally where the acts occurred.

The third category is children of approximately 7–10 years of age. Generally, children in this age group have begun learning sexual concepts and terms from various sources, often times in a school environment. They may have also begun sexual exploration or had discussions with parents, family members, friends, counselors, nurses, or doctors about sex. Some female children may also have begun menstruation and may have had discussions about their menstrual period and sex in general. This information does not decrease the reliability or accuracy of the child's report, but must be considered in light of the details contained in and surrounding the child's report. In short, the fact that a child has knowledge of or discussed sex and sexual behavior does not by itself tend to support or abrogate the accuracy of the child's report of sexual abuse in this category. However, it is important that the forensic interviewer obtains information about who perpetrated the abuse, where it occurred, what abuse occurred, and the time frames in which the abuse occurred.

The fourth category is children of approximately over 10 years of age to adulthood, otherwise known in simple terms as teenagers. In this category, sex has generally been discussed or learned through education, and even consensual acts. As in category three, the information the child has about sexual acts or sexual behavior does not decrease the reliability or accuracy of the child's report, but must be considered in light of the details contained in and surrounding the child's report. Lying is also a learned behavior and it is critical that the forensic interviewer recognizes that there may be additional motive to fabricate, but continue to treat the report as truthful. Again, it is important that the forensic interviewer obtains information about who perpetrated the abuse, where it occurred, what abuse occurred, and the time frames in which the abuse occurred.

The following represents a general list of the phases of a phased interview approach. It is important to remember that expert opinions vary as to the title, topic, and purpose of each phase. Some experts consolidate the purpose of the phases, or change the title of the phases. Some experts opine that the order of the phases should vary. However, as a general guideline, the phases of a forensic interview of a child reporting sexual abuse are as follows:

- Phase 1—Preparing the interview
- Phase 2—Introduction and developing rapport
- Phase 3—Establishing legal competency

- Phase 4—Establishing an interview structure
- Phase 5—Introducing the topic and information gathering
- Phase 6—Questioning and clarification
- Phase 7—Closing the interview

Each phase will be briefly addressed keeping in mind that this discussion does not include an exhaustive list of suggestions and prohibitions for each phase. However, it is intended to provide a general understanding of each phase of the interview taking into account a few considerations for the interviewer while conducting the phased interview. Again, as the interviewer moves through the interview with the child victim, certain phases may be skipped, addressed quickly, addressed out of order, or may take additional time. An example of this is where a child may skip prior phases and move right into phase 5, information gathering. In this case, the forensic interviewer will want to complete phase 5, and perhaps phase 6, questioning and clarifying, before moving back to phase 3, establishing legal competency.

It is also recommended and important that forensic interviewers attend and successfully complete current law enforcement recognized and approved forensic interview training or trainings in order to fully understand and apply each phase of the interview before attempting to conduct a forensic interview of a child who reports being a victim of sexual abuse.

Phase 1: Preparing the Interview

Many advocates adhere to the outdated philosophy that a child should have an attendant during a forensic interview. It is recommended that forensic interviews be conducted with one forensic interviewer with the child and without the presence of any other person. It should be noted that generally advocate groups become politically charged about being excluded from the interview. It is recommended that advocates be placed in an adjoining or nearby room to observe the interview through a one-way mirror or via live video. The forensic interview should be recorded, both audio and video if available. If there is no ability to record the interview, a second interviewer should be present simply as a witness but should not be involved in the interview in any way other than to witness and document the interview.

The room should be simple and friendly. There should be no distractions, toys, stuffed animals, food, or like objects. There should be a simple desk and comfortable chairs. Objects that may be used in the forensic interview should be stored in the room with easy access by the interviewer. The objects should not include anatomical dolls, which are not recognized as reliable and can be suggestive. Anatomic drawings may be necessary to be used on a case-by-case basis as will be discussed. The interviewer should not place the desk between the interviewer and the child, but should be comfortably arranged to facilitate discussion by the child. The interviewer should turn off all cell phones and other electronic equipment and ensure any weapons are not visible.

A therapy animal, usually a dog, also known as a service or courthouse dog, may be used depending on the laws and policy of the jurisdiction and if the child requests the animal after being offered the use of the animal. This prosecutor encourages the use of therapy dogs in interviews. Therapy dogs have been proven to provide a sense of comfort and friendliness to victims of any crime and assist the child in stating and describing the factual events about the sexual abuse. While therapy dogs are becoming more and more accepted in forensic interviews of child victims and during courtroom proceedings, their use, and legal concerns regarding their use in the courtroom, are still being vetted through the court systems in the United States.

It is important in this phase of the interview that the interviewer gathers as much information about the child from family and sources surrounding the report. The amount of time that should be dedicated to this task will vary on a case-by-case basis. Safety of the child and addressing any medical concerns is of paramount importance before any interviewing occurs. An interviewer should carefully evaluate the appropriate time and place in which to conduct a forensic interview on a case-by-case basis. Background information gathered should include, but is not limited to, information about the child such as age, date of birth, nicknames, developmental progress or delays, medical conditions, languages spoken, pets, the child's behaviors, the child's description of body parts if known, prior disclosures if any, family composition, household members, family dynamics, relatives, friends of the child, friends of the household members, household domestic violence, household drug use, household pornography, and possible motivations for false allegations.

Finally, it is important to remember that the overall length of an interview will vary depending on the category, development of the child, facts of each case, and the interview itself. However, as a general rule, children can become emotionally exhausted and wary during an interview and therefore it may be necessary to take breaks or schedule additional interviews. As a word of caution, too many interviews with a child can cause legal concerns for the prosecution and appeal of any conviction in a case.

Phase 2: Introduction and Developing Rapport

During the interview, the interviewer should be respectful of the child at any age, use simple terms, ask open-ended questions, and avoid legal, technical, or investigatory jargon. The interviewer should refrain from showing emotional reactions, making physical contact with the child, or making any promises to the child. The interviewer should not make negative statements about anyone. The interviewer should not make suggestive statements or statements that encourage or coach responses from the child. The interviewer should not reward the child or reinforce responses. The interviewer should refrain from asking "why" questions and should avoid excessively correcting the child. And perhaps one of the most difficult tasks to learn, the interviewer must exercise patience and refrain from interrupting a child. The interviewer should allow the child to answer open-ended questions.

During this phase of the interview, the interviewer should begin by introducing themselves and their job in a neutral manner. The interviewer should begin developing rapport with the child. Too often, interviewers spend entirely too much time developing rapport. The amount of time necessary to adequately develop rapport will vary with every case, every child, every interviewer, and every interview. The interviewer should ask open-ended questions that elicit responses that are generally comfortable for the child to speak about. For example, asking about pets, family, teachers, and school classes. During these questions, the interviewer must constantly assess the child's developmental level, ascertaining whether or not the child understands the interviewer's questions and is providing appropriate responses.

Phase 3: Establishing Legal Competency

In many cases the transition from one phase of the interview to the next will present itself naturally. However, in some cases, it may be necessary for the interviewer to force the transition from one phase to the next. While assessing the child's developmental level the interviewer will typically determine when to transition to establishing competency. Legal competency is generally a child's ability to "receive just impressions and articulate the difference between a truth and a lie." In layman's terms, the interviewer should be satisfied that the child understands questions, conduct, and consequences, and is able to discern and describe the difference between a truth and a lie.

There are many ways to accomplish this objective and it is recommended that an interviewer uses a variety of tasks depending on the age and developmental level of the child. For example, in interviewing a child from category two, the interviewer may hold up a blue piece of paper and ask the child what color the paper is. The interviewer may then ask "if I said the paper was yellow, would that be a truth or a lie?" Colors are generally learned early and therefore are a good reference; however, the interviewer should be cautious about using red or green in the event the child is colorblind.

In this phase, the interviewer can also ascertain information from the child that will assist the interviewer in later phases. For example, for a prosecutor to make certain charging decisions, it is necessary for the prosecutor to know whether or not there was actual penetration during the sexual abuse. It is therefore recommended that an interviewer takes the opportunity during this phase to covertly determine the child's understanding and description of penetration. This task is easily accomplished using a tissue box or envelope. For example, using a tissue box, the interviewer simply asks the child to place their hand on top of the tissue box, under the tissue box, and inside the tissue box. Nothing more is asked. The result confirms the child has the ability to receive just impressions and relate the information by action. Moreover, the child has just demonstrated that the child understands what it means to have something inside and therefore if the child later describes penetration that occurred during the sexual abuse, the interviewer already knows that child understands and is accurately describing penetration.

Phase 4: Establishing an Interview Structure

In this phase, the interviewer must establish certain ground rules that empower the child to be able to inform the interviewer they do not understand a question or may correct the interviewer. As previously stated, the goal of the forensic interview is to objectively obtain factual statements from the child victim about the sexual abuse that occurred. Objective factual statements are unbiased and strive to be in the words of the child victim without fear, anticipation of reward, coaching or suggestibility. Therefore it is important that the child not only understand but also accept that the child may not know an answer, may not understand a question, or may simply not remember a fact. Accordingly, it is recommended that the interviewer encourages the child to be truthful, not guess, and inform the interviewer if they do not understand a question.

Phase 5: Introducing the Topic and Information Gathering

Even the most trained professionals have difficulty introducing the topics of sexual abuse and transitioning to gathering information about the specific details about the abuse from the child. It is recommended that the forensic interviewer introduces the topic gently by prompting the child in a neutral manner. An example is as simple as asking the child to tell the interviewer why the child is there to talk to the interviewer. The interviewer should keep in mind that the child has been silent about the abuse until the report. This silence may have gone on for years with the abuser exercising authority over the child. That authority is best articulated by Leonardo da Vinci who is credited for stating "nothing strengthens authority so much as silence." A simple neutral prompt most often aids the child in overcoming reluctance and anxiety and allows the interviewer to transition into gathering the pertinent information from the child about the sexual abuse.

The interviewer should be cautious about their body language and responses. The interviewer should note any change in the child's affect that is exhibited, but should be careful to not react to the information from the child or any change in the child's affect the interviewer observes during the interview. There is no specific methodology, practice, checklist, or example that can be provided for gathering information from a child about the specific instances of abuse. In some cases, the child will remember the last or first incident with great detail, in other cases the child will remember something tangential to the abuse. In some cases, the child will remember specific details surrounding the abuse, such as the house they lived at, the room it occurred in, a vehicle, article of clothing, friend, season, birthday or other event that occurred surrounding the incident of abuse. In other cases, the child may remember only parts of the abuse or events surrounding the abuse. The interviewer should be patient, ask open-ended questions, encourage a free recall of the events, wait for the child to respond fully, and avoid suggestibility.

Phase 6: Questioning and Clarification

During this phase of the interview, the interviewer should transition into clarifying details the child provided during the information gathering phase. The interviewer should use developmentally appropriate words and use the child's descriptors of body parts or sexual acts. The interviewer should focus on details that will support a prosecutor's ability to charge and prosecute the case. During this phase, as previously discussed, the interviewer should establish jurisdiction, or in other words, where the crime occurred. It is recommended that even if the acts of abuse, or some of them, occurred outside the jurisdiction of the interviewer, the interviewer completes the interview fully obtaining as much information about the abuse irrespective of the jurisdiction in which the acts of abuse occurred.

The interviewer should determine whether or not there was penetration during the sexual abuse, how many times the abuse occurred, and the time line in which the abuse occurred. The interviewer should get as many details as possible about the abuse, including sensory details, and whether lotions, rags, or objects were used. The interviewer should get details about grooming, bribes, or threats. The interviewer should use open-ended questions. If the interviewer must ask direct questions to focus the child's memory, it is recommended that the interviewer follows up with open-ended questions. The interviewer should attempt to get clarification of any inconsistencies. Again, the interviewer should exercise patience, ask one question at a time and wait for the child to answer the question.

The interviewer should use appropriate protocols and tools. This may vary by jurisdiction and law enforcement policy. However, again, it is recommended the interviewer not use anatomical dolls as they are not proven reliable and could be subject to suggestibility. Anatomical drawings may be used. However, when used, the interviewer should follow policy, introduce the drawings only after disclosure of abuse has occurred, and have the child identify the body parts of the child. The drawings should be marked and retained by the interviewer as evidence.

Phase 7: Closing the Interview

Often neglected, this phase is important for the child, the interviewer, and the prosecutor. It is recommended that to the extent possible, the interviewer closes the interview on a positive note with child. To the extent the child had become upset or the interviewer noticed a change in the child's affect, closing the interview provides an opportunity for the interviewer to bring the child out of the traumatic event and for the child to regain composure. The interviewer should thank the child for participating, allow the child an opportunity to ask any questions or voice any concerns. In addition, the interviewer should provide an opportunity for the child to add anything they think is important that the interviewer had not asked. Closing the interview properly continues the rapport the interviewer developed with the child at the beginning of the interview. This rapport will provide the foundation for additional interviews the interviewer or any other experts may have with the child should it become necessary. The interviewer should leave that opportunity open with the child so that the child understands that there will be the possibility that they will have to speak more about the report of child abuse.

Charging and Prosecuting Considerations, Concerns, and Dynamics

Time

The single most difficulty a prosecutor faces in cases involving allegations of child sexual abuse is simply time. Generally, from the moment a report is made, child welfare services, law enforcement, household members, family, relatives, and friends of the child, will work closely to ensure the child's safety and maintain a distance from the suspect while the investigation is open. However, family composition, household members, family dynamics, domestic violence, relatives, friends of the child, friends of the household members, and the community play an important role in a child's fortitude in what will in almost every case, be a long time before the case is fully prosecuted.

Pressure

There is always a propensity and eagerness for volunteers, advocates, social workers, household members, family, relatives, friends of the child, teachers, counselors, clergy, and even community members, to want to discuss the facts of the report with the child. These individuals often mean well and in some ways it is simply human nature to want to help a child who has been hurt. In other cases, there may be a motive for others, such as family members or the suspect, to pressure the child to recant. Often times monetary concerns and stress created by the report, investigation, and possibly arrest of the suspect creates fear for family members and the victim. Fear, often times misplaced, may include the idea that the family will not have the ability to obtain food, shelter, or necessities, or may even face deportation. These have the potential to create pressure on the victim to falsely recant. These propensities and concerns only increase as time passes while the case is being investigated, charges are being considered, and if charges are filed, the time the case is pending in the court system.

Delay

If the prosecutor files charges, the case generally will not be tried for at least approximately a period up to an additional 2 years after the length of time it takes for law enforcement to investigate the case and the prosecutor files charges. Additional delays may be caused from the time charges are filed, an arrest warrant is issued, and the defendant is arrested. In addition, the court's busy calendar, prosecutor and defense calendar conflicts, expert calendar conflicts, and other factors contribute to the reasons for the delay. However, too often, the defense will simply state that they cannot possibly be prepared to go to trial for a variety of reasons, effectively forcing the court to postpone the trial or face reversal of any jury conviction for ineffective assistance of defense counsel.

The simple truth is that the persons involved in cases of child sexual abuse have an understanding and awareness that time affects the case for all the reasons discussed. In addition, the child is growing older, developing, healing, and becoming more reluctant to speak about the incident. With time, witnesses can become difficult to find and will forget details which affects their credibility when testifying. Moreover, financial hardship or fear can pressure the child to recant. Time can also affect how jurors perceive how the criminal system works and may question the time between the incident, investigation, and trial.

Victim Impact

It should be noted that victims of child sexual abuse can manifest a reaction to the abuse they endured in any number of ways. They may become increasingly promiscuous, begin or increase drug or alcohol use, run away, endanger themselves, become withdrawn or remissive, become argumentative or combatant, become silent or distant, have or increase nightmares, physical ailments, show a marked change in behavior, change in grades, to name only a few reactions or symptoms. However, these reactions, behavioral changes, or symptoms, denoted hereafter as "symptoms," alone are not indicative of child sexual abuse as there may be many other factors that could cause these same manifestations.

When considering a report of child sexual abuse and the presence of one or more of these symptoms, there is a strong indication that some if not all of the symptoms could be linked to the child sexual abuse. These factors should be considered, but not solely relied upon, in the totality of the prosecutor's evaluation of the case and charging decision. However, as time passes, these symptoms may manifest themselves in addition ways that affect the prosecutor's ability to proceed through trial. One such example that arises often is a female victim, who is well too often still a child herself, becoming pregnant through consensual sex. The prosecutor is often faced with having to now explain the victim's promiscuity to the jury to ensure the jury does not adversely judge the pregnant victim when testifying about being sexually abused.

Victim–Witness Advocates

For all of these reasons, it is important and recommended that jurisdictions utilize victim–witness advocates if available. Some victim–witness advocates work for the prosecution and are a liaison between the prosecutor and the victim, and often the victim's family. These advocates provide a source of comfort, resources, and communication for the victim and the family. The advocates provide a person who can speak with the victim and explain the legal process. The advocates provide information and resources about funding for victims of violent crime as well as other funding sources that can help defray concerns about housing, food, and other necessities. The advocates provide information about available counseling at little or no cost, to address ways to cope or heal from the abuse and emotional or physical damage the victim has suffered. The advocates also provide information, if necessary, about special visas to remain in the country as a victim of a violent crime. The advocates also provide communication between the victim and the prosecutor. Finally, the advocates provide a source of emotional comfort to the victim and their family as the long legal process proceeds.

Collateral Evidence

Child sexual abuse is a traumatic event for the child victim. Too often, prosecutors, the defense, courts, and juries become focused on intricate details surrounding the sexual abuse rather than the abuse itself. Those details include challenging and questioning the child about the child's memory as to the day, time, month, or even season of the abuse. They challenge and question the child's memory about the clothes the child was wearing when the abuse occurred, the clothes the perpetrator was wearing when the abuse occurred, or the physical description of the perpetrator's sexual organs. They may draw into question what the child ate the day of the abuse, or what bed sheets the child had, or what car a parent may have owned. However, a child may or may not remember these collateral details during the traumatic event of the sexual abuse itself. The fact that a child does not recall these details does not by itself abrogate the fact that the sexual abuse occurred.

In addition to the symptoms the victim may be exhibiting, the prosecutor should equally consider and balance other collateral evidence from the report of the sexual abuse. It may be necessary for the prosecutor to request that law enforcement follow-up and collect collateral evidence. For example, if the child reported that just prior to the abuse, the perpetrator showed the child pornography on a computer, law enforcement should attempt to obtain the computer for forensic examination for the existence or absence of pornography. Again, the existence or absence of pornography may or may not assist the prosecutor or jury in determining whether the abuse occurred, especially if the report is years later and a length of time passed allowing pornography to be deleted or destroyed. However, it can be extremely probative if the pornography does exist and corroborates the child's statements about the events surrounding the sexual abuse.

Case Example of the Use of Collateral Evidence

In one report of child sexual abuse, the victim, an 8-year-old, reported that the perpetrator gave the victim a choice on how to be abused, either orally, vaginally, or anally. The perpetrator used a lubricant when abusing the victim anally. The victim reportedly chose to be abused anally because of the use of the lubricant. The victim was able to describe the bottle of lubricant and draw a picture of the bottle. When questioned, the defendant admitted to possessing and using lubricant when having intercourse with the victim's mother. By itself, the lubricant carries little evidentiary value as lubricant is readably available and can be found in numerous households in the United States. However, in connection with the report that lubricant was used in the sexual abuse, the lubricant becomes important collateral evidence that should be collected by law enforcement. A prosecutor can further use the lubricant as a demonstrative tool during trial by showing the lubricant to the victim who can identify it and testify whether it was used and if so, how it was used. However, failure of law enforcement to collect or even attempt to collect the lubricant will leave law enforcement open to criticism and may become a challenge to the sufficiency or veracity of their investigation or testimony.

Equally important for law enforcement is the collection of evidence they find that may contain traces of bodily fluids, such as sexual fluids, semen, saliva, urine or blood. This evidence may be clothes, washcloths, tissue paper, napkins, etc. The bodily fluids may contain DNA of either the suspect or the victim or both. On their surface, the item may contain no evidentiary value. However, after forensic testing, the item may be direct evidence or contain collateral evidence of the sexual abuse.

For example, in a report of child sexual abuse by an adult male against a 12-year-old male child, the victim reported the suspect cleaned up the suspect's semen after he ejaculated with tissue. The victim likewise never reported that he ejaculated. However, law enforcement collected a washcloth from the location of the sexual abuse and had it analyzed for DNA. At the time of collection, the suspect admitted that the washcloth was his and was used to clean himself after he masturbated. The result of the DNA analysis was that the victim's DNA in the form of his semen was present on the washcloth. There was also the presence of another person's DNA. The washcloth becomes an important piece of evidence taken in conjunction with the report of abuse and the admission by the suspect that the washcloth would contain the suspect's DNA. The jury will be able to infer the unknown DNA is the suspects and can confirm that while the victim was mistaken that the washcloth was a tissue, the victim was correct in that the perpetrator cleaned himself after ejaculating the victim. The victim can also be asked in front of the jury whether or not he had ejaculated. That simple question often, and in this case did, trigger the memory for the victim that the perpetrator had ejaculated him.

In another example, a victim asserted that the perpetrator ripped a hole in her pajamas during the abuse. Law enforcement should make every effort to collect the pajamas and examine them to verify the presence of a hole. Law enforcement may even consider sending the pajamas for forensic testing to determine the presence of DNA. Again, the fact that DNA is not present does not abrogate the fact that abuse occurred, but depending on the facts, should be considered by the prosecutor in making a charging decision.

Failure of law enforcement to collect bodily fluids will affect the prosecutor's ability to prove a case of child sexual abuse. Moreover, failure of law enforcement to lawfully collect bodily fluids may cause evidence to be suppressed, which can prevent a prosecutor from proving the case. For example, in one case a mother walked in on her husband performing cunnilingus on her daughter. Her husband stopped immediately and spit on the floor. Law enforcement photographed the saliva but did not collect it or process it for the presence of DNA. To make matters worse, law enforcement obtained a buccal sample from the defendant without first obtaining a warrant after the defendant had retained an attorney. Law enforcement's errors not only thwarted justice, but also impacted the credibility of the testimony by the law enforcement officials.

In another example, a female victim, age 11, was told to go with the perpetrator in his truck in the evening after dark where the perpetrator gave her a lubricant he called "sperm killer" and instructed her to put it in her vagina. After which, the perpetrator put his penis in the child's vagina. The fact that the child did not remember the color of the truck or where the perpetrator took her when he committed the sexual abuse does not by itself abrogate the fact that the abuse occurred. An 11-year-old child would not be expected to know where she was taken in a truck in the dark. In contrast, the very collateral bazaar facts of the abuse itself, the use of "sperm killer," and the fact that the child remembered that it was a truck, irrespective of the color, makes the child victim's rendition of the abuse more probable that it occurred.

In some cases, the household continued to move and live in various locations, but the abuse assaults continued in every location in which they lived. It may be difficult for the victim to remember precisely what abuse occurred and in which location, especially if the abuse occurred essentially in the same manner each time it occurred. Law enforcement, and especially the forensic interviewer, should make every attempt to determine the specifics about the abuse in each location. Often times there may be details not associated with the abuse that will assist law enforcement in narrowing the time frame of the abuse. For example, obtaining school records if the victim changed schools or rental or lease agreements if the victim lived in a household that was rented or leased. In one case, the victim stated that one incident of abuse occurred the night before they painted her uncle's house. Law enforcement investigation should include interviews to determine what day, month, and year the house was painted and a search for store receipts to support purchase of painting materials. In some cases, it may be helpful to attempt to get photographs or apartment diagrams of the living quarters. These can be used by law enforcement with the victim for follow-up investigation or the prosecutor during the trial.

Issues Concerning the Prosecution of a Case Through a Trial

Jurisdiction and Time

A forensic interviewer and the prosecutor are faced with the challenge of determining jurisdiction and some degree of reliability as to the time the event occurred. Jurisdiction is essentially whether or not the sexual abuse occurred within the authority of the court in which the prosecutor is charging the crime. For example, determining whether the crime occurred within the county limits in which the prosecutor has authority to charge a crime.

Time is not an element of the crime of child sexual abuse. In simple terms, what that means is that the time of year, month, or day the sexual abuse occurred is not an element of the offense that the prosecution has to prove. However, the courts have determined that there must be some reliability as to the time the abuse occurred or the defense will not be in a position to defend against the charges. There is no general rule for the prosecution to establish a time frame. Some jurisdictions allow a prosecutor to charge an act over a 2-year time frame. Others are narrower. However, all parties are interested in being able to narrow the time frame to as close to the date the abuse occurred as possible in order to maintain fairness in the trial and judicial process.

Sometimes a victim will know the exact date the abuse occurred. However, often times there is a report of multiple instances of abuse occurring over a long span of time, often years. It is imperative that a forensic interviewer determines with as much detail from the child about each act of sexual abuse. This is done through the phased interview as discussed previously.

Prosecutors Versus Investigators

During the judicial process, it is important to note that prosecutors must remain in their role as prosecutors and not become investigators. What this means is that the role of a prosecutor is to seek justice and prosecute the case, not investigate and receive evidence in a case. Too often, prosecutors desire to discuss details and information with the victim and in so doing unwittingly begin an investigation into a case. Meeting and preparing a victim for testimony is acceptable practice for an attorney, and therefore a prosecutor. However, the line between witnesspreparation and investigation in cases of childsexual abuse can easily become blurred. The primary reason for this tenuous dynamic is the fact that the crime is one of secrecy. While preparing a victim to testify, the victim may suddenly remember a fact or event and blurt it out. The prosecutor will then find themselves in the awkward position of being required to turn that information over to the defense and potentially becoming a witness in the case.

To avoid these conflicts, it is recommended that the prosecutor meet with the victim only with the presence of a witness such as a victim–witness advocate or another prosecutor. Moreover, in preparing the victim to testify, it is recommended the prosecutor not delve into the specifics of the case with the victim, but simply provide general guidance about testifying and answer any questions or concerns the victim may have. Many prosecutors provide the following advice to all witnesses, including victims: "Tell the truth. Do not guess when answering a question. If you do not understand a question, simply state that you do not understand the question."

Juries and Considerations in Presenting a Child Sexual Abuse Case to a Jury

Each prosecutor will develop their own style in presenting a case to a jury. The jury is perhaps the most important factor in every case involving child sexual abuse. This is because crimes of child sexual abuse are crimes of secrecy and therefore in nearly every case, the jury will ultimately decide the credibility of the victim. If the jury does not believe the victim's testimony about the crime, the jury will acquit the defendant. Accordingly, every case is dependent on the selection of a neutral and impartial jury.

During the trial, a prosecutor will develop a strategy in presenting the case to the jury. That strategy will include the order of witnesses and other key decisions. One witness that must in almost every case testify is the victim. The victim's testimony will be difficult and emotional. Imagine being a young child and having to face a courtroom full of people. Now imagine being a young child that was sexually abused and having to face these same people and tell them how the defendant hurt you, often over and over again.

The people in the courtroom are a jury of approximately 14 people, usually 12 jurors who will decide the case and two alternate jurors, the judge, the court clerk, the court reporter, a bailiff, perhaps a few law enforcement officers, the prosecutor or prosecutors, the defense attorney or attorneys, the defendant who is the person who abused the child, and most likely a courtroom full of observers that may include the defendant's family who may be well known to the child. In face of all these people, the prosecutor will take the victim through their testimony in much the same manner that the forensic interviewer interviewed the child. Considerable time has passed by the time the child is testifying in front of the jury. The child is exhausted, tired of speaking about the sexual abuse, and now in face of all these people, must once again discuss what happened to him or her.

In one case example, a child was sexually abused repeatedly by the defendant and testified at trial when she was 8 years old. The defendant was convicted, but after the verdict and at the time of sentencing, a juror pronounced that the juror did her own independent investigation on an issue in the case and the verdict was reversed. The appeal took 4 years and the child, now 12 years old, testified again at the second trial. The child had already begun to heal, and when testifying about the abuse that occurred was distant and emotionally detached. The prosecutor made a decision to ask her a single question: "What did you think about when he did these things to you?" The reaction by the child was sudden, emotional, and nearly overwhelming. The victim froze, as if she had been hit and was stunned, tears welled in her eyes, she shook and blurted out "I put myself in a fantasy land and I had a pet dragon and the dragon's name was …" and she went on and on. The jury convicted the defendant. The victim's testimony demonstrated an overwhelming conviction that these crimes occur and the proper investigation and prosecution of them, ever mindful of error, results in justice.

Use of Expert Witnesses

The use of expert witnesses in a criminal jury trial is at the discretion of the prosecutor and the defense. Today, most likely from the influence of television programs and movies about crime scene investigation, courtroom antics, and legal conundrums, juries have become almost complacent in their expectation that there will be scientific or expert testimony in every jury trial. In some cases, as discussed previously, there is an obvious need for the prosecutor to introduce scientific evidence through expert testimony, such as the results of DNA testing. However, in other cases, where there is often no scientific evidence, the prosecutor may be prevented or limited in introducing expert testimony, or may risk introducing testimony that may cause the jury to become distracted from the testimony of the victim about the abuse that occurred.

Expert testimony is defined in legal jargon as:

> Opinion evidence of some person who possesses special skill or knowledge in some science, profession or business which is not common to the average [person] and which is possessed by the expert by reason of [the expert's] special study or experience.

Black's Law Dictionary, Black, Henry Campbell, 6th Edition, St., 1990, West Publishing Co., St. Paul, Minn. Essentially, an expert is a person, who has been trained, studied, or has experience in a particular field, and by way of that training, study, or experience, is permitted under the law to give an opinion relevant to an issue in the case during the expert's testimony. Other than through the testimony of an expert, there is simply no legal authority that allows a witness to give an opinion during a trial. This has the potential of giving the expert's testimony great deference for consideration by the jury. Moreover, the expert witness has the ability to explain their opinion on the relevant issue by providing hypothetical examples. Therefore, the introduction of expert testimony in a criminal jury trial concerning allegations of child sexual abuse is generally considered carefully by the prosecutor and the defense under the facts of each case and strategy of each party.

The prosecution will generally use the expert testimony of witnesses who conducted physical examinations, if any, of the victim reporting child sexual abuse. If an examination was conducted, the examination may or may not result in physical findings, and indeed in most cases do not result in physical findings. The statistics regarding physical findings have changed over the years as case studies are conducted and results analyzed. However, one fact that has remained constant is that there are very rarely any physical findings in children who are sexually abused. Physical findings include the obvious, such as semen, DNA, saliva, other bodily fluids, open wounds, abrasions, and like anomalies, if the abuse occurs within a short period of time of the physical examination. However, physical findings also include scaring and other anomalies that may be found during the examination when there is a lapse in time between the reported abuse and the examination. This information is critical for the prosecution to provide to the jury through the opinion testimony of the expert witness. A jury must understand that just because there are no physical findings does not mean the sexual abuse did not occur.

In addition, the prosecution will attempt to introduce statements made by the child during the examination through the expertwitness that conducted the examination, usually a nurse, nurse practitioner, or medical doctor. These statements are generally considered to be "hearsay" statements, statements the child told the expert during the examination but outside of the courtroom, and as such are not permitted to be told to the jury. As a general rule, called the hearsay rule, a witness is not permitted to tell a jury what someone else said to them outside of the courtroom. However, courts often allow the testimony of statements made to an expert during a medical examination because they are statements made in furtherance of medical diagnosis and treatment. This is important because society teaches children to be truthful in explaining to medical professionals what happened to them in order for the medical professionals to properly diagnose and treat the child. Therefore, there is a certain degree of reliability in the statements that are made by a child to a medical professional during an examination and for this reason the jury is often permitted to hear those statements. For the prosecution, the statements are important for the very same reason, they are reliable. The statements impress in the minds of the jury that the sexual abuse occurred or the child would not be telling the medical professional about the sexual abuse that occurred, and often, who and what hurt them.

A prosecutor is generally prohibited by the court from introducing excessive experttestimony that a child acted in conformity with a victim of sexual abuse. The reason for this is simply that courts are generally concerned about the reliability of the conduct and its relation to the sexual abuse. As discussed earlier, psychological, emotional, or physical reactions by a child to sexual abuse can manifest in a variety of ways, however those same reactions may also be attributable to other issues the child may be having, or both. If courts consistently or excessively allowed this opinion testimony, it could create an unfair advantage to the prosecution to convince a jury that the abuse must have occurred simply because the child has manifested certain conduct that can be consistent with sexual abuse.

The defense will use testimony of their retained experts to highlight any mistakes or failings of law enforcement, forensic interviewers, and other persons involved in the report and investigation of child sexual abuse allegations, which mistakes or failings impact the objectivity of the investigation, testing, and forensic interview or interviews. After highlighting these mistakes or failings, the expert will be able to testify to an opinion about the impact to the objectivity of the process which may cause the jury reasonable doubt as to whether the prosecution proved the abuse occurred.

It is important to remember that the standard the prosecutor has to prove is "beyond a reasonable doubt." These words, often heard and said with little gravity, create a very difficult burden for the prosecution to prove. It is for this reason one often sees statutes, depictions, or other artwork of a scale or the famous "lady justice" holding a scale that is off balance. The reason for this representation is that the prosecution has the increased burden of not only showing evidence to level the scale but also to show evidence which will tip the scale in favor of the prosecution. This also makes sense from the other side of the courtroom as our system of justice is one where the accused has a presumption that he or she is not only innocent, but also innocent until proven guilty beyond a reasonable doubt.

The most difficult task a prosecutor has to learn in the courtroom is cross examination. This is simply because the prosecutor, as the moving party, is most often in the position of being the side to call witnesses and therefore the prosecutor does not gain a lot of experience quickly in the art of cross examination. It should be noted that the defense is not required to call a single witness during the trial, the defendant has a constitutional right not to testify, and the prosecution is prohibited from making any comments or inferences about the defense not calling witnesses or the defendant not testifying. In addition, the jury is read a legal instruction that reminds them the defense is presumed innocent until proven guilty beyond a reasonable doubt and that no inferences may be drawn by the jury if the defense does not call any witnesses or the defendant does not testify.

It therefore follows that prosecutors can easily make mistakes in cross examination of expert witnesses. The propensity is for a prosecutor to try to "trip" the expert witness or "discredit" the expert witness. However, it is recommended that prosecutors understand that expert witnesses are generally skilled in testimony and are not subject to being tripped or discredited easily. To the contrary, it is recommended that prosecutors equally rely on the expertise of the defense expert witnesses in much the same manner as they rely on the expertise of their own expert witnesses. Generally, all expert witnesses will agree on certain issues, concerns, facts, elements, ideas, etc. A prosecutor should develop those agreed upon issues, concerns, facts, elements, ideas, etc. with the defense expert witness. Where the prosecutor, in consultation with their own expert, disagrees with the defenses expert, the prosecutor should simply call their own expert to establish the State's position with respect to the issues, concerns, facts, elements, ideas, etc. in which the two experts do not agree. It should be noted here that in nearly every state, expert witnesses for both the prosecution and defense are permitted to hear each other's testimony.

Defendant's Testimony

The prosecutor must also present their case with the knowledge that the defendant may or may not testify. The defendant has a constitutional right not to testify in a jury trial. If the defendant chooses not to testify, the prosecutor may not comment about the fact that the defendant did not testify. Therefore, the prosecutor must introduce evidence about any statements the defendant may have made to law enforcement and must further prepare to cross examine the defendant if the defendant testifies.

Conclusion

All reports of child sexual abuse should be treated as being truthful reports. As discussed, the primary function of the investigation and interviews that follow from the report is to objectively gather evidence. All interviews of children who report sexual abuse should be conducted by a person trained in forensic interviewing, in an established and coordinated manner, and following agency policy. Moreover, it is recommended that forensic interviewers use a phased interview approach to conduct a forensic interview of children who report child sexual abuse. Whenever possible, the use of therapy or service animals, usually dogs, in forensic interviewing of children reporting sexual abuse is encouraged if the child elects to have the animal during the interview.

A prosecutor's role in making charging decisions of child sexual abuse is to seek justice, not merely to convict. Prosecutors have a heavy emotional burden in making decisions to charge crimes of sexual abuse. However, prosecutors must be cognizant that the passage of time is the foremost difficulty a prosecutor faces in reviewing, charging, and prosecuting cases involving allegations of child sexual abuse.

Pressure from a multitude of sources as well as delays in prosecution will have an effect on the prosecution of cases involving child sexual abuse. Victims of child sexual abuse can have a variety of reactions and be impacted in many ways. Some of the impacts cause symptoms which can also affect the prosecution of the case; others will manifest themselves in a plethora of ways and create lasting effects for everyone involved. Treatment and counseling are recommended for the victim and household members in cases of reported sexual abuse. The use of a victim–witness advocate is important to provide a source of comfort, resources, and communication for the victim and the family, to understanding the legal process, providing information and resources about funding for victims of violent crime, and to bridge communication between the victim, victim's family, and the prosecutor.

Collateral evidence and follow-up should be performed by law enforcement. Prosecutors must develop skills in identifying and requesting the collection of evidence and follow-up. However, prosecutors should be mindful to not immerse themselves into an investigative role in examining and reviewing cases of child sexual abuse. Whenever meeting with a victim, prosecutors should utilize a witness, preferably a victim–witness advocate.

While each prosecutor will develop their own style for jury trial, the most important factor in every case involving child sexual abuse is selecting a jury. A crime of child sexual abuse is referred to as a crime of secrecy, which means there are generally no witnesses to the crime, and the jury will ultimately decide the credibility of the victim. In addition to the testimony of the victim, prosecutors often use expert witnesses in proving a crime of child sexual abuse.

The burden a prosecutor has is to prove the crime occurred is beyond a reasonable doubt. However daunting that task may appear, prosecutors must endeavor to bring justice to perpetrators who commit sexual abuse against children. Past successful prosecutions, appeals, skepticism, case law, criticism, challenges, developments, medical advancements, history, education, and human dignity constantly evolve to ensure the process is and remains fair.

Chapter 5
Childhood Memory: An Update from the Cognitive Neuroscience Perspective

Dwight J. Peterson, Kevin T. Jones, Jaclyn A. Stephens, Filiz Gözenman, and Marian E. Berryhill

The Emergence of Memory

Children are not simply miniature adults. As such, the memory of a child is significantly different from the memory of an adult. Furthermore, the ability to form memories is not innate and instead develops over the first nearly two decades of life. Consequently, memory researchers working in the developmental domain must carefully design studies to probe memory function using age-appropriate paradigms. This is especially true given the growing range of experimental approaches that can be leveraged to understand the neural underpinnings of memory and its development. Techniques such as functional near-infrared spectroscopy (fNIRS), functional magnetic resonance imaging (fMRI), and high-density electroencephalography (HD-EEG) join workhorse behavioral and neuropsychological methodologies to monitor many aspects of brain function and behavior during memory formation and retrieval.

In the following sections, we provide an overview of childhood memory development and retrieval of childhood memories. In particular, we focus on declarative,

D.J. Peterson, M.A., Ph.D.
Memory and Cognitive Aging Laboratory, Department of Psychological Sciences, University of Missouri, 9J McAlester Hall, Columbia, MO 65211-2500, USA
e-mail: dwight.peterson23@gmail.com

K.T. Jones, M.A., Ph.D.
Cognitive Neuropsychology Lab, Center for Aphasia Research and Rehabilitation, Georgetown University Medical Center, Building D, Suite 207D, 4000 Reservoir Road NW, Washington, DC 20057, USA
e-mail: kevjones22@gmail.com

J.A. Stephens, M.S.O.T., Ph.D. • F. Gözenman, M.S. • M.E. Berryhill, Ph.D. (✉)
Memory & Brain Laboratory, Program in Cognitive and Brain Sciences, Department of Psychology, University of Nevada, 1664 N. Virginia St., MS 296, Reno, NV 89557, USA
e-mail: jaclynanne09@gmail.com; filizg@gmail.com; mberryhill@unr.edu

W.T. O'Donohue, M. Fanetti (eds.), *Forensic Interviews Regarding Child Sexual Abuse*, DOI 10.1007/978-3-319-21097-1_5

or episodic, memory, the type of memory that most people think of when defining memory. More specifically, autobiographical memory is one class of episodic memory that is likely to be the most relevant to the types of questions posed by the forensic practitioner. Autobiographical memory refers to the retrieval of events from a person's life. The emergence of reliable autobiographical memory occurs during the first 10 years of childhood. In contrast, implicit memory, such as learning via conditioning, matures in infancy and shows little significant change during development (Murphy, McKone, & Slee, 2003). The development of episodic memory is interrelated with the development of working memory capacity as well. In general, across phonological, visual, and spatial working memory subcomponents, children's working memory capacity reaches adult levels around age 12 (Hulme, Muir, Thomson & Lawrence, 1984; Wilson, et al., 1987; Hitch et al., 1988).

We first briefly note challenges associated with studying memory in children before addressing the time course of neural development that underlies mnemonic function. We subsequently turn to several cognitive accounts of childhood amnesia before turning to the experimental literature to characterize the development of memory in children. Finally, we address the reliability of memory in children and what sorts of effects medical conditions and traumatic experiences may have on children's memory.

Studying Memory in Children

With adult participants it is reasonable to simply ask for freely recalled childhood memories to study events from childhood. For example, there are structured interviews, such as the Autobiographical Memory Interview (Kopelman, Wilson, & Baddeley, 1989) in which participants are asked to provide autobiographical memories and semantic information for different epochs over the life-span. This approach successfully identifies memory disorders such as dementia. More often, episodic memory paradigms classically involve the presentation of a set of memoranda during encoding with memory performance being tested by the accuracy of memory recall. This approach emerged with Ebbinghaus over a hundred years ago and remains in constant use today because it allows the experimenter complete control over the nature of the stimuli and easy ability to assess memory accuracy.

These approaches have limitations. List learning is not particularly ecologically valid and freely recalled memories are difficult to verify. Second, it is difficult to discriminate between memories retrieved from experience versus memories retrieved that were formed from hearing about events. This is true although there is some evidence suggesting that experienced events tend to have stronger imagery, sensory, and emotional components when compared to those acquired from others (Crawley & Eacott, 2006).

These challenges become more difficult when the participants are children. Probing autobiographical memories in children is complicated by a variety of factors including the child's age and emotional maturity, and emotional content of the event. Furthermore, interpreting young children's verbal accounts commonly requires a familiar, trustworthy adult. Such an adult may not always be available. Of primary importance to the issue of childhood autobiographical memory is infantile and childhood amnesia. Infantile amnesia, first described by Freud, encompasses the first 2 years of a child's life and is the complete absence of episodic memory (reviewed in Callaghan, Li, & Richardson, 2014). Childhood amnesia refers to the period of impoverished episodic memory, maturation of brain regions, self-awareness, theory of mind, and executive functioning until around age 7 (reviewed in Bauer & Larkina, 2013). Adults report almost no memories from early childhood and those early memories are impoverished with regard to detail (Usher & Neisser, 1993). But this does not mean that children do not remember events over time during childhood. Between ages 2 and 4 children begin to form lasting long-term memories (Bauer, Hertsgaard, & Dow, 1994; Mcdonough & Mandler, 1994; Rubin, 2000) and by around age 4 they begin to use narrative structure to recount autobiographical events (Fivush, Haden, & Adam, 1995). Events high in emotional content are better remembered. Three and 4-year-old children were tested on their memory for a tragic experience such as a fire (Pillemer, Picariello, & Pruett, 1994). Seven years later, the majority of the older group (57 %) was able to describe event, while only a small portion (18 %) of younger age group succeeded. Other examples of superior memory for emotionally valenced content include superior memory performance for unpleasant doctor's visits (Ornstein, 1995) and for a hurricane rather than an amusement park visit (Hamond & Fivush, 1991). Although memories are formed and shaped by various factors such as emotion, autobiographical memory performance in children does not reach adult levels of performance until around age 16 or older, with girls achieving more accurate performance than boys at this age (Willoughby, Desrocher, Levine, & Rovet, 2012). Indeed, there is some evidence to suggest that sophisticated memory organization such as segmenting events according to lifetime periods does not fully mature until age 18 (Chen, McAnally, & Reese, 2013).

Episodic Memory: Neural Necessities and Implications

Neural Development Underlies Mnemonic Capacity

The human brain is subject to an extended maturation process that continues beyond childhood and adolescence only reaching completion in our 20s (reviewed in Blakemore & Choudhury, 2006; Ofen, 2012). Appreciating this point is important because without an appropriately populated and interconnected brain there is no substrate for memory. Consequently, a primary reason for the absence of episodic memories during the period of infantile and childhood amnesia is due to immature brain function, particularly in prefrontal and medial temporal lobe structures essential for episodic memory. Of primary importance is that throughout the period of infantile amnesia there is immaturity of the hippocampus, particularly the dentate gyrus (reviewed in Ofen, 2012; Richmond & Nelson, 2007). Even more protracted is the maturation process of the inhibitory interneurons within the hippocampus, which continues until around age 8. Without a fully functional hippocampus there is poor memory encoding and retrieval (for a meta-analysis, see Svoboda, McKinnon, & Levine, 2006). Thus, the emergence of lasting episodic memories follows the neuronal development of hippocampal structures. This developmental sequence has been hypothesized to explain the apparent emergence of episodic memory from semantic memory (Mishkin, Suzuki, Gadian, & Vargha-Khadem, 1997). In contrast, semantic memory for factual knowledge about the world is less reliant on the hippocampus and can exist in those with congenitally impaired hippocampi (Vargha-Khadem et al., 1997) and inversely, episodic memory can remain intact in those with semantic memory deficits (Temple & Richardson, 2004).

In addition to hippocampal maturation there are essential increases in connectivity between brain regions and myelination of white matter tracts. The prefrontal cortex (PFC) is critical for executive functioning and the density and thickness of the gray matter in the PFC is significantly correlated with intelligence (Haier, Jung, Yeo, Head, & Alkire, 2004; Narr et al., 2007). During development, the rapid growth and subsequent pruning of neurons takes place later in the PFC than other regions of cortex (Huttenlocher & Dabholkar, 1997). This reduction of synaptic and neuronal density is followed by a growth of dendrites and increases in both gray and white matter density (Tsujimoto, 2008). The PFC continues to develop well into adolescence leading to an increase in executive function abilities (reviewed in Blakemore & Choudhury, 2006; Ofen, 2012). Furthermore, from 4 to 8 months of age there are significant cortical processing speed increases, reflecting the neuronal myelination process (Webb, Long, & Nelson, 2005). The continued maturation of brain regions as well as the increased efficiency in these regions is correlated with the offset of childhood amnesia.

Cognitive Requirements for Autobiographical Memory

Freud's now long abandoned proposal that repression explained infantile and childhood amnesia has been replaced by several competing hypotheses. Importantly, these perspectives are not mutually exclusive and they all require sufficient neural maturation for cognition (reviewed in Cycowicz, 2000). One explanation is based on the need for sufficient language skills to subserve encoding (Schachtel, 1947; recently reviewed in Josselyn & Frankland, 2012) and retrieval processes (Hayne & Rovee-Collier, 1995). For example, once children can verbally describe and discuss their experiences, even during the event itself, they are more likely to remember them and recall them accurately (Fivush, Kuebli, & Clubb, 1992; Tessler & Nelson, 1994). Language development is also influenced by the sophistication of speech heard in the household where exposure to sophisticated vocabulary facilitates the child's language skills (Huttenlocher, 1998; Huttenlocher, Haight, Bryk, Seltzer, & Lyons, 1991). In the classic "Magic Shrinking Machine" experiment, researchers placed large objects into the machine and the child removed a miniature version of the same item (Simcock & Hayne, 2003). Follow up testing 6 months and 1 year later, children were asked what items were shrunken in the machine. The children could only retrieve the names of the items they could verbally label at encoding, even if they had more recently learned the item's name. In other words, although they experienced the shrinking machine for all objects, only the ones they could name that day were later remembered.

A challenge for this perspective is the question of whether language performance can be extricated from the development of semantic memory. As mentioned previously, semantic memory refers to world knowledge, for instance, that a ball rolls, or that an apple is a fruit. Categorical representations emerge in infancy. For example, 3–4-month-old infants can discriminate between the categories of dogs and horses (Eimas & Quinn, 1994). Using semantic memory to group items makes it easier to remember a list of similar or semantically related words (Gathercole, 1995; Gathercole, Frankish, Pickering, & Peaker, 1999; Multhaup, Balota, & Cowan, 1996; Roodenrys, Hulme, & Brown, 1993).

A second explanation for childhood amnesia focuses on the development of cognitive abilities such as self-recognition (Howe & Courage, 1993), and theory of mind (Perner & Ruffman, 1995). According to this perspective, memory processes including context specificity, encoding speed, and the length of long-term memory retention must develop first to permit memory storage (reviewed in Hayne & Herbert, 2004). Support for this view comes from research revealing that the durability of long-term memories grows from 1 day in 1-year-olds, <1 week in 2-year-olds, <1 month in 3-year-olds, and up to 6 months in 4-year-olds (Morgan & Hayne, 2011). At a more advanced level, processing speed is linked to working memory span, reaches maturity in adolescence and facilitates episodic memory encoding (Kail, 1991). Both memory durability and the rapid processing of information facilitate memory formation.

A third account relates to the development of metamemory, which is the knowledge and awareness of one's own memory abilities (reviewed in Gathercole, 1998). Metamemory includes awareness of our ability to remember certain things more readily than others, and an understanding of the bounds of our own knowledge and a sense of our memory capacity. There is a strong positive relationship between metamemory and memory performance (reviewed in Gathercole, 1998; Ghetti, Lyons, Lazzarin, & Cornoldi, 2008; Isingrini, Perrotin, & Souchay, 2008). Even in children as young as 4 years old, metamemory knowledge is a strong predictor of memory performance on free recall tasks (Henry & Norman, 1996). This link becomes stronger over early elementary years and by third grade children are better predictors of whether they will remember something later (Henry & Norman, 1996). This is consistent with other observations demonstrating that 6–7-year-old children can distinguish between items that are fully recollected versus those that are simply familiar, but unlike adults they fail to report that false alarm trials contained items that felt familiar (Ghetti, Mirandola, Angelini, Cornoldi, & Ciaramelli, 2011).

A related executive function that is important for episodic memory is the ability to strategically organize information and rehearse memoranda in working memory. The ability to subvocally rehearse information does not mature until ~7 years

(Flavell, Beach, & Chinsky, 1966; Gathercole, Adams, & Hitch, 1994; Hitch, Halliday, Dodd, & Littler, 1989). This coincides with the maturation of organizational ability, which emerges during the elementary years and becomes stronger when children predict that a memory strategy will improve their performance (Moynahan, 1978). Younger children, even toddlers, will spontaneously use memory strategies, particularly in demanding situations (DeLoache, Cassidy, & Brown, 1985), even though they are not able to verbalize the merit of doing so (Henry & Norman, 1996; Schneider, 1986). By fourth grade, however, children apply appropriate grouping (e.g., fruits go together) whereas second graders do not (Schneider, 1986). This is consistent with fMRI data showing that 10-year-old children show activation in prefrontal regions more like adults do and significantly more than 7-year-olds do during challenging memory retrieval tasks in which memory strategy is useful (Chiu, Schmithorst, Brown, Holland, & Dunn, 2006). Importantly, the emergence of both metamemory and strategy use is influenced by the parents' literacy level and education (Grammer, Purtell, Coffman, & Ornstein, 2011). Thus, in cases where the parents' literacy and education is low may be associated with delayed memory development.

Clinical Conditions and Disorders in Children

Once children are able to form long-lasting memories there are a host of other factors that can impair memory. Children's memory function can be compromised by congenital factors including medical conditions, learning, developmental disabilities, and mental health conditions. It is also clear that memory and cognition are sensitive to exposure to alcohol and drugs prenatally or during adolescence, and childhood maltreatment. Because memory requires many other cognitive processes to function properly, e.g., attention, perception, it is possible that a child could have difficulty recalling facts or events without explicit *memory* impairment. In the following sections, we address the nature and implications of congenital and environmental factors.

Congenital Factors: Medical Conditions, Learning Disabilities, and Mental Health

Most medical conditions have primary physical manifestations. However, epilepsy, pediatric-onset multiple sclerosis, and diabetes mellitus are all also associated with cognitive deficits. Children with severe pediatric epilepsy have recurrent seizures, which disrupt cortical development and memory encoding (Widjaja et al., 2013). These children are at increased risk for verbal memory deficits (Hrabok, Sherman, Bello-Espinosa, & Hader, 2013). In pediatric-onset multiple sclerosis (MS), cognitive domains such as attention and visual memory are susceptible to deterioration over time as MS is a progressively degenerating disease (Till et al., 2013). Children diagnosed with type-1 diabetes mellitus are susceptible to deficits in selective attention, visual perception, and working memory (Tolu-Kendir et al., 2012). These cognitive deficits are not globally present in all children with type-1 diabetes, but rather, are modulated by factors such as early onset of diagnosis, frequency of hypoglycemia (i.e., low blood sugar levels), and poor glycemic control (Tolu-Kendir et al., 2012). Finally, very low birth weight children have reduced hippocampal volume and some memory sequelae (Isaacs et al., 2000). These medical conditions serve as examples of those that can directly and indirectly disrupt memory function.

A second congenital factor affecting memory is learning and developmental disability. Children identified as learning or developmentally disabled have cognitive deficits when compared to neurotypical children. For example, children with Williams and Down syndromes have deficits in sustained and selective attention (Costanzo et al., 2013). Children with specific language impairments (SLI) have difficulty encoding verbal information (Coady, Mainela-Arnold, & Evans, 2013), with severity correlating with the degree of memory impairment (Hesketh & Conti-Ramsden, 2013). Children may also have deficits specific to spatial information (Narimoto, Matsuura, Takezawa, Mitsuhashi, & Hiratani, 2013). Children with developmental disorders are susceptible to sleep disorders, which consequently disrupt memory consolidation (Urbain, Galer, Van Bogaert, & Peigneux, 2013) and further impair memory (Csabi, Benedek, Janacsek, Katona, & Nemeth, 2013).

A third congenital factor is mental health status. A number of psychiatric diagnoses are at greater risk for impaired cognitive function and/or impaired episodic memory (Ferreri, Lapp, & Peretti, 2011; Spinhoven, Bamelis, Molendijk, Haringsma, & Arntz, 2009), accompanied by atypical brain structure and function (Toga, Thompson, & Sowell, 2006). For example, children with Autism Spectrum Disorders (ASD) display deficits in executive functioning (e.g., initiating, planning, working memory) and with episodic memory attributed to dysfunction in hippocampal and prefrontal regions (reviewed in Boucher & Mayes, 2012; Boucher, Mayes, & Bigham, 2012). Children with high functioning autism have significantly impaired verbal recall compared to neurotypical children (Andersen, Hovik, Skogli, Egeland, & Oie, 2013). Oppositional defiant disorder is also associated with deficits in executive function and episodic memory (Rhodes, Park, Seth, & Coghill, 2012). It is also worth noting that children diagnosed with Asperger's Disorder recount memories with less detail, specifically with significantly *fewer* perceptual and emotional references (Brown, Morris, Nida, & Baker-Ward, 2012). Early-onset bipolar disorder is also associated with memory problems (Lera-Miguel et al., 2011; Udal et al., 2013; Udal, Oygarden, Egeland, Malt, & Groholt, 2012) and some data suggest that there are greater emotional memory deficits in those with type 1 diagnoses (Schenkel, West, Jacobs, Sweeney, & Pavuluri, 2012). One proposal is that abnormal activity in the fusiform gyrus impairs visual processing of emotional faces (Adleman et al., 2013). Obsessive-compulsive disorder (OCD) and Tourette syndrome both are linked with abnormal function in prefrontal and striatal regions, but OCD alone is associated with memory deficits in adults (Chang, McCracken, & Piacentini, 2007). Children with OCD have deficits in cognitive flexibility and planning and evidence of episodic memory deficits (Andres et al., 2007; Ornstein, Arnold, Manassis, Mendlowitz, & Schachar, 2010; but see Shin et al., 2008). Children with ADHD also show memory deficits (Rhodes et al., 2012) and abnormal patterns of neural activation in limbic and parietal regions during episodic memory retrieval (Krauel et al., 2007). Furthermore, many of the memory deficits linked with these diagnoses are compounded by comorbid attention deficit hyperactivity disorder (ADHD), including autism (Andersen et al., 2013; Yerys et al., 2009), oppositional defiant disorder (Rhodes et al., 2012), and early diagnosis bipolar disorder (Udal et al., 2012, 2013).

Environmental Factors: Drug/Alcohol Exposure and Use, Traumatic Experience

Children exposed to alcohol and illegal drugs in utero are vulnerable to lasting deleterious consequences (recently reviewed in Behnke & Smith, 2013) and broad changes to brain structure and function (reviewed in Toga et al., 2006). Prenatal drug exposure (PDE) to heroin and cocaine is related to changes in hippocampal structure that is negatively related to memory performance (Riggins et al., 2012). This may be primarily driven by heroin exposure, as there is limited evidence suggesting that prenatal cocaine exposure is associated with significant cognitiveproblems (Buckingham-Howes, Berger, Scaletti, & Black, 2013; reviewed in Bandstra, Morrow, Mansoor, & Accornero, 2010). Prenatal exposure to methylenedioxymethamphetamine (MDMA, "ecstasy") has dose-dependent effects with high exposures delaying motor (Singer et al., 2012) and cognitive development (reviewed in Chen & Lin, 2009).

Prenatal alcohol exposure occurs along a spectrum and when severe can cause fetal alcohol syndrome, central nervous system dysfunction, growth deficiencies, craniofacial anomalies, and a cognitive deficits (recently reviewed in Hoyme et al., 2005; Memo, Gnoato, Caminiti, Pichini, & Tarani, 2013; Pruett, Waterman, & Caughey, 2013). Children exposed to high levels of alcohol in utero may have significant difficulty with verbal encoding (Crocker, Vaurio, Riley, & Mattson, 2011), poor recognition and source memory (Kully-Martens, Pei, Job, & Rasmussen, 2012), deficits in memory and executive functioning (Pei, Job, Kully-Martens, & Rasmussen, 2011), and difficulty with language, visual perception, memory, learning, social functioning, and number processing tasks especially with difficult tasks (Kodituwakku, 2009). Neuroimaging studies reveal widespread anatomical brain abnormalities including a small or absent corpus callosum and irregular cortical thickness (Lebel, Roussotte, & Sowell, 2011; Lebel & Sowell, 2011). Functional neuroimaging suggests that some of the cognitive deficits observed in children with prenatal alcohol exposure may be related to widespread atypical activation patterns (reviewed in Coles & Li, 2011) and including prefrontal abnormalities (Norman et al., 2013).

The slow rate of brain maturation means that later adolescent drug and alcohol consumption may also impair memory performance. According to the Center for Disease Control, 70 % of adolescents in the USA have consumed alcohol and ~40 %

have experimented with marijuana (*Trends in the Prevalence of Marijuana, Cocaine, and Other Illegal Drug Use, National YRBS*: *1991–2011*, 2011). Compared to heavy alcohol use, marijuana has a targeted effect on memory and executive function ADDIN EN.CITE with concomitant structural changes in medial temporal lobe and frontal lobe (Batalla et al., 2013). In contrast, heavy alcohol use is associated with deficits in attention and executive function (Thoma et al., 2011). It is important to note that these findings are from a cross-sectional study; the long-lasting cognitive consequences of frequent marijuana use were not assessed. Adolescents who use inhalants have significant deficits in learning, memory, and executive functioning when compared to non-using age-matched peers (Takagi et al., 2011), as do those who use methamphetamine (King, Alicata, Cloak, & Chang, 2010). Little is known regarding the impact of these substances on adolescent brain development. As prenatal and adolescent exposure typically has dose-dependent effects, it is important to identify the extent of contact to predict the memory effects.

Traumatic childhood experiences may include abuse, maltreatment, or neglect. School-aged children who experience early trauma demonstrate worse performance on attention, working memory, and verbal recall tasks compared to matched control participants (Bucker et al., 2012; Chae, Goodman, Eisen, & Qin, 2011) and a series of brain changes including reduced hippocampal volume and changes in the corpus callosum (reviewed in Brietzke et al., 2012); see also De Bellis, Hooper, Woolley, & Shenk, 2010; De Brito et al., 2013). Memory for negative emotional experiences is heightened in maltreated children (Goodman, Quas, & Ogle, 2010; Howe, Toth, & Cicchetti, 2011). Children bullied by peers have more depressive symptoms and higher cortisol (a stress hormone) levels that negatively correlate with memory performance (Vaillancourt et al., 2011). More seriously affected children, and adults, diagnosed with post-traumatic stress disorder (PTSD) after witnessing violence have significantly greater deficits in learning, are more distractible, and impaired at memory rehearsal (Samuelson, Krueger, Burnett, & Wilson, 2010) and also have structural changes primarily in medial temporal lobe regions (reviewed in Bremner, 2006). Abuse may make children more susceptible to dissociative disorders and subsequently they may have greater inaccuracies in recounting personal events (Chae et al., 2011). Furthermore, children who are abused or neglected tend to have overgeneralized autobiographical memories with overrepresentation of negative self-representations than non-maltreated children (Valentino, Toth, & Cicchetti, 2009). Overall, children who have experienced abuse, maltreatment, or neglect are susceptible to various degrees of memory impairment, and memory impairment may revolve around the traumatic event itself.

The Accuracy of Children's Memory: Role as Eyewitnesses

Here, we turn from physical and environmental factors that can influence children's, and adults', memory function to factors that allow them to accurately report recollections of events. This is particularly important when children are providing testimony and are interacting with the judicial system.

Allegations of sexualabuse against children are taken with appropriate gravity. Given the legal ramifications associated with allegations of child sexual abuse, a variety of psychological factors become relevant during the course of an investigation and subsequent legal proceedings. For instance, given that corroborating evidence is often unobtainable, the only remaining available evidence in child sexual abuse cases may be the child's memory of the event (Roberts & Powell, 2001). Children are asked to recall details from the event in question during interviews with law enforcement, child psychologists, and, in testimony on the witness stand. Empirical evidence, however, indicates that similarly to adults, child eyewitness memory is susceptible to a variety of social and psychological factors that influence the process by which they encode, store, and retrieve information about events (Ceci & Bruck, 1993). Careful examination of this evidence is imperative to convict perpetrators while avoiding wrongful convictions of the innocent.

Post-event Suggestibility of Children

Events are not encapsulated in memory and instead are subject to interference and conflation from outside events. One source of contamination is post-event information, which can have long-lasting effects (London, Bruck, & Melnyk, 2009) and can occur during encounters such as formal interviews during which children are asked about an event (Zaragoza & Lane, 1994), conversations with parents (Poole & Lindsay, 2002) or conversations with peers (Schwarz & Roebers, 2006), or even by conflating life events involving some overlapping context (Powell, Roberts, Ceci, & Hembrooke, 1999). The types and sources of post-event information to which children are exposed during interviews has provided a wealth of knowledge pertaining to the social-cognitive factors contributing to accurate and inaccurate memory reports from children for past events.

Three leading experimental paradigms used to examine child suggestibility borrow from the work of cognitive psychologists in false memory and misinformation. In the misinformation effect paradigm, participants first witness an event (e.g., a car accident involving two cars). Second, they receive suggestive questions prompting exaggerated retrieval of details regarding the event (e.g., "how fast were the cars going when they: (a) smashed? (b) crashed? (c) bumped into one another?"). Finally, they are tested regarding their memory for the original event (Loftus, 1975; Loftus & Hoffman, 1989). Misinformation can distort memory, causing people to report exaggerated details regarding a previously witnessed event (e.g., answering (a) 65 mph, (b) 45 mph, (c) 25 mph to the example above). Implanting false memories, on the other hand, can involve scenarios similar to the now famous "lost in the mall" paradigm (Loftus & Pickrell, 1995). In this paradigm, participants are led to believe that they had been lost in a shopping mall when they were young. When interviewed by researchers, a significant proportion of participants produce details about an event that never occurred.

A frequently used laboratory approach to induce false memories involves the retrieval of verbal information and is referred to as the Deese-Roediger-McDermott

(DRM) paradigm (Deese, 1959; Roediger & McDermott, 1995). Here, participants are first presented with a list of semantically related words (e.g., *bed*, *dream*, *pillow*, *dark*, *nighttime*, and *drowsy*). After a delay, participants are asked to freely recall as many items as they can remember from the list of previously presented words. Importantly, many participants falsely recall words semantically related to words from the list, referred to as "critical lures" (e.g., *sleep*), which were never presented. Participants often feel highly confident that these critical lures were present in the list. Each paradigm has been used to probe the inconstancy and malleability of human memory in adults. Additionally, these paradigms have been applied to empirical investigations of child eyewitness memory, in particular to examine the suggestibility of children.

Child Suggestibility During Interviewing

A common finding from experiments employing variations of these paradigms is that suggestive or false information given to children prior to or during an interview can result in the inclusion of that information within the child's statement (Ceci & Bruck, 1993); reviewed in Ceci, Kulkofsky, Klemfuss, Sweeney, & Bruck, 2007). For example, mentioning a false, but plausible, detail (e.g., playing in the sandbox) that could have been part of a real past event (e.g., going to the beach) is likely to be incorporated into the child's subsequent report of the event (e.g., "I stopped to play in the sandbox"). Importantly, suggestibility decreases with development, as older (e.g., ages 5–6) children are more likely to report veridical information despite being exposed to suggestive statements compared to younger (e.g., ages 3–4) children (Leichtman & Ceci, 1995). Older (e.g., ages 11–12) children may still report false details that include plausible information (e.g., schoolmate choking on a piece of candy). However, they appear to be more resistant to implanted false information for highly implausible events (e.g., UFO abduction) compared to younger (e.g., ages 7–8) children (Otgaar, Candel, Merckelbach, & Wade, 2009).

Careful control over interactions with child eyewitnesses, however, can mitigate memory-related errors associated with child suggestibility to misinformation and leading questions. For instance, two main approaches are typically used during interviews with child eyewitnesses. The first, and more traditional category of approaches, involves a verbal-based interview, often conducted by law enforcement officials. To date, there are a variety of interviewing techniques, recommendations, and even protocol guidelines for conducting forensic verbal interviews with child eyewitnesses (Lamb, Hershkowitz, Orbach, & Esplin, 2008). For example, the National Institute of Child Health and Human Development (NICHD) has created structured interview protocols designed for use in real-world forensic interviews with children (Orbach et al., 2000). Empirical examination of the NICHD structured interview protocols indicates that these strategies are effective at extracting useful and accurate memory-related evidence during interviews with child witnesses (reviewed in Lamb, Orbach, Hershkowitz, Esplin, & Horowitz, 2007).

Other strategies are centered on techniques used by child psychologists and involve the use of props that are believed to serve as memory cues to facilitate retrieval of information regarding the event (Price et al., 2013).

Each approach entails a number of advantages and disadvantages with regard to obtaining accurate memory-related evidence from interviews with children. During verbal police interviews, which focus on free recall questions (e.g., "tell me what you remember from that day"), children have difficultly reinstating context when attempting to retrieve details from their memory of an event (Keary & Fitzpatrick, 1994). When police do ask specific questions during an interview, children often change their responses in the event that the same questions are repeated. For instance, an empirical investigation of question repetition on memory retrieval consistency found that children alter their responses to the same question even within the same interview (Krahenbuhl & Blades, 2006). Another problem with police interviews is that children may be apprehensive to share their memories of an event with law enforcement officials. In documented cases of sexual abuse, child victims often refuse to report details or admit that any abuse occurred during an initial interview with police (Leander, 2010). These authors suggest that two or three separate interviews with police are often necessary to build rapport and elicit thorough and accurate memory evidence from child victims of sexual abuse (Leander, 2010). On the other hand, repeated interviews can be problematic if misinformation is introduced and reinforced during subsequent interviews (Brainerd & Reyna, 1996; Melinder et al., 2010); reviewed in Brainerd, Reyna, & Ceci, 2008).

Aside from verbal reports taken by law enforcement officials, prop-assisted interviews are commonly used when interviewing child eyewitnesses in sexualabuse cases (review in Poole & Bruck, 2012). Children may have details stored in episodic memory from an event involving sexual abuse, but may not be able to retrieve those details without cues or may be too embarrassed to verbalize details from their traumatic experience (Russell, 2008). As such, forensic interviewers often employ props to elicit information from child eyewitnesses during interviews. The main concern regarding the use of props (e.g., anatomically detailed dolls, body diagrams/drawings) as retrieval cues during forensic interviews is that children may engage in fantasy play, increasing their suggestibility and potentially contaminating their memory of the event (Ceci & Bruck, 1995). Another issue with prop-assisted interviews regards the age of the child eyewitness. Three- and 4-year-olds often have a difficult time reporting details from events (e.g., "show me on the doll where they touched you") using both dolls and body diagrams (reviewed in (London, Bruck, & Wright, 2008). While 5–7-year-olds are relatively better than 3–4-year-olds at using props to retrieve details from memory regarding events involving sexual abuse, they still have issues understanding the purpose of the task and require correction and repeated instruction (Brown, Pipe, Lewis, Lamb, & Orbach, 2007). Moreover, even when older children understand the task demands, the introduction of props to facilitate questioning may lead to the generation of either suggested or spontaneous false responses (Poole & Bruck, 2012; Poole & Dickinson, 2011). Recent empirical comparisons of the traditional forensic verbal strategies and prop-assisted interviewing strategies have been conducted. This evidence suggests that, under certain conditions, prop-assisted strategies may produce more memory-related errors compared to carefully structured verbal interviews with child eyewitnesses (Melinder et al., 2010). As such, the benefits of prop-assisted interviewing strategies are limited and some suggest they are no better at eliciting accurate information from children than simply asking them questions about an event (Salmon, Pipe, Malloy, & Mackay, 2012). Clearly, the development of novel solutions is a necessary step toward improving the quality of child eyewitness memory reports obtained during the forensic interview process (review in Poole & Bruck, 2012).

Other Factors Influencing Child Suggestibility and Eyewitness Memory

Outside of formal interviews, children's memory for events can be contaminated via interaction with a variety of extra-interview factors (reviewed in Principe & Schindewolf, 2012). These social-cognitive influences on child suggestibility can influence memory retrieval accuracy even under unbiased, ideal interviewing conditions and typically emerge from post-event interactions with parents (Poole & Lindsay, 2002), peers (Schwarz & Roebers, 2006), co-witnesses (Principe & Ceci, 2002), or media exposure (e.g., television: Principe, Ornstein, Baker-Ward, & Gordon, 2000). Resulting from these interactions, children may incorporate details into their reports that they never experienced but someone else did, are completely false, or are highly exaggerated.

While many of these extra-interview factors (e.g., exposure to parents, peers, television) are difficult to control for in legal scenarios, limiting or preventing post-event exposure between children who were witnesses to the same event can control for co-witness influences. Witnesses to crimes and accidents often discuss the incident with other witnesses who are in close proximity to them after the event has occurred (Paterson & Kemp, 2006). Moreover, law enforcement officials often question witnesses simultaneously (Garven, Wood, Malpass, & Shaw, 1998). This contaminates eyewitness memories of the event. Indeed, when co-witnesses discuss their distinct memories of the same event, their reports are more likely to converge (Gabbert, Memon, & Allan, 2003). This "co-witness influence" can actually be more harmful to accurate memory recall than exposure to misinformation during a poorly conducted forensic interview (Paterson & Kemp, 2006; Principe, Guiliano, & Root, 2008; Principe & Schindewolf, 2012).

Like adults, child eyewitnesses are likely to discuss an event with their peers or other children who witnessed the same event (Candel, Memon, & Al-Harazi, 2007; Principe, Kanaya, Ceci, & Singh, 2006; Schwarz & Roebers, 2006). The relatively sparse number of empirical examinations of co-witness influence to date has found that children tend to conform to descriptions given by a co-witness. For instance, in a study in which child co-witnesses (ages 3–5) were exposed to different versions of an event, when child co-witnesses are interviewed together, the details they reported about the event converge (Bright-Paul, Jarrold, Wright, & Guillaume, 2012). Interestingly, when interviewed in private, the children still reported inaccurate information, even in the absence of social pressure to conform to co-witness reports.

As such, the influence of social conformity on the accuracy of child eyewitness reports only accounts for 32 % of the total amount of errors, leaving the remaining 68 % of errors made due to contaminated memory reconstruction of the event details based on prior social influence (Bright-Paul et al., 2012).

Another interesting form of suggestive social influence on child eyewitness memory comes in the form of rumors exchanged between child peers (Principe et al., 2006; Principe, Tinguely, & Dobkowski, 2007). In these instances, children produce false memory reports of an event that they overheard from another source, but never actually witnessed (Principe et al., 2006). For example, in the "magic trick" scenario used by Principe and colleagues (2006), four groups of preschool children (ages 3–5) received different levels of information about an event. One group witnessed a magic show involving a rabbit that never actually emerged from a magician's hat. Another group was exposed to false information by overhearing a conversation between two adults indicating that the rabbit escaped from the hat. The other two groups were either classmates of the group who overheard the rumor from adults or children who were not exposed to the rumor (control group). During either a neutral or suggestive interview nearly all of the children from each of the groups, with the exception of the control group, falsely reported that the rabbit was loose at the school (Principe et al., 2006).

Autosuggestibility and False Memory in Children

A related form of rumor-mongering that has recently been investigated relates to autosuggestibility, or rumors that emerge from the internal cognitive processes underlying the expectations or beliefs held by children (Brainerd & Reyna, 1995). In this form of child suggestibility, children create a rumor (akin to a false belief) based on observed evidence that converges with their recent experiences or preexisting beliefs about an event. For instance, Principe and colleagues (2008) developed a modified paradigm of the "magic trick" scenario used in one of their previous studies (Principe et al., 2008).

In this scenario, one group of children (ages 3–6) viewed the same "magic show" as previously described (false report of an escaped rabbit). After the magic show, the children walked back to class, one at a time, and passed by a bundle of carrots with bite marks (which nearby researchers confirmed the children noticed). A week later the children who viewed the magic show and clues, their classmates who did not view the magic show, and a control group of children at a different school were interviewed regarding the events that transpired on the day of the magic show. Compared to control subjects a significant proportion of both children who witnessed the magic show and the clues and their classmates falsely remembered details from the event (e.g., escaped rabbit ate the carrots). Not surprisingly, the 3–4-year-old classmate's memories were more susceptible than 5–6-year-olds to the influence of the rumors propagated by their classmates who witnessed the magic show and clues. Interestingly, compared to the 3–4-year-olds, a greater proportion of the 5–6-year-olds who witnessed the magic show and clues were more susceptible to autosuggestibility, and were responsible for generating the rumors from internal false memories of the event (Principe et al., 2008). Applied to real-world situations involving child co-witnesses, this evidence points to the need for to minimize co-witness influences on child eyewitness memory.

This pattern of results indicates a reverse developmental trend, wherein older children actually show greater susceptibility to the generation of false memories based on suggestive evidence (Principe et al., 2008). In the last decade, a wealth of research has produced evidence in support of developmental reversals within the child false memory literature. Similar to adults, children are susceptible to false memories when exposed to semantically associated lists of words as used in the DRM paradigm (Brainerd, Reyna, & Forrest, 2002; Sugrue, Strange, & Hayne, 2009).

Recent evidence, however, suggests that the commonly held perspective that younger, compared to older, children are more susceptible to the generation of false memories has not necessarily been validated empirically (reviewed in (Brainerd & Reyna, 2012). For example, in modified DRM paradigm tasks, older children (e.g., age 11) exhibit higher percentages of false recognition and recall compared to younger children (e.g., age 5) when tested on lists containing words from the same category (Brainerd, Holliday, & Reyna, 2004; Howe, 2006). Moreover, in ecologically pertinent examinations of child false memory, developmental reversals are observed. These ecologically valid examinations range from the generation of spontaneous false memories (e.g., using facial expressions, Fernandez-Dols, Carrera, Barchard, & Gacitua, 2008), false memories for complex events (e.g., false facts embedded in stories, Fazio & Marsh, 2008), as well as implanted false memories using modified versions of the Lofus (Loftus, 1975) misinformation paradigm (e.g., Ceci et al., 2007; Connolly & Price, 2006; Ross et al., 2006). In each of these examinations of false memory in children of various ages, older, rather than younger, children reported a higher proportion of false details. One explanation for these findings, borrowing from Fuzzy Trace Theory (FTT; Brainerd & Reyna, 1998; Ceci & Bruck, 1998), is that as children age, they develop a greater understanding of semantic "gist" and begin to store "gist-based" rather than verbatim episodic memory representations of events. As such, as children develop they are actually more susceptible to producing false memories of details of events due to a reliance on "gist-based" representations rather than verbatim representations (Reyna, 2012; Reyna & Brainerd, 1995). This theoretical explanation accounts for a great deal of empirical evidence from the extent literature regarding this reverse developmental trend showing that, under certain conditions, older children actually produce a greater amount of false memories than younger children.

Implications for Research in Child Eyewitness Memory

These recent findings are important, as existing dominant developmental, legal, and lay perspectives have adhered to the notion that young (e.g., preschool aged) children are the most susceptible to memory contamination and therefore are the least reliable eyewitnesses (Brainerd & Reyna, 2012). Indeed, empirical evidence regarding mock-juror perceptions of child eyewitnesses indicates that adults find the reports and testimony of children, younger children especially, to lack credibility (Melinder, Goodman, Eilertsen, & Magnussen, 2004; Newcombe & Bransgrove, 2007). The extant literature regarding child eyewitness memory, however, supports the notion that these perceptions of children as necessarily less reliable than older eyewitnesses are not entirely supported by empirical evidence. Our understanding of the malleability of human memory continues to evolve. Nevertheless, the goals of obtaining accurate memory reports from child sex abuse victims in order to enact justice, while simultaneously avoiding wrongful convictions of the innocent, remain at the forefront of these important areas of applied human memory research.

Conclusions

In closing, it is safe to say that there are many questions left to address regarding memory, both in children and adults. Here, cognitive neuroscience can serve as a bridge between psychological and neuroscientific observations and leverage new techniques to address the neural underpinnings of memory. The coming decades will then require clinicians to bring these findings into application. A real challenge going forward will be to foster interdisciplinary communication and research groups targeting the development of memory in children.

References

Adleman, N. E., Kayser, R. R., Olsavsky, A. K., Bones, B. L., Muhrer, E. J., Fromm, S. J., … Brotman, M. A. (2013). Abnormal fusiform activation during emotional-face encoding assessed with functional magnetic resonance imaging. *Psychiatry Research, 212*(2), 161–163. doi: 10.1016/j.pscychresns.2013.01.006.

Andersen, P. N., Hovik, K. T., Skogli, E. W., Egeland, J., & Oie, M. (2013). Symptoms of ADHD in children with high-functioning autism are related to impaired verbal working memory and verbal delayed recall. *PLoS One, 8*(5), e64842. doi:10.1371/journal.pone.0064842.

Andres, S., Boget, T., Lazaro, L., Penades, R., Morer, A., Salamero, M., & Castro-Fornieles, J. (2007). Neuropsychological performance in children and adolescents with obsessive-compulsive disorder and influence of clinical variables. *Biological Psychiatry, 61*(8), 946–951. doi: 10.1016/j.biopsych.2006.07.027.

Bandstra, E. S., Morrow, C. E., Mansoor, E., & Accornero, V. H. (2010). Prenatal drug exposure: Infant and toddler outcomes. *Journal of Addictive Diseases, 29*(2), 245–258. doi:10.1080/10550881003684871.

Batalla, A., Bhattacharyya, S., Yucel, M., Fusar-Poli, P., Crippa, J. A., Nogue, S., … Martin-Santos, R. (2013). Structural and functional imaging studies in chronic cannabis users: a systematic review of adolescent and adult findings. *PLoS One, 8*(2), e55821. doi: 10.1371/journal.pone.0055821.

Bauer, P. J., Hertsgaard, L. A., & Dow, G. A. (1994). After 8 months have passed: Long-term recall of events by 1- to 2-year-old children. *Memory, 2*(4), 353–382.

Bauer, P. J., & Larkina, M. (2013). Childhood amnesia in the making: Different distributions of autobiographical memories in children and adults. *Journal of Experimental Psychology. General, 143*(2), 591–611. 2013-28210-001 [pii]10.1037/a0033307.

Behnke, M., & Smith, V. C. (2013). Prenatal substance abuse: Short- and long-term effects on the exposed fetus. *Pediatrics, 131*(3), e1009–e1024. doi:10.1542/peds.2012-3931.

Blakemore, S. J., & Choudhury, S. (2006). Development of the adolescent brain: Implications for executive function and social cognition. *Journal of Child Psychology and Psychiatry, and Allied Disciplines, 47*(3–4), 296–312. doi:10.1111/j.1469-7610.2006.01611.x.

Boucher, J., & Mayes, A. (2012). Memory in ASD: Have we been barking up the wrong tree? *Autism, 16*(6), 603–611. doi:10.1177/1362361311417738.

Boucher, J., Mayes, A., & Bigham, S. (2012). Memory in autistic spectrum disorder. *Psychological Bulletin, 138*(3), 458–496. doi:10.1037/a0026869.

Brainerd, C. J., Holliday, R. E., & Reyna, V. F. (2004). Behavioral measurement of remembering phenomenologies: So simple a child can do it. *Child Development, 75*(2), 505–522.

Brainerd, C. J., & Reyna, V. F. (1995). Autosuggestibility in memory development. *Cognitive Psychology, 28*(1), 65–101. doi:10.1006/Cogp.1995.1003.

Brainerd, C. J., & Reyna, V. F. (1996). Mere memory testing creates false memories in children. *Developmental Psychology, 32*(3), 467–478. doi:10.1037/0012[--]1649.32.3.467.

Brainerd, C. J., & Reyna, V. F. (1998). Fuzzy-trace theory and children's false memories. *Journal of Experimental Child Psychology, 71*, 81–129.

Brainerd, C. J., & Reyna, V. F. (2012). Reliability of children's testimony in the era of developmental reversals. *Developmental Review, 32*(3), 224–267. doi:10.1016/j.dr.2012.06.008.

Brainerd, C. J., Reyna, V. F., & Ceci, S. J. (2008). Developmental reversals in false memory: A review of data and theory. *Psychological Bulletin, 134*(3), 343–382. doi:10.1037/0033-2909.134.3.343.

Brainerd, C. J., Reyna, V. F., & Forrest, T. J. (2002). Are young children susceptible to the false-memory illusion? *Child Development, 73*(5), 1363–1377.

Bremner, J. D. (2006). The relationship between cognitive and brain changes in posttraumatic stress disorder. *Annals of the New York Academy of Sciences, 1071*, 80–86. doi:10.1196/annals.1364.008.

Brietzke, E., Kauer Sant'anna, M., Jackowski, A., Grassi-Oliveira, R., Bucker, J., Zugman, A., … Bressan, R. A. (2012). Impact of childhood stress on psychopathology. *Revista brasileira de psiquiatria, 34*(4), 480–488.

Bright-Paul, A., Jarrold, C., Wright, D. B., & Guillaume, S. (2012). Children's memory distortions following social contact with a co-witness: Disentangling social and cognitive mechanisms. *Memory, 20*(6), 580–595. doi:10.1080/09658211.2012.690039.

Brown, B. T., Morris, G., Nida, R. E., & Baker-Ward, L. (2012). Brief report: Making experience personal—Internal states language in the memory narratives of children with and without Asperger's disorder. *Journal of Autism and Developmental Disorders, 42*(3), 441–446. doi:10.1007/s10803-011-1246-5.

Brown, D. A., Pipe, M. E., Lewis, C., Lamb, M. E., & Orbach, Y. (2007). Supportive or suggestive: Do human figure drawings help 5-to 7-year old children to report touch? *Journal of Consulting and Clinical Psychology, 75*(1), 33–42. doi:10.1037/0022-006x.75.1.33.

Bucker, J., Kapczinski, F., Post, R., Cereser, K. M., Szobot, C., Yatham, L. N., … Kauer-Sant'Anna, M. (2012). Cognitive impairment in school-aged children with early trauma. *Comprehensive Psychiatry, 53*(6), 758-764. doi: 10.1016/j.comppsych.2011.12.006.

Buckingham-Howes, S., Berger, S. S., Scaletti, L. A., & Black, M. M. (2013). Systematic review of prenatal cocaine exposure and adolescent development. *Pediatrics, 131*(6), e1917–e1936. doi:10.1542/peds.2012-0945.

Callaghan, B. L., Li, S., & Richardson, R. (2014). The elusive engram: What can infantile amnesia tell us about memory? *Trends in Neurosciences, 37*(1), 47–53. doi:10.1016/j.tins.2013.10.007. S0166-2236(13)00211-7 [pii].

Candel, I., Memon, A., & Al-Harazi, F. (2007). Peer discussion affects children's memory reports. *Applied Cognitive Psychology, 21*(9), 1191–1199.

Ceci, S. J., & Bruck, M. (1993). The suggestibility of children's recollections: An historical review and synthesis. *Psychological Bulletin, 113*, 403–439.

Ceci, S. J., & Bruck, M. (1995). *Jeopardy in the courtroom: A scientific analysis of children's testimony*. Washington, DC: American Psychological Association.

Ceci, S. J., & Bruck, M. (1998). The ontogeny and durability of true and false memories: A dual trace account. *Journal of Experimental Child Psychology, 71*, 165–169.

Ceci, S. J., Kulkofsky, S., Klemfuss, J. Z., Sweeney, C. D., & Bruck, M. (2007). Unwarranted assumptions about children's testimonial accuracy. *Annual Review of Clinical Psychology, 3*, 311–328. doi:10.1146/Annurev.Clinpsy.3.022806.091354.

Chae, Y., Goodman, G. S., Eisen, M. L., & Qin, J. (2011). Event memory and suggestibility in abused and neglected children: Trauma-related psychopathology and cognitive functioning. *Journal of Experimental Child Psychology, 110*(4), 520–538. doi:10.1016/j.jecp.2011.05.006.

Chang, S. W., McCracken, J. T., & Piacentini, J. C. (2007). Neurocognitive correlates of child obsessive compulsive disorder and Tourette syndrome. *Journal of Clinical and Experimental Neuropsychology, 29*(7), 724–733. doi:10.1080/13825580600966383.

Chen, C. Y., & Lin, K. M. (2009). Health consequences of illegal drug use. [Review]. *Current Opinion in Psychiatry, 22*(3), 287–292.

Chen, Y., McAnally, H. M., & Reese, E. (2013). Development in the organization of episodic memories in middle childhood and adolescence. *Frontiers in Behavioral Neuroscience, 7*, 84. doi:10.3389/fnbeh.2013.00084.

Chiu, C. Y. P., Schmithorst, V. J., Brown, R. D., Holland, S. K., & Dunn, S. (2006). Making memories: A cross-sectional investigation of episodic memory encoding in childhood using fMRI. *Developmental Neuropsychology, 29*(2), 321–340. doi:10.1207/S15326942dn2902_3.

Coady, J. A., Mainela-Arnold, E., & Evans, J. L. (2013). Phonological and lexical effects in verbal recall by children with specific language impairments. *International Journal of Language & Communication Disorders/Royal College of Speech & Language Therapists, 48*(2), 144–159. doi:10.1111/1460-6984.12005.

Coles, C. D., & Li, Z. (2011). Functional neuroimaging in the examination of effects of prenatal alcohol exposure. [Review]. *Neuropsychology Review, 21*(2), 119–132. doi:10.1007/s11065-011-9165-y.

Connolly, D. A., & Price, H. L. (2006). Children's suggestibility for an instance of a repeated event versus a unique event: The effect of degree of association between variable details. *Journal of Experimental Child Psychology, 93*, 207–223.

Costanzo, F., Varuzza, C., Menghini, D., Addona, F., Gianesini, T., & Vicari, S. (2013). Executive functions in intellectual disabilities: A comparison between Williams syndrome and Down syndrome. *Research in Developmental Disabilities, 34*(5), 1770–1780. doi:10.1016/j.ridd.2013.01.024.

Crawley, R. A., & Eacott, M. J. (2006). Memories of early childhood: Qualities of the experience of recollection. *Memory & Cognition, 34*(2), 287–294.

Crocker, N., Vaurio, L., Riley, E. P., & Mattson, S. N. (2011). Comparison of verbal learning and memory in children with heavy prenatal alcohol exposure or attention-deficit/hyperactivity disorder. *Alcoholism, Clinical and Experimental Research, 35*(6), 1114–1121. doi:10.1111/j.1530-0277.2011.01444.x.

Csabi, E., Benedek, P., Janacsek, K., Katona, G., & Nemeth, D. (2013). Sleep disorder in childhood impairs declarative but not nondeclarative forms of learning. *Journal of Clinical and Experimental Neuropsychology, 35*(7), 677–685. doi:10.1080/13803395.2013.815693.

Cycowicz, Y. M. (2000). Memory development and event-related brain potentials in children. *Biological Psychology, 54*, 145–174. S0301051100000557 [pii].

De Bellis, M. D., Hooper, S. R., Woolley, D. P., & Shenk, C. E. (2010). Demographic, maltreatment, and neurobiological correlates of PTSD symptoms in children and adolescents. *Journal of Pediatric Psychology, 35*(5), 570–577. doi:10.1093/jpepsy/jsp116.

De Brito, S. A., Viding, E., Sebastian, C. L., Kelly, P. A., Mechelli, A., Maris, H., & McCrory, E. J. (2013). Reduced orbitofrontal and temporal grey matter in a community sample of maltreated children. *Journal of Child Psychology and Psychiatry, and Allied Disciplines, 54*(1), 105–112. doi: 10.1111/j.1469-7610.2012.02597.x.

Deese, J. (1959). On the prediction of occurrence of particular verbal intrusions in immediate recall. *Journal of Experimental Psychology, 58*(1), 17–22.

DeLoache, J. S., Cassidy, D. J., & Brown, A. L. (1985). Precursors of mnemonic strategies in very young children's memory. *Child Development, 56*(1), 125–137.

Eimas, P. D., & Quinn, P. C. (1994). Studies on the formation of perceptually based basic-level categories in young infants. *Child Development, 65*(3), 903–917.

Fazio, L. K., & Marsh, E. J. (2008). Older, not younger, children learn more false facts from stories. *Cognition, 106*, 1081–1089.

Fernandez-Dols, J. M., Carrera, P., Barchard, K. A., & Gacitua, M. (2008). False recognition of facial expressions of emotion: Causes and implications. *Emotion, 8*(4), 530–539. doi:10.1037/A0012724.

Ferreri, F., Lapp, L. K., & Peretti, C. S. (2011). Current research on cognitive aspects of anxiety disorders. *Current Opinion in Psychiatry, 24*(1), 49–54. doi:10.1097/YCO.0b013e32833f5585.

Fivush, R., Haden, C. A., & Adam, S. (1995). Structure and coherence of preschoolers' personal narratives over time: Implications for childhood amnesia. *Journal of Experimental Child Psychology, 60*, 32–56.

Fivush, R., Kuebli, J., & Clubb, P. A. (1992). The structure of events and event representations: A developmental analysis. *Child Development, 63*(1), 188–201.

Flavell, J. H., Beach, D. R., & Chinsky, J. M. (1966). Spontaneous verbal rehearsal in a memory task as a function of age. *Child Development, 37*(2), 283. doi:10.1111/J.1467-8624.1966.Tb05387.X.

Gabbert, F., Memon, A., & Allan, K. (2003). Memory conformity: Can eyewitnesses influence each other's memory for an event? *Applied Cognitive Psychology, 17*, 533–543.

Garven, S., Wood, J. M., Malpass, R., & Shaw, J. S. (1998). More than suggestion: Consequences of the interviewing techniques from the McMartin preschool case. *Journal of Applied Psychology, 83*, 347–359.

Gathercole, S. E. (1995). Is nonword repetition a test of phonological memory or long-term knowledge? It all depends on the nonwords. *Memory & Cognition, 23*(1), 83–94.

Gathercole, S. E. (1998). The development of memory. *Journal of Child Psychology and Psychiatry, and Allied Disciplines, 39*(1), 3–27. doi:10.1017/S0021963097001753.

Gathercole, S. E., Adams, A. M., & Hitch, G. J. (1994). Do young children rehearse? An individual-differences analysis. *Memory & Cognition, 22*(2), 201–207.

Gathercole, S. E., Frankish, C. R., Pickering, S. J., & Peaker, S. (1999). Phonotactic influences on short-term memory. *Journal of Experimental Psychology. Learning, Memory, and Cognition, 25*(1), 84–95.

Ghetti, S., Lyons, K. E., Lazzarin, F., & Cornoldi, C. (2008). The development of metamemory monitoring during retrieval: The case of memory strength and memory absence. *Journal of Experimental Child Psychology, 99*(3), 157–181. doi:10.1016/j.jecp.2007.11.001.

Ghetti, S., Mirandola, C., Angelini, L., Cornoldi, C., & Ciaramelli, E. (2011). Development of subjective recollection: Understanding of and introspection on memory states. *Child Development, 82*(6), 1954–1969. doi:10.1111/J.1467-8624.2011.01645.X.

Goodman, G. S., Quas, J. A., & Ogle, C. M. (2010). Child maltreatment and memory. *Annual Review of Psychology, 61*, 325–351. doi:10.1146/annurev.psych.093008.100403.

Grammer, J. K., Purtell, K. M., Coffman, J. L., & Ornstein, P. A. (2011). Relations between children's metamemory and strategic performance time-varying covariates in early elementary school. *Journal of Experimental Child Psychology, 108*(1), 139–155. doi:10.1016/J.Jecp.2010.08.001.

Haier, R. J., Jung, R. E., Yeo, R. A., Head, K., & Alkire, M. T. (2004). Structural brain variation and general intelligence. *NeuroImage, 23*(1), 425–433. doi:10.1016/j.neuroimage.2004.04.025.

Hamond, N. R., & Fivush, R. (1991). Memories of mickey mouse—Young-children recount their trip to Disneyworld. *Cognitive Development, 6*(4), 433–448. doi:10.1016/0885[--]2014(91)90048-I.

Hayne, H., & Herbert, J. (2004). Verbal cues facilitate memory retrieval during infancy. *Journal of Experimental Child Psychology, 89*(2), 127–139. doi:10.1016/j.jecp.2004.06.002. S0022-0965(04)00092-X [pii].

Hayne, H., & Rovee-Collier, C. (1995). The organization of reactivated memory in infancy. *Child Development, 66*(3), 893–906.

Henry, L. A., & Norman, T. (1996). The relationships between memory performance, use of simple memory strategies and metamemory in young children. *International Journal of Behavioral Development, 19*(1), 177–199.

Hesketh, A., & Conti-Ramsden, G. (2013). Memory and language in middle childhood in individuals with a history of specific language impairment. *PLoS One, 8*(2), e56314. doi:10.1371/journal.pone.0056314.

Hitch, G. J., Halliday, M. S., Dodd, A., & Littler, J. E. (1989). Development of rehearsal in short-term-memory—Differences between pictorial and spoken stimuli. *British Journal of Developmental Psychology, 7*, 347–362.

Hitch, G. J., Halliday, S., Schaafstal, A. M., & Schraagen, J. M. (1988). Visual working memory in young children. *Mem Cognit, 16*(2), 120–132.

Howe, M. L. (2006). Developmentally invariant dissociations in children's true and false memories: Not all relatedness is created equal. *Child Development, 77*, 1112–1123.

Howe, M. L., & Courage, M. L. (1993). On resolving the enigma of infantile amnesia. *Psychological Bulletin, 113*(2), 305–326.

Howe, M. L., Toth, S. L., & Cicchetti, D. (2011). Can maltreated children inhibit true and false memories for emotional information? [Research Support, N.I.H., Extramural]. *Child Development, 82*(3), 967–981. doi:10.1111/j.1467-8624.2011.01585.x.

Hoyme, H. E., May, P. A., Kalberg, W. O., Kodituwakku, P., Gossage, J. P., Trujillo, P. M., … Robinson, L. K. (2005). A practical clinical approach to diagnosis of fetal alcohol spectrum disorders: clarification of the 1996 institute of medicine criteria. *Pediatrics, 115*(1), 39-47. doi: 10.1542/peds.2004-0259

Hrabok, M., Sherman, E. M., Bello-Espinosa, L., & Hader, W. (2013). Memory and health-related quality of life in severe pediatric epilepsy. *Pediatrics, 131*(2), e525–e532. doi:10.1542/peds.2012-1428.

Hulme, C., Thomson, N., Muir, C., Lawrence, A. (1984). Speech rate and the development of short-term memory span. *Journal of experimental child psychology, 38*(2), 241–253.

Huttenlocher, J. (1998). Language input and language growth. *Preventive Medicine, 27*(2), 195–199. S0091-7435(98)90301-2 [pii] 10.1006/pmed.1998.0301.

Huttenlocher, P. R., & Dabholkar, A. S. (1997). Regional differences in synaptogenesis in human cerebral cortex. *The Journal of Comparative Neurology, 387*(2), 167–178. 10.1002/(SICI)1096-9861(19971020)387:2<167::AID-CNE1>3.0.CO;2-Z [pii].

Huttenlocher, J., Haight, W., Bryk, A., Seltzer, M., & Lyons, T. (1991). Early vocabulary growth—Relation to language input and gender. *Developmental Psychology, 27*(2), 236–248. doi:10.1037/0012[--]1649.27.2.236.

Isaacs, E. B., Lucas, A., Chong, W. K., Wood, S. J., Johnson, C. L., Marshall, C., … Gadian, D. G. (2000). Hippocampal volume and everyday memory in children of very low birth weight. *Pediatric research, 47*(6), 713-720.

Isingrini, M., Perrotin, A., & Souchay, C. (2008). Aging, metamemory regulation and executive functioning. *Progress in Brain Research, 169*, 377–392. 10.1016/S0079-6123(07)00024-6S0079-6123(07)00024-6 [pii].

Josselyn, S. A., & Frankland, P. W. (2012). Infantile amnesia: A neurogenic hypothesis. *Learning & Memory, 19*(9), 423–433. 10.1101/lm.021311.11019/9/423 [pii].

Kail, R. (1991). Developmental change in speed of processing during childhood and adolescence. *Psychological Bulletin, 109*(3), 490–501.

Keary, K., & Fitzpatrick, C. (1994). Children's disclosure of sexual abuse during formal investigation. *Child Abuse & Neglect, 18*(7), 543–548. 0145-2134(94)90080-9 [pii].

King, G., Alicata, D., Cloak, C., & Chang, L. (2010). Neuropsychological deficits in adolescent methamphetamine abusers. *Psychopharmacology, 212*(2), 243–249. doi:10.1007/s00213-010-1949-x.

Kodituwakku, P. W. (2009). Neurocognitive profile in children with fetal alcohol spectrum disorders. *Developmental Disabilities Research Reviews, 15*(3), 218–224. doi:10.1002/ddrr.73.

Kopelman, M. D., Wilson, B. A., & Baddeley, A. D. (1989). The autobiographical memory interview: a new assessment of autobiographical and personal semantic memory in amnesic

patients. *Journal of Clinical and Experimental Neuropsychology, 11*(5), 724–744. doi:10.1080/01688638908400928.
Krahenbuhl, S., & Blades, M. (2006). The effect of question repetition within interviews on young children's eyewitness recall. *Journal of Experimental Child Psychology, 94*(1), 57–67. doi:10.1016/J.Jecp.2005.12.002.
Krauel, K., Duzel, E., Hinrichs, H., Santel, S., Rellum, T., & Baving, L. (2007). Impact of emotional salience on episodic memory in attention-deficit/hyperactivity disorder: A functional magnetic resonance imaging study. *Biological Psychiatry, 61*(12), 1370–1379. doi:10.1016/j.biopsych.2006.08.051.
Kully-Martens, K., Pei, J., Job, J., & Rasmussen, C. (2012). Source monitoring in children with and without fetal alcohol spectrum disorders. *Journal of Pediatric Psychology, 37*(7), 725–735. doi:10.1093/jpepsy/jsr123.
Lamb, M. E., Hershkowitz, I., Orbach, Y., & Esplin, P. W. (2008). *Tell me what happened: Structured investigative interviews of child victims and witnesses*. Chichester, England: Wiley.
Lamb, M. E., Orbach, Y., Hershkowitz, I., Esplin, P. W., & Horowitz, D. (2007). Structured forensic interview protocols improve the quality and informativeness of investigative interviews with children: A review of research using the NICHD Investigative Interview Protocol. *Child Abuse & Neglect, 31*, 1201–1231.
Leander, L. (2010). Police interviews with child sexual abuse victims: Patterns of reporting, avoidance and denial. *Child Abuse & Neglect, 34*(3), 192–205. 10.1016/j.chiabu.2009.09.011S0145-2134(10)00042-6 [pii].
Lebel, C., Roussotte, F., & Sowell, E. R. (2011). Imaging the impact of prenatal alcohol exposure on the structure of the developing human brain. *Neuropsychology Review, 21*(2), 102–118. doi:10.1007/s11065-011-9163-0.
Lebel, C., & Sowell, E. (2011). Diffusion tensor imaging studies of prenatal drug exposure: Challenges of poly-drug use in pregnant women. *The Journal of Pediatrics, 159*(5), 709–710. doi:10.1016/j.jpeds.2011.06.023.
Leichtman, M. D., & Ceci, S. J. (1995). The effects of stereotypes and suggestions on preschoolers' reports. *Developmental Psychology, 31*(4), 568–578.
Lera-Miguel, S., Andres-Perpina, S., Calvo, R., Fatjo-Vilas, M., Fananas, L., & Lazaro, L. (2011). Early-onset bipolar disorder: How about visual-spatial skills and executive functions? *European Archives of Psychiatry and Clinical Neuroscience, 261*(3), 195–203. doi:10.1007/s00406-010-0169-z.
Loftus, E. F. (1975). Leading questions and the eyewitness report. *Cognitive Psychology, 7*, 560–572.
Loftus, E. F., & Hoffman, H. G. (1989). Misinformation and memory: The creation of new memories. *Journal of Experimental Psychology. General, 118*(1), 100–104.
Loftus, E. F., & Pickrell, J. E. (1995). The formation of false memories. *Psychiatric Annals, 25*(12), 720–725.
London, K., Bruck, M., & Melnyk, L. (2009). Post-event information affects children's autobiographical memory after one year. *Law and Human Behavior, 33*(4), 344–355. doi:10.1007/s10979-008-9147-7.
London, K., Bruck, M., & Wright, D. B. (2008). Review of the contemporary literature on how children report sexual abuse to others: Findings, methodological issues, and implications for forensic interviewers. *Memory, 16*(1), 29–47. doi:10.1080/09658210701725732.
Mcdonough, L., & Mandler, J. M. (1994). Very long-term recall in infants—Infantile amnesia reconsidered. *Memory, 2*(4), 339–352. doi:10.1080/09658219408258954.
Melinder, A., Alexander, K., Cho, Y. I., Goodman, G. S., Thoresen, C., Lonnum, K., & Magnussen, S. (2010). Children's eyewitness memory: A comparison of two interviewing strategies as realized by forensic professionals. *Journal of Experimental Child Psychology, 105*, 156–177.
Melinder, A., Goodman, G. S., Eilertsen, D. E., & Magnussen, S. (2004). Beliefs about child witnesses: A survey of professionals. *Psychology, Crime & Law, 10*(4), 347–365. doi:10.1080/10683100001618717.
Memo, L., Gnoato, E., Caminiti, S., Pichini, S., & Tarani, L. (2013). Fetal alcohol spectrum disorders and fetal alcohol syndrome: The state of the art and new diagnostic tools. *Early Human Development, 89*(Suppl 1), S40–S43. doi:10.1016/S0378-3782(13)70013-6.

Mishkin, M., Suzuki, W. A., Gadian, D. G., & Vargha-Khadem, F. (1997). Hierarchical organization of cognitive memory. *Philosophical Transactions of the Royal Society of London. Series B, Biological Sciences, 352*(1360), 1461–1467. doi:10.1098/rstb.1997.0132.

Morgan, K., & Hayne, H. (2011). Age-related changes in visual recognition memory during infancy and early childhood. *Developmental Psychobiology, 53*(2), 157–165. doi:10.1002/dev.20503.

Moynahan, E. D. (1978). Assessment and selection of paired associate strategies: A developmental study. *Journal of Experimental Psychology, 26*, 327–333.

Multhaup, K. S., Balota, D. A., & Cowan, N. (1996). Implications of aging, lexicality, and item length for the mechanisms underlying memory span. *Psychonomic Bulletin & Review, 3*(1), 112–120. doi:10.3758/BF03210750.

Murphy, K., McKone, E., & Slee, J. (2003). Dissociations between implicit and explicit memory in children: The role of strategic processing and the knowledge base. *Journal of Experimental Child Psychology, 84*(2), 124–165.

Narimoto, T., Matsuura, N., Takezawa, T., Mitsuhashi, Y., & Hiratani, M. (2013). Spatial short-term memory in children with nonverbal learning disabilities: Impairment in encoding spatial configuration. [Research Support, Non-U.S. Gov't]. *The Journal of Genetic Psychology, 174*(1), 73–87.

Narr, K. L., Woods, R. P., Thompson, P. M., Szeszko, P., Robinson, D., Dimtcheva, T., … Bilder, R. M. (2007). Relationships between IQ and regional cortical gray matter thickness in healthy adults. *Cerebral Cortex, 17*(9), 2163-2171. 10.1093/Cercor/Bhl125

Newcombe, P. A., & Bransgrove, J. (2007). Perceptions of witness credibility: Variations across age. *Journal of Applied Developmental Psychology, 28*(4), 318–331. doi:10.1016/J.Appdev.2007.04.003.

Norman, A. L., O'Brien, J. W., Spadoni, A. D., Tapert, S. F., Jones, K. L., Riley, E. P., & Mattson, S. N. (2013). A functional magnetic resonance imaging study of spatial working memory in children with prenatal alcohol exposure: Contribution of familial history of alcohol use disorders. *Alcoholism, Clinical and Experimental Research, 37*(1), 132–140. doi: 10.1111/j.1530-0277.2012.01880.x.

Ofen, N. (2012). The development of neural correlates for memory formation. [Research Support, N.I.H., Intramural Review]. *Neuroscience and Biobehavioral Reviews, 36*(7), 1708–1717. doi:10.1016/j.neubiorev.2012.02.016.

Orbach, Y., Hershkowitz, I., Lamb, M. E., Sternberg, K. J., Esplin, P. W., & Horowitz, D. (2000). Assessing the value of structured protocols for forensic interviews of alleged child abuse victims. *Child Abuse & Neglect, 24*(6), 733–752. S0145-2134(00)00137-X [pii].

Ornstein, P. A. (1995). Children's long-term retention of salient personal experiences. *Journal of Traumatic Stress, 8*(4), 581–605.

Ornstein, T. J., Arnold, P., Manassis, K., Mendlowitz, S., & Schachar, R. (2010). Neuropsychological performance in childhood OCD: A preliminary study. *Depression and Anxiety, 27*(4), 372–380. doi:10.1002/da.20638.

Otgaar, H., Candel, I., Merckelbach, H., & Wade, K. A. (2009). Abducted by a UFO: Prevalence information affects young children's false memories for an implausible event. *Applied Cognitive Psychology, 23*, 115–125.

Paterson, H. M., & Kemp, R. I. (2006). Co-witnesses talk: A survey of eyewitness discussion. *Psychology, Crime & Law, 12*(2), 181–191. doi:10.1080/10683160512331316334.

Pei, J., Job, J., Kully-Martens, K., & Rasmussen, C. (2011). Executive function and memory in children with Fetal Alcohol Spectrum Disorder. *Child Neuropsychology, 17*(3), 290–309. doi: 10.1080/09297049.2010.544650.

Perner, J., & Ruffman, T. (1995). Episodic memory and autonoetic consciousness: Developmental evidence and a theory of childhood amnesia. *Journal of Experimental Child Psychology, 59*(3), 516–548. S0022096585710247 [pii].

Pillemer, D. B., Picariello, M. L., & Pruett, J. C. (1994). Very long-term memories of a salient preschool event. *Applied Cognitive Psychology, 8*(2), 95–106.

Poole, D. A., & Bruck, M. (2012). Divining testimony? The impact of interviewing props on children's reports of touching. *Developmental Review, 32*(3), 165–180. doi:10.1016/j.dr.2012.06.007.

Poole, D. A., & Dickinson, J. J. (2011). Evidence supporting restrictions on uses of body diagrams in forensic interviews. *Child Abuse & Neglect, 35*(9), 659–669. doi:10.1016/j.chiabu.2011.05.004. S0145-2134(11)00177-3 [pii].

Poole, D. A., & Lindsay, D. S. (2002). Reducing child witnesses' false reports of misinformation from parents. *Journal of Experimental Child Psychology, 81*(2), 117–140. doi:10.1006/jecp.2001.2648. S0022096501926487 [pii].

Powell, M. B., Roberts, K. P., Ceci, S. J., & Hembrooke, H. (1999). The effects of repeated experience on children's suggestibility. *Developmental Psychology, 35*(6), 1462–1477.

Price, J. S., Strong, J., Eliassen, J., McQueeny, T., Miller, M., Padula, C. B., … Lisdahl, K. (2013). Serotonin transporter gene moderates associations between mood, memory and hippocampal volume. *Behavioural Brain Research, 242*, 158–165. 10.1016/j.bbr.2012.11.013

Principe, G. F., & Ceci, S. J. (2002). "I saw it with my own ears": The influence of peer conversations and suggestive questions on preschoolers' event memories. *Journal of Experimental Child Psychology, 83*, 1–25.

Principe, G. F., Guiliano, S., & Root, C. (2008). Rumormongering and remembering: How rumors originating in children's inferences can affect memory. *Journal of Experimental Child Psychology, 99*, 135–155.

Principe, G. F., Kanaya, T., Ceci, S. J., & Singh, M. (2006). Believing is seeing—How rumors can engender false memories in preschoolers. *Psychological Science, 17*(3), 243–248. doi:10.1111/J.1467-9280.2006.01692.X.

Principe, G. F., Ornstein, P. A., Baker-Ward, L., & Gordon, B. N. (2000). The effects of intervening experiences on children's memory for a physical examination. *Applied Cognitive Psychology, 14*, 59–80.

Principe, G. F., & Schindewolf, E. (2012). Natural conversations as a source of false memories in children: Implications for the testimony of young witnesses. *Developmental Review, 32*(3), 205–223. doi:10.1016/J.Dr.2012.06.003.

Principe, G. F., Tinguely, A., & Dobkowski, N. (2007). Mixing memories: The effects of rumors that conflict with children's experiences. *Journal of Experimental Child Psychology, 98*, 1–19.

Pruett, D., Waterman, E. H., & Caughey, A. B. (2013). Fetal alcohol exposure: Consequences, diagnosis, and treatment. *Obstetrical & Gynecological Survey, 68*(1), 62–69. doi:10.1097/OGX.0b013e31827f238f.

Reyna, V. F. (2012). A new intuitionism: Meaning, memory, and development in Fuzzy-Trace Theory. *Judgment and Decision Making, 7*(3), 332–359.

Reyna, V. F., & Brainerd, C. J. (1995). Fuzzy-trace theory: An interim synthesis. *Learning and Individual Differences, 7*(1), 1–75. doi:10.1016/1041-6080(95)90031-4.

Rhodes, S. M., Park, J., Seth, S., & Coghill, D. R. (2012). A comprehensive investigation of memory impairment in attention deficit hyperactivity disorder and oppositional defiant disorder. *Journal of Child Psychology and Psychiatry, and Allied Disciplines, 53*(2), 128–137. doi:10.1111/j.1469-7610.2011.02436.x.

Richmond, J., & Nelson, C. A. (2007). Accounting for change in declarative memory: A cognitive neuroscience perspective. *Developmental Review, 27*(3), 349–373. doi:10.1016/j.dr.2007.04.002.

Riggins, T., Cacic, K., Buckingham-Howes, S., Scaletti, L. A., Salmeron, B. J., & Black, M. M. (2012). Memory ability and hippocampal volume in adolescents with prenatal drug exposure. *Neurotoxicology and Teratology, 34*(4), 434–441. doi:10.1016/j.ntt.2012.05.054.

Roberts, K. P., & Powell, M. B. (2001). Describing individual incidents of sexual abuse: A review of research on the effects of multiple sources of information on children's reports. *Child Abuse & Neglect, 25*(12), 1643–1659.

Roediger, H. L., & McDermott, K. B. (1995). False memories: Remembering words not presented in lists. *Journal of Experimental Psychology. Learning, Memory, and Cognition, 21*(4), 803–814.

Roodenrys, S., Hulme, C., & Brown, G. (1993). The development of short-term memory span: Separable effects of speech rate and long-term memory. *Journal of Experimental Child Psychology, 56*(3), 431–442. doi:10.1006/jecp.1993.1043.

Ross, D. F., Marsil, D. F., Benton, T. R., Hoffman, R., Warren, A. R., & Lindsay, R. C. L. (2006). Children's susceptibility to misidentifying a familiar bystander from a lineup: When younger is better. *Law and Human Behavior, 30*, 249–257.

Rubin, D. C. (2000). The distribution of early childhood memories. *Memory, 8*(4), 265–269. doi:10.1080/096582100406810.

Russell, A. (2008). Out of the woods: A case for using anatomical diagrams in forensic interviews. *Update, 21*(1), 2–6.

Salmon, K., Pipe, M., Malloy, A., & Mackay, K. (2012). Do non-verbal aids increase the effectiveness of 'best practice' verbal interview techniques? An experimental study. *Applied Cognitive Psychology, 26*(3), 370–380.

Samuelson, K. W., Krueger, C. E., Burnett, C., & Wilson, C. K. (2010). Neuropsychological functioning in children with posttraumatic stress disorder. *Child Neuropsychology, 16*(2), 119–133. doi:10.1080/09297040903190782.

Schachtel, E. G. (1947). On memory and childhood amnesia. *Psychiatry, 10*(1), 1–26.

Schenkel, L. S., West, A. E., Jacobs, R., Sweeney, J. A., & Pavuluri, M. N. (2012). Cognitive dysfunction is worse among pediatric patients with bipolar disorder Type I than Type II. *Journal of Child Psychology and Psychiatry, and Allied Disciplines, 53*(7), 775–781. doi:10.1111/j.1469-7610.2011.02519.x.

Schneider, W. (1986). The role of conceptual knowledge and metamemory in the development of organizational processes in memory. *Journal of Experimental Child Psychology, 42*(2), 218–236. doi:10.1016/0022[--]0965(86)90024-X.

Schwarz, S., & Roebers, C. M. (2006). Age differences in the effects of social influence on children's eyewitness performance and their metacognitive monitoring. *Journal of Experimental Child Psychology, 94*(3), 229–248. doi:10.1016/j.jecp.2006.01.003. S0022-0965(06)00013-0 [pii].

Shin, M. S., Choi, H., Kim, H., Hwang, J. W., Kim, B. N., & Cho, S. C. (2008). A study of neuropsychological deficit in children with obsessive-compulsive disorder. *European Psychiatry, 23*(7), 512–520. doi:10.1016/j.eurpsy.2008.03.010.

Simcock, G., & Hayne, H. (2003). Age-related changes in verbal and nonverbal memory during early childhood. *Developmental Psychology, 39*(5), 805–814.

Singer, L. T., Moore, D. G., Min, M. O., Goodwin, J., Turner, J. J., Fulton, S., & Parrott, A. C. (2012). One-year outcomes of prenatal exposure to MDMA and other recreational drugs. *Pediatrics, 130*(3), 407–413. doi: 10.1542/peds.2012-0666.

Spinhoven, P., Bamelis, L., Molendijk, M., Haringsma, R., & Arntz, A. (2009). Reduced specificity of autobiographical memory in Cluster C personality disorders and the role of depression, worry, and experiential avoidance. *Journal of Abnormal Psychology, 118*(3), 520–530. doi:10.1037/a0016393.

Sugrue, K., Strange, D., & Hayne, H. (2009). False memories in the DRM paradigm: Age-related differences in lure activation and source monitoring. *Experimental Psychology, 56*(5), 354–360. doi:10.1027/1618-3169.56.5.354.

Svoboda, E., McKinnon, M. C., & Levine, B. (2006). The functional neuroanatomy of autobiographical memory: A meta-analysis. *Neuropsychologia, 44*(12), 2189–2208. doi:10.1016/j.neuropsychologia.2006.05.023.

Takagi, M., Yucel, M., Cotton, S. M., Baliz, Y., Tucker, A., Elkins, K., & Lubman, D. I. (2011). Verbal memory, learning, and executive functioning among adolescent inhalant and cannabis users. [Research Support, Non-U.S. Gov't]. *Journal of Studies on Alcohol and Drugs, 72*(1), 96–105.

Temple, C. M., & Richardson, P. (2004). Developmental amnesia: A new pattern of dissociation with intact episodic memory. *Neuropsychologia, 42*(6), 764–781. doi:10.1016/j.neuropsychologia.2003.11.006.

Tessler, M., & Nelson, K. (1994). Making memories—The influence of joint encoding on later recall by young-children. *Consciousness and Cognition, 3*(3-4), 307–326. doi:10.1006/Ccog.1994.1018.

Thoma, R. J., Monnig, M. A., Lysne, P. A., Ruhl, D. A., Pommy, J. A., Bogenschutz, M., … Yeo, R. A. (2011). Adolescent substance abuse: The effects of alcohol and marijuana on neuropsychological performance. *Alcoholism, Clinical and Experimental Research, 35*(1), 39–46. doi: 10.1111/j.1530-0277.2010.01320.x

Till, C., Racine, N., Araujo, D., Narayanan, S., Collins, D. L., Aubert-Broche, B., … Banwell, B. (2013). Changes in cognitive performance over a 1-year period in children and adolescents with multiple sclerosis. *Neuropsychology, 27*(2), 210–219. doi: 10.1037/a0031665.

Toga, A. W., Thompson, P. M., & Sowell, E. R. (2006). Mapping brain maturation. *Trends in Neurosciences, 29*(3), 148–159. doi:10.1016/j.tins.2006.01.007.

Tolu-Kendir, O., Kiris, N., Temiz, F., Gurbuz, F., Onenli-Mungan, N., Topaloglu, A. K., & Yuksel, B. (2012). Relationship between metabolic control and neurocognitive functions in children diagnosed with type I diabetes mellitus before and after 5 years of age. *The Turkish Journal of Pediatrics, 54*(4), 352–71361.

Trends in the Prevalence of Marijuana, Cocaine, and Other Illegal Drug Use, National YRBS: 1991–2011. (2011). Atlanta.

Tsujimoto, S. (2008). The prefrontal cortex: Functional neural development during early childhood. *The Neuroscientist, 14*(4), 345–358. 10.1177/10738584083160021073858408316002 [pii].

Udal, A. H., Oygarden, B., Egeland, J., Malt, U. F., Lovdahl, H., Pripp, A. H., & Groholt, B. (2013). Executive deficits in early onset bipolar disorder versus ADHD: impact of processing speed and lifetime psychosis. *Clinical Child Psychology and Psychiatry, 18*(2), 284–299. doi: 10.1177/1359104512455181.

Udal, A. H., Oygarden, B., Egeland, J., Malt, U. F., & Groholt, B. (2012). Memory in early onset bipolar disorder and attention-deficit/hyperactivity disorder: Similarities and differences. *Journal of Abnormal Child Psychology, 40*(7), 1179–1192. doi:10.1007/s10802-012-9631-x.

Urbain, C., Galer, S., Van Bogaert, P., & Peigneux, P. (2013). Pathophysiology of sleep-dependent memory consolidation processes in children. *International Journal of Psychophysiology, 89*(2), 273–283. doi:10.1016/j.ijpsycho.2013.06.022.

Usher, J. A., & Neisser, U. (1993). Childhood amnesia and the beginnings of memory for four early life events. *Journal of Experimental Psychology. General, 122*(2), 155–165.

Vaillancourt, T., Duku, E., Becker, S., Schmidt, L. A., Nicol, J., Muir, C., & Macmillan, H. (2011). Peer victimization, depressive symptoms, and high salivary cortisol predict poorer memory in children. *Brain and Cognition, 77*(2), 191–199. doi: 10.1016/j.bandc.2011.06.012.

Valentino, K., Toth, S. L., & Cicchetti, D. (2009). Autobiographical memory functioning among abused, neglected, and nonmaltreated children: The overgeneral memory effect. *Journal of Child Psychology and Psychiatry, and Allied Disciplines, 50*(8), 1029–1038. doi:10.1111/j.1469-7610.2009.02072.x.

Vargha-Khadem, F., Gadian, D. G., Watkins, K. E., Connelly, A., Van Paesschen, W., & Mishkin, M. (1997). Differential effects of early hippocampal pathology on episodic and semantic memory. *Science, 277*(5324), 376–380.

Webb, S. J., Long, J. D., & Nelson, C. A. (2005). A longitudinal investigation of visual event-related potentials in the first year of life. *Developmental Science, 8*(6), 605–616. doi:10.1111/j.1467-7687.2005.00452.x.

Widjaja, E., Skocic, J., Go, C., Snead, O. C., Mabbott, D., & Smith, M. L. (2013). Abnormal white matter correlates with neuropsychological impairment in children with localization-related epilepsy. *Epilepsia, 54*(6), 1065–1073. doi:10.1111/epi.12208.

Willoughby, K. A., Desrocher, M., Levine, B., & Rovet, J. F. (2012). Episodic and semantic autobiographical memory and everyday memory during late childhood and early adolescence. *Frontiers in Psychology, 3*, 53. doi:10.3389/fpsyg.2012.00053.

Wilson, J. T. L., Scott, J. H., & Power, K. G. (1987). Developmental differences in the span of visual memory for pattern. *British Journal of Developmental Psychology, 5*, 249–255.

Yerys, B. E., Wallace, G. L., Sokoloff, J. L., Shook, D. A., James, J. D., & Kenworthy, L. (2009). Attention deficit/hyperactivity disorder symptoms moderate cognition and behavior in children with autism spectrum disorders. *Autism Research, 2*(6), 322–333. doi:10.1002/aur.103.

Zaragoza, M. S., & Lane, S. M. (1994). Source misattributions and the suggestibility of eyewitness memory. *Journal of Experimental Psychology. Learning, Memory, and Cognition, 20*(4), 934–945.

Chapter 6
The Process of Disclosure for Child Victims

Rachel Fondren Happel

A mother walks into her bedroom to see her 8 year old daughter being sexually abused by her husband, the young girl's stepfather. Mortified, she screams at her husband to leave and scoops up her little girl and rushes her to the emergency room. Her daughter participates in a Sexual Assault Forensic Examination (SAFE) and the medical findings are consistent with sexual abuse, which is rare, as less than 10 % of medical examinations are diagnostic of child sexual abuse (Frasier & Makaroff in Olafson & Lederman, 2006*). Child Protective Services (CPS) and local law enforcement arrive at the hospital and speak with the mother. A forensic interview is scheduled for the young girl for later in the afternoon.*

Upon arrival to the Children's Advocacy Center, the young girl is nervous. She doesn't know what to expect or how she will be able to talk about her experience. When asked by the forensic interviewer if someone has touched her in a way that made her feel uncomfortable or that she didn't like, she freezes. What will happen to her if she tells? What will happen to her stepfather if she tells? Will her stepfather go to jail? Will she go to jail for not stopping it? The young girl shakes her head to respond "no" and the forensic interviewer is concerned. Knowing the mother walked in and saw the abuse, why wouldn't the young girl disclose about her experience?

The above scenario is not uncommon as it relates to disclosure of childabuse. There are many reasons why children don't disclose, delay disclosure, or disclose about abuse and later recant, or take back their statements. This chapter will review these theories and data regarding the process of disclosure and how disclosure interacts with forensic interviewing.

Disclosure of abuse by child victims is an extremely difficult and important task. Children are often the only witnesses to child abuse crimes committed against them

R.F. Happel, M.S., L.P.C. (✉)
Department of Psychology, Missouri State University,
901 S National Avenue, Springfield, MO 65897, USA
e-mail: rachelhappel@missouristate.edu

W.T. O'Donohue, M. Fanetti (eds.), *Forensic Interviews Regarding Child Sexual Abuse*, DOI 10.1007/978-3-319-21097-1_6

and their statements can be a key piece in the investigation of their allegations. Understanding the disclosure process children often experience following abuse is crucial to increase the likelihood of gathering accurate statements from children while ensuring procedural fairness of the accused.

As human beings, it can be painful to discuss traumatic events that have happened to us and children are no exception. Similarly, children and adolescents may struggle to discuss their abuse because of the level of trauma experienced or because of the consequences or perceived consequences of discussing their abuse. Additionally, the support the children receive from family members, friends, and professionals during an investigation can influence their desire to cooperate and participate. If victims feel supported and believed, it often leads to a more compliance and engagement throughout the investigative process (Collins & Lincoln, 2002; Geiselman et al., 1984; Zulawski & Wicklander, 1993).

In a perfect world, all non-offending parents would be supportive and protective of their children when allegations of abuse existed. However, this isn't always the case and can complicate the disclosure process. According to Malloy and Lyon (2006), "non-offending caregivers' reactions are important not only in the aftermath of CSA (childsexualabuse) discovery, but also in terms of children's willingness to disclose in the first place," (p. 98). It can not only impact whether a disclosure occurs at all, but also may impact the timing, who the child discloses to, and the child's willingness to maintain their statements throughout the duration of an investigation (Malloy & Lyon, 2006). This suggests that early on, the reaction of individuals, particularly non-offending parents, can set the stage for the disclosure process of abused children. Even when things are done well, it does not guarantee children will disclose about abuse, and the remainder of this chapter will discuss some of the literature related to disclosure of child abuse experiences.

Introduction

Unfortunately, childabuse continues to be a widespread problem in the United States and around the world. The professional community recognized abuse as a social problem in the 1960s with Dr. Henry Kempe's suggestion that physicians should report observed cases of child abuse. Child abuse had previously been defined and identified, but not as a social problem. Over the years, the prevalence of child abuse and exploitation has increasingly become a major concern in our communities, "occupying a very high position on the social agendas of the United States and other countries," (Miller-Perrin & Perrin, 2012, p. 11). Through social constructionism, social conditions become social problems; essentially, when societal reactions of individuals, organizations, religious groups, and others are strong, they transform public perception about the importance of community problems (Miller-Perrin & Perrin, 2012; Perrin & Miller-Perrin, 2011). Child abuse became a social problem once communities started speaking out about their unwillingness to accept maltreatment and exploitation of children. When doctors began collaborating with other professionals in the field, the movement encouraged the development of laws related to mandated reporting of suspected child abuse. These laws were instrumental in bringing suspected child abuse victims to the attention of professionals who could help them and bring justice to the family.

A large percentage of childabuse cases go unreported for various reasons. Although we continue to have mandated reporter laws in each state, it does not mean that every child being abused is reported to social service agencies. Some families and/or professionals may have negative experiences following a report of child abuse and may choose to handle their concerns more informally, should future concerns arise. Some individuals still maintain they need "proof" before involving authorities in their concerns of child abuse, and this may delay or prevent the involvement of law enforcement and social service agencies.

Over 670,000 victims of childabuse and neglect were reported in fiscal year (FY) 2011. Some of these victims may have been subject to more than one report and when examining those numbers, over three million children were subject to at least one report in the same data examined. These numbers suggest there are approximately nine reported victims for every 1000 children in the United States (DHHS, 2011). Because of the volume of children who do not disclose or who delay their disclosure into adulthood, statistics regarding reported abuse may not accurately represent the true number of children who are victimized each year. Official statistics (actual cases reported to social service agencies) and self-report surveys often suggest different results, meaning that our estimation of child abuse is inaccurate and possibly by a significant number.

Data related to estimating the prevalence of abuse may be gathered by 1-year incidence studies, 1-year prevalence studies, child self-report studies, and adult self-report studies (Townsend & Rheingold, 2013). Each of these has limitations, due to the manner in which data is collected. Specifically, because children do not often report abuse at this time they are experiencing it and many cases of abuse are never reported to authorities, incidence and prevalence studies show statistics that do not fully account for all children who experience abuse (Broman-Fulks et al., 2007; London, Bruck, Ceci, & Shuman, 2005; Townsend & Rheingold, 2013).

According to Townsend and Rheingold (2013), there is no definitive research that can provide practitioners with a current prevalence statistic for children who have been sexually abused; the studies examined pointed to a childsexualabuse prevalence rate of 7.5–11.7 %, with the rate for girls as 10.7–17.4 % and for boys 3.8–4.6 %. Many prevalence rates that are currently reported are significantly outdated or misleading (Townsend & Rheingold, 2013). They propose an estimated rate of one in ten children is sexually abused before they turn 18.

Knowing that childabuse is such an epidemic, why don't all allegations of child abuse get reported to social service agencies? There are various reasons why reports don't make it to social services agencies, but one reason is related to the disclosure process. Children may not report abuse when it is occurring, may deny it, even when evidence exists that abuse has occurred, may make false reports, or may delay disclosure so significantly or provide such little detail, and their report may not be taken seriously.

There are certain situations where nondisclosure rates are more likely. For example, when images or videos exist that are associated with the perpetration, children are less likely to disclose. According to the Palmer and Stacey (2004), images or videos taken during abuse experiences may be the greatest inhibitor to children disclosing about their experiences. The images or videos make some victims feel like they are letting the abuse happen if they are smiling in the images, they fear they will be viewed as enjoying it, and they experience shame at being involved and being identifiable (Palmer & Stacey, 2004).

To assist with questioning children who are suspected victims of abuse, introducing evidence in a forensic interview may be necessary to invite the child to discuss his/her experience. The National Children's Advocacy Center (2012) states that most forensic interviewing protocols are designed for children who are actively disclosing or have previously disclosed abuse. All children are not actively disclosing, specifically those who were discovered as victims throughout the course of criminal investigations (i.e., images found on a subject's computer that provide identity of his/her victims). The sensitive introduction of evidence during a forensic interview may help reluctant children disclose about their experiences.

The child should be informed about the evidence that exists near the beginning of the forensic interview to assist in building rapport and provide them a framework for the interaction (NCAC, 2012). Additionally, being patient and developing a trusting relationship are important to set the stage for a successful forensic interview (von Weiler, Haardt-Becker, & Schulte, 2010).

If a child doesn't report abuse and there is reason to believe the child has been abused, it can create complex issues and the suspicion may not be investigated. This leaves not only this child at risk for future abuse, but also other children, who the perpetrator has access to, at risk. It is clear that understanding the disclosure process and how to improve our response to child abuse is crucial in protecting children and our communities.

Dynamics of Disclosure

When discussing the process of disclosure, we are often referring to childsexualabuse, although there may be disclosure issues related to other forms of abuse as well. Physical abuse and neglect often have physical signs and symptoms and may be discovered sooner than sexual abuse victimization, which may leave no physical evidence behind. Additionally, many forms of abuse co-occur, meaning some children are victims of multiple forms of abuse and neglect. Domestic violence, mental health diagnoses, lack of social support, and substance abuse are often thought of as individual problems; however, these risk factors impact parenting processes, productivity, and increase health care costs of both parents and children. Additionally, they can influence the parenting process which can impact children and hinder development and can lead to a lack of skills (i.e., cognitive, emotional) needed by children to succeed (NCCP, 2004). Essentially, many forms of abuse or a lack of resources can have deleterious effects on children's development and can pose threats to their overall well-being (NCCP, 2004).

Generally, research supports that various factors (i.e., non-offending caregiver support, relationship to the perpetrator, threats to child or family, age) can impact a child's disclosure in the forensic interview setting (Babiker & Herbert, 1998; Fanetti & Boles, 2004; Garven, Wood, Malpass, & Shaw, 1998; Malloy & Lyon, 2006; Myers, 2007; Olafson & Lederman, 2006). While this chapter will not discuss all possible explanations, it will touch upon some of the most common dynamics related to the disclosure process.

Research on the disclosure process has been gaining popularity over the last 30 years and can be first traced back to the early 1980s. In 1983, Roland Summit suggested a Child Sexual Abuse Accommodation Syndrome (CSAAS) which described why children may not disclose abuse experiences readily. While this syndrome has been met with some controversy (see London, Bruck, Ceci, & Shuman, 2007; London, Bruck, Wright, & Ceci, 2008; O'Donohue & Benuto, 2012), it was one of the first articles to discuss possible roadblocks in the disclosure process in children. One of the most problematic issues with this syndrome is that it is often used in forensic settings without consideration of the many concerns that have been presented in the literature (see O'Donohue & Benuto, 2012).

Summit (1983) proposed five reactions that children can exhibit who have been sexually abused. He does not suggest these reactions are diagnostic of abuse, but can provide investigators, therapists, and families with an understanding of behaviors that may be exhibited by child abuse victims. These reactions include: (1) *secrecy*, (2) *helplessness*, (3) *entrapment and accommodation*, (4) *delayed, unconvincing-disclosure*, and (5) *retraction*. As was previously mentioned, while this syndrome has been met with some controversy in the literature (London et al., 2005, 2008; O'Donohue & Benuto, 2012), some of the individual behavioral components Summit mentioned have been supported empirically (London et al., 2007).

Secrecy

Secrecy is fairly prevalent in childsexualabuse, either directly or indirectly (London et al., 2007; Olafson & Lederman, 2006). Children may be directly told to keep the abuse experience a secret or by the nature of the event, children may be embarrassed or assume they should keep it a secret. Due to popular media and television shows, it is often believed that children will be abused on a Monday evening and report their experience Tuesday morning, once they arrive at school. Due to the unknown nature of the consequences associated with disclosing about the abuse, shame, guilt, and confusion, secrecy or minimization about the abuse event is common (London et al., 2007; O'Donohue, Benuto, Fanetti, Fondren, & Vijay, 2013; Olafson & Lederman, 2006; Sjoberg & Lindblad, 2002).

Helplessness

Helplessness often arises in child sexual abuse due to the power differential that exists between the victim and the abuser. The child may feel powerless, or helpless, at not only ending the abuse, but also in reporting about the abuse. The perpetrator may directly or indirectly threaten the child and encourage the child not to tell or the fear of the unknown consequences may also create a sense of helplessness in the victim. There is lacking empirical evidence discussing the role of helplessness related to disclosure; however, helplessness or confusion may be a part of what leads children to delay or minimize abuse disclosures, which is supported in literature. One issue with CSAAS is the poorly defined concepts and lack of testing, thus, empirical support is lacking (O'Donohue & Benuto, 2012).

Entrapment and Accommodation

Entrapment and accommodation suggests the adaptation to the abuse that often occurs when a child recognizes that stopping the abuse would be difficult. Said another way, if the child feels trapped between stopping the abuse and sending the abuser to jail, the entrapment may be enough for the victim to dissociate during the abuse, justify the abuse, or accommodate their thoughts to avoid mental conflict about their experience. Abused children are often weighing the pros and cons of disclosing and trying to make sense of experiences that are overwhelming and confusing. Again, there is lacking empirical support for this behavioral reaction; however, it is possible that these factors may be related to the secrecy and minimization of abuse, which is supported in the literature (London et al., 2007; O'Donohue et al., 2013; Olafson & Lederman, 2006; Sjoberg & Lindblad, 2002).

Delayed Disclosure

Delayed disclosure suggests that children often wait years before they report abuse and when they do, their reports may be brief, unconvincing, or manifest in behavioral reactions. For example, a child has expressed to her father that she no longer wants to visit her mother and believes this is her way of reporting her victimization, although she doesn't specifically state what is happening at her mother's house. After a fight with her father where the child is grounded, the child blurts out, "Why do you keep sending me to mom's so Randy can rape me?" Of course, the statement will likely be a shock to her father and may appear suspicious due to the timing of her statement; the public often worries that children and adolescents make false accusations of abuse to avoid being in trouble, to seek revenge on someone they do not like, or during custody disputes (Faller, 2007).

Delayed or unconvincing disclosures should not be discredited; however, because regardless of when or how the disclosure takes place, follow-up should always take place.

According to Olafson and Lederman (2006), gradual disclosures among children are not unusual and multiple interviews may be necessary to gather information from victims. Thus, it is a misconception that children report abuse immediately after it occurs and some research suggests children may delay disclosure until adulthood (Lyon, 2014; Smith et al., 2000). Other research suggests that when children do report abuse in childhood, it often takes considerable time to do so (with some individuals delaying disclosure until adulthood, see Olafson & Lederman, 2006), with various factors like non-offending caregiver support, relationship to the perpetrator, and developmental and communication abilities influencing their behavior (London et al., 2005; Olafson & Lederman, 2006).

Retraction/Recantation

Retraction, or recantation, occurs when a child tries to "take back" what he/she has reported happened to him/her. Research does support that a "substantial minority of children recant abuse after initially admitting," (Faller, 2007, p. 185; see also Elliott & Briere, 1994). This is often seen as an attempt for things to "go back to the way they were," which may appear to be seemingly better than their life following the abuse disclosure. Often, following a report of abuse, an investigation ensues which can lead to arrests, individuals leaving their homes, court proceedings, medical examinations, etc. and the abuse may seem less devastating to a child than the process of interacting with criminal justice system. Additionally, there may be pressure from family members, the abuser, or internally, to retract their statements of abuse.

Over the years, research on disclosureand recantation has increased and has typically focused on prevalence rates, which vary significantly, ranging from 4 to 27 %, depending upon the study examined (Bradley & Wood, 1996; Gonzalez, Waterman, Kelly, McCord, & Oliveri, 1993). This is a large range and one reason for this may be some discrepancy on the inclusion criteria (London et al., 2005). For example, if false allegations are included in cases examined, the number of recantations will often be higher, (which doesn't support Summit's assertions in CSAAS) and this may be an artificial increase of the true number of recantations that occur.

The support of non-offending caretakers is negatively correlated with recantation (Elliott & Briere, 1994; Malloy & Lyon, 2006), while the number of interviews and lack of corroborative evidence appear to be predictors of recantation (Bradley & Wood, 1996; O'Donohue et al., 2013). In many cases, when recantation does occur, the allegation is eventually reaffirmed in formal interview settings (O'Donohue et al., 2013).

Age is supported empirically to have a relationship to recantation rates in child abuse literature, although research is somewhat mixed about the actual relationship. Malloy, Lyon, and Quas (2007) reported that significant predictors of recantation included age (with younger children more likely to recant than older), relationship with perpetrator (with parent/guardian leading to higher recantation rates), and lack of support from non-offending caregiver. Some studies suggest that older children may feel more culpable, or responsible, for the abuse event(s) (Goodman-Brown, Edelstein, Goodman, Jones, & Gordon, 2003). While age is an important consideration, we must also look at cognitive and developmental factors as these can vary significantly for a particular age.

Additionally, perceived consequences (negative emotions, physical harm/death to child or his/her family, and jail/legal to child or subject) can also impact disclosure and recantation rates (Malloy, Brubacher, & Lamb, 2011). Malloy et al. (2007) reported results from a study involving over 200 children randomly selected from substantiated child sexualabuse cases. They found that predictors of recantation were younger age, close relationship with perpetrator, and lack of maternal (non-offending) support. Factors not associated with recantation were corroborative evidence such as medical evidence or perpetrator confession, custody disputes, and prior history of offending of the offender (Faller, 2007).

Often, even when recantations do occur, statements will often be reaffirmed at some point. Recantation is not a reason to dismiss the child's previous statements because it does not necessarily mean the allegations are false; further exploration of the concerns is important to understand how to best proceed. It does mean that the child's statements are contradictory and it is important to address inconsistencies/ contradictory statements in a forensic interview setting to determine what occurred.

False Allegations

Do children lie? Of course, all humans have been known to lie at one time or another. Children lie about various things, but child abuse is typically not one of them. Dammeyer (1998) argues that when a child initiates a report of child sexual abuse, there is a high likelihood that the abuse actually took place and Faller (2007) supports this notion in stating that false allegations of sexual abuse by children are uncommon and more likely to come from adults (see Everson & Boat, 1989; Lanning, 2002).

When children are dishonest about abuse, they typically leave details out, or omit them (errors of omission), versus makeup events that did not happen to them (errors of commission). Errors of omission include factual information, but the information gathered is incomplete. On the other hand, errors of commission occur when incorrect details are also obtained, along with some factual information. Omission errors increase the likelihood of failing to detect abuse when it *did* happen and commission errors may increase the likelihood of suspecting abuse when it *did not* happen (Fanetti & Boles, 2004). Researchers suggest that the concern about children's memory comes from their errors of commission, rather than their errors of omission and a common gauge of recall accuracy is the amount of omission and commission errors present (Fanetti & Boles, 2004; Johnson & Foley, 1984). In free recall, more omission errors occur in younger children, although commission errors appear to occur equally in children and adults. Omission errors may lead some interviewers to use suggestive questioning techniques, which compromises the accuracy of the interview (Fanetti & Boles, 2004).

Some claim that society has become overly concerned with child maltreatment and this produces overreporting (Miller-Perrin & Perrin, 2012). Historically, concerns with overreporting are rooted in Besharov's (1986) claims that, "hundreds of thousands of innocent people are having their reputations tarnished and their privacy invaded," (Besharov, 1986, p. 32, in Miller-Perrin & Perrin, 2012). These figures came, in part, by the total difference of cases reported to child protection agencies versus the number of cases that are substantiated. Child abuse awareness is high, mandated reporting laws exist, and overall reports of child maltreatment have increased over the years (Miller-Perrin & Perrin, 2012).

There is a difference, however, between false allegations and those where suspicion remains, but cannot be proven, due to a lack of evidence (Faller, 2007). Statistically, there is little differentiation between these situations, thus the number of reports that were recorded as intentionally false was near zero in 2010 (U.S. DHHS, 2011). Researchers have attempted to estimate false allegation rates, and research is mixed and widely varies (Faller, 2007; Miller-Perrin & Perrin, 2012).

Society typically believes that false allegations occur more regularly than research supports (Miller-Perrin & Perrin, 2012). Media examples and well-publicized cases (McMartin Preschool, Kelly Michaels, custody disputes, etc.) cause the public to worry that false accusations/suggestive interviewing techniques are the norm. It is important to educate professionals and juries about research related to false allegations and how leading and suggestive interviewing techniques increase false reports. False allegations are not as common as unreported abuse (Faller, 2007), so this is a greater problem for professionals and communities. Failure to report abuse will be discussed in more detail in Chap. 18.

False negatives and false positives of alleged abuse can be equally challenging. According to Babiker and Herbert (1998), the cost of a false accusation is determined by decisions about the trade-off between the two potential types of error: the risk of misclassifying victims who are being abused and putting them and other children at risk for future abuse versus the risk of labeling children as victims who are not being abused and possibly subjecting them, their families, and others to unnecessary worry and stress; as well as potentially causing significant damage to the innocent adult, such as imprisonment or ruining of his/her reputation, (Fondren-Happel, Fanetti, & Visio, 2012; O'Donohue & Fanetti, 1996). Striking a balance of protecting victims and ensuring procedural fairness to the accused should be of the utmost importance in child abuse investigations. Conducting high-quality, legally defensible forensic interviews with suspected victims of abuse is one way to minimize challenges on the reliability of children's statements while also protecting individuals accused of crimes that are innocent. This will be discussed further in the section below.

Disclosure and Forensic Interviews

Following a research-based forensic interviewing protocol when questioning children is important for various reasons. According to Cirlugea and O'Donohue (2014), forensic interviewing protocols can be assessed for quality by examining interrater reliability, component construct validity, predictive (postdictive validity), incremental validity, sensitivity/specificity (see below), developmental appropriateness, cultural sensitivity, and implementation fidelity. When suspected victims of childabuse are questioned by individuals who are not trained in issues related to forensic interviewing including suggestibility, development, linguistics, or use questioning techniques/protocols that are not research-based and of good quality, it can have detrimental effects on investigations as well as the child's well-being.

Forensic interview protocols were developed to increase the likelihood that children interviewed will provide an accurate and detailed account to conclude whether a punishable offense did occur, while decreasing the likelihood that any personal/professional biases will enter the forensic interview. Forensic interviews are non-leading, objective, protocol-based interactions between a child and trained interviewer. There are multiple protocols used in the United States to conduct forensic interviews including, but not limited to: National Children's Advocacy Center (NCAC) Child Forensic Interview Structure (National Children's Advocacy Center, 2012), National Institute of Child and Human Development Protocol (NICHD) (Lamb, Orbach, Hershkowitz, Esplin, & Horowitz, 2007), and CornerHouse Forensic Interview Protocol (Anderson, 2013; Anderson et al., 2010). Following a protocol-based method of questioning and avoiding leading and suggestive questioning techniques can assist in gathering accurate details from children, buffer against coaching from outside sources, and assist children and adolescents who are struggling through the disclosure process. The sensitivity/specificity of a protocol (proportion of positive and negative cases identified) is important as it helps distinguish between children who have been abused and those who have not to avoid misidentification of victims or perpetrators (Cirlugea & O'Donohue, 2016).

Rapport is something that is important in facilitating a better outcome in many situations. From therapy to forensic interviewing, rapport can increase the comfort level of children, thus lessening stress and improving the ability to recall details. According to Collins and Lincoln (2002), a comfortable victim/witness will be more compliant and cooperative throughout the investigation (Collins & Lincoln, 2002; Geiselman et al., 1984; Zulawski & Wicklander, 1993). In the literature, rapport does appear to correlate with higher levels of accurate details (Boles, 2004; Fondren-Happel et al., 2012) Similarly, as rapport levels increase, the number of omissionerrors tends to decrease, suggesting that rapport does impact a child's ability to disclose information (Boles, 2004; Fondren-Happel et al., 2012). Rapport is one of the main components of all widely known forensic interview protocols due to its importance in creating a comfortable and appropriate environment for questioning children (Anderson, 2013; Anderson et al., 2010; Lamb et al., 2007; NCAC, 2012).

According to Fivush (1993), children may omit details from disclosures in forensic interviews because they may not be aware of their investigative importance. In forensic interviews, it is important to ask children to provide us with all details, even if they aren't sure if they are important, to attempt to gather as much forensically relevant detail as possible. Cued invitations ("Tell me more about that") can provide children an opportunity to provide additional information to already reported statements. Asking children to tell about "everything that happened from beginning to end" can also be another cue for children to not leave any details out about their experience.

One technique that is widely used in forensic interviewing protocols and childabuse investigations is the truth/lie discussion when gathering statements from children. This discussion is usually brief and may enhance the accuracy of child victim and witness reports and may buffer against false allegations and false denials. Typically, a discussion takes place to determine the child's ability to differentiate between statements that are true and false and seek agreement to talk about things that are true during the interaction. If a child struggles in this activity, the forensic interviewer can adjust his/her questioning to something more developmentally or cognitively appropriate. Sometimes adjusting the verbiage to right/wrong is an adjustment that can assist children in the conversation, particularly younger children who may have difficulty understanding the use of truth/lie terminology. Even when children lack the ability to fully participate in a truth/lie discussion, a promise to tell the truth appears to increase honest reporting (Lyon, 2014; Lyon, Malloy, Quas, & Talwar, 2008). Positive effects were noted in recall when interviewers engaged in conversations regarding the importance of truth-telling and avoiding reporting false information to authority figures (Huffman, Warren, & Larson, 1999; Saywitz & Moan-Hardie, 1994).

Coaching is another concern related to false allegations. It is a concern of childabuse investigators because it can take place prior to and throughout a formal investigation and can be difficult to control. Adult influence can negatively impact honesty, and some children may be particularly vulnerable to conceal or report information. Coaching can impair the accuracy of children's reports, and truth induction techniques may help offset the negative effects of coaching (Lyon et al., 2008). Non-suggestive questions in forensic interviews can buffer some of the effects of coaching, and asking children about possible coaching is an important task if there are concerns.

Unsubstantiated/unfounded cases and those that end in acquittals are not necessarily related to false allegations. A lack of evidence does not mean that abuse didn't occur. Criminal justice proceedings require evidence beyond a reasonable doubt and this is a high burden of proof. When this burden of proof is not met, the defendant should not be found guilty because the evidence doesn't support it; however, this does not necessarily mean that abuse did not occur; conversely, a conviction does not necessarily mean that abuse did occur.

Trauma and Disclosure

Trauma can impact the disclosure process (Berliner, Hyman, Thomas, & Fitzgerald, 2003). Specifically, the experience of trauma can influence a child's ability to recall detail. According to Berliner et al. (2003), memories for traumatic experiences are not always easily recalled and this may be due to the encoding process that often takes place when we experience negative events. Things that are shallowly encoded (possibly due to inattention or disassociation during the negative or traumatic experience, cannot be clearly recalled. Memories for traumatic or negative events often have less sensory detail (but more meaning and impact) than positive memories—which is likely due to cognitive avoidance strategies used while experiencing the event. In society, likely due to media and other factors, there is a perception that children will be able to recall and report a large amount of detail about abuse experiences and this is not always the case, due to the encoding and cognitive avoidance strategies discussed above. According to Koss et al. (1994), in a population who reported experiencing rape, those memories were hazier, lacked details, and were recalled less often than positive memories. Similarly, Hyman and Byrne (1999) found that college students had less detail for negative experiences than positive memories. Taken together, this suggests that the validity of traumatic memories should not be measured based upon the amount of detail or vividness of the report.

Cognitive avoidance strategies may be used when experiencing a negative event and this may account for memory loss or the ability to recall less detail (Berliner et al., 2003). Additionally, the way a negative event is encoded can also affect its salience in a child's memory and this, too, can influence a child's ability to recall details in a clear and concise manner. We cannot recall what we don't encode, thus, if a child has divided attention during an abusive/traumatic event, the event may not be encoded or may be shallowly encoded, causing difficulties with recall. Attention may not be focused on the specific components of the trauma and as suggested by Fivush et al. (2002), children may be more aware of negative internal states (how they are feeling) versus what is actually taking place during the event itself. Their research also suggests that the type of abuse may make some difference in the characteristics of memory and recall with sexual abuse/trauma as less vivid and coherent as compared to other forms of abuse (Berliner et al., 2003).

The use of technology during victimization can also complicate the disclosure process and potentially lead to additional trauma (Palmer, 2004). Of the 83 children identified, Palmer (2004) found that one of the greatest inhibitors to disclosure following being filmed or photographed is the humiliation of being recorded and fear that they will be recognized. The permanency of images and videos made during a child or adolescent's victimization can make disclosure difficult and may cause some victims to worry about their perceived culpability and may increase shame and guilt, specifically if the victim willingly provided the subject with the images or videos. This, of course, does not make the child or adolescent less of a victim, but they may fear that society perceives them as enjoying the victimization (especially if they were smiling when the image was produced). The images or videos may be discovered during the course of an investigation prior to the victim making a disclosure and because of this, some victims may show reluctance in talking about their victimization, since they are not actively disclosing. The National Children's Advocacy Center (NCAC) and the American Professional Society on the Abuse of Children (APSAC) do support the practice of introducing evidence in forensic interviews when such evidence exists (images, videos, chat logs, etc.), and this may be necessary for children who need cues to prod their memory and provide an opportunity to disclose about their experiences. It can give children the ability to clarify details about their experience and invite them to begin the disclosure and healing process.

Gender and Disclosure

When discussing gender and its relationship to disclosure, it is important to consider the gender of the child as well as gender of the forensic interviewer. Research is somewhat lacking in this area and methodology, and demographic differences such as age, gender, and relationship to the perpetrator lead to contradictory information. Overall, gender does not appear to be conclusively influential on disclosure rates, although more girls are reported as abuse victims in the literature. According to Fondren-Happel, Fanetti, and Visio (2012), in over 900 interviews examined, disclosure does not appear to be significantly related to gender of interviewer, gender of child, or age. This suggests that gender of the child or interviewer does not statistically have an impact on whether or not children make a disclosure in a forensic interview setting. As was mentioned previously, other factors such as perceived consequences to the child or perpetrator, non-offending caregiver support, and relationship to the perpetrator are likely more influential on disclosure/recantation than age alone. In agreement, Tang, Freyd, and Wang (2007) suggest the support for beliefs that males will be less likely to disclose than females, may not be as strong as previously reported, and may be related to the lower frequency with which males disclose child sexualabuse.

Overall, issues related to the disclosure process in children are complex and important. Research should continue to examine factors that increase and decrease the likelihood of children disclosing and continue refining techniques to gather information from children, while keeping the dynamics of disclosure in mind.

References

Anderson (2013). The CornerHouse Forensic Interview Protocol: An evolution in practice for almost 25 years. *APSAC Advisor*, Number 4.

Anderson, J., Ellefson, J., Lashley, J., Lukas-Miller, A., Olinger, S., Russell, A., … Weigman, J. (2010). The CornerHouse forensic interview protocol: RATAC. *T.M. Cooley Journal of Practical and Clinical Law, 12*, 194–331.

Babiker, G., & Herbert, M. (1998). Critical issues in the assessment of child sexual abuse. *Clinical Child and Family Psychology Review, 1*(4), 231–252.

Berliner, L., Hyman, I., Thomas, A., & Fitzgerald, M. (2003). Children's memory for trauma and positive experiences. *Journal of Traumatic Stress, 16*(3), 229–236.

Besharov, D. (1986). Vulnerable social worker: Liability for serving children and families. Washington, DC: National Association of Social Workers Practice.

Boles, R. (2004). The effects of rapport on child interviews. Unpublished manuscript.

Bradley, A. R., & Wood, J. M. (1996). How do children tell? The disclosure process in child sexual abuse. *Child Abuse & Neglect, 20*, 881–891.

Broman-Fulks, J., Ruggerio, K., Hanson, R., Smith, D., Resnik, H., Kilpatrick, D., & Saunders, B. (2007). Sexual assault disclosure in relation to mental health: Results from the National Survey of Adolescents. *Journal of Clinical & Adolescent Psychology, 36*(2), 260–266.

Cirlugea & O'Donohue (2016). This citation is from another chapter in this book. Unsure how to cite as I don't know the official title and placement of the chapter written by Olga and Bill and since it is within the same text. I have a partial citation below.Cirlugea, O. & O'Donohue, W. (2016). William T. O'Donohue and Matthew Fanetti (Eds): Forensic Interviews Regarding Child Sexual Abuse

Collins, R. & Lincoln, R. (2002). The effect of rapport in forensic interviewing. *Humanities and Social Sciences*, 1–16. Retrieved from http://epublications.bond.edu.au/hss_pub/18

CornerHouse Interagency Child Abuse Evaluation and Training Center. (2013). *CornerHouse child sexual abuse forensic interview training materials*. Minneapolis, MN: Author.

Dammeyer, M. D. (1998). The assessment of child sexual abuse allegations: Using research to guide clinical decision making. *Behavioral Sciences & the Law, 16*, 21–34.

Elliott, D. & Briere, J. (1994). Forensic sexual abuse evaluations of older children: Disclosures and symptomatology. *Behavioral Sciences and the Law, 12*, 21–31.

Everson, M. & Boat, B. (1989). False allegations of sexual abuse by children and adolescents. Journal of the American Academy of Child and Adolescent Psychiatry, 28, 230–235.

Faller, K. (2007). *Interviewing children about sexual abuse: Controversies and best practice*. New York, NY: Oxford University Press.

Fanetti, M., & Boles, R. (2004). Forensic interviewing and assessment issues with children. In W. O'Donohue & E. Levensky (Eds.), *Handbook of forensic psychology* (pp. 245–265). San Diego, CA: Elsevier Academic.

Fivush, R. (1993). Developmental perspectives on autobiographical recall. In G. S. Goodman & B. L. Bottoms (Eds.), *Child victims, child witnesses: Understanding and improving testimony* (pp. 1–24). New York, NY: Guilford.

Fivush, R., Hazzard, A., Sales, J., Sarfati, D., & Brown, T. (2002). Creating coherence out of chaos? Children's narratives of emotionally negative and positive events. *Applied Cognitive Psychology, 16*, 1–19.

Fondren-Happel, R., Fanetti, M., & Visio, M. (2012). Effects of gender on rate of disclosure in the forensic interviews of children. *American Journal of Forensic Psychology, 30*(1), 45–57.

Garven, S., Wood, J. M., Malpass, R. S., & Shaw, J. S. (1998). More than suggestion: The effect of interviewing techniques from the McMartin preschool case. *Journal of Applied Psychology, 83*(3), 347–359.

Geiselman, R., Fisher, R., Firstenberg, I., Hutton, L., Sullivan, S., Avetissian, I., & Prosk, A. (1984). Enhancement of eyewitness memory: An empirical evaluation of the cognitive interview. *Journal of Police Science and Administration, 12*(1), 74–80.

Gonzalez, L. S., Waterman, J., Kelly, R., McCord, J., & Oliveri, K. (1993). Children's patterns of disclosures and recantations of sexual and ritualistic abuse allegations in psychotherapy. *Child Abuse and Neglect, 17*, 281–289.

Goodman-Brown, T., Edelstein, R., Goodman, G., Jones, D., & Gordon, D. (2003). Why children tell: A model of children's disclosure of sexual abuse. *Child Abuse & Neglect, 27*, 525–540.

Huffman, M., Warren, A., & Larson, S. (1999). Discussing truth and lies in interviews with children: Whether, why, and how? *Applied Developmental Science, 3*, 6–15.

Hyman, I., Jr., & Byrne, C. (1999). *Differences between trauma memories and memories of other experiences*. Paper presented at the meeting of SARMAC: Society for Applied Research in Memory and Cognition, Boulder, CO.

Johnson, M., & Foley, M. (1984). Differentiating fact from fantasy: The reliability of children's memory. *Journal of Social Issues, 40*, 33–50.
Koss, M., Goodman, L., Browne, A., Fitzgerald, L., Keita, G., & Russo, N. (1994). *No safe haven: Male violence against women at home, at work, and in the community*. Washington, DC: American Psychological Association.
Lamb, M. E., Orbach, Y., Hershkowitz, I., Esplin, P. W., & Horowitz, D. (2007). A structured forensic interview protocol improves the quality and informativeness of investigative interviews with children: A review of research using the NICHD Investigative Interview Protocol. *Child Abuse and Neglect, 31*(11–12), 1201–1231.
Lanning, K. (2002). Criminal investigation of sexual victimization of children. In J. E. B. Myers, L. Berliner, J. Briere, C. Hendrix, C. Jenny, & T. Reid (Eds.), *The APSAC Handbook on child maltreatment* (2nd ed., pp. 329–347). Thousand Oaks, CA: Sage.
Lawrence, S., Chau, M., & Lennon, M. (2004). *Depression, substance abuse, and domestic violence: Little is known about co-occurrence and combined effects on low-income families* (National Center for Children in Poverty, New York, NY). Retrieved from www.nccp.org/publications/pdf/text_546.pdf
Loftus, E. (1996). *Eyewitness testimony*. Cambridge, MA: Harvard University Press.
London, K., Bruck, M., Ceci, S. J., & Shuman, D. W. (2005). Disclosure of child sexual abuse: What does the research tell us about the ways that children tell? *Psychology, Public Policy, and Law, 11*(1), 194–226.
London, K., Bruck, M., Ceci, S., & Shuman, D., (2007). Disclosure of child sexual abuse: A review of the contemporary empirical literature. In M.E. Pipe, M.E. Lamb, Y. Orbach, & A.C. Cederborg (Eds.), *Child Sexual Abuse: Disclosure, delay and denial* (pp 41–62). Mahwah, NJ: Lawrence Erlbaum Associates, Inc.
London, K., Bruck, M., Wright, D. B., & Ceci, S. J. (2008). Review of the contemporary literature on how children report sexual abuse to others: Findings, methodological issues, and implications for forensic interviewers. *Memory, 16*(1), 29–47.
Lyon, T. (2014). Interviewing children. *Annual Review of Law and Social Science, 10*, 73–89.
Lyon, T., Malloy, L., Quas, J., & Talwar, V. (2008). Coaching, truth induction, and young maltreatment children's false allegations and false denials. *Child Development, 79*(4), 914–929.
Malloy, L., Brubacher, S., & Lamb, M. (2011). Expected consequences of disclosure revealed in investigative interviews with suspected victims of child sexual abuse. *Applied Developmental Science, 15*(1), 8–19.
Malloy, L., & Lyon, T. (2006). Caregiver support and child sexual abuse: Why does it matter? *Journal of Child Sexual Abuse, 15*(4), 97–103.
Malloy, L., Lyon, T., & Quas, J. (2007). Recantation of child sexual abuse allegations. *Journal of the American Academy of Child and Adolescent Psychiatry, 46*, 162–170.
Miller-Perrin, C., & Perrin, R. (2012). *Child maltreatment: An introduction* (2nd ed.). Thousand Oaks, CA: Sage.
Myers, D. (2007). *Exploring psychology* (8th ed.). New York, NY: Worth Publishers.
O'Donohue, W. & Benuto, L. (2012). Problems with Child Sexual Abuse Accomodation Syndrome. *Scientific Review of Mental Health Practice, 9*(1), 20–28.
O'Donohue, W., Benuto, L., Fanetti, M., Fondren, R., & Vijay, A. (2013). Children's allegations of sexual abuse: What is unusual and what is not. *Journal of Forensic Psychology Practice 13(5)*, pp. 456–475.
O'Donohue, W., & Fanetti, M. (1996). Assessing the occurrence of child sexual abuse: An information processing, hypothesis testing approach. *Aggression and Violent Behavior, 1*(3), 269–281.
Olafson, E. & Lederman J. C. (2006). The state of debate about children's disclosure patterns in child sexual abuse cases. *Juvenile and Family Court Journal*, 27–40.
Palmer, T., & Stacey, L. (2004). *Just one click: Sexual abuse of children and young people through the internet and mobile phone technology*. Ilford, England: Barnardo's.
Perrin, R., & Miller-Perrin, C. (2011). *Child maltreatment: An introduction* (2nd ed.). Thousand Oaks, CA: Sage.

Saywitz, K., & Moan-Hardie, S. (1994). Reducing the potential for distortion of childhood memories. *Consciousness and Cognition, 3*, 257–293.
Sjoberg, R., & Lindblad, F. (2002). Delayed disclosure and disrupted communication during forensic investigations of child sexual abuse: A study of 47 corroborated cases. *Acta Paediatrica, 91*, 1391–1396.
Smith, D. W., Letourneau, E. J., Saunders, B. E., Kilpatrick, D. G., Resnick, H. S., & Best, C. L. (2000). Delay in disclosure of childhood rape: Results from a national survey. *Child Abuse and Neglect, 24*(2), 273–287.
Summit, R. (1983). The child sexual abuse accommodation syndrome. *Child Abuse and Neglect, 7*(2), 177–193.
Tang, S., Freyd, J., & Wang, M. (2007). What do we know about gender in the disclosure of child sexual abuse? *Journal of Psychological Trauma, 6*(4), 1–27.
The National Children's Advocacy Center History. (2012). Retrieved from www.nationalcac.org/history/history.html
Townsend, C. & Rheingold, A. (2013). *Estimating a child sexual abuse rate for practitioners: A Review of child sexual abuse prevalence studies* (Darkness to Light, Charleston, S.C.). Retrieved from www.D2L.org/1in10
U.S. Department of Health and Human Services, Administration for Children and Families, Administration on Children, Youth, and Families, Children's Bureau. (2011). *Child Maltreatment, 2010.* Retrieved from http://www.acf.hhs.gov/programs/cb/stats_research/index.htm#can
von Weiler, J., Haardt-Becker, A., & Schulte, S. (2010). Care and treatment of child victims of child pornographic exploitation (CPE) in Germany. *Journal of Sexual Aggression, 16*(2).
Zulawski, D., & Wicklander, D. (1993). *Practical aspects of interview and interrogation.* New York, NY: Elsevier.

Chapter 7
Disclosure Failures: Statistics, Characteristics, and Strategies to Address Them

Kathleen Coulborn Faller

Introduction

Provided in this chapter are estimates of the numbers of true sexual abuse cases in which children deny abuse, the reasons these children do not disclose, predictors of disclosure failure, and strategies that may facilitate disclosure of sexual abuse. The chapter relies upon both research and practice knowledge. The research is comprised of both quantitative and qualitative studies with a primary focus on field research rather than analogue studies. Much of the knowledge about denial of sexual abuse derives from literature on children and youth who eventually disclose their abuse. In the interest of parsimony, citations will not be exhaustive and will emphasize recent findings. Often, illustrative research, but not the entire body of supportive findings for an assertion or observation, will be presented.

Forensic Interviewers Should Be Aware the Child May Not Have Been Sexually Abused

As awareness of the phenomenon of child sexual abuse, its signs and symptoms, and the contexts in which there is risk for sexual abuse increase, more possible cases are being identified by parents and professionals. In this context, it is important to be ever-mindful that the child may not have been sexually abused. Moreover, advances in electronic access to sexual material render obsolete, or at least limited, some prior hallmarks of sexual abuse, for example, advanced sexual knowledge for the child's developmental stage and certain sexualized behaviors.

K.C. Faller (✉)
University of Michigan School of Social Work,
1080 S. University Ave., Ann Arbor, MI 48109-1106, USA
e-mail: kcfaller@umich.edu

W.T. O'Donohue, M. Fanetti (eds.), *Forensic Interviews Regarding Child Sexual Abuse*, DOI 10.1007/978-3-319-21097-1_7

What Can Evidence Tell Us About the Number of Sexually Abused Children Who Do Not Disclose?

The above points having been made, there is nevertheless research that indicates that a substantial minority of children, who have been sexually abused, do not disclose their abuse when forensically interviewed.

Pioneering work by the National Children's Advocacy Center (NCAC) determined that approximately a fourth of children who were evaluated for child sexuala-buse at NCAC did not disclose in a single interview. NCAC staff defined cases which warranted further evaluation as follows: (1) the child did not disclose but there was other compelling evidence of sexual abuse (e.g., medical findings, sexualized behaviors), (2) the child was not able to disclose the full extent of sexual abuse in a single interview, and (3) the allegations were still unresolved after a single interview. Based upon these observations, NCAC undertook several studies involving extended assessments as a method for resolving these cases, studies that will be discussed later in this chapter (Carnes, Wilson, & Nelson-Gardell, 1999, 2000; Carnes, Wilson, Nelson-Gardell, & Orgassa, 2001).

As noted in earlier chapters, the National Institute of Child Health and Human Development (NICHD) protocol is the most extensively researched child forensic interviewprotocol to date. Early studies focused on optimal strategies for eliciting narrative accounts from children who were willing and able to disclose their sexual abuse (e.g., Sternberg et al., 1997; Sternberg, Lamb, Esplin, & Baradaran, 1999). Disclosing children comprised about two-thirds of the children interviewed using the NICHD protocol (e.g., Sternberg, Lamb, Orbach, Esplin, & Mitchell, 2001). More recently, the research team studying the NICHD protocol has examined interviews of non-disclosing children (see Pipe, Lamb, Orbach, & Cederborg, 2007). Hershkowitz, Horowtiz, and Lamb (2005) report that, despite the demonstrated advantages of the NICHD protocol, about a third of children do not disclose in a single interview. They further examined cases when there was clear evidence that the children were sexually abused (Hershkowitz et al., 2006), again with about a third not reporting sexual abuse. Comparable findings were reported in a New Zealand case study involving four girls (8–15 years old at time of report) and eight adult men. In this study, there were photographs and audiotapes of the sexual abuse. The omission rate for documented sexual acts was of 36.9 % (Bidrose & Goodman, 2000).

Rates of non-disclosure have been found to be higher in specific situations. For example, disclosure rates for children with sexually transmitted diseases have been found to be 42–43 % in two studies (Lawson & Chaffin, 1992; Lyon, 2007). Similarly, an exploratory study involving a single offender who videotaped his abuse of ten victims (one girl and nine boys) found only half of children admitted to some of the videotaped acts when interviewed by police (Cederborg, Lamb, & Laurell, 2007; Sjoberg & Lindblad, 2002). These and other findings indicate that non-disclosing children represent a population whose interview needs warrant professional attention.

What Are the Reasons Children Fail to Disclose Sexual Abuse When Forensically Interviewed?

Both research and practice experience inform knowledge about why children do not disclose sexual abuse. Non-disclosing children with a history of sexual abuse fall into two general categories: (1) Children who do not know to disclose and (2) Children who do not want to disclose (Faller, 2007a).

Children Don't Know to Tell

There are a variety of reasons why children do not know to disclose sexual abuse. Chief among them that children lack general knowledge about sex and a range of sexual activities, as well as specific knowledge related to sexual abuse.

Children lack sexual knowledge. Young children, in particular, may have no knowledge about sexual behavior (Bussey & Grimbeek, 1995; Cederborg et al., 2007). Even children who have been taught "how babies are made" may lack knowledge about fondling behaviors, oral sex, and anal sex. Because of this, they do not relate sexual abuse to the knowledge they have about conception. Moreover, caretakers may not explain to children the pleasurable and other motivational aspects of sexual behavior. Sexual abuse, therefore, may be perceived as somewhat bewildering activity that does not fit into the child's knowledge base.

Children don't know sexual abuse is wrong. Even if children have sexual knowledge, they may not know that sexual behavior between an older person and a child is wrong (Schaeffer, Leventhal, & Asnes, 2011). For example, Sas and Cunningham (1995), who interviewed 138 children after their cases had been litigated, determined that 30 % of children did not know the abuse was wrong when they first experienced it. Efforts to educate children about "good touch/bad touch" may be inadequate because the sexual behavior is not experienced as touching.

Children don't understand the expectations for a forensic interview. Children do not know to tell because of the anomaly of a forensic interview (Faller, 2007a, 2007b, 2007c). For children, a forensic interview may be perceived as an encounter with a friendly (or not so friendly) stranger who asks the child open-ended questions which are foreign to the way most adults engage in discourse with children. In children's everyday encounters with adults, adults do most of the talking and expect short responses from children (Faller, 2007a). Especially for young children, open-ended questions may not trigger free recall of abusive events (Lyon, 2005).

Children don't perceive the abuse as noteworthy. Children may not know to tell because the abusive event may not be salient to the child. Forensic interviewers may focus on sexual abuse that happened sometime in the past, was disguised as childcare behavior, or occurred in the context of other more upsetting events, for example, living in a crack house. The child's perspective on saliency is often very different from the forensic interviewer's. As a consequence, open-ended prompts such as "Tell me the reason you came here today," or even "I understand something may have happened to you, tell me about it from the beginning to the end," (e.g., Lamb, Orbach, Hershkowitz, Esplin, & Horowitz, 2007) may not trigger the child's recollection.

Children Don't Want to Tell

Children who don't want to disclose pose great challenges to forensic interviewers. There are a number of reasons children are reluctant to disclose sexual abuse.

Children try to avoid being distressed. A typical child response to an upsetting topic is avoidance: avoidance of thinking about the topic and avoidance of talking about it. This response is often found in situations of documented sexualabuse (e.g., Hershkowitz et al., 2006; Leander, 2010).

Children may feel complicit. Children may be reluctant to disclose because they may feel they were complicit. When sexual abuse is discovered, sexually naïve children, who may have enjoyed the attention and/or the physical pleasure, discover that acts they thought were somewhat strange, in fact were very "bad." As a consequence, they come to believe they are bad for being involved in the abuse. These children do not want to admit that they were "bad." They are afraid they will be in trouble because of their involvement in the sexual abuse (Hershkowitz, Lanes, & Lamb, 2007). Children who were groomed or who were bribed may regard themselves as participants rather than victims and therefore not disclose (Alaggia, 2004; Goodman-Brown, Edelstein, Goodman, Jones, & Gordon, 2003; Staller & Nelson-Gardell, 2005).

Children feel they will label themselves "damaged goods." A related reason for not telling is that children may feel stigmatized, embarrassed, or ashamed (Deblinger & Runyon, 2005; Staller & Nelson-Gardell, 2005). Suzanne Sgroi (1982), a pioneer in the child sexual abuse field, described this phenomenon as "damaged goods syndrome," a common effect of sexual abuse. Older children may be very mindful of the stigma associated with having been a victim of sexual abuse and not want people to know (e.g., Staller & Nelson-Gardell, 2005).

Children are instructed not to talk to strangers. The expectation of professionals that children will disclose sexual abuse to a stranger in the context of a forensic interview is somewhat naïve. Many children are taught to be wary of strangers, which is who a forensic interviewer is. Older children may have had prior experience with the child welfare system and do not want to repeat this experience. In most instances, abused children harbor greater affinity for the offender than for the forensic interviewer.

Offenders manipulate children to keep the secret. Interviewers may fail to fully appreciate the impact on victims of having been admonished not to tell by the offender (Cederborg et al., 2007; Hershkowitz, 2006). Offender admonitions cover a wide spectrum (Malloy, Brubacher, & Lamb, 2011). Schaeffer et al. (2011) added questions about disclosure delays to the RATAC interview protocol (Vieth, 2006) and gathered information from 191 children who made disclosures. These researchers identified nine specific offender threats that were barriers to disclosure. Many researchers note that children may have been threatened with death, bodily hard, or harm to others, including caregivers, siblings, and pets (e.g., Faller, 2007a; Goodman-Brown et al., 2003; Schaeffer et al., 2011). In intrafamilial cases, the offender may have told the child that the family will break up, that he will go to jail, or that he won't love the child anymore (Faller, 2007a).

Children don't want to trouble the non-offending caregiver. Children may be influenced not to tell based upon their relationship with a non-offending caregiver. Research supports denial or delay in disclosure because of the lack of support of the non-offending caregiver (e.g., Malloy, Lyon, & Quas, 2007; Olafson & Lederman, 2006). On the other hand, children may fail to disclose because of reluctance to distress the non-offending parent. Schaeffer and colleagues (2011) found that children were fearful that the non-offending parent would be angry, harm the perpetrator, go crazy, be upset, be overwhelmed, be sad, or do something bad.

Children are apprehensive about the future if they tell. Finally, children may fail to disclose sexual abuse because they fear the unknown (Faller, 2007a). Although they are in an abusive situation, at least it is predictable. Even when they have not threatened with consequences if they tell, they simply do not know what might happen to them or to others if they tell (Goodman-Brown et al., 2003; Schaeffer et al., 2011).

Predictors of Non-disclosure

A number of studies have documented predictors of non-disclosure of sexual abuse during forensic interviews.

Gender. One predictor of denial of sexual abuse is gender. Disclosure rates for boys are generally lower than those for girls (e.g., DeVoe & Faller, 1999; Hershkowitz, Horowtiz, & Lamb, 2007; O'Leary & Barber, 2008). Because most offenders are male (e.g., Russell & Bolen, 2000), arguably male victims must overcome two taboos in order to disclose, being involved in sexual abuse and a same-gender sexual encounter (Finkelhor, 1984; Sorsoli, Kia-Keating, & Grossman, 2008). Moreover, the socialization of males to refrain from talking about their problems and vulnerabilities may contribute to their reluctance to disclose.

Proximity of the relationship with the offender. Many studies find that a close relationship between the child and the offender predicts denial of sexual abuse (e.g., Goodman-Brown et al., 2003; Schaeffer et al., 2011). Illustrative are findings from a very large sample study of interviews conducted by Israeli Youth Investigators, masters-level, trained forensic interviewers responsible for interviewing children with allegations of both physical and sexual abuse (Hershkowitz et al., 2005). The researchers report on data from over 25,000 interviews collected over a 5-year period, two-thirds involving parental figures. Although the overall disclosure rate for children alleged to have been sexually abused was 71 % (7812 sexual abuse disclosures), 8 % were of sexual abuse by parental figures and 92 % by non-parental figures. The researchers further examined 373 high certainty (cases with corroborating evidence) non-disclosing cases. Parents or parent figures were the alleged offenders in 85.5 % of these cases.

Non-supportive, non-offending caregiver. Having a non-supportive, non-offending parent predicts lack of willingness to tell the parent (Elliott & Carnes, 2001; Faller, 1988). Further, if the child does disclose to a parent but is not supported, there is increased risk for disclosure failure in a forensic interview (e.g., Hershkowitz, Lanes & Lamb, 2007; Lawson & Chaffin, 1992; Malloy & Lyon, 2006). Lack of trust of the caretaker (Schönbucher, Maier, Mohler-Kuo, Schnyder, & Landolt, 2012), especially with adolescents, and fear of being blamed are barriers to disclosure (Staller & Nelson-Gardell, 2005). Concern that the caretaker will not believe may delay or prevent disclosure (Alaggia, 2004; Faller, 1988; Schaeffer et al., 2011). If the caretaker is non-supportive or ambivalent (Bolen & Lamb, 2004, 2007a, 2007b), when the sexual abuse is revealed, the caretaker response may lead to recantation (Malloy et al., 2007) or failure to disclose in a forensic interview.

Age of the victim. Findings regarding age as a predictor of disclosure failure vary. Nonetheless, it appears that being very young and being an adolescent both are associated with decreased likelihood of disclosure. In a number of studies, disclosure rates are lower for younger children (e.g., Hershkowitz et al., 2005; Keary & Fitzpatrick, 1994). Lower disclosure rates can be explained by lack of knowledge about sex and sexual abuse, lack of understanding of expectations for a forensic interview, and less developed communication skills. Other research, however, finds lower disclosure rates among older children (e.g., Goodman-Brown et al., 2003; Hershkowitz, Lanes & Lamb, 2007), arguably because they can anticipate negative consequences emanating from telling.

Race and ethnicity. There is general recognition among practitioners that children from non-dominant racial and ethnic groups are potentially less likely to disclose sexual abuse in a forensic interview (e.g., Fontes, 2008; Fontes & Faller, 2007; Paine & Hansen, 2002). In addition, forensic interviewers are usually Caucasian (Williams, Nelson-Gardell, Faller, Cordisco-Steele, & Tishelman, 2014), and their interviewees are disproportionately children of color and increasingly children who are ethnically different from interviewers (Fontes & Faller). Despite the importance of race and ethnicity, there is little research that addresses racial/ethnic barriers and the role of racial and ethnic difference in forensic interviews (e.g., Paine & Hansen). There are some relevant studies, but with inconsistent findings.

Dunkerley and Dalenberg (1999) undertook an analogue study involving 128 children, ages 6–11 years, including 51 Black children and 43 Caucasian children. All children observed a male research assistant of the child's race engage in either a positive activity (providing a box of candy) or a negative activity (hiding a purse), both which they were told to keep secret. Children were asked about the secret either by a female graduate student, matched for race or cross race. Only 20 % of African–American children revealed the negative secret when interviewed by a white female, but 60 % did so when interviewed by an African–American female. Findings were comparable for Caucasian children but differences were less extreme.

Faller and Nelson-Gardell (2010) examined predictors of disclosure of sexuala-buse, using data from the NCAC multi-site study (to be described in greater detail under strategies that may facilitate disclosure). In this study, 22 interviewers provided data on 137 extended assessments. All but one of the interviewers were Caucasian (one was a Latina). Thirty-five (25 %) of the children were children of color, mostly African–American. In this study, children of color were less likely to disclose sexual abuse.

On the other hand, Springman, Wherry, and Notaro (2006) examined 220 archived forensic interviews for level of disclosure as it related to the race of the forensic interviewer. They reported that African–American children were more likely to disclose sexual abuse to a white interviewer, and white children were more likely to disclose sexual abuse to an African–American interviewer.

To date, there is recognition by practitioners that race matters (e.g., Fontes, 2008) as reflected in both practice guides (e.g., APSAC, 2012) and training of forensic interviewers (e.g., NCAC, 2014). More research is needed, however, to better understand the impact of race and ethnicity on non-disclosure of sexual abuse.

No priordisclosure. Finally, children who have not yet revealed their sexual abuse are less likely to do so in a formal forensic interview (e.g., Keary & Fitzpatrick, 1994; Olafson & Lederman, 2006; Paine & Hansen, 2002). For example, as noted earlier, children whose abuse is first identified by the presence of sexually transmitted disease (Lawson & Chaffin, 1992; Lyon, 2005) and children whose abuse is first identified by audiovisual evidence (Cederborg et al., 2007; Leander, 2010) have low rates of disclosure. Similarly, children thought to have been sexually abused because they exhibit sexualized behavior have lower disclosure rates (e.g., Olafson & Lederman, 2006).

Strategies that May Facilitate Disclosure

A number of strategies may facilitate disclosures from reluctant or non-disclosing children who have been sexually abused. These strategies derive from both research and practice.

Use the revised NICHD protocol. In their highly influential 2011 book, Lamb, La Rooy, Malloy, and Katz provide a revised NICHD protocol aimed at facilitating disclosure in reluctant and non-disclosing children. The NICHD protocol is a linear interview protocol; the revised protocol changes the order of rules and rapport by placing building rapport before providing interview rules. Hallmarks of the revised

NICHD protocol are instructing the interviewer to present a friendly, supportive demeanor, to use the child's name frequently during the interview, to acknowledge the child's feelings, but not to interpret them, and to provide non-contingent positive reinforcement. With regard to demeanor, Lamb and colleagues encourage smiling, leaning forward, and making eye contact. Because forensic interviewers are admonished to be neutral, they may be at risk for presenting as cold and unfriendly. Similarly, neutrality could result in failure to acknowledge the child's feelings. In the revised NICHD protocol, interviewers can acknowledge the child's feeling related to the interview process. The interviewer can say, for example, "I see you are upset." The interviewer may also say, "You are really doing a good job," but take care not to provide this feedback only when the child discloses abuse. Hershkowitz, Lamb, Katz, and Malloy (2013) report on a study in which 199 suspected victims of intrafamilial sexual abuse were randomly assigned to either the revised NICHD protocol or the standard NICHD protocol. The revised NICHD protocol elicited more disclosures (60 % compared to 50 %), disclosures to more open-ended prompts, reduced omissions (e.g., no answer, don't know, not sure), and fewer denials.

Extend the rapport-building phase of the interview. Extending the rapport-building portion of the interview with children who present as uncooperative in the early stages of the interview can increase the likelihood of disclosure. In a study that matched 50 high certainty, non-disclosing and 50 high certainty, disclosing children, Hershkowitz et al. (2006) report that non-disclosing children communicated less in the rapport-building phase of the interview, which continued into the abuse-related--> portion of the interview. Interviewers used fewer open-ended prompts and fewer supportive comments with these non-communicative children during rapport-building, suggesting an interactional phenomenon. That is, the less the child communicates, the fewer opportunities to offer support and the more the interviewer uses close-ended probes. One recommendation from this study was, when interviewers note a non-communicative pattern, interviewers extend rapport-building rather than moving on to the abuse-related part of the interview. Similarly, Hershkowitz (2011) offers this advice and provides a catalogue of non-suggestive, supportive comments that interviewers might use and examples. These include welcoming the child, expression of personal interest in the child, expression of care about the child's well-being, checking on the child's feelings during the interview process, reinforcement that the child is helping the interviewer understand, gestures of goodwill such as "Are you cold?" or "Here is a glass of water," and thanks at the end of the interview.

Ask the accompanying adult to give the child permission to talk. Interviewers can attempt to preempt reluctance and non-disclosure by asking the caregiver who brings the child to the forensic interview to give the child permission to answer the interviewer's questions. The adult gives this permission in the presence of the forensic interviewer. This strategy may be especially helpful in cases where the alleged offender is someone close to the child and in cases where the child is concerned about the impact of disclosure on the caregiver (Faller, 2007a).

Explain the expectations of a forensic interview. Because the forensic interview context is anomalous for most children, explaining the process is advised (e.g., Saywitz, Goodman, & Lyon, 2002). Setting the stage for the forensic interview has been shown in analogue research to result in increased free recall (e.g., Dorado & Saywitz, 2001). The interviewer should provide information about his or her role, about the method of recording (notes, audiotape, or videotape), and about the interview rules. A typical rule is a statement that the interviewer will be asking the child lots of questions and, if the child knows the answers, the child should answer the questions; if the child does not, the child should say, "I don't know." Additional rules are that if the child doesn't understand the question, the child should say so, and the interviewer will ask the question in a better way, and the child should talk about what really happened and not about pretend.

In addition, getting the child to promise to tell the truth and reassuring the child he/she will not get in trouble for telling the truth have been found to increase the likelihood of disclosure. Lyon and Dorado (2008) conducted analogue studies with latency-aged children who were under the jurisdiction of the dependency court. Children were interviewed about minor transgressions involving themselves and an adult confederate. Children in both the truth induction and the reassurance conditions were more likely to disclose the transgressions than children in the control condition.

Use facilitative strategies when the child has acknowledged something happened. There are a series of strategies derived from practice that may be useful in situations where the child acknowledges something happened but does not want to talk or says he/she does not remember much.

Focus on the context of abuse first. The interviewer may gather context information first. Contextual details include where the abuse happened, where others were at the time, when it happened, what the child and the offender were wearing, and what, if anything was said during the abusive encounter. When the interviewer has exhausted the child's report about the context, he/she then asks the child about the sexual acts (what?) and the perpetrator (who?) (Faller, 2007, Chapter 13).

Address reasons for denial. Another strategy, again if the child acknowledges something happened, the interviewer can explore reasons for non-disclosure and then address them. This can include reassurance that the child did nothing wrong and is not in trouble, but should not include promises that everything will be fine if the child discloses, because likely, things will not be fine (Faller, 2007a).

Attempt to motivate disclosure. A related strategy, again in circumstances in which the interviewer has information that the child has, in fact, been abused, is attempting to motivate disclosure. Children may be persuaded to disclose because they want the abuse to stop, they want to protect other vulnerable children, or they want the offender to suffer some consequences (e.g., Schaeffer et al., 2011). A question like "what do you think should happen?" may be appropriate (Faller, 2007a).

Normalize the disclosure process. Sometimes children can be motivated to tell by normalizing the disclosure process. The interviewer can say, "I talk to lots of kids when things have happened to them," or "This is a safe place for kids to talk."

Offer other media for disclosure. Finally, when children are reluctant to talk about abuse, the interviewer may suggest other modes of communication. The interviewer may present an anatomical drawing for the child to use to indicate where on the body abuse happened or what body part the offender used (Faller, 2007b). The interviewer may ask the child to draw a picture of the abusive event (Faller, 2007b). Older children may be given the option of writing their responses. In research on the NICHD protocol, both human figure drawings (Aldridge et al., 2004; Teoh, Yang, Lamb, & Larsson, 2010) and asking the child to draw a picture of the abuse (Katz & Hershkowitz, 2010) have been demonstrated to increase disclosures about sexual abuse. Interviewers can also employ dolls, including anatomical dolls to facilitate disclosure (e.g., Faller, 2007b; Goodman, Quas, Batterman-Faunce, Riddelsberger, & Kuhn, 1997; Saywitz, Goodman, Nicholas, & Moan, 1991).

For example, Goodman and colleagues (1997) studied reports of forty-six 3–10-year-old children who had experienced voiding cystourethrogram fluoroscopy (VCUG), an intrusive medical procedure for determining the source of urinary track problems. Most children explicitly revealed genital contact as part of the procedure using anatomical dolls but not in free recall. That said, because the research findings on anatomical dolls are mixed (e.g., Bruck, Ceci, & Francoeur, 2000; Bruck, Ceci, Francoeur, & Renick, 1995), forensic interviewers should be mindful that the use of anatomical dolls may be challenged.

Use externally derived information. If the interviewer has other information that supports sexual abuse, the interviewer can judiciously present this information to the child and ask the child to explain the inconsistency between the child's denial and the supportive information. Situations in which the child has made a prior disclosure or there is corroborating evidence such as medical findings, a confession, an eye witness, or physical evidence (e.g., video) are possible examples.

Employ more than a single interview. There is increasing support for conducting more than a single forensic interview with children whose sexual abuseallegations cannot be resolved in a single interview (e.g., Hershkowitz et al., 2006; La Rooy, Katz, Malloy, & Lamb, 2010; La Rooy, Lamb, & Pipe, 2009; Patterson & Pipe, 2009). Williams and colleagues conducted a web-based survey of professionals from the lists of the American Society on the Abuse of Children, the National Children's Advocacy Center, and the National Children's Alliance, on the need for extended assessments (also called extended forensic evaluations and extended forensic interviews) (Williams et al., 2014; Williams, Nelson-Gardell, Faller, Tishelman, & Cordisco-Steele, 2013). The 1294 child maltreatment professionals who responded to the survey reported that a not insignificant percentage of their caseloads (mean = 20 %, mode = 10 %; median = 10 %) during the past year could have benefited from an extended assessment. In terms of numbers of cases that could benefit, the respondents indicated a mean of 13, mode of 10, and a median of

6 children. Among the types of cases that could benefit from an extended assessment, 93.1 % of respondents identified "children/adolescents who deny sexual abuse when there is other persuasive evidence (medical indicators, audio or video evidence, offender confession)." There is an emerging body of research that supports both the value of more than a single interview and extended assessments.

Support for more than one interview. There are studies employing the NICHD protocol, with disclosing children who receive a second interview closely following the first (Hershkowitz & Terner, 2007; Katz & Hershkowitz, 2013). These studies found substantial additional information elicited in the second interview and only modest overlap in information from the first and second interviews. For example, Hershkowitz and Terner studied interviews with 30 children (ages 6–13) which occurred a half an hour apart. One-fourth of the details about sexual abuse derived from the second interview, and there was only a 47 % overlap in information from the first and second interviews. Moreover, in the second interview, the interviewers asked more open-ended questions, and the children's narratives were better organized.

Additional support for multiple interviews is provided by Leander (2010), who examined police interviews with 27 children whose sexual abuse was corroborated by video or photographs. Children were interviewed three times. Although children were avoidant and denied documented abuse in their initial interview, they provided twice as many new details about the abuse in second and third interviews than in the first and fewer denials than in their initial interview. Altogether these children provided 45 sexual details in the first interview, 100 in the second interview, and 103 in the third interview.

Support for extended assessments. Research on extended assessments conducted by the National Children's Advocacy Center (NCAC) demonstrates that they can resolve a substantial portion of cases when a single forensic interview cannot (Carnes et al., 1999, 2000, 2001). NCAC conducted a pilot study in which children, whose allegations had not been resolved in a single interview, received an eight session extended forensic evaluation (Carnes et al., 1999). Approximately half of these children's allegations were resolved with a conclusion the children had been sexually abused, about a fifth not sexually abused, and about a fourth still unresolved. The National Children's Advocacy Center then conducted a multi-site study (20 sites; 147 cases) comparing a four session protocol to an eight session protocol (Carnes et al., 2001). Later analysis of the data from the multi-site study demonstrated that the eight session protocol resulted in 56.6 % of cases being classified as credible disclosures, but the four session protocol only resulted in 29.5 % credible disclosures (Faller & Nelson-Gardell, 2010). Additional examination of disclosures in the eight session condition determined that 95 % of disclosures occurred before the seventh session, suggesting an extended assessment should consist of up to six sessions (Faller & Nelson-Gardell).

An extended assessment allows more time for rapport building and assessing the particular child's functioning; it adapts the pace and the structure of the inquiry to the child and gives the child more than a single chance to tell (Faller & Cordisco-Steele, 2014). Thus, it accommodates children who do not know to tell and children who don't want to tell. There are several models for extended assessments (Faller & Cordisco-Steele; J. N. Anderson, personal communication, May 15, 2014). Nevertheless, there is a need for more detailed articulation of the components of an extended assessment and research to document model efficacy.

Despite the support for extended assessments, there are two legitimate reasons for caution about them. First is expense in a context of scarce forensic interview resources. Even if extended assessments are used judiciously and with a small minority of allegations, Children's Advocacy Centers do not normally have funds (L. Cordisco-Steele, personal communication, Jan. 26, 2014) and federal child welfare funds are not easily accessible for this type of intervention. The second concern is that interviewers may, by virtue of "not taking no for an answer," induce children who have not been sexually abused to say that they have been. Research, however, demonstrates that the danger of inducing false positives results from leading and suggestive questioning in the context of multiple interviews, rather than from multiple interviews per se (Lyon, 1999).

Refer the child to abuse-focused therapy. A final strategy to address disclosure failures is abuse-focused treatment. Although non-disclosing children are routinely referred for treatment by child welfare professionals, this treatment has scant coverage in the literature. James, Everson, and Friedrich (n.d.) proposed an abuse-focused treatment model in which the clinician is mindful that the child may have been sexually abused and consciously switches from therapeutic to forensic mode if the child begins to disclose abuse. They advise this model for very young children, children who are reluctant to disclose, and children for whom the likelihood of sexual abuse is uncertain.

Best practice for abuse-focused treatment is for the clinician to use open-ended inquiry about possible abuse, provide opportunities for disclosure by structuring the treatment (e.g., using media or other materials that might trigger disclosure), and to avoid suggestive interpretations of the child's statements and behavior in treatment. If the child begins to disclose, the clinician gathers information using open-ended methods. Verbatim documentation of any disclosures and the clinician's mode of inquiry are important. Depending upon the characteristics of the case (e.g., relationship to the alleged offender, coherence of the child's disclosure, and safety issues), the clinician may prepare the child and then refer the child for a formal forensic interview.

Conclusions

Research and practice document that non-disclosing children who have likely been sexually abused comprise a significant minority of children and youth who come to professional attention because of sexual abuse allegations. There appear to be two distinct categories of denying children: (1) those who don't know to tell and (2) those who don't want to tell. Strategies to address these two categories of children can vary substantially. Research indicates there are factors that inhibit children's disclosures, including gender, relationship with the offender, having a non-supportive caretaker, age, race/ethnicity, and having not made an outcry before a formal forensic interview. Happily, both clinicians and researchers have begun to turn their attention to denying children and generate strategies that can assist them. Among these are the revised, more child-friendly NICHD protocol, extended rapport-building, practice-based strategies to be used within the interview itself, extended assessments, and abuse-focused treatment.

Nevertheless, there are no foolproof methods for eliciting information about abuse from denying children. Moreover, child abuse professionals must balance concerns about false negatives (children who have been victimized but do not disclose) and false positives (children who, because of interview strategies, falsely confirm sexual victimization).

References

Alaggia, R. (2004). Many ways of telling: Expanding conceptualizations of child sexual abuse disclosure. *Child Abuse & Neglect, 28*, 1213–1227.

Aldridge, J., Lamb, M. E., Sternberg, K. J., Orbach, Y., Esplin, P. W., & Bowler, L. (2004). Using a human figure drawing to elicit information from alleged victims of child sexual abuse. *Journal Of Consulting and Clinical Psychology, 72*(2), 304–316.

American Professional Society on the Abuse of Children (APSAC). (2012). *Practice guidelines: Forensic interviewing in cases of suspected child abuse.* Retrieved from www.apsac.org

Bidrose, S., & Goodman, G. (2000). Testimony and evidence: A scientific case study of memory for child sexual abuse. *Applied Cognitive Psychology, 14*, 197–213.

Bolen, R. M., & Lamb, J. L. (2004). Ambivalence in nonoffending guardians after child sexual abuse disclosure. *Journal of Interpersonal Violence, 19*(2), 185–211.

Bolen, R. M., & Lamb, J. (2007a). Can nonoffending mothers of sexually abused children be both ambivalent and supportive? *Child Maltreatment, 12*(2), 191–197.

Bolen, R. M., & Lamb, J. (2007b). Parental support and outcome in sexually abused children. *Journal of Child Sexual Abuse: Research, Treatment, & Program Innovations for Victims, Survivors, & Offenders, 16*(2), 33–54.

Bruck, M., Ceci, S., Francoeur, E., & Renick, A. (1995). Anatomically detailed dolls do not facilitate preschoolers' reports of a pediatric examination involving genital touching. *Journal of Experimental Psychology: Applied, 1*(2), 95–109.

Bruck, M., Ceci, S., & Francoeur, E. (2000). Children's use of anatomically detailed dolls to report genital touching in a medical examination: Developmental & gender comparisons. *Journal of Applied Experimental Psychology: Applied, 6*(1), 74–83.

Bussey, K., & Grimbeek, E. J. (1995). Disclosure processes: Issues for child sexual abuse victims. In K. Rotenberg (Ed.), *Disclosure processes in children and adolescents* (pp. 166–203). New York, NY: Cambridge University Press.

Carnes, C., Wilson, C., Nelson-Gardell, D., & Orgassa, U. (2001). Extended forensic evaluation when sexual abuse is suspected: A multi-site study. *Child Maltreatment, 6*(3), 230–242.

Carnes, C., Wilson, C., & Nelson-Gardell, D. (1999). Extended forensic evaluation when child abuse is suspected: A model and preliminary data. *Child Maltreatment, 4*(3), 242–254.

Carnes, C., Wilson, C., & Nelson-Gardell, D. (2000). Addressing the challenges and controversies in child sexual abuse interviewing: The forensic evaluation protocol and research project. In K. C. Faller (Ed.), *Maltreatment in early childhood: Tools for research-based intervention* (pp. 83–104). New York, NY: Haworth.

Cederborg, A., Lamb, M., & Laurell, O. (2007). Delay of disclosure, minimization, and denial of abuse even when the evidence in unambiguous: A multi-victim case. In M. E. Pipe, M. Lamb, Y. Orbach, & A. Cederborg (Eds.), *Child sexual abuse: Disclosure: Delay, and denial* (pp. 159–174). New York, NY: Psychology.

Deblinger, E., & Runyon, M. K. (2005). Understanding and treating feelings of shame in children who have experienced maltreatment. *Child Maltreatment, 10*(4), 364–376. doi:10.1177/1077559505279306.

DeVoe, E. R., & Faller, K. C. (1999). Characteristics of disclosure of children who may have been sexually abused. *Child Maltreatment, 4*(3), 217–227.

Dorado, J., & Saywitz, K. (2001). Interviewing preschoolers from low and middle income SES communities: A test of narrative elaboration recall improvement techniques. *Journal of Clinical Child Psychology, 30*(4), 566–578.

Dunkerley, G. K., & Dalenberg, C. J. (1999). Secret-keeping behaviors in Black and White children as a function of interviewer race, racial identity, and risk for abuse. *Journal of Aggression, Maltreatment & Trauma, 2*(2), 13–35. doi:10.1300/J146v02n02_02.

Elliott, A. N., & Carnes, C. N. (2001). Reactions of nonoffending parents to the sexual abuse of their child: A review of the literature. *Child Maltreatment, 6*(4), 314–331.

Faller, K. C. (1988). The myth of the 'Collusive Mother': Variability in the functioning of mothers of victims of intra-familial sexual abuse. *Journal of Interpersonal Violence, 3*(2), 190–196.

Faller, K. C. (2007a). Children who do not want to disclose. In K. C. Faller (Ed.), *Interviewing children about sexual abuse: Controversies and best practice* (pp. 175–190). New York, NY: Oxford University Press. Chapter 13.

Faller, K. C. (2007b). Media for interviewing children. In K. C. Faller (Ed.), *Interviewing children about sexual abuse: Controversies and best practice* (pp. 110–141). New York, NY: Oxford University Press. Chapter 9.

Faller, K. C. (2007c). *Interviewing children about sexual abuse: Controversies and best practice*. New York, NY: Oxford University Press.

Faller, K. C., & Cordisco-Steele, L. (2014, January). *Extended assessments/extended forensic interviews: Current state of the art and the science*. Presentation given at the 28th San Diego International Conference on Child and Family Maltreatment, San Diego, CA.

Faller, K. C., & Nelson-Gardell, D. (2010). Extended evaluations in cases of child sexual abuse: How many sessions are sufficient? *Journal of Child Sexual Abuse: Research, Treatment, & Program Innovations for Victims, Survivors, & Offenders, 19*(6), 648–668.

Finkelhor, D. (1984). *Child sexual abuse: New theory and research*. New York, NY: Free.

Fontes, L. (2008). *Interviewing clients across cultures: A practitioner's guide*. New York, NY: The Guildford.

Fontes, L., & Faller, K. C. (2007). Conducting culturally competent sexual abuse interviews with children from diverse racial, cultural, and socioeconomic backgrounds. In K. C. Faller (Ed.), *Interviewing children about sexual abuse: Controversies and best practice* (pp. 164–174). New York, NY: Oxford University Press. Chapter 12.

Goodman, G., Quas, J., Batterman-Faunce, J., Riddelsberger, M., & Kuhn, J. (1997). Children's reaction to and memory of a stressful event: Influences of age, anatomical dolls, knowledge, and parental attachment. *Applied Developmental Sciences, 1*, 54–75.

Goodman-Brown, T., Edelstein, R., Goodman, G., Jones, D. P. H., & Gordon, D. (2003). Why children tell: A model of children's disclosure of sexual abuse. *Child Abuse & Neglect, 27*, 525–540.

Hershkowitz, I. (2006). Delayed disclosure of alleged child abuse victims in Israel. *American Journal of Orthopsychiatry, 76*(4), 444–450.

Hershkowitz, I. (2011). Rapport-building in investigative interviews of children. In M. Lamb, D. La Rooy, L. Malloy, & C. Katz (Eds.), *Children's testimony: A handbook of psychological research and forensic practice* (2nd ed., pp. 110–128). Oxford, England: Wiley-Blackwell. Chapter 6.

Hershkowitz, I., Horowtiz, D., & Lamb, M. (2005). Trends in children's disclosure of abuse in Israel: A national study. *Child Abuse & Neglect, 29*(11), 1203–1214.

Hershkowitz, I., Horowtiz, D., & Lamb, M. (2007). Individual and family variables associated with disclosure and nondisclosure of child abuse in Israel. In M. E. Pipe, M. Lamb, Y. Orbach, & A. Cederborg (Eds.), *Child sexual abuse: Disclosure: Delay, and denial* (pp. 65–76). New York, NY: Psychology.

Hershkowitz, I., Lamb, M., Katz, C., & Malloy, L. (2013). Does enhanced rapport-building alter the dynamics of investigative interviews with suspected victims of intra-familial abuse? *Journal of Police and Criminal Psychology, 10*, 27–36.

Hershkowitz, I., Lanes, O., & Lamb, M. E. (2007). Exploring the disclosure of sexual abuse with victims and their parents. *Child Abuse & Neglect, 31*(2), 111–132.

Hershkowitz, I., Orbach, Y., Lamb, M., Pipe, M. E., Sternberg, K., & Horowitz, D. (2006). Dynamics of forensic interviews with suspected abuse victims who do not disclose. *Child Abuse & Neglect, 30*(7), 753–770.

Hershkowitz, I., & Terner, A. (2007). The effects of repeated interviewing on children's forensic statements of sexual abuse. *Applied Cognitive Psychology, 31*, 1131–1143.

James, B., Everson, M., & Friedrich, W. N. (n.d.). *Extended Evaluations of Allegations of Child Sexual Abuse*. Unpublished manuscript available from Mark Everson, Program on Child Trauma and Treatment, University of North Carolina, Chapel Hill, NC.

Katz, C., & Hershkowitz, I. (2010). The effects of drawing on children's accounts of sexual abuse. *Child Maltreatment, 15*(2), 171–179. doi:10.1177/1077559509351742.

Katz, C., & Hershkowitz, I. (2013). Repeated interviews with children who are the alleged victims of sexual abuse. *Research on Social Work Practice, 23*(2), 210–218.

Keary, K., & Fitzpatrick, C. (1994). Children's disclosure of sexual abuse during formal investigation. *Child Abuse & Neglect, 18*(7), 543–548.

La Rooy, D., Katz, C., Malloy, L., & Lamb, M. (2010). Do we need to rethink guidance on repeated interviews? *Psycholog McElvaney y, Public Policy, & the Law, 16*(4), 373–392.

La Rooy, D., Lamb, M., & Pipe, M. E. (2009). Repeated interviewing: A critical evaluation of the risks and potential benefits. In K. Kuehnle & M. Connell (Eds.), *Child sexual abuse: Research, evaluation, and testimony for the courts* (pp. 327–364). Hoboken, NJ: John Wiley.

Lamb, M., La Rooy, D., Malloy, L., & Katz, C. (2011). *Children's testimony: A handbook of psychological research and forensic practice*. London, England: Wiley Books.

Lamb, M. E., Orbach, Y., Hershkowitz, I., Esplin, P. W., & Horowitz, D. (2007). A structured forensic interview protocol improves the quality and informativeness of investigative interviews with children: A review of research using the NICHD Investigative Interview Protocol. *Child Abuse & Neglect, 31*(11–12), 1201–1231. doi:10.1016/j.chiabu.2007.03.021.

Lawson, L., & Chaffin, M. (1992). False negatives in sexual abuse disclosure interviews. *Journal of Interpersonal Violence, 7*(4), 532–542.

Leander, L. (2010). Police interviews with child sexual abuse victims: Patterns of reporting, avoidance and denial. *Child Abuse & Neglect, 34*(3), 192–205. doi:10.1016/j.chiabu.2009.09.011.

Lyon, T. D. (1999). *Questioning children: The effects of suggestive and repeated questioning*. Retrieved January 26, 2014, from C:USC/ARTICLES/guide/rethinkrev.wpd April 3, 2000.

Lyon, T. D. (2005). Speaking with children: Advice from investigative interviewers. In P. Talley (Ed.), *Handbook for the treatment of abused and neglected children* (pp. 65–81). Binghamton, NY: Haworth Social Work Practice.

Lyon, T. D. (2007). False denials: Overcoming methodological biases in abuse disclosure research. In M. E. Pipe, M. Lamb, Y. Orbach, & A. Cederborg (Eds.), *Disclosing abuse: Delays, denials, retractions, and incomplete accounts* (pp. 41–62). Mahwah, NJ: Laurence Earlbaum.

Lyon, T. D., & Dorado, J. S. (2008). Truth induction in young maltreated children: The effects of oath-taking and reassurance on true and false disclosures. *Child Abuse & Neglect, 32*(7), 738–748.

Malloy, L., Brubacher, S., & Lamb, M. (2011). Expected consequences of disclosure revealed in investigative interviews with suspected victims of child sexual abuse. *Applied Developmental Science, 15*(1), 8–19.

Malloy, L., & Lyon, T. (2006). Caregiver support and child sexual abuse: Why does it matter? *Journal of Child Sexual Abuse, 15*(4), 97–103.

Malloy, L., Lyon, T., & Quas, J. (2007). Filial dependency and recantation of child sexual abuse allegations. *Journal of the American Academy of Child and Adolescent Psychiatry, 46*(2), 162–170.

National Children's Advocacy Center (NCAC). (2014). *Advanced forensic interview training.* Retrieved from http://www.nationalcac.org/ncac-training/afi-training.html

O'Leary, P., & Barber, J. (2008). Gender differences in silencing following childhood sexual abuse. *Journal of Child Sexual Abuse, 17*(2), 133–143.

Olafson, E., & Lederman, C. (2006). The state of the debate about children's disclosure patterns of child sexual abuse. *Juvenile and Family Court Journal, 57*(1), 27–40.

Paine, M. L., & Hansen, D. J. (2002). Factors influencing children to self-disclose sexual abuse. *Clinical Psychology Review, 22*(2), 271–295.

Patterson, T., & Pipe, M. E. (2009). Exploratory assessments of child abuse: Children's responses to interviewer's questions across multiple interview sessions. *Child Abuse & Neglect, 33*(8), 490–504.

Pipe, M. E., Lamb, M., Orbach, Y., & Cederborg, A. (Eds.). (2007). *Child sexual abuse: Disclosure: Delay, and denial.* New York, NY: Psychology.

Russell, D. E. H., & Bolen, R. (2000). *The epidemic of rape and child sexual abuse in the United States.* Thousand Oaks, CA: Sage.

Sas, L., & Cunningham, A. (1995). *Tipping the balance to tell the secret: The public discovery of child sexual abuse.* Available from the London Court Clinic, 254 Pall Mall St., London. N6A 5P6 (519 679 7250).

Saywitz, K., Goodman, G., Nicholas, E., & Moan, S. (1991). Children's memory for a genital examination: Implications for child sexual abuse cases. *Journal of Consulting and Clinical Psychology, 59*, 682–691.

Saywitz, K. J., Goodman, G. S., & Lyon, T. D. (2002). Interviewing children in and out of court: Current research and practice implications. In J. B. Myers, L. Berliner, J. Briere, C. Hendrix, C. Jenny, & T. A. Reid (Eds.), *The APSAC handbook on child maltreatment* (2nd ed., pp. 349–377). Thousand Oaks, CA: Sage.

Schaeffer, P., Leventhal, J., & Asnes, A. G. (2011). Children's disclosures of sexual abuse: Learning from direct inquiry. *Child Abuse & Neglect, 35*, 343–352.

Schönbucher, V., Maier, T., Mohler-Kuo, M., Schnyder, U., & Landolt, M. (2012). Disclosure of child sexual abuse by adolescents: A qualitative in-depth study. *Journal of Interpersonal Violence, 27*(17), 3486–3515.

Sgroi, S. (1982). *Handbook of clinical intervention in child sexual abuse.* Lexington, MA: Lexington Books.

Sjoberg, R., & Lindblad, F. (2002). Limited disclosure of sexual abuse in children whose experiences were documented by videotape. *American Journal of Psychiatry, 159*(2), 312–314.

Sorsoli, L., Kia-Keating, M., & Grossman, F. (2008). "I keep that hush-hush": Male survivors of sexual abuse and the challenges of disclosure. *Journal of Counseling Psychology, 55*(3), 333–345.

Springman, R. E., Wherry, J. N., & Notaro, P. C. (2006). The effects of interviewer race and child race on sexual abuse disclosures in forensic interviews. *Journal of Child Sexual Abuse: Research, Treatment, & Program Innovations For Victims, Survivors, & Offenders, 15*(3), 99–116.

Staller, K., & Nelson-Gardell, D. (2005). "A burden on your heart": Lessons of disclosure from female preadolescent and adolescent survivors of sexual abuse. *Child Abuse & Neglect, 29*, 415–432.

Sternberg, K., Lamb, M., Esplin, P., & Baradaran, L. (1999). Using a scripted protocol in investigative interviews: A pilot study. *Applied Developmental Science, Special Issue, New Research on Child Witnesses, Part II, 3*(2), 70–76.

Sternberg, K., Lamb, M., Hershkovitz, I., Yudilevitch, L., Orbach, Y., Esplin, P., & Hovav, M. (1997). Effects of introductory style on children's abilities to describe experiences of sexual abuse. *Child Abuse and Neglect, 21*(11), 1133–1146.

Sternberg, K., Lamb, M., Orbach, Y., Esplin, P., & Mitchell, S. (2001). Use of a structured investigative protocol enhances young children's responses to free-recall prompts in the course of forensic interviews. *Journal of Applied Psychology, 86*(5), 997–1005.

Teoh, Y., Yang, P., Lamb, M., & Larsson, A. (2010). Do human figure diagrams help alleged victims of sexual abuse provide elaborate and clear accounts of physical contact with alleged perpetrators? *Applied Cognitive Psychology, 24*, 287–300.

Vieth, V. I. (2006). Unto the third generation: A call to end child abuse in the United States within 120 years. *Journal of Aggression, Maltreatment & Trauma, 12*(3–4), 5–54.

Williams, J., Nelson-Gardell, D., Faller, K. C., Cordisco-Steele, L., & Tishelman, A. (2014). Is there a place for extended assessments for evaluating concerns about child sexual abuse? perceptions of 1,294 child maltreatment professionals. *Journal of Forensic Social Work, 3*(2), 88–105.

Williams, J., Nelson-Gardell, D., Faller, K. C., Tishelman, A., & Cordisco-Steele, L. (2013). Is there a place for extended assessments in addressing child sexual abuse allegations? How sensitivity and specificity impact professional perspectives. *Journal of Child Sexual Abuse, 23*(2), 179–197.

Chapter 8
Understanding Suggestibility

Stephen Ceci, Amelia Hritz, and Caisa Royer

The concept of suggestibility is not new, with famous examples like the Salem Witch Trials that date back for centuries. These examples differ from the typical experimental studies of suggestibility that are carried out in the laboratory today, and they are occasionally mistakenly dismissed as instances of contagions, peer conformity, séances, or "mass hysterias," rather than as examples of suggestibility. However, there is merit to defining suggestibility broadly enough to include such phenomena. Doing so takes us beyond the purely cognitive factors involved in suggestibility to reveal the social and cultural influences and the diverse conditions that give rise to reporting errors. With such a broadened definition, suggestive forces can be seen through historical and cultural perspectives, rather than as an exclusively cognitive phenomenon.

At its core, suggestibility refers to behavior, images, or words in one's environment exerting an influence on their behavior. This depiction leaves unspecified the mechanism responsible for the influence, specifically whether it results from cognitive mechanisms (such as trace alteration or retrieval inhibition) or social mechanisms (such as peer pressure or cultural beliefs). We return to this distinction later, but first we provide an abbreviated tour of some celebrated examples of early suggestibility that illuminate its sociocultural component.

In research about child witnesses, no other topic has received as much attention as suggestibility. Hundreds of empirical studies of age differences in vulnerability to suggestions have been published (for early reviews, see Baxter, 1990; Ceci & Bruck, 1993). In what follows, we reprise and update the major trends in this vast corpus of findings. First, we will provide a brief historical context for research on suggestibility. Next, we will discuss how interviewer bias and suggestive interview techniques can lead to inaccurate reports in children. Finally, we will discuss new

S. Ceci (✉) • A. Hritz • C. Royer
Department of Human Development, Cornell University, Ithaca, NY 14853, USA
e-mail: sjc9@cornell.edu; sjc9@cornell.edu; sjc9@cornell.edu

W.T. O'Donohue, M. Fanetti (eds.), *Forensic Interviews Regarding Child Sexual Abuse*, DOI 10.1007/978-3-319-21097-1_8

research on suggestibility across age ranges that may inform how and when children may be particularly susceptible to suggestibility. This research will inform the care with which interviews with child witnesses should be performed.

A Brief History of Suggestibility

The historical record is replete with examples of suggestibility long before psychologists began to study it experimentally. For example, Sjoberg (1995) analyzed testimony given by approximately 600 Swedish youths to parish priests during an outbreak of witch hysteria in the late seventeenth century. Hundreds of these children testified to observing the sorcery of neighbors. As a result of their statements, 14 adults were burned at the stake in one community and another 27 adults were either beheaded or burned at the stake in an adjacent village. Analyses revealed that claims of witnessing acts of sorcery were more common among the youngest children; however, claims of a sexual nature were more common among older youth (Sjoberg, 1995), a point we shall revisit below in the context of what are now called "reverse age trends." Importantly, analyses also showed that the children's statements were influenced by whom they stood next to while waiting in line to give their testimony to parish priests. If children were discussing their observations of sorcery while in line, this often influenced those around them to describe similar acts when it was their turn to testify. Thus, the act of waiting in line was a suggestive influence. Although events such as this one are not historically viewed as instances of suggestibility, they bear striking resemblance to Solomon Asch's (1951, 1952) classic paradigm in which participants were likely to give an incorrect response after hearing others give the same answer. Most suggestibility researchers acknowledge this paradigm as a form of suggestion.

Likewise, accounts from Colonial America are rich with descriptions of what can be viewed as forms of suggestibility. The most notorious of these cases were the infamous witch trials that occurred in Salem, Massachusetts (and surrounding areas), during the final decade of the seventeenth century. In Salem, a group of children became known as the "circle girls" because they sometimes sat in a circle listening to an East Indian maid tell stories about witchcraft and sorcery. Later, these children claimed and testified in court that they witnessed townsfolk exhibiting the very behaviors that been described in the maid's stories, such as flying on broom sticks, celestial apparitions in the form of speaking animals, and the defendants instructing insects to fly into their mouths and deposit bent nails and pins in their stomachs. Based on their testimony, 19 defendants were convicted and put to death. A dozen more defendants were spared execution when they threw themselves on the mercy of the court and admitted their participation in witchcraft. Later in their lives, some of the former circle girls publicly recanted their accusatory testimony. Thus, it appears that the maid's suggestive stories influenced children's reports but not necessarily their memories, as the recanting children had never incorporated the stories into their memory.

Another historical example of mass suggestibility comes from the eighteenth century, during which time a man named Mesmer became wealthy for his magnetic therapies. His therapy technique involved treatment rooms containing large circular tubs around which several dozen people would stand with their hands linked. Each tub contained magnetized water in a star shape, and submerged in water were protruding magnetized iron rods. Initially, one patient would begin to writhe and speak in tongues, then the adjacent individual would become affected, and so on until everyone in the room was so affected:

> "Patients placed one hand on a rod and linked the other hand to their neighbor to form a "mesmeric chain." "These magnetic salons, were spectacular. As the "fluid" moved around the group, patients began to feel twinges and surges of pressure and release. First one, then another was swept up in the mysterious tide; people began writhing. Convulsing, speaking in tongues, often passing out. The commission appointed to study Mesmerism (Ben Franklin, included) concluded that there was no scientific basis to the alleged cures, just mass contagion and imitation. Cured patients were unable to discriminate between magnetized and nonmagnetized objects: "there is no proof of the existence of the animal magnetic fluid….the imagination without the aid of magnetism can produce convulsions., but magnetism without the aid of imagination can produce nothing." (Jay, 2003, p. 150)

As can be seen from these historical examples, individuals have always been prone to the influence of others, regardless of what this influence was called. However, it was not until the end of the nineteenth century that scientists began to study suggestibility under controlled conditions. The first recorded scientific report of suggestibility was made by Small (1896). In one of his suggestibility demonstrations, Small removed the cork from a vial of clear liquid while standing in front of a classroom of adolescents. He asked them to raise their hand if they could smell the fragrance emanating from the vial. After a few of the children seated closest to Small raised their hands, many others behind them also raised their hands. The vial contained only plain water, but the suggestive influence of seeing classmates raise their hands was evident.

Modern examples of mass suggestibility (or hysteria) outside of research also abound. In their book, *Connected*, the social network theorists Christakis and Fowler (2009) describe many cases of what they term "mass psychogenic illness" which resembles what we are calling suggestibility. At one high school in McMinnville, Tennessee a teacher claimed to smell gasoline, which caused shortness of breath, headaches, dizziness, and nausea. Witnessing her reaction (or even merely hearing about it from witnesses) resulted in students reporting similar symptoms. The school's alarm system was sounded and, in full view of the evacuated student body, the teacher and some students were taken by ambulance to a hospital. Over a hundred more students went to the hospital complaining of similar symptoms. Christakis and Fowler document the astonishingly extensive testing done by teams from OSHA, the CDC, and the EPA in the school as well as surrounding areas, all of which failed to reveal any physical basis to the students' complaints. They report:

> Two years later, a *New England Journal of Medicine* article described the extensive examination of possible environmental causes for the illness and …concluded that psychogenic factors were to blame. They found that the illness was associated with directly observing another ill person …The diagnosis was 'epidemic hysteria'. (p. 43)

Such instances of mass hysteria or contagion are similar to the mass allegation daycare sex abuse cases that received attention in the 1990s (Ceci & Bruck, 1995). In these cases, it was common for a "trigger child" to make the first allegation of satanic ritualistic abuse against a daycare worker (e.g., claiming to witness the worker slaughtering a horse and drinking its blood, or dismembering a live baby and eating it). Once the trigger child's allegation became public, numerous other children began "recollecting" similar stories.

Historically, suggestibility has been viewed in purely cognitive terms, a result of memory alteration or retrieval interference. Typical of the time, Gudjonsson (1986) describes suggestibility as the "extent to which individuals come to accept and subsequently incorporate post-event information into their memory recollections" (p. 195). However, in the course of synthesizing the large literature on suggestibility throughout modern research, this traditional definition was found to fail to capture important subtypes of suggestibility. This need led Ceci and Bruck (1993) to urge an expansion of the traditional definition to include social as well as cognitive mechanisms. They proposed that "suggestibility concerns the degree to which children's encoding, storage, retrieval, and reporting of events can be influenced by a range of social and psychological factors" (Ceci & Bruck, 1993, p. 404). Note that the inclusion of the word "reporting"; it extends suggestibility to sociocultural factors that are noncognitive, such as pressure on someone to misreport even though their memory (encoding, storage, and retrieval) is unaffected.

The Role of Interviewer Bias

Interviewer bias is the defining feature of many suggestive interviews (e.g., Ceci & Bruck, 1995). It refers to interviewers who hold a priori beliefs about the occurrence of certain events and, as a result, shape the interview to produce allegations that are consistent with these beliefs. One of the hallmarks of "interviewer bias" is the single-minded attempt to gather only confirmatory evidence and to avoid all avenues that may produce contradictory allegations. This means that the biased interviewer does not ask questions that might require alternate explanations. When provided with an inconsistent or ambiguous disclosure, biased interviewers either ignore the disclosure or interpret it within the framework of their initial hypothesis. The interviewer's biased belief is conveyed to the child through a variety of suggestive interviewing techniques (such as repeated questioning or affirmative responses) that have been shown to produce false reports. Consequently, the child may come to inaccurately report the belief of the interviewer rather than the child's own experience.

Interviewer bias has been the focus of research for the past two decades. The general findings of this research are that biased interviewers can elicit a number of false reports from the person being interviewed. In addition, biased interviewers will inaccurately report the contents of the interview; they will sometimes recall their a priori beliefs rather than the statements of the child. In what follows, we describe the type of evidence that supports these claims.

Langer and Abelson (1974) showed a videotaped interview of a man to two groups of therapists with different theoretical orientations. One group included behavior therapists who were trained to focus on the patient's presenting symptoms and to modify or alleviate them. The second group included therapists with a psychodynamic orientation who aimed to understand and interpret symptoms that are presumed to result from inner conflicts. Although all therapists viewed the same videotape, half were told that the man was applying for a new job and the rest were told he was a patient undergoing a psychiatric interview. After viewing the videotape, all the therapists were asked to assess the man's adjustment and behaviors. Psychodynamic therapists (who have a priori beliefs about the origins and meanings of behaviors) rated the job applicant more positively than they rated the patient. They viewed the job candidate as attractive, candid, and open, whereas they viewed the patient as tight, defensive, passive–aggressive, and having a conflict over homosexuality. In contrast, behavioral therapists who were trained to focus on the behavior without any attempt of interpretation (i.e., a priori beliefs) viewed the job candidate and the patient identically.

Thompson, Clarke-Stewart, and Lepore (1997) conducted a study in which children viewed a staged event that could be construed as either abusive or innocent. Some children interacted with a confederate named "Chester" as he cleaned some dolls and other toys in a playroom. Other children interacted with Chester as he handled the dolls roughly and in a mildly abusive manner. All of the children were then questioned about this event. The interviewer was either (1) "exculpatory" (suggesting that the janitor was just cleaning the toys and not playing), (2) "accusatory" (suggesting that the janitor had been inappropriately playing with the toys instead of working), or (3) "neutral" (nonsuggestive). In the first two types of interviews, the questions changed from mildly to strongly suggestive as the interview progressed. Following the first interview, all children were asked to tell in their own words what they had witnessed and then they were asked specific questions about the event. The children were also asked by their parents to recount what the janitor had done both immediately after the interview and 2 weeks later. When questioned by a neutral interviewer, or by an interviewer whose interpretation was consistent with the activity viewed by the child, children's accounts were both factually correct and consistent with the janitor's script. However, when the interviewer was biased in a direction that contradicted the activity viewed by the child, those children's stories quickly conformed to the suggestions or beliefs of the interviewer. In addition, children's answers to interpretive questions (e.g., "Was he doing his job or just being bad?") were in agreement with the interviewer's point of view, as opposed to what actually happened. Furthermore, when asked neutral questions by their parents, the children's answers remained consistent with the interviewers' biases.

Bruck, Ceci, Melnyk, and Finkelberg (1999) showed how interviewer bias can quickly develop in natural interviewing situations, and how interviewer bias taints not only the responses of child interviewees but also the reports of the adult interviewers. In this study, a special event—a surprise birthday party—was staged for 90 preschool children in their school. In groups of three and with the guidance of a research assistant, the children surprised a second research assistant for her birthday, played games, ate food, and watched magic tricks. Another 30 children did not attend the birthday party but in groups of two, they simply colored a picture with both research assistants instead. These children were also told that it was the second assistant's birthday. Interviewers (who were recruited from university graduate degree programs in social work or counseling and who had training and experience in interviewing children) were asked to question four children about what had happened when special visitors came to the school. The interviewers were not told about the events but were simply told to find out from each child what had happened. The first three children that each interviewer questioned attended the birthday party but the fourth child attended the coloring event. Immediately after the interview with the fourth child, the interviewers were asked to describe the special event that the children had attended. Several weeks later, the interviewers were again questioned about what they had learned from the children.

Bruck et al. found that the children who were interviewed last (all of whom attended the coloring event) produced twice as many errors as the children who attended the birthday party; 60 % of the children who only colored made false claims that involved a birthday party. This result suggests that the interviewers had built up a bias that all the children they interviewed had attended a birthday party. By the time they interviewed the fourth child, they structured their interviews in such a way as to elicit claims consistent with their primary hypothesis. Thus, if interviewers have the belief that all the children they interview have experienced a certain event, then it is probable that many of the children will come to make such claims even though they were nonparticipants (or nonvictims). Another important finding was that even when the child who only colored correctly denied attending a birthday party, 84 % of their interviewers still reported later that all the children they interviewed had attended a birthday party. These data suggest that regardless of what children actually say, biased interviewers may inaccurately report the child's claims in order to make them consistent with their own hypotheses.

The data highlight the dangers of having only one hypothesis about an event—especially when this hypothesis is incorrect. These studies demonstrate that interviewers' beliefs can influence their judgments as well as their style of questioning which, in turn, influences the accuracy of children's disclosures. Bruck and Ceci presented a model of the architecture of suggestive interviews (e.g., Ceci & Bruck, 1995). According to the model, interviewer bias influences the entire architecture of an interview and is revealed through a variety of suggestive practices.

One suggestive practice is the absence of open-ended questions (e.g., "tell me about the event," "then what happened?"). Biased interviewers do not enlist the child to tell a narrative but rather ask for series of monosyllabic responses to closed-ended questions (e.g., "did he ever touch you here?" "Did he do it on the sofa?" "Was it at your mother's house or your babysitter's?") The repetition of such questions within and between interviews can be highly suggestive because they supply a child with clues about the interviewer's own beliefs about happened. Other suggestive techniques include repeated interviews (especially when the child does not provide clear and unambiguous statements in the first interview), implicit or explicit threats, bribes, and inducements for telling the interviewer what the child assumes she wants to be told suggesting negative stereotypes (e.g., "Gary does bad things sometimes"), invoking peer pressure ("your classmates already told me and now I would like to hear it from you."), and visualizations ("close your eyes and form a picture of how you might feel if he did that to you," see Ceci et al. 1994a, b for evidence). The use of nonverbal props (including anatomically detailed dolls) can also be suggestive, especially with preschool-aged children (e.g., Bruck, Ceci & Francouer, 2000). All of these suggestive techniques can be associated with error, but the risk of making a false statement is increased when interviews contain a combination of these techniques.

Recent Updates on Age Differences in Suggestibility

If this chapter were written a decade ago it is safe to assume that it would contain a section on age differences in suggestibility which could be summarized as follows: suggestibility declines with age. In such a section, there might be a statement to the effect that the single strongest predictor of suggestibility errors is chronological age. No other factor—not personality, intelligence, need to conform, source monitoring, etc.—was as potent a predictor of suggestibility errors as was chronological age (e.g., Bruck & Melnyk, 2004; Chae & Ceci, 2005). Across myriad research paradigms the nearly invariant finding was that younger children were more suggestible than older children and adults (see Ceci & Bruck, 1993 for review). The magnitude of this age trend was nontrivial: in many studies, the youngest age group—usually preschoolers—made over 50 % more suggestion-induced errors than older children and adults (see Ceci, Ross, & Toglia, 1986, Figure 1).

Of course, even among the most vulnerable age groups, not all children succumb to suggestive influences. This awareness has led researchers to examine individual differences that could be used by legal professional to identify children who are either particularly susceptible or highly resistant to false suggestions. A large number of cognitive and social factors have been studied, including linguistic development, metacognitive awareness, intelligence, maternal attachment style, and temperament (Bruck & Melnyk, 2004). Clark-Stewart, Malloy, and Allhusen (2004) demonstrated that language skills, adaptive and inhibitory control, and the quality of parental relationships accounted for 32 % of variance in children's suggestiveness. Unfortunately, the effect of these factors is not large enough to warrant excluding the testimony of any particular child.

Chronological age remains the single most powerful predictor of suggestibility proneness. Recently, however, this strong developmental claim has been replaced by a more nuanced one that stipulates there are age trends in some situations but "reverse age trends" (with older children being more suggestible) in other situations (Brainerd, Reyna, & Ceci, 2008). This is the case with both interviewer-induced suggestibility (Finnila, Mahlberga, Santtilaa, Sandnabbaa & Niemib, 2003) and suggestibility that results from factors external to the interview (Principe et al., 2007). For example, Principe et al. (2008) showed that 5- and 6-year-olds were more likely than 3- and 4-year-olds to mistakenly report inferences about the causes of ambiguous events as actual experiences. This is probably because older children were more likely to generate plausible inferences that could be misinterpreted as memories for the observed event. Likewise, Ornstein et al. (1998) found that when asked to recall a doctor's exam that excluded some scripted medical procedures (e.g., the event purposely omitted the doctor's use of a stethoscope on the child's heart), 6-year-olds were more likely than 4-year-olds to wrongly "remember" this expected-but-nonexperienced procedure. Regardless of whether we are discussing developmental or reverse developmental trends, it is not age per se that is the driver, but underlying knowledge and strategies that may vary with age (see, e.g., Ceci, Papierno, & Kulkofsky, 2007).

An example of a situation in which reverse age trends should be expected is in "connected meaning" contexts. These are situations in which subjects are presented materials that are potentially semantically or thematically related, such as the list: *sugar, honey, candy, sour, chocolate, eat*. In research experiments testing connected meaning contexts, subjects may be read a list of similar words and then (after a delay) given a recognition task that includes a semantically related but unlisted word. In our example, this might be the word "sweet." When given this task, older individuals can be expected to mistakenly identify *sweet* as a listed word more often than young children (see Brainerd et al., 2008 for review and theoretical framework). This makes sense because they possess greater semantic knowledge than young children and their knowledge can be more readily activated (i.e., they automatically form associations with presented words). Thus, connected meaning paradigms such as this example will result in reverse age trends with older individuals making more suggestibility-induced errors than preschoolers.

In connected meaning paradigms a form of "autosuggestibility" occurs, with word meanings being automatically activated and their spreading activation results in falsely remembering the presence of semantically related foils. Such processes can be conscious or unconscious. A conscious process would be a situation in which the person recalling an event reviews all of the related knowledge they have and edits it to decide whether something was part of an experienced event. An example might be a repetitive exercise class that always begins with stretching exercises, followed by spinning, followed by a cooling down period, followed by a different aerobic exercise, and mat work at the end of the class. If someone familiar with this sequence of events is asked to recall a recent exercise class that omitted one of these exercises, she may consciously review all of the exercises in their routine temporal order to see if any were missing. In such situations, it is easy to falsely "remember" performing the missing exercise because, like the semantic activation described above, the presence of the other exercises activates the entire script for what usually occurs during class.

In general, whenever a situation invites the formation of relational structures (thematic, taxonomic, etc.), we can expect older subjects to engage in such formation to greater extent than their younger counterparts (Yim, Dennis, & Sloutsky, 2013). Going back to an example earlier in this chapter, the older children standing in line preparing to testify to parish priests made more claims of sexual abuse than did the younger children. This was precisely because they had more knowledge about what such events might typically include. Younger children had no such relational script so while they made more claims about sorcery, they were less likely to make claims about sexual abuse.

Having pointed out circumstances in which reverse age trends occur, the majority of contexts that bring individuals into contact with the justice system do not involve connected meaning (e.g., claims about whether their babysitter brandished a camera and took their photograph while bathing them). In such situations where there are no age-related differences in scripts, younger children are significantly more suggestible than older ones. Next we turn to a relatively new literature on how meaning gets represented in memory and how this affects suggestibility trends across age ranges.

Representational Complexity Theory

In a series of studies, it has been shown that the way knowledge is represented in memory can affect not only recall and recognition accuracy but even the subprocesses that underpin performance, such as metamemory, and thus suggestibility (Ceci et al., 2007; Ceci, Fitneva, & Williams, 2010). Usually, older individuals have more knowledge about an event and they represent this knowledge in more integrated and connected fashion. For example, a visit to a zoo may be cognitively represented along multiple dimensions (predators, arachnids, avians, etc.) that are unavailable for younger children simply because children do not yet understand the same complexities that adults do. Exceptions to this generality are situations in which younger children have greater knowledge, for example, about television programs they regularly watch (e.g., *Sesame Street*).

When material is manipulated so that some of it is represented more elaborately by younger children (more dimensions and greater semantic distance between them) and some is represented more elaborately by older children, then targeted predictions can be made about age trends. The results of such studies have confirmed predictions: older children are more suggestible about items whose representations were closely related to that of the suggestion, and the reverse was true of items whose representations were furthest from that of the suggestion. For instance, if younger children had a mental representation of the characters on *Sesame Street* that were close together, then they were more suggestible about those characters. Conversely, if types of weather were represented more closely by older children, they had greater suggestibility for it (see Table 1 of Ceci et al., 2007 for targeted predictions that were confirmed for both age trends and reverse age trends in suggestibility).

In Fig. 8.1, we see a spatial depiction of a typical 9-year-old's representation of a set of animals and foods. Note that "eagle" is as close to lion and bear as it is to other birds such as robin and sparrow. This is because by this age children often have a predator dimension they use to represent events such as a visit to the zoo and this means they associate eagles with other predators, such as lions and bears.

Fig. 8.1 A spatial depiction of a typical 9-year-old's representation of a set of animals and foods. The proximity between words represents how closely related the child believes these objects are

In contrast, the typical 4-year-old's representation for these same items would show eagle clustering only with other birds because they lack a predator dimension and don't associate eagles with other predators. Similar age differences can also be found for a dairy dimension, with older children clustering milk with other dairy items (e.g., cheese, butter, yogurt, ice cream) whereas 4-year-olds might cluster milk closer to other drinks. The same goes for a citrus dimension and other kinds of dimensions. Armed with the way different age groups actually represent their knowledge, targeted predictions have been made about age trends in suggestibility; for example, orange might be a stronger suggestion for lemon for an older child who posses a citrus dimension whereas it might be a stronger suggestion for apple for a younger child who only understands the fruit dimension.

The bottom line is that the nature and richness of the way events are represented influence suggestibility proneness, and sometimes this can lead to the expectation that older individuals will be more suggestible than younger ones, and at other times it can lead to the opposite prediction. This is important for understanding when children may be more susceptible to suggestive influences.

Conclusion

To date, hundreds of empirical studies have been published about children's vulnerability to suggestion (for reviews see Baxter, 1990; Ceci & Bruck, 1993). Historically, suggestibility was studied in purely cognitive terms, a result of memory alteration or retrieval interference. However, modern research has demonstrated that social factors influence suggestion, and this widening of the definition of suggestibility sheds new light on historical examples of suggestive behavior, such as the Salem Witch Trials. Furthermore, modern research has shown that social influences such as interviewer bias and suggestive interview techniques can lead to inaccurate reports in children. Suggestive techniques employed by interviewers with biases include asking close-ended questions, repeating questions, or providing affirmative responses. These techniques may cause the child to falsely report the belief of the interviewer rather than the child's own experience. Furthermore, biased interviewers may also recall their a priori beliefs rather than the statements of the child, causing them to inaccurately report the contents of the interview. All of these suggestive techniques can hinder the interviewer's ability to receive accurate reports from a child.

Research shows that the most powerful predictor of suggestibility proneness is chronological age, with young children being more prone to suggestive techniques. However, recent research has demonstrated that in some situations older children are actually more suggestible than younger children in situations that involve relational structures (Brainerd et al., 2008; Yim et al., 2013). Research examining these developmental reversals, including research on representational complexity theory, shows that suggestibility is complex. Suggestibility is not unique to extremely young children. Instead, the nature and richness of how events are represented in memory may influence susceptibility to suggestibility. When suggestive questioning targets a feature closely mentally represented to the event, anyone may be at risk for inaccurately recalling an event.

Overall, the research on suggestibility demonstrates that it is important for interviewers to consider both their own beliefs and the child's cognitive abilities. Interviewer bias and developmentally inappropriate questioning can lead to inaccurate reports by children, so interviewers should approach an interview with an open mind and an awareness for what the child understands and associates.

The single most important precaution an interviewer can take is to test an alternative hypothesis in the course of conducting an interview with a child. All interviewers harbor hunches and pet theories about what happened. There is nothing wrong with this; it is the way the human mind works. The alternative to having a hunch is to go into an interview "blind," without any hypothesis about what occurred. This would not be productive because it would result in missed opportunities to follow-up on potentially relevant lines of inquiry because the interviewer lacked the relevant hypothesis to recognize the child's statement as potentially important. On the other hand, having a hypothesis runs its own risk, particularly in a case where the interviewer is strongly biased in favor of it. This can result in a confirmatory bias in which the interviewer pursues a line of questioning that validates a favored hypothesis and ignores or misinterprets statements that contradict it (Ceci & Bruck, 1995). This can be seen in the surprise party experiment described earlier when the interviewer assumed the fourth child attended the party and proceeded to shape the child's answers to support this. It has been documented in a number of studies that even when a child tells such an interviewer something counter to the favored hypothesis, the latter reinterprets it to be consistent with it.

The best defense against a confirmatory bias is to plan to test the most plausible alternative hypotheses. These will depend on the case facts but can include probing whether the allegation is false, the product of coaching or suggestion. Asking about alternative hypotheses protects the integrity of an interview.

References

Asch, S. E. (1951). Effects of group pressure upon the modification and distortion of judgments. In H. Guetzkow (Ed.), *Groups, leadership and men* (pp. 177–190). Pittsburgh, PA: Carnegie.

Asch, S. E. (1952). Group forces in the modification and distortion of judgments. In S. E. Asch (Ed.), *Social Psychology* (pp. 450–501). Englewood Cliffs, NJ: Prentice Hall.

Brainerd, C., Reyna, V., & Ceci, S. J. (2008). Developmental reversals in false memory: A review of data and theory. *Psychological Bulletin, 134*, 334–375.

Baxter, J. (1990). Children's suggestibility. *Applied Cognitive Psychology, 3*, 1–15.

Bruck, M. & Ceci, S. J. (1999). The suggestibility of children's memory. *Annual Reviews of Psychology 50*: 419–439.

Bruck, M, Ceci, S. J., & Francoeur, E. (2000). Children's use of anatomically detailed dolls to report genital touching in a medical examination: Developmental and gender comparisons. *Journal of Experimental Psychology: Applied, 6(1)*: 74–83.

Bruck, M., & Melnyk, L. (2004). Individual differences in children's suggestibility: A review and synthesis. *Applied Cognitive Psychology, 18*(8), 947–996. Also see Special issue: Individual and developmental differences in suggestibility.

Ceci, S. J., & Bruck, M. (1993). The suggestibility of children's recollections: An historical review and synthesis. *Psychological Bulletin, 113*, 403–439.

Ceci, S. J., Huffman, M. L. C., Smith, E., & Loftus, E. F. (1994a). Repeatedly thinking about a non-event -source misattributions among preschoolers. *Consciousness and Cognition, 3*, 388–407. doi.org/10.1006/ccog.1994.1022.

Ceci, S. J., Loftus, E. F., Leichtman, M. D., & Bruck, M. (1994b). The possible role of source misattributions in the creation of false beliefs among preschoolers. *International Journal of Clinical and Experimental Hypnosis, 42*, 304–320. doi.org/10.1080/00207149408409361.

Ceci, S.J., Ross, D. and Toglia, M. (1987). Suggestibility of children's memory: Psycholegal implications. *Journal of Experimental Psychology: General*, 116. 38–49.

Clarke-Stewart, K. A., Malloy, L. C., & Allhusen, V. D. (2004). Verbal ability, self-control, and close relationships with parents protect children against misleading suggestions. *Applied Cognitive Psychology, 18(8)*, 1037–1058. doi: 10.1002/acp.1076.

Ceci, S. J., & Bruck, M. (1995). *Jeopardy in the courtroom: A scientific analysis of children's testimony*. Washington, DC: APA Books.

Ceci, S. J., Fitneva, S. A., & Williams, W. M. (2010). Representational Constraints on the Development of Memory and Metamemory: A Developmental-Representational-Theory. *Psychological Review, 117*, 464–495.

Ceci, S. J., Papierno, P. B., & Kulkofsky, S. C. (2007). Representational Constraints on Children's Memory and Suggestibility. *Psychological Science, 18*, 503–509.

Chae, Y. J., & Ceci, S. J. (2005). Individual differences in children's recall and suggestibility. *Journal of Applied Cognitive Psychology, 19*, 383–407.

Christakis, N. A., & Fowler, J. H. (2009). *Connected: How your friend's friend affects everything you think, feel and do*. New York, NY: Little, Brown.

Finnila K, Mahlberga N, Santtilaa P, Sandnabbaa K, Niemib P. (2003). Validity of a test of children's suggestibility for predicting responses to two interview situations differing in their degree of suggestiveness. *Journal of Experimental Child Psycholology, 85*, 32–49.

Gudjonsson, G (1986), The Relationship Between Interrogative Suggestibility and Acquiescence: Empirical Findings and Theoretical Implications. *Personality & Individual Differences, 7*, 195–205.

Langer, E., J., & Abelson, R. (1974). A patient by any other name… Clinician group difference in labeling bias. *Journal of Consulting and Clinical Psychology, 42*, 4–9.

Principe, G. F., Tinguely, A., & Dobkowski, N. (2007). Mixing memories: The effects of rumors that conflict with children's experiences. *Journal of Experimental Child Psychology, 98*, 1–19.

Principe, G. F., Guiliano, S., & Root, C. (2008). Rumormongering and remembering: How rumors originating in children's inferences can affect memory. *Journal of Experimental Child Psychology, 99*. 135–155.

Ornstein, P. A., Baker-Ward, L., Gordon, B. N., & Merritt, K. A. (1998). Children`s memory for medical experiences: Implications for testimony. *Applied Cognitive Psychology, 11*, 87-104. doi.org/10.1002/(SICI)1099-0720(199712)11:7<S87::AID- ACP556>3.0.CO;2-Z.

Thompson, W.C., Clarke-Stewart, K.A., & Lepore, S (1997). What did the janitor do? Suggestive interviewing and the accuracy of children's accounts. *Law & Human Behavior, 21(4)*, 405-426

Jay, M. (2003). *The Air Loom Gang: the strange and true story of James Tilly Matthews and his visionary madness*. London, England: Bantam.

Sjoberg, R. L. (1995). Child testimonies during an outbreak of witch hysteria: Sweden 1670–1671. *Journal of Child Psychology and Psychiatry, 36*, 1039–1051.

Small, W. S. (1896). Suggestibility of children. *Pedagogical Seminary, 13*, 176.

Yim, H., Dennis, S. J., & Sloutsky, V. M. (2013). The development of episodic Memory items, contexts, and relations. *Psychological Science*. doi:10.1177/0956797613487385.

Chapter 9
Forensic Interviewing for Child Sexual Abuse: Why Psychometrics Matters

Scott O. Lilienfeld

The aim of science is not to open the door to everlasting wisdom, but to set a limit on everlasting error.

Bertolt Brecht (1955), Life of Galileo

It goes without saying that interviewers are human. As a consequence, they are susceptible to error. Nevertheless, because of *bias blind spot* (Pronin, Lin, & Ross, 2002), a phenomenon whereby most of us are keenly aware of biases in others but oblivious to the same biases in ourselves, interviewers may erroneously assume themselves to be largely immune to clinical mistakes that afflict their fellow interviewers. In light of research on bias blind spot, I offer the following bold proposition. The forensic interviewers who operate in the most scientific and ethical manner are *not* those who are free from error; instead, they are those who are cognizant of their propensities toward error and make tireless efforts to combat or compensate for them.

Errors that arise when interviewing children for potential child sexual abuse can be serious, even disastrous (Cronch, Viljoen, & Hansen, 2006). *False positive* errors, in which abuse is deemed to be present when it is absent, can contribute to unjustified allegations against parents and other caregivers; needless emotional suffering and stress for children and adults; inestimable damage to the reputations of innocent individuals; and wasteful expenditures of valuable legal, financial, and personal resources (Wood & Garven, 2000). *False negative* errors, in which abuse is deemed to be absent when it is present, can allow abusers to go free, and thereby increase the risk of abuse to other children. Of course, both types of errors can erode the credibility of the legal and mental health systems. For all of these reasons, it is imperative that psychologists, psychiatrists, social workers, and other would-be interviewers strive to minimize the risk of both types of error when conducting forensic assessments of child sexual abuse.

S.O. Lilienfeld, Ph.D. (✉)
Department of Psychology, Emory University, Room 473, Psychology and Interdisciplinary Sciences Building, 36 Eagle Row, Atlanta, GA 30322, USA
e-mail: slilien@emory.edu

W.T. O'Donohue, M. Fanetti (eds.), *Forensic Interviews Regarding Child Sexual Abuse*, DOI 10.1007/978-3-319-21097-1_9

Virtually all measures, including interviews, contain a certain degree of error. According to classical test theory, observed scores on a measure consist of two components: true score and error (Whiston, 2012). All things being equal, the lower the level of error, technically called *measurement error*, the more likely our instrument will be to detect the phenomenon of interest. Our fundamental goal as interviewers, both scientifically and ethically, should be to minimize error, and thereby maximize our odds of arriving a genuine picture of nature.

As the great American psychologist E. L. Thorndike (1918, p. 16) famously proclaimed, "Whatever exists at all exists in some amount. To know it thoroughly involves knowing its quantity as well as its quality." Hence, Thorndike maintained, if we assume that a phenomenon exists, we can in principle measure it to some extent. For example, if we believe that a child is experiencing "underlying emotional conflicts" following sexual abuse, we should in principle be able to measure these conflicts, albeit imperfectly. To do so, we would first develop an *operationalization* of underlying emotional conflicts, followed by a measure of this operationalization (note that I used the term "operationalization" rather than the commonly used term, "operational definition," because the latter term implies erroneously that the operationalization is a strict dictionary-type definition of its intended construct; see Green, 1992). This measure would almost certainly be fallible, but it should hopefully be sufficiently saturated with the true score to be psychologically meaningful.

If a clinician were to aver that "I am certain that the child is experiencing underlying emotional conflicts, but there is no way to measure them," he or she would be in violation of Thorndike's dictum. Just as important, he or she would be operating unscientifically, because he or she would be advancing an assertion that is impossible to falsify (Popper, 1959). One major advantage of psychological measurement is that it forces us to be explicit in our assertions; more colloquially, it forces us to "put up or shut up" (see also O'Donoghue & Henderson, 1999). If our construct of "underlying emotional conflicts" is so nebulous and difficult to pin down that we cannot conceive of any way to operationalize, let alone measure, it, this should give us second thoughts regarding whether it is meaningful to begin with.

In this chapter, I review the basic principles of psychometrics, an applied technology that can help us to reduce, although not eliminate, the risk of error in clinical settings. I focus on classical test theory given its widespread use in forensic assessment; readers interested in generalizability theory, item response theory, and other more contemporary developments in psychometrics are referred elsewhere (e.g., Brennan, 2001; Embretson & Reise, 2000). Furthermore, I examine widespread sources of error in the forensic assessment of abuse and delineate constructive strategies for minimizing errors with the aid of psychological science.

The premise of this chapter is straightforward: Essentially all psychological measures are fallible, but we can minimize this fallibility by turning to psychometric methods, which are partial safeguards against errors. Furthermore, by relying on these safeguards, we can enhance the likelihood of accurate clinical decisions (Garb, 1998; Wood, Garb, & Nezworski, 2007). Paul Meehl (1997), the most influential clinical psychologist of the second half of the twentieth century, referred to psychometrics as one of the few 'noble' tradiitions. in clinical psychology, largely because it is among the best established bodies of knowledge in our field (Wood et al., 2007). In this respect, it is sobering that the quality and quantity of psychometric training in most psychology departments, which is already grossly suboptimal, has stagnated or deteriorated in recent decades (Aiken, West, & Millsap, 2008; see also Borsboom, 2006). I hope that this chapter will play a modest role in reversing this trend.

The Bread and Butter of Psychometrics: Implications for Forensic Interviewing for Child Sexual Abuse

Psychometrics is the science of mental measurement. Sir Francis Galton, a cousin of Charles Darwin who is commonly regarded as the "father of psychometrics," was among the first to develop psychological tests to detect individual differences in intellect and personality. Galton was well aware of the problems posed by measurement error in individuals' observations of phenomena (Fancher, 2009). For example, Galton advocated the use of aggregation across multiple observers, which helps to cancel out random deviations in observations, to minimize error. In a classic demonstration in 1906, he asked 787 individuals at a livestock fair in England to estimate the weight of an ox on display. Although most individual estimates were wildly inaccurate, the mean of all estimates (1197 lb) was only 1 lb away from the ox's actual weight (1198 lb; see Surowiecki, 2005). In addition, recognizing that virtually all of us are poor at detecting covariation with our unaided eyes, Galton developed the technique of correlation, which his student Karl Pearson elaborated into a now-famous and widely used product–moment formula (Stigler, 1989). Galton's seminal contributions to mental testing and psychometrics fueled scholarly interest in the development of more sophisticated psychological measures, as well as of statistical techniques for evaluating them.

Because forensic interviews are interpersonal interactions that typically entail a substantial amount of subjectivity, it is easy to forget that they are first and foremost psychological measures. Hence, they are subject to the same psychological criteria as are all other measures. Virtually all students of psychology, as well as other mental health professionals, are well aware of the fundamental benchmarks, such as reliability and validity, needed to evaluate psychological measures, including forensic interviews. Nevertheless, many of these psychometric criteria are considerably more complex and nuanced than is commonly appreciated.

In the following section, I review fundamental psychometric principles relevant to forensic interviewing, with a particular emphasis on widely held misconceptions and misunderstandings that can impede scientifically grounded clinical assessment (see also Haynes, Smith, & Hunsley, 2011). Many standard psychometrics texts focus largely or exclusively on reliability and validity, but this duo is incomplete. We also need to consider the utility of psychological measurement (Haynes et al., 2011), often regarded as the undeservedly neglected stepchild of psychometrics.

Accordingly, I focus on the psychometric triad of reliability, validity, and utility. These three criteria are nested hierarchically: Reliability is necessary but not sufficient for validity, and validity is necessary but not sufficient for utility.

Reliability: Consistency of Measurement

In psychology, the term *reliability* refers to consistency of measurement. This term can generate all manner of confusion in forensic contexts, because in the legal system, "reliability" typically refers to the extent to which a measure is statistically associated with important outcomes, such as a deception, criminal risk, or childabuse (e.g., Leo, Drizin, Neufeld, Hall, & Vatner, 2006). Hence, in the courtroom, reliability generally means something more akin to what psychologists call validity.

Reliability: An Insider's Guide

The relation between reliability and validity is less straightforward than is typically assumed. Because reliability places constraints on validity, a measure that contains no reliable variance cannot be valid. Within classical test theory, scores on a measure that contains no reliable variance are composed entirely of random—that is, unsystematic—error (unsystematic errors are uncorrelated with each other). As a consequence, this measure cannot relate systematically to other variables.

Conversely, a measure that is extremely reliable can still be invalid for its intended purpose, as its reliable variance consists largely or entirely of error, namely systematic error (in contrast to unsystematic errors, systematic errors are intercorrelated). For example, imagine that we attempted to detect a history of child sexualabuse by inspecting children's figure drawings for signs of long, narrow objects, such as bullets or missiles; let us further imagine that children tended to be extremely consistent over time in whether they included such objects in their drawings. Our judgments of child sexual abuse would be highly reliable but entirely invalid, because there is no evidence that long, narrow objects are valid indicators of a history of sexual abuse. More generally, children's figure drawings are well-nigh useless for detecting sexual abuse (Lilienfeld, Wood, & Garb, 2000). Note, however, that I wrote "for its intended purpose" in the opening sentence of this paragraph. A measure that is highly reliable is almost certainly a valid measure of *something*, but it may not be a valid measure of the construct that the clinician or researcher has in mind (Sechrest, 1984).

Although higher reliability will, *all things being equal*, lead to higher validity, all things are not necessarily equal. Indeed, in some cases, increasing reliability can actually lower the validity of a measure, an important but little-known phenomenon called the *attenuation paradox* (Loevinger, 1954; see also Clark & Watson, 1995). This paradox can arise when a researcher attempts to boost a measure's reliability by making it more homogeneous in content. For example, she might begin with a measure of childhood depression whose reliability (specifically, its internal consistency; see section "Internal Consistency") is deemed to be too low. To increase its reliability, she might write additional items designed to assess depressed mood and anhedonia (pervasive loss of pleasure), and jettison items designed to assess features of depression she regards as less central to the construct, such as concentration disturbances or psychomotor retardation (slowing). By doing so, she would probably end up with a more reliable but less valid measure of depression, because this measure would neglect to encompass the full range of signs and symptoms of this condition.

A further complexity is that validity is technically limited not by reliability per se but by the square root of reliability (Sechrest, 1984). Reliability can therefore technically exceed validity. For example, a psychiatric diagnosis can possess a reliability as low as $r=0.6$ and in principle still display validities, as ascertained by correlations with other measures, as high as $r=0.77$. This often overlooked point is potentially important, because some scholars have contended that as a field, we have sometimes overestimated the importance of reliability when evaluating psychological measures (Meehl, 1986). For example, the DSM-5 field trials almost exclusively emphasized reliability rather than validity (Regier et al., 2013), leaving open the possibility that a number of newly introduced diagnoses in the psychiatric manual are consistent but largely invalid measures of their intended constructs.

In reality, reliability and validity are not as distinct as we often imply. Instead, reliability and validity almost certainly lie on a continuum, namely, a dimension of *generalizability* (Campbell & Fiske, 1959; Cronbach, Rajaratnam, & Gleser, 1963). By generalizability, we mean the extent to which scores on the test can be extrapolated outside of the testing situation, such as to other measures, settings, or raters. At one extreme on the continuum, which comprises the "extreme" cases of reliability, one examines the association between maximally similar measures of the same construct. For example, across multiple adolescents, we might inquire about the levels of clinical depression twice within the same interview. Our resulting measure of association would be a prototypical measure of reliability, namely test–retest reliability (see section "Test–retest reliability"). At the other end of the continuum, the "extreme" cases of validity, one examines the association between maximally *dissimilar* measures of the same construct (Campbell & Fiske, 1959). For example, across multiple adolescents, we might inquire about their depression levels in an interview and also attempt to detect their levels of depression by administering an implicit association test. Our resulting measure of association would be an index of the validity of one or both measures. Between these two extremes, we often find cases that fall into the murky middle ground between reliability and validity. For example, if we attempt to detect adolescents' levels of clinical depression by administering an interview to them and then administering the same interview to their mothers (whom we ask to report on their child's depression levels), would the resulting index of association be an index of reliability or validity? From a scientific perspective, the answer is not especially important, because reliability and validity fall on a dimension of generalizability, with no clear line of demarcation between them.

Making matters still more complicated, measures can be consistent or inconsistent in different ways (Schmidt & Hunter, 1996). Hence, reliability is not a unitary concept (Sechrest, 1984). Moreover, for a given measure, different subtypes of reliability do not necessarily coincide in magnitude; levels of one form of reliability can be high while another is low. For example, scores derived from the Thematic Apperception Test, a widely used projective technique that asks respondents to tell stories in response to a series of ambiguous pictures, frequently display moderately high levels of test–retest reliability but low levels of internal consistency (Lundy, 1985). As a final complexity, we cannot assume that reliability values in one sample will necessarily generalize to other samples. For example, a self-report measure of attention-deficit hyperactivity disorder (ADHD) may display high reliability in an outpatient child disorders clinic, in which there is substantial variance in ADHD features, but low reliability in an undergraduate sample, in which the variance in ADHD features will presumably be lower (Haynes et al., 2011). As a consequence, reliability should be viewed as potentially conditional on our samples.

Hence, the commonly invoked, but hopelessly imprecise, phrase "this measure has been found to be reliable" should probably be forever banned from the pages of psychology journals, not to mention all courts of law. Authors and expert witnesses who are describing the reliability of their measures should instead be required to specify the form of reliability to which they are referring, as well as the sample from which it was derived.

Test–Retest Reliability

The best known form of reliability, *test–retest reliability*, refers to the stability of scores over time. In general, high levels of test–retest reliability for a measure are desirable. Nevertheless, this is only the case if one anticipates that the attribute being assessed should be reasonably stable over time, such as a personality trait (e.g., neuroticism) or a cognitive capacity (e.g., verbal ability). If one instead anticipates that the attribute in question should change over time, high levels of test–retest reliability would actually be undesirable. This distinction underscores a crucial point that holds for both test–retest reliability and the form of reliability I discuss next, namely, internal consistency: *The proper interpretation of reliability can only occur within a theoretical context*. That is, whether we expect or desire high levels of reliability hinges on our conceptualization of the construct being measured.

The question of the proper test–retest interval for a measure does not lend itself to a simple answer (Sechrest, 1984). Too brief a test–retest interval, such as one day, can be problematic, in part because individuals may recall their previous answers to questionnaires or interviews (Lord & Novick, 1968). Conversely, too lengthy a test–retest interval, such as several months, may also be problematic, as some of the changes in scores over time could reflect alterations in levels of true scores (the underlying attributes being measured, such as personality traits) rather than measurement error. Researchers and forensic assessors should be therefore certain to report the test–retest intervals used when presenting the test–retest reliability of a measure.

Internal Consistency

Measures of internal consistency address the question of how well the items on a measure "hang together" or, more precisely, assess the same construct. By definition, internal consistency applies only to measures that consist of multiple items. As in the case of test–retest reliability, high levels of internal consistency are generally desirable. Nevertheless, there are again exceptions. For example, a measure of independent life events, which are occurrences (e.g., death of a parent, experiencing an earthquake) that are presumably independent of the individual's behavior (Hammen, 1991), would be expected to display low internal consistency, because the events in question should be essentially random. Indeed, we might legitimately call into question an ostensible measure of independent life events that was highly internally consistent. Such high levels of internal consistency might suggest that the life events measure is contaminated by an unmeasured variable, such as negative emotionality (Watson & Clark, 1984).

One of the oldest measures of internal consistency is the *split-half coefficient*, which is calculated by dividing the test in half, and then correlating the two halves (Callender & Osburn, 1977). Most often, this procedure is accomplished by taking the odd numbered items on the test (1, 3, 5, etc.) and summing them, the even numbered items on the test (e.g., 2, 4, 6, etc.) and summing, and then correlating these two subtotals, yielding a statistic called *odd–even reliability*. Nevertheless, because there are many ways of divvying up a test into two halves, this procedure is somewhat arbitrary and can yield unstable results.

Hence, the preferred metric today for calculating internal consistency is Cronbach's alpha (Cronbach, 1951). Given some assumptions that we need not address here, Cronbach's alpha can be interpreted as the mean of all possible split-half coefficients (Cortina, 1993). Technically, we can interpret Cronbach's alpha within the context of parallel-forms reliability, the reliability reflecting the correlation between two parallel forms of the same test (Tavakol & Dennick, 2011). Specifically, if a measure has an alpha of 0.75, that value means that a measure consisting of the same number of psychometrically parallel items should correlate with the original measure at $r=0.75$. Cronbach's alpha is regarded as a "lower bound estimate" of internal consistency, because for multidimensional measures it will typically underestimate the interrelatedness among test items (Haynes et al., 2011).

Probably the most frequent error made in evaluating internal consistency estimates is to interpret them as indices of homogeneity (Cortina, 1993; Tavakol & Dennick, 2011). In fact, Cronbach's alpha is a notoriously poor indicator of homogeneity, especially for tests that contain many items. That is because Cronbach's alpha is affected substantially by test length. All things being equal, tests that contain more items will display higher internal consistencies as assessed by Cronbach's alpha and related metrics. Particularly for lengthy tests, authors should routinely report the mean inter-item correlation (MIC), which is simply the mean pairwise correlation among all items. In contrast to Cronbach's alpha, the MIC offers a direct index of homogeneity. For reasons that are unclear, MICs are rarely reported in published psychological research.

Inter-rater Reliability

The form of reliability most relevant to forensic interviews of child abuse is *inter-rater reliability*, the relation between the scores of two (or more) individuals, such as interviewers or other observers, on the same measure. Inter-rater reliability statistics address a fundamental question: Do the ratings of one interviewer generalize to those of other interviewers? If they do not, it raises the possibility that the scores of this interviewer are idiosyncratic.

When computing the inter-rater reliability of dimensional scores on interviews, such as interviewees' levels of anxiety or thought disorder, the preferred metric of agreement is the *intraclass correlation* (ICC). The ICC measures the amount of variance in scores attributable to the individuals being rated rather than to the raters themselves. If all of the variance in scores is attributable to the individuals being rated, the ICC will be 1.0; conversely, if all of the variance in scores is attributable to the raters, the OCC will be 0. In contrast to the Pearson product–moment correlation, which takes into account only the *relative* ranking and spacing of scores, most versions of the ICC are also influenced by the *absolute* levels of scores (McGraw & Wong, 1996). As a consequence, they will be influenced by differences in rater thresholds. For example, if two interviewers differ in their thresholds for labeling acts of physical aggression against children as "child abuse," with one requiring more severe or overt aggression than the other before labeling the behavior as abuse, the ICC, but not the Pearson correlation, will be affected by this difference.

When computing the inter-rater reliability of categorical scores on interviews, such as the presence or absence of child sexual abuse or the presence or absence of a psychiatric diagnosis (e.g., posttraumatic stress disorder), the preferred metric is the kappa coefficient, which measures the levels of chance-corrected agreement (Cohen, 1968; Fleiss & Cohen, 1973). By chance-corrected agreement, we mean agreement that is not attributable to the *base rates* (prevalences) of the phenomenon of interest (Brennan & Prediger, 1981). If we do not correct for chance-corrected agreement, we risk overestimating the level of inter-rater reliability. Imagine a case of two interviewers evaluating whether participants in an outpatient mood disorders clinic, in which the base rate of the diagnosis of major depression is 85 %, meet criteria for major depression. The interviewers could agree 85 % of the time merely by guessing that everyone in the sample meets criteria for major depression. By correcting for agreement that is potentially due to base rates, kappa addresses this problem. Nevertheless, because kappa may sometimes penalize raters for their shared expertise, it provides a statistically conservative estimate of rater agreement (Lilienfeld, Smith, & Watts, 2013).

Threats to the Reliability of Forensic Interviews

In a user-friendly and engaging analysis, Shea (1998) delineated a number of common threats to the reliability of interviews; most or all of these threats apply to forensic interviews. I examine three such threats here. It should be borne in mind, however, that because reliability sets limits on validity, these errors also bear implications for the validity of interviews.

Cannon Questions

First, interviewers may engage in *cannon questions*, in which they "fire off" (Shea, 1998, p. 45) multiple queries in rapid succession, typically in the context of a single question (e.g., "Do you often feel extremely sad, tense, uptight, agitated, even suicidal?"). Such questions should almost always be avoided, because either positive or negative replies can be ambiguous or misleading. A "yes" reply could mean that the individual often experiences one of the emotions listed, some of them, or all of them; conversely, a "no" reply could mean that the individual denies experiencing one, some, or all of the emotions listed. Making matters worse, either a "yes" or "no" response could simply mean that the individual forgot some or all of the descriptors listed in the question. Cannon questions are especially ill-advised with children, who may misunderstand such questions, and with individuals with memory or concentration difficulties, including those with depression (see Watts, MacLeod, & Morris, 1988).

Phrasing Questions in the Negative

Second, phrasing questions in the negative (e.g., "You haven't thought about killing yourself, have you?"), which is a common error when inquiring about sensitive topics, can also diminish the reliability of interviews. Such questions, which again should almost always be avoided, can readily engender demand characteristics (Orne, 1962) in interviewees, as they can imply that the interviewer looks down on the behavior in question or is hoping for a denial of the undesirable behavior (Shea, 1998).

Altering Verbal or Nonverbal Behavior

Third, interviewers may subtly—or not so subtly—alter their verbal or nonverbal behaviors when asking certain questions during the interview (Shea, 1998). For example, when inquiring about sensitive topics, such as sexual abuse, physical abuse, drug use, or suicidal or homicidal ideation, they may lower their voice or change their pitch or speed of delivery of questions. Alternatively, they might inadvertently respond with signs of surprise, concern, or disapproval when the interviewee provides them an answer that is not to their liking. In all these cases, interviewers may unknowingly elicit inconsistent responses within respondents, across respondents, or both (Shea, 1998).

Validity: An Insider's Guide

Validity, as every psychology student learns, refers to the extent to which a measure assesses what it purports to measure; some students joke that the best way to answer a multiple choice question that concerns the definition for validity is simply to look for the word "purports." Recent years have witnessed the emergence of lively debates concerning the meaning and interpretation of validity (e.g., Borsboom, Mellenbergh, & van Heerden, 2004). I do not intend to revisit these at times arcane debates here, although I encourage interested readers to consult several recent discussions (e.g., Braun, 2012; Newton, 2012; Sechrest, 2005; Strauss & Smith, 2009).

The most crucial point for our purposes is that like reliability, validity is a multifaceted concept (Nunnally & Bernstein, 1994). Moreover, like reliability, validity is potentially conditional on the sample examined. Therefore, as in the case of reliability, the hackneyed phrase "this measure has been found to be valid" should be forever banished from psychological and psychiatric journal articles. I briefly review the major subtypes of validity here.

Content Validity

A measure's content validity refers to the extent to which it samples adequately from the "universe" of content comprising the construct of interest. For example, if I believe that psychopathic personality (psychopathy) is paradoxical constellation of characteristics that includes both psychologically adaptive features, such as superficial charm, interpersonal poise, and absence of anxiety, as well as psychologically maladaptive features, such as self-centeredness, guiltlessness, callousness, dishonesty, manipulativeness, and poor impulse control (see Cleckley, 1941; Hare, 1991/2003), a measure of psychopathy that consists only of maladaptive features would be of dubious content validity (see Lilienfeld, Patrick, Benning, Berg, Sellbom, & Edens, 2012, for a discussion). Although some authors have attempted to develop metrics to quantify content validity (see Polit, Beck, & Owen, 2007), these metrics have not caught on in most quarters. Hence, for better or worse, content validity is generally evaluated subjectively.

Content validity should not be confused with *face validity*, which is arguably not a form of validity at all (Lynn, 1986). Face validity refers to the extent to which test takers can infer the construct measured by the test. Face validity has long been a fraught concept in psychometrics, and for good reason. First, what may strike one test taker as obvious may strike another as obscure; hence, whereas one test taker may correctly surmise that the Beck Depression Inventory (Beck, Steer, & Brown, 1996) is a measure of clinical depression, another may assume that it is designed primarily to detect anxiety, suicide propensity, maladjustment, or negative emotionality. Second, in part for this reason, there is no standard quantitative metric for ascertaining face validity. Third, it is not even clear whether face validity is an advantage or disadvantage for psychological measures. On the one hand, we might assume that *low* face validity would be advantageous, as this property should render it difficult for individuals to detect the purpose of the assessment and distort their responses accordingly (Bornstein, Rossner, Hill, & Stepanian, 1994). On the other hand, face validity is often associated with empirical validity. Indeed, efforts to generate self-report items with high empirical validity but low face validity, so-called *subtle items*, have typically been disappointing (Sechrest, 1984; Weed, Ben-Porath, & Butcher, 1990).

Criterion-Related Validity

Criterion-related validity is a broad concept that refers to the extent to which a measure relates to nontest variables (Maroof, 2012). The term "criterion-related validity" is typically preferable to the more traditional term "criterion validity" because there are precious few genuine "criteria"—infallible indicators or "gold standards"—in clinical psychology, personality, and allied fields (Cronbach & Meehl, 1955). For example, to ascertain the criterion-related validity of a measure of child sexual abuse, we might examine the extent to which it is associated with objectively corroborated indicators of abuse.

Criterion-related validity can itself be decomposed into several subtypes, corresponding to two overarching distinctions. First, we can subdivide criterion-related validity into subtypes corresponding to *when* the external variable was measured relative to the administration of the test. *Concurrent validity* examines whether the extent to which a test is associated with variables measured at about the same time the test was administered; *predictive validity* examines the extent to which a test is associated with variables measured long (e.g., months or years) after the test was administered; and *postdictive validity*, which is more rarely investigated, examines the extent to which a test is associated with variables measured long before the test was administered. For example, we might examine the concurrent validity of an interview-based measure of major depression by determining whether it correlates with a self-report measure of depression administered during the same session; we might examine its predictive validity by determining whether it correlates with future depressive episodes; and we might examine its postdictive validity by determining whether it correlates with past depressive episodes. In this case, both predictive and postdictive validity are premised on the fact that major depression tends to be an episodic and often recurrent disorder. Note that many authors misuse the term predictive validity, using it to refer to the extent to which a measure correlates with any nontest variable. This use is incorrect; this term should be reserved for the capacity of a measure to *forecast* future outcomes.

Criterion-related validity can be subdivided in another important way (Campbell & Fiske, 1959; Cole, 1987). *Convergent validity* examines whether a test correlates with measures of variables with which we would theoretically expect it to correlate. In contrast, *discriminant validity*, sometimes also called divergent validity, examines whether a test is uncorrelated (or largely uncorrelated) with measures of variables with which we would theoretically expect it not to correlate (or to correlate minimally). For example, if we were to develop a novel measure of posttraumatic anxiety for children, it would be important to demonstrate not only that the measure correlates positively with other measures of posttraumatic symptoms—convergent validity—but that the measure correlates less highly with variables that are theoretically unrelated or largely independent of such symptoms, such as intelligence or a social undesirability response style (see section "Threats to the validity of forensic interviews")—discriminant validity.

Given that most measures of psychopathology tend to be at least moderately positively correlated, tests of the discriminant validity of new measures of mental disorder are in many respects even more important than are tests of convergent validity (Tellegen, 1985). Virtually any measure of psychopathology will correlate at least moderately with other measures of psychopathology, even if it does not validly detect the construct of interest. For example, if I were to develop a new measure of depression that was actually more of a measure of anxiety, it would nonetheless correlate moderately with other measures of depression, because depression and anxiety measures are highly correlated (Dobson, 1985). As a result, I could be misled into concluding that my measure is a valid indicator of depression. If, however, I also administered a measure of anxiety, I would soon discover that my ostensible measure of depression correlated more highly with the anxiety measure than with another depression measure, revealing an absence of discriminant validity and forcing me to go back to the test construction drawing board. Nevertheless, discriminant validity tends to be underemphasized in the psychological literature.

Incidentally, many authors misuse the term discriminant validity to describe the capacity of a measure to discriminate between or among diagnostic groups. For example, many would describe the capacity of a measure of posttraumatic stress disorder (PTSD) to distinguish individuals diagnosed with PTSD from individuals diagnosed with another condition, such as major depression, as indicator of the measure's discriminant validity. In fact, it is an indicator of the test's convergent validity, because we are examining whether the measure correlates positively with another variable, namely, the presence versus absence of PTSD. The precise term for this psychometric property is *discriminative validity* (Haynes et al., 2011), which is a variant of convergent validity.

Construct Validity

Construct validity is the extent to which a measure detects a construct, which is a hypothesized attribute of individuals (Cronbach & Meehl, 1955; Loevinger, 1957). Constructs in clinical psychology include general intelligence, executive functioning, personality traits (e.g., extraversion), and psychiatric disorders (e.g., schizophrenia). None of these phenomena can be observed directly and can only be inferred. Because all of the forms of validity I have already reviewed bear on the capacity of a measure to detect constructs, construct validity subsumes them. Hence, whenever we are measuring constructs—latent attributes—construct validity *is* validity (Messick, 1995; Sechrest, 1984; Waldman, Lilienfeld, & Lahey, 1995). Accordingly, authors who state that "this measure possesses good content, criterion-related, and construct validity" are asserting a pleonasm, not to mention committing a logical error. Construct validity supersedes these other forms of validity.

Construct validation requires test developers to postulate an explicit *nomological network*, a system of hypotheses that includes convergent and discriminant linkages among constructs, among variables, and between constructs and variables (Cronbach & Meehl, 1955; Waldman et al., 1995). For example, a researcher who developed a new measure of psychopathy should posit up front which variables he or she expects the measure to correlate with (e.g., current and future violence, diminished empathy as reported by self and others, psychophysiological indicators of fear insensitivity) as well as which variables he or she expects the measure to correlate weakly or at least less highly with (e.g., intelligence, depression, psychophysiological indicators of baseline arousal). The more evidence we amass over time that our measure correlates with theoretically predicted variables (convergent validity) and correlates weakly or not all with theoretically unpredicted variables (discriminant validity), the most compelling is the evidence for this measure's construct validity. Although provisional efforts have been made to quantify construct validity (Westen & Rosenthal, 2003), the evaluation of construct validity, like that of content validity, is almost always subjective.

Note that I wrote "explicit" in the first sentence of the previous paragraph. One of the hazards of construct validation, especially when it is performed in a less than rigorous manner, is that we can too easily accrue evidence for our measure in a post hoc fashion (Bechtoldt, 1959; Lynam & Miller, 2012). In other words, we can often "retrofit" evidence after the fact and claim that it was consistent with our initial hypotheses. Hence, it is incumbent on test developers to be as explicit as possible regarding which findings would falsify, or at least call into question, their assertion that their measure is a valid indicator of the intended construct.

Because construct validation, like the process of validating scientific theories, is in principle a continual and never-ending endeavor, we should avoid referring to measures as "validated." Instead, the best we can say is that extant evidence supports the assertion that our measure validly detects the latent attribute of interest.

Threats to the Validity of Forensic Interviews

A host of variables, some stemming from interviewers and others stemming from interviewees, can adversely affect the validity of interviews, including forensic interviews. Here I discuss three particularly important threats to interview validity. The first and third threats originate largely from interviewer behaviors, whereas the second threat originates largely from interviewee behavior. Nevertheless, because the interview is a dyadic interaction, all three errors can derive in part from the actions of both interviewer and interviewee.

Inadequate Probing

Inexperienced interviewers, and occasionally experienced interviewers who are experiencing intense time pressure, may commit the error of inadequate probing of interviewee responses. This mistake is especially likely when interviewers assume that they understand certain words or phrases on the part of interviewees, such as "depressed," "panicky," "aggressive," or "manic." As the American psychiatrist Harry Stack Sullivan (1954) noted in his classic book, *The Psychiatric Interview*, this assumption is almost always unwarranted, because these words or phrases do not necessarily have identical or even similar meanings across interviewees. One interviewee may say "I am feeling depressed" to refer to a mild state of sadness following a rough day at work, whereas another may use this phrase to refer to profound feelings of psychological agony. Similarly, one interviewee may report that "I was aggressive with my wife last night" to describe his interrupting her during an argument, whereas another may use this phrase to describe his physically assaulting her with a closed fist.

Perhaps the best antidote to this error is the use of *behavioral incidents* (Pascal, 1983; Shea, 1998), which are concrete behavioral examples or details. When eliciting behavioral incidents, interviewers probe interviewees' ambiguous terms and phrases by inquiring about specific actions. For example, rather than assuming that one understands what the interviewee means by "being aggressive," the skilled forensic interviewer would follow up with such probes as "In what ways were you aggressive?," "When you say 'aggressive', what do you mean?," "Tell me what you did," "What happened first?," "Then what happened?," and so on. Behavioral incidents can minimize the risk of error in interviews and thereby enhance their validity by enhancing the odds that interviewer judgments are grounded in reasonably objective behavioral indicators. Of course, the interviewees' selection of terms may itself sometimes be of clinical interest. An interviewee who habitually describes the physical abuse of his child as "being a bit rough with my kid every once in a while" may be engaging in minimization, a characteristic that may be tied to certain clinically important personality traits or personality disorders, such as psychopathy (Porter & Woodworth, 2007). Nevertheless, interviewers should not rely exclusively on the interviewers' choice of terms, as this reliance can be misleading.

Response Sets and Response Styles

Response sets and *response styles* are ways of responding to questions that are largely independent of content (Paulhus, 1991). Response sets and response styles fall on a continuum, with sets being primarily situational (e.g., a response to an insanity evaluation) and styles being primarily dispositional.

Response sets and styles, in turn, can be largely unsystematic or systematic (Piedmont, McCrae, Riemann, & Angleitner, 2000). Unsystematic response sets and styles, which are more relevant to self-report measures than to interviews, include random or careless responding. Systematic response sets and styles, which are relevant to both self-report measures and interviews, include acquiescence/counteracquiescence, social desirability, and malingering. *Acquiescence*, colloquially called "yea-saying," reflects a propensity to answer yes to questions independent of their content; *counteracquiescence*, colloquially called "nay-saying," reflects a propensity to answer no to questions independent of their content. Acquiescence is a particular threat to the validity of forensic interviews with children, who are especially vulnerable to the effects of suggestive questioning (Bruck & Ceci, 2000; Ceci & Bruck, 1993). *Social desirability* is a propensity to provide answers that make oneself appear "good" in the eyes of others and to deny trivial faults (Ones, Viswesvaran, & Reiss, 1996). For example, a "yes" response to an item such as "I have no bad habits" would give a respondent a point on most standard social desirability scales. *Malingering* is virtually the opposite of social desirability and is a tendency to make oneself appear ill or psychologically disturbed. Many malingering scales consist of items designed to assess seemingly plausible features of psychopathology that are in fact exceedingly rare (e.g., Lilienfeld & Andrews, 1996). For example, a malingering item on a self-report scale might be "At times I see large fish, birds, or other animals floating in front of my eyes."

One often unappreciated advantage of self-report measures is that they can detect response sets and styles systematically, usually by means of embedded validity scales (Widiger & Frances, 1987). In keeping with the core theme of this chapter, the principle here is that *if one cannot eliminate a source oferror, one can at least attempt to measure it*. In turn, one can use systematic measures of response sets and response styles to compensate for error, such as by treating them analytically as moderators or suppressors of the validity of measures (see McGrath, Mitchell, Kim, & Hough, 2010, for a discussion). Interviews can in principle also be used to detect response sets and response styles, such as malingering, although relatively few systematic efforts have been undertaken in this regard (see Rogers, 2010, for a notable exception). Nevertheless, there is presently an active debate regarding whether controlling for social desirability and other response styles leads to clinically significant increases in net validity (McGrath et al., 2010; Piedmont et al., 2000; Rohling et al., 2011).

Suggestive or Leading Questions

Forensic interviewers can compromise validity by engaging in suggestive or leading questions, which fall on a dimension, with leading questions (e.g., "Daddy touched you there, right?") being more suggestive than suggestive questions (e.g., "I heard that Daddy touched you there. Is that right?"). Such questions can inadvertently end up providing interviewers with the answers they are looking or hoping for (Geiselman, Fisher, Cohen, & Holland, 1986). Nevertheless, these answers may be inaccurate. Suggestive or leading questioning can also contribute to low levels of inter-rater reliability, especially when some interviewers but not others engage in this practice. Ironically, a team of researchers or clinicians all trained to engage in suggestive or leading questioning could exhibit high levels of inter-rater reliability but low levels of validity.

Utility

Just as reliability does not ensure validity, validity does not ensure utility. Utility refers to the extent to which a measure is useful for clinical purposes. Utility addresses several important pragmatic questions, such as whether a measure enhances treatment outcomes (Hayes, Nelson, & Jarrett, 1987) or contributes to the statistical prediction of events, such as child abuse, above and beyond already collected data (Meehl, 1959). In the case of forensic interviews, an assessment of child sexualabuse should be clinically useful: It should help us to assign abused children to appropriate treatment, decrease their risk for subsequent psychopathology, and so on.

For reasons that are insufficiently appreciated, even a measure with extremely high validity may be virtually useless in certain clinical settings. This paradoxical state of affairs can arise in two major ways.

Base Rates

First, a measure that possesses high levels of criterion-related validity in one sample may be virtually clinically useless in a sample with an extremely low base rate of the phenomenon of interest (Meehl & Rosen, 1955; see also Finn & Kamphuis, 1995); as noted earlier, base rates refer to the prevalence of a phenomenon. Incidentally, it will also be virtually clinically useless in the rarer case of a sample with an extremely high base rate of this phenomenon. To take an extreme example, a measure with high validity for detecting sexual abuse will be clinically useless in a sample in which no one has been abused. Note, however, that this measure will similarly be clinically useless in a sample in which everyone has been abused. A measure cannot make differentiations if there is nothing to differentiate.

More commonly, of course, practitioners are tasked with the job of identifying a clinical phenomenon, such as sexual abuse, in a sample in which the base rate is not zero, but is very low. In such cases, a valid test may still yield little or virtually no clinically useful information. The mathematical formula known as *Bayes' theorem* reminds us that our proportion of correct identifications will be a joint function of (1) the test's validity and (2) the base rate of the phenomenon of interest (see Wood, 1996, for a superb tutorial on using Bayes theorem to inform child abuse evaluations). Although the mathematics of Bayes' theorem need not concern us here, suffice it to say that as base rates decrease, the rates of false positive identifications will increase. Moreover, if the base rates are sufficiently low, the use of a test with only modest validity can sometimes result in an *increase* in overall classification errors. In such situations, we would have been better off just "playing the base rates" and not using the test at all (Meehl & Rosen, 1955)!

Incremental Validity

Second, a valid measure may not be worth administering if it is redundant with other information, especially information that is already available to us. One of the most crucial criteria for establishing clinical utility is *incremental validity* (Sechrest, 1963), the extent to which a measure is associated with clinically important outcomes above and beyond other measures. Given these considerations, it is surprising and perhaps disconcerting how rarely test developers attempt to demonstrate the incremental validity of newly constructed measures above and beyond extant measures (Garb, 2003; Hunsley & Meyer, 2003; Wood et al., 2007). For example, if an investigator were to develop a novel self-report measure for detecting child sexualabuse, the onus should be on him or her to demonstrate that this measure possesses "added value" above and beyond existing measures, especially measures that are less expensive and more easily administered. The lone major exception to this requirement is when new measures are designed to be briefer and more easily administered versions of existing measures with well-demonstrated validity. In such cases, a measure may not possess incremental validity above and beyond an extant measure; but if it is equally valid for detecting relevant phenomena, it should generally be preferred because it is more economical.

An important but rarely invoked distinction is that between *statistical* and *clinical* incremental validity. Statistical incremental validity refers to the extent to which a measure contributes additional statistical information, often quantified as a change in the amount of variance accounted for in a multiple regression equation, above and beyond extant information. Statistical incremental validity cannot be negative; at worse, it will zero. If a measure does not contribute additional statistical information above and beyond other measures, it will merely "drop out" of a regression equation, as all of its variance will have been soaked up by other measures.

In contrast, clinical incremental validity refers to the extent to which clinical judgments and predictions are enhanced by the addition of a new measure to an existing set of measures. Unlike statistical incremental validity, clinical incremental validity *can* be negative (Wedding & Faust, 1989). How? The literature on social cognition has identified a "dilution effect" whereby the provision of additional information sometimes results in an overall decrease in the accuracy of judgments (Nisbett, Zukier, & Lemley, 1981). This effect is especially likely to occur when the novel information is (1) more salient ("eye catching") than the existing information but (2) of lower validity than the existing information. Imagine that a forensic practitioner interested in ascertaining whether a client has been adversely affected by sexual abuse has collected a large body of psychometric data—biographical information, well-validated self-report measures of psychopathology, cognitive and other neuropsychological measures, observations from relatives and coworkers—and concluded that the evidence is inconclusive. Nevertheless, based on a brief, informal interview with the client that suggests maladjustment, the practitioner may be inclined to override the other data and place undue weight on the less systematic, and perhaps less valid, interview impressions. Indeed, the classic review of Sawyer (1966) suggested that the addition of interviews to additional psychometric information sometimes contributes to a net *decrease* in the accuracy of clinical judgments (see also Dana, Dawes, & Peterson, 2013).

This critical point is commonly misunderstood by individuals who reflexively recommend "more testing" whenever the answer to a clinical question (e.g., "What is the client's diagnosis?" "Was the client sexually abused?") is unclear. They may assume that "more information is always better than less." Nevertheless, from the standpoint of clinical integration, this assumption is erroneous (Lilienfeld, Wood, & Garb, 2007). More information, especially if it is of lower validity than existing information, can inadvertently lead practitioners to rearrange their "mental regression weights" and accord unjustified emphasis to less valid data.

Norms and Standardization

Two other important, and closely related, means of reducing error in certain clinical inferences are the use of norms and standardization. Psychometricians commonly distinguish *criterion-referenced* from *norm-referenced* assessment (Popham & Husek, 1969). In criterion-referenced assessments, we are concerned only with *whether* a skill has been acquired or an attribute is present; we are not concerned with how the level of this skill or attribute compares with that of other individuals. A driver's test is a classic example of a criterion-referenced assessment. The governing body granting individuals a driver's license does not care how well a given driver performs relative to others drivers; all it cares about is whether the driver meets the established threshold for safe driving. Similarly, when assessing a child for a history of potential sexual abuse, the forensic interviewer is typically concerned only with whether this abuse is present.

In contrast, in norm-referenced assessment, we are preoccupied with the "compared with what" question (see Dawes, 1994). That is, we want to answer the question, "How do this person's scores compare with those of other people?" For example, when conducting a forensic interview, we may be interested in ascertaining how anxious a child is relative to other children of his or her age, and perhaps his or her gender. Or we may wish to determine whether a child who has been physically abused is experiencing more impaired executive functioning relative to nonabused children who have comparable overall levels of intelligence.

In such circumstances, accurate *norms* become crucial. Norms are average population baselines that form a basis of comparison with other scores (Cicchetti, 1994). Typically, norms are expressed in standard scores, such as scores that have a mean of 100 and a standard deviation of 15, as is the case with most standardized intelligence tests. In some cases, psychological tests may also be normed within specific subgroups, such as gender, race, or specific age subgroups.

The history of psychological assessment offers a powerful reminder of the need for accurate norms, as well as of the hazards of inaccurate norms. For example, the norms on some early intelligence tests were badly flawed, leading to numerous misclassifications of people with average of even above-average intelligence as intellectually disabled (Wood et al., 2007). Ironically, David Wecshler, the developer of the most widely used intelligence test used today, was classified as "feebleminded" by early intelligence tests. A more recent example comes from clinical practice and research on the Rorschach Inkblot Test. Data strongly suggest that the norms for the Comprehensive ("Exner") system, still the most widely used scoring and interpretative scheme for this test, are seriously in error and tend to misclassify many psychologically healthy individuals as pathological (Wood, Nezworski, Garb, & Lilienfeld, 2001).

Standardization of administration, which increases the chances that measures are administered in a comparable fashion across respondents, is essential for accurate norms. For norms to be meaningful, we need to be certain that error variance relevant to methods of administration is minimized, and that the resulting scores on measures faithfully reflect individual differences in the construct of interest, such as intelligence.

In the case of forensic interviews for child abuse and other psychological phenomena, standardization per se is rarely relevant given that these interviews tend to be individually tailored to respondents. Nevertheless, forensic interviews, like other interviews, vary on a continuum from *unstructured* to *structured*. Unstructured interviews have few or no standard questions, probes, or algorithms (scoring criteria), whereas structured interviews fall on the opposite end of this dimension. Interviews that fall in between these two extremes are commonly called *semistructured*. In general, meta-analyses (mathematical syntheses of the literature) suggest that structured interviews possess higher inter-rater reliability and construct validity than do unstructured interviews (Schmidt & Zimmerman, 2004; Wiesner & Cronshaw, 1988), almost certainly because they reduce psychometric error arising from interviewer differences in (a) the initial questions and probe questions asked and (b) interpretation and scoring of answers.

Concluding Thoughts

The forensic interview, when well conducted, can yield remarkable amounts of clinically useful information. At the same time, the forensic interview is inevitably a fallible psychological instrument, conducted by fallible human beings. Fortunately, by attending carefully to psychometric principles, interviewers can reduce their risk of clinical errors and harmful outcomes, and hopefully arrive at a closer approximation of the state of nature. Psychometric principles help to keep us humble: They remind us of our propensities toward errors (see also McFall, 1997; O'Donohue & Lilienfeld, 2007). At the same time, these principles also steer us away from the abyss of nihilism, as they remind us that these errors can be partly remediated with the aid of the finely honed tools of clinical science.

References

Aiken, L. S., West, S. G., & Millsap, R. E. (2008). Doctoral training in statistics, measurement, and methodology in psychology: Replication and extension of Aiken, West, Sechrest, and Reno's (1990) survey of PhD programs in North America. *American Psychologist, 63*, 32–50.

Bechtoldt, H. P. (1959). Construct validity: A critique. *American Psychologist, 14*, 619–629.

Beck, A. T., Steer, R. A., & Brown, G. K. (1996). *Beck depression inventory*. San Antonio, TX: The Psychological Corporation.

Bornstein, R. F., Rossner, S. C., Hill, E. L., & Stepanian, M. L. (1994). Face validity and fakability of objective and projective measures of dependency. *Journal of Personality Assessment, 63*, 363–386.

Borsboom, D. (2006). The attack of the psychometricians. *Psychometrika, 71*, 425–440.

Borsboom, D., Mellenbergh, G. J., & van Heerden, J. (2004). The concept of validity. *Psychological Review, 111*, 1061–1071.

Braun, H. (2012). Conceptions of validity: The private and the public. *Measurement: Interdisciplinary Research & Perspective, 10*(1–2), 46–49.

Brennan, R. L. (2001). *Statistics for social science and public policy: Generalizability theory*. New York, NY: Springer.

Brennan, R. L., & Prediger, D. J. (1981). Coefficient kappa: Some uses, misuses, and alternatives. *Educational and Psychological Measurement, 41*, 687–699.

Bruck, M., & Ceci, S. J. (2000). The suggestibility of children's memory. *Annual Review of Psychology, 50*, 419–439.

Callender, J. C., & Osburn, H. G. (1977). A method for maximizing split-half reliability coefficients. *Educational and Psychological Measurement, 37*, 819–825.

Campbell, D. T., & Fiske, D. W. (1959). Convergent and discriminant validation by the multitrait-multimethod matrix. *Psychological Bulletin, 56*, 81–205.

Ceci, S. J., & Bruck, M. (1993). Suggestibility of the child witness: A historical review and synthesis. *Psychological Bulletin, 113*, 403–439.

Cicchetti, D. V. (1994). Guidelines, criteria, and rules of thumb for evaluating normed and standardized assessment instruments in psychology. *Psychological Assessment, 6*, 284–290.

Clark, L. A., & Watson, D. (1995). Constructing validity: Basic issues in objective scale development. *Psychological Assessment, 7*, 309–319.

Cleckley, H. (1941). *The mask of sanity*. St. Louis, MO: Mosby.

Cohen, J. (1968). Weighted kappa: Nominal scale agreement provision for scaled disagreement or partial credit. *Psychological Bulletin, 70*, 213–220.

Cole, D. A. (1987). Utility of confirmatory factor analysis in test validation research. *Journal of Consulting and Clinical Psychology, 55*(4), 584–594.

Cortina, J. M. (1993). What is coefficient alpha? An examination of theory and applications. *Journal of Applied Psychology, 78*, 98–104.

Cronbach, L. J. (1951). Coefficient alpha and the internal structure of tests. *Psychometrika, 16*, 297–334.

Cronbach, L. J., & Meehl, P. E. (1955). Construct validity in psychological tests. *Psychological Bulletin, 52*, 281–302.

Cronbach, L. J., Rajaratnam, N., & Gleser, G. C. (1963). Theory of generalizability: A liberalization of reliability theory? *British Journal of Statistical Psychology, 16*, 137–163.

Cronch, L. E., Viljoen, J. L., & Hansen, D. J. (2006). *Forensic interviewing in child sexual abuse cases: Current techniques and future directions* (Faculty Publications, Department of Psychology, Paper 6). Lincoln, NE: University of Nebraska-Lincoln. Retrieved from http://digitalcommons.unl.edu/psychfacpub/6

Dana, J., Dawes, R. M., & Peterson, N. (2013). Belief in the unstructured interview: The persistence of an illusion. *Judgment and Decision Making, 8*, 512–520.

Dawes, R. D. (1994). *House of cards: Psychology and psychotherapy built on myth*. New York, NY: Free.

Dobson, K. S. (1985). The relationship between anxiety and depression. *Clinical Psychology Review, 5*, 307–324.

Embretson, S. E., & Reise, S. P. (2000). *Item response theory for psychologists*. Mahwah, NJ: Erlbaum.

Fancher, R. E. (2009). Scientific cousins: The relationship between Charles Darwin and Francis Galton. *American Psychologist, 64*, 84–92.

Finn, S. E., & Kamphuis, J. H. (1995). What a clinician needs to know about base rates. In J. N. Butcher (Ed.), *Clinical personality assessment: Practical approaches* (pp. 224–235). New York, NY: Oxford University Press.

Fleiss, J. L., & Cohen, J. (1973). The equivalence of weighted kappa and the intraclass correlation coefficient as measures of reliability. *Educational and Psychological Measurement, 33*, 613–619.

Garb, H. N. (1998). *Studying the clinician: Judgment research and psychological assessment*. Washington, DC: American Psychological Association.

Garb, H. N. (2003). Incremental validity and the assessment of psychopathology in adults. *Psychological Assessment, 15*(4), 508–520.

Geiselman, R. E., Fisher, R. P., Cohen, G., & Holland, H. (1986). Eyewitness responses to leading and misleading questions under the cognitive interview. *Journal of Police Science and Administration, 14*, 31–39.

Green, C. D. (1992). Of immortal mythological beasts: Operationism in psychology. *Theory and Psychology, 2*, 291–320.

Hammen, C. (1991). Generation of stress in the course of unipolar depression. *Journal of Abnormal Psychology, 100*, 555–561.

Hare, R. D. (2003). *Manual for the Psychopathy Checklist-Revised (PCL-R)*. Toronto, Ontario: Multi-Health Systems (Original work published 1991).

Hayes, S. C., Nelson, R. O., & Jarrett, R. B. (1987). The treatment utility of assessment: A functional approach to evaluating assessment quality. *American Psychologist, 42*, 963–974.

Haynes, S. N., Smith, G. T., & Hunsley, J. D. (2011). *Scientific foundations of clinical assessment*. New York, NY: Routledge.

Hunsley, J., & Meyer, G. J. (2003). The incremental validity of psychological testing and assessment: Conceptual, methodological, and statistical issues. *Psychological Assessment, 15*, 446–453.

Leo, R. A., Drizin, S. A., Neufeld, P. J., Hall, B. R., & Vatner, A. (2006). Bringing reliability back in: False confessions and legal safeguards in the twenty-first century. *Wisconsin Law Review, 2006*(2), 479–538.

Lilienfeld, S. O., & Andrews, B. P. (1996). Development and preliminary validation of a self-report measure of psychopathic personality traits in noncriminal population. *Journal of Personality Assessment, 66*, 488–524.

Lilienfeld, S. O., Patrick, C. J., Benning, S. D., Berg, J. M., Sellbom, M., & Edens, J. F. (2012). The role of fearless dominance in psychopathy: Confusions, controversies, and clarifications. *Personality Disorders: Theory, Treatment, and Research, 3*, 327–333.

Lilienfeld, S. O., Smith, S. F., & Watts, A. L. (2013). Issues in diagnosis: Conceptual issues and controversies. In W. E. Craighead, D. J. Miklowitz, & L. W. Craighead (Eds.), *Psychopathology: History, diagnosis, and empirical foundations* (2nd ed., pp. 1–35). Hoboken, NJ: Wiley.

Lilienfeld, S. O., Wood, J. M., & Garb, H. N. (2000). The scientific status of projective techniques. *Psychological Science in the Public Interest, 1*(2), 27–66.

Lilienfeld, S. O., Wood, J. M., & Garb, H. N. (2007). Why questionable psychological tests remain popular. *Scientific Review of Alternative Medicine, 10*, 6–15.

Loevinger, J. (1954). The attenuation paradox in test theory. *Psychological Bulletin, 51*, 493–504.

Loevinger, J. (1957). Objective tests as instruments of psychological theory: Monograph supplement 9. *Psychological Reports, 3*, 635–694.

Lord, F. M., & Novick, M. R. (1968). *Statistical theories of mental test scores*. Reading, MA: Addison-Wesley.

Lundy, A. (1985). The reliability of the thematic apperception test. *Journal of Personality Assessment, 49*, 141–145.

Lynam, D. R., & Miller, J. D. (2012). Fearless dominance and psychopathy: A response to Lilienfeld et al. *Personality Disorders: Theory, Research, and Treatment, 3*, 341–353.

Lynn, M. R. (1986). Determination and quantification of content validity. *Nursing Research, 35*, 382–386.

Maroof, D. A. (2012). *Statistical methods in neuropsychology: Common procedures made comprehensible*. New York, NY: Springer.

McFall, R. M. (1997). Making psychology incorruptible. *Applied and Preventive Psychology, 5*(1), 9–15.
McGrath, R. E., Mitchell, M., Kim, B. H., & Hough, L. (2010). Evidence for response bias as a source of error variance in applied assessment. *Psychological Bulletin, 136*, 450–470.
McGraw, K. O., & Wong, S. P. (1996). Forming inferences about some intraclass correlation coefficients. *Psychological Methods, 1*, 30–46.
Meehl, P. E. (1959). Some ruminations on the validation of clinical procedures. *Canadian Journal of Psychology, 13*, 102–128.
Meehl, P. E. (1986). Diagnostic taxa as open concepts: Metatheoretical and statistical questions about reliability and construct validity in the grand strategy of nosological revision. In T. Millon & G. L. Klerman (Eds.), *Contemporary directions in psychopathology* (pp. 215–231). New York, NY: Guilford.
Meehl, P. E. (1997). Credentialed persons, credentialed knowledge. *Clinical Psychology: Science and Practice, 4*, 91–98.
Meehl, P. E., & Rosen, A. (1955). Antecedent probability and the efficiency of psychometric signs, patterns, or cutting scores. *Psychological Bulletin, 52*, 194–216.
Messick, S. (1995). Validity of psychological assessment: Validation of inferences from persons' responses and performances as scientific inquiry into score meaning. *American Psychologist, 50*, 741–749.
Newton, P. E. (2012). Clarifying the consensus definition of validity. *Measurement: Interdisciplinary Research and Perspective, 10*(1–2), 1–29.
Nisbett, R. E., Zukier, H., & Lemley, R. E. (1981). The dilution effect: Nondiagnostic information weakens the implications of diagnostic information. *Cognitive Psychology, 13*, 248–277.
Nunnally, J. C., & Bernstein, I. H. (1994). *Psychometric theory*. New York, NY: McGraw-Hill.
O'Donohue, W., & Lilienfeld, S. O. (2007). The epistemological and ethical dimension of clinical science. In T. A. Treat, R. R. Bootzin, & T. B. Baker (Eds.), *Psychological clinical science: Papers in honor of Richard M. McFall* (pp. 29–52). New York, NY: Routledge.
O'Donohue, W., & Henderson, D. (1999). Epistemic and ethical duties in clinical decision-making. *Behaviour Change, 16*(1), 10–19.
Ones, D. S., Viswesvaran, C., & Reiss, A. D. (1996). Role of social desirability in personality testing for personnel selection: The red herring. *Journal of Applied Psychology, 81*, 660–679.
Orne, M. T. (1962). On the social psychology of the psychological experiment: With particular reference to demand characteristics and their implications. *American Psychologist, 17*, 776–783.
Pascal, G. R. (1983). *The practical art of diagnostic interviewing*. Homewood, IL: Dow Jones-Irwin.
Paulhus, D. L. (1991). Measurement and control of response bias. In J. P. Robinson & P. R. Shaver (Eds.), *Measures of personality and social psychological attitudes* (pp. 17–59). San Diego, CA: Academic.
Piedmont, R. L., McCrae, R. R., Riemann, R., & Angleitner, A. (2000). On the invalidity of validity scales: Evidence from self-reports and observer ratings in volunteer samples. *Journal of Personality and Social Psychology, 78*, 582–593.
Polit, D. F., Beck, C. T., & Owen, S. V. (2007). Is the CVI an acceptable indicator of content validity? Appraisal and recommendations. *Research in Nursing & Health, 30*, 459–467.
Popham, W. J., & Husek, T. R. (1969). Implications of criterion-referenced measurement. *Journal of Educational Measurement, 6*, 1–9.
Popper, K. R. (1959). *The logic of scientific discovery*. New York, NY: Basic Books.
Porter, S., & Woodworth, M. (2007). "I'm sorry I did it… but he started it": A comparison of the official and self-reported homicide descriptions of psychopaths and non-psychopaths. *Law and Human Behavior, 31*, 91–107.
Pronin, E., Lin, D. Y., & Ross, L. (2002). The bias blind spot: Perceptions of bias in self versus others. *Personality and Social Psychology Bulletin, 28*, 369–381.
Regier, D. A., Narrow, W. E., Clarke, D. E., Kraemer, H. C., Kuramoto, S. J., Kuhl, E. A., & Kupfer, D. J. (2013). DSM-5 field trials in the United States and Canada, part II: test-retest reliability of selected categorical diagnoses. *American Journal of Psychiatry, 170*, 59–70.
Rogers, R. (2010). *Structured interview of reported symptoms*. New York, NY: Wiley.

Rohling, M. L., Larrabee, G. J., Greiffenstein, M. F., Ben-Porath, Y. S., Lees-Haley, P., Green, P., & Greve, K. W. (2011). A misleading review of response bias: comment on McGrath, Mitchell, Kim, and Hough (2010). *Psychological Bulletin, 137*, 708–712.

Sawyer, J. (1966). Measurement and prediction, clinical and statistical. *Psychological Bulletin, 66*, 178–200.

Schmidt, F. L., & Hunter, J. E. (1996). Measurement error in psychological research: Lessons from 26 research scenarios. *Psychological Methods, 1*, 199–223.

Schmidt, F. L., & Zimmerman, R. D. (2004). A counterintuitive hypothesis about employment interview validity and some supporting evidence. *Journal of Applied Psychology, 89*, 553–561.

Sechrest, L. (1963). Incremental validity: A recommendation. *Educational and Psychological Measurement, 23*, 153–158.

Sechrest, L. (1984). Reliability and validity. In I. A. S. Bellack & M. Hersen (Eds.), *Research methods in clinical psychology* (pp. 24–54). New York, NY: Pergamon.

Sechrest, L. (2005). Validity of measures is no simple matter. *Health Services Research, 40*, 1584–1604.

Shea, S. (1998). *Psychiatric interviewing: The art of understanding*. Baltimore, MD: Saunders.

Stigler, S. M. (1989). Francis Galton's account of the invention of correlation. *Statistical Science, 4*, 73–79.

Strauss, M. E., & Smith, G. T. (2009). Construct validity: Advances in theory and methodology. *Annual Review of Clinical Psychology, 5*, 1–25.

Sullivan, H. S. (1954). *The psychiatric interview*. New York, NY: W.W. Norton & Company.

Surowiecki, J. (2005). *The wisdom of crowds*. New York, NY: Random House.

Tavakol, M., & Dennick, R. (2011). Making sense of Cronbach's alpha. *International Journal of Medical Education, 2*, 53–55.

Tellegen, A. (1985). Structures of mood and personality and their relevance to assessing anxiety, with an emphasis on self-report. In A. H. Tuma & J. D. Maser (Eds.), *Anxiety and the anxiety disorders* (pp. 681–706). Hillsdale, NJ: Erlbaum.

Thorndike, E. L. (1918). Fundamental theorems in judging men. *Journal of Applied Psychology, 2*, 67–76.

Waldman, I. D., Lilienfeld, S. O., & Lahey, B. B. (1995). Toward construct validity in the childhood disruptive behavior disorders: Classification and diagnosis in DSM-IV and beyond. In T. H. Ollendick & R. J. Prinz (Eds.), *Advances in clinical child psychology* (Vol. 17, pp. 323–364). New York, NY: Plenum.

Watson, D., & Clark, L. A. (1984). Negative affectivity: the disposition to experience aversive emotional states. *Psychological Bulletin, 96*, 465–490.

Watts, F. N., MacLeod, A. K., & Morris, L. (1988). Associations between phenomenal and objective aspects of concentration problems in depressed patients. *British Journal of Psychology, 79*, 241–250.

Wedding, D., & Faust, D. (1989). Clinical judgment and decision making in neuropsychology. *Archives of Clinical Neuropsychology, 43*, 233–265.

Weed, N. C., Ben-Porath, Y. S., & Butcher, J. N. (1990). Failure of Wiener and Harmon Minnesota Multiphasic Personality Inventory (MMPI) subtle scales as personality descriptors and as validity indicators. *Psychological Assessment, 2*, 281–285.

Westen, D., & Rosenthal, R. (2003). Quantifying construct validity: Two simple measures. *Journal of Personality and Social Psychology, 84*, 606–618.

Whiston, S. (2012). *Principles and applications of assessment in counseling*. Belmont, CA: Cengage Learning.

Widiger, T. A., & Frances, A. (1987). Interviews and inventories for the measurement of personality disorders. *Clinical Psychology Review, 7*, 49–75.

Wiesner, W. H., & Cronshaw, S. F. (1988). A meta-analytic investigation of the impact of interview format and degree of structure on the validity of the employment interview. *Journal of Occupational Psychology, 61*, 275–290.

Wood, J. M. (1996). Weighing evidence in child sexual abuse evaluations: An introduction to Bayes' theorem. *Child Maltreatment, 1*, 25–36.

Wood, J. M., Garb, H. N., & Nezworski, M. T. (2007). Psychometrics: Better measurement makes better clinicians. In S. O. Lilienfeld & W. T. O'Donohue (Eds.), *The great ideas of clinical science: 17 principles that every mental health professional should understand* (pp. 77–92). New York, NY: Routledge.

Wood, J. M., & Garven, S. (2000). How sexual abuse interviews go astray: Implications for prosecutors, police, and child protection services. *Child Maltreatment, 5*, 109–118.

Wood, J. M., Nezworski, M. T., Garb, H. N., & Lilienfeld, S. O. (2001). The misperception of psychopathology: Problems with the norms of the comprehensive system for the Rorschach. *Clinical Psychology: Science and Practice, 8*, 350–373.

Chapter 10
Basic Principles of Interviewing the Child Eyewitness

Jonni L. Johnson, Kelly McWilliams, Gail S. Goodman, Alexandra E. Shelley, and Brianna Piper

In this chapter, we discuss basic principles of interviewing alleged child victims of sexual abuse. We have divided our review into three distinct yet complementary (and at times, somewhat overlapping) sections: the interviewee, the interviewer, and the interview. Issues for forensic interviewers to consider when questioning child victims are outlined. In this paper, we assume the interview goal is to elicit accurate eyewitness accounts. We acknowledge that child forensic interviewing is a large and growing field of study; therefore, the topics included in each section are not exhaustive of all factors examined in the extant literature. Moreover, despite the vast research base, there are still many factors that can affect actual forensic investigations that remain largely unexplored. For present purposes, we consider *who* is being interviewed, *who* is conducting the interview, and *how* the interview is conducted. Before discussing our selected factors, we briefly summarize evidence regarding children's memory for *stressful* events as these are inherently the types of events interviewers ask children to recount.

J.L. Johnson • G.S. Goodman (✉) • A.E. Shelley • B. Piper
Department of Psychology, University of California,
1 Shields Avenue, Davis, CA 95616, USA
e-mail: jonjonson@ucdavis.edu; ggoodman@ucdavis.edu

K. McWilliams
Gould School of Law, University of Southern California,
699 Exposition Blvd., Los Angeles, CA 90089, USA

W.T. O'Donohue, M. Fanetti (eds.), *Forensic Interviews Regarding Child Sexual Abuse*, DOI 10.1007/978-3-319-21097-1_10

Children's Memory for Stressful Events

The existing literature indicates that children, even as young as age 2 or 3 years of age, form memories of highly arousing, personally significant, stressful events (e.g., Fivush, 2002; Peterson, 2011; Tustin & Hayne, 2010), and can often accurately recall such memories later, sometimes even after long delays (Jack, Simcock, & Hayne, 2012; Quas et al., 1999). Compared to young children, older ones typically provide more detailed accounts and answer questions about such events with greater accuracy (e.g., Eisen, Goodman, Qin, Davis, & Crayton, 2007; Jack et al., 2012; Morris & Baker-Ward, 2007; Peterson, 2011; Usher & Neisser, 1993). The high arousal that even relatively young children experience during stressful events may help them attend to details that are central to the event, thus resulting in particularly accurate reports of *central* information, potentially at the cost of poorer memory for *peripheral* information (Chae, Goodman, Eisen, & Qin, 2011; Christianson, 1992; Eisen et al., 2007; Quas et al., 1999). However, children also may attend to and recall idiosyncratic or peripheral information, likely because it was personally significant, represents "the worst moment," or was otherwise distinctive for the children's young minds (Goodman, Rudy, Bottoms, & Aman, 1990; Howe, 2006; Pynoos & Eth, 1984). Errors in memory for stressful events can also occur in children and adults (e.g., Eisen et al., 2007).

The legal system often requires "particularization" of memory, that is, the child being able to describe each assault. This can be a difficult task for anyone, but experiencing multiple or repeated traumatic events may cause more blending of memories in young children's (e.g., 4-year-olds) reports than it does for older children (e.g., 7-year-olds) and adults, making it more difficult for young children to recall a specific event (Howe, Courage, & Peterson, 1995; Terr, 1988; but see Goodman, Quas, Batterman-Faunce, Riddlesberger, & Kuhn, 1994). However, interview strategies (e.g., "What happened the last time?") can benefit children in "sourcing" details to specific events, helping children report separate events accurately (Brubacher, Powell, & Roberts, 2014; Drohan-Jennings, Roberts, & Powell, 2010; Lyon, 2005). Some researchers are finding that asking children what "usually happens" is helpful when later probing specific instances (Brubacher et al., 2014).

Although even very young children (2-year-olds) are capable of remembering core information from personally significant stressful events, it is likely that over time, "infantile amnesia" will increasingly block access to recall of experiences, including stressful ones, that occurred in infancy or toddlerhood (Usher & Neisser, 1993). Moreover, there is little to no evidence that preschoolers, older children, or adults can verbally recall events from their first year of life regardless of the traumatic nature of the event (but see Myers, Clifton, & Clarkson, 1987), although remnants of the early experiences may show in their behavior (Terr, 1988). Furthermore, a number of socioemotional factors can affect children's motivation, ability, and willingness to share traumatic information. These socioemotional factors in child sexual abuse cases include shame and embarrassment; fear of retribution, getting in trouble, and implicating a loved one or even a stranger; the distress produced by recalling and thus "reliving" a traumatic event; and intimidation by or lack of rapport with an interviewer (e.g., Bidrose & Goodman, 2000; Cederborg, Lamb, & Laurell, 2007; Goodman-Brown, Edelstein, Goodman, Jones, & Gordon, 2003; Pynoos & Eth, 1984; Saywitz, Goodman, Nicholas, & Moan, 1991).

Knowledge about stress and memory in children, combined with age-appropriate, child-friendly tactics, can be used to help children provide their eyewitness accounts accurately. In the next sections, additional factors are discussed that may also affect the quality of children's memory reports.

The Interviewee

Researchers have examined children's eyewitness abilities in laboratory and forensic settings for several decades (Goodman, 2006; Goodman & Melinder, 2007; Lamb, Orbach, Hershkowitz, Esplin, & Horowitz, 2007; Lamb, Orbach, Warren, Esplin, & Hershkowitz, 2007; Paz-Alonso, Ogle, & Goodman, 2013). This has increased our understanding of children's developing capabilities to be reliable and accurate eyewitnesses and has uncovered important individual differences for forensic interviewers to consider when questioning children about child sexual abuse. Here we discuss findings regarding children's age, gender, psychopathology, and maltreatment histories.

Age and Gender

With age, children's memory abilities improve. Likely due to their cognitive growth in knowledge base, memory organization, retrieval strategies, and language acquisition (Bjorklund, 2011; Howe, 2011), older children tend to remember more information and make fewer errors compared to younger children about stressful events and nonstressful events (e.g., Eisen et al., 2007; Eisen, Qin, Goodman, & Davis, 2002; Jack, Leov, & Zajac, 2014; Tustin & Hayne, 2010). Older compared to younger children have better source memory (e.g., remembering whether they witnessed something or heard someone talk about it) with sometimes vast improvements occurring between ages 3 and 8 years (Brubacher et al., 2014; Foley, 2014). The general trend is that as children age, they become better eyewitnesses, at least in terms of their memory abilities, by providing greater amounts of correct information and succumbing less often to false suggestions (Malloy, Johnson, & Goodman, 2013; McWilliams, Narr, Goodman, Ruiz, & Mendoza, 2013; but see Brainerd, Reyna, & Ceci, 2008, regarding reverse developmental trends in memory).

However, *remembering* and *disclosing* details about child sexual abuse are not identical processes. Younger children may fail to disclose child sexual abuse for several reasons, such as because they do not understand the importance or point of a forensic interview, because they think the interviewer already knows what happened, or due to short attention span or intimidation. Moreover, they are less likely than older children to consistently disclose sexual abuse (Keary & Fitzpatrick, 1994). Older children may be particularly at risk of reluctance to disclose due to fearing consequences of disclosure; they may also recant sexual abuse details, particularly in intrafamilial abuse cases (e.g., Malloy, Brubacher, & Lamb, 2011; Malloy, Lyon, & Quas, 2007). Regardless of age, children who have been sexually victimized at times even deny that the abuse occurred (Pipe, Lamb, Orbach, & Cederborg, 2007). Older children have greater cognitive ability to remember and recount events accurately, but they may struggle with the social components of disclosing what occurred, whereas younger children may experience both cognitive and social difficulties during forensic interviews. Interviewers may avoid age-related problems by reducing cognitive demands (e.g., avoiding ambiguous or complex questioning, offering reminders to children to correct interviewers if they make mistakes) and providing social support and sufficient rapport building.

Regarding child gender, it remains unclear if memory accuracy for traumatic events differs between boys and girls, and if gender differences exist in willingness to disclosure and discuss past emotional events (e.g., Areh, 2011; Grysman & Hudson, 2013). A small subset of boys (younger than 5) have been observed in research studies to confabulate reports of touch (e.g., Poole, Dickinson, Brubacher, Liberty, & Kaake, 2014). Girls tend to provide more complete accounts than boys in their descriptions of past emotional events (e.g., Buckner & Fivush, 1998; Fivush & Zaman, 2014). However, gender may serve as only a proxy indicator; that is, other variables, such as verbal ability and cognitive control, likely serve as better predictors of memory performance and mitigate gender differences (e.g., Grysman & Hudson, 2013; Poole et al., 2014). Although gender difference in such abilities may exist at young ages (e.g., Bornstein, Han, & Haynes, 2004; Wallentin, 2009), these differences tend to disappear with age such that gender differences in the ability to recall traumatic details and answer questions accurately do not typically exist later on (Eisen et al., 2007; Quas et al., 1999). However, boys report fearing more consequences (e.g., Malloy et al., 2011), may be more reluctant to disclose sexual abuse details (e.g., Malloy et al., 2007), and provide less complete reports (e.g., Eisen et al., 2002; Grysman & Hudson, 2013) than do girls.

Taken together, findings indicate that boys and girls can report their (traumatic and nontraumatic) pasts at comparable rates of accuracy when additional factors are considered (e.g., verbal ability, cognitive control). Yet in the absence of considering additional factors, when gender differences are found, they typically show young girls to report past events with greater accuracy than young boys (Poole et al., 2014). Moreover, boys, compared to girls, may feel more social stigma or embarrassment, experience reluctance to disclose abuse-related details, or provide minimal details or less complete reports about sexual abuse.

Child Psychopathology, Maltreatment History, and Memory

Research suggests that trauma-related psychopathology and children's maltreatment histories can affect how children attend to, interpret, consolidate, and recall traumatic details later. We briefly discuss each topic in turn while acknowledging that the evidence reported needs replication as well as experimental and longitudinal study designs.

Trauma-related psychopathology. Perhaps the most well-known trauma-related psychopathology is posttraumatic stress disorder (PTSD). Surprisingly, few eyewitness memory studies have explicitly focused on PTSD in children and adolescents; evidence from related studies appears to be mixed as to whether children and adolescents with PTSD have poorer or better memory abilities compared to children and adolescents without PTSD (Beers & De Bellis, 2002; de Decker, Hermans, Raes, & Eelen, 2003; Eisen et al., 2007; Moradi, Taghavi, Neshat-Doost, Yule, & Dalgleish, 2000; Ogle et al., 2013; Yasik, Saigh, Oberfield, & Halamandaris, 2007). Although some findings suggest that the children and adolescents with PTSD have difficulty in accessing the specific details of autobiographical memories (e.g., Moradi et al., 2008), other studies indicate the opposite pattern: Adolescents who reported child sexual abuse as their most traumatic life event and who evinced greater PTSD symptomatology were observed to have more specific memory reports than adolescents with lower PTSD symptomatology (Ogle et al., 2013). Moreover, at least by older adolescence, PTSD is associated with particularly accurate memory of child sexual abuse (Alexander et al., 2005). Nevertheless, symptoms may be present in children and adolescents with PTSD that affect interview responses, such as inattentiveness, impulsivity, and lower working memory abilities (Beers & De Bellis, 2002; Ogle et al., 2013).

When different standardized measures of trauma-related symptoms (e.g., PTSD, depression, dissociation) are combined to form a single dimension of psychopathology, memory for positive information seems to be more consistently affected adversely than is memory for negative information (Goodman et al., in press). That said, in a study of maltreated children's memory, clinicians' appraisals of children as having lower adaptive functioning were significantly correlated with the children's memory errors for a stressful event (Eisen et al., 2007).

Maltreatment histories. As was just discussed, the psychopathology resulting from traumatic experiences, such as child maltreatment, can possibly affect children's memories. Trauma-related psychopathology is not always differentiated from maltreatment history in existing studies (e.g., Carrion, Weems, & Reiss, 2007). Forensic interviewers should take into account possible effects that maltreatment histories could have on children's cognitive and socioemotional functioning, as these effects may influence how maltreated children remember and recount traumatic events to others (see Cicchetti & Toth, 2005; Goodman, Quas, & Ogle, 2010).

Prolonged or chronically elevated levels of stress, like those experienced by some maltreated children, may lead to dysregulation of the Hypothalamic-Pituitary Adrenal (HPA) axis, the stress hormone system responsible for releasing cortisol (Cicchetti, Rogosch, Howe, & Toth, 2010; Sapolsky, 1996), and may eventually (e.g., in adulthood) have an effect on hippocampal functioning (a region of the brain that is important for memory). However, there is conflicting evidence of HPA axis effects on children's eyewitness memory (see Goodman et al., in press, for review). Maltreatment histories may affect, however, how children attend to and process trauma-related details. Some researchers have found that maltreated children are particularly attentive to negative stimuli (e.g., Masten et al., 2008; Pollak, Messner, Kistler, & Cohn, 2009), which could lead to stronger memory representations for negative events, such as abuse (see Goodman et al., 2010). Yet basic memory processes (e.g., associative memory) for maltreated and nonmaltreated children appear to be quite similar (e.g., Cicchetti et al., 2010; Howe, Cicchetti, & Toth, 2006), and both groups can report details accurately about positive and negative events (e.g., Eisen et al., 2007). In other words, it appears that children with maltreatment histories can be just as accurate when recounting details about their lives as children without maltreatment histories.

An important consideration, like the one we addressed in the PTSD discussion, is that children with maltreatment histories, on average, display delays or deficits in several cognitive processes other than memory, such as executive function, language abilities, and IQ compared to children without maltreatment histories (Goodman et al., 2010; Lyon & Evans, 2014; Porter, Lawson, & Bigler, 2005; Veltman & Browne, 2001). Deficits in these cognitive areas could have implications for maltreated children in reporting their abuse episodes. For example, deficits in language comprehension and production (e.g., Veltman & Browne, 2001) may interfere with maltreated children's understanding of an interviewer's questions or phrasing, impinge on children's abilities to articulate and describe details, and decrease the ability to monitor reports for errors while recounting their abuse (e.g., Lyon & Evans, 2014).

A relatively new avenue of research has revealed that children may benefit from truth induction procedures prior to their interviews (e.g., taking a child-friendly version of an oath to tell the truth); these procedures seem to increase disclosure of information while not increasing false details or false reports for both maltreated and nonmaltreated children (Evans & Lee, 2010; Lyon & Evans, 2014). However, although research reveals that maltreated children benefit from truth induction procedures, interviewers may need to simplify such procedures due to possible language deficits exhibited by the children (Lyon & Evans, 2014).

The Interviewer

Child forensic interviewers play a crucial role in investigations of child sexual abuse. It is not an easy job. With increasing frequency, child forensic interviewers are expected to master and use science-based interview protocols; to obtain in a nonleading way (e.g., "So tell me why you are here today?") the legally specified (and often quite precise) information needed by child protection workers, law enforcement officers, and/or district attorneys to pursue or drop a case; to question children while being videotaped, observed, and evaluated by professionals in an adjoining room; to remain calm and supportive, and yet unbiased, even when children are recounting horrific experiences; to build rapport with traumatized children within minutes of meeting them; to interview a wide array of children, from 3-year-olds, who have no idea why they are there and can barely sit in a chair for more than a few minutes, to 14-year-olds, who know exactly why they are there and would rather be anywhere else; to work quickly because the children's attention may not last long and anyway, the professionals observing have little time before they have to leave to investigate other crimes; and to be able to defend their interviews in court. It's a lot to ask of anyone, and yet, seasoned child forensic interviewers (often specially trained social workers) do their jobs with apparent ease, interviewing hundreds of children each year—often thousands of children across the interviewer's career.

Perhaps the most important, and yet understudied, interviewer skill is the ability to build rapport with children quickly. Children who are intimidated are more likely to "shut down" and refuse to talk, or to be suggestible (e.g., Saywitz & Nathanson, 1993). Science-based protocols uniformly begin with a rapport-building phase, which often consists of having children recount everyday events. Yet the interpersonal interactions that take place during that recounting, not often the subject of research, are likely crucial for making the child feel at ease, open up, resist false suggestions, and trust the interviewer enough to disclose what may be highly personal, distressing, and embarrassing information. To date, research indicates that females and males can be equally proficient in obtaining accurate memory reports from children, as long as sufficient rapport is built (Schaaf, Alexander, & Goodman, 2008). In addition to a supportive stance by the interviewer, a supportive interview context (one where children feel safe and comfortable discussing traumatic pasts) has been shown to be helpful for children of all ages when recounting events, including when disclosing abuse details (Brubacher et al., 2014; Lamb, Orbach, Hershkowitz et al., 2007; Lamb, Orbach, Warren et al., 2007; Saywitz & Nathanson, 1993).

The age appropriateness of the language used by the interviewer can also influence children's responses. Language that is too complex for a given age, such as using words or sentence constructions that children do not understand, can result in greater memory error, especially when combined with intimidation (Carter, Bottoms, & Levine, 1996). Forensic interviewers may be able to account for possible cognitive deficits, like language difficulties, in maltreated children by adapting questions and interview formats to accommodate the children's language needs (e.g., asking open-ended questions, keeping questions simple). Similarly, interviewers may want to use specific labels that are spontaneously generated by children, after clarifying what the children mean by the terms (e.g., Brubacher et al., 2014).

Another important skill for interviewers to possess is the ability to maintain neutrality and not reinforce specific types of answers or specific types of content (Garven, Wood, Malpass, & Shaw, 1998; Saywitz, Lyon, & Goodman, 2010). Interviewers are advised to keep an open mind about what may have occurred and to test alternative hypotheses through their questioning, rather than assume child sexual abuse took place (Ceci & Bruck, 1993). Although interviewer factors are important, when Gilstrap and Ceci (2005) analyzed interviews of children conducted by professional interviewers, these researchers reported that "interviewers' use of leading questions did not result in increased acquiescence as previously found… analyses showed that it was possible to predict directly from child-to-child behavior, effectively skipping the intervening adult behavior." (p. 40). These results imply that individual differences among children in their willingness to acquiesce to or counter misleading questions were more important than the interviewer's behavior, at least for the interviews studied, which were likely not highly leading.

In any case, interviewers should keep in mind that they are not usually the first people to interview the alleged child victim. Especially with young children, the first person to suspect sexual abuse and to whom the child has disclosed is likely to be the parent, particularly the mother. Research indicates that children are less suggestible about abuse when interviewed by their mothers versus strangers, and that children can maintain accuracy in later forensic-like interviews even when parents are wrongly suspicious that something bad happened (Goodman, Sharma, Thomas, & Considine, 1995; McWilliams, 2014). That said, with sufficient pressure, coaching, or misinformation, some children may clam up or provide false information (e.g., Bottoms, Goodman, Schwartz-Kenney, & Thomas, 2002; Poole & Lindsay, 1995). Interviewers often ask children if anyone told the children to say something or not to say something, in an effort to sort out possible contamination. Although there is little research to validate this practice, asking children such questions may help fact finders feel more comfortable evaluating children's statements.

It is incumbent on child forensic interviewers to be conversant with the laws governing their counties, state, and countries. Increasingly in the United States, the courts are considering child forensic interviews to fall within the realm of law enforcement and for the interviews therefore to be considered "testimonial." This means that, at trial in criminal proceedings, it is likely that the child victim will have to testify face-to-face with the defendant in order for the videotaped forensic interview to be entered into evidence and shown to the jury, as the videotape is considered a form of "hearsay" (Myers, 2011). In other types of hearings (and in other countries), however, the videotape might be more easily shown even without the child appearing. When shown, the interviewer and the interview will likely be scrutinized as to whether proper rapport was established, whether the language used was age appropriate, and so forth—but perhaps especially, the types of instructions given, the interview questions asked, and interview methods used. We turn to these topics next.

The Interview

The cognitive and emotional demands of the interview conducted with child witnesses must be considered when assessing their reports. Laboratory and field studies reveal that young children are particularly sensitive to interview conditions that overburden their cognitive abilities, introduce social pressures that promote lack of disclosure or tainted testimony, and neglect their socioemotional needs and concerns (Brubacher et al., 2014; Lamb, Orbach, Hershkowitz et al., 2007; Lamb, Orbach, Warren et al., 2007; Lyon & Evans, 2014). We focus on three components of the interview that may influence children's eyewitness abilities: interview instructions, interview questions, and interview props.

Interview Instructions

For children, the expectations and conversational rules governing child forensic interviews differ from those of natural conversations with adults. For example, in their day-to-day lives, children are accustomed to being questioned by parents and teachers who often already know the answers to questions; and, in some cultures, children are not supposed to disagree with or correct adults. Given the uniqueness of child forensic interviews, children need instructions on how to proceed. Fortunately, researchers have developed instructions to aid children's performance.

Based on the research, science-based forensic interview protocols typically provide a set of instructions that interviewers are told to state toward the start of the interview. For example, in Lyon's Ten Step Interview protocol, instructions to be provided include the following: the Don't Know Instruction (e.g., "If I ask you a question and you don't know the answer, then just say, 'I don't know'."); the Don't Understand Instruction (e.g., "If I ask you a question and you don't know what I mean or what I'm saying, you can say, 'I don't know what you mean'."); and the You're Wrong Instruction (e.g., "Sometimes I make mistakes or say the wrong thing. When I do, you can tell me that I am wrong."). To be effective, such instructions need to be provided with children being able to practice each one, as specified in the protocols. Even young children can profit from such instructions (e.g., Cordon, Goodman, & Saetermoe, 2005).

Interview Questions

One of the most widely studied topics on child forensic interviewing concerns the influence of question type on children's memory reports. Question format can influence both the accuracy and the amount of information that children provide (Bjorklund, Bjorklund, Brown, & Cassel, 1998; Lamb, Orbach, Hershkowitz et al., 2007; Lamb, Orbach, Warren et al., 2007). Open-ended questions and prompts such as "I heard you saw a policeman last week, tell me more about that" (Lyon, 2005) are widely recognized as the most ideal format for children, typically resulting in more accurate responses than specific closed-ended questions (Eisen et al., 2007; Poole & Lindsay, 1995). Open-ended questions are preferred because they do not limit children's options for a response and are typically not leading (or at least are often less leading than other types of questions). Instead, open-ended questions allow children to give their own account without significant amounts of information being provided or implied by the interviewer (Lamb, Orbach, Hershkowitz et al., 2007; Lamb, Orbach, Warren et al., 2007; Saywitz et al., 1991).

Unfortunately for forensic interviewers, children, especially preschool-aged children, do not always offer a significant amount of information when solely asked open-ended questions (Goodman et al., 1994). Often, children need memory cues to recall certain information, or children may assume adults already know the information and thus the children fail to include it in their reports. To obtain the amount of information needed for most forensic situations, open-ended questions must be followed up with direct questioning. Direct questioning can be a beneficial strategy when working with younger witnesses; however, interviewers must be careful when posing direct questions to young children. Direct questions, when formatted in certain ways, can be leading and introduce misinformation (Peterson & Biggs, 1997).

Researchers have theorized that exposure to misinformation and suggestion can alter children's actual memories, rather than just the children's responses. One such theory specifies that memory errors result from misinformation when children fail to engage in source monitoring efforts to differentiate an experienced event from what was implied in the misleading question (Ceci, Loftus, Leichtmen, & Bruck, 1994). However, misinformation and suggestion may not alter children's actual memories but rather create social pressures that influence children's responses. During forensic interviews, children are questioned about sensitive information, usually by authority figures. Some children acquiesce to questioning in an attempt to please the interviewer, rather than reporting their true memory. Awareness of how misinformation and suggestion can be inadvertently introduced during a forensic interview may permit interviewers to avoid such influence on children's testimony and on children's credibility down the legal road.

Two types of direct questions that should be avoided are yes/no ("Did your dad touch you?") and forced choice questions ("Was the person who hurt you your mom or your dad?"). These types of questions can be problematic for young children for a variety of reasons. First, yes/no and forced choice questions limit the options children have for a response. Children could interpret these forms of questioning to indicate that adults already know the correct answer. As a result, children may falsely affirm or choose one of the options, respectively, due to social pressure rather than relying on their own memory. Second, to pose a yes/no or forced choice question, an interviewer may provide false information in the question itself, which could introduce misinformation.

To avoid introducing suggestion into an interview with direct questioning, some researchers have recommended that forensic interviewers attempt to utilize a "Wh-" question format for their specific questions (Peterson, Dowden, & Tobin, 1999). For example, after a child discloses, "My dad touched me," a useful "Wh-" questions would be, "Where did your dad touch you?" The former structure of the question allows interviewers to probe for more specific details during their investigations, while avoiding many of the problems elicited by yes/no and forced choice questions (Peterson & Biggs, 1997). These specific questions should be followed up with open-ended questions, such as "Tell me more" or "Then what happened?" However, many researchers recognize that avoiding all specific (and therefore potentially leading) questions during forensic interviews with children can be difficult, and structured forensic interview protocols have been developed to address this issue, permitting use of some specific questioning (e.g., NICHD Protocol, Ten Step Investigative Interview; a discussion of these protocols is provided in a later chapter of this book). Moreover, misleading questions do not necessarily led to error in children's later reports (Peterson, Parsons, & Dean, 2004).

The frequency with which an interviewer asks a child about specific information is also important to consider, although the influence of repeated questioning on children's memory reports is complex (Goodman & Quas, 2008). Repeated questioning presents a risk, within or across interviews, if children interpret these repetitions as insinuations that their initial accurate reports were not desired responses. However, repeated questioning also has the potential to benefit memory. Questions that are repeated in sequential interviews can give children the opportunity to rehearse memories which can potentially strengthen their memory traces and representations, and keep such memories from fading over time (e.g., Quas et al., 2007). In some instances, repeated questioning can also lead to hypermnesia, where additional details of traumatic memories are recalled after a delay (La Rooy, Pipe, & Murray, 2005; Payne, 1987).

Over time, memories are subject to forgetting and distortion as delay increases between when events were experienced and when events are described; in this regard, it is important to conduct interviews as soon as possible. Laboratory studies reveal that the completeness of children's memory reports may remain constant over time; however, the amount of detail has been shown to change, accuracy decreases, and children have increased risk of exposure to misinformation (e.g., La Rooy et al., 2005; McWilliams et al., 2013; Waterman & Blades, 2013; but see Quas et al., 1999). Additionally, delays have been linked to children's willingness to guess in response to unanswerable questions with longer delays associated with increased willingness to guess (e.g., Waterman & Blades, 2013), which could lead to the possibility of errors in a forensic situation. To minimize this risk, ideally interviews should be conducted as soon as possible to tap into children's memory while it is still robust. It is also, possible, however, that with development, some children will be better able to recount events (e.g., have the words, retrieval strategies, and concepts) when they are older than when they were younger.

Interview Props

Research on the use of forensic interviewing props, such as anatomically detailed dolls, body diagrams, and comfort drawings, has revealed mixed results. Although such tools have been used by investigators to interview children of all ages in nearly half of child sexual abuse cases (Hlavka, Olinger, & Lashley, 2010), the effectiveness of these props at eliciting accurate details and minimizing false reports remains in question (e.g., Goodman & Melinder, 2007). Professionals reportedly prefer these tools as they are believed to help children clarify prior disclosures, overcome communication barriers, and support coping strategies to help children discuss traumatic details (e.g., "You said the man touched you; Point to where he touched you."; Hlavka et al.), although their effectiveness may not supersede that of other empirically based interviewing methods (e.g., Salmon, Pipe, Malloy, & Mackay, 2012).

Particularly for younger children (3- to 5-year-olds) who may lack cognitive abilities to understand the dual-representational function of dolls and diagrams, interviewing tools such as these may be ineffective at eliciting additional correct information (e.g., Salmon et al., 2012). Children (approximately 6 years and older) tend not to report false details with the use of dolls or diagrams; however, the use of these props does not always result in children providing additional accurate details when compared to the use of verbal prompts (e.g., "You mentioned 'X', Tell me more about 'X'."; Salmon et al., 2012). For child forensic interviewers, verbal prompts (e.g., "Tell me more") and effective interview strategies (e.g., NICHD protocol, Ten Step Interview, Narrative Elaboration Technique; Saywitz & Comparo,

2013) may be preferred over use of dolls and diagrams given the lack of empirical validation of props; if used, it is often recommended that body diagrams should be presented after a disclosure (e.g., at the end of the interview) to provide clarification of prior disclosures and with cognitively competent children.

Evidence does support, however, use of comfort drawings (i.e., allowing children to draw freely while they answer questions) as this may serve, in effect, as a coping strategy to provide comfort while disclosing traumatic details and also by keeping children engaged, facilitating more opportunities for interviewers to ask nonleading open-ended questions (Katz, Barnetz, & Hershkowitz, 2014; Patterson & Hayne, 2011). Comfort drawing has been shown to increase the amount of information reported (although it may not increase the number of accurate details), but of importance, it did not increase errors (e.g., Patterson & Hayne, 2011); children are merely comforted while disclosing. Props that do not adversely affect the accuracy of children's reports but provide emotional support could be of interest because children feel more comfortable disclosing traumatic details when emotionally supported (Katz et al., 2014; Malloy et al., 2011). If comfort drawings are used, interviewers are cautioned against interpreting meaning of details within the drawing (e.g., colors chosen to represent specific people) as these details are not necessarily related to the emotional content or memory for the event (Crawford, Gross, Patterson, & Hayne, 2012).

Conclusion

It is challenging to conduct forensic interviews with children, especially young children or children who are hesitant to disclose. Although scientific researchers continue to examine and identify effective ways to interview children in child sexual abuse cases, many factors can influence children's memories and reports, some of which are still in need of research and others of which will always be difficult for researchers to study ethically. For example, there is little scientifically sound research on children's memory and suggestibility regarding their parents' actions, regarding situations about which children feel shame or fear retribution, regarding reporting of events with anatomical dolls alone (apart from other props) or human figure drawings that show naked bodies, and so forth. There is still much to learn.

Nevertheless, our review, although not exhaustive, illustrates some of the main issues that should be considered, based on research at this point in time, when interviewing children about sexual abuse in relation to the interviewee, interviewer, and interview. A list of basic principles interviewers might review prior to interviewing children include:

- The amount of information children provide increases with age.
- Preschool children on average tend to report less information on their own in free recall and also to be more suggestible than older children. For this and other reasons, very young children (e.g., 3-year-olds) can be especially difficult to interview, even with scientifically based protocols.

- Carefully consider both cognitive and socioemotional abilities and needs of children, and that these needs change with development.
- Individual characteristics of each child should be considered, including for young children their level of cognitive control and verbal ability.
- Psychopathology factors may result in less accurate reports (e.g., for positive information). Nevertheless, children with certain symptoms of psychopathology (e.g., PTSD) are likely to have intact memory abilities, yet potential deficits related to other domains (e.g., inattentiveness, impulsivity), which could impinge on answering questions accurately.
- Maltreated children's basic memory abilities are similar to that of nonmaltreated children, but effects of maltreatment may influence the content of memory and other domains (e.g., language).
- Interviewers should ensure they can develop rapport with children quickly.
- Interviewers should remain neutral and unbiased in their questioning of children and be cognizant of current laws regarding child forensic interviews and child sexual abuse in their jurisdictions.
- Open-ended, nonsuggestive questions can help circumvent misinformation effects and augment accurate reports; children's credibility is also less likely to be questioned if the interview is not overly leading.
- Interview props do not necessarily increase reporting of accurate details over empirically supported interviewing methods, particularly for preschool-aged children.

References

Alexander, K., Quas, J., Goodman, G. S., Ghetti, S., Edelstein, R., Redlich, A., Cordon, I., & Jones, D. P. H. (2005). Traumatic impact predicts long-term memory of documented child sexual abuse. *Psychological Science, 16*, 33–40.

Areh, I. (2011). Gender-related differences in eyewitness testimony. *Personality and Individual Differences, 50*(5), 559–563.

Beers, S. R., & De Bellis, M. D. (2002). Neuropsychological function in children with maltreatment-related posttraumatic stress disorder. *The American Journal of Psychiatry, 159*(3), 483–486.

Bidrose, S., & Goodman, G. S. (2000). Testimony and evidence: A scientific case study of memory for child sexual abuse. *Applied Cognitive Psychology, 14*, 197–214.

Bjorklund, D. F. (2011). *Children's thinking: Cognitive development and individual differences* (5th ed.). Belmont, CA: Wadsworth, Cengage Learning.

Bjorklund, D. F., Bjorklund, B. R., Brown, R. D., & Cassel, W. S. (1998). Children's suggestibility to repeated questions: How misinformation changes children's answers and their minds. *Applied Developmental Science, 2*, 99–111.

Bornstein, M. H., Han, C. H., & Haynes, O. M. (2004). Specific and general language performance across early childhood: Stability and gender considerations. *First Language, 24*, 267–304.

Bottoms, B. L., Goodman, G. S., Schwartz-Kenney, B., & Thomas, S. (2002). Understanding children's use of secrecy in the context of eyewitness reports. *Law and Human Behavior, 26*, 285–313.

Brainerd, C. J., Reyna, V. F., & Ceci, S. J. (2008). Developmental reversals in false memory: A review of data and theory. *Psychological Bulletin, 134*(3), 343–382.

Brubacher, S. P., Powell, M. B., & Roberts, K. P. (2014). Recommendations for interviewing children about repeated experiences. *Psychology, Public Policy, and Law, 20*(3), 325–335.

Buckner, J. P., & Fivush, R. (1998). Gender and self in children's autobiographical narratives. *Applied Cognitive Psychology, 12*(4), 407–429.

Carrion, V. G., Weems, C. F., & Reiss, A. L. (2007). Stress predicts brain changes in children: A pilot longitudinal study on youth stress, posttraumatic stress disorder, and the hippocampus. *Pediatrics, 119*(3), 509–516.

Carter, C. A., Bottoms, B. L., & Levine, M. (1996). Linguistic and socioemotional influences on the accuracy of children's reports. *Law and Human Behavior, 20*, 335–358.

Ceci, S. J., & Bruck, M. (1993). Suggestibility of the child witness: A historical overview and synthesis. *Psychological Bulletin, 113*, 403–439.

Ceci, S. J., Loftus, E. F., Leichtmen, M. D., & Bruck, M. (1994). The possible role of source misattributions in the creation of false beliefs among preschoolers. *International Journal of Clinical and Experimental Hypnosis, 42*, 304–320.

Cederborg, A.-C., Lamb, M., & Laurell, O. (2007). Delay of disclosure, minimization and denial when the evidence is unambiguous. A multi victim case. In M.-E. Pipe, M. Lamb, Y. Orbach, & A.-C. Cederborg (Eds.), *Child sexual abuse: Disclosure, delay and denial* (pp. 159–174). Hillsdale, NJ: Lawrence Erlbaum.

Chae, Y., Goodman, G. S., Eisen, M. L., & Qin, J. (2011). Event memory and suggestibility in abused and neglected children: Trauma-related psychopathology and cognitive functioning. *Journal of Experimental Child Psychology, 110*(4), 520–538.

Christianson, S. (1992). Emotional stress and eyewitness memory: A critical review. *Psychological Bulletin, 112*(2), 284–309.

Cicchetti, D., Rogosch, F. A., Howe, M. L., & Toth, S. L. (2010). The effects of maltreatment and neuroendocrine regulation on memory performance. *Child Development, 81*(5), 1504–1519.

Cicchetti, D., & Toth, S. L. (2005). Child maltreatment. *Annual Review of Clinical Psychology, 1*(1), 409–438.

Cordon, I., Goodman, G. S., & Saetermoe, C. (2005). Facilitating children's accurate responses: Conversational rules and interview style. *Applied Cognitive Psychology, 19*, 249–266.

Crawford, E., Gross, J., Patterson, T., & Hayne, H. (2012). Does children's color use reflect the emotional content of their drawings? *Infant and Child Development, 21*(2), 198–215.

de Decker, A., Hermans, D., Raes, F., & Eelen, P. (2003). Autobiographical memory specificity and trauma in inpatient adolescents. *Journal of Clinical Child and Adolescent Psychology, 32*, 22–31.

Drohan-Jennings, D., Roberts, K. P., & Powell, M. B. (2010). Mental context reinstatement increases resistance to false suggestions after children have experienced a repeated event. *Psychiatry, Psychology and Law, 17*(4), 594–606.

Eisen, M. L., Goodman, G. S., Qin, J., Davis, S., & Crayton, J. (2007). Maltreated children's memory: Accuracy, suggestibility, and psychopathology. *Developmental Psychology, 43*(6), 1275–1294.

Eisen, M. L., Qin, J., Goodman, G. S., & Davis, S. L. (2002). Memory and suggestibility in maltreated children: Age, stress arousal, dissociation, and psychopathology. *Journal of Experimental Child Psychology, 83*(3), 167–212.

Evans, A. D., & Lee, K. (2010). Promising to tell the truth makes 8- to 16-year-olds more honest. *Behavioral Sciences & the Law, 28*(6), 801–811.

Fivush, R. (2002). The development of autobiographical memory. In H. L. Westcott, G. M. Davies, & R. H. C. Bull (Eds.), *Children's testimony: A handbook of psychological research and forensic practice* (pp. 3–19). Chichester, England: Wiley.

Fivush, R., & Zaman, W. (2014). Gender, subjective perspective, and autobiographical consciousness. In P. Bauer & R. Fivush (Eds.), *The handbook on the development of children's memory* (Vol. I-II, pp. 586–604). Chichester, England: Wiley-Blackwell.

Foley, M. A. (2014). Children's memory for source. In P. J. Bauer & R. Fivush (Eds.), *The handbook on the development of children's memory* (Vol. I II, pp. 427–452). Chichester, England: Wiley-Blackwell.

Garven, S., Wood, J., Malpass, R., & Shaw, J. (1998). More than suggestion: The effect of interview techniques from the McMartin Preschool Case. *Journal of Applied Psychology, 83*, 347–359.

Gilstrap, L. L., & Ceci, S. J. (2005). Reconceptualizing children's suggestibility: Bidirectional and temporal properties. *Child Development, 76*, 40–53.

Goodman, G. S. (2006). Children's eyewitness memory: A modern history and contemporary commentary. *Journal of Social Issues, 62*(4), 811–832.

Goodman, G. S., Goldfarb, D., Quas, J. A., Narr, R., Milojevich, H., & Cordon, I. M. (in press). Memory development, trauma-related psychopathology, and memory. In D. Cicchetti (Ed.), *Developmental psychopathology*. New York, NY: Wiley.

Goodman, G. S., & Melinder, A. (2007). Child witness research and forensic interviews of young children: A review. *Legal and Criminological Psychology, 12*(1), 1–19.

Goodman, G. S., & Quas, J. A. (2008). Repeated interviews and children's memory. *Current Directions in Psychological Science, 17*, 386–390.

Goodman, G. S., Quas, J. A., Batterman-Faunce, J. M., Riddlesberger, M. M., & Kuhn, J. (1994). Predictors of accurate and inaccurate memories of traumatic events experienced in childhood. *Consciousness and Cognition, 3*, 269–294.

Goodman, G. S., Quas, J. A., & Ogle, C. M. (2010). Child maltreatment and memory. *Annual Review of Psychology, 61*, 325–351.

Goodman, G. S., Rudy, L., Bottoms, B. L., & Aman, C. (1990). Children's concerns and memory: Issues of ecological validity in the study of children's eyewitness testimony. In R. Fivush & J. Hudson (Eds.), *Knowing and remembering in young children* (pp. 249–284). New York, NY: Cambridge University Press.

Goodman, G. S., Sharma, A., Thomas, S. F., & Considine, M. (1995). Mother knows best: Effects of relationship status and interviewer bias on children's memory. *Journal of Experimental Child Psychology, 60*, 195–228.

Goodman-Brown, T. B., Edelstein, R., Goodman, G. S., Jones, D. P. H., & Gordon, D. (2003). Why children tell: A model of children's disclosure of sexual abuse. *Child Abuse & Neglect, 27*, 525–540.

Grysman, A., & Hudson, J. A. (2013). Gender differences in autobiographical memory: Developmental and methodological considerations. *Developmental Review, 33*(3), 239–272.

Hlavka, H. R., Olinger, S. D., & Lashley, J. L. (2010). The use of anatomical dolls as a demonstration aid in child sexual abuse interviews: A study of forensic interviewers' perceptions. *Journal of Child Sexual Abuse, 19*(5), 519–553.

Howe, M. L. (2006). Developmental invariance of distinctiveness effects in memory. *Developmental Psychology, 42*, 1193–1205.

Howe, M. L. (2011). *The nature of early memory: An adaptive theory of the genesis and development of memory*. New York, NY: Oxford University Press.

Howe, M. L., Cicchetti, D., & Toth, S. L. (2006). Children's basic memory processes, stress, and maltreatment. *Development and Psychopathology, 18*(3), 759–769.

Howe, M. L., Courage, M. L., & Peterson, C. (1995). Intrusions in preschoolers' recall of traumatic childhood events. *Psychonomic Bulletin and Review, 2*, 130–134.

Jack, F., Leov, J., & Zajac, R. (2014). Age-related differences in the free-recall accounts of child, adolescent, and adult witnesses. *Applied Cognitive Psychology, 28*(1), 30–38.

Jack, F., Simcock, G., & Hayne, H. (2012). Magic memories: Young children's verbal recall after a 6-year delay. *Child Development, 83*(1), 159–172.

Katz, C., Barnetz, Z., & Hershkowitz, I. (2014). The effect of drawing on children's experiences of investigations following alleged child abuse. *Child Abuse & Neglect, 38*(5), 858–867.

Keary, K., & Fitzpatrick, C. (1994). Children's disclosure of sexual abuse during formal investigation. *Child Abuse & Neglect, 18*, 543–548.

La Rooy, D., Pipe, M. E., & Murray, J. E. (2005). Reminiscence and hypermnesia in children's eyewitness memory. *Journal of Experimental Child Psychology, 90*, 235–254.

Lamb, M. E., Orbach, Y., Hershkowitz, I., Esplin, P. W., & Horowitz, D. (2007). Structured forensic interview protocols improve the quality and informativeness of investigative interviews with children: A review of research using the NICHD Investigative Interview Protocol. *Child Abuse & Neglect, 31*, 1201–1231.

Lamb, M. E., Orbach, Y., Warren, A. R., Esplin, P. W., & Hershkowitz, I. (2007). Enhancing performance: Factors affecting the informativeness of young witnesses. In M. P. Toglia, J. D. Read, D. F. Ross, & R. C. L. Lindsay (Eds.), *The handbook of eyewitness psychology: Memory for events* (Vol. 1, pp. 429–451). Mahwah, NJ: Lawrence Erlbaum.

Lyon, T. D. (2005). Ten step investigative interview. Los Angeles. Retrieved from http://works.bepress.com/thomaslyon/5/

Lyon, T. D., & Evans, A. D. (2014). Young children's understanding that promising guarantees performance: The effects of age and maltreatment. *Law and Human Behavior, 38*(2), 162–170.

Malloy, L. C., Brubacher, S. P., & Lamb, M. E. (2011). Expected consequences of disclosure revealed in investigative interviews with suspected victims of child sexual abuse. *Applied Developmental Science, 15*(1), 8–19.

Malloy, L., Johnson, J. L., & Goodman, G. S. (2013). Children's memory and event reports: The current state of knowledge and best practice. *Journal of Forensic Social Work, 3*, 1–30.

Malloy, L. C., Lyon, T. D., & Quas, J. A. (2007). Filial dependency and recantation of child sexual abuse allegations. *Journal of the American Academy of Child and Adolescent Psychiatry, 46*(2), 162–170.

Masten, C. L., Guyer, A. E., Hodgdon, H. B., McClure, E. B., Charney, D. S., Ernst, M., … Monk, C. S. (2008). Recognition of facial emotions among maltreated children with high rates of post-traumatic stress disorder. *Child Abuse & Neglect, 32*(1), 139–153.

McWilliams, K. (2014). *Parent-child discussion and children's eyewitness memory*. (Unpublished doctoral dissertation). University of California, Davis, CA.

McWilliams, K., Narr, R., Goodman, G. S., Ruiz, S., & Mendoza, M. (2013). Children's memory for their mother's murder: Accuracy, suggestibility, and resistance to suggestion. *Memory, 21*, 591–598.

Moradi, A. R., Herlihy, J., Yasseri, G., Shahraray, M., Turner, S., & Dalgleish, T. (2008). Specificity of episodic and semantic aspects of autobiographical memory in relation to symptoms of posttraumatic stress disorder (PSTD). *Acta Psychologica, 127*(3), 645–653.

Moradi, A. R., Taghavi, R., Neshat-Doost, H., Yule, W., & Dalgleish, T. (2000). Memory bias for emotional information in children and adolescents with posttraumatic stress disorder: A preliminary study. *Journal of Anxiety Disorders, 14*(5), 521–534.

Morris, G., & Baker-Ward, L. (2007). Fragile but real: Children's capacity to use newly acquired words to convey preverbal memories. *Child Development, 78*, 448–458.

Myers, J. E. B. (2011). *Myers on evidence of interpersonal violence: Child maltreatment, intimate partner violence, rape, stalking, and elder abuse cases*. Amsterdam, The Netherlands: Wolters Kluwer Law & Business.

Myers, N. A., Clifton, R. K., & Clarkson, M. G. (1987). When they were very young: Almost-threes remember two years ago. *Infant Behavior & Development, 10*(2), 123–132. Retrieved from http://search.proquest.com/docview/617311362?accountid=14505.

Ogle, C. M., Block, S. D., Harris, L. S., Goodman, G. S., Pineda, A., Timmer, S., … Saywitz, K. J. (2013). Autobiographical memory specificity in child sexual abuse victims. *Development and Psychopathology, 25*(2), 321–332.

Patterson, T., & Hayne, H. (2011). Does drawing facilitate older children's reports of emotionally laden events? *Applied Cognitive Psychology, 25*(1), 119–126.

Payne, D. G. (1987). Hypermnesia and reminiscence in recall: A historical and empirical review. *Psychological Bulletin, 10*, 5–27.

Paz-Alonso, P., Ogle, C. M., & Goodman, G. S. (2013). Children's memory and testimony in "scientific case studies" of child sexual abuse: A review. In M. Ternes, D. Griesel, & B. Cooper (Eds.), *Applied issues in investigative interviewing, eyewitness memory, and credibility assessment* (pp. 143–172). New York, NY: Springer.

Peterson, C. (2011). Children's memory reports over time: Getting both better and worse. *Journal of Experimental Child Psychology, 109*, 275–293.

Peterson, C., & Biggs, M. (1997). Interviewing children about trauma: Problems with "specific" questions. *Journal of Traumatic Stress, 10*, 279–290.

Peterson, C., Dowden, C., & Tobin, J. (1999). Interviewing preschoolers: Comparisons of yes/no and wh- questions. *Law and Human Behavior, 23*, 539–555.

Peterson, C., Parsons, T., & Dean, M. (2004). Providing misleading and reinstatement information a year after it happened: Effects on long-term memory. *Memory, 12*, 1–13.

Pipe, M-E., Lamb, M. E., Orbach, I., & Cederborg, A-C. (Eds.). (2007). *Disclosure, delay, and denial*. New York, NY: Routledge.

Pollak, S. D., Messner, M., Kistler, D. J., & Cohn, J. F. (2009). Development of perceptual expertise in emotion recognition. *Cognition, 110*(2), 242–247.

Poole, D. A., Dickinson, J. J., Brubacher, S. P., Liberty, A. E., & Kaake, A. M. (2014). Deficient cognitive control fuels children's exuberant false allegations. *Journal of Experimental Child Psychology, 118*, 101–109.

Poole, D., & Lindsay, D. S. (1995). Interviewing preschoolers: Effects of nonsuggestive techniques, parental coaching, and leading questions on reports of nonexperienced events. *Journal of Experimental Child Psychology, 60*, 129–154.

Porter, C., Lawson, J. S., & Bigler, E. D. (2005). Neurobehavioral sequelae of child sexual abuse. *Child Neuropsychology, 11*(2), 203–220.

Pynoos, R., & Eth, S. (1984). The child as witness to homicide. *Journal of Social Issues, 40*, 87–108.

Quas, J. A., Goodman, G. S., Bidrose, S., Pipe, M., Craw, S., & Ablin, D. S. (1999). Emotion and memory: Children's long-term remembering, forgetting, and suggestibility. *Journal of Experimental Child Psychology, 72*(4), 235–270.

Quas, J. A., Malloy, L. C., Melinder, A., Goodman, G. S., D'Mello, M., & Schaaf, J. (2007). Developmental differences in the effects of repeated interviews and interviewer bias on young children's event memory and false reports. *Developmental Psychology, 43*, 823–837.

Salmon, K., Pipe, M., Malloy, A., & Mackay, K. (2012). Do non-verbal aids increase the effectiveness of 'best practice' verbal interview techniques? An experimental study. *Applied Cognitive Psychology, 26*(3), 370–380.

Sapolsky, R. M. (1996). Why stress is bad for your brain. *Science, 273*, 749–750.

Saywitz, K. J., & Comparo, L. (2013). *Evidence-based child forensic interviewing: The developmental narrative elaboration interview*. New York, NY: Oxford University Press.

Saywitz, K. J., Goodman, G. S., Nicholas, E., & Moan, S. (1991). Children's memories of physical examinations involving genital touch: Implications for reports of child sexual abuse. *Journal of Consulting and Clinical Psychology, 59*, 682–691.

Saywitz, K. S., Lyon, T., & Goodman, G. S. (2010). Interviewing children. In J. E. B. Myers (Ed.), *APSAC handbook on child maltreatment* (3rd ed., pp. 337–360). Newbury Park, CA: Sage.

Saywitz, K. J., & Nathanson, R. (1993). Children's testimony and perceived stress in and out of the courtroom. *Child Abuse & Neglect, 17*(5), 613–622.

Schaaf, J., Alexander, K., & Goodman, G. S. (2008). Predictors of children's true disclosure and false memory. *Journal of Experimental Child Psychology, 100*, 157–185.

Terr, L. C. (1988). What happens to early memories of trauma? A study of twenty children under age five at the time of documented events. *Journal of the American Academy of Child and Adolescent Psychiatric, 27*, 96–104.

Tustin, K., & Hayne, H. (2010). Defining the boundary: Age-related changes in childhood amnesia. *Developmental Psychology, 46*(5), 1049–1061.

Usher, J. A., & Neisser, U. (1993). Childhood amnesia and the beginnings of memory for four early life events. *Journal of Experimental Psychology: General, 122*(2), 155–165.

Veltman, M. W. M., & Browne, K. D. (2001). Three decades of child maltreatment research: Implications for the school years. *Trauma, Violence & Abuse, 2*(3), 215–239.

Wallentin, M. (2009). Putative sex differences in verbal abilities and language cortex: A critical review. *Brain and Language, 108*, 175–183.

Waterman, A. H., & Blades, M. (2013). The effect of delay and individual differences on children's tendency to guess. *Developmental Psychology, 49*, 215–226.

Yasik, A. E., Saigh, P. A., Oberfield, R. A., & Halamandaris, P. V. (2007). Posttraumatic stress disorder: Memory and learning performance in children and adolescents. *Biological Psychiatry, 61*(3), 382–388.

Chapter 11
Planning the Forensic Interview

Monica Rohrabaugh, Kamala London, and Ashley K. Hall

Imagine a criminal sexual conduct case that was brought to the attention of authorities when a mother found sexually explicit photographs of her 7-year-old son. Upon questioning by his mother, the boy said his biological father had taken the photos. The boy's mother and stepfather immediately contacted the police. In a single video-recorded interview session, the boy was forthcoming in providing detailed accounts of severe and repeated physical and sexual maltreatment by his biological father that took course over the past 2 years. The boy denied sexual touching by anyone outside of his biological father. Given the nature of the suspected abuse, a medical examination was performed. A physician assistant concluded signs of anal trauma were present. The biological father confessed to the abuse. He was arrested and eventually found guilty, and there was no further contact between the boy and his biological father. All of these details provide an extremely strong case that abuse truly did take place.

However, imagine further that the boy was seen for a follow-up medical exam 3 months after the arrest of his father. The physician assistant opined that the boy's anus still showed signs of trauma and surely such trauma would have healed over the past 3 months. He concluded the boy must have suffered additional and more recent sexual trauma. The physician assistant forwarded his opinion along to detectives. Detectives interviewed the boy, honing in on the boy's stepfather (since he was the only other male who had consistent contact with the boy). During an initial

M. Rohrabaugh (✉) • K. London
Department of Psychology, University of Toledo,
Mail Stop # 948, 2801 West Bancroft Street, Toledo, OH 43606-3390, USA
e-mail: monica.rohrabaugh@rockets.utoledo.edu; kamala.london@utoledo.edu

A.K. Hall
Department of Psychology, University of Southern Indiana,
8600 University Blvd., Evansville, IN 47712, USA
e-mail: ahall4@usi.edu

W.T. O'Donohue, M. Fanetti (eds.), *Forensic Interviews Regarding Child Sexual Abuse*, DOI 10.1007/978-3-319-21097-1_11

unrecorded interview with the boy at his school, he repeatedly denied maltreatment by anyone besides his biological father. Two days after the school interview, detectives picked up the boy from school and brought him to the police department. They interviewed him from about 3:30 to 6:30 in an unrecorded session without breaks or any food or drinks. Little is known about the 3 h of unrecorded interviewing, though the detectives did note the boy repeatedly denied abuse by his stepfather. After 3 h of nonstop interviewing, the child relayed a story that was similar to the earlier substantiated report involving his biological father. After the boy began to make allegations, the detectives brought him to an interview room where the interview was conducted again "for the purposes of video recording." At that time, the boy made allegations of sexual abuse against his stepfather. He claimed that his stepfather began abusing him during the investigation against his biological father.

In the recorded interview, the detectives used many forced-choice questions and selectively reinforced incriminating statements the boy made about his stepfather. When the boy said he could not remember, the detectives suggested details, telling him it was a scary thing to talk about and maybe he buried some of the memories. At trial, the boy retracted his allegations against his stepfather. However, an expert testified for the prosecution, saying prior abuse makes the boy more susceptible to later abuse and that such patterns of denial and recantation are seen in *all* sexually abused children. Combined with the medical evidence proffered by the physician assistant (later shown to be without foundation), the jury yielded a guilty verdict. Twenty years later, the stepfather is still in prison. The boy (now a man) maintains his biological father truly abused him, but his stepfather never did. He says he felt forced to make accusations against his stepfather because he was tired, hungry, and scared. He claims the detectives kept questioning him and he had no choice but to make allegations against his stepfather. He says he has been wracked by guilt over his stepfather's imprisonment.

Most readers probably agree that the criminal case against the biological father is much stronger than the case against the stepfather. The same medical and law enforcement team investigated both cases, yet the circumstances of the investigations greatly differ. In the first case against the biological father, the investigation appeared to be conducted in a sound and unbiased manner. However, in the second case, the unfolding of the investigation largely was influenced by the misguided belief that physical signs indicated a more recent sexualtrauma. The investigative team prepared for both cases in drastically different fashions. This variation in preparation for the interview could be costly. In this chapter, we discuss best practice guidelines for forensic interview preparation.

The overarching goal of a forensic interview is one of seeking the truth. Although forensic interviewers often are considered part of the "prosecution team" the goal is to uncover whether abuse did or did not occur and, if it did, by whom and how. The goal is not one of increasing *all* prosecutions, but rather increasing *valid* prosecutions. Interview preparation is a crucial part of the forensic evaluation process and should not be overlooked.

This chapter is divided into three main sections. In the first section, we address the issue of interviewer bias and whether interviewers should gather child and case-specific knowledge versus conducting "blind" interviews. In the second section, we discuss the importance of taking a hypothesis-testing approach to forensic interviews. In the third section, we provide specific recommendations for preparing for the interview, including the importance of video recording and what type of case information to gather before the interview. In the conclusion, we return to evaluate the above case in light of the recommendations and the scientific evidence pertaining to interview preparation.

Currently, there is disagreement among researchers and professionals concerning the scope of information the interviewer should gather before conducting the forensic interview. More research is needed to clearly understand the potential costs and benefits that preinterview knowledge exerts on the reliability of children's forensic reports. Research findings regarding interviewer bias are reviewed next as a means to understand the potential harm that inaccurate preinterview knowledge can inflict on the investigation.

Interviewer Bias and Expectancy Effects Can Negatively Shape Investigation Outcomes

Interviewer bias occurs when the interviewer formulates questions in a manner to gather information consistent with their prior beliefs. Biased interviewers tend to disregard contradictory evidence the child provides. For example, if the interviewer holds the belief that a nondisclosing child is simply too frightened to disclose, then the child's repeated denials of abuse may be interpreted as reluctance that must be overcome. The interviewer may proceed in order to "help the child" reveal the abuse that the interviewer is convinced must have occurred. Unfortunately, if the interviewer's intuition or beliefs were incorrect, then the child's reports become tainted. The biased interviewer can have benevolent intentions yet inadvertently elicit false reports from the child. A biased interviewer can be anyone who questions the child, from formal interviewers (e.g., police, social workers, therapists, physicians, representatives from the Department of Health) to people who interview children in an informal setting such as concerned parents, siblings, or teachers.

Laboratory studies have found that interviewers can shape children's reports to coincide with the interviewers' beliefs (for reviews, see Bruck & Ceci, 2004; Ceci, Bruck, & Battin, 2000). For example, in Thompson, Clarke-Stewart, and Lepore (1997), 5- and 6-year-old children interacted with a confederate, purportedly a janitor, as he handled some toys in a playroom. Half of the children saw the janitor play with the dolls, and half of the children saw the janitor clean the dolls. When questioned by a neutral interviewer, or by an interviewer whose interpretation was consistent with the activity, children were very accurate in their event reports. However, when the interviewer was biased in a direction that contradicted the activity viewed by the child, those children's stories quickly conformed to the suggestions or beliefs of the interviewer. In addition, children's answers to interpretive questions (e.g., "Was he doing his job or just being bad?") were in agreement with the interviewer's point of view, as opposed to what actually happened.

Principe and colleagues have demonstrated that interviewer bias can exert deleterious effects in an informal context via family members (see Principe & Schindewolf, 2012, for a review). For example, mothers in Principe, DiPuppo, and Gammel (2013) either were not given information (i.e., neutral) or were provided with false information (i.e., mislead) regarding a failed trick that occurred during a staged magic event with their children. All mothers were instructed to question their child a week after the magic show. Children interviewed by misled mothers provided significantly more inaccurate information about the magic show compared to children interviewed by neutral mothers. Furthermore, the amount of accurate information provided during the mother–child interview regarding the event was correlated to the amount of accurate information the child provided during a second neutral interview ($r = .42$). These results indicate that mothers' prior knowledge of an event (particularly when this information is inaccurate) can influence the child's report of the previous event while reminiscing with their mother and also when interviewed later by a neutral interviewer (also see Goodman, Sharma, Thomas, & Considine, 1995; Poole & Lindsay, 2001, 2002).

Bruck, Ceci, Melnyk, and Finkelberg (1999a, 1999b) documented how interviewer bias can develop in natural situations. In this study, an event was staged for 90 preschool children. In one condition, children experienced a "surprise birthday party" (with games, food, and magic tricks) for one of the research assistants. In the other condition, children were informed it was one of the research assistant's birthday, but they simply colored pictures with the research assistants.

Interviewers were recruited from graduate programs in counseling and social work and had experience with interviewing children. Interviewers were asked to question four children about what happened when the visitors came to their school. The interviewers were not told about the events but were simply told to find out from each child what had happened. The first three children that each interviewer questioned attended the birthday party and the fourth child attended the coloring event. Immediately after the interview with the fourth child, the interviewers were asked to report what they learned from all four children. Several weeks later, the interviewers were again questioned about what they had learned from the children.

Bruck and her colleagues (1999a, 1999b) found that the fourth children interviewed (those that attended the coloring event) produced twice as many errors as the children who attended the birthday party. The majority of the children (60 %) who only colored made false claims that involved a birthday party. This result suggests that the interviewers had built up a bias that all the children had attended a birthday party. By the time they interviewed the fourth child, the interviewers structured their interviews in such a way as to elicit claims consistent with their hypothesis. Another important finding was that when the fourth child denied attending a birthday party, 84 % of their interviewers later reported that all the children they interviewed had attended a birthday party. These data suggest that, regardless of what children actually say, biased interviewers inaccurately interpret the child's claims, making them consistent with their own beliefs.

Additionally, police officers are not immune to the downfalls of interviewer bias. Powell, Hughes-Scholes, and Sharman (2012) examined the effect of preinterview knowledge on police officers' questioning of children about a staged event. The police officers had extensive training on the importance of employing a nonsuggestive questioning style while interviewingchildwitnesses. Police officers were designated as either *good* or *poor* interviewers based on their usage of open-ended and nonleading questions in an independent hypothetical interviewing scenario. Additionally, interviewers were either blind to the "allegation" (i.e., the staged event) or were given accurate and inaccurate information regarding the staged event before interviewing the children. Police officers interviewed children a week after the event. Powell et al. (2012) found that poor biased interviewers asked a lower proportion of open-ended questions and a higher proportion of yes/no questions compared to poor non-biased interviewers. However, preinterview knowledge did not significantly affect the performance of good interviewers. Unfortunately, Powell et al. (2012) did not discuss how interviewers' questioning affected the reliability of children's reports. While this study is a good start toward understanding the role of preinterview knowledge and interviewer bias, more work is needed.

In summary, interviewers' preconceived beliefs are not always accurate; this is the very reason a forensic interview must be conducted. If interviewers' preconceived intuitions were largely correct, then forensic interviews would not be necessary. Unfortunately, if an interviewer holds prior (and incorrect) beliefs regarding an event, then the interview may be structured in a way to extract confirmatory evidence from the child. During the interviewing process, children often conform to the interviewer's prior beliefs, even inaccurate depictions of what actually happened. Additionally, conflicting evidence provided by the child is often ignored. Interviewers tend to interpret children's reports consistent with their a priori beliefs, and information consistent with these beliefs seeps into their reports. While preparing for the interview, interviewers need to keep in mind the potential for interviewer bias when having prior knowledge of the child and/or allegations.

To be Blind or Not to be Blind: That is the Question

Given the robust and deleterious effects of interviewer bias, a question that begs to be asked is whether (and how much) interviewers should gather information before conducting the interview. In the United States, several states (Idaho, Arizona, Wisconsin, and Pennsylvania) have instituted interviewing practices aimed to reduce preinterview knowledge in interviewing childwitnesses. Additionally, the Idaho v. Wright (1989) Supreme Court ruling suggested that allegation blind forensic interviewing could act as a legal safeguard for interviewing child witnesses. However, the Supreme Court did not provide specific practice recommendations. Blind interviewing is not the norm in forensic interviews with children, and most protocols recommend that interviewers gather information before conducting the interview. However, in many areas of professional practice outside of child forensic interviews, blind assessment procedures are practiced.

Blind assessment procedures have been used as a staple in medical and social science research methodology for over 200 years. The rationale is that blind procedures are necessary to isolate data founded on the scientific truth rather than external influences (e.g., confirmation bias and expectancy effects) (Kaptchuck, 1998). Blind procedures originated in the late eighteenth century as a means to challenge the true effectiveness of unconventional medical and psychological treatments (e.g., mesmerism) aside from personal beliefs in therapy. Blind assessments became mainstream in the medical community by the mid-nineteenth century and grew in popularity among experimental psychologists in the late-nineteenth century. Today, blind assessments are a normative infrastructure in medical, psychological, neurological, and pharmacological research designs, with double-blind placebo-controlled studies being the gold standard in science (Kaptchuck, 1998).

A large body of work led by Rosenthal (e.g., Rosenthal, 1994; Rosenthal & Rubin, 1978) demonstrates that the experimenter's expectations prior to conducting the experiment result in participants demonstrating the expected behaviors. Experimenter expectancy effects are robust and have been replicated in various areas of research (e.g., learning, reaction time, judgment, perception) (Canter, Hammond, & Youngs, 2012). Blind research designs are employed in efforts to avoid contaminating the data with experimenters' expectations.

Professionals and researchers interested in best practice procedures for forensic investigations also have been concerned with experimenter expectancy effects. Much of this concern in the forensic arena has focused on eliminating expectancy effects while conducting lineups (e.g., Wells et al., 1998). Double-blind lineup procedures, in which the witness and investigator are blind to the suspects' location within the lineup, are considered the best practice safeguard for reducing any unintentional bias in the witness' selection (International Association of Chiefs of Police, 2013). The double-blind lineup procedure is an empirically validated method for reducing expectancy effects and is endorsed by policy makers and the American Psychology and Law Society (Wells et al., 1998).

Additionally, forensic researchers have advocated for blind hypothesis testing while processing evidence from a crime scene (see Kassin, Dror, & Kukucka, 2013, for a review). Blind testing is common in matching shoe prints, firearms, bloodstains, handwriting, teeth marks, and fingerprints. Myriad procedures for processing forensic evidence do not have systematic and objective *yes or no* tests, but rather rely on expert opinion in determining if the evidence from the crime scene matches evidence from a suspect (Dror & Cole, 2010). Research has shown that this area of the forensic investigation is not immune to experimenter bias. In fact, evidence-processing experts often provide contradictory conclusions when examining the same fingerprints when given external information versus no information (Dror & Cole, 2010).

While some forensic investigation tools have been empirically evaluated and adjusted for expectancy effects (e.g., lineups), one area in which expectancy effects are surprisingly underresearched is forensic interviewing. The potential for bias in forensic interviewing could be especially problematic in cases involving childsexualabuse, as most cases lack physical indicators, and the child often is the only witness to the alleged abuse. In these cases, children's statements provide the central and possibly sole evidence. Bias produced by interviewers' prior knowledge might contaminate the reliability of statements made during the forensic interview.

To our knowledge, only one field study has evaluated the effect of preinterview knowledge on disclosure rates of childsexualabuse. In Cantlon, Payne, and Erbaugh (1996), interviewers were either blind to the allegation at the start of the interview or they had knowledge of the allegations prior to the interview. Though "allegation blind interviewers" were initially blind to the allegations, they were allowed to review case-specific information as the interview progressed. In this study, preinterview blind interviews resulted in a higher disclosure rate compared to interviews conducted by preinterview informed interviewers. Cantlon et al. (1996) posited that preinterview blind interviewers had to be patient with the child, which may have facilitated rapport and subsequent disclosures. While findings from Cantlon et al. (1996) shed some light on the issue of preinterview knowledge, there are limitations to their study such as a lack of random assignment and an unbalanced design ($n = 196$ preinterview informed interviews and $n = 1330$ preinterview blind interviews). Additionally, since Cantlon et al. (1996) was a field study, the veracity of the disclosures is unknown. As such, these findings need to be taken with caution.

Some researchers and practitioners hold that it is impractical for interviewers to be completely blind prior to conducting the interview. Child-specific knowledge is often necessary to create a developmentally appropriate interview according to the child's developmental trajectory (Poole & Lamb, 1998; Saywitz & Camparo, 1998). Information about the child's family composition, living arrangements, and caretaking schedule can be collected prior to the interview to aid in creating a comfortable interviewing environment for the child (Morgan, 1995; Poole & Lamb, 1998). Some professionals argue that prior knowledge of the child and the child's family environment creates a context for the interviewer to interpret the behaviors of child witness, especially for very young children (e.g., Hewitt, 1999). Many researchers and child protection professionals agree that child-specific knowledge is necessary to conduct a developmentally appropriate forensic interview (e.g., Anderson et al., 2010).

The more controversial debate regarding preinterview information spurs from the interviewer's prior knowledge of allegation-specific information. Some professionals argue allegation blind interviews are not conducive to eliciting a complete interview in which alternative hypotheses are explored and the necessary information to judge the validity of the allegation is obtained (e.g., Raskin & Esplin, 1991). Under this assumption, most child welfare researchers and professionals recommend the interviewer should gather knowledge regarding the events in question (Anderson et al., 2010; Great Britain Ministry of Justice, 2011; Hewitt, 1999; Morgan, 1995; Poole & Lamb, 1998; State of Michigan Governor's Task Force on Children's Justice and Department of Human Services, 2004) and any past reports of abuse (Hewitt, 1999; Morgan, 1995). Interviewers are advised to gather allegation-specific information by carefully reviewing police reports (Morgan, 1995), contacting child protective services (Poole & Lamb, 1998), and interviewing family members as well as the adult who made the report (Morgan, 1995). Some professionals contend an understanding of the child's abuse history (Hewitt, 1999; Morgan, 1995), the current allegation (Hewitt, 1999; Morgan, 1995), and offender-specific information (Morgan, 1995) is particularly important to conducting a complete interview. In fact, Morgan (1995) states that collecting necessary background information prior to conducting the interview leads to a better interview compared to blind interviews as learning information about the child and allegations can assist the interviewer in planning and testing alternate hypotheses.

Forensic interviewers are in a difficult position. On one hand, confirmation bias and expectancy effects can unwittingly shape the architecture of the interview. On the other hand, some information about the child and allegations seems necessary for interviewers to focus their questioning and to develop alternative hypotheses. Until additional data establish the effectiveness of blind interview processes with children, we agree that gathering information about the child and the allegations is warranted. However, a wealth of scientific data highlights the dangers of having only one hypothesis about the event in question—especially when this hypothesis is incorrect. In the next section, we discuss the importance of alternative hypothesis testing during the forensic interview as a means of countering expectancy effects.

Minimizing Interviewer Bias and Expectancy Effects: Taking a Hypothesis-Testing Approach

Given the robust literature demonstrating interviewer bias and expectancy effects, great care must be taken to ensure the interviewer takes a hypothesis-testing versus a hypothesis-confirming approach. However, as just reviewed, the interviewers' prior beliefs can exert an influence without malice or intent on the part of the interviewer. Therefore, a crucial part of the interview is planning out alternative hypotheses.

A number of worldwide forensic interviewprotocols agree on the importance of adopting hypothesis-testing approach with childwitnesses. The State of Michigan protocol cites hypothesis testing as one of the central features of a sound evidence-based-->interview (State of Michigan Governor's Task Force on Children's Justice and Department of Human Services, 2004). Similarly, the American Professional Society on the Abuse of Children (APSAC) guidelines caution interviewers to weigh alternative justifications for any allegations or inconsistencies in children's report (APSAC Task Force on Investigative Interviews in Cases of Alleged Child Abuse, 2002). The CornerHouse/RATAC protocol reminds interviewers that children are the experts in the interview setting and interviewers' assumptions regarding the child's experiences must be avoided (Anderson et al., 2010).

Exploring alternative hypothesis during the interview is crucial in attempting to combat interviewer bias. For specific information on developing alternative hypotheses, see State of Michigan Governor's Task Force on Children's Justice and Department of Human Services (2004) and Poole and Lamb (1998).

Unfortunately, little scientific evidence exists to date testing whether interviewers can control their preexisting beliefs when properly warned to do so. Lamb and colleagues have conducted extensive training with forensic interviewers regarding the importance of employing open-ended and nonleading questioning techniques (see Lamb, Hershkowitz, Orbach, & Esplin, 2008). Despite a great deal of training and despite the interviewers' intentions, they unwittingly dropped into leading and directive questioning techniques when they were simply provided with these guidelines. Importantly, interviewers tend to believe they are using best-practice questioning methods despite videotaped interview transcripts indicating otherwise. Guidelines generally are not enough to lessen interviewer bias. Several prominent interview protocols in the United States, however, do just that: the guidelines caution interviewers against using directive and suggestive questioning strategies but do not provide a structured protocol. Most likely, forensic interviewers adhere to the guidelines at varying levels according to their preexisting beliefs. If they believe children will be resistant and need to be *helped* (which may translate to children being pressured or even badgered), then their methods will deviate from best practice. One of the authors of this chapter (KL) has seen an unfortunate number of forensic interviews resembling coercive suspect interviews rather than developmentally sensitive child interviews. In one such case, a nationally prominent academic social worker violated almost every interview principle in *her own* forensic interview books.

So what can policy makers and practitioners do? Lamb and colleagues have conducted over two decades of developmental studies demonstrating interviewers can be trained to successfully follow best-practice interviewing protocols which can help reduce the effects of interviewer bias. The National Institute of Child Health and Human Development (NICHD) protocol is a structured interviewing protocol that provides a flexible road map for the interviewer (see Lamb, Orbach, Hershkowtiz, Esplin, & Horowitz, 2007). While many interview "protocols" provide guidelines based on sound developmental research, the question of their actual effectiveness in the field has not been established. Decades of laboratory research and scientific collaboration among developmental researchers, childabuse professionals, and police served as the foundation of the NICHD protocol (Lamb, La Rooy, Malloy, & Katz, 2011). The NICHD protocol has been shown to increase the quality of both interviewers' questioning behavior (e.g., Lamb et al., 2008; Sternberg, Lamb, Orbach, Esplin, & Mitchell, 2001) and children's statements, even among preschoolers (Hershkowitz, Fisher, Lamb, & Horowitz, 2007). Due to the fact that the NICHD protocol has undergone rigorous testing worldwide (Bull, 2010; Lamb et al., 2008), we strongly recommend this protocol for interviewing children. Combined with alternative hypotheses developed in advance of the interview, the NICHD protocol (or others similar to it) provides the best means of countering expectancy effects that result from interviewer bias. In the next section, we turn our attention to practical considerations of planning the interview.

Planning the Interview: Practical Considerations

Contemporary forensic interview guidelines share common features for interview-preparation. Many of these factors deal with planning the actual interview, while others focus on information to be gained and arrangements to be made before the interview takes place. Here, we will focus on four basic areas of preparation: (1) video recording/documentation, (2) interview context, (3) information about the child, and (4) information about the alleged event.

Video Recording

Interviewers will need to determine how they are going to document the interview. Two primary reasons for documentation of the interview include (1) obtaining a detailed and objective record of the child's report, and (2) verifying the child was questioned in an appropriate manner. Most forensic interview guidelines recommend videotaping the interview (e.g., American Professional Society on the Abuse of Children, 2012; Anderson et al., 2010; Bottoms, Najdowski, & Goodman, 2009; Great Britain Ministry of Justice, 2011; Home, 2007; Lamb et al., 2008; Pence & Wilson, 1994; Poole & Lamb, 1998; Smith & Milne, 2011).

The rationale for videotaping forensic interviews with children parallels the logic behind video recording interviews with criminal suspects: fact finders and experts must be able to evaluate the extent to which the statements arose voluntarily or as the result of pressure from the interviewer. In the United States, as of February 2014, 19 states and Washington, DC now have recording laws for suspect interviews (http://www.reid.com/pdfs/20140331a.pdf). In 2013, President Obama issued a statement encouraging videotaping in all capital cases. In June 2014, Deputy Attorney General James M. Cole mandated that interviews with individuals detained in federal custody must be electronically recorded (Office of the Attorney General, 2014). Deputy Attorney Cole stated that electronic recording will ensure individuals' constitutional rights are protected and also will help federal investigating agencies (FBI, DEA, ATF, and US Marshals) show they employed proper techniques with a clear and indispensable record of important statements and confessions. The bottom-line rationale for electronically recording interviews, whether with suspects or child victims and witnesses, is that electronic records are necessary to provide veridical documentation of the interview procedures and individuals' statements. Certainly if adults can succumb to social pressure from investigators, then children as young as 3-years-old deserve similar protection during forensic interviews (see "Childhood Memory: An Update from the Cognitive Neuroscience Perspective", this volume). Very high stakes are involved in CSA cases, so it is imperative that proper investigative methods are followed.

Many interviewers opt to take notes during the interview as their form of documentation rather than video recording the interview. However, note taking is not an adequate form of documentation of childforensic interviews for a number of reasons. First, note taking during the interview may disrupt the flow of conversation and may distract both the interviewer and the child. Second, the child and the interviewer's affect and nonverbal communication cannot be clearly documented in written notes. Third, notes reflect the gist of the interview, but do not fully capture the details necessary to assess whether the interview included suggestive features (for a review, see Bruck, Ceci, & Principe, 2006).

Major errors can be made in replicating the content and structure (what questions were asked, how many times, with what response from the interviewer, how the child's statements were elicited) of the conversation in handwritten records. Even highly trained and motivated interviewers perform quite poorly in recounting the verbatim questions and statements made during the interview, and rather tend to recall the gist. Lamb, Orbach, Sternberg, Hershowitz, and Horowitz (2000) compared audiotaped recordings of 20 forensic interviews to contemporaneous "verbatim" notes taken by highly trained interviewers. More than half of the interviewers' utterances and 25 % of the children's incident relevant details were not reported in the so-called verbatim notes. Less than half of the details provided by children were attributed to the correct eliciting question. Even when taking highly detailed notes during the interview, well-intentioned professionals leave out a great deal of information.

Information on the exact wording of each question asked of children during interviews, as well as the number of times questions are repeated and the tone of the questions, is necessary to evaluate the reliability of the children's allegations. Like with suspect interviews, experts and fact finders must be able to evaluate the extent to which statements were brought about by social pressure versus using scientifically supported interview techniques. The lack of such information from the initial interviews makes it impossible to make such a determination and therefore makes a reliability assessment untenable.

Some professionals have argued that videotaping is not necessary because the child will provide testimony at the trial, and the jurors can evaluate whether the child's statements were improperly influenced at that time. Once children have been suggestively interviewed, their later reports may continue to show the initial suggestive influence even when interviewed with open-ended neutral techniques (e.g., London, Bruck, & Melnyk, 2009). Unfortunately, laypeople and professionals cannot reliably distinguish between true and false reports based on the content of children's statements. One body of scientific work has shown that laypeople and professionals do poorly in distinguishing true versus false reports, whether the false reports stem from intentional deception (see Talwar & Crossman, 2012, for a review) or from suggestive interview techniques (Ceci, Huffman, Smith, & Loftus, 1994; Leichtman & Ceci, 1995).

In a second area of study, researchers have systematically compared children's true and false narratives. The general paradigm in these studies involves staging an event for children and later exposing children to some sources of false suggestions. Children's subsequent narratives are then coded for a number of characteristics including number of spontaneous utterances, details, contradictory statements, narrative cohesion, and improbable details. Surprisingly, the results generally reveal that false narratives were actually more elaborate than children's true narratives (see Bruck, Ceci, & Hembrooke, 2002; Powell, Jones, & Campbell, 2003; Principe & Ceic, 2002). For example, Kulkofsky and Klemfuss (2008) found that increases in narrative quality were associated with decreases in accuracy. These two areas of research dispute the notion that jurors can separate unreliable from reliable testimony provided by the child witnesses during trial. In fact, this research provides increasing support that interviews should be videotaped.

Video recording the childforensic interview has additional benefits. By recording the interview, the investigationteam can help minimize the number of times the child is questioned (Pence & Wilson, 1994; Poole & Lamb, 1998). Furthermore, video recording allows interviewers to review their own interviewing skills and improve their techniques (Lamb et al., 2002; Pence & Wilson, 1994). Lamb and colleagues (2002) found that interviewers can be trained to follow the NICHD protocol, but this training involves a feedback process in which the interviewer watches their prior interviews as a means to improve upon their previous performance. This reviewing process is an integral component of training, and videotapes of prior interviews are necessary.

Taken together, these data provide an empirical basis for the importance of obtaining electronic copies of interviews with children. If the investigator has a bias that the child was sexually abused prior to the interview, confirmation bias could color his or her interpretations of what the child said or did; and it is this interpretation that appears in interviewer's notes rather than a factual account of what transpired. If a number of children are interviewed and the reports are not immediately written, then the investigator may confuse which child said what (Bruck et al., 1999a, 1999b). This literature highlights the problem with relying on reports of children's behaviors and statements that occurred in the past and that were not recorded at the time of their occurrence.

Interviewers and child protection agencies should be transparent about the investigative techniques they employ. Just like the evidence technician must show they employed proper techniques in finger print collection, investigators must show they employed proper techniques in interviewing children. If the interviewer fails to electronically record the interview, like a car wash, they wash away the evidence of what occurred to produce statements from the child. If interviewers generally employ proper techniques, then the videotape should provide excellent evidence that the interview was conducted in a sound manner that allows optimal assessment of the abuse suspicions.

When audio or visual recording equipment is used, it will be necessary to regulate who will have access to the records, how they will be stored, and how they will eventually be destroyed and by whom (Poole & Lamb, 1998). Some states require certain information is recorded at the onset of the recording such as the name of people in the room and the time and date of the interview. Video recording equipment can be small and very discreetly placed. Refer to requirements in your jurisdiction.

Interview Context

Location. Interviewers must decide where the interview is going to take place. A neutral location is ideal as it reduces any power the alleged offender may have over the child (Pence & Wilson, 1994). Child advocacy centers (CAC) are becoming increasingly more common hosts for child interviews and are the preferred location (State of Michigan Governor's Task Force on Children's Justice and Department of Human Services, 2004). These centers typically are already child appropriate and equipped with the necessary video recording equipment (Pence & Wilson, 1994; Poole & Lamb, 1998). Adjoining rooms where other adults can view the interview through a two-way mirror is recommended.

Child-friendly environment. The interview location must be private, child friendly, and free from distraction. Privacy is necessary in order to establish rapport and help the child feel safe in their environment (APSAC Task Force on Investigative Interviews in Cases of Alleged Child Abuse, 2002; Saywitz, Lyon, & Goodman, 2011). The interview room must be physically safe and childproof (Russell, 2004). Child-appropriate seating should be available which does not encourage roaming or bouncing around by the child (Anderson et al., 2010; Bohannan et al., 2004; Poole & Lamb, 1998; Russell, 2004; Saywitz & Camparo, 1998). A simple set of table and chairs (avoid swivel chairs) should suffice (Poole & Lamb, 1998). If the child has special needs, the interview room and location must be fully accessible to the child (Russell, 2004).

Interviewers should be sure the child is comfortable. Interviewers should avoid scheduling the interview during the child's naptime and ensure the child is not hungry or thirsty before initiating the interview. Ideally, bathroom facilities should be available to children directly from the interview room so children do not have to pass through the waiting area mid-interview.

In the past, forensic interviews frequently were conducted in private rooms at locations such as a public library or the child's school. Children are typically comfortable at their school, which may foster rapport building. If the interview is to take place at the child's school, interviewers must work to ensure that unnecessary attention will not be drawn to the child (Pence & Wilson, 1994). Additionally, extra care should be taken to remove all distractions such as toys and computers from the interview room at the child's school (Poole & Lamb, 1998).

Most formal forensic interview guidelines suggest that interview rooms are free of all toys and other distractions, including drawing materials, phone calls, or other possible interruptions (American Professional Society on the Abuse of Children, 2012; Anderson et al., 2010; Bottoms et al., 2009; Lamb et al., 2008; Saywitz & Camparo, 1998). However, many professionals agree that a play area with neutral toys in a waiting room might be beneficial in helping children feel more at ease and helping interviewers to establish rapport prior to the interview (Poole & Lamb, 1998; Russell, 2004; Zwiers & Morrissette, 1999).

Interviewers sometimes allow children to continue playing with toys or to draw during substantive questioning. Sometimes the interviewer also draws or plays along with the child throughout the interview, oscillating between discussing the suspected abuse and the fantasy drawings. We discourage this practice as it distracts the child and disrupts the flow of the conversation when the discussion flops back and forth from the drawings to the event questions. Additionally, the play activity could be suggestible by encouraging pretend play.

Multidisciplinary teams. Interviewers should act as a part of a multidisciplinary team (American Professional Society on the Abuse of Children, 2012; Russell, 2004). The team approach can help keep interview sessions to a minimum and help ensure complete questioning occurs during the first session.

Number of interviewers in the room. The investigationteam must decide who will be present during the interview. Most forensic interview guidelines recommend that a single person conducts the interview (American Professional Society on the Abuse of Children, 2012; Anderson et al., 2010; Lamb et al., 2008; Saywitz & Camparo, 1998; Smith & Milne, 2011). Having more than one adult in the room may be intimidating to children, creating difficulties in rapport building or leading to an atmosphere that engenders children's compliance with the adults.

Ideally, other adults on the investigationteam can watch the interview through a one-way mirror. Additionally, many CAC centers are now set up where the forensic interviewer wears an earpiece so that observers on the investigation team can communicate with the interviewer. Alternatively, the interviewer can take a break toward the end of the interview and leave the room briefly to conference with the other investigation members. Multiple perspectives may be helpful in producing additional alternative hypotheses or interview questions. At the same time, the interviewer has to be careful the proposed questions do not introduce bias.

Support persons. Interviewers must also decide whether support persons will be allowed in the interview room (Saywitz et al., 2011). Support persons are not recommended as they may interfere with the interview by interrupting the conversation, prompting or distracting the child, or preventing the child from using sexually explicit language (American Professional Society on the Abuse of Children, 2012; Poole & Lamb, 1998; State of Michigan Governor's Task Force on Children's Justice and Department of Human Services, 2004). We recommend that, if at all possible, support persons should not be allowed in the interview room. Support persons particularly should not be allowed in the room if one plausible hypothesis is that family members may be exerting influence upon the child. An interviewer can establish some rapport in the waiting area, which may help children who refuse to separate from their caregiver.

Timing and number of interviews. Interviews should be conducted as close in time to the alleged event as possible, taking both the child's mental and emotional state as well as their immediate safety into account (American Professional Society on the Abuse of Children, 2012; Smith & Milne, 2011). Interviewing the child as soon as suspicions arise may help to lessen the likelihood that other people in the child's life influence the child's report.

A single interview is recommended though this may not be possible due to child characteristics, particularly their routine, age, and medical, mental, or emotional condition (Smith & Milne, 2011). In some cases, more than one interview may be necessary (American Professional Society on the Abuse of Children, 2012; Lamb et al., 2008). Much caution must be used if conducting more than one interview to avoid suggestive questions or queries about a specific topic involving a specific person. Researchers have found that repeatedly asking children if a nonexperienced event occurred produces elaborate free recall reports from some children (Leichtman & Ceci, 1995). Repeated interviews may promote additional information from children but do so at the expense of accuracy (Bruck et al., 1997; Peterson, Moores, & White, 2001; Pipe, Gee, Wilson, & Egerton, 1999; Salmon & Pipe, 2000). Furthermore, interviewers can implicitly convey interviewer bias if they continue to interview children who repeatedly deny abuse until an allegation is forthcoming. Much more research is needed to establish how repetitive interviewing could be conducted in order to promote additional details without compromising the accuracy of the details provided by children (see La Rooy, Katz, Malloy, & Lamb, 2010).

Use of props. Interviewers should start the interview with open-ended questions that do not rely on props or other types of symbols (Home Office in conjunction with Department of Health, 1992; Lamb et al., 2007; Lyon, 2005; Poole & Dickinson, 2011; Steward et al., 1996). Though some forensic interviewprotocols place a large emphasis on human-figure drawings (HFDs), the use of such drawings has not been empirically validated (for details, see Poole & Bruck, 2012; Poole & Dickinson, 2011). Open-ended prompts produce more substantive and complete reports even from young children (Lamb et al., 2007). The continued use of dolls and HFDs is a potentially dangerous practice (Lytle, London, & Bruck, 2015) and is inconsistent with past and current research examining children's understanding and use of such props.

Information About the Child

Developmental history. Basic information about the child (e.g., age, history of injury or illness, developmental milestones) may be helpful in planning the interview (American Professional Society on the Abuse of Children, 2012; Great Britain Ministry of Justice, 2011; Saywitz & Camparo, 1998; Smith & Milne, 2011; Sternberg et al., 2001). This information can be obtained by working as part of a multidisciplinary team, particularly with family physicians, medical or mental health care providers, teachers, caretakers, detectives, and social workers.

Cultural sensitivity. Some interview protocols recommend the interview is adapted according to the child's cultural background and language (American Professional Society on the Abuse of Children, 2012; Russell, 2004). The NICHD protocol has been shown to be effective with children across various countries (e.g., United States,

Canada, England, Scotland, Sweden, New Zealand, and Australia). The interviewer should be aware of any factors that could act as barriers in developing rapport and eliciting sensitive information (American Professional Society on the Abuse of Children, 2012). Children should be interviewed in their first language (Smith & Milne, 2011). However, if this is not feasible or the child is deaf/hard of hearing, an extra familial interpreter may be necessary and should be arranged prior to the interview (American Professional Society on the Abuse of Children, 2012; Smith & Milne, 2011).

Special needs. Consider and accommodate any special needs of the child prior to the interview, including physical and developmental disabilities (American Professional Society on the Abuse of Children, 2012). The interview room should be accessible and the interviewer should be receptive to the child's needs. If developmental delays are present, it may be necessary to consult with guardians or other professionals working with the child in order to determine the child's developmental level (American Professional Society on the Abuse of Children, 2012). As with any population, children with special needs should be encouraged to make reports in their own words. If a child has severely limited language abilities due to a developmental disorder, the interviewer needs to be careful not to resort to a barrage of forced-choice questions. Just like typical populations, such directive and suggestive questions run an increased risk of eliciting erroneous information (see London, Henry, Conradt, & Corser, 2010, for a review). Further work is needed on a variety of special populations such as children with atypical development of varying etiologies, suspected victims of familial abuse, and suspected victims of the commercial sex trade industry.

Developmentally appropriate language. Some forensic interviewprotocols recommend that the adults' language should be tailored to the child's developmental level (American Professional Society on the Abuse of Children, 2012). Vocabulary, sentence structure, and complexity should be continually assessed throughout the interview and adapted where appropriate (American Professional Society on the Abuse of Children, 2012). Rapport building that comes before the substantive portion of the interview is an ideal time to assess the child's linguistic abilities. The interviewer should also be careful to use kinship and anatomical terms with which the child is familiar (American Professional Society on the Abuse of Children, 2012). One of the advantages of the NICHD protocol is that it has been extensively tested (both in field studies and in laboratory studies) and shown to produce reliable reports even from children as young as age four (Lamb et al., 2008). The NICHD protocol leaves less to subjective judgment on what language is appropriate for children at different ages by providing a semistructured protocol.

Information About the Alleged Event

Information about the alleged event and history of the allegations can be informative in guiding the questioning, particularly in the formation of alternative hypotheses (Poole & Lamb, 1998; State of Michigan Governor's Task Force on Children's

Justice and Department of Human Services, 2004). Obtaining information about the allegations may be particularly important in cases involving divorce and custody disputes so that such information can be used with generating alternative hypotheses about the provenance of the allegations. Information needed in order to set clear goals for the interview may include:

- The nature of the alleged event
- Timing, duration, and location of the alleged event
- How the child came to be interviewed
- Any threats or psychological factors used to intimidate the child
- The child's relationship to the suspected perpetrator
- Any history of abuse
- The alleged victim's usual routine

Conclusions

At the beginning of this chapter, we outlined a scenario where a 7-year-old boy made allegations of abuse against his biological father and later against his stepfather. In the first scenario, the boy was forthcoming about the abuse perpetrated by his biological father. In the second case, the boy was questioned due to a physician assistant's medical opinion that was without scientific foundation. This belief propelled law enforcement to continue to interview the boy despite his repeated denials.

In the first case involving his biological father, the boy had not come forward to make allegations. The abuse was discovered when the mother and the stepfather found a sexually explicit photograph of the child. When questioned briefly by police at his residence on the day of the photo's discovery, the boy relayed details about abuse by his biological father. The boy was interviewed the next day in a single video-recorded session. He gave detailed reports about severe physical and sexual abuse by his biological father that had taken place over the past 2 years. The boy's reports were consistent with the medical evidence and the photograph. The biological father was found guilty and remains imprisoned.

In the second case, the same investigationteam employed very different tactics. Driven by their misguided belief that the medical evidence proved the boy had been abused more recently than by his biological father, two detectives repeatedly interviewed the boy in hours of unrecorded sessions. The detectives do not appear to have approached the case with a plan, but rather continued to interview the boy until he gave statements consistent with their belief that the stepfather had abused him. No discernable interview protocol was followed. When the boy denied abuse or said he could not remember, the detectives told the boy he probably blocked out the memories due to trauma. In all likelihood, the detectives had the boy's best interest in mind: due to the faulty medical opinion, they believed the boy had been abused by the stepfather and conducted their investigation to extract abuse-consistent information.

The danger that interviewers face when repeatedly interviewing a child who denies abuse is that suggestive methods may produce allegations. Of course, if the interviewer's initial intuition or the reporting parent's concerns of abuse were valid, then the report may be predominately accurate. However, if intuition were enough, we would not need forensic interviews. Instead, we would allow the forensic interviewer to make decisions according to their intuition. Unfortunately, some interviewers do continue to operate in this fashion, where they develop a belief prior to the interview and continue to conduct the (often unrecorded) interview until allegations consistent with their prior beliefs are elicited. In a recent case on which one of the authors (KL) served as a consultant, the interviewer conducted 18 unrecorded interviews with a child beginning at age 2 years 9 months. Of course, interviewers do this for a reason. He or she believes their intuition regarding the child's abuse status is correct. Therefore, the interviewer may lead the child down a path of false reports in the interest of "helping the child." In such cases where abuse did not occur, however, the interviewer is actually exploiting the child and perhaps unjustifiably taking the child away from his or her parents. Forensic interviewers must remember the interview takes place for a reason: truth seeking. Well-planned investigation procedures can help maximize the odds that the truth will prevail.

References

American Professional Society on the Abuse of Children. (2012). *Forensic interviewing in cases of suspected child abuse*. Practice guidelines.

Anderson, J., Ellefson, J., Lashley, J., Lukas Miller, A., Olinger, S., Russell, A., ... Weigman, J. (2010). The CornerHouse forensic interview protocol: RATAC®. *Thomas M. Cooley Journal of Practical and Clinical Law, 12*(2), 193–331.

APSAC Task Force on Investigative Interviews in Cases of Alleged Child Abuse. (2002). *Practice guidelines: Investigative interviewing in cases of alleged child abuse*. Elmhurst, IL: American Professional Society on the Abuse of Children. Retrieved from: https://www.cornerhousemn.org/images/CornerHouse_RATAC_Protocol.pdf.

Bohannan, S., Chianello, T., Flagor, R., Gallagher, J., Kettner, D., Sieg, C., ... Van Ness, P. (2004). *Oregon interviewing guidelines* (2nd ed.). Salem, OR: Oregon Department of Justice. Retrieved from http://www.doj.state.or.us/crimev/pdf/orinterviewingguide.pdf

Bottoms, B. L., Najdowski, C. J., & Goodman, G. S. (Eds.). (2009). *Children as victims, witnesses, and offenders: Psychological science and the law*. New York, NY: Guilford Press.

Bruck, M., & Ceci, S. J. (2004). Forensic developmental psychology. *Current Directions in Psychological Science, 13*(6), 229–232. doi:10.1111/j.0963-7214.2004.00314.x.

Bruck, M., Ceci, S. J., Melnyk, L., & Finkelberg, D. (1999, April). *The effect of interviewer bias on the accuracy of children's reports and interviewer's reports*. Paper presented to the biennial meeting of the Society of Research in Child Development, Albuquerque, NM.

Bruck, M., Ceci, S. J., Melnyk, L., & Finkelberg, D. (1999, April). *Does interview bias create tainted reports?* Paper presented at the biannual meeting of the Society of Research in Child Development, Albuquerque, NM.

Bruck, M., Ceci, S. J., & Hembrooke, H. (1997). Children's reports of a pleasant and unpleasant events. In D. Read & S. Lindsay (Eds.), *Recollections of Trauma: Scientific Research and Clinical Practice* (pp. 199–219). New York, NY: Plenum.

Bruck, M., Ceci, S. J., & Hembrooke, H. (2002). The nature of children's true and false narratives. *Developmental Review, 22*(3), 520–554. doi:10.1016/S0273-2297(02)00006-0.

Bruck, M., Ceci, S. J., & Principe, G. F. (2006). The child and the law. In W. Damon & R. M. Lerner (Series Eds.), & K. A. Renniger & I. E. Sigel (Vol. Eds.), *Handbook of child psychology: Vol. 4. Child psychology in practice* (6th ed., pp. 776–816). New York, NY: Wiley.

Bull, R. (2010). The investigative interviewing of children and other vulnerable witnesses: Psychological research and working/professional practice. *Legal and Criminological Psychology, 15*(1), 5–23. doi:10.1348/014466509X440160.

Canter, D., Hammond, L., & Youngs, D. (2012). Cognitive bias in line-up identifications: The impact of administrator knowledge. *Science and Justice, 53*(2), 83–88. doi:10.1016/j.scijus.2012.12.001.

Cantlon, J., Payne, G., & Erbaugh, C. (1996). Outcome-based practice: Disclosure rates of child sexual abuse comparing allegation blind and allegation informed structured interviews. *Child Abuse & Neglect, 20*(11), 1113–1120. doi:10.1016/0145-2134(96)00100-7.

Ceci, S. J., Bruck, M., & Battin, D. B. (2000). The suggestibility of children's testimony. In D. F. Bjorklund (Ed.), *False-memory creation in children and adults: Theory, research, and implications*. Mahwah, NJ: Lawrence Erlbaum Associates.

Ceci, S. J., Huffman, M. L. C., Smith, E., & Loftus, E. F. (1994). Repeatedly thinking about a non-event: Source misattributions among preschoolers. *Consciousness and Cognition, 3*(3-4), 388–407. doi:10.1006/ccog.1994.1022.

Dror, I. E., & Cole, S. A. (2010). The vision in blind justice: Expert perception, judgment, and visual cognition in forensic pattern recognition. *Psychonomic Bulletin & Review, 17*(2), 161–167. doi:10.3758/PBR.17.2.161.

Goodman, G. S., Sharma, A., Thomas, S. F., & Considine, M. G. (1995). Mother knows best: Effects of relationship status and interviewer bias on children's memory. *Journal of Experimental Child Psychology, 60*(1), 195–228. doi:10.1006/jecp.1995.1038.

Great Britain Ministry of Justice. (2011). *Achieving best evidence in criminal proceedings: Guidance on interviewing victims and witnesses, and guidance on using special measures.* London, England: Ministry of Justice.

Hershkowitz, I., Fisher, S., Lamb, M. E., & Horowitz, D. (2007). Improving credibility assessment in child sexual abuse allegations: The role of the NICHD investigative interview protocol. *Child Abuse & Neglect, 31*(2), 99–110. doi:10.1016/j.chiabu.2006.09.005.

Hershkowitz, I., Lamb, M. E., Katz, C., & Malloy, L. C. (2013). Does enhanced rapport-building alter the dynamics of investigative interviews with suspected victims of intra-familial abuse? *Journal of Police and Criminal Psychology, 30*(1), 6–14. doi:10.1007/s11896-013-9136-8.

Hewitt, S. K. (1999). *Assessing allegations of sexual abuse in preschool children*. Thousand Oaks, CA: Sage.

Home Office (2007). *Achieving best evidence in criminal proceedings: Guidance on interviewing victims and witnesses and using special measures.* London, England: Author.

Home Office in conjunction with Department of Health. (1992). *Memorandum of good practice on video recorded interviews with child witnesses for criminal proceedings*. London, England: HMSO.

Idaho v. Wright, 166 Idaho 382, 775 P.2d 1224. (1989).

International Association of Chiefs of Police. (2013). *National summit on wrongful convictions: Building a systemic approach to prevent wrongful convictions.* Washington, DC: U.S. Government Printing Office.

Kaptchuck, T. J. (1998). Intentional ignorance: A history of blind assessment and placebo controls in medicine. *Bulletin of the History of Medicine, 72*(3), 389–433. Retrieved from http://muse.jhu.edu/journals/bulletin_of_the_history_of_medicine/v072/72.3kaptchuk.html

Kassin, S. M., Dror, E. E., & Kukucka, J. (2013). The forensic confirmation bias: Problems, perspectives, and proposed solutions. *Journal of Applied Research in Memory and Cognition, 2*(1), 42–52. doi:10.1016/j.jarmac.2013.01.001.

Kulkofsky, S., & Klemfuss, J. Z. (2008). What the stories children tell can tell about their memory: Narrative skill and young children's suggestibility. *Developmental Psychology, 44*(5), 1442–1456. doi:10.1037/a0012849.

La Rooy, D., Katz, C., Malloy, L. C., & Lamb, M. E. (2010). Do we need to rethink guidance on repeated interviews? *Psychology, Public Policy, and Law, 16*(4), 373–392. doi: 10.1037/a0019909.

Lamb, M. E., Hershkowitz, I., Orbach, Y., & Esplin, P. W. (2008). *Tell me what happened: Structured investigative interviews of child victims and witnesses.* Chichester, England: Wiley.

Lamb, M. E., La Rooy, D. J., Malloy, L. C., & Katz, C. (Eds.). (2011). *Children's testimony: A handbook of psychological research and forensic practice* (Vol. 52). Chichester, England: Wiley.

Lamb, M. E., Orbach, Y., Hershkowtiz, I., Esplin, P. W., & Horowitz, D. (2007). A structured forensic interview protocol improves the quality and informativeness of investigative interviews with children: A review of research using the NICHD Investigative Interview Protocol. *Child Abuse & Neglect, 31*(11–12), 1201–1231. doi:10.1016/j.chiabu.2007.03.021.

Lamb, M. E., Orbach, Y., Sternberg, K. J., Hershowitz, I., & Horowitz, D. (2000). Accuracy of investigators' verbatim notes of their forensic interviews with alleged child abuse victims. *Law and Human Behavior, 24*(6), 699–708. doi:10.1023/A:1005556404636.

Lamb, M. E., Sternberg, K. J., Orbach, Y., Hershowitz, I., Horowitz, D., & Esplin, P. W. (2002). The effects of intensive training and ongoing supervision on the quality of investigative interviews with alleged sex abuse victims. *Applied Developmental Science, 6*(3), 114–125. doi:10.1207/S1532480XADS0603_2.

Leichtman, M. D., & Ceci, S. J. (1995). The effects of stereotypes and suggestions on preschoolers' reports. *Developmental Psychology, 31*(4), 568–578. doi:10.1037/0012-1649.31.4.568.

London, K., Bruck, M., & Melnyk, L. (2009). Post-event information affects children's autobiographical memory after one year. *Law and Human Behavior, 33*(4), 344–355. doi:10.1007/s10979-008-9147-7.

London, K., Henry, L. A., Conradt, T., & Corser, R. (2010). Suggestibility and individual differences in typically developing and intellectually disabled children. In A. M. Ridley, F. Gabbert, & D. J. LaRooy (Eds.), *Suggestibility in legal contexts: Psychological research and forensic implications* (pp. 129–148). Hoboken, NJ: Wiley-Blackwell.

Lyon, T. D. (2005). Speaking with children: Advice from investigative interviewers. In P. F. Talley (Ed.), *Handbook for the treatment of abused and neglected children* (pp. 65–82). Binghamton, NY: Haworth.

Lytle, N., London, K., & Bruck, M. (2015). Young children's ability to use 2-dimensional and 3-dimensional symbols to show placements of body touches and hidden objects. *Journal of Experimental Child Psychology, 134*, 30–42. doi:10.1016/j.jecp.2015.01.010.

Morgan, M. (1995). *How to interview sexual abuse victims.* Thousand Oaks, CA: Sage. Office of the Attorney General (2014, May 22). Attorney General Holder Announces Significant Policy Shift Concerning Electronic Recording of Statements. Retrieved from http://www.justice.gov/opa/pr/attorney-general-holder-announces-significant-policy-shift-concerning-electronic-recording

Office of Attorney General (2014). *Policy concerning electronic recording of statements.* Washington, DC: U.S. Government Printing Office.

Pence, D., & Wilson, C. (1994). *Team investigation of child sexual abuse: The uneasy alliance.* Thousand Oaks, CA: Sage.

Peterson, C., Moores, L., & White, G. (2001). Recounting the same event again and again: Consistency across multiple interviews. *Applied Cognitive Psychology, 15*(4), 353–371. doi:10.1002/acp.708.

Pipe, M.-E., Gee, S., Wilson, J. C., & Egerton, J. M. (1999). Children's recall 1 or 2 years after an event. *Developmental Psychology, 35*(3), 781–789. doi:10.1037/0012-1649.35.3.781.

Poole, D. A., & Bruck, M. (2012). Divining testimony? The impact of interviewing props on children's reports of touching. *Developmental Review, 32*(3), 165–180. doi:10.1016/j.dr.2012.06.007.

Poole, D. A., & Dickinson, J. J. (2011). Evidence supporting restrictions on uses of body diagrams in forensic interviews. *Child Abuse & Neglect, 35*(9), 659–669. doi:10.1016/j.chiabu.2011.05.004.

Poole, D. A., & Lamb, M. E. (1998). *Investigative interviews of children: A guide for helping professionals.* Washington, DC: American Psychological Association.

Poole, D. A., & Lindsay, D. S. (2001). Children's eyewitness reports after exposure to misinformation from parents. *Journal of Experimental Psychology: Applied, 7*(1), 27–50. doi:10.1037/1076-898X.7.1.27.

Poole, D., & Lindsay, D. S. (2002). Reducing child witnesses' false reports of misinformation from parents. *Journal of Experimental Child Psychology, 81*(2), 117–140. doi:10.1006/jecp.2001.2648.

Powell, M. B., Hughes-Scholes, C. H., & Sharman, S. J. (2012). Skill in interviewing reduces confirmation bias. *Journal of Investigative Psychology and Offender Profiling, 9*(2), 126–134. doi:10.1002/jip.1357.

Powell, M. B., Jones, C. H., & Campbell, C. (2003). A comparison of preschooler's recall of experienced events versus non-experienced events across multiple interviews. *Applied Cognitive Psychology, 17*(8), 935–952. doi:10.1002/acp.932.

Principe, G. F., & Ceic, S. J. (2002). "I saw it with my own ears": The effects of peer conversations on preschoolers' reports of nonexperienced events. *Journal of Experimental Child Psychology, 83*(1), 1–25. doi:10.1016/S0022-0965(02)00120-0.

Principe, G. F., DiPuppo, J., & Gammel, J. (2013). Effects of mothers' conversation style and receipt of misinformation on children's event reports. *Cognitive Development, 28*(3), 260–271. doi:10.1016/j.cogdev.2013.01.012.

Principe, G. F., & Schindewolf, E. (2012). Natural conversations as a source of false memories in children: Implications for the testimony of young witnesses. *Developmental Review, 32*(3), 205–223. doi:10.1016/j.dr.2012.06.003.

Raskin, D. C., & Esplin, P. W. (1991). Statement validity assessment: Interview procedures and content analysis of children's statements of sexual abuse. *Behavioral Assessment, 13*(3), 265–291. Retrieved from http://psycnet.apa.org/psycinfo/1992-33513-001.

Rosenthal, R. (1994). Interpersonal expectancy effects: A 30-year perspective. *Current Directions in Psychological Science, 3*(6), 176–179. doi:10.1111/1467-8721.ep10770698.

Rosenthal, R., & Rubin, D. B. (1978). Interpersonal expectancy effects: The first 345 studies. *Behavioral and Brain Sciences, 1*(3), 377–415. doi:10.1017/S0140525X00075506.

Russell, A. (2004). Forensic interview room set-up. *Half a nation: The newsletter of the state & national finding words courses*, 1–8. Retrieved from https://www.cornerhousemn.org

Salmon, K., & Pipe, M.-E. (2000). Recalling an event one year later: The impact of props, drawing and a prior interview. *Applied Cognitive Psychology, 14*(2), 99–120. doi:10.1002/(SICI)1099-0720(200003/04)14:2<99::AID-ACP639>3.0.CO;2-5.

Saywitz, K. J., & Camparo, L. (1998). Interviewing child witnesses: A developmental perspective. *Child Abuse & Neglect, 22*(8), 825–843. doi:10.1016/S0145-2134(98)00054-4.

Saywitz, K. J., Lyon, T. D., & Goodman, G. S. (2011). Interviewing children. In J. E. B. Myers (Ed.), *The APSAC handbook on child maltreatment* (3rd ed.). London, England: Sage.

Smith, K., & Milne, R. (2011). Planning the interview. In M. E. Lamb, D. J. La Rooy, L. C. Malloy, & C. Katz (Eds.), *Children's testimony: A handbook of psychological research and forensic practice* (2nd ed.). Chichester, England: Wiley.

State of Michigan Governor's Task Force on Children's Justice and Department of Human Services. (2004). *State of Michigan Governor's Task Force on Children's Justice and Department of Human Services forensic interviewing protocol*. Retrieved from http://www.mi.gov/documents/dhs/DHS-PUB-0779_211637_7.pdf

Sternberg, K. J., Lamb, M. E., Orbach, Y., Esplin, P. W., & Mitchell, S. (2001). Use of a structured investigative protocol enhances young children's responses to free-recall prompts in the course of forensic interviews. *Journal of Applied Psychology, 86*(5), 997–1005. doi:10.1037/0021-9010.86.5.997.

Steward, M. S., Steward, D. S., Farquhar, L., Myers, J. E. B., Reinhart, M., Welker, J., … Morgan, J. (1996). Interviewing young children about body touch and handling. *Monographs of the Society for Research in Child Development, 61*(4–5), 1–214. doi:10.2307/1166205

Talwar, V., & Crossman, A. M. (2012). Children's lies and their detection: Implications for child witness testimony. *Developmental Review, 32*(4), 337–359. doi:10.1016/j.dr.2012.06.004.

Thompson, W. C., Clarke-Stewart, K. A., & Lepore, S. J. (1997). What did the janitor do? Suggestive interviewing and the accuracy of children's accounts. *Law and Human Behavior, 21*(4), 405–426. doi:10.1023/A:1024859219764.

Wells, G. L., Small, M., Penrod, S. J., Malpass, R. S., Fulero, S. M., & Brimacombe, C. A. E. (1998). Eyewitness identification procedures: Recommendations for lineups and photospreads. *Law and Human Behavior, 22*(6), 603–647. doi:10.1023/A:1025750605807.

Zwiers, M. L., & Morrissette, P. J. (1999). *Effective interviewing of children: A comprehensive guide for counselors and human service workers*. Ann Arbor, MI: Edwards Brothers.

Chapter 12
Avoiding Problems in Child Abuse Interviews and Investigations

Misty C. Duke, Elizabeth R. Uhl, Heather Price, and James M. Wood

In 1983 a mother suffering from serious mental illness alleged that Raymond Buckey, a teacher at the McMartin Preschool in Manhattan Beach, California, had molested her 2½-year-old son (Nathan & Snedeker, 2001). The accusations set off a highly publicized investigation and eventually led to the longest-running criminal trial in United States history. Based on accusations by dozens of children, Buckey, his mother Peggy, and five other preschool workers were charged with multiple counts of sexualabuse. Many children claimed that they had been forced to participate in bizarre events, such as being spirited into tunnels below the school to carry out satanic rituals. Eventually, Raymond and Peggy Buckey were acquitted by a jury and charges against the other defendants were dropped. At the Buckeys' trial their attorneys presented video-recorded interviews of the alleged victims. Jurors later stated that these recordings, which showed interviewers questioning the children in a highly suggestive manner, heavily influenced their verdict to acquit.

Similar stories played out across America in the 1980s and early 1990s at other daycare centers and schools. In many cases, children made bizarre accusations of

M.C. Duke (✉)
Intelligence and National Security Studies, National Security Studies Institute, University of Texas at El Paso, Kelly Hall, 500 W. University Ave., El Paso, TX 79968, USA
e-mail: mcduke@utep.edu

E.R. Uhl
Georgia Southwestern State University, Americus, GA, USA

H. Price
Department of Psychology, University of Regina,
3737 Wascana Parkway, Regina, SK, Canada, S4S 0A2
e-mail: Heather.price@uregina.ca

J.M. Wood
Department of Psychology, University of Texas at El Paso,
500 W. University Ave., El Paso, TX 79968, USA
e-mail: jawood@utep.edu

W.T. O'Donohue, M. Fanetti (eds.), *Forensic Interviews Regarding Child Sexual Abuse*, DOI 10.1007/978-3-319-21097-1_12

satanic abuse against teachers and daycare workers that were eventually discredited, although only after the defendants had spent years in prison. These cases raised important questions: Why would children fabricate such bizarre, detailed stories about child abuse? How could social workers and law enforcement be convinced that the stories were true despite little or no evidence to corroborate them? And perhaps most importantly, what role did suggestive interviewing play in creating these children's allegations of abuse?

In the following years, social scientists have generated a large body of research that sheds light on the factors that contribute to children's suggestibility, that is, their acquiescence to suggestions made by interviewers or other individuals. It is now widely recognized that although child witnesses and victims are often capable of giving reliable reports of their experience, suggestive influences and interviewer pressure can alter these reports and even induce children to make false criminal allegations.

This chapter reviews the kinds of missteps that can contribute to children's suggestibility in cases of suspected sexual abuse. The first part of the chapter explains the dangers of interviewer bias and how it can lead to suggestive questioning. The second part describes the four suggestive questioning techniques that are most commonly used by biased interviewers. The third part discusses additional ways that child abuse investigations can go awry. All three parts of the chapter include recommendations to help interviewers and investigators in sexual abuse cases avoid the pitfalls that we describe. A central task of sexual abuse investigations is to uncover the truth about whether or not abuse has occurred. To achieve this goal, interviewers and investigators must be able to recognize and avoid the mistakes that lead to suggestible responding by children.

Interviewer Bias

According to Maggie Bruck and Stephen Ceci, ground-breaking researchers in the field of suggestibility, interviewer bias constitutes the central and most important characteristic of suggestive child interviews (Bruck & Ceci, 2011). A biased interviewer enters the interviewing room with preconceived ideas—for instance, that the child has been abused. If the child violates these expectations—for instance, by denying abuse—the interviewer may resort to suggestive questioning until the child's reports become more consistent with what the interviewer expects to hear.

Interviewer bias is an example of what psychologists call "confirmation bias," the tendency to one-sidedly seek evidence that confirms one's own preexisting beliefs while ignoring evidence that disconfirms them (Cialdini, 2009; see also Kassin, Dror, & Kukucka, 2013, and following commentaries). Confirmation bias is a common human failing that can be observed every day, for example, when people discuss political topics. However, in a child forensic interview, it can have disastrous effects. A child's statement that confirms the interviewer's preconceived ideas may be accepted uncritically even if it is vague or improbable, whereas a statement disconfirming these ideas is likely to be ignored or discounted.

Confirmation bias can easily give rise to many undesirable interviewer behaviors. A study by Bruck, Ceci, Melnyk, and Finkelberg (1999, as cited by Bruck & Ceci (2011)) demonstrated how a biased interviewer can unwittingly encourage children to give false statements. Participants in the study were 120 preschool children, 90 of whom attended a birthday party with a visitor. The remaining 30 children were not at the party but instead spent time coloring with a visitor.

Interviewers in the study were graduate students recruited from social work and counseling programs who knew that the children had participated in an activity with a visitor but not what it was. Each interviewer was asked to individually question four children to discover what they had done with the visitor. Unknown to the interviewer, the first three children he or she questioned had been at the birthday party but the fourth had not.

The study found that, after questioning the first three children who had attended the party, most interviewers wrongly assumed that the fourth child had also been there. The interviewers then engaged in biased questioning to confirm their faulty preconceptions. In response to these suggestive questions, 60 % of children who had not actually attended the party made false claims to have been there, and 85 % of interviewers wrongly concluded that all four of the children they questioned had attended the party. As this study showed, even well-intentioned child interviewers can become biased and then use suggestive techniques to extract false statements.

Another study by White, Leichtman, and Ceci (1997) illustrates the negative effects of bias. Two professionals, a teacher and social worker, were given a list of activities that had supposedly occurred during a play session by a group of preschoolers. Unknown to the professionals, half of the activities were bogus and had not really occurred. The professionals then questioned the children to learn what had happened during the play session. The study found that interviewers repeatedly used suggestive questions to ask the children about the bogus activities. In response, the children falsely agreed that they had engaged in about 30 % of these activities, some of which involved bodily touch. Further, some children who initially denied that the bogus event occurred later changed their accounts and provided false details about it.

Avoiding Interviewer Bias

Avoiding interviewer bias is not a simple matter because, like any kind of confirmation bias, it is typically accompanied by a lack of awareness. Biased interviewers usually do not realize that they have lost their objectivity or engaged in suggestive questioning, and thus a mere admonition to "avoid bias" is unlikely to be effective in altering their behavior. Instead, law enforcement and child protection agencies should establish training requirements and other procedures to prevent bias (Powell, Hughes-Scholes, & Sharman, 2012), as set forth in the following three recommendations:

1. Agencies should ensure that child interviews are conducted only by individuals who have received formal training in the principles and practice of good interviewing. Because child forensic interviewing is a specialized professional skill, it requires more expertise than can be provided by only on-the-job training and brief workshops. Interviewers need to be closely familiar with professional guidelines (Lamb, 1994) and books (Ceci & Bruck, 1995; Lamb, Hershkowitz, Orbach, & Esplin, 2008; Poole & Lamb, 1998) that provide an in-depth understanding of the child interviewing process and the dangers of suggestiveness.
2. Agencies should develop clear and detailed protocols for child interviews that are based on best practices and consistent with the scientific literature. A structured interview developed at the National Institute of Child Health and Development (NICHD; Lamb et al., 2008) is presently the only interview protocol that has received extensive support in the scientific literature. It can be used without charge and agencies should consider adopting it or using it as a model for their own protocol.
3. Agencies should ensure that all child interviews are recorded. Video recording that clearly shows both parties should be the default, although audio recording is acceptable for brief initial interviews conducted in the field. Experts recommend such recording to ensure that all details in a child's statement are preserved, to reduce the number of times the child is interviewed, and to provide a record which allows assessment of whether or not the interviewer has engaged in biased or suggestive questioning (Lamb, 1994; Poole & Lamb, 1998).

   In some cases investigated by child protection and law enforcement agencies, legitimate doubts can arise regarding the reliability of a particular child's allegations of sexual abuse, either because the child makes vague or improbable statements or because there is reason to suspect that the child has been coached or unduly influenced to make a false report. A common failing of biased interviewers is to ignore obvious indications that a child's statements are unreliable. To avoid such bias, we offer the following additional recommendations.
4. When a child makes statements that are vague, confusing, contradictory, or improbable, the interviewer should follow up by using open-ended questions to clarify the child's statement. Books on interviewing explain how to discuss apparent contradictions with children in a gentle, nonconfrontational way.
5. Sometimes abuse reports are vague and unconvincing because they fail to include a detailed description of any specific incident. For instance, a child may state simply that she was touched by a certain person, but without specifying the surrounding context, the events that led up to the incident, or the words that were spoken. To avoid this problem we recommend that whenever abuse has been alleged, the interviewer should ensure that the child describes at least one specific incident of abuse from beginning to end and with as much detail as possible. For instance, the interviewer might say, "Tell me everything about the last time it happened. Start at the beginning. Tell me where you were and everything that happened." After the child has given a free narrative response, appropriate follow-up questions should be asked to clarify details of the incident and when it occurred.

6. In many agencies it is a common practice for observers to watch child forensic interviews through closed-circuit television from another room. For instance, a police officer may observe an interview and recommend additional questions that may later help in the investigation or prosecution of the case. We recommend that if a child interview is observed in this way, one of the observers should be formally assigned the task, among their other duties, of identifying any problematic aspects of the child's statement and recommending appropriate follow-up questions. For example, if the child has made inconsistent statements, or if there is a possibility that the child has been unduly influenced by an adult to make false allegations, the observer should be responsible for identifying these issues and reminding the interviewer to address them during the interview. Similarly, if the interviewer has failed to get the child to describe a specific incident of abuse the observer should remind the interviewer to do so.
7. Before ending an interview in which a child has disclosed abuse, the interviewer should routinely ask if the child has previously talked with anyone else about the abuse and, if so, to whom and under what circumstances. Such questions are included in the NICHD interview mentioned earlier in this section and can help clarify whether the child may have been exposed to suggestive influences before the interview.
8. Child protection and law enforcement agencies should routinely interview the "first confidante," that is, the first person to whom a child has made a report of abuse (Wood, Nathan, Nezworski, & Uhl, 2009). The first confidante should be asked to describe the circumstances of the disclosure, including his or her recollection of questions posed and what the child said. Recording such interviews is important to preserve details that may later prove essential for evaluating the possibility of undue influence.

Four Suggestive Techniques Commonly Used by Biased Interviewers

Interviewer bias can lead to two characteristic kinds of mistakes: the interviewer may fail to adequately explore evidence that a child's statement is unreliable or may engage in suggestive questioning. The first kind of mistake was discussed in the previous section. Suggestive questioning is the topic of the present section.

A study by Nadja Schreiber and her colleagues (2006) provides a framework for our discussion. These researchers examined interview transcripts from the McMartin Preschool case described at the beginning of this chapter and another case and identified four suggestive techniques used by interviewers: Positive and Negative Consequences, Other People, Inviting Speculation, and Introducing Information.

Extensive research has shown that these four suggestive techniques can lead children to make false statements, including false allegations of wrongdoing against adults (e.g., see Finnila, Mahlberg, Santtila, Sandnabba, & Niemi, 2003; Garven, Wood, Malpass, & Shaw, 1998). The following pages describe each technique in detail, with citations to the relevant research and recommendations for avoiding them.

Positive and Negative Consequences

Positive Consequences and *Negative Consequences* are both suggestive interviewing techniques that involve the use of reinforcement. Positive Consequences involve giving praise or rewards to a child, or indicating that the child can earn such praise or rewards, in return for providing information concerning abuse. Negative Consequences involve expressing disappointment or giving other negative feedback to a child for making statements that the interviewer deems inadequate. Schreiber et al. (2006, p. 27) provide the following examples of *Positive Consequences* from the McMartin Preschool case:

> Interviewer: Oh, you're so smart. I knew you'd remember….
> Interviewer: So I bet if you guys put on your thinking caps, you can help remember it. Now let's make a test of your brain and see how good your memories are.

Garven et al. (1998, p. 349) provide the following example of Negative Consequences, also from the McMartin case:

> Interviewer: "Are you going to be stupid, or are you going to be smart and help us here?"

Negative Consequences can also include expressing doubt about what the child has said ("Are you sure?") or repeating questions in a way that implies that the child's prior statements are incorrect.

A study by Garven, Wood, and Malpass (2000) found that reinforcement in the form of Positive and Negative Consequences can have a strong impact on suggestibility. Preschool children were visited at school by a man introduced as Paco Perez and were later questioned about what he had done. Half of the children received reinforcement for making false allegations of wrongdoing against Paco. Within a few minutes reinforced children acquiesced to 35 % of false allegations whereas non-reinforced children acquiesced to only 12 %. A similar study by Uhl, Wood, and Scullin (2014) found that Positive Consequences and Negative Consequences can affect older children as well, with 40 % of reinforced fourth graders acquiescing to false allegations as compared with only 4 % of non-reinforced children.

Avoiding problems with Positive and Negative Consequences. Many researchers agree that Positive Consequences can be helpful at the very beginning of child interviews if they are used to build rapport and encourage the child to talk (Poole & Lamb, 1998; Seidler & Howie, 1999). However, once the topic of abuse is introduced into an interview, it is important to discontinue giving the child any further positive or negative feedback.

Other People

The Other People technique involves telling a child what other witnesses have already said concerning the events that the child is being questioned about. Schreiber et al. (2006, p. 28) provide the following example from the McMartin Preschool transcripts:

> Interviewer: You see all the kids in this picture? Every single kid in this picture has come here and talked to us. Isn't that amazing? … These kids came to visit us and we found out they know a lot of yucky old secrets from that old school. And they all came and told us the secrets. And they're helping us figure out this whole puzzle of what used to go on in that place …

The Other People technique can influence a child's reports in two ways. First, it can pressure the child to conform with the statements of other witnesses. The child, believing that the other witnesses are correct (Cialdini, 2009) or feeling reluctant to contradict them, may wrongly confirm what they have said. Several studies have shown that both adults and children can be influenced to make false statements if they are exposed to inaccurate information from other witnesses (Carol, 2014; Jones, 2013; Paterson, Kemp, & Ng, 2011; Shaw, Garven, & Wood, 1997).

The Other People technique can also influence a child's statements by increasing the plausibility of a false event. A child must consider a false event plausible before he or she can develop a mistaken memory that it occurred (Mazzoni, Loftus, & Kirsch, 2001). Studies have demonstrated that increasing the plausibility of a false event, even one that is highly improbable, can increase the likelihood that children wrongly believe that it occurred (Otgaar, Smeets, & Peters, 2012; Strange, Sutherland, & Garry, 2006). For example, Otgaar, Candel, Merckelbach, and Wade (2009) told children 7–8 years old that they were abducted by a UFO when they were 4 years old and then provided them with false newspaper articles that discussed the prevalence of UFO abductions. Children who read the newspaper article were twice as likely to report having been abducted by a UFO as were children who did not read it.

Similarly, telling a child that his or her peers have reported abuse may increase the child's belief that he or she *could* have been abused. As the event becomes more plausible, the child may come to accept suggestions of abuse as actual memories. The studies cited earlier have shown that younger children are more susceptible to this effect than older children.

Avoiding problems with Other People. Interviewers sometimes use the Other People technique because they hope to make a child feel more comfortable about disclosing abusive incidents. However, this technique becomes highly suggestive when child witnesses are told the details of other children's reports, thus pressuring them to provide information that is consistent with these reports. While it might be acceptable for an interviewer to inform a child witness at the very beginning of an interview that other children have been questioned, no information should be provided about what these children have said.

Inviting Speculation

Inviting Speculation involves asking a child to offer opinions or speculations about what *could* have happened during an event or to *pretend* that an event occurred. Schreiber et al. (2006, p. 29) provide the following example from the McMartin Preschool transcripts:

Interviewer: Now, I think this is another one of those tricky games. What do you *think*, Rags?

Child: Yep.

Interviewer: Yes. Do you *think* some of that yucky touching happened, Rags, when she was tied up and she couldn't get away? Do you *think* some of that touching that—Mr. Ray *might* have done some of that touching? Do you think that's *possible*? Where do you *think* he *would have* touched her? Can you use your pointer and show us where he *would have* touched her? [Emphasis added]

Several studies have examined the effects of Inviting Speculation on children's memories. For instance, in a study by Ackil and Zaragoza (1998) half of the children interviewed about a video were forced to make up false answers in response to unanswerable questions. For example, when asked "What present did the boy get for his birthday?" these children had to provide a response, even though the video did not depict a boy receiving a present for his birthday. The remaining children in the study were asked the same unanswerable questions but allowed to answer "I don't know."

When children were interviewed a second time by a different interviewer, they were informed that the first interviewer had made some mistakes and that the children needed to help the new interviewer find out what really happened in the video. Children who had been forced to generate false answers made twice as many memory errors during this second interview than children who were allowed to say "I don't know." Several other studies have found similar negative effects of Inviting Speculation on children's accuracy, even when they are no longer being encouraged to speculate (Krähenbühl & Blades, 2006; Poole & White, 1991; Schreiber & Parker, 2004; Shapiro & Purdy, 2005; Stolzenberg & Pezdek, 2013). These findings indicate that children will make up responses to questions if asked to do so and may later misinterpret these fabricated details as actual memories.

Avoiding problems with Inviting Speculation. Garven et al. (1998) note that Inviting Speculation was typically used by the interviewers in the McMartin Preschool case after other techniques had failed to elicit accusations from children. However, rather than yielding accurate information, this technique yields fabricated information that children may later come to believe is true. Therefore, interviewers should refrain entirely from asking children to speculate or pretend. If a child witness has repeatedly denied the occurrence of abuse, interviewers should normally accept the denials at face value rather than resorting to a technique that is likely to produce false memories.

Introducing Information

The technique of Introducing Information is similar to what lawyers call "leading questions." It involves the introduction into an interview of accurate or inaccurate information that has not been previously mentioned by the child. Schreiber et al. (2006, p. 29) provide the following example from the McMartin Preschool transcripts:

Interviewer: How about Naked Movie Star? You guys remember that game?
Child: No.
Interviewer: Everybody remembered that game. Let's see if we can figure it out.

As noted by Schreiber et al. (2006), Introducing Information overlaps with some of the other suggestive techniques that have already been discussed here. Referred to by some researchers as *suggestive questioning* or *postevent misinformation*, it has been studied extensively with both adults (see Garry & Loftus, 1994 and Ayers & Reder, 1998 for reviews) and children (Otgaar, Candel, Smeets, & Merckelbach, 2010; Sutherland & Hayne, 2001; see Bruck & Ceci, 1999 for a review). For example, in a study by Leichtman and Ceci (1995) a fictional character named Sam Stone visited nursery schools for a brief staged event. Children were interviewed about true and false aspects of the visit using one of four types of interviews: (a) the *control* interview, which used nonsuggestive questions; (b) the *stereotype* interview, which repeatedly introduced children to a stereotype about Sam as clumsy and used nonsuggestive questions; (c) the *highly suggestive* interview, which used suggestive questions (i.e., "When Sam Stone got that bear dirty did he do it on purpose or was it an accident?"); or (d) the *stereotype plus highly suggestive* interview, in which children were given a stereotype about Sam and interviewed using suggestive questions. Children given the *stereotype plus highly suggestive* interview were most likely to agree with inaccurate details about Sam's visit. Children given the *suggestive* interview were more likely than children given the *control* interview to agree with these inaccurate details. Other studies have generally produced similar results, showing that Introducing Information reduces the accuracy of children's reports and that younger children are especially vulnerable to its negative effects.

Avoiding problemswith Introducing Information. Interviewers rarely know "ground truth" when questioning a child about abuse. Thus, when they introduce information during an interview, they cannot be sure whether or not the information is accurate. Inaccurate information can become part of the child's report because some children, particularly preschoolers, misinterpret it as real memories (see *Introducing Imagery* for a description of reality monitoring). To avoid creating inaccurate memories, interviewers should refrain from using this technique.

Speaking more generally, the same agency procedures recommended earlier in this chapter to prevent interviewer bias can also help prevent the use of Introducing Information and other suggestive techniques: (1) rely on well-trained interviewers who are familiar with professional guidelines and standard textbooks on child interviewing, (2) formally adopt a scientifically tested interview protocol, and (3) make video or audio recordings of all interviews.

Other Problems in Child Abuse Interviews and Investigations

Interviewer bias and suggestive questioning, the topics covered in the preceding sections, account for a large proportion of the problems that occur in child abuse investigations. However, other less common mistakes sometimes lead child abuse investigations astray, as discussed in this section.

Failure to Consider Disconfirming Evidence

Some child abuse cases go awry because investigators have uncritically accepted children's statements as true without considering other physical, medical, and documentary evidence. For example, in the McMartin Preschool case some children claimed to have been taken into tunnels underneath their school and made to participate in satanic rituals. Extensive searches by law enforcement officials, including digs conducted by teams of archeologists, failed to uncover any tunnels. Despite this disconfirming evidence, officials and many members of the community steadfastly maintained their belief in the children's reports (Nathan & Snedeker, 2001), an example of confirmation bias as discussed earlier in this chapter.

In more than half of child sexual abuse cases, the child's statement is the only evidence of abuse. However, in a substantial minority of cases there is additional evidence to confirm the child's statement. In a review of 894 cases of alleged child abuse, Herman (2010) found that when a child made an allegation of abuse there was a 40 % probability that it was corroborated by external evidence such as a confession by the perpetrator, statements from another eyewitness, or medical evidence.

In cases of alleged child abuse, it is important to consider evidence that tends to either confirm or disconfirm the child's statement. For example, in a high-profile case in Bakersfield, California, two parents were accused of bizarre abuse (Nathan & Snedeker, 2001). At trial their children described being hung from hooks impaled in their backs. If these allegations were true there should have been scarring on the children's backs, but no such evidence was presented by prosecutors. This lack of corroborating physical evidence should have raised grave questions concerning the reliability of the children's testimony. Especially in cases that involve bizarre or improbable accusations, investigators should actively seek and evaluate corroborative and noncorroborative evidence before evaluating the allegations.

Multiple Interviews

There is no doubt that multiple interviews with a biased interviewer can lead to inaccurate statements and create false memories (see Ceci, Huffman, Smith, & Loftus, 1994, and Ceci, Loftus, Leichtman, & Bruck, 1994 for early research on this issue). In fact, research has demonstrated that just one interview with a biased interviewer can lead to false accusations, especially when some of the other techniques identified in this chapter, such as reinforcement, have been used (Garven et al., 2000).

However, some research suggests that multiple interviews may have neutral or even positive effects on memory if they are conducted without any bias or suggestive techniques. For example, La Rooy, Pipe, and Murray (2005) found that repeated interviews of 5- and 6-year-olds with open-ended prompts produced a reminiscence effect, that is, new information was obtained in subsequent interviews. More research is necessary to clarify the impact of repeated interviews. Goodman and

Quas (2008) suggest that merely examining the impact of repeated interviews may not be enough, and that other factors, such as bias, social pressure, and delays must also be considered in order to understand the impact of repeated interviews on children's accuracy.

Suggestive Therapy

In a small proportion of cases seen by protective agencies, children deny victimization to interviewers even though there is strong suspicion that abuse has occurred (e.g., the child may have privately made allegations to a friend). Occasionally, the children in such cases are assumed to be "in denial" and referred for therapy to help them "disclose."

There are several reasons why it is inadvisable to put "strongly suspected" children in therapy for the purpose of encouraging disclosure. First, many of these children may not have been abused. A strong suspicion is not the same as certainty, and thus in some unknown proportion of suspected cases, even the "strongly suspected" ones, the suspicion is wrong.

Second, therapy to encourage disclosure is questionable from an ethical point of view. Such therapy typically has the covert goal of producing evidence that can be used in legal proceedings. However, this *forensic* goal can interfere with *therapeutic* goals, such as making the child felt understood and providing emotional support in difficult circumstances.

Third, a therapist who sets out to elicit a disclosure is by definition engaging in a form of confirmation bias and thus is likely to engage in suggestive techniques. Suggestive questioning by a therapist is particularly problematic from a legal perspective because therapy sessions, unlike child forensic interviews, are not usually recorded.

For these reasons, we strongly recommend against referring children to therapy in order to encourage disclosure. Instead, we recommend an alternative procedure adopted by many agencies: if a child is strongly suspected of having been abused but has not made an allegation to investigators, a referral should be made to a well-trained therapist for supportive counseling. The goal of therapy should be to provide a secure relationship in which the child can discuss important problems and worries. The therapist should not attempt to elicit a disclosure from the child, initiate discussions of abuse, or imply that the child may have been victimized. Instead, by focusing on the child's current concerns, a skilled therapist can provide practical guidance and emotional support, thus creating a safe space in which the child may eventually feel comfortable enough to disclose abuse, if abuse has in fact occurred.

If a child has not made allegations, it is also important to protect her or him from other suggestive or biased influences. For example, parents and other caregivers should be advised to provide emotional support to the child but without initiating discussions of abuse. If the child initiates a discussion of abuse, parents should arrange for the child to discuss the topic with the therapist.

Encouraging Children to Create Imagery

Child interviewers and child therapists sometimes ask children to imagine, draw, or spend time thinking about an event in order to help them remember its details. All these activities create mental imagery (Ceci, Huffman et al., 1994; Ceci, Loftus et al., 1994; Quas, Schaaf, Alexander, & Goodman, 2000).

Reality monitoring refers to a person's ability to distinguish between events they have actually experienced versus events they have only imagined. Research has demonstrated that the reality monitoring skills of young children are much poorer than those of older children and adults (Markham, Howie, & Hlavacek, 1999; Welch-Ross, 1995). For instance, a study by Foley and Johnson (1985) had children imagine, pretend, or "think real hard" about performing some actions and actually perform other actions. For example, children imagined making a sad face but actually did a jumping jack. The children also imagined and watched other people performing certain actions. For example, they imagined a person touching his or her own nose but actually witnessed a person running in place.

Later the children were asked to identify which actions actually happened and which were imagined. Compared with adults, 6- and 9-year-old children were equally poor in discriminating between performed and imagined actions. In other words, the children confused real actions with actions they only imagined. This and other studies on reality monitoring indicate that asking a child to imagine or pretend that a false event occurred can cause the child to believe that the event actually occurred. Other techniques involving the creation of imagery, such as drawing pictures or providing children with photographs of an event, can also cause children to believe that imagined events really occurred (Bruck, Melnyk, & Ceci, 2000; Strange, Garry, & Sutherland, 2003; Strange, Hayne, & Garry, 2008). For this reason, it is inadvisable to gather forensically relevant information from children by encouraging creation of imagery.

Anatomical Dolls

The use of anatomical dolls in forensic interviews with children has generated considerable controversy. On the one hand, experts advocating the use of anatomical dolls have pointed to their use in aiding memory retrieval and making children feel comfortable disclosing abuse (Everson & Boat, 1997). On the other hand, researchers opposed to the use of anatomical dolls express doubts whether the dolls are useful for generating accurate information and argue that the dolls may increase children's suggestibility, particularly if combined with suggestive questioning methods (Ceci & Bruck, 1994; Everson & Boat, 1997).

Research on the usefulness of anatomical dolls has yielded mixed results (see Aldridge, 1998; Everson & Boat, 1997; Salmon, 2001 for reviews). Most studies have found that nonabused children rarely use the dolls for explicit sex play, although they may explore the dolls in a manner that could be misconstrued as sexual, for example, by exploring the doll's anus. Some studies have found that children interviewed using anatomical dolls reveal more information about events than children interviewed without the dolls (i.e., Goodman, Quas, Batterman-Faunce, Riddlesberger, & Kuhn, 1997), but other studies have not found such an effect (i.e., Lamb, Hershkowitz, Sternberg, Boat, & Everson, 1996).

Part of the disagreement regarding the use of anatomical dolls stems from the disparate ways in which they are used. In a study examining actual forensic interviews with anatomical dolls, Thierry, Lamb, Orbach, and Pipe (2005; see also Santila, Korkman, & Sandnabba, 2004) found that different interviewers introduced the dolls at different points in the interview and used different approaches when questioning children about them. These variations in use create difficulty in assessing the reliability and validity of anatomical dolls as a tool for identifying abuse.

Despite the mixed findings, research on anatomical dolls tends to converge on one important point: the dolls should not be used with children ages 3½ years or younger (Ceci & Bruck, 1994; Everson & Boat, 1997). These young children are especially likely to produce inaccurate reports when anatomical dolls are used (Thierry, Lamb, Orbach, & Pipe, 2005).

There is no conclusive evidence that anatomical dolls elicit more information, or more accurate information, than can be gathered during a well-conducted child interview, nor is there convincing evidence that abuse can be diagnosed by watching children play with the dolls. On the other hand, very little research shows that the dolls can cause a child to report inaccurate sexual details, unless the child is questioned suggestively or is 3½ years old or younger. In addition, the available research indicates that the dolls may be helpful for very limited purposes, such as a memory stimulus for older children (Everson & Boat, 1997). Given the limited usefulness of anatomical dolls and the controversy surrounding them, we recommend against their routine use in child interviews, especially with younger children. If the dolls are used, interviewers should be careful not to engage in suggestive questioning and should not attempt to diagnose abuse based on the child's doll play.

Social Contagion, Community Panic, and "Reporter Zero"

Social contagion and community panic occur when highly disturbing and "contagious" false ideas are spread among members of a community or other social group (Harrigan, Achananuparp, & Lim, 2012). Such contagion often occurs in high-profile sexual abuse cases that involve schools, day care centers, multiple alleged victims, or multiple alleged perpetrators. Although such cases occur only infrequently, they typically have devastating consequences for everyone concerned, including children, parents, and the accused.

The McMartin case described at the beginning of this chapter illustrates the way that social contagion can occur (Wood et al., 2009). After receiving an initial allegation against Raymond Buckey, police mailed letters to more than 200 parents urging them to question their children about possible molestation at the preschool. The letters set off a panic within the community. Many distraught parents engaged in suggestive questioning of their children that generated numerous false accusations of abuse against Buckey and the other McMartin teachers. These accusations were shared among parents, who then engaged in even more suggestive questioning and generated even more false accusations. Thus, through a process of social contagion, many parents and law enforcement officials became convinced that the children were victims of sinister organized abuse. The fact that the children's reports were often bizarre, inconsistent, and lacked corroborating evidence did little to reduce the effects of the contagion. The panic was further inflamed by a flurry of sensationalist media reports about the prevalence of ritual satanic abuse (Nathan & Snedeker, 2001; see also Beckett, 1996).

Epidemics involving cholera or other infectious diseases can often be traced back to a single person, referred to by epidemiologists as "patient zero," who is the initial source of infection. Similarly, community panics involving sexual abuse accusations can usually be traced back to a single adult of questionable credibility who reported the first false allegations or induced a child to make them. We will refer to this person as "reporter zero." For instance, "reporter zero" in the McMartin case was a parent suffering from schizophrenia. In other high-profile cases, the role of "reporter zero" has been played by a parent involved in a bitter custody dispute, a woman who held a long-standing grudge against the accused perpetrator, or a "serial accuser" who previously had made ill-founded allegations of abuse against other individuals.

Panics involving sexual abuse, like deadly epidemics, are relatively rare. However, because of their devastating consequences they call for a thoughtful and effective response. We offer six recommendations to child protection and law enforcement agencies to help prevent panics and minimize the effects of social contagion.

1. Before broadening an investigation of sexual abuse accusations involving multiple victims or multiple perpetrators, agency officials should carefully evaluate the credibility of the initial allegations. Extreme caution is appropriate if (a) the initial victim has supposedly reported abuse outside the interviewing room but failed to repeat the allegations when formally interviewed; (b) the alleged victim has sometimes denied abuse or made seriously inconsistent statements; (c) the accusations are vague, bizarre, or improbable; (d) there is reason to suspect that the accusations are the result of coaching, suggestive questioning, or other undue influence by an adult ("reporter zero"); or (e) the accusations lack corroborating evidence or are inconsistent with known facts.
2. We have already recommended that the first confidante—that is, the first person to whom a child discloses abuse—should always be interviewed about how the disclosure was made and the exact wording of what was said, including the questions of the first confidante and the statements of the child. The same recommendation applies to "reporter zero" in cases that have a potential for creating community panic. Investigators should consider the psychosocial history and credibility of "reporter zero" when evaluating evidence in the case.

3. If investigators deem it necessary to broaden the investigation and interview additional children regarding the accusations, these new interviews should be carried out individually by well-trained interviewers and within a very short period of time. Established agency procedures should be carefully followed and interviews should be recorded. Parents should be notified only after interviews are complete.
4. In such interviews, interviewers should systematically inquire not only about the alleged abuse but also about possible social contagion, for instance, by asking "Who else have you talked with about [the alleged perpetrator]? Have you heard about [the alleged perpetrator] doing bad things to other people? How did you hear? Tell me everything you heard."
5. Information released to parents and the media should be free from specific details about the allegations, including any inflammatory information that could create a panic. Additionally, when releasing information, investigators should request that parents *not* interview their children about the abuse.
6. Any additional accusations that are made after the release of information should be evaluated with special care because they are likely to have been influenced by social contagion.

Conclusions

In this chapter, we have tried to inform interviewers and investigators in child abuse cases about factors that can create serious errors in sexual abuse investigations. Interviewer bias was identified as the central characteristic of suggestive interviewing, and four suggestive techniques used by biased interviewers were discussed. Several other problematic procedures were described that can lead to erroneous decisions in child sexual abuse investigations.

This chapter presented examples from high-profile abuse investigations in which a convergence of poor investigation methodology, biased interviewers, suggestive interviewing, and social contagion led to false accusations of abuse against multiple perpetrators. Such cases are fairly rare. However, investigators and interviewers can learn from the mistakes made during these investigations and become better equipped to protect children from those who would do them harm.

References

Ackil, J. K., & Zaragoza, M. S. (1998). Memorial consequences of forced confabulation: Age differences in susceptibility to false memories. *Developmental Psychology, 34*(6), 1358–1372. doi:10.1037/0012-1649.34.6.1358.

Aldridge, N. C. (1998). Strengths and limitations of forensic child sexual abuse interviews with anatomical dolls: An empirical review. *Journal of Psychopathology and Behavioral Assessment, 20*(1), 1–41. doi:10.1023/A:1023084525733.

Ayers, M. S., & Reder, L. M. (1998). A theoretical review of the misinformation effect: Predictions from an activation-based memory model. *Psychonomic Bulletin & Review, 5*(1), 1–21. doi:10.3758/BF03209454.

Beckett, K. (1996). Culture and the politics of signification: The case of child sexual abuse. *Social Problems, 43*(1), 57–76. doi:10.1525/sp.1996.43.1.03x0336x.

Bruck, M., & Ceci, S. J. (1999). The suggestibility of children's memory. *Annual Review of Psychology, 50*, 419–439. doi:10.1146/annurev.psych.50.1.419.

Bruck, M., & Ceci, S. J. (2011). Forensic developmental psychology in the courtroom. In D. Faust (Ed.), *Coping with psychiatric and psychological testimony* (6th ed., pp. 723–736). New York, NY: Oxford University Press.

Bruck, M., Ceci, S. J., Melnyk, L., & Finkelberg, D. (1999, March). *The effect of interviewer bias on the accuracy of children's reports and interviewers' reports.* Paper presented at the Biennial Meeting of the Society for Child Development. Albuquerque, NM.

Bruck, M., Melnyk, L., & Ceci, S. J. (2000). Draw it again Sam: The effect of drawing on children's suggestibility and source monitoring ability. *Journal of Experimental Child Psychology, 77*(3), 169–196. doi:10.1006/jecp.1999.2560.

Carol, R. (2014). *'Other people' and suggestibility: A child's age predicts a source's influence.* Manuscript in preparation.

Ceci, S. J., & Bruck, M. (1994). How reliable are children's statements? It depends. *Family Relations, 43*(3), 255–257. doi:10.2307/585411.

Ceci, S. J., & Bruck, M. (1995). *Jeopardy in the courtroom: A scientific analysis of children's testimony.* Washington, D.C.: American Psychological Association.

Ceci, S. J., Huffman, M. L. C., Smith, E., & Loftus, E. F. (1994). Repeatedly thinking about a non-event: Source misattributions among preschoolers. *Consciousness and Cognition, 3*(3–4), 388–407. doi:10.1006/ccog.1994.1022.

Ceci, S. J., Loftus, E. F., Leichtman, M. D., & Bruck, M. (1994). The possible role of source misattributions in the creation of false beliefs among preschoolers. *International Journal of Clinical and Experimental Hypnosis, 42*(4), 304–320. doi:10.1080/00207149408409361.

Cialdini, R. B. (2009). *Influence: Science and practice* (5th ed.). Boston, MA: Pearson. ISBN 9780205609994.

Everson, M. D., & Boat, B. W. (1997). Anatomical dolls in child sexual abuse assessments: A call for forensically relevant research. *Applied Cognitive Psychology, 11*, S55–S74. doi:10.1002/(SICI)1099-0720(199712)11:7<S55::AID-ACP521>3.0.CO;2-P.

Finnila, K., Mahlberg, N., Santtila, P., Sandnabba, K., & Niemi, P. (2003). Validity of a test of children's suggestibility for predicting responses to two interview situations differing in their degree of suggestiveness. *Journal of Experimental Child Psychology, 85*, 32–49. doi:10.1016/S0022-0965(03)00025-0.

Foley, M. A., & Johnson, M. K. (1985). Confusions between memories for performed and imagined actions: A developmental comparison. *Child Development, 56*, 1145–1155.

Garry, M., & Loftus, E. F. (1994). Pseudomemories without hypnosis. *International Journal of Clinical and Experimental Hypnosis, 42*(4), 363–378. doi:10.1080/00207149408409365.

Garven, S., Wood, J. M., Malpass, R. S., & Shaw, J. S., III. (1998). More than suggestion: The effect of interviewing techniques from the McMartin preschool case. *Journal of Applied Psychology, 83*(3), 347–359. doi:10.1037/0021-9010.83.3.347.

Garven, S., Wood, J. M., & Malpass, R. S. (2000). Allegations of wrongdoing: The effects of reinforcement on children's mundane and fantastic claims. *Journal of Applied Psychology, 85*(1), 38–49.

Goodman, G. S., & Quas, J. A. (2008). Repeated interviews and children's memory: It's more than just how many. *Current Directions in Psychology Science, 17*(6), 386–390. doi:10.1111/j.1467-8721.2008.00611.

Goodman, G. S., Quas, J. A., Batterman-Faunce, J., Riddlesberger, M. M., & Kuhn, J. (1997). Children's reactions to and memory for a stressful event: Influences of age, anatomical dolls, knowledge, and parental attachment. *Applied Developmental Science, 1*(2), 54–75. doi:10.1207/s1532480xads0102_1.

Harrigan, N., Achananuparp, P., & Lim, E. (2012). Influentials, novelty, and social contagion: The viral power of average friends, close communities, and old news. *Social Networks, 34*(4), 470–480. doi:10.1016/j.socnet.2012.02.005.

Herman, S. (2010). The role of corroborative evidence in child sexual abuse evaluations. *Journal of Investigative Psychology and Offender Profiling, 7*, 189–213. doi:10.1002/jip.122.

Jones, R. L. (2013). *The effect of co-witness information and individual differences in cognitive abilities on the suggestibility of pre-school children* (Doctoral dissertation). UMI number 3609492.

Kassin, S. M., Dror, I. E., & Kukucka, J. (2013). The forensic confirmation bias: Problems, perspectives, and proposed solutions. *Journal of Applied Research in Memory and Cognition, 2*, 42–52.

Krähenbühl, S., & Blades, M. (2006). The effect of question repetition within interviews on young children's eyewitness recall. *Journal of Experimental Child Psychology, 94*(1), 57–67. doi:10.1016/j.jecp.2005.12.002.

La Rooy, D., Pipe, M. E., & Murray, J. E. (2005). Reminiscence and hypermnesia in children's eyewitness memory. *Journal of Experimental Child Psychology, 90*, 235–254. doi:10.1016/j.jecp.2004.11.002.

Lamb, M. E. (1994). The investigation of child sexual abuse: An interdisciplinary consensus statement. *Child Abuse & Neglect, 18*, 1021–1028.

Lamb, M. E., Hershkowitz, I., Orbach, Y., & Esplin, P. W. (2008). *Tell me what happened: Structured investigative interviews of child victims and witnesses*. Mahwah, NJ: Wiley. ISBN 978-0-470-51866-3.

Lamb, M. E., Hershkowitz, I., Sternberg, K. J., Boat, B., & Everson, M. D. (1996). Investigative interviews of alleged sexual abuse victims with and without anatomical dolls. *Child Abuse & Neglect, 20*(12), 1251–1259. doi:10.1016/S0145-2134(96)00121-4.

Leichtman, M. D., & Ceci, S. J. (1995). The effects of stereotypes and suggestions on preschoolers' reports. *Developmental Psychology, 31*(4), 568–578. doi:10.1037/0012-1649.31.4.568.

Markham, R., Howie, P., & Hlavacek, S. (1999). Reality monitoring in auditory and visual modalities: Developmental trends and effects of cross-modal imagery. *Journal of Experimental Child Psychology, 72*(1), 51–70. doi:10.1006/jecp.1998.2476.

Mazzoni, G. A. L., Loftus, E. F., & Kirsch, I. (2001). Changing beliefs about implausible autobiographical events: A little plausibility goes a long way. *Journal of Experimental Psychology: Applied, 7*(1), 51–59. doi:10.1037/1076-898X.7.1.51.

Nathan, D., & Snedeker, M. (2001). *Satan's silence: Ritual abuse and the making of the modern American witch hunt*. San Jose, CA: Author's Choice Press. ISBN 0-595-18955-5.

Otgaar, H., Candel, I., Merckelbach, H., & Wade, K. A. (2009). Abducted by a UFO: Prevalence information affects young children's false memories for an implausible event. *Applied Cognitive Psychology, 23*(1), 115–125. doi:10.1002/acp.1445.

Otgaar, H., Candel, I., Smeets, T., & Merckelbach, H. (2010). 'You didn't take Lucy's skirt off': The effect of misleading information on omissions and commissions in children's memory reports. *Legal and Criminological Psychology, 15*(2), 229–241. doi:10.1348/135532509X471951.

Otgaar, H., Smeets, T., & Peters, M. (2012). Children's implanted false memories and additional script knowledge. *Applied Cognitive Psychology, 26*(5), 709–715. doi:10.1002/acp.2849.

Paterson, H. M., Kemp, R. I., & Ng, J. R. (2011). Combating co-witness contamination: Attempting to decrease the negative effects of discussion on eyewitness memory. *Applied Cognitive Psychology, 25*(1), 43–52. doi:10.1002/acp.1640.

Poole, D. A., & Lamb, M. E. (1998). *Investigative interviews of children: A guide for helping professionals*. Washington, D.C.: American Psychological Association.

Poole, D. A., & White, L. T. (1991). Effects of question repetition on the eyewitness testimony of children and adults. *Developmental Psychology, 27*, 975–986. doi:10.1037/0012-1649.27.6.975.

Powell, M. B., Hughes-Scholes, C. H., & Sharman, S. J. (2012). Skill in interviewing reduces confirmation bias. *Journal of Investigative Psychology and Offender Profiling, 9*, 126–134.

Quas, J. A., Schaaf, J. M., Alexander, K. W., & Goodman, G. S. (2000). Do you really remember it happening or do you only remember being asked about it happening? Children's source monitoring in forensic contexts. In K. P. Roberts & M. Blades (Eds.), *Children's source monitoring*. Mahwah, NJ: Lawrence Erlbaum Associates.

Salmon, K. (2001). Remembering and reporting by children: The influence of cues and props. *Clinical Psychology Review, 21*(2), 267–300. doi:10.1016/S0272-7358(99)00048-3.

Santila, P., Korkman, J., & Sandnabba, N. K. (2004). Effects of interview phase, repeated interviewing, presence of a support person, and anatomically detailed dolls on child sexual abuse interviews. *Psychology Crime and Law, 10*, 21–35. doi:10.1080/1068316021000044365.

Schreiber, N., Bellah, L. D., Martinez, Y., McLaurin, K. A., Strok, R., Garven, S., & Wood, J. M. (2006). Suggestive interviewing in the McMartin Preschool and Kelly Michaels Daycare abuse cases: A case study. *Social Influence, 1*(1), 16–47. doi:10.1080/15534510500361739

Schreiber, N., & Parker, J. F. (2004). Inviting witnesses to speculate: Effects of age and interaction on children's recall. *Journal of Experimental Child Psychology, 89*, 31–52.

Seidler, K. M., & Howie, P. M. (1999). Motivational factors in children's reporting of events: The influence of age and expected reinforcement contingency. *Journal of Applied Developmental Psychology, 20*, 101–118. doi:10.1016/S0193-3973(99)80006-9.

Shapiro, L. R., & Purdy, T. L. (2005). Suggestibility and source monitoring errors: Blame the interview style, interviewer consistency, and the child's personality. *Applied Cognitive Psychology, 19*(4), 489–506. doi:10.1002/acp.1093.

Shaw, J. S. I., II, Garven, S., & Wood, J. M. (1997). Co-witness information can have immediate effects on eyewitness memory reports. *Law and Human Behavior, 21*(5), 503–523. doi:10.1023/A:1024875723399.

Stolzenberg, S., & Pezdek, K. (2013). Interviewing child witnesses: The effect of forced confabulation on event memory. *Journal of Experimental Child Psychology, 114*(1), 77–88. doi:10.1016/j.jecp.2012.09.006.

Strange, D., Garry, M., & Sutherland, R. (2003). Drawing out children's false memories. *Applied Cognitive Psychology, 17*(5), 607–619. doi:10.1002/acp.911.

Strange, D., Hayne, H., & Garry, M. (2008). A photo, a suggestion, a false memory. *Applied Cognitive Psychology, 22*(5), 587–603. doi:10.1002/acp.1390.

Strange, D., Sutherland, R., & Garry, M. (2006). Event plausibility does not determine children's false memories. *Memory, 14*(8), 937–951. doi:10.1080/09658210600896105.

Sutherland, R., & Hayne, H. (2001). Age-related changes in the misinformation effect. *Journal of Experimental Child Psychology, 79*(4), 388–404. doi:10.1006/jecp.2000.2610.

Thierry, K. L., Lamb, M. E., Orbach, Y., & Pipe, M. (2005). Developmental differences in the function and use of anatomical dolls during interviews with alleged sexual abuse victims. *Journal of Consulting and Clinical Psychology, 73*(6), 1125–1134. doi:10.1037/0022-006X.73.6.1125.

Uhl, E. R., Wood, J. M., & Scullin, M. H. (2014). *The effect of reinforcement on suggestibility among older children*. Manuscript submitted for publication.

Welch-Ross, M. (1995). Developmental changes in preschoolers' ability to distinguish memories of performed, pretended, and imagined actions. *Cognitive Development, 10*(3), 421–441. doi:10.1016/0885-2014(95)90005-5.

White, T. L., Leichtman, M. D., & Ceci, S. J. (1997). The good, the bad, and the ugly: Accuracy, inaccuracy, and elaboration in preschoolers' reports about a past event. *Applied Cognitive Psychology, 11*, S37–S54. doi:10.1002/(SICI)1099-0720(199712)11:7<S37::AID-ACP546>3.0.CO;2-4.

Wood, J. M., Nathan, D., Nezworski, M. T., & Uhl, E. (2009). Child sexual abuse investigations: Lessons learned from the McMartin and other daycare cases. In B. L. Bottoms, C. J. Najdowski, & G. S. Goodman (Eds.), *Children as victims, witnesses, and offenders: Psychological science and the law* (pp. 81–101). New York, NY: Guilford Press.

Chapter 13
Review of Psychometrics of Forensic Interview Protocols with Children

Olga Cirlugea and William T. O'Donohue

Review of Psychometrics of Forensic Interview Protocols with Children

There is a misperception that if a child has been sexually abused there usually will be medical evidence corroborating the abuse (Frasier & Makoroff, 2006). If that were the case, there would be less need to subject children to an interview; however, research indicates that only about 4 % of all child sexual abuse (CSA) investigations produce medical evidence such as genital anomalies, bruising and cuts supporting the occurrence of the abuse (e.g., Berenson et al., 2000; Heger, Ticson, Velasquez, & Bernier, 2002). Even with physical evidence key questions remain: Who was the perpetrator? How many times did the abuse occur? In what jurisdiction did the abuse occur? When did the abuse occur? Did any adult know of this abuse and failed to stop it? This key information can only be gathered through an interview with the child. The forensic interview also can provide a safe and supportive environment for disclosure to occur and can facilitate disclosure. Children sometimes do not disclose abuse, at least not immediately. For example, Malloy and colleagues (Malloy, Brubacher, & Lamb, 2011) found that 20 % disclosures occurred within 1 month of the alleged abuse, and an additional 57 % occurred up to several years after the event.

O. Cirlugea, B.A. (✉)
Department of Psychology, University of Nevada, Reno, MS 0296, Reno, NV 89557, USA
e-mail: olgacirlugea@gmail.com

W.T. O'Donohue, Ph.D.
Department of Psychology, Victims of Crime Treatment Center, University of Nevada, Reno, MS 0296, Reno, NV 89557, USA
e-mail: wto@unr.edu

W.T. O'Donohue, M. Fanetti (eds.), *Forensic Interviews Regarding Child Sexual Abuse*, DOI 10.1007/978-3-319-21097-1_13

Egregious Examples of Problems in Interviewing

Even though the American Educational Research Association encourages that "those who select tests and interpret test results should refrain from introducing biases that accommodate individuals or groups with a vested interest in decisions affected by the test interpretation," (1999, p. 131) CSA interviewers can bring personal biases into the interview and may even have their own agenda for the interview. The purpose of the interview should always be to elicit accurate and complete information (whatever this may be), but interviewers can have affiliations that may lead to biases (e.g., ultimately be employed by prosecutors), or have biases that the child was abused or not abused before the interview has even begun (Ceci & Bruck, 1995). In fact, history is replete with high-profile trials involving very poorly conducted CSA interviews that focused on only one hypothesis—that the child was sexually abused—and that had severe negative consequences for all concerned (e.g., millions of dollars spent, innocent people serving many years in prison, etc.; Rabinowitz, 2003). The infamous McMartin trial, which lasted from 1987 until 1990, is probably the most notorious and was one of the first to expose widespread concerns regarding suggestive techniques used in forensic interviews with children (Ceci & Bruck, 1995). Seven teachers at a Manhattan Beach, California preschool were charged with kidnapping and sexually abusing hundreds of children. Extensive interviews conducted by child advocate Kee MacFarlane led to allegations of satanic rituals, for example, children being forced to drink blood, watching babies being beheaded, flights over the Pacific Ocean where babies were fed to sharks, and thousands of counts of sexual abuse including group sex and sodomy. However, reviews of videotapes of the interviews indicated that MacFarlane had relied heavily on suggestive interview techniques that elicited allegations of sexual abuse (Schreiber et al., 2006). The recognition of this problematic interviewing eventually led to the seven teachers being cleared of all charges, however, not before some had spent years in prison and had lost their homes, their families, and their reputations (Rabinowitz, 2003).

In the early 1990s, Edenton, North Carolina experienced a similar trial involving several preschool workers at the Little Rascals Daycare (Ceci & Bruck, 1995). The owner, Bob Kelly, his wife, and 5 other caregivers were accused of raping and sodomizing 29 preschool children. Initially no child made any allegations of sexual abuse or satanic rituals taking place at the daycare. However, after months of repeated interviews during therapy sessions, persistent questioning at home and attending "court school" in preparation for testimony in court, the children began disclosing details of satanic rituals during which children were allegedly vaginally and anally penetrated with various objects (e.g., pins and markers), thrown into pools of sharks, and beaten. The children's statements also included fantastical stories of being flown in spaceships and hot air balloons. Unlike the case of the McMartin trial, no videotapes of the interviews were available for review—which in itself is quite problematic—as the therapists conducting the interviews had lost or destroyed them (Anderson, 2007). However, an important part of the problem seemed to be that interviewers and other officials associated with these cases appeared to be more concerned about false negatives (e.g., acquittal of guilty perpetrators) and showed little or no concerns about false positives (e.g., conviction of innocent defendants; Ceci & Bruck, 1995).

On the other hand, children may fail to be interviewed and their abuse can remain undetected and this can set the stage for the perpetrator to continue to abuse them or to abuse others. For example, in the infamous recent Penn State case, former coach Jerry Sandusky was convicted of 45 counts of abuse he had perpetrated from 1994 to 2009. The investigation was prompted by the first victim's disclosure in 2008 and many of his victims did not come forward until the trial.

The Heterogeneity of Interview Protocols

Poor forensic interviewing techniques like those utilized in the McMartin and Edenton cases created a need for successful interviewing protocols that minimize suggestive questioning, as well as avoiding other mistakes in order to maximize the accuracy of information elicited and subsequently a number of such interview protocols have been attempted. While the American Education Research Association (1999, p. 43) requires that all "tests and testing programs should be developed on a sound scientific basis," additional controversy is created because some forensic protocols still use less than supported techniques (e.g., sexually anatomically correct dolls and anatomical drawings; Elliott, O'Donohue, & Nickerson, 1993). Nevertheless, because these protocols are still widely used in the United States, it is necessary to critically review them based on a set of criteria proposed in a later section.

A thorough search of the literature has identified the following three protocols as the most influential forensic protocols for CSA interviewing:

1. National Institute of Child Health and Human Development (NICHD) Investigative Interview Protocol (Orbach et al., 2000; Lamb, Orbach, Hershkowitz, Esplin, & Horowitz, 2007)
2. RATAC Forensic Protocol (CornerHouse, 1990; 2003; 2007)
3. Step-wise interview (Yuille, Hunter, Joffe, & Zaparniuk, 1993)

The rate at which these protocols, combinations, variants, or wholly idiosyncratic interviews are actually used is currently unknown, although the NICHD Investigative Interviewing Protocol, or some variant of it, seems to be the most often used. The fidelity of the interviewers in the field adhering to these protocols is also unknown. Additionally, because there are a wide variety of professionals interviewing children, in a wide variety of jurisdictions, with varied backgrounds (e.g., police, social workers, psychologists, interview specialists, etc), varied levels of experience in forensic interviewing and levels of training, variability in the content of the interviews will inevitably be produced.

Evaluation Criteria for Forensic Interviews with Children

In order to assess the quality of interview protocols, one needs a reasonable set of evaluative criteria. A set of criteria for evaluating CSA protocols is proposed below. Some of these criteria have been drawn from the Standards for Educational and Psychological Testing developed by the American Educational Research Association (1999) while others have been taken from the extent literature on CSA.

1. *Interrater Reliability.* Interrater reliability indicates the "degree of agreement between scores or ratings obtained from different sources (observers, instruments, and clinicians)" (Haynes, Smith, & Hunsley, 2011). Every interview protocol should be tested for interrater reliability prior to its use outside of a research setting. It is important to know that the interview results would not have varied significantly if another interviewer were to have conducted the interview. Results should indicate that the protocol has high interrater reliability to ensure that two or more raters are able to agree on the inferences made based on the child's statements, for example that the child was sexually abused. Because there are multiple inferences made in an interview (e.g., whether the child was abused; what the abuse consisted of; where it occurred, etc.) there is actually a series of interrater reliabilities to be examined in an interview.
2. *Component Construct Validity.* Construct validity is the "degree of validity of inferences about unobserved variables (constructs) based on observed indicators" (Haynes et al., 2011). In the context of a forensic interview, one inference made is about whether adequate rapport has been established with the child. Assessing this construct often relies on multiple indicators regarding the child's behavior such as the child's general affect, his or her willingness to have a parent leave the room, his or her willingness to discuss details surrounding the abuse, as well as other indicators. However, eventually the interviewer comes to some sort of general conclusion that "sufficient" rapport was or was not attained and the accuracy of this inference must be determined. Forensic protocols are comprised of a number of distinct components constructs (e.g., rapport building; understanding of the meaning of telling the truth versus a lie; lack of threats or bribes; prepositional competence) and psychometrically there is an interest in the degree of validity of each inference that is made about each of these constructs.
3. *Predictive (Postdictive) Validity.* Once the construct validity of the individual components of a protocol is established, the inferences made based on the integration of information gathered from a forensic interview become relevant. It is important to determine the accuracy of inferences involved in conclusions that may be drawn from the interview such as, "The interview suggests that this child was anally penetrated on four separate occasions in Sacramento California by her Uncle Joe between March 2011 and August 2011 and no one knew of this abuse, and no other acts or actors were involved." Because these events are in the past, they fall under the psychometric term of "postdictive validity." Postdictive validity may be defined as the accuracy of inferences made about historical

events and there are a number of inferences about the past that the forensic interviewer seeks to make, including:

(a) Abuse Status (that the child was or wasn't sexually abused)
(b) Who the child has identified as the alleged perpetrator
(c) What type of sexual abuse it was (contact or noncontact, and whether penetration took place is particularly important)
(d) Where and when the abuse took place
(e) How many times the abuse was perpetrated
(f) If anyone else knew of the abuse and was complicit in it

As mentioned in an earlier section, these details play a large role in the charging and sentencing of the perpetrator and could mean the difference between a lighter and a more severe judgment.

4. *Incremental Validity.* Incremental validity is defined as the degree to which data from one or more measures "increase validity or utility of a judgment beyond what can be accomplished with other sources of data" (Haynes et al., 2011). When conducting forensic interviews it is important, given previous pieces of information gathered during the CSA investigation from the medical examination, interrogation of the alleged perpetrator, collateral contacts, etc., to what extent information elicited by the interviews adds to the judgment facilitated by those data. Interviews are time-consuming and costly, and it is important that these costs be justified.
5. *Sensitivity/Specificity.* Sensitivity is described as the "proportion of positive cases so identified on the basis of a measure from a particular assessment instrument" while specificity refers to "the proportion of negative cases so identified by an assessment instrument" (Haynes et al., 2011). The reason interview protocols were developed in the first place was to increase the likelihood that the child will provide the most accurate and detailed narrative possible in order to most precisely determine whether sexual abuse did in fact occur or not, while at the same time decreasing the likelihood that any personal biases will enter the professional judgment of the interviewer. Therefore, it is extremely important that research reveals that an interview protocol has adequate sensitivity and specificity and is thus able to distinguish between children who have been abused and those who have not. Not doing so can have serious consequences for persons involved in the allegation. In the case of false positives, the alleged perpetrators may be falsely accused of sexually abusing a child and may end up serving time, have to register as a sex offender, pay monetary compensation, etc., because of a crime he did not commit. When a protocol results in false negatives the perpetrator is not correctly identified and brought to justice for his crimes and this increases the likelihood that he will have the opportunity to reoffend and hurt more children before finally being caught.
6. *Developmental Appropriateness.* In attending to a child's age during forensic interviews, we are in fact interested in the child's cognitive development. Two-year-olds have different cognitive capacity from 12-year-olds, and this difference

must be taken into consideration when asking questions and when evaluating the child's statement. For example, investigators interviewing younger children must use simpler words and shorter sentences. Research indicates that younger children provide fewer details when free narratives are elicited (e.g., Ceci & Bruck, 1993). Additionally, they are also more susceptible to suggestibility and the formation of false memories than older children and adults, although research has shown that even adults are capable of falsely accepting events that never happened as true (Loftus & Pickrell, 1995). Having certain disabilities (e.g., developmental disabilities) may also complicate forensic interviews. An autistic child, for example, may have reduced cognitive ability, problems verbalizing, attention issues, etc., and all these would affect the accuracy and completeness of the child's report and the inferences made based on information elicited during the interview. If modifications are made to accommodate disabilities in the protocol, "the validity of inferences made from test scores and the reliability of scores on tests administered to individuals with various disabilities should be investigated and reported by the agency or publisher that makes the modification" (American Educational Research Association, 1999, p. 107).

7. *Cultural Sensitivity.* The APA (2003) stresses that due to a growing population that is increasingly multicultural, psychologists should demonstrate cultural competence in their practice. A number of issues, ranging from language barriers to different attitudes toward authorities, could emerge when conducting forensic interviews with such populations. In fact, American Educational Research Association (1999) affirms that "testing practice should be designed to reduce threats to the reliability and validity of test score inferences that may arise from language differences" (p. 97). If a forensic protocol has been translated into other languages, it is important to outline "the methods used in establishing the adequacy of the translation," and "empirical and logical evidence should be provided for score reliability and the validity of the translated test's score inferences for the uses intended in their linguistic groups to be tested" (American Educational Research Association 1999, p. 99). Cultural differences may pose additional barriers when interviewing a child. Talking about sexual abuse is difficult for any child, but children from certain cultures may be less likely to disclose abuse to an interviewer because such events are usually kept "in the family" and are not discussed with authorities (Fontes & Plummer, 2010). It is also useful to know if a protocol has evaluated with other populations (e.g., people with disabilities, people from a different culture) and if the studies indicate that the protocol is appropriate for use with those populations.
8. *Trainable Successfully* (*Implementation Fidelity*). The American Educational Research Association (1999) advises that "those who use psychological tests should confine their testing and related assessment activities to their areas of competence, as demonstrated through education, supervised training, experience, and appropriate credentialing" (p. 131). Any successful protocol must include a successful training that ensures the desired level of competence. Because a variety of professionals, from psychologists to law enforcement personnel, are trained to conduct forensic interviews, protocol developers must keep

the users and their differences in mind. One cannot assume that a psychologist with a background in child development will have the same knowledge about memory, suggestibility, behavioral principles, etc., as a police officer who may have never taken relevant courses and read relevant research. Therefore, it is probably more prudent to err on the side of caution and provide sufficient background knowledge to any training course in CSA interviewing. Finally, drift and supervision issues must be also addressed. Research shows that even though professionals spend valuable time and money getting trained in CSA interviewing, over time some just fail to adhere to the protocol (Lamb, Sternberg, Orbach, Esplin, & Mitchell, 2002; Lamb, Sternberg, Orbach, Hershkowitz et al., 2002). Drift and nonadherence to the protocol may demonstrate a need for continued supervision and help with difficult cases. Therefore, it is imperative that field studies be conducted to evaluate the effectiveness of training by assessing fidelity of protocol adherence.

Description and Evaluation of Major Protocols

National Institute of Child Health and Human Development Investigative Interview Protocol

The NICHD Investigative Interview Protocol (Orbach et al., 2000; Lamb et al., 2007) is the best-researched and most widely used forensic protocol for CSA interviewing. This structured protocol is divided into two stages, the presubstantive and substantive portions of the interview. The interviewer introduces him/herself, discusses the child's duty during the interview (i.e., tell the truth), and covers the rules and expectations (e.g., use of "I don't know" responses) during the introductory phase. During the rapport phase, the interviewer seeks to build rapport with the child in a comfortable environment. The narrative training phase helps the child get accustomed to responding to open-ended questions about a neutral event. A transitional phase occurs between the presubstantive and the substantive phase of the interview in which the interviewer orients the child to the target event/s under investigation through the use of prompts. If the transitional phase elicits a disclosure, the interviewer moves on to the free-recall phase and, once the interviewer has gathered as many possible details through free-recall prompting, the transition is made to directive questioning about information previously provided by the child. At this time, the child may take a break. After the break, the interviewer continues to ask direct questions about the disclosure. When the required information has been elicited, the interviewer may go on to the closing phase, and a neutral topic (for example, asking the child about his/her plans for the day) may also be discussed with the child.

Two memory enhancing techniques, Physical Context Reinstatement (child is interviewed at the scene of the alleged crime) and Mental Context Reinstatement (guided mental reconstruction of the setting of the alleged crime) have both been used in conjunction with the NICHD protocol (Orbach et al., 2000; Hershkowitz et al., 2001; Hershkowitz, 2002). Both of these techniques appear to have elicited additional details from the children. Studies conducted in Israel, United States, United Kingdom, and Canada all have demonstrated that interviewers using the NICHD Investigative Interview Protocol as opposed to those using non-protocol methods used more open-ended and free-recall prompts, and used fewer focused, directive, and option-posing questions (Orbach et al., 2000; Sternberg et al., 2001; Lamb et al., 2006; Cyr & Lamb, 2009). However, results relevant to amount of information provided by the children in response to these questions revealed no differences between conditions in the number of informative information given by the child, although children in the protocol condition did provide most of their information in response to open-ended and free-recall prompts (Lamb et al., 2009).

Interrater Reliability. Hershkowitz et al. (2007) evaluated the interrater reliability of the judgments of 42 Israeli youth investigators. Twenty-four forensic interviews were selected, of which half were classified as plausible and half as implausible based on the Horowitz et al. (1995) "ground truth" scale that utilized independent evidence to corroborate allegations made during an interview. Half of the interviews used the NICHD Investigative Interview Protocol, while the other half did not follow a protocol (non-protocol condition). In order to elicit an interrater reliability coefficient, "seven child investigators independently judged the credibility of each of the transcribed interviews" using a 4-point scale to indicate how likely it was that each alleged incident had really taken place (p 103). Results indicated that there was a difference between the interrater reliability of investigators rating non-protocol interviews (a=.764) and the interrater reliability of those rating the NICHD Investigative Interview Protocol interviews (a=.874). Additionally, a significant difference emerged when rating cases involving implausible allegations (a=.338 versus a=.642 for non-protocol and NICHD Investigative Interview Protocol interviews respectively).

Component Construct Validity. While the protocol was developed by experts in the field of child interviewing, there is no evidence that it has undergone subsequent content validation. Several studies reveal that interviewers using the NICHD Investigative Interview Protocol were more likely to engage in the recommended techniques (e.g., to explain the ground rules and utilize rapport building techniques) than those using a non-protocol interview (Sternberg et al., 2001). Additionally, the use of the protocol increased the number of open-ended utterances posed by the interviewers (Orbach et al., 2000; Sternberg et al., 2001; Lamb et al., 2006; Cyr & Lamb, 2009).

Postdictive Validity. There is no research available evaluating the accuracy of inference made about the alleged CSA and details surrounding it.

Incremental Validity. While no studies specifically examined the incremental validity of the NICHD protocol, Darvish et al. (2005, as described in Lamb et al., 2008) evaluated the amount of investigative leads provided by NICHD Investigative Interview Protocol interviews versus non-protocol interviews.

Investigative leads were categorized as information about the suspect, witnesses, medical leads, material leads, and "miscellaneous" and as "very strong" to "very weak" on a 6-point scale. Details elicited were classified as either central or peripheral, and the verifiability of entire statement of the child was rated from "very low" to "very high" on a 4-point scale. Results indicated that the NICHD Investigative Interview Protocol interviews yielded significantly more leads categorized as "very strong," and statements that were more highly verifiable than the non-protocol interviews.

Sensitivity/Specificity. The Hershkowitz and colleagues (2007) study described in the Interrater Reliability section above examined the accuracy of judgments made by investigators in addition to the reliability of their judgments. Results revealed that 59.5 % of the judgments of the NICHD Investigative Interview Protocol interviews were accurate (95.2 % of judgments about plausible statements and 23.8 % of judgments about implausible statements), while only 29.6 % of the judgments of non-protocol interviews were accurate (38.1 % of judgments about plausible statements and 11.9 % of judgments about implausible statements). These findings indicated that, while the NICHD Investigative Interview Protocol interviews had better outcomes when interviewers rated plausible statements, interviewers rating statements elicited by both NICHD Investigative Interview Protocol and non-protocol interviews failed to accurately rate those when the judgments were made about statements that were implausible.

Developmental Appropriateness. Multiple studies have been conducted examining the ability of interviewers using the NICHD Investigative Interview Protocol to elicit accurate and detailed information from children of different ages. The typical study compared the effects of NICHD Investigative Interview Protocol interviews to non-protocol interviews on interviewer utterances (invitations, directive, option-posing, and suggestive) and on amount and accuracy of details given by the children. Some of the studies (e.g., Sternberg et al., 2001; Hershkowitz, 2001) have failed to identify any differences among age groups. However, Orbach et al. (2000) found that older children gave more details than younger children in both the NICHD Investigative Interview Protocol and non-protocol conditions. Additionally, Lamb et al. (2003) found that 8-year-old children provided a greater amount of details than 4-year-old children, although there were no differences in the amount of information elicited by each type of utterance. Alridge et al. (2004) noted that when Human Figure Drawings were added to the protocol, younger children (ages 4–7) provided 27 % more details after having allegedly exhausted their memories, versus 19 % for 8–10-year-olds and 12 % for 11–13-year-olds. The authors caution that these additional details may have come at the expense of less accurate information. When Mental Context Reinstatement was added to the protocol (Hershkowitz et al., 2001), all children provided proportionally more details in response to invitations than to other prompts, with children ages 4–6 reporting more free-recall information (41 %) than children ages 7–9 (15 %) and 10–13 (17 %), although the overall number of details did not increase.

Additionally, the protocol has been evaluated in children with developmental disabilities. Dion and Cyr (2008) examined 34 forensic interviews of children with low verbal abilities (LVA) as indicated by low scores on the Vocabulary subtest of the WISC III. Half of the interviews were conducted with the NICHD Investigative Interview Protocol and half without a protocol. Findings indicate that interviewers using the protocol provided significantly more invitations and significantly less suggestive utterances than those not using the protocol, and there was no significant difference in amount of directive and option-posing utterances. Furthermore, when compared to children of average verbal ability (AVA), children with LVA interviewed with the NICHD Investigative Interview Protocol gave more details than children with AVA interviewed without the use of a protocol. When both sets of children were interviewed using the protocol, children with AVA provided more details than their LVA counterparts. Brown et al. (2012) assessed the ability of intellectually disabled children (mild-IQ below 80, and moderate-IQ 40-55) to provide reliable accounts of an experienced event. The children witnessed a classroom event and were subsequently interviewed in a supportive manner 1 week or 6 months after the event using the NICHD Investigative Interview Protocol. Suggestive questions were added at the end of each interview. Results revealed that the mildly intellectually disabled children were able to provide highly accurate information about the experienced event, particularly to open-ended prompts. However, moderately intellectually disabled children required more specific prompting and more focused questions, and had poorer performance overall. All children provided more inaccurate information in response to the suggestive questions.

Cultural Sensitivity. The protocol has been tested in four countries, Israel, United States, United Kingdom, and Canada. Cyr and Lamb (2009) found that Canadian interviewers using the NICHD Investigative Interview Protocol utilized significantly more open-ended prompts and significantly less suggestive and option-posing questions than interviewers conducting a non-protocol interview with French-speaking children. Additionally, the children provided more details per prompt when the NICHD Investigative Interview Protocol was used, and these results were replicated by Lamb et al. (2009) in a British sample.

Trainable Successfully. Several studies have been conducted on the effects of training on the quality of forensic interviews. Examined 192 interviews conducted by 21 Israeli youth investigators. The authors tested the following four conditions: validation; rapport building; "victims" protocol in which the interviewers were trained in the NICHD protocol; and "suspects" protocol condition. The validation and rapport building trainings consisted of brief workshops while the "victims" and "suspects" protocol conditions consisted more intensive training followed by continued supervision and case reviews in the "victims" protocol condition. Interviews conducted in one of the four conditions were compared to interviews in baseline conditions (that is, interviews previously conducted by the same interviewers). Results demonstrated that interviewers in the "victims" protocol condition performed significantly better as evidenced by using more open-ended prompts and fewer focused prompts. This indicates that the more intensive training and subsequent supervision increased the quality of the forensic interviews. Lamb, Sternberg, Orbach, Esplin et al. (2002) and

Lamb, Sternberg, Orbach, Hershkowitz et al. (2002) conducted a similar study in which the interviews conducted by eight experienced forensic investigators while they were receiving ongoing supervision were compared to the interviews conducted by the same group of investigators after supervision had ended. Results indicated that the termination of supervision had an adverse effect on the interviewers' behavior, as interviewers used significantly fewer invitations and more option-posing and suggestive prompts after supervision had ended. In light of these findings, the authors suggested that continued supervision may be required to ensure that investigators maintain a high quality of forensic interviews.

RATAC Forensic Protocol

The RATAC forensic protocol (CornerHouse, 1990, 2003, 2007, described in Anderson et al., 2007) is a semi-structured interview protocol comprised of five stages: Rapport; Anatomy Identification; Touch Inquiry; Abuse Scenario; and Closure. The first stage, Rapport, seeks to establish the child's comfort, communication, and competence. The second stage, Anatomy Identification, utilizes anatomical drawings for a number of different purposes depending on the child's age. The drawings are used with young children to assess whether they can identify their own gender as well as to capture the child's idiosyncratic language for different body parts. The protocol also allows the use of drawings as memory cues. Stage three, Touch Inquiry, assesses the child's understanding of good touches and unwanted touches. Children are asked to define a touch, "identify who gives the touch, and to indicate" what body part has been touched (Anderson et al., 2007, p. 297). If the child has made a disclosure, the interviewer proceeds to the Abuse Scenario phase in which information is gathered about the child's experience including who the perpetrator was and how many times the abuse took place. During this phase, the use of interview aids such as drawings, anatomical drawings, and anatomical dolls is allowed, the latter that are introduced after disclosure has occurred in order to clarify details or get a visual demonstration of the child's experience. The protocol recommends that interviewers take into account the child's developmental level when employing such aids. The last stage of the protocol, Closure, is a time for the child to share any other information he/she may have about the alleged abuse; to validate the child's emotions surrounding the disclosure; to address any questions the child may have about the interview; and to thank the child for his/her participation in the interview. This stage also incorporates education about personal safety, about reporting future experiences, and exploration of safety options should abuse occur in the future. Interviewers may modify or eliminate any one of these stages to better address the child's developmental level.

Interrater Reliability. No research has examined the interrater reliability of the RATAC forensic protocol.

Component Construct Validity. RATAC components include Rapport, Anatomy Identification, Touch Inquiry, Abuse Scenario, and Closure. However, none of these components have been evaluated to ensure that they have each been adequately addressed during the forensic interview and they have not been validated for content by experts in the field. Additionally, some of the stages utilize questionable techniques (for example, the multitude of interviewing aids) that have not been validated for use with potential victims of CSA.

Postdictive Validity. No studies are available examining the predictive validity of the RATAC forensic protocol.

Incremental Validity. There are no studies assessing the incremental validity of the RATAC forensic protocol.

Sensitivity/Specificity. No research has been conducted on the sensitivity and specificity of the RATAC forensic protocol.

Developmental Appropriateness. There are no studies examining the use of the protocol with children of different ages. However, the protocol aims to take a developmentally appropriate approach to interviewing children that takes into consideration differences in children's memory functions, attention span, comprehension, simple versus complex language, and concrete versus abstract concepts. Additionally, it provides general guidelines for age-appropriate questions (e.g., using only "who" and "what" questions with 3-year-olds, adding "where" questions with 4-year-olds, and omitting the use of "why" questions with all children). The protocol also discusses question type (e.g., open-ended, focused, etc.) in the context of child development and recommends that more direct questions be used with younger children.

Cultural Sensitivity. No studies have been conducted examining the validity of the protocol with individuals from different cultures. However, the protocol does indicate that culture plays a role in how children disclose given the cultural differences in narrative models (e.g., children from Western cultures may discuss their feelings, thoughts, and preferences more than those from Eastern cultures).

Trainable Successfully. There is no empirical evidence that the protocol can be trained successfully and that interviewers who have undergone the RATAC training conduct superior interviews to those who have not. Nevertheless, the protocol cites case after case in which expert testimony has been admitted in court because the expert witness was trained in this protocol (Anderson et al., 2007). Additionally, Vieth (2009) notes that interviewers trained in the RATAC forensic protocol receive continued supervision, technical assistance, etc., although none of these claims have been evaluated.

Step-Wise Interview

The Step-wise interview (Yuille et al., 1993) was developed in order to attain the following goals: minimize trauma experienced by the child during the interview; maximize the information provided by the child about the alleged abuse; minimize contamination of the child's information; and "maintain the integrity of the investigative process" (Yuille et al., 1993, p. 100). This protocol proceeds in nine phases: rapport building, requesting recall of two specific events, telling the truth, introducing the topic of concern, free narrative, general questions, specific questions (if necessary), interview aids (if necessary), and concluding the interview. The interview begins with a rapport building phase in which the investigator discusses neutral topics with the child in order to develop rapport. During this phase, the child is asked to describe two past experiences, the goal being to assess how much detail the child can be expected to provide as well as to model the form of the interview for the child. The next phase assesses the child's ability to define truth and lies, to identify whether specific statements are truth or lies, and to determine the child's understanding of the consequences for lying. Next, the topic of concern is introduced in a step-wise manner. Open-ended questions are first used to elicit a disclosure, then more specific prompts are utilized such as "Has anyone done something to you" and "Has anything happened to you which you would like to tell me about?" However, the authors advise against using the name of the alleged perpetrator or suggesting what happened during the alleged abuse. Drawings of both genders may also be used to determine if the child can name and describe the functions of all body parts from head to toe, and to assess if the child has seen any of the private parts (genitals and anus) on another person or if anyone has touched those parts on the child. After the child is oriented to the topic of concern, prompts such as "tell me what happened" are used to elicit a free narrative from the child. General questions based on the information provided by the child can be used to elicit additional details about the event. The authors advise against using leading or suggestive questions. The specific questions phase should only be covered if the free-narrative and open-questions phase have not extracted sufficient details and there is a need for further clarification or extension of the child's answers. This is also a time for resolving any inconsistencies in the child's statement. The authors suggest that interview aids may be used with young children or children with language or emotional difficulties. Although they allow the use of anatomical dolls, they do so with a cautionary statement that they only be used after the child has made a disclosure in order to clarify what sexual act has taken place. In the case that the child appears to acquiesce to suggestion, the authors also recommend asking a few leading questions not related to the event to determine the child's suggestibility. The final phase is the conclusion of the interview. The child's questions are answered, and he/she is thanked for his/her participation. The protocol strongly advises against making any promises to the child, for example, that the abuse will not happen again.

This protocol was developed in conjunction with the Statement Validity Analysis (SVA; Raskin & Yuille, 1989), a technique for the assessment of the credibility of children's statements. SVA is made up of two sections, the criteria for content-based criterion analysis (CBCA) that assumes that certain elements are present in a true disclosure and a validity checklist. The CBCA assesses the following 19 elements of a child's statement: coherence, spontaneous reproduction, sufficient detail, contextual embedding, description of interactions, reproduction of conversation, unexpected complications during the interview, unusual details, peripheral details, accurately reported details not understood, related external associations, accounts of subjective mental state, attribution of perpetrator's mental state, spontaneous corrections, admitting lack of memory, raising doubts about one's testimony, self-deprecation, pardoning the perpetrator, and reports of other's action. In addition, the validity checklist addresses the following factors: statement-related factors, psychological characteristics, appropriateness of language and knowledge, presence of affect, spontaneous gestures, susceptibility to suggestion, interview characteristics, and adequacy of the interview. There is little evidence for the validity of SVA in evaluating the veracity of children's statements; however, because it is meant to be used simultaneously with the Step-wise interview, we will be at times referring to it when evaluating the protocol for the proposed criteria.

Interrater Reliability. No research has been conducted on interrater reliability of the Step-wise interview.

Component Construct Validity. Step-wise interview phases include rapport building, requesting recall of two specific events, telling the truth, introducing the topic of concern, free narrative, general questions, specific questions (if necessary), interview aids (if necessary), and concluding the interview. These components have not been validated for content by experts in the field. Additionally, there is no research examining whether these phases are appropriately addressed by interviewers trained in this protocol.

Postdictive Validity. Zaparniuk and colleagues (1995) evaluated the ability of trained coders to accurately identify statements elicited from interviews guided by the Step-wise protocol as true or false utilizing the CBCA portion of the SVA. Coders followed set decision rules that would help them differentiate true from false statements, for example, having criteria 1 to 5 present, as well as any other 2 criteria from the CBCA. Results indicated that the coders only performed slightly better than chance at distinguishing true from false statements, demonstrating the difficulties in making accurate inferences about historical events.

Incremental Validity. There are no studies evaluating the incremental validity of the protocol.

Sensitivity/Specificity. No research has been conducted examining the sensitivity and specificity of the Step-wise interview.

Developmental Appropriateness. The Step-wise interview has a few factors build in that directly address developmental appropriateness. The phase in which the child is asked to describe two neutral events was developed to obtain a baseline of the child's memory and language skills which can then be compared to the details provided during the disclosure of the sexual abuse. There is also an optional phase in which the interviewer may test the child's prepositional understanding. A set of interview rules are also provided, but are not recommended for use with preschool-aged children. Several studies analyzed the developmental appropriateness of the protocol. Hardy and Van Leeuwen (2004) examined four variations of the Step-wise interview with children ages 3–8. The children watched performances of *The Beast with a Thousand Teeth* given by undergraduate students in their classrooms and preschools. The children were subsequently interviewed in one of four interview conditions: "a. direct probes with past event talk; b. direct probes with general event rapport talk; c. indirect probes with past even talk; and d. indirect probes with general event talk" (p. 159). Some children were also given four suggestive and ambiguous probes to test their ability to resist suggestion. Results indicated that older children provided more information than the younger children. These results were significant in the indirect probes conditions. Additionally, younger children provided fewer accurate details when questioned about specific past events. No age differences were found in children's ability to resist suggestive probes except for in the condition using indirect probes, in which older children were less suggestible. Porter, Yuille, and Bent (1995) compared the eyewitness accounts of deaf and hearing children using a procedure based on the Step-wise interview. The children were shown a set of slides that depicted a story in which a man wearing a cowboy hat stole a woman's wallet after bumping into her. The participants were subsequently interviewed using free recall and direct questions, and accuracy scores were collected. Results revealed no significant difference between amount of detail recalled by deaf and hearing children. Additionally, both deaf and hearing children recalled details with similar accuracies during the free-recall phase. However, when direct questions were used, the details of hearing children were significantly more accurate than those of deaf children.

Cultural Sensitivity. No studies have been conducted that examine the validity of the protocol with different ethnic groups. Additionally, the Step-wise interview has not been translated in any other languages.

Trainable Successfully. Yuille et al. (1983) conducted a field study examining three aspects of the training: the trainee's satisfaction with the training at the end of the 4-day workshop; a follow-up session 6 months after the training in which trainees rated how often they used the protocol; and "ratings of the quality of the taped interviews of trained and untrained workers" (p. 111). Child Protective Services workers, law enforcement personnel, and prosecutors from two districts attended a 4-day workshop on the Step-wise interview. Professionals from a third district served as the control group and did not receive training in the protocol. Results revealed that participants reported they had a positive view of the training and adequate information was provided. At the 6-month follow up, most participants indicated that they used the protocol "sometimes to always" when conducting CSA interviews. When the control and experimental groups were compared in regard to adequacy of interviews, 30 % of the interviews in the control condition were deemed inadequate due to scant or contaminated information versus 5 % in the experimental groups, illustrating problems in training and implementation of forensic protocols. Additionally, the manuscript did not mention whether the raters were blind, posing additional problems regarding the interpretation of the results.

Conclusions

There are several major protocols for forensic interviews of children who may have been sexually abused. Although these protocols share some key similarities (e.g., the importance of rapport building), they also demonstrate significant divergences. We have proposed criteria of adequacy for the content of these protocols and although no interview currently meets all criteria, future research needs to be conducted to evaluate the importance of each of these domains in impacting the reliability and validity of a protocol.

Of particular importance is the missing psychometric information on each of these protocols. For example, very little is known about the interrater reliability of these protocols—a key question because this sets a limit on validity but also because the field would like the results not to be interviewer dependent (i.e., that another interview would have produced very different information and have come to different conclusions.) Of even greater concern is that there is limited information on the postdictive validity of these protocols (e.g., what are the error rates of these interviews?). Knowing error rates is a key piece of information in rendering a technique admissible in court proceedings. Finally, the extent to which training in these protocols is effective is unknown as there are few data showing fidelity to any protocol in actual practice in the field. The NICHD Investigative Interview Protocol has the most psychometric data but also appears to have significant gaps in this psychometric information as well as content.

There are other major pieces of missing information: the incremental validity of these interviews; how to adapt to the developmental variability of children; the cultural appropriateness of these protocols; and the extent to which component domains are validly executed (e.g., rapport, truth/lie distinction, prepositional competence). Clearly much more research is needed to further understand the abilities of protocols to achieve these ends. For example, a common procedure to establish prepositional competence is to have the child demonstrate that they know prepositions like "in" and "on top of" with objects such as a marker and a Kleenex box. However, questions can be raised regarding the extent to which generalizations can be made from this demonstration to whether a child knows whether a finger went "in" his or her vagina or anus.

A key issue is that these protocols can at best be "semi-structured." Because each child and each potential abuse situation is unique, the interviewer must be given leeway to adapt general principles to the individual situation. For example, there is no mechanical process that can be followed to develop rapport and thus, there will also be an "art" of interviewing. Research will be needed to understand what interviewer characteristics seem relevant to making these decisions on the fly in actual interviews as it may reveal that some individuals are better suited than others to conduct these interviews.

It should be noted that some of this psychometric research is extremely difficult to conduct. There are important ethical constraints that will limit the research that can be done. For example, conducting multiple interviews with actual cases to determine interrater reliability may be both forensically and ethically complicated.

It may also be difficult to conduct this research in analog settings as asking children the kind of questions required in a sexual abuse investigation will raise legitimate ethical concerns. However, without finding a way to address these questions, it is difficult for the field to claim that its practice is evidence based and difficult for investigators to demonstrate adequate psychometrics of their interviews.

These protocols are being asked to accomplish a lot including to be applicable to a wide range of developmental stages, to explore very sensitive information, with a wide range of child characteristics (e.g., withdrawn to hyperactive; Caucasian versus Hispanic), in a wide range of jurisdictions (some even internationally), in a wide range of individual contexts (e.g., a non supportive, poorly functioning mother), and to achieve a wide range of objectives (e.g., establish rapport, not be leading, be sensitive to the presence of threats or bribes, and most importantly to gather complete and accurate information about acts that may have occurred years earlier in a developmentally not fully developed individual). These complexities are important and illustrate the major issues in forensic interviewing. It might be that multiple protocols may need to be developed or that the evaluative questions regarding these interviews need to be more nuanced, i.e., more along the lines of Gordon Paul's (1967) "ultimate question" regarding psychotherapy, "What protocol, by whom, is most effective for this individual, with this specific situation, and why?"

Finally, it may be best practice to place both these protocols and the field interviews into a quality improvement system. Since there is so much to be known about the quality of the interviews themselves as well as the quality of a particular interview protocol, it may be best practice for data to be continuously gathered on several quality dimensions. Fidelity to the protocol can be measured in each interview and interviewers can be given feedback on problems or stuck points. This feedback should be provided, as in all quality improvement procedures, in a supportive manner. Conducting forensic interviews well is an extremely difficult task given the idiosyncratic nature of each child and case, the complexity of the protocols, as well as functioning in a rather complex legal and even clinical context. In addition, the protocols themselves need to be constantly evaluated and improved. Interviewer feedback can be gained regarding issues such as ambiguities or areas where more support is needed. Feedback from other stakeholders can also be systematically gathered, e.g., from parents, prosecuting attorneys, and defense attorneys. In addition, this quality improvement system ought to gather some of the key psychometric data that are missing, benchmark these numbers, and constantly try to improve them.

References

Aldridge, J., Lamb, M. E., Sternberg, K. J., Orbach, Y., Esplin, P. W., & Bowler, L. (2004). Using a human figure drawing to elicit information from alleged victims of child sexual abuse. *Journal of Consulting and Clinical Psychology, 72*, 304–316.

American Educational Research Association, W. C., American Psychological Association, W. C., & National Council on Measurement in Education, W. C. (1999). *Standards for Educational and Psychological Testing*. Washington, DC: American Educational Research Association.

American Psychological Association. (2003). Guidelines on multicultural education, training, research, practice, and organizational change for psychologists. *American Psychologist, 58*(5), 377–402.

Anderson, W. L. (2007). *The trials of the Edenton Seven, or how Joseph Goebbels became the standard for North Carolina justice*. In LewRockwell.com. Retrieved June 26, 2012.

Anderson, J., Ellefson, J., Lashley, J., Miller, A. L., Olinger, S., Russell, A., … Weigman, J. (2007). *The CornerHouse forensic interview protocol: RATAC*. Retrieved from http://www.ncptc.org/vertical/Sites/%7B8634A6E1-FAD2-4381-9C0D-5DC7E93C9410%7D/uploads/%7B0CB5FDDE-6496-40B7-8D70-E4EE6498903D%7D.PDF

Brown, D. A., Lewis, C., Lamb, M. E., & Stephens, E. (2012). The influences of delay and severity of intellectual disability on event memory in children. *Journal of Consulting and Clinical Psychology, 80*, 829–841. doi:10.1037/a0029388.

Berenson, A. B., Chacko, M. R., Wiemann, C. M., Mishaw, C. O., Friedrich, W. N., & Grady, J. J. (2000). A case-control study of anatomic changes resulting from sexual abuse. *American Journal of Obstetrics and Gynecology, 182*(4), 820–834.

Ceci, S. J., & Bruck, M. (1993). Suggestibility of the child witness: A historical review and synthesis. *Psychological Bulletin, 113*(3), 403–439.

Ceci, S. J., & Bruck, M. (1995). *Jeopardy in the courtroom: A scientific analysis of children's testimony*. Washington, DC: American Psychological Association.

Cyr, M., & Lamb, M. E. (2009). Assessing the effectiveness of the NICHD investigative interview protocol when interviewing French-speaking alleged victims of child sexual abuse in Quebec. *Child Abuse & Neglect, 33*(5), 257–268.

Darvish, T., Hershkowitz, I., Lamb, M. E., & Orbach, Y. (2005, Jan). The production of investigative leads in child sexual abuse interviews using the NICHD protocol. Paper presented to the Society for Applied Research on Memory and Cognition; Victoria, New Zealand.

Dion, J., & Cyr, M. (2008). The use of the NICHD Protocol to enhance the quantity of details obtained from children with low verbal abilities in investigative interviews: A pilot study. *Journal of Child Sexual Abuse, 17*(2), 144–162.

Elliott, A. N., O'Donohue, W. T., & Nickerson, M. A. (1993). The use of sexually anatomically detailed dolls in the assessment of sexual abuse. *Clinical Psychology Review, 13*(3), 207–221.

Fontes, L., & Plummer, C. (2010). Cultural issues in disclosures of child sexual abuse. *Journal of Child Sexual Abuse, 19*(5), 491–518.

Frasier, L. D., & Makoroff, K. L. (2006). Medical evidence and expert testimony in child sexual abuse. *Juvenile and Family Court Journal, 57*(1), 41–50.

Hardy, C. L., & Van Leeuwen, S. A. (2004). Interviewing young children: Effects of probe structures and focus of rapport-building talk on the qualities of young children's eyewitness statements. *Canadian Journal of Behavioural Science, 36*(2), 155–165.

Haynes, S. N., Smith, G. T., & Hunsley, J. D. (2011). *Scientific foundations of clinical assessment*. New York, NY: Routledge.

Heger, A., Ticson, L., Velasquez, O., & Bernier, R. (2002). Children referred for possible sexual abuse: Medical findings in 2384 children. *Child Abuse & Neglect, 26*(6/7), 645.

Hershkowitz, I. (2001). Children's responses to open-ended utterances in investigative interviews. *Legal and Criminological Psychology, 6*(1), 49.

Hershkowitz, I. (2002). The role of facilitative prompts in interviews of alleged sex and abuse victims. *Legal and Criminological Psychology, 7*(1), 63.

Hershkowitz, I., Fisher, S., Lamb, M. E., & Horowitz, D. (2007). Improving credibility assessment in child sexual abuse allegations: The role of the NICHD investigative interview protocol. *Child Abuse & Neglect, 31*(2), 99–110.

Hershkowitz, I., Orbach, Y., Lamb, M. E., Sternberg, K. J., & Horowitz, D. (2001). The effects of mental context reinstatement on children's accounts of sexual abuse. *Applied Cognitive Psychology, 15*(3), 235–248.

Horowitz, S. W., Lamb, M. E., Esplin, P. W., Reiter-Lavery, L., & Krispin, C. (1995). Establishing ground truth in studies of child sexual abuse. *Expert Evidence, 4*, 42–51.

Lamb, M. E., Hershkowitz, I., Orbach, Y., & Esplin, P. W. (2008). *Tell me what happened: Structured investigative interviews of child victims and witnesses*. Hoboken, NJ: Wiley.

Lamb, M., Orbach, Y., Hershkowitz, I., Esplin, P. W., & Horowitz, D. (2007). A structured forensic interview protocol improves the quality and informativeness of investigative interviews with children: A review of research using the NICHD investigative interview protocol. *Child Abuse & Neglect, 31*(11-12), 1201–1231.

Lamb, M. E., Orbach, Y., Sternberg, K. J., Aldridge, J., Pearson, S., Stewart, H. L., … Bowler, L. (2009). Use of a structured investigative protocol enhances the quality of investigative interviews with alleged victims of child sexual abuse in Britain. *Applied Cognitive Psychology, 23*(4), 449–467.

Lamb, M. E., Sternberg, K. J., Orbach, Y., Aldridge, J., Bowler, L., Pearson, S., & Esplin, P. W. (2006, July). *Enhancing the quality of investigative interviews by British police officers.* Paper presented at the Second International Investigative Interviewing conference, Portsmouth, England.

Lamb, M. E., Sternberg, K. J., Orbach, Y., Esplin, P. W., Stewart, H., & Mitchell, S. (2003). Age differences in young children's responses to open-ended invitations in the course of forensic interviews. *Journal of Consulting and Clinical Psychology, 71*(5), 926–934.

Lamb, M. E., Sternberg, K. J., Orbach, Y., Esplin, P. W., & Mitchell, S. (2002). Is ongoing feedback necessary to maintain the quality of investigative interviews with allegedly abused children? *Applied Developmental Science, 6*(1), 35–41.

Lamb, M. E., Sternberg, K. J., Orbach, Y., Hershkowitz, I., Horowitz, D., & Esplin, P. W. (2002). The effects of intensive training and ongoing supervision on the quality of investigative interviews with alleged sex abuse victims. *Applied Developmental Science, 6*(3), 114–125.

Loftus, E. F., & Pickrell, J. E. (1995). The formation of false memories. *Psychiatric Annuals, 25*(12), 720–725.

Malloy, L. C., Brubacher, S. P., & Lamb, M. E. (2011). Expected consequences of disclosure revealed in investigative interviews with suspected victims of child sexual abuse. *Applied Developmental Science, 15*(1), 8–19.

Orbach, Y., Hershkowitz, I., Lamb, M. E., Sternberg, K. J., Esplin, P. W., & Horowitz, D. (2000). Assessing the value of structured protocols for forensic interviews of alleged child abuse victims. *Child Abuse & Neglect, 24*(6), 733–752.

Paul, G. L. (1967). Strategy of outcome research in psychotherapy. *Journal of Consulting Psychology, 31*, 109–118.

Porter, S., Yuille, J. C., & Bent, A. (1995). A comparison of the eyewitness accounts of deaf and hearing children. *Child Abuse & Neglect, 19*(1), 51–61.

Rabinowitz, D. (2003). *No crueler tyrannies*. New York, NY: Free Press.

Raskin, D. C., & Yuille, J. C. (1989). Problems in evaluating interviews of children in sexual abuse cases. In M. P. Toglia, S. J. Ceci, & D. F. Ross (Eds.), *Adult perceptions of child testimony*. New York, NY: Springer.

Schreiber, N., Bellah, L. D., Martinez, Y., McLaurin, K. A., Strok, R., Garven, S., & Wood, J. M. (2006). Suggestive interviewing in the McMartin Preschool and Kelly Michaels Daycare abuse cases: A case study. *Social Influence, 1*(1), 16–47.

Sternberg, K. J., Lamb, M. E., Orbach, Y., Esplin, P. W., & Mitchell, S. (2001). Use of a structured investigative protocol enhances young children's responses to free-recall prompts in the course of forensic interviews. *Journal of Applied Psychology, 86*, 997–1005.

Vieth, V. I. (2009). Forensic interviewer at trial: Guidelines for the admission and scope of expert witness testimony concerning an investigative interview in a case of child abuse. *William Mitchell Law Review, 36*, 186.

Yuille, J. C., Hunter, R., Joffe, R., & Zaparniuk, J. (1983). Interviewing children in sexual abuse cases. In G. S. Goodman, B. L. Bottoms (Eds.), Child victims, child witnesses: Understanding and improving testimony (pp. 95–115). New York, NY US: Guilford Press.

Yuille, J. C., Hunter, R., Joffe, R., & Zaparniuk, J. (1993). Interviewing children in sexual abuse cases. In G. S. Goodman & B. L. Bottoms (Eds.), *Child victims, child witnesses: Understanding and improving testimony* (pp. 95–115). New York, NY: Guilford Press.

Zaparniuk, J., Yuille, J. C., & Taylor, S. (1995). Assessing the credibility of true and false statements. *International Journal of Law and Psychiatry, 18*(3), 343–352.

Chapter 14
Psychological and Investigative Pathways to Untrue Allegations of Child Sexual Abuse

William T. O'Donohue, Olga Cirlugea, Natalie Bennett, and Lorraine T. Benuto

When an allegation of child sexual abuse is made, law enforcement often immediately becomes involved and some kind of investigation regarding the child's allegations is undertaken. O'Donohue, Benuto, and Fanetti (2010) previously proposed a systematic model of pathways to false allegations whereby they identified two major pathways to a false allegation of child sexual abuse: (1) the child is lying and (2) the child has a false memory due to his or her problems in information processing. In this chapter, we discuss this model alongside additional sub-pathways that could lead to a false allegation. In particular, we discuss in much more detail the possible role of child psychopathology in the genesis of false allegations.

However, before these topics are discussed further, a few important points need to be made to set the proper context for what follows:

1. There is a wide degree of heterogeneity in these investigations. Some of this variance are created by variance in the laws and regulations defining what constitutes sexual abuse or what is a properly constituted investigation. Some of this variance are due to the heterogeneity of professionals and professional training: sometimes these investigations are multidisciplinary; sometimes these are just lead by law enforcement; at other times a mental health professional may be the investigator. Additional variance is due to pragmatics such as the availability of professionals (e.g., in rural or frontier settings); and some variance can be due to issues such as expense. Finally, still additional variance may be due to psycho-

W.T. O'Donohue, Ph.D. (✉) • N. Bennett, B.S. • L.T. Benuto, Ph.D.
Department of Psychology, University of Nevada, Reno, MS 0296, Reno, NV 89557, USA
e-mail: wto@unr.edu; nmbennett06@gmail.com; dr.benuto@gmail.com

O. Cirlugea, B.A.
Department of Psychology, University of Nevada, Reno,
1693 Ordway Ave., Reno, NV 89509, USA
e-mail: olgacirlugea@gmail.com

W.T. O'Donohue, M. Fanetti (eds.), *Forensic Interviews Regarding Child Sexual Abuse*, DOI 10.1007/978-3-319-21097-1_14

logical differences in the people involved; personal variables such as beliefs about the frequency of false allegations, or even sexism, or political ambitions can affect how investigations proceed.

2. As a field, we know too little about the accuracy of these investigations. It can be generally agreed that all interested parties to this want to minimize both false positives and false negatives. However, there is not a research or quality improvement data for us to decide what "best practices" consist of in order to minimize these errors. For example, Cirlugea and O'Donohue (in press) recently reviewed the psychometrics of the major forensic interview protocols with children and found that key information is missing regarding the inter-rater reliability of these, the sensitivity of these, the specificity of these, what training conditions are necessary for faithful implementation, and so on. Given this lack of data, there are a lot of opinions about what constitute best practices and how well any proposed best practices are actually sufficiently supported by data. What is most disconcerting is that there appears to be no emerging trends to correct this: it is highly likely that in a decade the field will be in much the same position.
3. Research in this area is quite difficult. There is very little grant funding. The ethics of the research is complicated: if one uses real-world cases to maximize external validity, then one can be mucking about in actual legal procedures with procedures of unknown (by definition) quality. It is an open question what limitations institutional review boards will place on research in this area.
4. Theory is underdeveloped in this area. In an important sense this volume and this chapter are attempts at partially filling this void. Key questions are, "What considerations in principle does an investigator need to account for when evaluating a allegation of child sexual abuse?" "What is the justification for these as opposed to others?" and "Even in principle, what are reasonable ways of accounting for these considerations?"
5. Finally, there are hosts of what might be called practical-political issues relevant to these. For example, "Can a consensus emerge about answers to these questions, particularly among parties with diverse interests (e.g., prosecutors and defense attorneys)?" "How is any best practice scaled and quality assurance procedures undertaken to assure fidelity across settings and time?" "How can we learn from experience to see the limitations of these and improve these so harm is minimized?" and "What is the cost of these practices and are these affordable and cost-effective?"

We turn now to an initial attempt at addressing point 4 above: i.e., a theoretical model to account for some of the factors that must be examined to more thoroughly understand a child's sexual abuse allegation.

The Child Is Lying

Most Allegations Are Arguably True

The question regarding the veracity of the child's allegation can arise in several contexts. Parents can wonder about their children's allegations or even lack thereof (e.g., given other children's allegations or worrying "signs" such as genital rashes but also see Penix and O'Donohue (2003) for problems in reasoning from symptoms to abuse status). Law enforcement facing decisions about arrest and prosecution will also need to make some perhaps preliminary decisions about the veracity of the child. Forensic interviewers and clinicians deciding on treatment needs also can be concerned about either the child's allegations or lack thereof. Finally, child protective services facing decisions about removal and safety of children can also be interested in the veracity of the allegations. However, establishing whether a child's allegation is true is not an easy task as medical evidence is only found in approximately 4 % of all child sexual abuse investigations (e.g., Berenson, Chacko, & Wiemann, 2000; Heger, Ticson, & Velasquez, 2002), and this is due to both temporal factors (e.g., abuse is not immediately reported and thus any physical evidence, such as bruising has had time to heal) and differences in sexual abuse acts (e.g., acts such as kissing and touching the breasts would not leave any physical markers). And it must be remembered that there are many parameters of "truth"—the right perpetrator, the right number of acts, the right descriptions of the abusive behavior, the right location and date, and even the right witnesses. The lack of medical evidence in child sexual abuse investigations as well as the little information provided by medical exams (e.g., even if physical evidence is present, unanswered questions remain such as who the perpetrator was, where the abuse occurred, how many times?, etc.) highlight the need for alternative methods of gathering information to support or refute the sexual abuse allegations which may include forensic interviews with the child, interviews with collateral contacts, and interviews with the alleged perpetrator, all which come with their own set of problems. Thus, determining whether a particular child is lying about being sexually abused is an important yet difficult task.

Complicating this matter is that some have taken an *a priori* position on the issue. For example, during the infamous McMartin preschool trial an "advocacy" organization *Believe the Children* was formed by the parents involved and one of the central claims of this organization was that "children never lie" about being sexually abused (De Young, 2004). Indeed their actual position was more nuanced, in that they countenanced that the possibility that children's *denials* may be lies, and this belief was used to justify aggressive, repetitive, and leading forensic interviewing with the children (Schreiber et al., 2006). Thus, they promoted the idea that children's allegations should be believed without question and when a child denies abuse this denial should, at least in many cases, be interpreted as a lie. Admittedly, currently it seems that fewer are explicitly promoting this sort of belief system; however, it seems to be the case that some individuals involved in understanding abuse allegations can have an inchoate form of this belief. For example, in some jurisdictions (such as California) the Child Sexual Abuse Accommodation Syndrome is admissible evidence. This problematic theory (for a critique of the CSAAS see O'Donohue et al., 2010) claims (falsely) that most children recant their original abuse allegations. Thus, even if a child is currently strenuously and perhaps plausibly denying their initial allegation, experts in CSAAS are called to "explain" that these recantations are expected but always false, according to CSAAS, in all allegations of child sexual abuse.

How Often Do Children Lie About Abuse?

In order for a child to make a false allegation, by definition he or she must *knowingly* state a falsehood. This is in contrast to a *false memory* that entails that although the child is stating a falsehood, he or she (incorrectly) believes that what he or she is stating is true, and thus is not knowingly stating a falsehood—a necessary definitional condition for lying. This key distinction has at times been ignored in the false allegation literature.

When these two pathways are not distinguished, studies on the rates of false allegations have yielded results ranging from 1 to 9 % (e.g., Everson & Boat, 1989; Jones & McGraw, 1987; Kendall-Tackett, 1991; Trocmé et al., 2005). For example, Kendall-Tackett (1991) surveyed 201 professionals in the Boston area about their judgments regarding whether the children made false child sexual abuse allegations. Results revealed that most professionals suspected lying to have occurred in fewer than 5 % of cases. Similarly Everson and Boat (1989) interviewed 100 Child Protective Service workers at the Department of Social Services in North Carolina and determined that false allegations of sexual abuse by children were made in an average of 4.7 % of CPS cases.

A few studies have directly examined cases regarding whether intent to lie was present in the false allegation. For example, Goodwin, Sahd, and Rada (1978) reviewed 46 cases of alleged child sexual abuse that they had encountered in their work at a child abuse agency as well as an undisclosed number of cases from professionals working at other agencies in the Albuquerque area. Results indicated that of the 46 cases, only one was a false accusation made by a child (2 %). This case involved a 13-year-old child who began exhibiting suspicious behavioral problems after her mother remarried. Similarly Jones and McGraw (1987) evaluated 573 reports of child sexual abuse made to the Denver Department of Social Services in 1983 and determined that only 1 % of accounts were false reports made by a child ($N=8$), defined as containing deliberate falsification, misperceptions, or an adult coaching the child to make a false report (this conflates lying with false memories). More recently, the Public Health Agency of Canada conducted a large-scale incidence study of reported child abuse and neglect and published its major findings in 2003. Of the 6244 unsubstantiated child sexual abuse reports, most were considered to be non-malicious while a small number were deemed malicious (9 %) and the intent to lie was unknown in 1046 (16.8 %). Of course these percentages are dependent on the validity of the criteria for determining an allegation is false—and there is no infallible criterion.

The literature reviewed above suggests that most allegations of sexual abuse do not involve lies. Nonetheless it is important to note that in certain contexts, there can be higher rates of false allegations. For example, studies evaluating allegations in the context of child custody evaluations have yielded higher rates of false allegations. Specifically, Green (1986) evaluated 11 cases of alleged child sexual abuse referred to the author (a psychiatrist) who concluded that four of the 11 children (35 %) had falsely accused their fathers of sexually abusing them. Similarly,

Benedek and Schetky (1985) presented 18 cases of alleged child sexual abuse they had encountered in psychiatric practice, ten of which they judged to be false (56 %). Caution must be taken when interpreting the Benedek and Schetky findings as it was not specified whether it was children or adults making the false allegations. Despite context-specific false allegation rates, it is clear that arguably most allegations are not due to the child lying. However, it is also equally clear that this sometimes happens and needs to be countenanced and evaluated in any case.

The studies above also highlight the difficulty of measuring a child's intent in making a false allegation (e.g., that he or she knowingly stated a falsehood) given that most studies have been unable to make this distinction clearly. Some studies have used professional judgment, some the child's retraction of the original allegation, and some the presence of a sexually transmitted infection in order to classify allegations yet other studies have failed to even go as far as determining whether it was the parent or the child making the false allegation. The diversity in decision criteria used to determine intent makes it difficult to determine accurately measure this dimension and thus it is fair to say that the extant research in this area is flawed and thus conclusions must be drawn very tentatively. In addition, in these studies the sample sizes examined are quite small, while in other cases it is not clear that these were representative. It seems fair to say at this point there are too few data from well-controlled studies to accurately describe the rate of lying in child sexual abuse allegations. Importantly we must also acknowledge the possibility that these rates may vary according to some key parameters, e.g., it may be the case these rates are higher in adjudicated cases than in cases that are more easily resolved.

Suggestive Contacts: Another Key Pathway to False Allegations

Several high-profile trials in the late 1980s sometimes dubbed "the satanic ritual trials" first exposed concerns regarding suggestive techniques used in forensic interviews with children. In addition to suggestive contacts with forensic interviewers, it is important to note that children may also come into contact with parents or caregivers who may suggest misleading information and these pathways will be described in the Adult Pathology section of this chapter.

A study conducted by Poole and Lindsay (2001) examined the effects of misinformation and misleading suggestions from parents on children's eyewitness reports in children aged 3–8 years old. Families were recruited from a daycare and 114 children participated, including 19 three-year-olds, 19 four-year-olds, 18 five-year-olds, 18 six-year-olds, 18 seven-year-olds, and 22 eight-year-olds. Children participated in a science demonstration where they interacted with "Mr. Science" for approximately 16 min. During this interaction, Mr. Science would demonstrate an activity (e.g., spinning tops and then reaching for them with and without a prism glass) and encourage the child to participate. After the first session, children were interviewed about their experience in a nonsuggestive manner. Approximately 3.5 months later, their parents read them a story that described events that were experienced and not experienced by the child. The second and third sessions were 1 month apart. Both of these sessions involved interviews in the child's home that included open-ended questions, direct yes-no questions, and a source-monitoring procedure. The results suggested that fictitious events were evident in children's narratives during the early, nonsuggestive stages of the interview, indicating that the use of open-ended prompts does not guarantee accuracy when a child has been exposed to misinformation. Although both problematic forensic interviews and caregiver (intentional or inadvertent) suggestions refer to suggestive contacts with other individuals, the child's contact with certain stimuli in his or her environment may also lead to a false allegations and two pathways through which this may occur are described below.

Misinterpretation of Nonsexual Events as Sexual

Children may falsely allege sexual abuse when they have experienced events that could be mistaken as sexually abusive even when that was not the case. How children categorize their experience depends on a number of factors but their cognitive development may limit or bias their judgments. For example, Oates et al. (2000) examined erroneous accounts of sexual abuse alleged by children and found that in three cases, the false allegation was due to the child being confused or misinterpreting nonsexual events (e.g., a child had a nightmare about being abused and then believed it was real).

Other circumstances may lead to a child falsely alleging sexual abuse. For example, bathing a young child obviously is not necessarily exploitive or abusive, and is a normative activity for young children. However, there are situations where there is some reason to suspect that bathing a young child may be sexually abusive, for example if the child is reporting some unusual circumstances of the bath—e.g., a lot of time spent bathing of genitals. Additionally, bathing older children is more questionable as children are expected to be able to care for their own hygiene past a certain age.

A study conducted by Krackow and Lynn (2003) evaluated whether innocuous touch in the games of Twister and Shapes (the latter being made up by the authors) increased the likelihood of children falsely affirming "abuse touch" questions. Additionally, the authors were interested whether suggestive tag questions such as, "Amy touched your bottom, didn't she?" were more likely to elicit inaccurate information out of children than less suggestive questions such as "Did Amy touch your bottom?" (p. 589). The researchers hypothesized that children who were touched would be more likely to confirm that they had been touched in a sexual manner. The researchers enlisted 48 children ages 48–70 months to participate in the study. Half of the children played Twister and half played Shapes, a game in which the researcher drew imaginary shapes on different body parts, and for each game there were two conditions, touch and non-touch. In the touch condition, the experimenter touched the children on their hand, arm, calf, and foot. Seven days later the children were interviewed about their experiences and were asked to explain how the games were played in free recall, then were asked specific questions, and finally they had to answer 30 yes or no questions, and some of these questions were forensic in nature. Results showed that children who were asked the specific yes or no questions elicited more false assents to "touch questions" compared to the nearly 100 % accuracy of the children who had been asked the direct questions. Children also falsely affirmed that they had been touched inappropriately to "twice as many forensic questions when they were tag questions" (p. 597).

Children also play games with each other that involve touch or other elements that may or may not be indicative of sexual abuse. Some abuse allegations involve other children, often older children as the perpetrator. Normative sexual behavior including inspecting another child's body and simulating the roles of parents has been observed in young children playing games such as "house" or "doctor" (Poole & Wolfe, 2009) and such behavior among children of similar ages should not necessarily be considered sexual abuse. Friedrich, Fisher, and Broughton (1998) evaluated normative sexual behavior including self-stimulation, exhibitionism, voyeurism, kissing, and discussing sexual knowledge in a sample of 1114 male children aged 2–12 years old. Results indicated that every one of the 38 sexual behavior items were endorsed by at least a few parents and of those behaviors, self-stimulation and exhibitionism were the most frequently endorsed ones. It is currently unclear how a valid distinction is made between "normal" sex play and "child abuse" between two children.

Confabulation of Different Experiences

In addition to misinterpreting nonsexual contact as sexual, children may also incorporate abuse-related events into neutral (nonsexual) experiences resulting in a false memory and false allegations. It is possible that a false allegation of abuse can result from the confabulation of experiences (Ceci & Bruck, 1993). Children may be exposed to sexual content in a variety of settings (e.g., sexual abuse prevention programs in school, websites or photos on the internet, sexual discussions among children, disclosure of sexual abuse by a friend or family member, etc.) and such information may be distorted and personalized by the child. For example, a child who was an altar boy watches a news program exposing child sexual abuse perpetrated by a priest and incorporates this sexual content into his or her own nonsexual experiences with the church, thus producing a false memory of sexual abuse at the hands of priest.

Problematic Forensic Interviews

In addition to the misinterpretation of nonsexual events as sexual and confabulation of different experiences, children may develop false memories as a result of suggestive techniques being used during a forensic interview. Because suggestibility is discussed in other chapters of this book, we will only briefly mention interviewing techniques determined by the literature to increase the likelihood of a child making a false allegation. Nonetheless, there are a few points we wish to make here regarding problematic interviews. Garven, Wood, Malpass, and Shaw (1998) reviewed the scientific literature on pathways to false allegations and found that the majority of interviewer techniques that were likely to result in children making false allegations fell into one of four major categories: suggestiveness, "other people" technique, reinforcement, and removal from direct experience. Suggestiveness was defined as the interviewer introducing new information into the interview that was not previously disclosed by the child. Context is necessary whether a question is suggestive or not. For example, the question "What was he wearing when he was in your room that night?" is only considered to be suggestive if the child has not yet disclosed that the man was in his or her room. The "other people" technique refers to interviewers informing the child about what other people have already said regarding the allegations (e.g., that another child has already disclosed abuse) and may function to put pressure on the child to conform to those statements. Fanetti, O'Donohue, and Bradley (2006) in their Protocol for the Evaluation of Forensic Interviews with children (PEFIC) called this factor "conformity press".

Differential reinforcement of certain responses, that is, responses that are in line with the interviewer's expectations that the child had been abused, also increased the likelihood that children would falsely allege abuse. Positive and negative consequences are behavioral principles utilized to increase or decrease the likelihood of a behavior occurring again in the future. In the context of a forensic interview, this technique can be used to shape a child's responses by selectively rewarding desired answers, for example, using social praise or promises of a tangible reward such as "You're a good boy, I'll make sure you get a toy at the end of this interview" when a child names an alleged perpetrator, while inhibiting undesired answers, for example, saying "Are you sure that didn't happen?" or the interviewer looking unhappy or frowning when the child denies abuse. Removal from direct experience, including inviting speculation from the child (i.e., by asking the child to guess about what may have happened while aiding the child in constructing a story to fit the interviewer's interpretation of the events) through the use of anatomically correct dolls (Elliott, O'Donohue, & Nickerson, 1993) and other problematic methods, was an indirect interviewing technique that functioned to remove the child from the direct experience of the interview. Additional biasing techniques including failure to establish the child's competency in using "I don't know" responses, interviewer's inappropriate use of close-ended questions, and repetitive questions are described in Fanetti et al.'s (2006) Protocol for Evaluating Forensic Interviews of Children.

Grooming

Sexual grooming is understood to be the tactics through which child abusers gain access to their future victims and prepare them to be compliant with the abuse (Brackenridge, 2001; Gillespie, 2002). Sexual grooming is not found to be used by all child abusers, but studies show that prevalence rates of these behaviors in cases of abuse can range from 35 % (Gallagher, 2000) to much higher (e.g., 53 %, Elliott, Browne, & Kilcoyne, 1995; 61 %, Berliner & Conte, 1990). The exact prevalence rates of grooming are difficult to know, as many definitions of the construct exist (for a full review, see Bennett & O'Donohue, in press) as well as other terms that are used to describe the behavior such as "entrapment" (Gallagher, 1999) or "subjection" (Spiegel, 2003).

Current grooming definitions include varying criteria such as preparing a child for the abuse, gaining the child's trust, or making it difficult for the child to resist or disclose the abuse. Additionally, some definitions include concrete examples (e.g., "the use of an array of material, illicit and emotional 'inducements'," Gallagher, 1999), whereas others include more abstract properties (e.g., "the process of predisposing a boy to sexual abuse by means of subtle or blatant interactions that lead to boundary diffusion and role confusion," Spiegel, 2003). The heterogeneity of these definitions can lead to the classification of behaviors as grooming under certain definitional criteria but not under others, thus leading to difficulty in identifying such behaviors. Currently, no valid assessments exist that can aid in determining whether or not an alleged perpetrator's behaviors were indeed grooming.

Bennett and O'Donohue (in press) presented a solution to this definitional confusion: grooming should be defined as "antecedent inappropriate behavior that functions to increase the likelihood of future sexual abuse." According to this definition, the assessment of grooming would involve a two-step process: (1) determining that the adult's behavior is inappropriate in and of itself; and (2) that it can be reasonably argued that the function of this inappropriate behavior is to increase the likelihood of future abusive contact. It is proposed that this definition will aid in correct identification of sexual grooming behaviors prior to the abuse occurring, rather than the identification of grooming behaviors being an entirely post hoc process (i.e., only after abuse is alleged are the behaviors seen as inappropriate). The identification of such behaviors is not an easy task, however. Sexual grooming behaviors used by perpetrators may appear to be normal to some outsiders (Hartill, 2009). This is why many sex offenders use certain kinds of grooming behaviors; children do not necessarily recognize them to be inappropriate and sometimes caregivers also fail to recognize their problematic nature. For example, giving a child a piece of candy does not necessarily mean that sexual abuse will follow, although it could be intended as a bribe to coerce the child into complying with the abuse.

It is possible that false conclusions regarding the sexual grooming of could lead to false conclusions about the veracity of an allegation of sexual abuse. Within an interview context, if a child discloses that the suspected adult has been buying him gifts over the past few months, the interviewer may conclude this behavior to be sexual grooming and thus be more likely to question the child with the bias in mind that sexual abuse did indeed occur. This type of suggestive interviewing could then result in a false allegation. It could also be the case that a parent notices an adult performing such behaviors as giving gifts to the child and thus repeatedly questions the child as to whether or not sexual abuse occurred. In these cases, the child would be more likely to falsely allege abuse due to biased interviewing.

Child Pathology: A Relatively Unexplored Pathway

Above, we covered how suggestive contacts can lead to a false allegation. In this section, we have categorized these under child pathology and we detailed how certain childhood diagnoses can be related to the development of a false allegation. The general premise is that psychopathological process can distort reality contact or the interpretation of reality. A possible distortion can be that the child claims that they were abused when in fact they were not. Or this pathology can create a diathesis in which other pathways can be more frequently involved, e.g., lying (because of Conduct Disorder) or suggestibility (because of a psychotic disorder, for example). The role of some pathologies in reality distortion is relatively uncontroversial but the implications for forensic contexts are often not fully understood. For example, an individual with a dog phobia has incorrect beliefs about reality, namely that even safe dogs will inevitably bite them. An individual who is depressed may also have a host of false beliefs: that they are worthless, that no one values them, that it is impossible for them to feel better in the future. A person suffering from Narcissist Personality Disorder also has a host of false beliefs: about, for example, how much attention others pay to them and about their attractiveness or competence in a variety of contexts. Finally, to use the most common example, an individual with a psychotic disorder may believe a host of delusions or hallucinations. We turn now to an understanding of how psychopathology in children may impact whether or not they hold false beliefs about whether they have been abused.

Conduct Disorder

There are a number of DSM-5 (American Psychiatric Association (APA), 2013) diagnoses that are linked to the child's propensity to lie and even lie about important matters that can hurt others. Conduct Disorder is characterized by behavior that violates either the rights of others or major societal norms. One of the diagnostic criteria for this disorder is deceitfulness [or theft] (American Psychiatric Association; APA, 2013). Given this criterion, it is plausible that if a child has a history of lying and either has had or merits a diagnosis of Conduct Disorder, it is important to rule out conduct disorder as a pathway to a false allegation. Specifically if the child has a long history of being deceitful and makes an allegation, this history of deceit should be considered: the question: *is the child being deceitful in the allegation that s/he is making?* should be ruled assessed. Moreover because of the antisocial nature of conduct disorder (conduct disorder is believed to be a precursor to antisocial personality disorder (ASPD): Daversa, 2013), deceit could be used to hurt others. As illustrated throughout this chapter, there can be severe adverse consequences for an individual who is accused of CSA. Thus, in instances where a diagnosis of Conduct Disorder is merited, stake (does the child have something to gain by hurting the alleged perpetrator) should be carefully considered. At the same time, it is worth noting that if a child has Conduct Disorder it does not necessarily mean that the child was not abused. It simply signals that the hypothesis that the child is making a false allegation (lying) should be explored given that the child likely has a history of extreme behavior problems and lying.

Oppositional Defiant Disorder

While Opposition Defiant Disorder (ODD) has been described as less severe than conduct disorder it nonetheless is characterized by vindictiveness and consists of a presentation, whereby the child is oppositional towards authority figures (APA, 2013) and as such is likely to violate rules. While stake factors leading to lying are described below, it is worth noting here that if a child has a diagnosis of ODD, it should be ruled out as a pathway to a false allegation. Similar to what we discussed above under Conduct Disorder, if a child resents with ODD his/her allegations should be considered in light of this diagnosis—does the child have a history of being deceitful? Is there a stake involved? Is the allegation only coming to light when the child is in trouble or has broken a rule? Again, we are not advocating that a child who manifests severe behavioral problems could not be sexually abused (in fact, the opposite could be true as one of the sequelae of child sexual abuse is the manifestation of behavioral problems) but rather that children who have a history of behavioral problems may have a higher propensity to lie.

Personality Disorders

Although children are typically not given Personality Diagnoses the DSM permits this if they meet criteria for more than 2 years. The highest concern is with Cluster B diagnoses: Anti-Social Personality Disorder, Histrionic Personality Disorder, Narcissistic Personality Disorder, and Borderline Personality Disorder. These all have disturbances in interpersonal relationships and with belief formation that can give rise to a false allegation. Antisocial personality disorders do not care if they hurt others, and perhaps even enjoy these sorts of rule violations. Thus, if they feel vindictive or even they see some sort of personal gain, they will have less inhibition to make a false allegation of abuse. Histrionic personality disordered individuals can enjoy the attention an allegation of abuse gives them. Individuals suffering from borderline personality disorder (BPD) can, according to the DSM-V, have some paranoid ideation and this can result in misinterpreting reality and causing a false allegation. Finally individuals with Narcissistic Personality Disorder can see themselves as sexually attractive to others when this is not the case.

Developmental Delays

Developmental delays by definition signify problems in cognitive and information processing. It is certainly the case that there is some evidence that these individuals have a higher rate of sexual victimization (Hershkowitz, Lamb, & Horowitz, 2007), but it is also the case that their information processing problems can have two problematic effects: (1) they can be more prone to suggestibility than their chronological age would suggest as their mental age is not congruent; and (2) they can have more problems correctly interpreting reality: their understanding of what a good touch or a bad touch is may not be as accurate as their same age peers. A clear example of the first pathways occurred with the use of Facilitated Communication with children suffering from autism (Jones, 1994). There were numerous reports of noncommunicative autistic children suddenly making allegations of sexual abuse against their teachers and caregivers when their communication was being "facilitated" with computers and aids. These are shown to be impossible because all the communications were being authored by the aids.

Other Problematic Conditions

Stake factor for the child. In some cases, the child may lie about being abused due to some sort underlying personal motivation (O'Donohue et al., 2010). Examining the contextual factors in which the child first alleges the sexual abuse is thus important. Did the child make the initial outcry when getting in trouble for something else (e.g., an adolescent who discloses abuse to a parent right after being punished for misbehavior?) or, did the child first allege the abuse after seeing another child receive secondary gains for alleging abuse (e.g., a child discloses abuse and receives love and attention from a supportive parent)? These stake factors surrounding the initial outcry should be examined to determine whether they might have played a role in the abuse allegation.

Adult (Caregiver/Guardian) Pathology

Given the information provided above, it is evident that there are factors related to childhood pathology that could lead to a false allegation. The same is true with regard to adult pathology. In this pathway, the genesis of the false allegation is seen to being with the parent's pathology. Indeed there are a number of factors by which a parent (or caregiver) could either overtly or inadvertently suggest to the child that abuse was perpetrated against them. This suggestion could lead to the child developing a false memory.

When assessing pathways to false allegations, the mental health of the parent or caregiver of the child can be an important consideration. Namely the presence of certain mental health diagnoses could lead the parent/caregiver to make statements to the child that could lead to the formation of a false memory leading to a false allegation.

Psychotic Disorders

There are several disorders classified as psychotic disorders in the Diagnostic and Statistical Manual V (DSM-V). These include schizophrenia, delusional disorder, and schizoaffective disorder (APA, 2013). If the parent/caregiver presents with a psychotic disorder, a potential pathway to a false allegation exists if the parent/caregiver has delusions regarding events (i.e., abuse) that were perpetrated against the child. If the parent/caregiver shares these with the child, the child is at risk of forming a false memory. Thus mental health history of the parent or caregiver should be carefully evaluated. Indeed at times, individuals who are experiencing psychosis may develop delusions that are sexual in nature and/or experience hallucinations that may lead them to believe that certain events have occurred. Specific to this chapter and topic, if the parent or caregiver of a child is experiencing delusions that somebody wants to harm the child, he or she may share this with the child and the child may in turn interpret this as being sexual abuse—this could present a pathway to a false allegation that is perhaps part of a false memory. More directly, the parent or caregiver who is psychotic could share delusions or hallucinations with that child that directly implicates someone in an allegation of CSA. Arguably such situations are likely uncommon but nonetheless, could constitute a pathway to a false allegation.

Personality Disorders

Within the DSM-V (APA, 2013), there are several personality disorders that could contribute to pathways of false allegations. For example, ASPD is characterized by failure to conform to social norms, deception, impulsivity, irritability and aggressiveness, reckless disregard for safety of self or others, consistent irresponsibility, and lack of remorse. Several of these traits at face value alone could possess a person (i.e., parent/caregiver) to lie (e.g., create a false allegation) and many of the other traits (e.g., impulsivity, reckless disregard for the safety of self or others) could lead a person to make a false allegation either with the intention of influencing a child to make the false allegation or without regard for the possibility that certain statements could influence the child's beliefs about events that did or did not occur.

Similar to ASPD, BPD is also characterized by traits that could lead to a person making false statements to the child that are either overtly suggestive or statements that are inadvertently suggestive. Regarding the former, individuals with BPD tend to display inappropriate, intense anger or difficulty controlling anger (APA, 2013). Arguably such traits could lead a person to engage in behavior that is vindictive. Thus, an additional pathway to a false allegation could be an angry reaction-response from a parent/caregiver with the intention of harming the other parent/caregiver with a false allegation. Moreover, individuals with BPD tend to have a pattern of unstable and intense interpersonal relationships characterized by alternating between extremes of idealization and devaluation. If the caregiver/parent is devaluing the other parent/caregiver he or she could make comments in front of the child that could be misinterpreted by the child and result in a false memory/false allegation.

Depressed Mood

While the diagnostic criteria for a mood disturbance are not as overt in terms of the manner in which it could lead to a false allegation, there is some relevance. If the parent or caregiver is experiencing depressed mood (whether attributable to a life adjustment such as a divorce or simply to Major Depression), he or she may be feeling hopeless and or irritable (APA, 2013) and could make statements to the child about another individual that could be unintentionally leading or suggestive. For example, if a couple is going through a break-up and the mother makes comments to the child such as, "Your dad is such a bad person, he's done terrible things to our family. He's been a terrible father to you," the child could misinterpret these statements as meaning that the father has perpetrated against him/her. Similarly if a parent or caregiver is feeling hopeless due to a depressed mood, he or she could make hopeless statements to the child such as, "Bad things always happen to us. This is just like it always is, one bad thing happening after another." If the child hears this and interprets "bad thing" to mean someone has done something "bad" to him or her, the child could develop a false memory of CSA. While the above examples may not be common, they highlight the importance of understanding the context and factors that led up to an initial outcry.

Other Problematic Conditions

Stake factor for the parent. It is possible that a child alleging sexual abuse has been coached to do so by an adult who has a hidden agenda in the outcome surrounding the case. According to O'Donohue et al. (2010) and O'Donohue, Benuto, and Cirlugea (2013), an adult may have complex motivations that can lead to pressuring a child to falsely allege abuse (e.g., a mother going through a high-conflict divorce who is seeking revenge against the father; an aunt who wants custody of the children, etc.). Additionally, the motivations for the adult to encourage the child to falsely allege abuse could be financial in nature (e.g., a parent who wants to receive money for damages from a high-profile individual or institution).

Summary and Conclusions

As evidenced throughout our discussion, when a child alleges sexual abuse law enforcement immediately becomes involved and an investigation regarding the child's allegations is (ideally) promptly undertaken. From the research reviewed in this chapter, it is evident that while some children do lie about abuse, the rates of false allegations are relatively low (Everson & Boat, 1989). Nonetheless, there is evidence that suggests that at times children do make false allegations either knowingly stating a falsehood or because there has been some suggestive contact that led the child to believe that he or she was abused. In sum, the pathways to false allegations of sexual abuse can be categorized as follows: (1) suggestive contacts; (2) child pathology; and (3) adult/caregiver/parent pathology. These pathways should be examined when a child does make an allegation to ensure that all hypotheses for why the allegation was made have been explored.

In spite of the multiple pathways through which false allegations are produced, a limitation of most forensic interviewing protocols is that few hypotheses are tested beyond the one seeking to confirm that the child was in fact abused and in order to address this shortcoming, Cirlugea, O'Donohue, and Fanetti (2014) have developed the Sexual Abuse Structured Interview for Children-Revised (SASIC-R), a protocol that takes a hypothesis-testing approach to child sexual abuse interviewing. Each section of the protocol includes hypotheses to be tested as the interviewer gathers information. For example, during the Ground Rules section, the interviewer attempts to explore plausible rival hypotheses such as that the child did not know that he or she could say "I don't know" in response to a question rather than guessing, that the child did not understand the meaning of telling the truth versus a lie, and that the child … The SASIC-R also evaluates the suggestive contacts pathway in one of two ways: suggestive contacts with caregivers, law enforcement personnel, mental health professionals, etc., are all explored by the interviewer through nonleading questions designed to assess the content of the conversations with such individuals; and the protocol is designed to elicit accurate information from the child while minimizing suggestibility and any potential biases introduced during the interview are to be included in the report (e.g., "the child did not appear to understand the difference between the truth and a lie and therefore this may have biased his or her allegation.")

References

American Psychiatric Association (APA). (2013). *Diagnostic and statistical manual of mental disorders* (5th ed.). Arlington, VA: American Psychiatric Publishing.

Benedek, E. P., & Schetky, D. H. (1985). Allegations of sexual abuse in child custody and visitation disputes. In D. H. Schetky & E. B. Benedek (Eds.), *Emerging issues in child psychiatry and the law*. New York, NY: Brunner/Mazel.

Bennett, N. & O'Donohue, W. (in press). Sexual grooming: Conceptual and assessment issues. *Journal of Child Sexual Abuse.*

Berenson, A. B., Chacko, M. R., & Wiemann, C. M. (2000). A case-control study of anatomic changes resulting from sexual abuse. *American Journal of Obstetrics and Gynecology, 182*(4), 820–834.

Berliner, L., & Conte, J. R. (1990). The process of victimization: The victims' perspective. *Child Abuse and Neglect, 14*, 29–40.

Brackenridge, C. H. (2001). *Spoilsports: Understanding and preventing sexual exploitation in sport*. London, England: Routledge.

Ceci, S. J., & Bruck, M. (1993). Suggestibility of the child witness: A historical review and synthesis. *Psychological Bulletin, 113*(3), 403–439.

Cirlugea, O., & O'Donohue, W. (in press). Review of psychometrics of forensic interview protocols with children: Forensic and research implications of missing data. In W. T. O'Donohue & M. Fanetti (Eds.), Forensic interviews regarding child sexual abuse—A guide to evidencebased practice. New York: Springer.

Cirlugea, O., O'Donohue, W., & Fanetti, M. (2014). Sexual Abuse Structured Interview for Children-Revised (SASIC-R). Unpublished manuscript.

Daversa, M. T. (2013). Development of criminal and antisocial behavior in children and adolescents. In J. B. Helfgott (Ed.), *Criminal psychology: Vol. 1. Theory and research; Vol. 2. Typologies, mental disorders, and profiles; Vol. 3. Implications for forensic assessment, policing, and the courts; Vol. 4. Implications for juvenile justice, corrections, and reentry* (pp. 3–33). Santa Barbara, CA: Praeger/ABC-CLIO.

De Young, M. (2004). *The day care ritual abuse moral panic*. Jefferson, NC: McFarland & Company.

Elliott, M., Browne, K., & Kilcoyne, J. (1995). Child sexual abuse prevention: What offenders tell us. *Child Abuse and Neglect, 19*(5), 579–594.

Elliott, A. N., O'Donohue, W. T., & Nickerson, M. (1993). The use of sexually anatomically detailed dolls in the assessment of sexual abuse. *Clinical Psychology Review, 13*(3), 207–221.

Everson, M. D., & Boat, B. W. (1989). False allegations of sexual abuse by children and adolescents. *Journal of the American Academy of Child and Adolescent Psychiatry, 28*(2), 230–235.

Fanetti, M. N., O'Donohue, W. T., & Bradley, A. R. (2006). A method for evaluating child forensic interviews. *American Journal of Forensic Psychology, 24*(3), 5–27.

Friedrich, W. R., Fisher, J., & Broughton, D. (1998). Normative sexual behavior in children: A contemporary sample. *Pediatrics, 101*(4), 9.

Gallagher, B. (1999). The abuse of children in public care. *Child Abuse Review, 8*, 357–365.

Gallagher, B. (2000). The extent and nature of known cases of institutional child sexual abuse. *British Journal of Social Work, 30*(6), 795–817.

Garven, S., Wood, J. M., Malpass, R. S., & Shaw, J. (1998). More than suggestion: The effect of interviewing techniques from the McMartin Preschool case. *Journal of Applied Psychology, 83*(3), 347–359.

Gillespie, A. (2002). Child protection on the internet: Challenges for criminal law. *Child and Family Law Quarterly, 14*(4), 411–425.

Goodwin, J., Sahd, D., & Rada, R. T. (1978). Incest hoax: False accusations, false denials. *Bulletin of the American Academy of Psychiatry and the Law, 6*(3), 269–276.

Green, A. H. (1986). True and false allegations of sexual abuse in child custody disputes. *Journal of the American Academy of Child Psychiatry, 25*, 449–456.

Hartill, M. (2009). The sexual abuse of boys in organized male sports. *Men and Masculinities, 12*, 225–249.

Heger, A., Ticson, L., & Velasquez, O. (2002). Children referred for possible sexual abuse: Medical findings in 2384 children. *Child Abuse & Neglect, 26*(6–7), 645–659.

Hershkowitz, I., Lamb, M. E., & Horowitz, D. (2007). Victimization of children with disabilities. *American Journal of Orthopsychiatry, 77*(4), 629–635.

Jones, D. P. H. (1994). Autism, facilitated communication and allegations of child abuse and neglect. *Child Abuse & Neglect, 18*(6), 491–493.

Jones, D., & McGraw, J. J. (1987). Reliable and fictitious accounts of sexual abuse to children. *Journal of Interpersonal Violence, 2*(1), 27–45.

Kendall-Tackett, K. A. (1991). How many children make false allegations of sexual abuse?: A survey of mental health and law enforcement professionals. *Family Violence Bulletin, 7*, 19–21.

Krackow, E., & Lynn, S. J. (2003). Is there touch in the game of Twister®? The effects of innocuous touch and suggestive questions on children's eyewitness memory. *Law and Human Behavior, 27*(6), 589–604.

O'Donohue, W., Benuto, L., & Fanetti, M. (2010). Children's allegations of sexual abuse: A model for forensic assessment. *Psychological Injury and Law, 3*(2), 148–154.

Oates, R. K., Jones, D. P. H., Denson, D., Sirotinak, A., Gary, N., & Krugman, R. D. (2000). Erroneous concerns about child sexual abuse. *Child Abuse & Neglect, 24*, 149–157.

O'Donohue, W., Benuto, T., & Cirlugea, O. (2013). Analyzing child sexual abuse allegations. *Journal of Forensic Psychology Practice, 13*(4), 296–314. doi:10.1080/15228932.2013.822245.

Penix, T., & O'Donohue, W. (2003). Post hoc reasoning in possible cases of child sexual abuse: Symptoms of inconclusive origins. *Clinical Psychology: Science and Practice, 10*(3), 320–334. doi:10.1093/clipsy/bpg029.

Poole, D. A., & Lindsay, S. D. (2001). Children's eyewitness reports after exposure to misinformation from parents. *Journal of Experimental Psychology, 7*(1), 27–50.

Poole, D. A., & Wolfe, M. A. (2009). Child development: Normative sexual and nonsexual behaviors that may be confused with symptoms of sexual abuse. In K. Kuehnle & M. Connell (Eds.), *The evaluation of child sexual abuse allegations: A comprehensive guide to assessment and testimony* (pp. 101–128). Hoboken, NJ: Wiley.

Schreiber, N., Bellah, L., Martinez, Y., McLaurin, K., Strok, R., Garven, S., & Wood, J. (2006). Suggestive interviewing in the McMartin Preschool and Kelly Michaels daycare abuse cases: A case study. *Social Influence, 1*(1), 16–47.

Spiegel, J. (2003). *Sexual abuse of males: The SAM model of theory and practice*. New York, NY: Brunner-Routledge.

Trocmé, N., Fallon, B., MacLaurin, B., Daciuk, J., Felstiner, C., Black, T., … Barter, K. (2005). Canadian incidence study of reported child abuse and neglect—2003: Major findings. Ottawa, Ontario: Minister of Public Works and Government Services Canada.

Chapter 15
How Often Do Children Lie About Being Sexually Abused?

William T. O'Donohue and Olga Cirlugea

The question of the child's veracity regarding sexual abuse can arise in several contexts. Parents can wonder about their children's allegations or lack thereof (e.g., given other children's allegations or worrying signs such as genital rashes). Law enforcement facing decisions about arrest and prosecution also may want to understand this question. Forensic interviewers can be concerned about either about the child's allegations or lack of allegations. Child protective services facing decisions about removal of children and the safety of children can also wonder about the answer to this question.

These key individuals may also want to understand the base rate of lying about sexual abuse to make an informed decision about the likelihood or truth telling in an individual case. For example, the reasoning can be, "If only 1 % of children who make a claim of sexual abuse are lying, and this child is alleging abuse then, we ought to proceed with prosecution." On the other hand, if the base rate is much higher, say, 40 %, then a more cautious approach would be warranted. And the converse is also important, "If x% of children denying abuse are lying when they indicate that they have not been abused but it is actually the case that they have been abused, then perhaps further (maybe even repetitive) questioning and investigation is still warranted."

We must also recognize two other situations. First, sometimes children allege logically inconsistent states of affairs: at one time they say they have not been abused and at another time they say they were. Because of the logical law of the

W.T. O'Donohue, Ph.D. (✉)
Department of Psychology, Victims of Crime Treatment Center,
University of Nevada, Reno, MS 0296, Reno, NV 89557, USA
e-mail: wto@unr.edu

O. Cirlugea, B.A.
Department of Psychology, University of Nevada, Reno, MS 0296, Reno, NV 89557, USA
e-mail: olgacirlugea@gmail.com

W.T. O'Donohue, M. Fanetti (eds.), *Forensic Interviews Regarding Child Sexual Abuse*, DOI 10.1007/978-3-319-21097-1_15

excluded middle we know that both cannot be true and thus there is interest finding which is true. Finally, a sexual abuse allegation is actually a series of claims. Claims typically involve who abused them, what the abuse consisted of, how many times each kind of abuse occurred, who witnessed this, if anyone, where the abuse occurred (which can be important regarding jurisdiction), etc. We must also countenance that some of these claims can be truthfully put forward while others could be lies.

Further complicating this issue is that some have taken positions on this issue. For example, during the infamous McMartin preschool trial an advocacy organization, "Believe the Children," was formed by parents involved. One of the central claims of this organization was that "children never lie" about being sexually abused (De Young, 2004). It seems to be the case that their actual position was more (problematically) nuanced, in that they countenanced the possibility that children's denials may be lies, and this belief was used to justify aggressive, repetitive, and leading forensic interviewing with the children (Schreiber et al., 2006). Thus, they promoted the idea that children's allegations should be believed without question; while their denials could be lies. In addition, classical psychoanalytic theory (Freud, 1900/1991) suggests that all children go through an Oedipinal stage of psychosexual development in which they want to have sex with their opposite sex parent and may at times confuse fantasy with fact (although as we shall see this may be more indicative of false memories rather than intentionally lying).

A few key distinctions need to be made at the outset. First, children can lie in either making a allegation (e.g., "My father touched my privates") or lie in denying this ("My father did not touch my privates"). It is much more common in the literature to recognize and be concerned the latter possibility than the former (see e.g., Summit, 1983 but also see O'Donohue & Benuto, 2012). Second, it is important to point out that lying is only one pathway for a false allegation. Some naively think something along the lines that "if the child utters a claim that they have been sexually abused that is false, then he or she must be lying." However, this inference is false. What the field has shown over the past three decades or so is that a variety of suggestive influences (e.g., leading questions, repetitive questions, social conformity press, etc) can cause the child to have false memories (e.g., Poole & Lindsay, 1995; Ceci & Bruck, 1993; Quas et al., 2007, see Chaps. 5 and 8 in this volume.). That is, the child "remembers" that x happened to him or her, when in fact, x did not occur. However, it is important to point out that in this case the child is not *lying*, i.e., intentionally and knowingly stating a falsehood but rather has made a memory error—an error of commission, rather than the more commonly recognized error of omission—forgetting.

Thus, more formally, a key distinction needs to be made. When the question is asked, "How often do children *lie* about being sexually abused?" we assert the following two criteria need to be met:

1. The child is stating a falsehood.
2. The child is *knowingly* stating this falsehood.

This is in direct contrast to a *false memory* that instead would meet these criteria:

1. The child is stating a falsehood.
2. The child believes (albeit incorrectly) that what he or she is stating is true.

This second situation is consistent with the false memory research (e.g., Steffens & Mecklenbräuker, 2007, Chaps. 5 and 8 this volume). It is again important to point out that not all false allegations made by children are lies.

As previously stated, a final distinction needs to be made regarding the scope of the lie. Allegations of sexual abuse usually involve many subsidiary claims, e.g., who did it; exactly what did they do; when did they do it;, where did they do it; how many times did they do it; who witnessed it; did they offer any threats or bribes?, etc. The child may lie (or have a false memory) about any or all of these dimensions. This adds a complexity to this question as in an individual case the child's allegations may involve a combination of true statements, lies, and/or false memories.

Thus, we are now in a position to see some of the key complexities that need to be addressed before reviewing what is known regarding the question of children's lying about sexual abuse. Research that attempts to provide information relevant to this question must include:

1. Use of a methodology to reasonably conclude that the child's claims are, in fact, false. That is, if the child claims that an uncle touched her on the chest in August of 2007; that there is a valid method for determining whether or not this in fact did not occur. As there is no perfect lens into history, researchers need to argue on pragmatic grounds that sufficient sound information was gathered to make a reasonably accurate inference regarding this historical matter.
2. Use of a methodology for determining the child's state of mind at the time of the claim, namely that the child made a certain claim and knew when he or she was making this claim that it was false. That is, researchers need to distinguish a lie from a false memory as discussed above; and in order to do this, they need to establish with some reasonable amount of evidence that the child was *knowingly* stating a falsehood.
3. Ideally, these two criteria would need to apply to each subclaim in the child's allegation. That is, researchers need to countenance the possibility that the child's claim that their uncle did this was true, but they may be lying about the number of times the uncle abused them.

Meeting these three criteria is not an easy matter and to date we shall argue that extant research has not done a particularly good job in dealing with these.

We also want to briefly address possible motivations for why a child may lie about being sexually abused:

1. The child may be seeking to hurt someone by the allegation. For example, they may be angry at this person for a parenting decision.
2. The child may be afraid to make the accusation because the perpetrator has threatened them or fail to make the accusation because the perpetrator has bribed them.
3. The child may know their accusation could disrupt family life (e.g., financially) and thus falsely deny actual abuse.

4. The child may be influenced by an adult who has a stake in the child's accusation, e.g., a vengeful mother in a custody dispute; or a mother worried about the financial consequences if a perpetrator is incarcerated.
5. The child may have a history of lying and this is just one more example of a chronic problem in telling the truth.
6. The child may suffer from a mental disorder such as Conduct Disorder in which they disregard societal rules and they do not have normal internalized morality.
7. The child may like the attention gained from the false allegation.
8. The child may like the secondary gain received from the allegation, e.g., different living situation, etc.

We will now critically review research that has attempted to address this question. In order to find all relevant studies, we used several EBSCOhost databases including PsychINFO and E-Journals, with the search terms "false" + "allegations + sexual + abuse," "false + denials + sexual + abuse" "lie + sexual abuse," and "recantations + sexual + abuse." This search yielded few relevant results. In fact, we found most of the articles we chose to review in the reference sections of the articles found through EBSCOhost databases. In selecting studies to review, we picked those that utilized participants ages 18 and under and that reported rates of false allegations, false denials and/or recantations in child sexual abuse allegations. No studies specifically looked at rates of false denials; therefore, we chose to include studies that reported rates of denials in validated cases of child sexual abuse, and we referred to those as rates of false denials given that the sexual abuse was considered to have occurred and the child was denying that the abuse took place. We will now examine the criteria used to determine factual accuracy as well as intentionality.

False Allegations

Studies Involving Surveys of Professional Judgments

Kendall-Tackett and New Hampshire Univ. (1991) surveyed 74 law enforcement professionals and 127 mental health professionals to determine what percentage of child sexual abuse allegations were false. The 201 Boston area participants took part in a standardized telephone interview in which they were ask to provide the percentages of children below the age of 6, 6–9, and 10–12 whom they believed to have made false accusations about being sexually abused. Results suggested that most professionals suspected that lying about sexual abuse occurred in less than 5 % of cases, and that children ages 10–12 made more false accusations than their younger counterparts. Eighty-two percent of professionals endorsed that more than 5 % of 10–12 year-olds had lied versus 71 % of professionals for 6–9-year-olds and 59 % professionals for 6-year-olds. Additionally, findings indicated that female professionals reported significantly fewer fictitious allegations than their male peers.

This study has several important limitations and results should be interpreted with caution. First, lying was defined as a child stating that the abuse occurred when in fact it did not (i.e., false positives). Thus, this study did not assess the child's intentionality and thus failed to distinguish lying from false memory. In addition, the definition used in the study excluded any instances of abuse where the child claimed that the abuse didn't take place when it clearly did (i.e., false negatives). Second, the only method for determining the percentage of children that had lied about being abused was to ask law enforcement and mental health workers to offer their opinions. No information was provided on how these judgments were made, the correctness of these judgments, or whether the professionals distinguished between telling a falsehood that the child knew to be fallacious and telling a falsehood that the child believed to be true (e.g., false memories). In addition, there is no evidence that a professional's opinion about rates of lying is a valid indicator of actual rates of lying. Instead, it may be a better index of professionals' preconceptions about this issue. Additionally, no evidence was presented providing support for the specific reasons the professionals came to their judgments in individual cases, for example that the child was involved in a custody battle where one of the parents had a stake in the allegation. It would also have been useful for professionals to rate the same cases to at least determine interrater agreement on this, i.e., whether multiple professionals agreed that lying did or did not occur in a specific case.

Everson and Boat (1989) interviewed 100 Child Protective Service workers in the Department of Social Services in North Carolina to estimate the rate of false allegations of sexual abuse in CPS cases. In phase 1 of the study, the participants were required to provide estimates of total number child sexual abuse cases in which the CPS worker had participated, number of substantiated cases, and number of cases determined to contain false allegations of child sexual abuse. Eighty-eight of 100 CPS workers returned completed questionnaires. Results indicated that CPS workers reported a total of 1249 cases of child sexual abuse. The mean rate of substantiation, defined as the percentage of cases of child sexual abuse confirmed to be reliable by a CPS investigation, was 56 % across four different age groups (children under 3, between 3 and 6, elementary school aged children, and adolescents). Children were determined to have made false allegations in an average of 4.7 % of the cases. However, there were large discrepancies across age groups, as children under 3 were believed to have lied about being sexually abused in 1.6 % of cases while those older than 12 were thought to have lied in 8 % of the cases.

In Phase 2 of the study, 24 of the 34 CPS workers who had reported fictitious allegations of child sexual abuse were selected and placed in the "False Reports" subgroup while 24 of the 54 workers who had reported no false allegations were placed in the "True Reports" subgroup. The participants were asked to approximate what percentage of any 100 children making allegations of sexual abuse would lie about being abused. Results indicated that the workers in the False Reports subgroup expected more children to make false allegations (12.2 %) than those in the True Reports subgroup (5.2 %). The 24 CPS workers in the False Reports subgroup were also interviewed about details of the false reports of abuse in a sample of 29 cases and were asked to explain their judgment that the allegations of abuse were false.

The participants judged the allegations to be false in a majority of the cases because the children had retracted their statements. They also determined that 14, or almost half of the children's accounts, lacked credibility for reasons other than recantation. This consisted of unsubstantiated claims of sexual abuse made by the children in the past, statements that included fantastical and implausible details, insufficient amount of details for the child's age and developmental level, inconsistencies in the statements, presence of contradicting evidence as well as absence of supportive medical evidence, lack of fear toward the perpetrator, and, in one case, the passing of a polygraph test by the alleged perpetrator. However, again, legitimate questions can be raised about the validity of some of these criteria, and it was unclear how many criteria were used in an individual case or how multiple criteria were combined.

Again, this study did not report the criteria for determining falsehood in each individual case, although they did attempt to uncover some of the criteria that were generally used. Like much of the research described above, this study relied on professional judgment that again may be prone to antecedent bias. Again, most of the criteria described, for example, complexity of statement, polygraph results, absence of medical evidence, etc., have not been shown to validly indicate that the claims are fictitious. Additionally, children have been known to falsely recant their statements, so retractions may also not be valid indicators of fictitious allegations. Finally, the authors provided no methodology for determining the child's intentionality. Thus, the study did not provide evidence that the child knowingly stated a falsehood, i.e., had lied.

The Public Health Agency of Canada conducted a large-scale incidence study of reported child abuse and neglect and published its major findings in 2003. The agency obtained data on 217, 319 child maltreatment investigations from 63 child welfare services areas across Canada (excluding Quebec) in five areas of interest: physical abuse, sexual abuse, neglect, emotional maltreatment, and exposure to domestic violence. Of these investigations, 47 % were substantiated (103,297). The findings excluded cases that were investigated only by the police, and reports that were screened out (that is, never investigated), either because of insufficient information about the child's location or because they weren't considered "to be within the defined mandate of the child welfare services" (p. 19). The investigation was the basis for judging whether reports were eventually substantiated, suspected, or unsubstantiated. Reports were considered "substantiated" if there was additional evidence corroborating the abuse, "suspected" if there was not enough evidence to substantiate maltreatment but in which maltreatment couldn't be disregarded, and "unsubstantiated" if there was more evidence contradicting the abuse. Unsubstantiation was determined by the investigation worker and did not connote that the report was malicious. There were 12,468 child sexual abuse investigations conducted, of which only 21 % of these reports were considered substantiated (2935), while 15 % (1702) were suspected and 64 % (6244) were unsubstantiated. Caution is recommended when interpreting these findings, as children and other sources of referral were all included in the different categories. Of the 6244 unsubstantiated reports, most were considered to be non-malicious while a small number were deemed malicious (9 %) and the intent was unknown in 1046 (16.8 %). Once again there is no indication whether it was children or other sources of referral making the malicious reports. Three percent of all referrals (for all types of maltreatment) were unsubstantiated malicious reports by a child; unfortunately the study does not tease apart malicious reports by primary category of abuse.

The study presents a number of problems that limit interpretations of the findings. First, it does not differentiate between child sexual abuse allegations made by a parent, teacher, police, etc., and those made by the child. The numbers indicated that a relatively large number of reports were unsubstantiated; however, it is not known that children made those reports. Also unsubstantiated does not mean a false report, let alone a false report related to a child's lie. Second, while the study does report rates of unsubstantiated malicious reporting by a child (this would more closely meet the criteria of a lie as "knowingly stating a falsehood"), the study lumps together all forms of abuse and does not indicate what percentage of unsubstantiated malicious reports were due to allegations of sexual abuse. Third, the findings also fail to report how "maliciousness" was defined. Fourth, the Public Health Agency of Canada relied on the professional judgment of the investigation workers to determine whether the abuse was substantiated, suspected, or unsubstantiated. This again introduces bias in such a judgment. Finally, there was no explication of the validity of the criteria used to determine that a report was substantiated, thus concerns about false positive rates are valid.

Studies Involving the Child's Statement

Goodwin, Sahd, and Rada (1978) reviewed 46 cases of alleged child sexual abuse they had encountered in their work at a child abuse agency as well as an undisclosed number of cases from professionals working at other agencies in the Albuquerque area. All alleged abuse was perpetrated by a family member or someone living within the family. The authors found that of the 46 cases only 1 was a false accusation made by a child (2 %). This case involved a 13-year-old child who began exhibiting behavioral problems after her mother remarried. The girl had run away from her home and sought shelter from a friend whose father was a policeman. When questioned about why she ran away, the girl disclosed that she had been sexually abused by her stepfather. She later revealed that she had made up the story after reading about incest in a book. Two of the cases (4 %) were deemed false retractions of a true accusation made by a child. The two sisters ages 11 and 8 had run away and made claims of physical abuse. When those claims were investigated, one of the sisters also revealed that sexual abuse had taken place. A medical examination indicated that the older sister had "a ruptured hymen and a wide vaginal canal." In a subsequent interview, the sisters recanted their story, calling it a hoax and revealing that they had been coached to make false allegations by an older girl. One of the sisters refused to provide more information about the hoax while the other cried and confessed that the mother had made up the retraction.

The authors only provided the child's statement as a means of verifying that the child knowingly lied about being sexually abused, e.g., in the case of the girl who admitted fabricating the story after reading about incest. Additionally, none of the methods utilized to determine that the child lied (either by stating that the sexual abuse took place when it didn't or by recanting a true allegation) can be taken as conclusive evidence that lying occurred. In the case where a child made a false accusation, the criteria for concluding that the child's claims were in fact false consisted of (a) the general circumstances of the initial outcry and (b) the child's subsequent statement retracting the allegation. In the two cases where the study concluded that the children made false recantations, the criteria for establishing that the children's recantations were truly false were limited to the children's statements and some medical evidence that may or may not be indicative of sexual abuse. In addition, conclusions from this study are limited by sampling technique as there is no reason to believe that the original sample was representative. Finally, no methodology was used to establish that the child was knowingly stating false information.

Studies Involving Surveys of Professional Judgments and the Child's Statement

Jones and McGraw (1987) examined the rates of false reports of child sexual abuse and features of fictitious reports in a two-part study. Part One reviewed reports of suspected child sexual abuse in 1983 to the Denver Department of Social Services (DDS) (N=573). The Sexual Abuse Team of Denver DDS placed each report in one of five categories: reliable accounts, recantations, unsubstantiated suspicion, insufficient information, fictitious reports by adults, and fictitious reports by children. These five classifications were assessed by the researchers to ensure validity. Results indicated almost half of all reports (49 %) were reliable. Recantations, defined as reliable accounts that were taken back by the child under duress, made up 4 % of reports (N=25). Insufficient information was provided in 24 % of reports (N=37), while unsubstantiated suspicion made up 17 % of the cases (N=96). Fictitious reports were made by adults 5 % of the time (N=26) and only 1 % of accounts were deemed false reports made by a child (N=8). The latter were judged to be fictitious if they contained deliberate falsification, misperceptions, or an adult coaching the child to make a false report.

Part Two of the study focused on establishing the validity of statements in 21 fictitious cases reported to the Denver DDS between 1983 and 1985, of which five were reports made by children, nine by adults, and the remainder were mixed cases in which it was not possible to determine who had made the initial allegation. Accounts indicated that four of the five children making false allegations had been sexually abused in the past and were currently suffering from PTSD symptoms while one was currently involved in a custody battle. The authors used the following criteria for determining the veracity of the children's statements: presence of explicit as well as unusual and distinguishing details, age appropriateness of the child's' words and sentence formation, perspective, emotion expressed, psychological response, pattern of abuse and elements of secrecy due to coercion or threats. Supporting features such as family history, child's behavior, disclosure, statement to other people, consistency of the report, use of toys and other play materials, knowledge of sexual anatomy and function, and the presence of other children that may have been part of the abuse (e.g., as victims or witnesses) were also investigated as factors taken to provide further evidence for/against the truthfulness of the child's statement. Additionally, the quality of the investigative interviews was considered and the authors determined that in 8 of the 21 cases no interviews were conducted, while of the remaining interviews only two met the adequacy criteria (length and developmental level of interview, exclusion of leading questions and of anatomically correct dolls). An evaluation of the children's statements according to the criteria described above indicated that the false statements lacked emotion as well as distinguishing or unusual details, descriptions of threats, and the perspective of the child. The authors noted that the absence of emotion in the statements may at times be a symptom of unresolved PTSD. Contrary to what the authors anticipated about the amount and content of details in the fictitious reports (i.e., that fictitious reports were more likely to have insufficient details), a large number of details were present in the children's false reports. The authors hypothesized that the information provided was a result of the child being coached by a parent or the child's previous victimization. Finally, the researchers cautioned that the presence or absence of a particular feature does not make for a false report; rather, it takes multiple such features to be able to distinguish truthful reports from fictitious ones. However, they fail to specify the exact weighting of these or how many factors need to be present for such a determination. In addition, they failed to provide any information about the inter rater reliability of this key judgment.

Findings of the study are restricted by the lack of valid methods to reasonably decide that the children's claims were in fact false. The authors did not specify a way to determine whether the child had knowingly made a fictitious claim, or if he or she truly believed the claim to be legitimate. Additionally, while the first part of the study took into consideration multiple types of fictitious accounts (recantations as well as false allegations declaring that the abuse did occur), it left out cases in which the child falsely denied that the sexual abuse took place. The second part of the study ignored all instances of lying which did not include a child claiming that the abuse occurred when in reality it did not. Furthermore, in both parts of this study "fictitious report" was defined as a report regarded by a professional to be false. Reliance on professional judgment may lead to a misestimate of true rates of fictitious accounts, even in cases where support was provided for the professionals' decisions. Again, no assessment of the child's intentionality was made.

Green (1986) assessed 11 cases of alleged child sexual abuse referred to the author (a psychiatrist) in the context of child custody evaluations. Results indicated that 4 of the 11 children (35 %) had falsely accused their fathers of sexually abusing them. The first case illustrated a little boy who disclosed to the author that he had seen his father ejaculate. The author concluded that child's narrative lacked emotion and that his interactions with his father were positive, except for when the mother was present, when the child would behave in an angry and hostile way toward the father. The second case portrayed a mother who brought charges of sexual abuse against her ex-husband after her daughter came home with bloodstained underwear. The child reported that her father had rubbed against her, but later recanted her allegation and stated that she was only trying to please her mother and to stop her from the repeated questioning about alleged sexual abuse. The third case involved a 4-year-old boy whose mother suspected had been sexually abused after the child allegedly played a sexualized game that he claimed he learned from his father. The child later retracted his story, declaring that he had only made the allegations to stop his mother's persistent inquiring. The fourth case depicted the maternal grandmother of a young girl who brought the child to be examined after the child protested to going to visit her father and complained of rectal and vaginal pain. The author decided that the alleged sexual abuse did not occur as evidenced by the child's warm interaction with her father, lack of signs and symptoms of sexual molestation, and the pediatrician's confirmation that the child had a chronic irritation on her bottom not due to sexual abuse. There was no mentioning of whether the child made any of the allegations of sexual abuse herself, or if they were all brought up by the grandmother.

The author relied on the child's statement to establish that the children in fact knew they were lying about the allegations of sexual abuse, for example, when they admitted to "making up" the stories to terminate their mothers' questioning. The following criteria were used to determine that the sexual abuse allegations were fictitious: spontaneous disclosure without negative affect, child use of sexual terminology, discussion of the abuse by the child after checking-in with the mother, confrontation of the father by the child in the mother's presence, positive interactions of child and father, paranoid and hysterical mothers who brainwashed their children into making the accusations, and signs and symptoms of child sexual abuse (e.g., PTSD symptoms).

Corwin, Berliner, Goodman, and Goodwin (1987) critiqued Green's method of judging whether child sexual abuse allegations were true or false. Specifically, they criticized his use of a psychoanalytically derived technique that lacked empirical support, employment of his own clinical experience and anecdotal case reports and limited sample size. Additionally, the authors disagreed with Green's judgment of the case of the 4-year-old boy presented above as later evidence revealed that the sexual abuse had in fact occurred. We agree with the authors that Green's methodology was seriously flawed as most of his criteria for determining that the alleged abuse was false were not supported by the research. This study is a prime illustration of the dangers of relying on professional judgment, especially when basis of that judgment is Freud's controversial theory regarding sexuality. In addition, it is clear that Green's sample was not representative.

Benedek and Schetky (1985) presented 18 cases of alleged child sexual abuse they had encountered in psychiatric practice, ten of which they judged to be false (56 %). All cases were reviewed as part of child custody evaluations. Care must be taken when interpreting Benedek and Schetky's findings due to the small and highly unrepresentative sample utilized by the authors. Furthermore, since it was not specified whether it was children or adults making the false allegations, it is unclear how many children, if any, made false allegations of sexual abuse. Therefore it cannot be determined how many children made false accusations of child sexual abuse. Due to this omission, it cannot be determined if there were any criteria utilized for establishing intentionality, namely whether the child knowingly and intentionally stated a lie.

The authors did, however, employ a variety of methods to assist their professional judgment of whether the child sexual abuse allegations were true or false. First they evaluated the child's ability to distinguish fact from fantasy and assessed at the developmental appropriateness of the language used by the child. They cautioned that using precocious sexual vocabulary isn't necessarily indicative of child sexual abuse, and that such language may be a result of the child having been "sexually overstimulated" by adults (i.e., witnessing parents interacting in a sexualized manner with each other) or coached by one of the parents. Next they evaluated potential "brainwashing" by the nonoffending parent. They also employed children's play and drawings in the assessment of CSA under the assumption that this would help the children both in their disclosure of and coping with the sexual abuse. Additionally, they assessed for preoccupation with sex and displays of seductive behavior, which the authors once again indicate may be evidence of sexual abuse or of "sexual overstimulation" by adults. Finally, they engaged in direct questioning, evaluation of both parents, observation of parent–child interactions, and collateral information.

While the use of multiple methods of assessment is recommended for analyzing child sexual abuse allegations, many of the methods listed above have not been shown to accurately categorize whether child sexual abuse has occurred or not. The authors themselves admitted that precocious sexual language, preoccupation with sex, and seductive behavior are not always indicative of child sexual abuse. The use of any type of drawings and dolls are not supported by the literature, and sexually anatomically detailed dolls are particularly problematic as research examining their use (e.g., Elliott, O'Donohue, & Nickerson, 1993) indicated that a large number of nonabused children do engage in sexualized play with the dolls, increasing the risk of false positive identifications. Lastly, the accuracy of any observations and evaluations of the parents may be compromised by a variety of factors (e.g., parental stake in the outcome of a child sexual abuse investigation). There is also no indication for what behaviors, histories, and disorders are good indicators of CSA and should be the focus of assessment (i.e., criminal record in alleged offending parent).

False Denials of Sexual Abuse and Recantations

None of the studies that we reviewed specifically looked at the rates of false denials of sexual abuse, that is, that children knowingly and falsely denied being sexually abused. Nevertheless, some of the studies do report rates of denial in cases substantiated by various agencies like CPS, and we will refer to those as false denials of sexual abuse. A large limitation of the research conducted on the topic is that none of the studies assessed for intentionality, and most utilized professional judgment as their criteria for evaluation of the child's statement validity. Because of this, we have only chosen to briefly review a few of the studies and found that false denials ranged from 2 (Malloy, Lyon, & Quas, 2007) to 72 % (Sorensen & Snow, 1991) and those of recantations from 4 (Bradley & Wood, 1996) to 27 % (Gonzalez, Waterman, Kelly, McCord, & Oliveri, 1993). Table 15.1 provides a more comprehensive list of published studies.

Sorensen and Snow (1991) proposed a disclosure process of denial that developed in four stages: denial (initial statement indicating that no sexual abuse occurred), disclosure (tentative—acknowledgement of sexual abuse or active—personal admission by the child of being sexually abused), recant (retraction of the disclosure of sexual abuse), and reaffirm (reassertion that the abuse did in fact occur). The authors evaluated 630 cases of alleged child abuse they had encountered in their practice and selected 116 cases that they judged fit their proposed disclosure process. All of these cases were considered substantiated by one or more of the following: offender's confession (80 %), conviction of offender (14 %), and substantial corroborative medical evidence (6 %). Results indicated that a majority of the children initially denied being sexually abused (72 %) and that most of these denials took place when the children were interviewed by a parent or other adult figure or in the context of a forensic interview. Of those children who initially denied being the abuse, 7 % went on to make active disclosures while 78 % provided tentative disclosures. Eventually 90 % of the children had gone on to make active disclosures. Children recanted their previous allegations in 22 % of the cases, and of those 92 % later reaffirmed the abuse.

Lawson and Chaffin (1992) evaluated false negative disclosures, defined as cases in which sexual abuse occurred but there was no verbal disclosure by the child, in a sample of 28 children aged 3 to puberty diagnosed with one or more STDs. The authors found that 12 children (43 %) provided a verbal disclosure during an investigated interview conducted by a social worker, while 16 (57 %) provided no verbal disclosure. The latter group fits the authors' standard for false negative disclosures of sexual abuse due to the supporting medical findings of the STDs. Caregiver's level of supportiveness was associated with disclosure by the child, given that 63 % of children with caregivers deemed supportive disclosed while only 17 % of children with caregivers considered unsupportive disclosed.

Bradley and Wood (1996) assessed 234 cases of CSA validated by Protective Services. About half of the cases (52 %) met Sorensen and Snow's (1991) criteria for inclusion (medical evidence, conviction of offender and offender's confession). Results indicated that of the entire sample, 13 of cases were denials (6 %) and 8 were recantations (4 %). Similar results were found when only the cases meeting Sorensen and Snow's inclusion criteria were analyzed. Since the cases were considered validated, we can understand the percentage of denials as that of false denials, although we recognize that the accuracy of this number is limited by the accuracy with which Protective Services validated the cases. The authors determined that child's mother had played a large role in the child's recantations in five of the eight cases through repeated pressuring of the child to take back the allegations of abuse.

Gonzalez et al. (1993) examined recantation rates in a sample of 63 children who had disclosed sexual and ritualistic abuse after attending preschool. The 63 children

Table 15.1 Recantation and Denial Rates from Child Clinic Studies

Study	*N*	Age (range)	Disclosures (%)	Recantations (% of total sample)	False denials (% of total sample)	Lying		Type of interview
						Intentionality assessment	Validity criterion	
Sorensen and Snow (1991)	116	3–17	28	22	72	None	Offender's confession/ conviction, medical evidence	Therapy
Lawson and Chaffin (1992)	28	3 to puberty	43		57	None	Presence of STD (medical evidence)	Social worker
Bybee and Mowbray (1993)	106	2–11	58	7		None	Statement validity analysis	CPS and therapy records
Gries, Goh, and Cavanaugh (1996)	96	3–17	64	10		None	Professional judgment	CSA clinic
Gonzalez et al. (1993)	63	2–12	74	27		None	Professional judgment	Therapy
Gordon and Jaudes (1996)	141	3–14	73	12	1	None	Professional judgment	CSA team
Elliott and Briere (1994)	399	8–15	85	5	5	None	External evidence (e.g., medical evidence)	Clinician
DeVoe and Faller (1999)	76	5–10	87		5	None	Previous disclosure/corroborative evidence independent of previous statements	Social worker
Bradley and Wood (1996)	234	1–18	96	4	6	None	Professional judgment, Sorensen and Snow's criteria	CPS

(continued)

Table 15.1 (continued)

Study	*N*	Age (range)	Disclosures (%)	Recantations (% of total sample)	False denials (% of total sample)	Lying		Type of interview
						Intentionality assessment	Validity criterion	
Malloy et al. (2007)	257	2–17	99.98	23[a]	2	None	Professional judgment	CPS, medical, police and psych records
Faller and Henry (2000)	323	3–21		6.5		None	Professional judgment	CPS/police
Weighted mean				23.8	19.4			

[a]$n = 252$, after the 5 cases of nondisclosure were thrown out

were evaluated by psychotherapists, and all disclosures were made in the therapy sessions. Results indicated that 76.2 % of children disclosed CSA in the first month of therapy, and of those 27 % recanted their allegations of sexual abuse, but most (88 %) later reaffirmed the statements. The therapists identified events related to system response (e.g., having to tell police, testifying in court) and events related to parent–child variables (e.g., parental pressure) as factors possibly associated with recantation. While the authors don't label the recantations as "false" in this study, the overall sentiment is that the children falsely retracted their statements due to outside pressures, and that recantations should not be associated with false allegations (i.e., the child retracts his or her initial statement because that statement was fictitious) but rather seen as "a phase within the disclosure process for some children" (p. 288).

Malloy et al. (2007) analyzed rates of recantation of child sexual abuse allegations in 257 substantiated cases of CSA. Disclosures of sexual abuse were drawn from multiple formal (conducted by a professional, e.g., law enforcement personnel) and informal interviews (conducted by nonprofessionals, for example parents). Results indicated that in five cases (2 %) children never disclosed abuse. Because those cases were considered substantiated and there had been an attempt made during the interview to discuss sexual abuse, it can be concluded that this percentage to be demonstrative of false denials of CSA. Recantation occurred in 23.1 % of the interviews, at times within the same interview. Rates varied based on type of interview (formal vs. informal), informal interviews eliciting a slightly larger number of recantations than the formal ones.

As mentioned above, there are no criteria presented in any of the studies that indicates that any of the authors evaluated for the intentionality of the children's statements concerning the sexual abuse. Thus, again, it cannot be said that the child lied about being sexually abused as knowingly stating a falsehood is required for this determination. Criteria for determining falsehood, that is that the children falsely denied or recanted sexual abuse even though the abuse did take place, varies from professional judgment (e.g., in the studies on disclosures and recantations in therapy sessions) to a consideration of medical findings to the offender's confession and/or conviction. Some of these measures are more valid than others. For example, if a medical examination finds that a 5-year-old child is infected with gonorrhea, one can safely infer that sexual abuse must've taken place for the child to contract a sexually transmitted disease. However, studies relying on the professional judgment of therapists, social workers, etc., introduce too much observer bias, therefore reducing the accuracy of the reported rates of denials and recantations. If one cannot accurately determine whether the abuse did in fact occur or not, one cannot accurately assess the recantation and/or false denial rates.

Discussion and Conclusions

Because of methodological limitations of existing studies, we reach the Socratic conclusion that we do not know the rates at which children lie about sexual abuse. That is, we know neither how often children lie about being abused when they have not been, nor do we know how often children lie about not being abused when they in fact have been. The principle methodological shortcoming that prevents such conclusions involves a lack of a valid method to determine whether or not the child is intentionally stating a falsehood. Thus, present studies are more relevant to the question of the frequency of false reporting as opposed to the question of lying—although again due to lack of representative samples and sound assessment of historical accuracy, even conclusions about this are problematic.

Studies, with all their methodological flaws, generally reported low rates of lying and false reports. There is some evidence to suggest that lying may be more associated with older children than younger children—which is interesting as younger children have been shown in the literature to be more suggestive (see Chap. 5 in this volume) and thus there may be differences based on age on pathways to false allegations. There is also some evidence to suggest that lying about abuse not occurring may be more common than lying that abuse did occur. However, again, given the significant methodological limitations of studies reviewed, these conclusions are very tentative.

However it is also notable that studies vary tremendously on their criteria used to determine historical accuracy. Some simply use professional "judgment" and usually even fail to explicate the details of this judgment. In addition, the studies reviewed fail to show the interrater reliability of these judgments. This metric would be useful as reliability sets a constraint on validity (Haynes, Smith, & Hunsley, 2011), that is, if any lack of reliability indicates a limitation on validity. Other studies use the confession or conviction of the offender; however, we know that people have falsely confessed of crimes, and that a conviction does not guarantee that the abuse took place as people have been falsely convicted of child sexual abuse. Other studies use a variety of criteria, many of which have not been shown empirically to be valid indicators and most studies also fail to show how multiple criteria were combined to make ultimate judgments. In addition, no study examined the subcomponents of the child's claims individually to determine which were false and which were true. All studies took a rather global perspective and either judged all the children's claims as true or all as false.

This knowledge gap is important because it calls into question certain lines of reasoning that may be used in actual cases. This knowledge gap certainly questions the reasoning of advocacy organizations such as Believe the Children and their claims that children never lie. This strong claim clearly has not been established in the empirical literature. However, it also calls into question more nuanced claims that use the reasoning that because the rate of children's lying is trivially low (say 1 or 4 %) and that therefore these very low base rates suggest that some particular case of child abuse ought to be believed. Conversely, our review of the literature suggests that the same sort of argumentation is flawed regarding denials of abuse, i.e., that since we do not know the rates of lying about this, we also have to be cautious of the use of percentages in our arguments regarding this. This is particularly true in actual court cases as there have been no studies of the rattles of lying in actively adjudicated samples. However, we must also quickly say that there is no evidence to suggest that lying is a highly frequent phenomena—certainly there is no evidence that the majority of even a sizable minority of allegations are lies.

This review suggests that more research is needed. Future research ought to seek representative samples as well as to examine samples involved in judicial proceedings as there are reasons to believe that the rates of lying in these samples may differ from those in the general population For example, one reason why these rates may be different is that there may be an increased motivation for falsely accused individuals to adjudicate rather than accept a plea bargain. In addition, future research should examine special samples of children, for example, an interesting partition may be children with a history of lying about other issues or children with significant psychopathology; or children who have been threatened by their possible perpetrator. In addition, research ought to more carefully handle the question of the child's intentionality as well as more carefully address the question of historical accuracy. Finally, we suggest a more molecular approach be used and accuracy judgments be made about individual components of the child's allegations, e.g., who was the perpetrator, how many times this occurred, etc., as these are key components of the child's allegations and have important consequences, e.g., the jurisdiction and the number of counts.

The implications for forensic interviewing are also unclear. The research suggests that professionals do not have a better rate of detecting lying than nonprofessionals. In addition, there are not valid gross indicators of lying (gaze, blushing, etc), especially as these may also occur when discussing sensitive matters like sexual abuse. Thus, one caution would be to take a skeptical stance of interviewers who come to strong conclusions about lying in their interviews. Finally, it is not clear what methods ought to be adopted in the forensic interview. Most protocols incorporate whether the child knows the difference between a truth and a lie, but knowing this differences does not mean that the child will not then tell a lie. Some protocols attempt to emphasize the importance of truth during the interview but again, there is no evidence that this has any effect on increasing the probability of truth. Intentionality is a notoriously difficult construct for an outside observer to accurately assess and thus will always present a conundrum in forensic interviews.

References

Benedek, E. P., & Schetky, D. H. (1985). Allegations of sexual abuse in child custody and visitation disputes. In D. H. Schetky & E. B. Benedek (Eds.), *Emerging issues in child psychiatry and the law*. New York, NY: Brunner/Mazel.

Bradley, A. R., & Wood, J. M. (1996). How do children tell? The disclosure process in child sexual abuse. *Child Abuse & Neglect, 20*, 881–891.

Bybee, D., & Mowbray, C. T. (1993). An analysis of allegations of sexual abuse in a multi-victim day-care center case. *Child Abuse & Neglect, 17*, 767–783.

Ceci, S. J., & Bruck, M. (1993). Suggestibility of the child witness: A historical review and synthesis. *Psychological Bulletin, 113*(3), 403–439.

Corwin, D. L., Berliner, L., Goodman, G., & Goodwin, J. (1987). Child sexual abuse and custody disputes: No easy answers. *Journal of Interpersonal Violence, 2*(1), 91–105.

De Young, M. (2004). *The day care ritual abuse moral panic*. Jefferson, NC: McFarland.

DeVoe, E. R., & Faller, K. C. (1999). The characteristics of disclosure among children who may have been sexually abused. *Child Maltreatment, 4*, 217–227.

Elliott, D. M., & Briere, J. (1994). Forensic sexual abuse evaluations of older children: Disclosures and symptomatology. *Behavioral Sciences & the Law, 12*, 261–277.

Elliott, A. N., O'Donohue, W. T., & Nickerson, M. A. (1993). The use of sexually anatomically detailed dolls in the assessment of sexual abuse. *Clinical Psychology Review, 13*(3), 207–221.

Everson, M. D., & Boat, B. W. (1989). False allegations of sexual abuse by children and adolescents. *Journal of the American Academy of Child and Adolescent Psychiatry, 28*(2), 230–235.

Faller, K. C., & Henry, J. (2000). Child sexual abuse: A case study in community collaboration. *Child Abuse & Neglect, 24*, 1215–1225.

Freud, S. (1991). *The interpretation of dreams* (The Penguin Freud Library, Vol. 4). London, England: Penguin (Original work published 1900).

Gonzalez, L. S., Waterman, J., Kelly, R., McCord, J., & Oliveri, K. (1993). Children's patterns of disclosures and recantations of sexual and ritualistic abuse allegations in psychotherapy. *Child Abuse & Neglect, 17*, 281–289.

Goodwin, J., Sahd, D., & Rada, R. T. (1978). Incest hoax: False accusations, false denials. *Bulletin of the American Academy of Psychiatry and the Law, 6*(3), 269–276.

Gordon, S., & Jaudes, P. K. (1996). Sexual abuse evaluation in the emergency department: Is the history reliable? *Child Abuse & Neglect, 20*, 315–322.

Green, A. H. (1986). True and false allegations of sexual abuse in child custody disputes. *Journal of the American Academy of Child Psychiatry, 25*, 449–456.

Gries, L. T., Goh, D. S., & Cavanaugh, J. (1996). Factors associated with disclosure during child sexual abuse assessment. *Journal of Child Sexual Abuse, 5*, 1–20.

Haynes, S. N., Smith, G., & Hunsley, J. (2011). *Scientific foundations of clinical assessment*. New York, NY: Routledge.

Jones, D., & McGraw, J. J. (1987). Reliable and fictitious accounts of sexual abuse to children. *Journal of Interpersonal Violence, 2*(1), 27–45.

Kendall-Tackett, K. A., & New Hampshire Univ., D. b. (1991). *How many children lie about being sexually abused?: A survey of mental health and law enforcement professionals*.

Lawson, L., & Chaffin, M. (1992). False negatives in sexual abuse disclosure interviews: Incidence and influence of caretaker's belief in abuse in cases of accidental abuse discovery by diagnosis of STD. *Journal of Interpersonal Violence, 7*, 532–554.

Malloy, L. C., Lyon, T. D., & Quas, J. A. (2007). Filial dependency and recantation of child sexual abuse allegations. *Journal of the American Academy of Child and Adolescent Psychiatry, 46*(2), 162–170.

O'Donohue, W. T., & Benuto, L. (2012). Problems with the child sexual abuse accommodation syndrome. *Scientific Review of Mental Health Practice, 9*(1), 20–28.

Poole, D. A., & Lindsay, D. (1995). Interviewing preschoolers: Effects of nonsuggestive techniques, parental coaching, and leading questions on reports of nonexperienced events. *Journal of Experimental Child Psychology, 60*(1), 129–154.

Quas, J. A., Malloy, L. C., Melinder, A., Goodman, G. S., D'Mello, M., & Schaaf, J. (2007). Developmental differences in the effects of repeated interviews and interviewer bias on young children's event memory and false reports. *Developmental Psychology, 43*(4), 823–837.

Schreiber, N., Bellah, L., Martinez, Y., McLaurin, K., Strok, R., Garven, S., & Wood, J. (2006). Suggestive interviewing in the McMartin Preschool and Kelly Michaels daycare abuse cases: A case study. *Social Influence, 1*(1), 16–47.

Sorensen, T., & Snow, B. (1991). How children tell: The process of disclosure of child sexual abuse. *Child Welfare, 70*, 3–15.

Steffens, M. C., & Mecklenbräuker, S. (2007). False memories: Phenomena, theories, and implications. *Zeitschrift für Psychologie/Journal of Psychology, 215*, 12–24.

Summit, R. C. (1983). The child sexual abuse accommodation syndrome. *Child Abuse and Neglect, 7*, 177–193.

Chapter 16
Truth, Lies, and Recantation

April R. Bradley, John-Paul Legerski, Katie Thomas, and Kristin E. Matson

Survey data indicate that, globally, 20 % of women and up to 10 % of men report experiencing sexual abuse during childhood (Stoltenborgh, van IJzendoorn, Euser, & Bakermans-Kranenburg, 2011). In 2012, US rates of sexual abuse reports were approximately 63,000 or 9.3 %. This is likely a low estimate given the stigma often associated with child sexual abuse (CSA) and reluctance to report abuse. It is clear that CSA occurs at a significant rate in both the United States and around the world. It poses a serious risk to children and adults, with the accompanying negative psychological effects and impact on health.

The negative effects of CSA have been documented extensively in the literature, including the development of post-traumatic stress disorder, depression, anxiety disorders, and sexual problems during childhood, adolescence, and continuing into adulthood (Murray, Nguyen, & Cohen, 2014; Subica, 2013) . The stress and trauma related to CSA also makes victims more vulnerable to the negative effects of future stressful and traumatic events. Therefore, prevention efforts, identification of CSA as early as possible, and prosecution and/or rehabilitation of offenders is greatly needed. While there have been great strides in prevention and identification efforts, prosecution of offenders remains difficult.

In many cases of reported CSA, the only evidence is the child's report (London, Bruck, Wright, & Ceci, 2008). Physical evidence is present in only a minority of cases (Bays & Chadwick, 1993; Berenson et al., 2000). Victims often appear psychologically similar to non-abused children (Poole & Lindsay, 1998; Wood & Wright, 1995). Therefore, the victim's report becomes the most important piece of

A.R. Bradley, Ph.D. (✉) • J.-P. Legerski, Ph.D.
Psychology, University of North Dakota, Box 8380, Grand Forks, ND 58202, USA
e-mail: April.bradley@und.edu; Johnpaul.legerski@und.edu

K. Thomas, M.A. • K.E. Matson, M.S.
University of North Dakota, 3939 SW Bond Ave, Apt 330, Portland, OR 97239, USA
e-mail: Katie.miller.2@my.und.edu; Kristin.e.matson@my.und.edu

W.T. O'Donohue, M. Fanetti (eds.), *Forensic Interviews Regarding Child Sexual Abuse*, DOI 10.1007/978-3-319-21097-1_16

evidence in prosecuting offenders of CSA, and the validity and reliability of the child's report is often called into question.

Taking precautions to maximize the accuracy of reporting is especially important given what is at stake for both the victim and perpetrator. Faulty information collected during the assessment process can lead to intervention efforts (or the lack thereof) that can be harmful in a number of different ways (Lilienfeld, 2007). False negatives, produced when victims deny or recant abuse that has indeed occurred, can interfere, disrupt, and prohibit access to adequate care; potentially reuniting the child with family members or friends that perpetrated the abuse. In turn, false positives resulting from false allegations (intentional or not) can disrupt families, and result in criminal action, unemployment, significant financial loss, social stigma, and other negative outcomes. This chapter will review factors that impact denials, recantations, lies, and accurate statements by victims of CSA.

Theories of Denial and Recantation

CSA was not acknowledged before the late nineteenth century (Bolen, 2001). Although Freud initially reported the occurrence of CSA in several of his patients, he later came to believe that CSA had never actually occurred. Rather, he suggested that the patients desired sexual attention from their fathers (Bolen, 2001). This view was widely held until the twentieth century, when Sandor Ferenczi discussed the occurrence of CSA (Bolen, 2001). Interest in CSA increased significantly in the 1970s, after the first nationally funded study on child abuse and neglect was released (Bolen, 2001). Through the 1980s, researchers and practitioners not only acknowledged CSA to exist and to cause psychological harm, but there was also a prevalent belief that a child is unlikely to report CSA and is, in fact, likely to initially deny CSA during a formal interview (Lyon, 1995; Sorenson & Snow, 1991; Summit, 1983). Therefore, during the 1970s and 1980s, if a child initially denied abuse, the child was questioned again. In addition, if a child disclosed experiencing CSA, he or she was generally assumed to be providing a reliable and accurate version of events.

Summit (1983) proposed a model for the process of disclosing CSA, which he called the Child Sexual Abuse Accommodation Syndrome (CSAAS). According to this model, the pattern of victim–perpetrator interactions produce behaviors that seemingly discount the possibility that CSA occurred when viewed from the perspective of adult evaluators and caregivers. In the first stage, the perpetrator commands the victim to keep the abuse secret (often with threats of harm or other means). The child feeling helpless during the abuse and perceiving the abuse as unavoidable, refrains from engaging in resistance behaviors, contrary to what adults might expect. Children often believe that adults are to be trusted and obeyed, so the abused child may subsequently adopt the belief that they must have done something that warranted the abuse. The child victim may then experience a "double-bind" regarding abuse disclosure—believing that adults will react negatively if he or she discloses, but also respond negatively if he or she delays disclosure. If the victim eventually discloses in a delayed or unconvincing manner, he or she may experience alienation from caregivers and feelings of self-blame. The child therefore receives a negative reaction from adults at the time that he or she mostly needs love and support (Summit, 1983).

Summit emphasized that disclosure is rare, typically happening by accident, and characterized as being delayed, conflicted, and unconvincing. The disclosure results in alienation and loss of emotional support, ultimately increasing the likelihood of a retraction. He posited that retraction occurs because the child has experienced negative reactions to the disclosure (such as being disbelieved or blamed by parents, being removed from the home, etc.). Therefore, the child tries to restore normalcy in the family and home. However, this retraction subsequently supports the assumption made by caregivers and other adults that the child is lying about the abuse (Summit, 1983).

Summit's CSAAS model has been very influential, albeit not without its critics (McCann, Lynn, Lilienfeld, Shindler, & Hammond Natof, 2014; O'Donohue & Benuto, 2012; Weiss & Alexander, 2013). CSAAS has influenced case law, mental health practice, and policy related to handling of CSA cases. Many researchers and clinicians (e.g., Carnes, 2000; Conte, Sorenson, Fogarty, & Rosa, 1991) agreed with the model and based their CSA assessment guidelines off of its suggestions. These guidelines were adopted into official policy that still is used today, and many professionals consider CSAAS in forensic evaluations and court testimony (London, Bruck, Ceci, & Shuman, 2005). Furthermore, although CSAAS was not intended as a diagnostic tool, many professionals use it as a basis for determining the presence or absence of CSA (London et al., 2005).

Researchers have examined why children may deny and, later, recant their allegations. Koverola and Foy (1993) hypothesized that sexually abused children engage in an "avoidance phase" in which they deny or recant because they do not wish to experience the emotional distress associated with the abuse. Another explanation for recantation, more consistent with the CSAAS model, has been proposed by Gonzalez, Waterman, Kelly, McCord, and Oliveri (1993). Based on their research, they postulate that children often recant allegations to cease the family discord and social support network disruption that resulted from the disclosure. Similar research has found that concerns about family reactions or loyalty to the family may be influential in children denying or recanting abuse allegations (Lawson & Chaffin, 1992). In addition, a study by Fontes (1993) indicated that CSA victims may recant if their culture holds particular beliefs about sexual abuse. Lyon (1995) also reported that a child may be even less likely to report CSA if the offender is a parent, as many children are unwilling to accuse parents of any wrongdoing.

Although CSAAS has been very influential, some have raised concerns regarding the validity of CSAAS (for a detailed critique, see O'Donohue & Benuto, 2012). These concerns stem from evidence that children who have not been sexually abused have been known to make inconsistent statements when describing events, as well as the inherent difficulty in falsifying the model (London et al., 2008; McCann et al., 2014). In essence, CSAAS proposes that almost any response offered by a child at any point in time—a denial, accusation, or recantation—can be interpreted to suggest exposure to sexual abuse. This makes it difficult to empirically investigate and refute the model. As such, the model provides a means for child examiners and other service providers holding preconceived notions of a given youth's sexual abuse exposure to always find what they are looking for. Furthermore, the belief that children follow a pattern of responding to sexual abuse, where disclosure of the abuse at times is unlikely, may lead interviewers to use certain interview techniques that are more likely to support their assumption that sexual abuse has occurred. This may include the use of repeated or suggestive questions, projective techniques, anatomically detailed dolls, or the use of recovered memory techniques that have little empirical support and may place children at risk for making false accusations and developing false memories (Hunsley, Lee, Wood, & Taylor, 2014; London et al., 2008; McCann et al., 2014).

One approach that may exist for empirically evaluating the CSAAS model is to examine the frequency of denial, accusation, or recantation of sexual abuse. The model postulates that these behaviors follow a pattern, beginning with a denial, followed by an accusation, and ending with a recantation. The presence of this pattern would suggest that denials and recantations would be common and be present in relatively equal frequency. We have provided an overview of the research exploring the frequencies of these response types below.

Research on Denial

When discussing research in this area, it is important to distinguish denial of CSA from not disclosing CSA. Not disclosing involves not volunteering information related to the abuse, whereas denial is not admitting to being abused when asked directly (O'Donohue & Benuto, 2012). In terms of disclosure, most researchers and clinicians would agree that CSA is something that is underreported by victims and their families. London et al. (2008) noted in their review of studies using retrospective report from adult survivors of CSA that between 55 and 69 % of the study participants did not report the CSA during their childhood. Furthermore, only a marginal percentage of adults reported disclosing their CSA to authorities (5–13 %). Additional research has shown that victims often report failing to make accusations of abuse due to feelings of shame, believing they may have been at fault, fears that they will be judged harshly or punished from others, being threatened or bribed, wanting to protect the perpetrator, and memory lapses or failure (Connolly & Don Read, 2007). Clearly, many individuals fail to disclose abuse. However, the number of children who deny abuse when asked is significantly smaller.

Subjective reports of memory lapses of sexual abuse, particularly repressed memories, have produced a long history of debate (see Chap. 1, Laney & Loftus, 2015). Beliefs that children repress and later accurately recover memories contradict findings that, even after a significant delay, traumatic events can often be described in vivid detail (Cordón, Pipe, Sayfan, Melinder, & Goodman, 2004; Fivush, McDermott Sales, Goldberg, Bahrick, & Parker, 2004). A recent study also found evidence of a positive correlation between post-traumatic adjustment and the level of detail of children's description of circumstances related to a traumatic event (Legerski, Greenhoot, Vernberg, La Greca, & Silverman, 2014). Specifically, Legerski and colleagues found that children who disclose their emotions, perceptions, and cognitions when describing circumstances related to a traumatic event tended to also have the highest levels of post-traumatic stress symptoms. This seemingly contradicts the assumption that children severely impacted by a traumatic event repress memories as a means of avoiding distress.

Research on the denial of CSA is very difficult given that a child's denial may stem from either the actual absence of abuse or a false denial of abuse in situations, where abuse has indeed occurred. Two early studies, published by Sorenson and Snow (1991) and Gonzalez et al. (1993) each showed patterns of denial that show a number of consistencies with the CSAAS model described above. In 1991, Sorenson and Snow reviewed the files of 116 children seen by the authors in either private practice or in an outpatient sexual abuse treatment clinic. All cases were considered substantiated with a confession or plea by the offender, a conviction for the offense, or medical evidence consistent with sexual abuse (Sorenson & Snow, 1991). Through their review of these cases, Snow and Sorenson determined that disclosure of CSA was a process, with stages of denial, tentative disclosure, and then active disclosure. Sorenson and Snow's results suggested that 72 % of their sample initially denied that any abuse had occurred. Seventy-eight percent of the sample either began the disclosure process in tentative disclosure, or moved from denial to the tentative disclosure phase. In total, 96 % of the participants eventually actively disclosed the CSA, either initially or after denying and then tentatively disclosing.

Shortly after the Sorenson and Snow study, Gonzalez and colleagues examined the patterns of abuse disclosures and recantations of 63 preschool children who were also seen by the authors in private psychotherapy practice. The children were seen in therapy due to reports that ritualistic abuse (e.g., sexual abuse that is repetitive and bizarre and has religious or supernatural undertones; London et al., 2005) had occurred within their school setting. The authors concluded that, within one month of therapy, 76.2 % of the participants had disclosed the CSA. The authors also found that their participants first made vague comments about sexual abuse before disclosing any specific experiences. For example, a participant would make a comment about an adult touching his/her bottom before he/she would disclose intrusive sexual and ritualistic abuse (Gonzalez et al., 1993).

A number of concerns have been raised regarding the validity and generalizability of the two studies above. The participants in both studies were recruited from the private psychotherapy practices of the authors, and there have been concerns that the authors/practitioners engaged in "biased suggestive interviewing practices" (p. 213, London et al., 2005). Further, the participants in both studies were involved in widely publicized sexual abuse allegations that have since been criticized for the way in which children were interviewed and disclosure was handled (Nathan & Snedekor, 1995). Without any taped psychotherapy sessions to review, it is unclear if the nature of the practitioners' therapeutic style contributed to their results. Tentative disclosure is characterized by Gonzalez et al. study as participants providing vague or nondescript description of events that occurred. These findings are contrary to more recent research by O'Donohue et al. (2013), which examined allegations made by children with substantiated claims of abuse. According to their research, allegations included few instances of logistical implausibilities, impoverished details, fantastical details, or reports or repressed memories.

More recent research has failed to replicate many of the findings of Sorenson and Snow (1991) and Gonzalez et al. (1993). In particular, evidence suggests that denying CSA has occurred is rare, despite assertions that proponents of the CSAAS have made that it is relatively common (O'Donohue & Benuto, 2012). Based on findings presented in a comprehensive review of the literature, London et al. (2008) have shown that among children undergoing forensic evaluation for CSA, disclosure rates were between 24 and 96 %, with the pooled disclosure rate at 85 %. According to this data, it appears the denial of CSA is relatively rare among children who are directly evaluated.

While initial studies led to widespread belief that disclosure follows a specified pattern from denial to tentative disclosure to active disclosure, the majority of subsequent research has refuted this claim. Unfortunately, the impact of this initial research on human services and legal systems remains.

Research on Recantation

Recantation of disclosed abuse can be an attempt to rectify an initial false disclosure of abuse that did not actually occur, or an attempt to undo a true disclosure of abuse. Children who have experienced CSA may recant their initial disclosure for a variety of reasons. Children may feel pressure from family to recant if their initial disclosure brought about major family changes, such as the removal of the offending parent from the home and the loss of financial resources provided by the offender (Lovett, 2004; Malloy, Lyon, & Quas, 2007; Reiser, 1991).

The studies that have specifically addressed rates of recantation of CSA have come to differing conclusions. Sorenson and Snow (1991) found that 22 % of the participants in their study recanted their initial disclosure. However, 93 % of those individuals who recanted reaffirmed their initial disclosure. This data led Sorenson and Snow to conclude that recantation is a part of the disclosure process that can resolve in an active disclosure. Similar rates were found in the Gonzalez et al. (1993) study with 27 % of those children who had disclosed recanting. Among those that recanted, all but two of the children eventually reaffirmed their initial disclosure (Gonzalez et al., 1993).

In contrast to the disclosure and recantation rates of the previous studies, Bradley and Wood (1996) examined court records of 234 CSA cases that were validated by the Department of Protective and Regulatory Services (DPRS) in El Paso, Texas. In the Bradley and Wood sample, 96 % of the children had made disclosures of CSA to either DPRS or law enforcement. The majority of the children had initially disclosed the abuse to a family member or friend before reporting to law enforcement or DPRS.

Only 3 % of their sample recanted initial disclosures of CSA. Of the eight participants who recanted their disclosures, four of the cases showed documentation that the children were pressured to recant by their caretaker. They also found that 10 % of the participants evidenced reluctance to discuss specific aspects of the abuse. The authors rejected the previously proposed theory that disclosure occurs in stages that start in denial of abuse and progress towards active disclosure. Seventy-eight percent of the Bradley and Wood sample started with active disclosure and did not go through stages of denial, tentative disclosure, or recantation. With a small minority of participants recanting (3 %) or denying (6 %) the validated CSA, the authors suggested that recantation and denial of true abuse is a relatively uncommon event. However, while uncommon, of cases in which recantation did occur, the authors noted the existence of some of the characteristics of CSAAS.

More recently, Faller and Henry (2000) reviewed 323 cases of Criminal Sexual Conduct between 1988 and 1998. Though the study was designed to evaluate a community collaboration program between Child Protective Services, law enforcement, and the criminal justice system, the authors also addressed rates of disclosure, denial, and recantation found in their case reviews. Because the child's disclosure of CSA was necessary for criminal prosecution in the jurisdiction, the authors found a 100 % disclosure rate. The child initially denied the CSA in 4.6 % of the cases, and they recanted or changed the account of the abuse in 6.5 % of the cases.

The rates of recantation and denial found in the previously described studies are significantly lower than the rates found in the Sorenson and Snow (1991) and Gonzalez et al. (1993) studies (Bradley & Wood, 1996; Faller & Henry, 2000). One criticism of the high rates of disclosure and the low rates of recantation is the type of cases that were considered substantiated and included in the analyses. For example, suspicion bias occurs when samples only include children who have previously disclosed abuse and exclude cases of abuse in which the child does not disclose the abuse, or when the disclosure is not considered substantiated. For example, retrospective reports have indicated that approximately 15 % of CSA cases were disclosed to law enforcement or child protective services. Thus, studies that only include cases that have been substantiated by the courts or child protective services could be overestimating the rates of disclosure of CSA.

Estimating rates of disclosure and recantation in CSA is difficult because there are no diagnostic criteria or assessments that can offer definitive proof of CSA. There are few ways to ensure that suspected child abuse did indeed occur. A Swedish case allowed researchers the rare opportunity to study disclosure and recantation in the presence of very strong evidence of CSA; law enforcement was able to confiscate video documentation of the CSA from videotapes made by the perpetrator (Cederborg, Lamb, & Laurell, 2007). A total of ten children were abused by the perpetrator and six of the children experienced abuse that the authors deemed "memorable" or "severe," which included physical touching of the child's genitals or making the child touch the perpetrator's genitals. The remaining four cases involved the perpetrator filming the child's genitals without contact, or touching the child's genitals during activities such as diaper changing or helping the child use the bathroom (Cederborg et al., 2007). The four children whose abuse was considered "nonsevere" either denied any abuse or admitted to being touched by the perpetrator but did not disclose much detail about the incident. Of the six children whose abuse was considered severe, half of them denied that abuse had occurred. The perpetrator was related to five of the children and known by all of the children, as a daycare provider, babysitter, or caregiver. In the six severe abuse cases, the perpetrator instructed the child not to disclose the abuse, and used bribes or threats to coerce the child to participate in the abuse and maintain silence. Only half of the six children whose abuse was deemed severe disclosed abuse activities. This study indicates that even when CSA had clearly occurred, children may not necessarily provide detailed disclosures. However, none of the children who disclosed recanted their disclosure, which supports the notion that recantation of actual abuse is a rare occurrence.

Most researchers and clinicians today agree that denial and recantation can be understandable reactions to the turmoil and distress that follow CSA, but that they do not necessarily characterize the majority of children who have been abused (e.g., London et al., 2005). However, false recantations do occur in a small minority of CSA victims. Therefore, it is important to understand the factors that contribute to false recantations. Malloy et al. (2007) examined 257 case files of substantiated CSA. Documents used in the study revealed that 23.1 % of cases recanted CSA in formal and informal interviews. A number of factors were identified as increasing the risk of recantation, with children most likely to recant if they were younger, they were abused by a parent figure, or they were encouraged by the non-offending caregiver.

False Reports

During the 1980s, child abuse became a prevalent topic in books, television, movies, and popular culture in general. As more and more individuals began to report that they had been victims of CSA, there also was an increase in the number of professional therapists and counselors who purported to be experts in sexual abuse. There were also multiple allegations of ritual and sexual abuse that caught national attention, many of which were aimed at daycare providers. Many of these cases involved claims of ritual abuse, which is generally thought to be "sexual in nature," involving children being raped and forced to participate in satanic ceremonies that can include, but are not limited to, cannibalism, human sacrifice, live burials, forced impregnations, and blood-drinking (DeYoung, 2004).

One of the most famous cases occurred in 1983. Daycare providers at the McMartin Preschool in Manhattan Beach, California were accused of sexually abusing children who attended the daycare. The allegations also included claims that the providers forced the children to participate in ritualistic abuse, including burying a child in a coffin, stapling a child's eyes shut, and burning the brains of a decapitated baby. The providers were indicted and prosecuted. The preschool itself was dismantled as authorities searched for secret tunnels described by the children. In the end, the charges were dropped due to lack of evidence and inconsistencies in the children's reports. This case is particularly important with regard to CSA interviewing, as many of the techniques used to interview the children were later considered to be suggestive (DeYoung, 2007).

The Georgian Hills Day Care Center case involved another situation in which a daycare employee was accused of abusing children in a ritualistic manner, after a little girl told her mother that she "hurt down there" (DeYoung, 2007, p. 55). Allegations from other children soon followed, which included claims that the day-care provider had flown them in a helicopter and filmed them having sex in the mountains. The provider was convicted and sentenced to prison for 5 years. Later, her sentence was overturned (DeYoung, 2007).

In addition to concerns about false negatives in CSA reports, there also exists the possibility of a false positive—that a child's report is inaccurate. False or inaccurate reports can occur for many reasons, including conscious efforts to provide inaccurate information (lies), confusion, misleading or bias-producing interviews, and false memories of abuse, among others. Lipian, Mills, and Brantman (2004) propose three possible scenarios that would lead to a false report: (1) the child is being pressured to report by an authority figure; (2) the child has false memories; (3) the false reports are the result of avoiding honest responses (Lipian et al., 2004). Interestingly, the possibility of a child lying for malicious reasons is not included as a possibility. Empirical studies on false reports support this idea, in that most intentionally false reports that were examined involved another adult. For instance, Bala, Mitnick, Trocme, and Houston (2007) found that only 2 % of false reports were made by the children themselves. Furthermore, none of the reports involved sexual abuse.

As many professionals believe that false negatives are more prevalent than false positives, there exist relatively few studies on false reports. Bala et al. (2007) found that the rate of intentionally providing false reports was 4 %, although false allegations tended to be higher when made by a noncustodial parent. Furthermore, 13 % of the allegations were suspected to be false, and 27 % were not found to have enough evidence (Bala et al., 2007). In a separate study, Faller (2007) found that 189 or 80 % of professionals indicated that they had worked on a child abuse case in which they believed that the child was coached by an adult, leading to a false allegation of abuse. The research that has been conducted indicates that, while intentionally false reports likely do occur, they are very infrequent. This number becomes even smaller when identifying children who make an intentionally false report on their own, with little parent involvement.

Future Research

Although much research has been conducted in the CSA area, more remains to be done. Relatively little is known about recantation and even less about children who lie to authorities about abuse. Understanding conditions in which recantation occurs should be studied in laboratory settings (Lyon & Saywitz, 2006), which would allow more specificity in findings.Research on ways to distinguish true from false reports is still in its infancy. While it is often difficult to obtain data on children who lie to authorities about abuse, some research has identified risk factors in which false reports are more likely to occur, such as parental divorce or conflict (McGraw & Smith, 1992). More efforts to determine risk of making false claims should be conducted.

Also needed is further research on the interview process. Individual differences in suggestibility and assessment of suggestibility should continue to be conducted to better determine who is most susceptible to poor interview technique and more likely to produce inaccurate reports. Goodman and others have conducted initial research on "inoculation procedures," or procedures to reduce susceptibility in children. More research should be conducted in this area.

Implications for Practice

While denials, recantations, and false reports can and do occur in allegations of CSA, there are steps that can be taken to decrease the likelihood of these events. While CSAAS, as proposed by Summit, does not appear to be fully substantiated by research, there is evidence to indicate that, in a small minority of cases, children do deny or recant abuse due to pressure related to family, stigma, culture, and other environmental factors. Professionals working with abused children, such as police, legal personnel, and mental health professionals should make attempts to assess these pressures early, and to provide the support the child may need. Children making allegations in high risk contexts, such as a contested custody case, should be scrutinized.

The research on child interviewing is substantial. However, first responders still lack training in appropriate interviewing technique. Even when performed by professionals, interview protocols should be followed and interviews should be regularly reviewed in order to give the interviewer feedback on their performance. In addition, educators, such as primary teachers, should receive training in talking to children about abuse, as part of their mandatory training curriculum.

Very little effort has been made to educate the general public about bias in child interviews. What little information that is out there is often disregarded because parents and friends do not view talking to their loved one about an abuse event to be an "interview." Information about what to say or not say when a parent suspects abuse of their child should be made available through the schools and other public information sources.

The number of abuse allegations rises substantially during custody disputes (McGraw & Smith, 1992; Wakefield & Underwager, 1991). This may be due to active coaching or repeated questioning by a concerned parent. Efforts can be made to reduce this risk, such as offering free mediation for parents to resolve custody issues. Making parents aware that this is a concern may also reduce the likelihood of a parent attempting to coach a child.

Conclusion

In summary, research indicates that recantation does occur in CSA cases, and that recantation alone does not prove that the CSA allegations are false. Reasons for children recanting can include trying to decrease family discord, concern about family living arrangements or finances, cultural stigma or embarrassment about sexual abuse, and anxiety about the abuse or the upcoming trial. However, the studies that have been conducted suggest that recantation and denial is not as common as Summit (1983) and others proposed, in fact it occurs in only a minority of cases.

Research also suggests that false reports are generally rare, but do occur. However, it appears that false reports may be more prevalent when allegations are made during a custody or visitation dispute, and when they are made by the noncustodial parent. In addition, false reports may be the result of coaching, suggestive interviewing techniques, or false memories. Research is lacking on children who independently make purposeful false allegations (lie). This is primarily due to the fact that it is likely a rare occurrence.

References

Bala, N. M. C., Mitnick, M., Trocme, N., & Houston, C. (2007). Sexual abuse allegations and parental separation: Smokescreen or fire? *Journal of Family Studies, 13*(1), 2–37.

Bays, J., & Chadwick, D. (1993). Medical diagnosis of the sexually abused child. *Child Abuse & Neglect, 17*, 91–110.

Berenson, A. B., Chacko, M. R., Wiemann, C. M., Mishaw, C. O., Friedrich, W. N., & Grady, J. J. (2000). A case-control study of anatomic changes resulting from sexual abuse. *American Journal of Obstetrics and Gynecology, 182*, 820–831.

Bolen, R. M. (2001). *CSA: Its scope and our failure*. New York, NY: Kluwer Academic/Plenum.

Bradley, A. R., & Wood, J. M. (1996). How do children tell? The disclosure process in child sexual abuse. *Child Abuse & Neglect, 20*, 881–891.

Carnes, C. N. (2000). *Forensic evaluation of children when sexual abuse is suspected* (2nd ed.). Huntsville, AL: National Children's Advocacy Center.

Cederborg, A.-C., Lamb, M., & Laurell, O. (2007). Delay of disclosure, minimization and denial when the evidence is unambiguous: A multi victim case. In M. Pipe, M. Lamb, Y. Orbach, & A.-C. Cederborg (Eds.), *Child sexual abuse: Disclosure, delay and denial* (pp. 159–174). Hillsdale, NJ: Lawrence Erlbaum.

Connolly, D. A., & Don Read, J. (2007). Canadian criminal court reports of historic child sexual abuse: factors associated with delayed prosecution and reported repression. In M. E. Pipe, M. E. Lamb, Y. Orbach, & A. C. Cederborg (Eds.), *Child sexual abuse: Disclosure, delay, and denial* (pp. 195–217). Mahwah, NJ: Lawrence Erlbaum.

Conte, J. R., Sorenson, E., Fogarty, L., & Rosa, J. D. (1991). Evaluating children's reports of sexual abuse: Results from a survey of professionals. *American Journal of Orthopsychiatry, 61*, 428–437.

Cordón, I. M., Pipe, M. E., Sayfan, L., Melinder, A., & Goodman, G. S. (2004). Memory for traumatic experiences in early childhood. *Developmental Review, 24*(1), 101–132.

DeYoung, M. (2004). *The day care ritual abuse moral panic*. Jefferson, NC: McFarland.

DeYoung, M. (2007). Two decades after McMartin: A follow-up of 22 convicted day care employees. *Journal of Sociology and Social Welfare, 34*, 9–33.

Faller, C. F. (2007). Coaching children about sexual abuse: A pilot study of professionals' perceptions. *Child Abuse & Neglect, 31*(9), 947–959.

Faller, K. C., & Henry, J. (2000). Child sexual abuse: A case study in community collaboration. *Child Abuse & Neglect, 24*(9), 1215–1225.

Fivush, R., McDermott Sales, J., Goldberg, A., Bahrick, L., & Parker, J. (2004). Weathering the storm: Children's long-term recall of Hurricane Andrew. *Memory, 12*(1), 104–118.

Fontes, L. A. (1993). Disclosures of sexual abuse by Puerto Rican children: Oppression and cultural barriers. *Journal of Child Sexual Abuse, 2*, 21–35.

Gonzalez, L. S., Waterman, J., Kelly, R. J., McCord, J., & Oliveri, M. K. (1993). Children's patterns of disclosures and recantations of sexual and ritualistic abuse allegations in psychotherapy. *Child Abuse & Neglect, 17*, 281–289.

Hunsley, J., Lee, C. M., Wood, J. M., & Taylor, W. (2014). Controversial and questionable assessment techniques. In S. O. Lilienfeld, S. J. Lynn, & J. M. Lohr (Eds.), *Science and pseudoscience in clinical psychology* (pp. 42–82). New York, NY: Guilford.

Koverola, C., & Foy, D. (1993). Post traumatic stress disorder symptomatology in sexually abused children: Implications for legal proceedings. *Journal of Child Sexual Abuse, 2*(4), 119–128.

Laney, C., & Loftus, E. (2015). History of Forensic Interviewing. In W. O'Donohue & M. Fanetti (Eds.), *Forensic interviews regarding child sexual abuse: A guide to evidence-based practice*. New York, NY: Springer.

Lawson, L., & Chaffin, M. (1992). False negatives in sexual abuse disclosure interviews: Incidence and influence of caretaker's belief in abuse in cases of accidental abuse discovery of STD. *Journal of Interpersonal Violence, 7*(4), 532–542.

Legerski, J. P., Greenhoot, A. F., Vernberg, E. M., La Greca, A. M., & Silverman, W. K. (2014). Longitudinal analysis of children's internal states language and posttraumatic stress symptoms following a natural disaster. *Applied Cognitive Psychology, 29*(1), 91–103. doi:10.1002/acp.3081.

Lilienfeld, S. O. (2007). Psychological treatments that cause harm. *Perspectives on Psychological Science, 2*(1), 53–70.

Lipian, M. S., Mills, M. J., & Brantman, A. (2004). Assessing the verity of children's allegations of abuse: A psychiatric overview. *International Journal of Law and Psychiatry, 27*(3), 249–263.

London, K., Bruck, M., Ceci, S. J., & Shuman, D. (2005). Children's disclosure of sexual abuse: What does the research tell us about the ways that children tell? *Psychology, Public Policy, and Law, 11*, 194–226.

London, K., Bruck, M., Wright, D. B., & Ceci, S. J. (2008). Review of the contemporary literature on how children report sexual abuse to others: findings, methodological issues, and implications for forensic interviewers. *Memory, 16*(1), 29–47.

Lovett, B. B. (2004). Child sexual abuse disclosure: Maternal response and other variables impacting the victim. *Child and Adolescent Social Work Journal, 21*(4), 355–371.

Lyon, T. D. (1995). False allegations and false denials in child sexual abuse. *Psychology, Public Policy, and Law, 1*, 429–437.

Lyon, T. D., & Saywitz, K. J. (2006). From post-mortem to preventive medicine: Next steps for research on child witnesses. *Journal of Social Issues, 62*(4), 833–861.

Malloy, L. C., Lyon, T. D., & Quas, J. A. (2007). Filial dependency and recantation of child sexual abuse allegations. *Journal of the American Academy of Child and Adolescent Psychiatry, 46*(2), 162–170.

McCann, J. T., Lynn, S. J., Lilienfeld, S. O., Shindler, K. L., & Hammond Natof, T. R. (2014). The science and pseudoscience of expert testimony. In S. O. Lilienfeld, S. J. Lynn, & J. M. Lohr (Eds.), *Science and pseudoscience in clinical psychology* (pp. 83–112). New York, NY: Guilford.

McGraw, J. M., & Smith, H. A. (1992). Child sexual abuse allegations amidst divorce and custody proceedings: Refining the validation process. *Journal of Child Sexual Abuse, 1*(1), 49–62.

Murray, L. K., Nguyen, A., & Cohen, J. A. (2014). Child sexual abuse. *Child and Adolescent Psychiatric Clinics of North America, 23*(2), 321–337.

Nathan, D., & Snedekor, M. (1995). *Satan's silence: Ritual abuse and the making of a modern American witch hunt*. New York, NY: Basic Books.
O'Donohue, W., & Benuto, L. T. (2012). Problems with child sexual abuse accommodation syndrome. *Scientific Review of Mental Health Practice, 9*(1), 20–28.
O'Donohue, W., Benuto, L. T., Fondren, R. N., Tolle, L., Vijay, A., & Fanetti, M. (2013). Dimensions of child sexual abuse allegations: What is unusual and what is not? *Journal of Forensic Psychology Practice, 13*(5), 456–475.
Poole, D. A., & Lindsay, D. S. (1998). Assessing the accuracy of young children's reports: Lessons from the investigation of child sexual abuse. *Applied and Preventative Psychology, 7*, 1–26.
Reiser, M. (1991). Recantation in child sexual abuse cases. *Child Welfare, 70*, 611–621.
Sorenson, Y., & Snow, B. (1991). How children tell: The process of disclosure in child sexual abuse. *Child Welfare, 70*(1), 3–15.
Stoltenborgh, M., van IJzendoorn, M. H., Euser, E. M., & Bakermans-Kranenburg, M. (2011). A global perspective on child sexual abuse: Meta-analysis of prevalence around the world. *Child Maltreatment, 16*, 79–101.
Subica, A. M. (2013). Psychiatric and physical sequelae of childhood physical and sexual abuse and forced sexual trauma among individuals with serious mental illness. *Journal of Traumatic Stress, 26*, 588–596.
Summit, R. C. (1983). The child sexual abuse accommodation syndrome. *Child Abuse & Neglect, 7*, 177–193.
Wakefield, H., & Underwager, R. (1991). Sexual abuse allegations in divorce and custody disputes. *Behavioral Science & the Law, 9*, 451–468.
Weiss, K. J., & Alexander, J. C. (2013). Sex, lies, and statistics: Inferences from the child sexual abuse accommodation syndrome. *Journal of the American Academy of Psychiatry and the Law, 41*(3), 412–420.
Wood, J. M., & Wright, L. (1995). Evaluation of children's sexual behaviors and incorporation of base rates in judgments of sexual abuse. *Child Abuse & Neglect, 19*, 1263–1273.

About the Authors

April R. Bradley is a licensed psychologist and Associate Professor of Clinical and Forensic Psychology at the University of North Dakota. She conducts research and clinical work in the areas of child sexual abuse and forensic assessment.

John-Paul Legerski is a licensed child psychologist and Assistant professor at the University of North Dakota. He conducts research in the areas of emotional development, memory, and PTSD in children and adolescents within a developmental psychopathology framework. His clinical work focuses on children with PTSD and behavioral problems.

Katie Thomas is a doctoral candidate at the University of North Dakota. She conducts research and clinical work in the areas of trauma, NSSI, and PTSD in children and adults.

Kristin E. Matson is a doctoral candidate at the University of North Dakota. She conducts research and clinical work in the areas of forensic assessment and PTSD.

Chapter 17
Child Abuser's Threats and Grooming Techniques

Natalie Bennett and William T. O'Donohue

"Grooming" (also known as "entrapment," "engagement," "subjection," etc.) might be thought of as a seduction stage which can precede incidences of child sexual abuse (e.g., Budin & Johnson, 1989; Burgess & Holmstrom, 1980; Conte, Wolf, & Smith, 1989; Elliott, Browne, & Kilcoyne, 1995). During this stage, child molesters may use various techniques which function to gain access to the child, increase the child's compliance with the sexual abuse, and also decrease the likelihood of the child disclosing the abuse to anyone. Child abusers may also use threats during the grooming process and subsequently during the abuse to keep the child compliant as well as prevent the child from disclosing (e.g., Elliott et al., 1995; Faller, 1988). It is unclear what percentage of abusive acts are preceded by a grooming process and what percentage are not. For example, it may be the case that grooming processes are used by some abusers initially and then are abandoned. Obviously, not all abuse incidents are preceded by grooming and thus the absence of grooming does not mean that abuse has not taken place. In addition it is not known what variables affect whether a grooming process is present or not or the details of the grooming processes. These are important empirical questions.

Although there is no current consensus on a definition of grooming, several empirical studies have examined the various techniques that child molesters commonly use to aid in committing abuse (for a more complete discussion, see Bennett & O'Donohue, in press). Sexual grooming can be conceptualized at the techniques through which child abusers gain access to their future victims and prepare them to be compliant with the abuse (Brackenridge, 2001; Gillespie, 2002). The current grooming definitions used in the field vary, including criteria such as preparing the child for the abuse, gaining the child's trust, or making it difficult for the child to resist or disclose the abuse. Some definitions rely on concrete examples

N. Bennett, B.S. (✉) • W.T. O'Donohue, Ph.D.
Department of Psychology, University of Nevada, Reno, MS 0296, Reno, NV 89557, USA
e-mail: nmbennett06@gmail.com; wto@unr.edu

W.T. O'Donohue, M. Fanetti (eds.), *Forensic Interviews Regarding Child Sexual Abuse*, DOI 10.1007/978-3-319-21097-1_17

(e.g., "presenting the activity as a game or something that is 'special' and fun"; Sgroi, 1982). Other definitions are much more abstract (e.g., "the process of predisposing a boy to sexual abuse by means of subtle or blatant interactions that lead to boundary diffusion and role confusion" Spiegel, 2003). The correct identification of grooming behaviors thus suffers from the definitional confusion. That is, behaviors considered grooming under one definition may not be classified as such under another definition.

Partly due to this confusion, the exact prevalence rates of grooming are not known. Additionally, CSA tends to be underreported in general, and thus many grooming techniques may exist of which we have limited knowledge. From cases that have been reported, studies show that prevalence rates of grooming behaviors in cases where sexual abuse occurred can range from 35 (Gallagher, 2000) to 61 % (Berliner & Conte, 1990). In addition, as we will discuss more below, no matter what definition of grooming is used, currently there is not an attendant psychometrically sound assessment methodology to measure the presence or absence of grooming behaviors.

Recently, Bennett and O'Donohue (in press) presented a proposed solution to the definitional problems of the grooming construct: grooming should be defined as "antecedent inappropriate behavior that functions to increase the likelihood of future sexual abuse." Thus, according to this definition, assessment of a grooming behavior would include: (1) determining that the adult's behavior is inappropriate in and of itself; and (2) reasonably arguing that the function of this inappropriate behavior is to increase the likelihood of future abusive contact. Ideally, this definition should help interviewers and clinicians correctly identify grooming behaviors.

The offender's use of such grooming and threatening methods may affect how a child victim presents during a forensic interview. The child may not entirely realize that what the offender did was wrong either in the grooming process or possibly even the abusive contact, especially if the offender groomed the child to believe as such. It is also possible that the child wholeheartedly believes the any threats the offender made and is thus willing to deny the abuse occurred in order to protect him or herself or a loved one. This chapter will review the empirical literature regarding what is known about grooming and threatening techniques, as well as provide suggestions on what to look for in a forensic interview regarding evidence of such techniques.

What to Look for in a Forensic Interview

It is important to recognize that determining whether or not an alleged offender's behaviors can be considering grooming is a complicated task. In general, many grooming behaviors can appear to be normal within the context of a healthy adult–child relationship (Hartill, 2009). For example, gift giving and compliments can be normal, but it is also possible that they are intended to coerce the child into complying with the abuse. Offenders tend to engage in grooming techniques that are as "normal" as possible in order to gain the child's compliance and later silence, as well as to mitigate any suspicions that the child's family or caregivers may hold.

The identification of grooming or threatening behaviors can help aid the investigation of a sexual abuse allegation. Thus, when conducting a forensic interview, it may be important to ask the child about his or her relationship with the perpetrator prior to the abuse. For example, did the alleged offender give the child special attention or bribes? Did he or she engage in lots of physical, but maybe not sexual, acts such as wrestling or other touching with the child? The following categories are areas that have been identified in the empirical literature as common areas where grooming may occur.

Special Attention or Bribery

Common techniques that many sex offenders admit to using to gain the compliance of their victims include some use of inappropriate attention or bribery. Specifically, some offenders have admitted to using a nice and nonthreatening voice and listening to the child as a grooming strategy (Conte et al., 1989). Additionally, in one study, over three-quarters of the sample of 72 sex offenders admitted to acting like the child's friend (Budin & Johnson, 1989). Furthermore, Gallagher (2000) reviewed 65 cases of substantiated institutional abuse (i.e., sexual abuse that occurs between a child and a person who works with them in a residential home). He found that in 22 % of these cases, the offender admitted to giving the child extra attention.

Offenders may also offer to teach the child how to play a game, sport, or musical instrument. Additionally, offenders may use gifts or bribes such as money, toys, candy, cigarettes, beer, or drugs (Budin & Johnson, 1989; Gallagher, 2000). These gifts may be given with the intent of gaining the child's trust or possibly in exchange for sexual favors. The offender may also offer to take the child out for an outing or to drive the child home (Elliott et al., 1995; Gallagher, 2000). In one study, prevalence rates for such attention and bribery grooming behaviors (in sample of 91 child molesters) ranged from 46 to 53 %, meaning that nearly half of these offenders engaged the use of these grooming techniques prior to committing their abusive acts (Elliott et al., 1995).

Offenders have also admitted to purposefully using love and affection to gain the child's trust (Elliott et al., 1995). They may also use phrases such as "If you love me you'd let me do it" in order to coerce the child into complying with the abusive acts (Conte et al., 1989). However, the attention that offenders give may also take on a negative tone. Spiegel (2003) noted that primarily in male victims, perpetrators may use name-calling words such as "fag" or "whore" to put the child down and make him feel ashamed and thus less likely to disclose the abuse.

Finally, it should be noted that CSA victims as well report high rates of being groomed prior to the abuse occurring. For example, Berliner and Conte (1990) interviewed 23 CSA victims and found that the almost all of the victims reported some type of experience of being bribed or coerced into compliance with the abuse.

For instance, over half of the victims in this study reported that their abusers made excuses to spend time alone with them; were told that they were special, different, or the only one who understood the abuser; or reported that their abusers gave them special privileges which made them feel obligated to be compliant in the abuse. About one-third of the victims reported that their abuser prevented them from having friends or doing activities that other children do; or that their abuser treated them "meaner" than other children.

Sexual Desensitization

Another common strategy that offenders may use to make a child compliant with sexual abuse is sexual desensitization. According to Berliner and Conte (1990), sexual desensitization tends to occur gradually. Normal physical or affectionate contact such as bathing, snuggling, or tickling may eventually progress into sexual touching and then possibly into more intrusive forms of sexual abuse. In fact, almost two-thirds of the children in this study reported that at first the genital touching seemed accidental. It should be noted, however, that a few of the victims in this study reported that the shift from normal touching to sexual abuse was abrupt and thus the period of gradual sexual desensitization was either small or nonexistent,

Offenders have also endorsed using the sexual desensitization tactic. For example, the offender may start talking to the child about sex or offer to bathe or clothe the child alone (Elliott et al., 1995). In this same study, about a quarter of offenders who babysat their victims admitted to using these grooming techniques. Additionally, almost a third of the offenders admitted to asking the child for help with something, such as undressing. Almost half admitted to talking about sex with the child or "accidentally" touching the child.

Offenders also admitted to using pornographic videos and magazines to desensitize the child to sex. Interestingly, Spiegel (2003) noted that the use of pornography in sexually desensitizing children is more common with male victims than with female victims. Sometimes the offender may tell the child that he or she is teaching the child sex education and will engage the use of pornography and touching the child's body to do so (Berliner & Conte, 1990). However, it is also the case that showing pornography to a child is abuse in and of itself and not a part of a grooming process preparatory to abuse. It may however be preparatory to more severe abuse such as contact abuse.

Commonly, offenders will gradually increase physical contact to increase the child's compliance with the abuse (Gallagher, 2000). For example, the offender may begin by wrestling, kissing, massaging, or snuggling the child, all while evaluating the child's reaction to the touching. If the child feels uncomfortable and asks the offender to stop, the offender may stop for a little while and then gradually increase contact again (Conte et al., 1989; Elliott et al., 1995). Offenders also admit to making a game out of the abuse, e.g., Red Light, Green Light. In this situation, the offender may begin touching up the child's leg until the child protests (Conte et al., 1989).

Other common techniques that the offender may use to desensitize the child include the offender "accidentally" showing his or her naked body to the child, making sexual comments about the child's body or clothing, or telling the child about previous sexual encounters that he or she has had (Berliner & Conte, 1990).

Boundary Violations

Offenders may also use techniques that violate the child's privacy and personal boundaries. For example, in the Berliner and Conte (1990) interviews, 70 % of victims reported that their abuser "accidentally" came into their bedroom or bathroom while the child was undressing. Additionally, if the offender is a caregiver for the child, he or she may refuse to allow the child to close doors for privacy. The offender may also inspect the child's body "to see how it is developing." Almost a quarter of the victims also indicated that their abusers put lotion or ointment on them when they were alone.

Furthermore, particularly in father–daughter incest, offending fathers may insist on being the sole person to bathe their daughters (Christiansen & Blake, 1990). These baths will then frequently involve inappropriate sexual behavior. Offending fathers may also insist on dressing their daughters or on watching them get dressed or use the bathroom.

Grooming the Child's Environment

Offenders may not focus grooming techniques solely on the victim; indeed they may also attempt to groom those in the child's environment (e.g., parents or family). Nearly half of offenders in one study admitted to isolating their victims through babysitting (Elliott et al., 1995). Twenty percent of the offenders in this study also admitted to purposefully gaining the trust of the child's family in order to abuse the child. Additionally, offenders may use strategies such as the "foot in the door technique" to win over the parents of an intended victim (Van Dam, 2001). For example, the offender may attend the child's birthday party uninvited but appear very friendly and play games with the children there. The child's parents would most likely allow the offender to stay as asking him to leave might appear rude.

Common Threats Used

Offenders may also commonly use threats to make the child compliant or to keep him or her from telling anyone about the abuse. The offender may threaten physical harm to the child. These threats may range from any type of physical injury to the child (e.g., "I'll cut off your fingers") to threats of death (Berliner & Conte, 1990). The offender may also threaten physical harm or death to a family member or friend of the child (Faller, 1988). Threats of physical harm may also take the form of the child witnessing the offender be physically violent with another person. For example, if the offender is a father, the child victim may see him be violent towards the child's mother. Offenders may also use their physical size to intimidate the child or hold the child still (Conte et al., 1989). Additionally, this type of physical harm threat may take the form in which the offender harms an animal and tells the child the same will happen to him or her if the abuse is disclosed. For example, in one study, one victim disclosed that the offender made her eat stew made from a pet rabbit, threatening that he would make a stew out of her if she disclosed the abuse (Faller, 1988).

Furthermore, the offender may threaten the child with abandonment, rejection, or other emotional consequences, e.g., "Your mother will be mad at you" (Berliner & Conte, 1990). The offender may also threaten that the child will lose friends or the offender's love if the child does not comply with the abuse. Additionally, the offender may threaten that the child will be institutionalized if he or she discloses the abuse (Budin & Johnson, 1989). Conversely, the offender may threaten the child with negative consequences to him or herself. For example, the offender may threaten suicide, or that the offender will be thrown in jail or murdered if the child tells (Berliner & Conte, 1990).

The offender may also use "scary person" or "scary place" threats (Faller, 1988). In "scary person" types of threats, the offender makes statements in which he or she takes on special powers. For example, an offender may say that he is "stronger than the Incredible Hulk" (p. 293) and thus the child should not attempt to be noncompliant or to disclose the abuse. This type of threat could also take the form of the offender dressing in a certain way to scare the child (e.g., the offender dresses herself as a witch). In "scary place" type threats, the offender tells the child that he or she will be sent to a frightening place if the abuse is disclosed. Using Faller (1988)'s example, the offender may make a child crawl inside an oven and threaten to cook the child if he or she discloses the abuse.

Finally, the offender may threaten that the child's family will suffer emotional consequences. For example, the offender may tell the child that his or her family will be forever shamed if they find out that their child was abused (Berliner & Conte, 1990). Offenders may also tell the child that his or her parents will get divorced if the child does not cooperate (Budin & Johnson, 1989).

Special Case: Teacher Sexual Abuse

Although many of the grooming techniques used in teacher sexual abuse cases are similar to that of other cases, subtle differences exist. In particular, the grooming behaviors may seem particularly normal in this type of abuse case, as students are expected to spend time with their teachers and many parents are in fact grateful when a teacher gives a student extra attention (Shakeshaft, 2004), as this seems likely to further the student's education. An additional complexity that Shakeshaft pointed out is that in teacher sexual abuse, even if there is suspicion of grooming behaviors, a teacher giving attention to a student is legitimate within the responsibilities of the occupation, and thus cannot lead to any disciplinary action.

Similar to other types of grooming behaviors, teacher sexual offenders often use bribery against their intended victims. They tend to give their intended victims special attention or rewards. While the use of bribery is occurring, these offenders also typically begin to converse about sexual matters with their intended victims (Knoll, 2010). Teacher sexual offenders also tend to coerce their victims by providing additional help on projects or taking them for outings (Shakeshaft, 2004). Finally, teacher sexual offenders may also attempt to groom the student's environment by manipulating the relationship with the intended victim's parents, thus gaining approval to spend time alone with the student (Knoll, 2010).

Questions to Ask During the Forensic Interview

Examination of the NICHD Investigative Interview Protocol (taken from Lamb, Orbach, Hershkowitz, Esplin, & Horowitz, 2007) revealed that there are no specific questions related to grooming in the current protocol. It is important to elicit information about grooming from the child within the forensic interview without assuming that grooming did or did not take place. If within the interview the child mentions some sort of incident that *could* be grooming-related (e.g., "He asked me to play red light green light") it would be important to respond with an open-ended query, such as "Tell me all about that."

If the child does not mention any incidents that sound like grooming, it may still be possible to ask about such occurrences towards the end of the interview, as not to contaminate any part of the allegation about the abusive incidents. Open-ended prompts such as "Tell me about your relationship with [the alleged perpetrator] before [the incidents] happened" can be utilized. However, if the child does not give a detailed response, it may be reasonable to ask more focused questions such as:

- "Did you and [the alleged perpetrator] play games where you touched each other? Tell me everything about that."
- "Did [the alleged perpetrator] ever give you presents? Tell me all about that."
- "Did [the alleged perpetrator] give you baths or help you get undressed? Tell me all about that."
- "Did [the alleged perpetrator] tell you something bad would happen if you told someone what he was doing? Tell me about that."
- "Did [the alleged perpetrator] tell you that you would get in trouble if you told someone what he was doing? Tell me everything about that."

It is important to remember is that once such questions are asked, an answer of "yes" does not mean that grooming necessarily occurred. Many of these behaviors, such as bathing or dressing, occur within the context of normal adult–child relationships.

As discussed in Bennett and O'Donohue (in press), to be considered grooming, the behavior should be shown to be inappropriate in and of itself and that the function of this inappropriate behavior is to increase the likelihood of future abusive contact.

Again, no grooming assessment with valid psychometric properties currently exists. Bennett & O'Donohue are now working on developing a measure based on their proposed definition. This assessment device will be a clinical tool, similar to a decision tree, in which the possible grooming behavior is subjected to various questions (e.g., "Is it inappropriate?" or "Were there alternative choices?"). Ultimately, the behavior would fall into one of three categories: (1) definitely grooming, (2) definitely not grooming, or (3) unclear. Furthermore, it is planned that this device will be subjected to empirical study to determine sensitivity and specificity, as well as reliability and validity.

Mistakes to Avoid

Common judgment and decision-making errors may result in a biased forensic interview. An important error to avoid when conducting a forensic interview, especially with regards to grooming behavior, is that of confirmation bias. Confirmation bias has been defined as "the tendency to prefer information that is consistent with a hypothesis rather than to information that opposes it" (Plous, 1993, p. 233). This means that if an interviewer questions the child with a hypothesis already in mind (e.g., that the child was sexually abused), then the interviewer may pay more attention to and be more likely to believe any information that the child offers which confirms the interviewer's hypothesis. The interviewer may also be less likely to believe or attend to any information that contradicts the hypothesis. In terms of grooming, it could be easy for such an interviewer to attend to the instances in which the alleged offender gave the child gifts and to ignore other crucial information such as the fact that the gifts were given only on birthdays and holidays. Leading questions can be a result of confirmation bias within an interview, and have been shown to lead to an increased risk of false testimony (Powell, Garry, & Brewer, 2009).

Another possible problem in assessing whether or not grooming has taken place is the common use of the representativeness heuristic. Kahneman and Tversky (1972) explained that people use the representativeness heuristic when they judge the probability of an event by its characteristics' similarity to those of the parent population. A frequently used example demonstrating this heuristic is "Nancy is a shy, single woman who loves to read. Is Nancy more likely to be a lawyer or a librarian?" Most people would answer that she is more likely to be a librarian, as her characteristics seem similar to that of a prototypical librarian. However, in terms of sheer probabilities, Nancy is more likely to be a lawyer as there are many more lawyers than librarians. In terms of grooming, a father's lavish birthday gift to his young daughter may appear similar to grooming techniques that are used by offenders—i.e., special attention and bribery. The problem here is that the giving of lavish birthday gifts occurs much more frequently as an act of kindness rather than a grooming behavior. Thus, one must be wary of the tendency to ignore base rates when judging the probability of an event.

Additionally, the use of the "post hoc ergo propter hoc" fallacy (i.e., "after this, therefore because of this") can contribute to problems that arise during forensic interviews regarding grooming techniques. To clarify, if a child alleges sexual abuse, and then it is discovered that the offender had been giving the child candy prior to the alleged abuse, many people would come to the conclusion that the candy-giving was obviously a grooming technique and thus abuse must have occurred. Candy-giving does not predictably result in sexual abuse (i.e., not all adults who give a child candy go on to sexually abuse that child); however, it is a technique that may be used by offenders. Thus, it is important to interpret such grooming behaviors with caution—questioning the child about the offender's grooming behaviors may help guide understanding of the allegation but cannot confirm that abuse did in fact occur.

Conclusion

The exact prevalence rates of grooming behaviors in cases of sexual abuse are not currently known, as CSA in general tends to be underreported and even then the allegations may not include details of the grooming behaviors. However, considerable support from empirical studies shows that rates of grooming generally tend to fall between 35 (Gallagher, 2000) to 61 % (Berliner & Conte, 1990). Additionally, in one study, 39 % of offenders admitted to using threats against their victims (Elliott et al., 1995). Thus, it is fairly likely that in any particular CSA case, any type of grooming or threatening technique was used. Within a forensic interview context, it would be important to ask the child if any of the behaviors covered in this chapter occurred during his or her relationship with the alleged perpetrator. Importantly, common errors in judgment and decision-making such as confirmation bias, representativeness heuristic, and post hoc reasoning should be avoided.

References

Bennett, N., & O'Donohue, W. (in press). Sexual grooming: Conceptual and assessment issues. *Journal of Child Sexual Abuse*.

Berliner, L., & Conte, J. R. (1990). The process of victimization: The victims' perspective. *Child Abuse & Neglect, 14*, 29–40.

Brackenridge, C. H. (2001). *Spoilsports: Understanding and preventing sexual exploitation in sport*. London, England: Routledge.

Budin, I. E., & Johnson, C. F. (1989). Sexual abuse prevention: Offenders' attitudes about their efficacy. *Child Abuse & Neglect, 13*, 77–87.

Burgess, A. W., & Holmstrom, L. L. (1980). Sexual trauma of children and adolescents: Pressure, sex, secrecy. In L. G. Schultz (Ed.), *The sexual victimology of youth* (pp. 67–82). Springfield, IL: Charles C Thomas.

Christiansen, J. R., & Blake, R. H. (1990). The grooming process in father-daughter incest. In A. L. Horton (Ed.), *The incest perpetrator: A family member no one wants to treat* (pp. 88–98). Thousand Oaks, CA: Sage.

Conte, J. R., Wolf, S., & Smith, T. (1989). What sexual offenders tell us about prevention strategies. *Child Abuse & Neglect, 13*(2), 293–301.

Elliott, M., Browne, K., & Kilcoyne, J. (1995). Child sexual abuse prevention: What offenders tell us. *Child Abuse & Neglect, 19*(5), 579–594.

Faller, K. C. (1988). The spectrum of sexual abuse in daycare: An exploratory study. *Journal of Family Violence, 3*(4), 283–298.

Gallagher, B. (2000). The extent and nature of known cases of institutional child sexual abuse. *British Journal of Social Work, 30*(6), 795–817.

Gillespie, A. (2002). Child protection on the internet: Challenges for criminal law. *Child and Family Law Quarterly, 14*(4), 411–425.

Hartill, M. (2009). The sexual abuse of boys in organized male sports. *Men and Masculinities, 12*, 225–249.

Kahneman, D., & Tversky, A. (1972). Subjective probability: A judgment of representativeness. *Cognitive Psychology, 3*(3), 430–454.

Knoll, J. (2010). Teacher sexual misconduct: Grooming patterns and female offenders. *Journal of Child Sexual Abuse, 19*, 371–386.

Lamb, M. E., Orbach, Y., Hershkowitz, I., Esplin, P. W., & Horowitz, D. (2007). Structured forensic interview protocols improve the quality and informativeness of investigative interviews with children: A review of research using the NICHD Investigative Interview Protocol. *Child Abuse & Neglect, 31*(11–12), 1201–1231.

Plous, S. (1993). *The psychology of judgment and decision making*. Philadelphia, PA: Temple University Press.

Powell, M. B., Garry, M., & Brewer, N. D. (2009). Eyewitness testimony. In I. Freckelton & H. Selby (Eds.), *Expert evidence* (pp. 1–42). Sydney, New South Wales, Australia: Thompson Reuters.

Sgroi, S. M. (1982). *Handbook of clinical intervention in child sexual abuse*. Lexington, MS: Lexington Books.

Shakeshaft, C. (2004). *Educator sexual misconduct: A synthesis of existing literature* (U.S. Department of Education Document No. 2004-09). Washington, DC: U.S. Department of Education.

Spiegel, J. (2003). *Sexual abuse of males: The SAM model of theory and practice*. New York, NY: Brunner-Routledge.

Van Dam, C. (2001). *Identifying child molesters: Preventing child sexual abuse by recognizing the patterns of the offenders*. Binghamton, NY: Haworth Maltreatment and Trauma Press/The Haworth Press.

Chapter 18
Assessing the Quality of Forensic Interviews with Child Witnesses

Becky Earhart, David La Rooy, and Michael Lamb

Overview

The child's account of what happened is often the only evidence available in investigations of child sexualabuse. Whenever there is a lack of physical or corroborating evidence, the child's testimony and ensuing legal decisions can have far-reaching consequences for all those involved. Even when there is physical evidence of abuse, it often remains important to have an account from the child so that what happened and who was involved can be fully clarified. Obtaining and evaluating the evidence provided in these cases presents a challenge for many legal systems that were not designed to deal with the complexities of proceedings that involve children. Most importantly, those referred to simply as "children" actually represent a very broad categorization including infants, toddlers, young children, older children, and adolescents. Indeed, in many jurisdictions children and young persons are considered vulnerable until the age of 18 years. The accounts that children provide in forensic interviews must thus be viewed and assessed within the context of their social, emotional, and cognitive development by appropriately qualified experts. A substantial

B. Earhart (✉)
Department of Psychology, Wilfrid Laurier University,
75 University Avenue W, Waterloo, ON, Canada, N2L 3C5
e-mail: earh9100@mylaurier.ca

D. La Rooy
University of Abertay, Dundee, UK

School of Law, Royal Holloway, University of London, Egham TW20 0EX, UK
e-mail: david@larooy.net

M. Lamb
Department of Psychology, University of Cambridge,
Free School Lane, Cambridge CB2 3RQ, UK
e-mail: mel37@cam.ac.uk

W.T. O'Donohue, M. Fanetti (eds.), *Forensic Interviews Regarding Child Sexual Abuse*, DOI 10.1007/978-3-319-21097-1_18

amount of scientific evidence guides our understanding and approach to many issues surrounding forensic interviews with children, informing us about how investigative interviews should be conducted and the pitfalls that should be avoided (e.g., Lamb, Hershkowitz, Orbach, & Esplin, 2008; Lamb, La Rooy, Malloy, & Katz, 2011; Poole & Lamb, 1998; and this volume).

In this chapter, we discuss key aspects of assessing the quality of forensic interviews conducted with childwitnesses. We begin by discussing the quality of the case material, before reviewing the key components of investigative interviews and methods of assessing the quality of each of these components. The overall structure of the interview is discussed with reference to the use of "ground rules" and the effectiveness of rapport building and episodic memory training during the presubstantive phase of the interview. Issues surrounding the identification of appropriate and inappropriate questions and prompts are examined in relation to the strengths and weaknesses of memory. Additional issues that can influence the effectiveness of an interview, such as the use of repeated questions, the specific vs. generic nature of accounts, and the use of anatomical dolls, are also considered in light of the impact they may have on children's responses.

Who Should Conduct Assessments of Interview Quality?

Requests for assessments of forensic interviews are often made by lawyers defending accused individuals in criminal and civil court cases to determine whether or not interviews were conducted fairly. An expert witness will often be asked to prepare a report for the parties involved that can inform fact finders of any concerns with the way the interviews were conducted, and thus affect the weight that should be placed on the interviews as evidence. Given what is currently known about the laws of memory and how they apply to child forensic interviewing, combined with the social, linguistic, and emotional factors that are involved, it is not surprising that professionals turn to psychologists to provide these assessments. Expert witness interview as evidence. Sometimes, however, there is heated debate about exactly who should be considered an expert, especially when issues to do with memory and suggestibility are to be considered.

In many jurisdictions judges themselves decide who should be considered an expert, but there are also professional standards and ethical considerations, about which psychologists should be particularly aware. Some experts are so considered because they are recognized by their peers as scholars in the field. The easiest way to assess this "recognition" is through publications in peer-reviewed journals. The peer-review process functions to improve the quality and coherence of scientific research and demonstrates that the expert's reasoning is consistent with that of scholars who have had the opportunity to evaluate their work. Although qualified experts may still have differences of opinion, selecting suitably qualified expert witnesses decreases the chance that there will be "battles of the experts" in court. In reality, many professionals are willing to put themselves forward as memory experts based on their professional experience and training rather than an understanding of the dynamics of memory and scientific research about interviewing children. Thus, disagreements between experts are often better understood with reference to individual training and qualifications. For this reason, whenever experts provide court reports it is advisable to provide up-to-date curricula vitae so that professional qualifications are transparent.

Case Material to be Assessed

There is widespread agreement that both electronic records and verbatim transcripts should be examined in order to appropriately assess the quality of forensic interviews (La Rooy & Block, 2013; Lamb, Orbach, Sternberg, Hershkowitz, & Horowitz, 2000; Warren & Woodall, 1999). The advantage of having electronic recordings of interviews is that children's evidence is accurately preserved so that systematic analyses can take place. Electronic recordings and written transcripts are equally important, and thus, the first step is to have the recording fully transcribed so that all of the interviewer's questions and child's responses can be easily examined.

In some jurisdictions interviews are not routinely recorded and transcribed, and interviewers instead rely on contemporaneous or retrospectively written notes. It is difficult to understand why this practice persists because note taking is unlikely to result in an accurate record of the exact questions posed and the information elicited from children. Lamb and colleagues (2000) directly compared handwritten notes taken by experienced interviewers with electronic recordings of the same interviews. The results showed that more than half of the questions and prompts posed by the investigators were not recorded verbatim, and a quarter of the details reported by the interviewees were not recorded. Importantly, details of the children's accounts were often incorrectly attributed to being elicited by higher quality interviewer prompts, (i.e., the interviewers were recording the interviews as being of a higher standard than they actually were). Notes from interviews often include the gist of what each person has said rather than the exact wording of the questions and answers. Therefore, analysis of interviewer notes is somewhat problematic, and this issue should be clearly identified for fact finders if a transcript is not available.

Following transcription, the interview must be carefully inspected to identify aspects of the interview that are conducted in accordance with best practice, as well as any areas of concern surrounding the nature and appropriateness of questioning. The transcript allows for a more accurate examination than the electronic recording alone because it is possible to move backward and forward through the interview quickly to determine where information was introduced, and whether it was introduced by the child or the interviewer. It is not possible to do this type of detailed analysis in "real time" by simply viewing a recording of the interview, and it is too time consuming and difficult to rewind and fast forward electronic recordings to verify this type of information with any degree of accuracy.

A video recording is ideal because it allows consideration of nonverbal cues provided by both the interviewer and the child. Children may nod in response to prompts or indicate body parts in a way that cannot be captured in a typed transcript; it is only through careful viewing of a video that one can clarify the children's responses. Interviewers also use nonverbal cues, such as gestures, intonation, and pauses, which may affect the child's responses, so examining a video may help to put interviewer prompts in context. For example, if a transcript states "child nods," it is important to check whether this was indeed a clear gesture or whether the child appeared to be mimicking the interviewer. The video cannot, however, be used to make judgments about truthfulness based on the child's demeanor. Although some experts may claim that they are proficient at detecting nonverbal cues to lying and truth telling, research shows that adults' accuracy at detecting children's lies is at chance levels (i.e., they are no better than guessing; see Vrij, 2008, for a comprehensive review of this issue).

Rapport Building

During investigative interviews children may feel apprehensive about discussing highly personal experiences with strangers (Saywitz, Goodman, Nicholas, & Moan, 1991). This is especially true when discussing experiences of sexualabuse, which are intimate and embarrassing. It is recommended that interviewers begin by building rapport with interviewees to put them at ease, make them feel more comfortable disclosing sensitive information, and set a supportive context that encourages children to trust interviewers (Collins, Lincoln, & Frank, 2002; Goodman, Bottoms, Schwartz-Kenney, & Rudy, 1991; Lamb, Orbach, Warren, Esplin, & Hershkowitz, 2007; Sternberg et al., 1997). This can be done by discussing neutral or positive personal topics, such as friends and family, school, hobbies, etc., to get to know the children better (Lamb, Sternberg, & Esplin, 1998; Poole & Lamb, 1998).

There is evidence that rapport building improves both the amount and accuracy of information that children provide about personal experiences, especially if it is established using open-ended prompts (Roberts, Lamb, & Sternberg, 2004; Sternberg et al., 1997). Rapport building is especially important for reluctant children (Wood, McClure, & Birch, 1996), making it more likely that they will disclose abuse and provide more details about their experiences (Hershkowitz, Lamb, & Katz, 2014; Hershkowitz, Lamb, Katz, & Malloy, 2013). Overall, high levels of interviewer supportiveness help to improve the accuracy of children's reports (Almerigogna, Ost, Bull, & Akehurst, 2007; Carter, Bottoms, & Levine, 1996; Davis & Bottoms, 2002; Goodman et al., 1991; Quas & Lench, 2007), but in practice interviewers do not often use open-ended questions during the rapport building phase (Warren, Woodall, Hunt, & Perry, 1996), or they may not do enough rapport building (Sternberg, Lamb, Esplin, & Baradaran, 1999). If rapport building is not done effectively, the benefits for children's testimony will not be evident as seen in laboratory studies.

Although creating a supportive environment is an important goal of rapport building, interviewers must be cautious about how they express their support to children. Normal responses to the disclosure of abuse, such as shock or surprise, might be seen as attempts to overempathize and shape the testimony. Thus, empathetic responses, such as, "That must have hurt," could be seen as examples of interviewers suggesting information that was not provided by the children. Research also shows that children are sensitive to positive reinforcement and praise for answers that they think interviewers want to hear, so even comments like, "Aren't you wonderful?" can be seen as ways of shaping testimony. While it is undesirable that interviewers overempathize with children in interviews, support can be provided in a more neutral manner that does not attract criticism. Commenting on the effort a child is making by saying, "I can tell you are trying hard," and small acts of kindness such as offering a glass of water or a tissue should not be considered attempts by interviewers to alter the content of the child's testimony, but can nonetheless help an interviewer build rapport with a reluctant child.

Ground Rules

Interviewers often establish "ground rules" or interview instructions early on that indicate what is expected of children during the interviews and define the conversational rules. Although they are often communicated at the beginning of an interview, they may also be communicated after rapport building or at any time during the interview when appropriate. Investigative interviews are strange for children, who most often interact with more informed adults who ask questions of them to assess their knowledge (Lamb et al. 2007a; Lamb, Orbach, Hershkowitz, Esplin, & Horowitz, 2007b; Lyon, 2010). Children must understand that interviewers do not know what happened, and communication of the ground rules is designed to help children become aware that they are in control and should not feel pressured to answer questions (Lamb, Orbach, Hershkowitz et al., 2007; Lyon, 2010; Saywitz, Camparo, & Romanoff, 2010; Sternberg, Lamb, Esplin, Orbach, & Hershkowitz, 2002). Commonly recommended ground rules include (a) communicating that it's important to tell the truth/promise to tell the truth (Evans & Lee, 2010; Lyon & Dorado, 2008; Talwar, Lee, Bala, & Lindsay, 2002); (b) asking the child to demonstrate that s/he understands the difference between telling the truth and telling a lie; (c) it is okay to tell the interviewer if you do not understand (Saywitz, Snyder, & Nathanson, 1999); (d) it is okay to say "I don't know" (Gee, Gregory, & Pipe, 1999; Saywitz & Moan-Hardie, 1994; Waterman & Blades, 2011); (e) it is okay to correct the interviewer (Krackow & Lynn, 2010; Saywitz & Moan-Hardie, 1994); and (f) if questions are repeated, it does not mean that that the interviewer was unhappy with the previous answer.

The ground rules are considered an important part of the presubstantive phase of the interview because they are designed to remove implicit pressure on interviewees to guess if they are not sure about what happened, and/or to acquiesce to interviewer suggestions. If the ground rules are not explained, children may answer in the way they think interviewers want to hear in order to seem cooperative (Ceci & Bruck, 1993, 1995; Ceci, Kulkofsky, Klemfuss, Sweeney, & Bruck, 2007; Melnyk, Crossman, & Scullin, 2007). The ground rules are intended to reduce the effects of poor quality questions, such as misleading or closed questions, because children will feel comfortable indicating that they do not know the answer or do not agree with the interviewers' suggestions (e.g., see Lamb et al., 2008, pp. 85–87). The ground rules help to discourage children from hazarding a guess when they are actually unsure about the answer and are also associated with how informative children are during the substantive phase (Teoh & Lamb, 2010).

In sum, the research makes clear that it is desirable to see ground rules communicated to children at the start of forensic interviews; however, ground rules are not always communicated, and there is variation both within and across jurisdictions about how many are communicated and which ones are perceived to be most important. For example, testing a child's understanding of the truth and lies is a legal requirement in some jurisdictions, but not in others.

The Practice Interview

Interviewers commonly extend rapport in the presubstantive phase of the interview by conducting what is known as a "practice interview" (sometimes referred to in academic writing as "episodic memory training"; e.g., Orbach et al., 2000). The practice interview ideally involves interviewers using open prompts to elicit detailed accounts of *neutral, specific, real experiences* from interviewees. The purpose of this phase is to provide children with practice at remembering specific experiences in detail rather than recalling the gist of what happened. Importantly, this is when interviewers should introduce open prompts and continue building rapport. Children thus have a chance to feel successful at providing information and feel in control. Practice interviews also provide good opportunities for interviewers to better understand the cognitive abilities and communicative styles of the children they are interviewing (Roberts, Brubacher, Price, & Powell, 2011).

Research on the benefits of practice interviews has shown that, after practice phases, children's reports in the substantive phase are longer and contain more details (Brubacher, Roberts, & Powell, 2011; Hershkowitz, 2009; Price, Roberts, & Collins, 2013; Sternberg et al., 1997), and are also more accurate (Roberts et al., 2004). Even a low quality practice interview is better than not conducting a practice interview at all, but in particular, a practice interview containing open-ended questions is more likely to increase the amount of information provided during the substantive phase of the interview than one using closed questions (Anderson, Anderson, & Gilgun, 2014; Price et al., 2013; Sternberg et al., 1997).

While practice interviews are desirable features of forensic interviews, there may be circumstances in which the practice interview is omitted. For example, if a child seems eager to disclose or discuss why they came to the interview, an interviewer might not include aspects of the presubstantive phase and instead allow the child to discuss substantive events. It is important to remember that the absence of a practice interview does not mean that information elicited using open prompts in the substantive phase is less likely to be accurate (Brubacher et al., 2011).

When assessing forensic interviews it is important to be aware that interviewers often think that they have conducted practice interviews when they have not done so. Interviewers sometimes ask children for descriptions of fantasy-based topics such as television shows, movies, and video games. This is undesirable because it could adversely affect the child's testimony (based on the literature on suggestibility and false memory, discussed below) or the credibility of the witness, whose ability to distinguish between fantasy and reality may be questioned (Woolley & Ghosaini, 2013). Interviewers may also ask for general descriptions of repeated or highly scripted events (e.g., dance lessons, sports, or a birthday party). Though children are describing real events, it does not provide them with the opportunity to practice discussing specific episodic memories, as they may instead report general details about what usually happens in such events. In neither case would interviewers be using the practice interview in the way that it is intended and supported by research.

Transition Phase

Building rapport, explaining ground rules, and conducting practice interviews are all things that can be done in the presubstantive phase to prepare children for their roles as informative witnesses. Once these phases are complete, interviewers should introduce the substantive topic non-suggestively. It is crucial to assess the transition from the presubstantive to the substantive phase of the interview. How was the allegation elicited? Did the child make an allegation free from any pressure, or was it necessary for the interviewer to use direct questions and/or to introduce the allegation? Most research-based protocols recommend that the transition be initiated by the interviewer using a neutral prompt such as, "I'd like to talk about why you came to see me today." As vague as this seems, research shows that most children who have already made a prior disclosure will make an allegation when given this opportunity (Hershkowitz, Fisher, Lamb, & Horowitz, 2007).

Some children do not provide any information about alleged events in response to these initial open prompts. When this happens, depending on the case characteristics, it may be necessary for the interviewer to ask a very direct or suggestive question like, "Did somebody hit you?" On one hand there may be physical evidence and/or strong suspicions that abuse has occurred that appear to justify such direct suggestions. On the other hand, the suggestibility of childwitnesses and evidence that even neutrally posed suggestions can elicit inaccurate information are causes for concern (Ceci et al., 2007). In some cases, interviewers' suggestions have resulted in descriptions of entire false events (e.g., Bruck, Ceci, & Hembrooke, 2002; Ceci, Huffman, Smith, & Loftus, 1994; Ceci, Loftus, Leichtman, & Bruck, 1994; Quas et al., 2007; Strange, Garry, & Sutherland, 2003). However, in these cases interviews were considered to be very suggestive, and in the vast majority of forensic interviews with children, issues surrounding false allegations and false memory surface rarely.

The Substantive Phase: Assessing the Questions and Prompts

A consistent and clear message that has emerged from research on investigative interviews with children is that the manner in which children are questioned, and the types of questions that they are asked, can dramatically affect the accuracy of the information they provide. Therefore, those tasked with assessing the quality of interviews must be able to identify different types of interviewer utterances and be familiar with research informing us about their strengths and weaknesses. Although different researchers/protocols sometimes use different terminology to identify the types of prompts and questions that interviewers ask, there is strong agreement based on both memory and linguistic factors about the types of questions that are the safest to use and those that are more risky (Kassin, Tubb, Hosch, & Memon, 2001).

Open prompts. Memory experts agree that children ought to be allowed to describe events in their own words, free from pressure and any suggestive influence. For this reason, interviewers are advised to use as many *open prompts* as possible (see Lamb et al., 2008 for a review). The most common example of an open prompt is, "Tell me what happened." Other examples of open prompts that are also desirable in forensic interviews are, "Tell me more about that," "Tell me everything about that," "Then what happened?," and "What happened next?" When reviewing a forensic interview a useful rule to use is, "Does the prompt allow the child to respond using a narrative, rather than just a few words?" If the answer is "yes" then the interviewer utterance is likely to be open.

It is also acceptable to use open prompts to enquire about specific information, especially relating to elaboration of information that the child has already provided (Lamb et al., 2003). One way this can be achieved is using anchor points in time as components of open prompts. For example, "*Tell me what happened* from the moment he came in to your room to the moment that he left your room," is an acceptable way of refocusing a child to provide more details about a critical element of the account. Similarly, combining information that the child has provided with open prompts is another method of increasing the specificity of a question in a non-suggestive manner; e.g., "You said he hit you, *tell me more about that*." Because information obtained using open prompts comes from free recall memory it is more likely to be accurate than information elicited using other question types (e.g., Dent & Stephenson, 1979; Hutcheson, Baxter, Telfer, & Warden, 1995; Lamb & Fauchier, 2001; Oates & Shrimpton, 1991).

Focused questions. Prompts for specific details using "wh-" questions (who, when, where, etc.) need to be considered carefully given the known risks associated with them. Ideally, these types of questions are intended to refocus the child's attention on topics that have already been mentioned and request specific additional details; for example, "What time did that happen?" Questions of this nature are often answered using only a few words and often contain concepts and words that children have emerging abilities to understand (e.g., times, dates, and numbers representing ages, event frequency, etc.; Evans, Lee, & Lyon, 2009; Walker & Kenniston, 2013; Zajac & Hayne, 2003; Friedman, 1991, 1993; Orbach & Lamb, 2007; Sharman, Powell, & Roberts, 2011; Wandrey, Lyon, Quas, & Friedman, 2012).

Those assessing the quality of interviews need to be mindful that young children's vocabularies are limited (Dale, 1976; de Villiers & de Villiers, 1999). It is normal for children to use words before they understand their adult meanings, and there is a risk that they will not indicate when they have not understood questions that are asked of them. Moreover, some children may not realize that they did not understand questions and thus fail to see the need to ask interviewers for clarification. Because children sometimes try to answer questions they do not understand (Gee et al., 1999; Waterman, Blades, & Spencer, 2000, 2001, 2004), responses to these types of questions need to be viewed in light of the cognitive abilities of the children concerned. As mentioned above, the ground rules may help with this issue by emphasizing that it is okay to say "I don't know" and seek clarification.

Some interviewers use focused question as "memory tests," attempting to determine whether events really happened by identifying contradictions and gaps in knowledge that could be evidence of fabrication. Psychological research is able to explain that contradictory and apparently "missing" information are common when these types of questions are asked, regardless of the truthfulness of the report. When children are asked focused questions, the questions themselves may be enquiring about information that was not encoded in memory.

Sometimes contradictions are provided in response to poorly conceived questions, and thus, questions need to be carefully examined to illuminate apparent contradictions. For example, in a case reported by Jones and Krugman (1986), a 3-year-old child reported that the perpetrator's car was black when it was actually orange. In fact, the child may have been accurately describing the color of the upholstery, as opposed to the outside of the car as intended by the questioner. Questions like these often need to be considered carefully to determine whether there is potential for misunderstanding. Importantly, inaccurate answers in response to focused questions are not diagnostic of the accuracy of information elicited freely in response to open prompts.

Option posing and yes/no questions. These types of prompts focus the child's attention on details that the child has not previously mentioned, asking the child to select an interviewer-given option, or to answer by saying "Yes" or "No." This type of question can normally be answered using one word or only a few words. Option-posing questions are sometimes referred to as leading questions. Similar to focused questions, they may also contain concepts and words that children have emerging abilities to understand.

When very specific yes/no questions are asked, there is a risk that children will make acquiescence errors, tending to agree or "go along" with what is being said by answering "yes" when they do not really remember what happened; this tendency increases at long recall delays and is more problematic for younger children (5 years and younger) than older children (Ahern, Lyon, & Quas, 2011; Fivush, Peterson, & Schwarzmueller, 2002; Peterson, Dowden, & Tobin, 1999). The more closed a question is, the riskier it is because there is more potential for misunderstanding to occur or for interviewers to introduce inaccurate information.

Suggestive questions. It is vitally important to assess the impact of suggestive questions in forensic interviews with children, and for experts to be able to identify both subtle and overt influences on children's responses. By definition, suggestive questions are stated in such a way that the interviewer communicates what response is expected, assumes details that have not already been provided by the child, or introduces information that has not been provided by the child (Ceci & Bruck, 1993). When questioned suggestively, children may go along with the interviewers' suggestions and so it is important to identify the impact on children's reports. For example, the child may incorporate words introduced by the interviewer into subsequent narratives, and in some cases children have been shown to provide elaborate descriptions of events that have not actually happened (e.g., Bruck et al., 2002; Ceci, Huffman et al., 1994; Ceci, Loftus et al., 1994; Strange et al., 2003). Alternatively, children may simply disagree with interviewers' suggestions; thus, it is important to identify the effect that suggestive questions might have had on the interviews as a whole.

Repeated Questions

Another well-studied aspect of focused questions such as those discussed above revolves around the potential effects of repeating questions (for reviews, see Fivush & Schwarzmueller, 1995; Poole & White, 1993). It has been relatively easy to study the effects of repeated questions in laboratory studies because questions are precisely constructed and read to children word for word (e.g., Fivush & Schwarzmueller, 1995). When assessing forensic interviews, questions are rarely repeated verbatim so it is necessary to broaden the definition of "repeated questions" to include all interviewer questions and prompts that refocus children on their previous responses in the same way that repeated questions would. For example, "When did it happen?" followed by, "When did you say it happened?" should be considered repeated questions. In contrast, interviewer prompts that are identical should not always be considered repetitions. For example, if an interviewer asks, "What did he do?" and a child replies, "He didn't do anything it was my brother," the next question, "What did *he* do?" ought not to be considered a repetition for obvious reasons. Ultimately, decisions about repeated questions should focus on the content of interviewer prompts, rather than the exact language used.

In some cases repeated questions are necessary, and the reasons for repeating questions may be clear from examining the interview; for example, a need to refocus children on their previous responses because initial answers were incomplete or unclear, to summarize and check details about topics already discussed, or after reassuring reluctant witnesses that it is safe to disclose information. However, generally speaking, interviewers are trained not to repeat focused questions in interviews because doing so may pressure children to change their answers and these inconsistencies may reduce their credibility as witnesses (Andrews & Lamb, 2014; Bruck, Fisher, & Cutler, 1999; Bruck, Ceci, & Hembrooke, 1998; Gilbert & Fisher, 2006; Poole & Lamb, 1998; Poole & White, 1993). Therefore, it is important to assess whether contradictions within a child's statement arose due to question repetition. As a safeguard against inadvertently suggesting that children's previous responses are incorrect, professional guidelines often recommend that children be told why questions may be repeated in order to minimize the risk that they feel pressured to change their responses.

Episodic vs. Generic Language

Child abuse is often a repeated experience (e.g., Connolly & Read, 2006), but children may be required to describe specific instances of abuse (i.e., particularization) in order for charges to be laid and so that defendants have a fair opportunity to challenge allegations (Guadagno, Powell, & Wright, 2006). When children experience events repeatedly, they create a script, or general representation of what usually happens during these types of events. Scripts can guide memory recall, leading to a general account of the gist of events, rather than a specific account of one instance. Identifying and describing one instance of a repeated event requires source monitoring, which is difficult for young children (see Roberts, 2002, for a review).

If it has been established that the alleged abuse has occurred multiple times, it is recommended that interviewers ask about the first time, the last time, and another time in order to elicit accounts of individual instances. Another strategy that interviewers can use to assist children in describing specific instances is to use episodic language (asking about what happened on specific times) rather than generic language (asking about what usually happens; Brubacher, Malloy, Lamb, & Roberts, 2013; Powell, Roberts, & Guadagno, 2007). Children tend to respond in kind when faced with episodic or generic questions; therefore, using more episodic prompts encourages children to use more episodic language and describe specific episodic memories.

Information About the Initial Disclosure

Forensic investigations begin following children's statements that cause alarm to the adults in their lives. Children initially disclose their experiences in contexts over which we have no control; prior to a formal investigation, children may often have conversations with adults who ask closed or suggestive questions about the alleged events. This cannot be prevented, so the best strategy is to conduct open interviews to clarify what has happened. Research-based interviewing protocols suggest asking children about the conversations they have had about the abuse, how the allegations were disclosed, and to whom. Asking about the initial disclosure provides more information about the potential abuse and also about whether children have been coached by adults about what to say.

Anatomically Detailed Dolls and Other Props

The use of anatomically detailed dolls was initially thought to be a promising means of facilitating the communication of children's experiences by allowing them to demonstrate what occurred. However, anatomically detailed dolls have caused significant controversy and their use has been, and continues to be, heavily criticized (e.g., Poole, Bruck, & Pipe, 2011). One issue relates to the possibility that the dolls themselves are inherently suggestive because they inadvertently encourage certain types of play. A second concern is that they might simply encourage "make believe" play that is interpreted as actual experience. Given that there are no specific behaviors that reliably diagnose sexualabuse (Bridges, Faust, & Ahern, 2009) it is widely agreed that the risk of inaccurate conclusions being drawn from observations of children's interactions with anatomically detailed dolls is too high to support their use in investigations of child abuse. Importantly, research investigating the use of anatomically detailed dolls has shown adverse effects on the accuracy of the information obtained, even within a single interview (Bruck, Ceci, Francoeur, & Renick, 1995; Goodman & Aman, 1990). There is no evidence that the content of children's interactions or play with dolls provides a reliable diagnostic indicator of abuse. Evidence for the use of anatomically detailed dolls comes largely from practitioners who are not aware of the risks.

Although in theory the value of anatomical dolls seems plausible, it is extremely difficult to assess their use and impact in interviews. An important requirement is that the interactions with the dolls be recorded in minute detail. In practice, this is not typically achieved and many of the interactions are "off camera," or happen too quickly, which prevents any assurance about what actually happened and the potential for suggestion. There is a risk that interviewers could shape interactions by preempting the actions of the child. The requirement to have a video recording and to be able to determine the sequence of child actions and interviewer utterances makes assessment of this practice very time consuming. Using interview aids such as human figure drawings and props create similar problems when assessing forensic interviews.

Recall Delay

We should not be surprised that very young children can provide clear descriptions of their experiences when they have occurred recently, yet forget those details when questioned months and years later. Researchers have studied the effects of recall delay on children's memory in great detail. For example, Jones and Pipe (2002) documented the rate at which memory declines over time by asking different groups of 5- and 6-year-old children about a visit to a "friendly pirate" either immediately, 1 day, 1 week, 1 month, or 6 months later. When the results were graphed, it became apparent that forgetting is most rapid soon after the event; as more time passes, the amount of forgetting decreases, until there is very little further forgetting. Children not only remember less over time, but there are also increases in the number of errors in their reports (Bruck et al., 2002; La Rooy, Pipe, & Murray, 2007; Melnyk & Bruck, 2004). Younger children forget event details more quickly than older children do (Brainerd, Reyna, Howe, & Kingma, 1990). Because forgetting is most drastic early on, every attempt should be made to conduct interviews in a timely fashion and not delay interviewing witnesses.

The Issue of Psychometrics

Interview protocols are not subject to traditional psychometric testing; each interview has unique questions and the quality of interviews cannot be assessed using a scale. It would be ideal if there were psychometrically valid tests to determine whether or not children have been abused or whether or not they are telling the truth, but these do not exist. Because researchers do not know what has happened to children who have been interviewed, they cannot tell if children's responses are "valid" (in the traditional way that the concept of validity is described).

One tool that was initially thought to be potentially useful for this purpose is Criteria-Based Content Analysis (CBCA) (Raskin & Esplin, 1991; Steller & Koehnken, 1989). Lamb et al. (1997) used the CBCA procedure to assess the testimonies of 98 children, some of whom were known to have been describing incidents that were improbable, while others described events for which there was strong corroborating evidence. CBCA scores significantly differentiated between the plausible and implausible accounts, but there was considerable overlap between the scores and the technique was clearly not precise enough to be used in forensic contexts. Lamb et al. (1997) noted that most of the testimonies included few narratives, making it difficult for raters to identify the crucial criteria. In a later study, Hershkowitz, Fisher, Lamb, and Horowitz (2007) showed that investigators assessed credibility more accurately when the children provided more narratives and the interviews had been conducted in accordance with best-practice guidelines, although, as in previous studies, the raters correctly identified plausible statements much more accurately than they identified implausible ones. Though this may be the closest researchers have come to developing a measure for the validity of children's reports, it is not accurate enough to be used to determine the outcomes of real cases involving children's interviews.

Therefore, the only way to assess interviews is to focus not on whether the children are telling the truth, but on what the interviewers have done during the interviews, and whether the conditions are right for obtaining accurate statements. There is extensive evidence that interviewers have profound effects on what children say, so experts can examine what interviewers have done to determine if that may have affected children's statements in any way, positively or negatively.

Conclusion

Determining whether or not abuse happened is the job of the jury and the judge, not an expertwitness. The question that expert witnesses can answer is, "Was the interview itself conducted in a way that meets the standards that are agreed upon in the scientific literature?" Experts should assess whether the interviews were conducted appropriately and explain the possible impact of the practices followed so that fact finders can come to reasoned decisions about the evidence. For example, if no ground rules were laid out, no open prompts were used, and suggestive questions abounded, experts need to make clear that the evidence is of poor quality because well-established research-based guidelines were not followed.

High quality interviewing is not an art form; it is a science. The evidence about interviewquality is highly consistent and it is important to follow these guidelines in order to increase the ability of interviewers, experts, and fact finders to evaluate the usefulness of the information elicited. Good reports about interview practices can also help to prevent unnecessary court exposure for children when cases are resolved out of court and/or more quickly.

As explained above, there are many interviewing principles that are consistently agreed upon and supported by scientific evidence. If interviews meet these agreed upon criteria, they should be taken seriously because they are likely to yield accurate accounts of what has happened. The expert's role is to describe the issues about which there is a consensus and to address whether the interviews in question were conducted in accordance with relevant interviewing guidelines. If childwitnesses are interviewed under ideal conditions, we can have reasonable faith in what they have said; their testimony ought to convince the public, and may also convince accused persons that the testimony will be persuasive in court.

References

Ahern, E. C., Lyon, T. D., & Quas, J. A. (2011). Young children's emerging ability to make false statements. *Developmental Psychology, 47*, 61–66. doi:10.1037/a0021272.

Almerigogna, J., Ost, J., Bull, R., & Akehurst, L. (2007). A state of high anxiety: How non-supportive interviewers can increase the suggestibility of child witnesses. *Applied Cognitive Psychology, 21*, 963–974. doi:10.1002/acp.1311.

Anderson, G. D., Anderson, J. N., & Gilgun, J. F. (2014). The influence of narrative practice techniques on child behaviors in forensic interviews. *Journal of Child Sexual Abuse, 23*, 615–634. doi:10.1080/105387/12.2014.932878.

Andrews, S. J., & Lamb, M. E. (2014). The effects of age and delay on responses to repeated questions in forensic interviews with children alleging sexual abuse. *Law and Human Behavior, 38*, 171–180. doi:10.1037/lhb0000064.

Brainerd, C. J., Reyna, V. F., Howe, M. L., & Kingma, J. (1990). The development of forgetting and reminiscence. *Monographs of the Society for Research in Child Development, 55*, 1–109. doi:10.2307/1166106.

Bridges, A. J., Faust, D., & Ahern, D. C. (2009). Methods for the identification of sexually abused children: Reframing the clinician's task and recognizing its disparity with research on indicators.

In K. Kuehnle & M. Connell (Eds.), *The evaluation of child sexual abuse allegations: A comprehensive guide to assessment and testimony* (pp. 21–47). Hoboken, NJ: Wiley.

Brock, P., Fisher, R., & Cutler, B. (1999). Examining the cognitive interview in a double-test paradigm. *Psychology, Crime & Law, 5*, 29–45. doi:10.1080/10683169908414992.

Brubacher, S. P., Malloy, L. C., Lamb, M. E., & Roberts, K. P. (2013). How do interviewers and children discuss individual occurrences of alleged repeated abuse in forensic interviews? *Applied Cognitive Psychology, 27*, 443–450. doi:10.1002/acp.2920.

Brubacher, S. P., Roberts, K. P., & Powell, M. (2011). Effects of practicing episodic versus scripted recall on children's subsequent narratives of a repeated event. *Psychology, Public Policy, and Law, 17*, 286–314. doi:10.1037/a0022793.

Bruck, M., Ceci, S. J., Francoeur, E., & Renick, A. (1995). Anatomically detailed dolls do not facilitate pre-schoolers' reports of a paediatric examination involving genital touch. *Journal of Experimental Psychology. Applied, 1*, 95–109.

Bruck, M., Ceci, S. J., & Hembrooke, H. (1998). Reliability and credibility of young children's reports: From research to policy and practice. *American Psychologist, 53*, 136–151. doi:10.1037/0003-066X.53.2.136.

Bruck, M., Ceci, S. J., & Hembrooke, H. (2002). The nature of children's true and false narratives. *Developmental Review, 22*, 520–554. doi:10.1016/S0273-2297(02)00006-0.

Carter, C. A., Bottoms, B. L., & Levine, M. (1996). Linguistic and socioemotional influences on the accuracy of children's reports. *Law and Human Behavior, 20*, 335–356. doi:10.1007/BF01499044.

Ceci, S. J., & Bruck, M. (1993). Suggestibility of the child witness: A historical review and synthesis. *Psychological Bulletin, 113*, 403–439. doi:10.1037/0033-2909.113.3.403.

Ceci, S. J., & Bruck, M. (1995). *Jeopardy in the courtroom: A scientific analysis of children's testimony*. Washington, DC: American Psychological Association. doi:10.1037/10180-000.

Ceci, S. J., Huffman, M. L. C., Smith, E., & Loftus, E. F. (1994). Repeatedly thinking about a non-event: Source misattributions among preschoolers. *Consciousness and Cognition, 3*, 388–407. doi:10.1006/ccog.1994.1022.

Ceci, S. J., Kulkofsky, S., Klemfuss, J. Z., Sweeney, C. D., & Bruck, M. (2007). Unwarranted assumptions about children's testimonial accuracy. *Annual Review of Clinical Psychology, 3*, 311–328. doi:10.1146/annurev.clinpsy.3.022806.091354.

Ceci, S. J., Loftus, E. F., Leichtman, M. D., & Bruck, M. (1994). The possible role of source misattributions in the creation of false beliefs among preschoolers. *International Journal of Clinical and Experimental Hypnosis, 42*, 304–320.

Collins, R., Lincoln, R., & Frank, M. G. (2002). The effect of rapport in forensic interviewing. *Psychiatry, Psychology and Law, 9*, 69–78. doi:10.1375/132187102760196916.

Connolly, D. A., & Read, J. D. (2006). Delayed prosecutions of historic child sexual abuse: Analyses of 2064 Canadian criminal complaints. *Law and Human Behavior, 30*, 409–434. doi:10.1007/s10979-006-9011-6.

Dale, P. S. (1976). *Language development: Structure and function*. New York, NY: Holt, Rinehart, & Winston.

Davis, S., & Bottoms, B. (2002). Effects of social support on children's eyewitness reports: A test of the underlying mechanism. *Law and Human Behavior, 26*, 185–214.

de Villiers, J. G., & de Villiers, P. A. (1999). *Language development*. Mahwah, NJ: Lawrence Erlbaum Associates.

Dent, H. R., & Stephenson, G. M. (1979). An experimental study of the effectiveness of different techniques of questioning child witnesses. *British Journal of Social and Clinical Psychology, 18*, 41–51. doi:10.1111/j.2044-8260.1979.tb00302.x.

Evans, A. D., & Lee, K. (2010). Promising to tell the truth makes 8- to 16-year olds more honest. *Behavioral Sciences & the Law, 28*, 801–811. doi:10.1002/bsl.960.

Evans, A. D., Lee, K., & Lyon, T. D. (2009). Complex questions asked by defense lawyers but not prosecutors predicts convictions in child abuse trials. *Law and Human Behavior, 33*, 258–264. doi:10.1007/s10979-008-9148-6.

Fivush, R., Peterson, C., & Schwarzmueller, A. (2002). Questions and answers: The credibility of child witnesses in the context of specific questioning techniques. In M. L. Eisen, J. A. Quas, & G. S. Goodman (Eds.), *Memory and suggestibility in the forensic interview* (pp. 331–354). Mahwah, NJ: Erlbaum.

Fivush, R., & Schwarzmueller, A. (1995). Say it once again: Effects of repeated questions on children's event recall. *Journal of Traumatic Stress, 8*, 555–580.

Friedman, W. J. (1991). The development of children's memory for the time of past events. *Child Development, 62*, 139–155. doi:10.2307/1130710.

Friedman, W. J. (1993). Memory for the time of past events. *Psychological Bulletin, 113*, 44–66. doi:10.1037/0033-2909.113.1.44.

Gee, S., Gregory, M., & Pipe, M. E. (1999). 'What color is your pet dinosaur?' The impact of pre-interview training and question type on children's answer. *Legal and Criminal Psychology, 4*, 111–128. doi:10.1348/135532599167716.

Gilbert, J. A. E., & Fisher, R. P. (2006). The effects of varied retrieval cues on reminiscence in eyewitness memory. *Applied Cognitive Psychology, 20*, 723–739. doi:10.1002/acp.1232.

Goodman, G. S., & Aman, C. (1990). Children's use of anatomically detailed dolls to recount an event. *Child Development, 61*, 1859–1871. doi:10.2307/1130842.

Goodman, G. S., Bottoms, B. L., Schwartz-Kenney, B. M., & Rudy, L. (1991). Children's testimony about a stressful event: Improving children's reports. *Journal of Narrative and Life History, 1*, 69–99.

Guadagno, B. L., Powell, M. B., & Wright, R. (2006). Police officers' and legal professionals' perceptions regarding how children are, and should be, questioned about repeated abuse. *Psychiatry, Psychology and Law, 13*, 251–260. doi:10.1375/pplt.13.2.251.

Hershkowitz, I. (2009). Socioemotional factors in child sexual abuse investigations. *Child Maltreatment, 14*, 172–181. doi:10.1177/1077559508326224.

Hershkowitz, I., Fisher, S., Lamb, M. E., & Horowitz, D. (2007). Improving credibility assessment in child sexual abuse allegations: The role of the NICHD investigative interview protocol. *Child Abuse & Neglect, 31*, 99–110. doi:10.1016/j.chiabu.2006.09.005.

Hershkowitz, I., Lamb, M. E., Katz, C. & Malloy, L. C. (2013). Does enhanced rapport-building alter the dynamics of investigative interviews with suspected victims of intra-familial abuse? *Journal of Police and Criminal Psychology, 30*, 6–14.

Hershkowitz, I., Lamb, M. E., & Katz, C. (2014). Allegation rates in forensic child abuse investigations: Comparing the revised and standard NICHD protocols. *Psychology, Public Policy, and Law, 20*, 336–344. doi:10.1037/a0037391.

Hutcheson, G. D., Baxter, J. S., Telfer, K., & Warden, D. (1995). Child witness statement quality: Question type and errors of omission. *Law and Human Behavior, 19*, 641–648. doi:10.1007/BF01499378.

Jones, D. P., & Krugman, R. D. (1986). Can a three-year-old child bear witness to her sexual assault and attempted murder? *Child Abuse & Neglect, 10*, 253–258. doi:10.1016/0145-2134(86)90086-4.

Jones, C. H., & Pipe, M.-E. (2002). How quickly do children forget events? A systematic study of children's event reports as a function of delay. *Applied Cognitive Psychology, 16*, 755–768. doi:10.1002/acp.826.

Kassin, S. M., Tubb, V. A., Hosch, H. M., & Memon, A. (2001). On the "general acceptance" of eyewitness testimony research: A new survey of the experts. *American Psychologist, 56*, 405–416. doi:10.1037/0003-066X.56.5.405.

Krackow, E., & Lynn, S. J. (2010). Event report training: An examination of the efficacy of a new intervention to improve children's eyewitness reports. *Applied Cognitive Psychology, 24*, 868–884. doi:10.1002/acp.1594.

La Rooy, D., & Block, S. (2013). The importance of scientifically analysing the quality of joint investigative interviews (JIIs) conducted with children in Scotland. *Scots Law Times, 10*, 77–78.

La Rooy, D., Pipe, M., & Murray, J. E. (2007). Enhancing children's event recall after long delays. *Applied Cognitive Psychology, 21*, 1–17. doi:10.1002/acp.1272.

Lamb, M. E., & Fauchier, A. (2001). The effects of question type on self-contradictions by children in the course of forensic interviews. *Applied Cognitive Psychology, 15*, 483–491. doi:10.1002/acp.726.

Lamb, M. E., Hershkowitz, I., Orbach, Y., & Esplin, P. W. (2008). *Tell me what happened: Structured investigative interviews of child victims and witnesses*. Hoboken, NJ: Wiley. doi:10.1002/9780470773291.

Lamb, M. E., La Rooy, D., Malloy, L. C., & Katz, C. (2011). *Children's testimony: A handbook of psychological research and forensic practice* (2nd ed.). Chichester, England: Wiley.

Lamb, M. E., Orbach, Y., Warren, A. R., Esplin, P. W., & Hershkowitz, I. (2007a). Enhancing performance: Factors affecting the informativeness of young witnesses. In M. P. Toglia, J. D. Read, D. F. Ross, & R. C. L. Lindsay (Eds.), The handbook of eyewitness psychology (Memory for events, Vol. 1, pp. 429–451). Mahwah, NJ: Erlbaum.

Lamb, M. E., Orbach, Y., Hershkowitz, I., Esplin, P. W., & Horowitz, D. (2007b). A structured forensic interview protocol improves the quality and informativeness of investigative interviews with children: A review of research using the NICHD investigative interview protocol. *Child Abuse & Neglect, 31*, 1201–1231. doi:10.1016/j.chiabu.2007.03.021.

Lamb, M. E., Orbach, Y., Sternberg, K. J., Hershkowitz, I., & Horowitz, D. (2000). Accuracy of investigators' verbatim notes of their forensic interviews with alleged child abuse victims. *Law and Human Behavior, 24*, 699–708.

Lamb, M. E., Orbach, Y., Warren, A. R., Esplin, P. W., & Hershkowitz, I. (2007). Enhancing performance: Factors affecting the informativeness of young witnesses. In M. P. Toglia, J. D. Read, D. F. Ross, & R. C. L. Lindsay (Eds.), *The handbook of eyewitness psychology* (Memory for events, Vol. 1, pp. 429–451). Mahwah, NJ: Erlbaum.

Lamb, M. E., Sternberg, K. J., Esplin, P. W., Hershkowitz, I., Orbach, Y., & Hovav, M. (1997). Criterion-based content analysis: A field validation study. *Child Abuse & Neglect, 21*, 255–264. doi:10.1016/S0145-2134(96)00170-6.

Lamb, M. E., Sternberg, K. J., Orbach, Y., Esplin, P. W., Stewart, H., & Mitchell, S. (2003). Age differences in young children's responses to open-ended invitations in the course of forensic interviews. *Journal of Consulting & Clinical Psychology, 71*, 926–934. doi:10.1037/0022006X.71.5.926.

Lamb, M. E., Sternberg, K. J., & Esplin, P. W. (1998). Conducting investigative interviews of alleged sexual abuse victims. *Child Abuse & Neglect, 2*, 813–823.

Lyon, T. D. (2010). Investigative interviewing of the child. In D. N. Duquette & A. M. Haralambie (Eds.), *Child welfare law and practice* (2nd ed., pp. 87–109). Denver, CO: Bradford.

Lyon, T. D., & Dorado, J. S. (2008). Truth induction in young maltreated children: The effects of oath- taking and reassurance on true and false disclosures. *Child Abuse & Neglect, 32*, 738–748.

Melnyk, L., & Bruck, M. (2004). Timing moderates the effects of repeated suggestive interviewing on children's eyewitness memory. *Applied Cognitive Psychology, 18*, 613–631. doi:10.1002/acp.1013.

Melnyk, L., Crossman, A. M., & Scullin, M. H. (2007). The suggestibility of children's memory. In D. F. Ross, R. C. L. Lindsay, M. P. Toglia, & J. D. Read (Eds.), *The handbook of eyewitness psychology* (Memory for events, Vol. 1, pp. 401–427). Mahwah, NJ: Erlbaum.

Oates, K., & Shrimpton, S. (1991). Children's memories for stressful and non-stressful events. *Medical Science and Law, 31*, 4–10.

Orbach, Y., Hershkowitz, I., Lamb, M. E., Sternberg, K. J., Esplin, P. W., & Horowitz, D. (2000). Assessing the value of structured protocols for forensic interviews of alleged child abuse victims. *Child Abuse and Neglect, 24*, 733–752. doi:10.1016/S0145-2134(00)00137-X.

Orbach, Y., & Lamb, M. E. (2007). Young children's references to temporal attributes of allegedly experienced events in the course of forensic interviews. *Child Development, 78*, 1100–1120. doi:10.1111/j.1467-8624.2007.01055.x.

Peterson, C., Dowden, C., & Tobin, J. (1999). Interviewing preschoolers: Comparisons of yes/no and wh- questions. *Law and Human Behavior, 23*, 539–555. doi:10.1023/A:1022396112l9.

Poole, D. A., Bruck, M., & Pipe, M.-E. (2011). Forensic interviewing aids: Do props help children answer questions about touching? *Current Directions in Psychological Science, 20*, 11–15. doi:10.1177/0963721410388804.

Poole, D. A., & Lamb, M. E. (1998). *Investigative interviews of children: A guide for helping professionals*. Washington, DC: American Psychological Association.

Poole, D. A., & White, L. T. (1993). Two years later: Effects of question repetition and retention interval on the eyewitness testimony of children and adults. *Developmental Psychology, 29*, 844–853. doi:10.1037/0012-1649.29.5.844.

Powell, M. B., Roberts, K. P., & Guadagno, B. (2007). Particularisation of child abuse offences: Common problems when interviewing child witnesses. *Current Issues in Criminal Justice, 19*, 64–74.

Price, H. L., Roberts, K. P., & Collins, A. (2013). The quality of children's allegations of abuse in investigative interviews containing practice narratives. *Journal of Applied Research in Memory and Cognition, 2*, 1–6. doi:10.1016/j.jarmac.2012.03.001.

Quas, J. A., & Lench, H. C. (2007). Arousal at encoding, arousal at retrieval, interviewer support, and children's memory for a mild stressor. *Applied Cognitive Psychology, 21*, 289–305. doi:10.1002/acp.1279.

Quas, J. A., Malloy, L. C., Melinder, A., Goodman, G. S., D'Mello, M., & Schaaf, J. (2007). Developmental differences in the effects of repeated interviews and interviewer bias on young children's event memory and false reports. *Developmental Psychology, 43*, 823–837. doi:10.1037/00121649.43.4.823.

Raskin, D. C., & Esplin, P. W. (1991). Statement validity assessment: Interview procedures and content analysis of children's statements of sexual abuse. *Behavioral Assessment, 13*, 265–291.

Roberts, K. P. (2002). Children's ability to distinguish between memories from multiple sources: Implications for the quality and accuracy of eyewitness statements. *Developmental Review, 22*, 403–435. doi:10.1016/S0273-2297(02)00005-9.

Roberts, K. P., Brubacher, S. P., Price, H. L., & Powell, M. B. (2011). Practice narratives. In M. E. Lamb, D. La Rooy, C. Katz, & L. Malloy (Eds.), *Children's testimony: A handbook of psychological research and forensic practice* (pp. 129–145). West Sussex, England: Wiley-Blackwell.

Roberts, K. P., Lamb, M. E., & Sternberg, K. J. (2004). The effects of rapport building style on children's reports of a staged event. *Applied Cognitive Psychology, 18*, 189–202. doi:10.1002/acp.957.

Saywitz, K., Camparo, L. B., & Romanoff, A. (2010). Interviewing children in custody cases: Implications of research and policy practice. *Behavioral Sciences and the Law, 28*, 542–562. doi:10.1002/bsl.945.

Saywitz, K. J., Goodman, G. S., Nicholas, E., & Moan, S. F. (1991). Children's memories of a physical examination involving genital touch: Implications for reports of child sexual abuse. *Journal of Consulting and Clinical Psychology, 59*, 682–691. doi:10.1037/0022-006X.59.5.682.

Saywitz, K. J., & Moan-Hardie, S. (1994). Reducing the potential for distortion of childhood memories. *Consciousness & Cognition, 3*, 408–425.

Saywitz, K. J., Snyder, L., & Nathanson, R. (1999). Facilitating the communicative competence of the child witness. *Applied Developmental Science, 3*, 58–68. doi:10.1207/s1532480xads0301_7.

Sharman, S. J., Powell, M. B., & Roberts, K. P. (2011). Children's ability to estimate the frequency of single and repeated events. *International Journal of Police Science & Management, 13*, 234–242. doi:10.1350/ijps.2011.13.3.243.

Steller, M., & Koehnken, G. (1989). Criteria-based statement analysis. In D. C. Raskin (Ed.), *Psychological methods in criminal investigation and evidence* (pp. 217–245). New York, NY: Springer.

Sternberg, K. J., Lamb, M. E., Esplin, P. W., Orbach, Y., & Hershkowitz, I. (2002). Using a structured interview protocol to improves the quality of investigative interviews. In M. L. Eisen, J. A. Quas, & G. S. Goodman (Eds.), *Memory and suggestibility in the forensic interview* (pp. 409–436). Mahwah, NJ: Erlbaum.

Sternberg, K. J., Lamb, M. E., Esplin, P. W., & Baradaran, L. P. (1999). Using a scripted protocol in investigative interviews: A pilot study. *Applied Developmental Science, 3*, 70–76. doi:10.1207/s1532480xads0302_1.

Sternberg, K. J., Lamb, M. E., Hershkowitz, I., Yudilevitch, L., Orbach, Y., Esplin, P. W., & Hovav, M. (1997). Effects of introductory style on children's abilities to describe experiences of sexual abuse. *Child Abuse and Neglect, 21*, 1133–1146. doi:10.1016/S0145-2134(97)00071-9.

Strange, D., Garry, M., & Sutherland, R. (2003). Drawing out children's false memories. *Applied Cognitive Psychology, 17*, 607–619. doi:10.1002/acp.911.

Talwar, V., Lee, K., Bala, N., & Lindsay, R. C. L. (2002). Children's conceptual knowledge of lying and its relation to their actual behaviors: Implications for court competence examinations. *Law and Human Behavior, 26*, 395–415.

Teoh, Y.-S., & Lamb, M. E. (2010). Preparing children for investigative interviews: Rapport-building, instruction, and evaluation. *Applied Developmental Psychology, 14*, 154–163. doi:10.1080/10888691.2010.494463.

Vrij, A. (2008). *Detecting lies and deceit: Pitfalls and opportunities* (2nd ed.). Chichester, England: Wiley.

Walker, A. G., & Kenniston, J. (2013). *Handbook on questioning children: A linguistic perspective* (3rd ed.). Washington, DC: American Bar Association.

Wandrey, L., Lyon, T. D., Quas, J. A., & Friedman, W. J. (2012). Maltreated children's ability to estimate temporal location and numerosity of placement changes and court visits. *Psychology, Public Policy & Law, 18*, 79–104. doi:10.1037/a0024812.

Warren, A. R., & Woodall, C. E. (1999). The reliability of hearsay testimony: How well do interviewers recall their interviews with children? *Psychology, Public Policy, and Law, 5*, 355–371.

Warren, A. R., Woodall, C. E., Hunt, J. S., & Perry, N. W. (1996). "It sounds good in theory, but…" Do investigator interviewers follow guidelines based on memory research? *Child Maltreatment, 1*, 231–245.

Waterman, A. H., & Blades, M. (2011). Helping children correctly say "I don't know" to unanswerable questions. *Journal of Experimental Psychology, 17*, 396–405. doi:10.1037/a0026150.

Waterman, A. H., Blades, M., & Spencer, C. (2000). Do children try to answer nonsensical questions? *British Journal of Developmental Psychology, 18*, 211–225. doi:10.1348/026151000165652.

Waterman, A. H., Blades, M., & Spencer, C. (2001). Interviewing children and adults: The effect of question format on the tendency to speculate. *Applied Cognitive Psychology, 15*, 521–531. doi:10.1002/acp.741.

Waterman, A. H., Blades, M., & Spencer, C. (2004). Indicating when you do not know the answer: The effect of question format and interviewer knowledge on children's 'don't know' responses. *British Journal of Developmental Psychology, 22*, 335–348. doi:10.1348/0261510041552710.

Wood, J. M., McClure, K. A., & Birch, R. A. (1996). Suggestions for improving interviews in child protection agencies. *Child Maltreatment, 1*, 223–230.

Woolley, J. D., & Ghosaini, M. E. (2013). Revisiting the fantasy–reality distinction: Children as naïve skeptics. *Child Development, 84*, 1496–1510. doi:10.1111/cdev.12081.

Zajac, R., & Hayne, H. (2003). I don't think that's what really happened: The effect of cross-examination on the accuracy of children's reports. *Journal of Experimental Psychology. Applied, 9*, 187–195. doi:10.1037/1076-898X.9.3.187.

Chapter 19
Psychometric Analysis of Forensic Interviews and Post Hoc Interview Evaluations

William T. O'Donohue and Matthew Fanetti

Evaluating Forensic Interviews with Children Who May Have Been Sexually Abused

Adults in many settings sometimes question children with the goal of discovering information about their experiences. When a variety of professionals (e.g., police officers, social workers, clinical psychologists, physicians) engage in this for the purpose of gaining information that is legally relevant this process is generally called "a forensic interview." When the goal of the forensic interview is to discover from the child some information about whether or not he or she has been sexually abused, and if so, details about this abuse, this process may be called "a forensic interview of a child regarding sexual abuse status."

These have had a long and some might even say a notorious history (Rabinowitz, 2004). There have been cases—most notably the McMartin case in the 1980s in Manhattan Beach, California—but also others (e.g., a daycare case in Edenton, NC and the Kelly Michaels case in New Jersey) where these forensic interviews were done so shoddily that in all likelihood false allegations were created by these interviews or the interview failed to uncover the truth that the children had not been sexually abused by the adult or adults in question. As a result of these problematic interviews, a variety of harm was done—reputations were ruined, innocent individuals were prosecuted, some innocent individuals were imprisoned for several years, families were stressed and even torn apart, millions of dollars were needlessly spent,

W.T. O'Donohue
Department of Psychology, University of Nevada, Reno, MS 0296, Reno, NV 89557, USA

M. Fanetti (✉)
Department of Psychology, Missouri State University,
901 S. National Ave., Springfield, MO 65897, USA
e-mail: mfanetti@missouristate.edu

W.T. O'Donohue, M. Fanetti (eds.), *Forensic Interviews Regarding Child Sexual Abuse*, DOI 10.1007/978-3-319-21097-1_19

and children were given false identities as abuse victims. On the other hand, errors certainly have also occurred in forensic interviews in which children who actually have been abused but the interview failed to elicit this information. Not only is this a failure of the interview to accurately uncover actual abuse status, and not only is there a grievous failure of justice, but these children can be returned to environments where they can be further victimized.

No one disputes that these forensic interviews ought to be done well. What is less clear is how exactly should these interviews be conducted so that they are indeed done well. This clearly involves a meta-question: By what standards ought the quality of a forensic interview with a child who may have been sexually abused be evaluated? A related question is what kind of, or how much, error can one of these forensic interviews contain and still be used to make reasonably accurate conclusions about the child's abuse standards? This chapter will examine these issues. We will examine various criteria for evaluating interviews. We will conclude that there is much missing evaluative information regarding these interviews, that there is reason to be concerned about gaps in what is currently known about the psychometrics of forensic interviews, and there are other issues that are also troubling when evaluating these interviews. We call for a prioritization of corrective action on these problems.

Partly in response to the question of quality of the interview, interview protocols have been developed (see Cirlugea and O'Donohue (2015) for reviews of the major interview protocols). The basic idea behind the development and use of an interview protocol is to provide some standardization—certain stages or moves in the interview will always occur—certain moves will be avoided, and a certain temporal sequencing will occur. Without this standardization, psychometric properties cannot be determined; for example, reliability and validity need to be of some relatively fixed measurement process. Interview protocols attempt to decrease heterogeneity in these interviews. If interviewing were a "free for all"—any interviewer could make up anything as they go along—there would simply be no fixed process that can be evaluated for its strengths and weaknesses. It is important to note that a certain amount of forensic interviews of children do not follow any protocol—they are in fact—"make it up as you go" and a weakness of this is that the accuracy of these is entirely unknown. A final caveat is called for—if an interview protocol is modified then its psychometrics are also unknown. That is, if some entity modifies a known psychometric protocol, the interview becomes different and one cannot assume the psychometrics of the original protocol remain unchanged.

In addition, the basic idea is that these interview protocols would also contain the "best thinking" about how these interviews of children ought to be conducted so that accuracy is maximized—for example, the best thinking suggests that it is important to initially establish rapport with the child so this is a first stage in most interview protocols; and the best thinking generally includes the importance of avoiding suggestive questioning, so interview guidelines define suggestibility and define strategies to avoid this. However, it is also important to note that all these interviews protocols are what is called *semistructured*—these do not contain an invariant script that the interviewer must follow. Rather some flexibility and hence heterogeneity must be allowed to accommodate the wide range of unique values of key variables encountered in the interview (e.g., the child's prior answers, the developmental level of the child, the nature of the abuse itself, unique difficulties the child may have).

One other preliminary matter ought to be quickly addressed. First, some might claim that these interviews of children ought not to be evaluated—these are simply "hearing what the child has to say." This view is false and more than a bit naïve for three reasons: (1) this ignores the vast literature of child suggestibility (see x this volume) as well as the past record of problematic interviews resulting in false conclusions about child abuse status. Interviewing is a complex, protracted, interpersonal process that involves memory, information processing, interpersonal influence, and other psychological processes; and (2) this view ignores the fact that even if the interview is construed as "just hearing what the child has to say" this is still a measurement task—we want to detect "what the child has to say" and we can make errors in doing this. It is a basic principle of psychometrics that all measurement contains error—although certainly some contain more than others—and the goal of psychometrics is to understand the kind and degree of error of any measurement task—even if the measurement task is "just hearing what the child has to say" (Haynes, Smith, & Hunsely, 2011). Finally, the view that there is little concern about the degree of accuracy of these interviews is perplexing because it assumes that no matter what the interviewer does, the interview will invariably and inevitably produce accurate information from the child. This seems implausible particularly because we know that children can contradict themselves across interviews and by logic contradictory statements cannot both be true.

Evaluative Criteria for a Forensic Interview

How should forensic interviews of children who may have been sexually abused be evaluated? Is it sufficient to show that if the interviewer has earned some sort of general professional credentials that the interview was sound—and if so, what credentials—a mental health license in the state, a certificate of some sort of training completion? Is it sufficient for some interviewer to simply show that they have some sort of general past experience in some area relevant to interviewing children who may have been sexually abused, say in childsexualabuse or clinical interviewing? These seem to be the de facto standards of competence in the field—perhaps because these kinds of credentials generally can pass legal muster during a voir dire process. However, psychometrically these seem quite inadequate.

One can raise obvious questions about these sorts of standards:

1. Which credentials exactly? No credentials have been shown to actually assure accuracy of the forensic interview of the child.
2. To what extent does the typical generic training in a variety of professions (social work, clinical psychology, pediatrics, police work) actually make one a competent forensic interviewer of children? Most of this generic training would

give short shrift to this particular domain and thus would be unlikely to produce competence.
3. How much training in the forensic interviewing of children who may have been sexually abused is sufficient? No training has been shown to be necessary or sufficient for assuring accuracy of these interviews.
4. Does this training need to be refreshed—as drift is often the case in faithfully following protocols? Very little information is available on the durability of training on interview fidelity.
5. Ought there be some sort of rigorous test to show that the training was at least initially successful—and if so what is an adequate test of this competence and what should the cut score for competence be? Again, these sorts of questions have been ignored in the literature and in practice. No test score on any test has been shown to assure forensic interview accuracy.
6. Which of the variety of interview protocols ought interviewers be trained in, and why? How psychometrically sound is the protocol? Cirlugea and O'Donohue (2015) point out the vast amounts of missing psychometric information on the protocols used to interview children who may have been sexually abused.
7. Does one become globally competent after this training, that is, competent to interview a child of any age, any child from any culture, and even a child with any special circumstances (e.g., being developmentally delayed)? This question has very little data and is unsettled.

These are tough questions that are generally ignored in the "x was trained in a protocol" or the "x is a licensed professional with some sort of experience in childsexualabuse" views of competency. Thus, we conclude that this standard of evaluation is unsatisfactory.

An Interview Protocol's Sensitivity and Specificity

Typically in medicine a fairly quick and dirty evaluation of a test's overall quality can be given by the metrics of *sensitivity* and *specificity*. A measure's sensitivity is the probability that it will detect x if x is actually present. That is, it is the probability that if x is present (say cancer) that the test will indicate that the cancer is present. Alternatively, a test's sensitivity can be said to be the probability of a false negative—a test has failed to be sensitive if it says that no cancer is present, when in fact cancer is present. Obviously in this case, a forensic interview would fail to be sensitive if it concludes that abuse has NOT occurred, when in fact it has.

Specificity is the converse and equally important. A test can assure perfect sensitivity if the test always indicates "X is present"—after all if the test says x is always present then the measure would never miss an actual incidence of presence. However, the problem with this strategy is that the test would produce a number of false positives—the test would indicate that x is present when it is in fact not. The probability of a false positive is a test's *specificity*—a desirable characteristic for a test to have is to say x is NOT present when in fact x is NOT present. Obviously in a forensic interview with children who may have been sexually abused it is important to conclude that the child has not been sexually abused when the child has not been sexually abused.

As Cirlugea and O'Donohue (2015) have pointed out as a field we do not know the sensitivity or the specificity of the protocols we use to interview children who may have been sexually abused. This is a serious gap in our knowledge. As previously stated this gap becomes even more of a concern when interviews are made up on the fly—that is, that the interviewer fails to follow any protocol—because in principle this *ad hoc* process can have no known sensitivity or specificity—it is not sufficiently constant or fixed to become an object of study. Thus, currently, if an interviewer is questioned along the following lines:

1. What is the rate of false negatives of the interview you administered?
2. What is the rate of false positives of the interview you administered?

The interviewer unfortunately would simply have to say, "These are unknown." This is quite problematic as we do not know if one or both of these are high—and perhaps so high as to render serious concerns about the interview's error rates. Moreover, as a field we don't know which is higher for a particular protocol—false negatives or false positives and this for a variety of reasons seems important to know. If for example, when false negatives of an interview protocol are high—we ought to be more cautious about concluding a child has not been abused even though this is the conclusion of the interview.

In addition, it must also be recognized that there actually might be a series of sensitivities and specificities of a forensic interviewprotocol that ought to be known. For example, in oncology there is not simply a single sensitivity of biopsies, the sensitivity can vary to the type of cancer, the size of the mass examined, etc. There is a parallel situation here—there may be a range of sensitivities and specificities depending on variables such as the age of the child being interviewed, the experience of the interviewer, the severity of the abuse, the relationship between the abuser and the child, etc.

Finally, it must be recognized that the use of a particular protocol actually involves two separate issues: (1) the sensitivity and specificity of the interview protocol but also (2) evidence that the interviewer faithfully followed the interview protocol. Thus, the actual interview must be examined to determine the extent to which it faithfully followed the interview protocol. It is a difficult question—and again unsettled in the field—of how much deviation is permissible? More basically there is little known about how to assess fidelity to a protocol. However, it should not simply be assumed that a particular interviewer faithfully followed a protocol.

What is probably most concerning currently is that there has not been and there currently seems to be little urgency in the field for addressing this critical knowledge gap. Forensic practice seems to be relatively complacent with the ignorance of the sensitivity and specificity of forensic interviews of children who may have been sexually abused. Admittedly, this research can be difficult to conduct but the question raised in a clinical science approach to practice is, "Are these research difficulties sufficient to excuse practice that may contain a level of error that is injurious to our consumers?" This is particularly perplexing because the Daubert criterion of legal admissibility is that the instrument or theory must have a known error rate and these interview protocols do not meet this criterion, yet surprisingly these interviews are routinely admitted in court.

Other Important Psychometric Properties

It is fair to say that the Standard for Educational and Psychological Testing is an important but underutilized document in the field of interviewing children who may have been sexually abused. This document lists several other important evaluative criteria that ought to be known about any measure including:

1. Interrater reliability (the extent to which two different interviewers will arrive at the same conclusions)
2. Test–retest reliability (the extent to which two interviews given at two different times will have the same results)
3. Split half reliabilities (the extent some half of a test agrees or is consistent with some other half)
4. Construct validity (the extent to which the score of this measure agrees with the score of another measure of the same construct—there can be a variety of constructs involved in a forensic interview of a child—rapport, truth knowledge, prepositional competence, etc.)
5. Postdictive validity (the extent to which the score of the measure agrees with some criterion in the past, e.g., actual abuse history)
6. Incremental validity (the extent to which some measure adds or subtracts to the accuracy of some criterion, e.g., the extent to which the forensic interview adds or subtracts accuracy from other information such as medical tests)

Cirlugea and O'Donohue (2015) reviewed psychometric information on several of the protocols and find much missing information although clearly the NICHD protocol has the most known psychometrics known at this point in time. Again, it must be emphasized that "adaptations" of some known protocol or free-form interviews would be missing this key evaluative information.

In addition, the suggests other key information ought to be present for a measure. For example:

1. A manual that will aid the administrator in proper administration procedures, offer information on limitations of the test, and provide information on correct scoring and interpretation.
2. The provision of information related to fair testing and limitations of this (e.g., perhaps testing with some cultural groups results in decreased validity).

In general, there are two other issues raised by the Standards for Educational and Psychological testing. First, there is little information about proper scoring and interpretation of the results of the forensic interview with children who may have been sexually abused. For example, consider the following situations:

(a) A child in the initial part of an interview says that she has not been sexually abused but in a later part of the interview says that she has been abused. How is the interviewer to interpret this inconsistency? What if the sequencing were reversed—initially the child says she was abused but in a subsequent part of the interview she says she was not? Does this order affect the conclusions? How is the interviewer to interpret these inconsistencies?
(b) How is the interviewer to interpret a child's report that contains fantastical details, for example, a teacher touched them inside their underwear and while this was occurring real witches were flying around the room?
(c) What kind of conclusions is the interviewer to make in an interview in which the child gives very little detail about the abuse, for example, "My stepfather touched my chest" but can elaborate no further—cannot recall the number of times, who was present in the home when this allegedly occurred, how many times this occurred, how long it occurred, and cannot give a time of day or date, etc. How much does this lack of detail affect the conclusions of the interview? Of course it would seem that this would partly depend on the child's age but exactly how? Exactly how much detail can we expect from an average 5 year old vs. an average 9 year old?
(d) What kind of conclusions is the interviewer to make in an interview in which implausible details are given, for example, when a 4-year-old child reports that an adult anally penetrated them but that he or she felt no pain?
(e) How is an interviewer to interpret an interview when a parent engaged in suggestive interviewing practices before the interview took place (e.g., repeatedly asking several dozen times if an uncle touched them before the child made an outcry)?
(f) What kind of conclusions is the interviewer to make in an interview in which a child claims that they completely forgot the abuse for several years but then suddenly remembered all of the abuse—a so-called recovered memory?
(g) How is the interviewer to interpret a child's denial of abuse when several other witnesses say they saw the child being abused?
(h) What kind of conclusions is the interviewer to make in an interview that contains a child's responses when English is not their first language and they displayed some difficulties either comprehending or expressing themselves in English—yet there was no interpreter in their native language available?
(i) Finally, how does an interviewer interpret a child's statements in the interview when the child has a rather extensive history of lying—perhaps even displayed in the interview about topics other than abuse (e.g., prizes the child has won)?

These are difficult questions—and no doubt depend on a number of other details surrounding the particular case. However, it is too infrequently recognized that there is in fact an interpretation task at the end of a forensic interview of a child who may have been sexually abused—and these interpretations have a potential for error. Rarely do these interview data "speak for themselves." These conclusions can even be more problematic if the interviewer has a bias—is prone to interpret data in one way or another (exculpatory vs. incriminating)—this issue will be discussed more below.

The second issue to be recognized is there are actually multiple components of an interview and each of these can have their own psychometric properties. Psychometrics refer to the accuracy of inferences being made and a typical interview actually results in a number of inferences. This of course adds considerably to the complexity of an evaluation of the forensic interview with a child who may have been sexually abused. For example, a forensic interview protocol of a child who may have been sexually abused has several components and inferences can be made about each of these—and these inferences can be correct or incorrect.

(a) Rapport building phase of the interview—can result in the inference, "Adequate report was established"
(b) Knowledge of the truth—can result in the inference, "Adequate knowledge was displayed"
(c) Prepositional competence phase—can result in the inference, "The child knew key propositions such as 'inside' and 'underneath'"
(d) "I don't know" responses are permissible—can result in the inference, "The child knew that it was permissible and important to say that they did not know an answer to a question, when in fact they don't know"

Each of these inferences can be correct or incorrect. Note there are several other key elements in most protocols (e.g., the special importance of saying the truth in this context, the importance of correcting the interviewer if they say something wrong, etc.). It is important to note that inferences concerning each of these components can have their own psychometrics.

Was the Interviewer Unbiased?

Another way a forensic interview can be evaluated is to ask, "Was the interviewer objective and unbiased?" This question has been too infrequently asked and may be a core reason why some cases have gone so awry—the interviewer was working for a side that had a vested interest and may have been intentionally or intentionally attempting to please their employer. Ideally, an interviewer ought to have no allegiance to any side—say the prosecution or the defense—they ought to be fully committed to finding out the truth and what the child has to say. However, not all interviewers in all situations may meet this standard and the degree to which this standard of objectivity is met needs to be assessed.

Indicated how a biased interviewer can unintentionally influence children to provide false statements. Subjects were 120 preschool children, 90 of whom attended a birthday party with a visitor. The remaining 30 children did not attend the party but instead spent time coloring with a visitor. Interviewers were graduate students from social work and counseling programs who knew that the children had participated in an activity with a visitor but not what it was. Each interviewer individually questioned four children to discover what the child had done with the visitor. Unknown to the interviewer, the first three children that he or she interviewed had been at the birthday party but the fourth had not.

This study found that interviewers after questioning the first three children who had attended the party wrongly assumed that the fourth child had also attended the party. The interviewers then (unintentionally) engaged in biased questioning with the fourth child in an apparent attempt to confirm their faulty preconceptions. What is particularly interesting is that in response to these suggestive interviews, 60 % of children who had not actually attended the birthday party made false claims to have been there, and 85 % of interviewers wrongly concluded that all four of the children they questioned had attended the party. Thus, even well-intentioned child interviewers can become biased based on their expectations and background beliefs and then use suggestive techniques to extract false statements from children. A key question is to what extent does this sort of phenomena occur in centers that routinely interview children who may have been sexually abused? What steps can occur to assure that it does not?

Another study by can depict that these sorts of problems can occur even before the forensic interview takes place. It is often the case that other professionals have contact with the child—perhaps to hear their initial outcry before the forensic interview takes place. In this study, two professionals, a teacher and social worker, were given a list of activities that had supposedly occurred during a play session in a group of preschoolers. Unknown to these professionals, half of the activities had not really occurred. These professionals then questioned the children to learn what had happened during the play session. Data from the study indicated that interviewers repeatedly used suggestive questions to ask the children about the bogus activities. In response, these children falsely agreed that they had engaged in about 30 % of these bogus activities, some of which involved bodily touch. Further, some children who initially denied that the bogus event occurred later changed their accounts and provided false details about it. This study shows both accounting for the possible biases of any adult who interviews the child can be critical and again shows the inculcating of false memories by biased professionals.

One other study shows the importance of bias in adults. Had preschool-aged children witness four science demonstrations in a university laboratory. Four months later parents were mailed stories that contained descriptions of their children's visit to the lab. Two of the stories were true and two were false (i.e., described experiments that the children had not seen). Each story finished with a fabricated account of what happened when it was time to leave the lab: "Mr. Science wiped (child's name) hands and face with a wet-wipe. The cloth got close to (child's name) mouth and tasted really yucky." Parents read the story to their children three times. Later, children told the experimenters that they had participated in demonstrations that they had not (i.e., the false stories read by their parents). More than half of the participants said that Mr. Science had wiped their mouths and many elaborated on their "yes" answers. When asked if Mr. Science had actually wiped their mouths or did their mother just read the story 71 % of the children maintained that it really happened. This study was replicated using children from a wider age range (3–8-year-olds). Findings were similar except they found that when asked if Mr. Science wiped their mouths or if their mother just read the story the older children tended to recant their claims and said that their mother told them.

Thus, ascertaining potential biases of anyone who has questioned the child about their possible abuse seems important. Duke, Uhl, Wood, and Price (2015) recommend that the forensic interview be expanded so that the individual or individuals who heard the child's initial outcry be interviewed to understand if their questions could have been suggestive and thus biasing. In addition, it should be asked, who is the interviewer working for? Who is paying the interviewer?

McMartin Mistakes vs. Suggestive Pathways Before the Forensic Interview

Another incorrect view currently held in the field seems to be along the lines of "if no McMartin type mistakes—repeated questions, conformity pres, suggestive questions are made then the interview is good." We shall argue that this view is incorrect—it sets too low of a bar. We argue that this is a necessary criterion of adequacy but not a sufficient one. The interview also needs to meet two other criteria.

First, it must attempt to understand and resolve any problems in the key dimensions of the allegation. Suggested that a forensic interview with a child who may have been sexually abused in order to be comprehensive attempt to understand the following dimensions:

1. *Outcry analysis*—the general circumstances of the child's initial accusations should be determined and analyzed for possible bias
2. *Stake analysis*—whether or not anyone who had significant contact with the child has a hidden agenda relevant to a guilty or not guilty verdict toward the accused should be established
3. *Parental/Significant Other suggestion*—whether or not a caregiver or parent has made leading statements or engaged in leading questioning with the child and thus the child has developed a false memory should be evaluated
4. *Forensic Interview analysis*—whether or not biased interviewing techniques were practiced should be evaluated
5. *Memory analysis*—whether or not memory errors (e.g., errors of omission or commission) may have occurred should be determined
6. *Sufficiency of details provided by the child*—whether the child can describe in an age-appropriate manner events that occurred before, during, and after in a way that makes a coherent, understandable, narrative should be assessed

7. *Inconsistencies analysis*—a contradictory statement by logic contains falsehoods, thus whether or not the child has provided inconsistent core details between or within statements should be assessed
8. *Logistical detail analysis*—whether or not the allegation contains logistical implausibilities should be assessed. For example, claims that the child was anally raped but did not experience pain would make the report logistically problematic
9. *Fantastical details analysis*—the presence or absence of fantastical details in the allegations should be examined
10. *Personological analysis*—whether the child suffers from any mental health problems or history that may indicate an increased probability of either truth telling or problematic reports should be assessed

The basic idea is that these dimensions of a sexualabuse allegation are central to understanding what the child is indeed saying or attempting to say. Children due to a variety of factors may not be articulate clearly what happened and the interviewer needs to be mindful and probe key dimensions of a possible sexual abuse allegation so that the interview provides as much clarity and as much detail as possible. Moreover problems with the child's statements need to be identified and disclosed and not ignored or swept under the rug—doing this is not consistent with objectivity. Thus, the degree to which the interview actually addresses these dimensions and attempts to resolve any problems with these, and objectively admits any of these in the conclusions is part of a forensic interview's being comprehensive and objective.

The Protocol for Evaluating Forensic Interviews of Children

Rising general awareness of potentially problematic interviewing practices necessitates the post hoc evaluation of forensic interviews of children for the presences or absence of these practices. However, because these evaluations are yet another form of assessment, they too are bound by the need to establish at least minimal reliability and validity. Unfortunately, very few methods currently exist to identify the presence of problematic interviewing practices and necessary assessments. Furthermore, only one method has been published in peer-reviewed journals with explication of the manner in which it established reliability and validity. That method is the Protocol for Evaluation of Forensic Interviews of Children (PEFIC; Fanetti, O'Donohue, & Bradley, 2006; O'Donohue, Benuto, & Fanetti, 2010).

The PEFIC is an observational behavioral rating system. The PEFIC lists 17 ways, referred to as "biasing factors," that a child's event recall or verbal report may be skewed away from accuracy. Some of these are intra-interview factors—those specifically exhibited by the interviewer in the course of the interview. Others are extra-interview and represent other ways (e.g., including child beliefs) that a child's report or event recall may be biased. For this second set, the interviewer is not responsible for the presence of the potential problem, but rather is responsible for the *assessment of its presence or absence*. Below is a list of each of the factors specifically identified in the PEFIC.

Intra-interview Factors

1. *Difficulties in establishing rapport*: Does the interviewer maintain sufficient rapport to facilitate a successful interview?
2. *The presence of leading questions*: Does the interviewer, at any point, provide forensically relevant details to the child before the child has iterated said details?
3. *Interviewer disconfirmations of child responses*: Does the interviewer provide either direct or functional disconfirmations of the child's responses?
4. *Inappropriate styles of reinforcement*: Does the interviewer provide a differential form of responding to the child's answers (e.g., accusatory vs. exculpatory)?
5. *Repetitive questions/questioning style*. Does the interviewer repeat questions directly or functionally without providing a justification?
6. *Communication modality inconsistencies*. Does the interviewer fail to observe or note potential disagreements between the child's verbal, paraverbal, and nonverbal responses?
7. *Encouraging the child to speculate*. Does the interviewer encourage or endorse a child's stated speculation while answering questions?
8. *Conformity pressure*. Does the interviewer mention prior or existing reports by the child or other individuals during the context of the interview?
9. *Response class focus*. Did the interviewer redirect the child to a specific individual or class of behavior?

Extra-interview Factors

10. *Outside Contamination*. Did the interviewer assess for the nature of external or outside communication that the child has experienced regarding the allegations?
11. *Understanding of role and purpose*. Did the interviewer assess for the child's understanding of the purpose of the interview and the child's role in the interview?
12. *External threats or bribes*. Did the interviewer assess for possibility that the child's report may have been influenced by threats and or bribes?
13. *Concept oftruth*. Did the interviewer assess for the child's understanding of the meaning of truth?
14. *Importance of truth*. Did the interviewer assess for the child's knowledge that the truth is especially important in this forensic context?
15. *"I don't know" responses*. Did the interviewer assess for the child's understanding of how and when to answer questions with a phrase such as, "I don't know"?
16. *Authority pleasing*. Did the interviewer assess for the possibility that the child may be answering questions in a way thought to be pleasing to important individuals?
17. *Discomfort*. Did the interviewer assess for the possibility that the child may not feel sufficiently comfortable or free to discuss forensic details in this setting? This is separate from general rapport.

Those trained to reliably identify these interviewproblems and assessments are then able to state whether they existed in a specific interview, but not whether they actually influenced the child's responses in that interview. Conclusions are limited to the presence or absence of these factors. If absent, it can be argued that they could not have influenced the child. If present, it can be argued that they may have influenced the child or may not. That influence could simply be not ruled out. Without knowing how the child *would have responded in the absence* of those influences, we cannot know the extent of their effect.

Reports related to this form of interviewevaluation should contain a rationale for the way the assessment is done, a complete observational explication of the positive indicators related to each factor (e.g., including quoted interactions from the interview), detailed analyses of why each passage is thought to be an indicator of a problem (or of a sufficient assessment), and conclusions about the breadth and extent of identified problems and strengths. Important in the discussion is the idea that the conclusions to not indicate any level (or lack) of veracity related to the child's report. Decisions of veracity of allegations are primarily the responsibility of the jury and or judge. Evaluations of the forensic interview only serve to highlight the context(s) in which those allegations arose.

Conclusions

Forensic interviews of children are assessment procedures. As such, they are bound by the same principles that guide the development of other psychological assessments. In that way, they will be prone to yield results with some degree of error, even if well-controlled interviews are administered with a high degree of adherence. However, we know that humans that use assessment tools sometimes do so incorrectly. Thus, it is our view that forensic science should focus more closely on the psychometric properties of the assessments utilized, so that the errors rates and adherence problems become known quantities, rather than remaining unknown—and thus a source of debate or contention in applied settings. Without psychometric evaluation, descriptions of the utility, adherence, and quality of interviews are often not much more than an appeal to authority. Authority is not a more convincing replacement for scientific psychometric analysis.

Even without the daunting task of measuring adherence to forensic childinterview protocols (which are designed to assess events of nearly unlimited variance), the field has reached some agreement on basic problems that occur in interviews that may harm a child's accuracy and likely do not help it. We suggest as a minimal first step that we ensure an ability to identify when these things have happened in an interview. After all, if we cannot agree that certain problems have or have not occurred, how are we then to make the argument that they are or are not a problem in the first place? We think that methods for such observational agreement have existed in the literature for decades, but only as hidden components of other studies—as functional "procedures" used in studies of memory and suggestibility. We argue that these procedures have merit in their own space and should be developed and psychometrically evaluated as stand-alone assessment methods. This is the goal and application of the PEFIC mentioned above.

References

Cirlugea, O., & O'Donohue, W. (2015). Review of psychometrics of forensic interview protocols with children. In W. O'Donohue & M. Fanetti (Eds.), *Forensic interviews regarding child sexual abuse: A guide to evidence-based practice*. New York, NY: Springer.

Duke, M. C., Uhl, E. R., Wood, J. M., & Price, H. L. (2015). Avoiding problems in child abuse interviews and investigations. In W. O'Donohue & M. Fanetti (Eds.), *Forensic interviews regarding child sexual abuse: A guide to evidence-based practice*. New York, NY: Springer.

Fanetti, M., O'Donohue, W., & Bradley, A. (2006). A method for evaluating child forensic interviews. *American Journal of Forensic Psychology, 24*(5), 5–27.

Haynes, S., Smith, G. T., & Hunsely, J. (2011). *Scientific foundations of assessment*. New York, NY: Academic Books.

O'Donohue, W., Benuto, L., & Fanetti, M. (2010). Children's allegations of sexual abuse: A model for forensic assessment. *Psychological Injury and Law, 3*, 148–154.

Rabinowitz, D. (2004). *No crueler tyrannies*. New York, NY: Free Press.

Chapter 20
Cultural Considerations in Forensic Interviewing of Children

Lorraine T. Benuto and Jena Garrick

The field of psychology is currently focused on evidence-based practice (Ollendick & King, 2012) and experts have noted that research on ethnic minority individuals are underrepresented in the scientific literature (Bernal & Scharró-del-Río, 2001). For example, despite that African Americans constitute 13.1 % of the United States population (U.S. Census Bureau, 2013), they are not commensurately represented in the literature (Coley & Barton, 2004). Reasons for this disparity have been cited as being due to distrust of the medical/scientific community, poor access to care, poor recruiting strategies, etc. (Shavers-Hornaday, Lynch, Burmeister, & Torner, 1997). With regard to Asian-Americans, in many studies Asians are not listed as participants (likely because they are categorized as "other") and when they are listed they constitute a small minority of the research samples; studies that are exclusively focused on Asian-Americans are few and far in between (Benuto, Thaler, & Leany, 2014). While research on Hispanics is slightly more abundant, this group also remains underrepresented in the literature (Benuto, 2013). This underrepresentation is even more pronounced in the forensic literature. Indeed, with the exception of how demographic factors interplay with risk evaluations, there is little literature on forensic assessment practices with ethnic minority individuals (Carter & Forsyth, 2007).

Because the information gleaned from a forensic evaluation can have such important consequences, understanding how cultural factors interplay with forensic evaluations is of utmost importance. While there are *not* circumstances where the results of an evaluation are *unimportant*, there are instances where the results of a forensic evaluation can carry substantially more weight than others (Benuto, 2013). Specific to this chapter is the issue of forensic interviewing with children.

The consequences associated with the results of a forensic interview are monumental. The findings from an investigation (in which a forensic interview plays a

L.T. Benuto, Ph.D. (✉) • J. Garrick, B.A.
Department of Psychology, University of Nevada, Reno, MS 0296, Reno, NV 89557-0296, USA
e-mail: dr.benuto@gmail.com

W.T. O'Donohue, M. Fanetti (eds.), *Forensic Interviews Regarding Child Sexual Abuse*, DOI 10.1007/978-3-319-21097-1_20

large role) can have huge implications for the child who made the allegation as well as for the accused. If the child's allegation is found to be true, the perpetrator can suffer substantial legal consequences. Forensic interviews with children must be carried out in a manner that minimizes suggestibility and maximizes the chance that true and accurate information is obtained during the interview as both false positives and false negatives can have deleterious consequences. A false positive could result in unjust and substantial legal consequences for the accused and a false negative could place the perpetrator back in contact with the child. In this chapter, we provide an overview of cultural factors that are relevant to forensic interviewing of children. We also provide specific guidelines for individuals who work with ethnic minority children who have made an allegation of abuse.

Crimes Committed Against Children

According to the CDC, over 3.7 million reports were made to Child Protective Services (CPS) of children being abused or neglected. It is suspected that CPS reports underestimate the actual occurrence of child abuse, and that one in every seven children will experience abuse in their lifetimes (CDC, 2013). Child abuse encompasses a host of crimes including sexual abuse; neglect; child maltreatment; and physical, emotional, and/or psychological abuse; children are the most victimized segment of the population (Finkelhor, 2011). Haboush and Alyan (2013) described child sexual abuse in particular to be widely documented as occurring across all racial, cultural, ethnic, and socioeconomic groups illustrating the importance of understanding cultural characteristics that may have relevance in forensic interviewing. Table 20.1 includes the prevalence of child abuse in different racial/ethnic groups throughout the United States. Given that ethnic minority children are not exempt from experiencing abuse, examining cultural considerations for forensic interviewing is necessary.

Sociodemographic Factors and Suggestibility, Memory, and Disclosure

There are a number of factors that require special consideration in the context of forensic interviewing of children. These include suggestibility, memory and accuracy of recall, age and maturity level of the child, interviewing questioning technique (e.g., open vs. close ended), and the benefit on single interviews over multiple interviews. Not surprisingly, research on ethnic minorities and the aforementioned variables is essentially absent.

For example, research examining demographic variables (e.g., ethnic differences) and suggestibility is virtually nonexistent. In terms of other factors that may be related to suggestibility (e.g., demographic, psychosocial, and cognitive factors:

Table 20.1 Child maltreatment prevalence among different U.S. Cultural Groups (CDC, 2013)

Victim characteristics	Rate of victimization (per 1000 children)
African Americans	14.3
American Indian/Alaska Natives	11.4
Pacific Islanders	8.5
Hispanics	8.6
Whites	7.9
Asian-Americans	1.7

Bruck & Melnyk, 2004), suggestibility is related to age, with preschool-aged children having the highest level of influence. Interestingly, McFarlane et al. (2004) found that children from lower socioeconomic status (SES) are more suggestible than children from higher SES, although other studies during this time could replicate this finding (Alexander et al., 2002; Clarke-Stewart, Malloy, & Allhusen, 2004; London & Bruck, 2004) suggesting that SES may hold no relationship to suggestibility and/or that confounds in the McFarlane et al. (2004) study might the differences between SES groups observed. While some researchers have found that girls are more suggestible than boys (e.g., McFarlane, Powell, & Dudgeon, 2002) others have presented conflicting results (e.g., Crossman, 2001) or no results at all (Quas & Schaaf, 2002; Vrij & Bush, 2000; Young, Powell, & Dudgeon, 2003) suggesting that there is likely not a relationship between gender and suggestibility.

With regard to memory processing, given the biological basis by which memory is run, it is unlikely that ethnic differences in memory processing exist. However, Geddie, Fradin, and Beer (2000) revealed that race and SES were significantly related to total recall, with Caucasian children correctly recalling more information than African American children, and higher recall rates in children of higher SES backgrounds (Geddie, Fradin, & Beer, 2000). A review of the extant literature on truth, lies, and recantations did not reveal any studies on cultural differences. Given the conflicting results and limited research on suggestibility and memory and sociodemographic factors, it does not appear that considerations or exceptions need to be made beyond those normally made in regard to forensic interviewing (e.g., not asking leading or repetitive questions).

Research surrounding the disclosure process of children during interviewing is abundant, but much of the research focuses on the individual's experience, social reactions, and implications of the two combined. The disclosure process is an integral part of the psychological recovery for sexual abuse victims. Since child sexual abuse is found to occur across ethnicities (Putnam, 2003), being culturally sensitive is important although the relationship between ethnicity and child sexual abuse is unclear (Van Toledo & Seymour, 2013). While empirically it remains unclear whether cultural factors impact the disclosure process, experts have offered some theoretical perspectives. For example, Lovett (2004) stated that disclosure may be influenced by race, ethnicity, culture, and gender. In fact, Fontes and Faller (2006) asserted that cultural differences between the interviewer and the child may hinder the disclosure process in children.

Interestingly, Stoltenborgh, Van Ijzendoorn, Euser, and Bakermans-Kranenburg, (2011) identified cross-cultural differences in CSA prevalence rates with Asia countries having the lowest prevalence. Stoltennorgh and colleagues hypothesized that the differences could be attributed to rates of disclosure affected by shame, guilt, or other culturally sensitive experiential elements rather than a real reflection of prevalence. This is consistent with findings by Foynes, Platt, Hall, and Freyd, (2014) who indicated that close victim–perpetrator relationships are more likely to delay disclosure or eliminate disclosure. Foynes et al. hypothesized that nondisclosure may serve to protect the relationship among families, in particular traditional Asian families due to their cultural values of interdependence. Often the demographic variables studied regarding disclosure are not directly linked to ethnic differences in the disclosure process. For example, a study involving African American and Latina girls found that age was the only demographic characteristic that was linked to disclosure, although African American girls reported more severe cases of CSA and more later-in-life outcomes resulting in depression and PTSD (Glover et al., 2010). As illustrated above, empirically speaking it does not appear that cultural characteristics impact the disclosure process. The above being said there are some cultural norms that may impact the decision to disclose or not to disclose. For example, in some cultures, it is not uncommon for a young adolescent to date a much older adolescent. While in certain states this may be illegal and therefore a reportable sex crime, if it is considered to be an acceptable practice because of cultural norms, the crime may not be reported or the adolescent may not perceive that a crime has occurred. Consider the following case example: Sandra is a 13-year-old Hispanic female. She began a relationship with a 19-year-old male (Hector) unbeknown to her parents. She felt “in love” with Hector and knowing that her mother had married her father when she was merely 14, she did not consider her age or Hector’s age to be a problem. One day Sandra skipped school to spend the day with Hector and her parents and the school found out about it. It came to light that Sandra had been having sex with Hector and the police were contacted. Her parents were upset but did not anticipate the legal ramifications that followed. Hector was arrested and during the investigation Sandra continually expressed confusion over why Hector had been arrested and was not cooperative during the forensic interview as she did not perceive that a crime had been committed. This case example highlights that cultural norms may influence the disclosure process.

Cultural Considerations and the Forensic Interview

In an attempt to catalog and explore how interviews can be used with ethnic minorities in a culturally sensitive manner, a number of authors have evaluated the literature on the use of such interviews with ethnic minority clients (Mestre, Rossi, & Torrens, 2013; Zink, Lee, & Allen, 2015). Clinical interviews are often used as forensic assessment tools, with interviews categorized as structured, semistructured, and unstructured. In an unstructured interview, the psychologist does not use a specific set of questions but rather seeks to gather preliminary data. Unstructured interviews are key in rapport building and in-depth information gathering, but they lack consistency across interviewers due to their flexibility in question formatting (Huss, 2009; Grisso, 2003). A semistructured interview consists of predetermined questions but allows for flexibility in follow-up or clarification questions by the interviewer. The semistructured interview style is considered more consistent than the unstructured interview due to its reliability across interviewers from its more rigid question sets (Craig, 2005). A structured interview requires the psychologist to ask specific questions without deviating from the interview protocol. These interviews are designed to test specific items and should be used when consistency and reliability are most important (Huss, 2009). Given the structured nature of forensic interviewing protocols for children, an important cultural consideration is with regard to language. Table 20.2 includes a list of the major forensic interviews that are used with children and the languages that those interviews are available in.

Language

As illustrated at the outset of this chapter the cultural panorama of the United States is diverse. Within this diversity is a wide variety of languages. According to the United State Census Bureau's 2011 Language Mapper report, within the United States four main language categories exist: Spanish, other Indo-European languages, Asian and Pacific Island languages, and All Other languages. The data from this report showed the following languages are predominately spoken next to English: French, French Creole, Italian, Russian, Portuguese, German, Arabic, Japanese, Tagalog, Chinese, Vietnamese, Korean, Persian, Polish (U.S. Census Bureau, 2011).

Among cultural minorities, it has been documented that not all cultural minorities speak English. For example, approximately 78 % of Hispanics age five and older speak Spanish as their primary language in the home (Weil, 2010) and less than half of Hispanic immigrants residing in the United States have *even* limited English language proficiency (Pew Hispanic Center, 2012). Given that 20.8% of the population does not speak English "well," nor is English the language they speak in their households (U.S. Census Bureau, 2010) when conducting a forensic interview, the child's language preference and proficiency level should be considered.

Preference vs. *Proficiency*. Language is an important element to assess given that the child will need to understand somewhat complex questions and be able to provide answers to these questions during the forensic interview. This obviously is reliant on the child's ability to understand the language. Because working memory and language learning are related (Baddeley, 2003) and higher order executive functions contribute to language abilities like encoding and comprehension (de Abreu, Baldassi, Puglisi, & Befi-Lopes, 2013) ensuring that there is a consistency between

Table 20.2 Forensic interviews

Protocol	Language
NICHD	• French (Cyr, Lamb, 2009)
	• English (Boser, La Roy, & Wilson, 2014)
	• Portuguese (Boser, La Roy, & Wilson, 2014)
	• Japanese (Boser, La Roy, & Wilson, 2014)
	• Brazilian Portuguese (Boser, La Roy, & Wilson, 2014)
	• French Canadian (Boser, La Roy, & Wilson, 2014)
	• Italian (Boser, La Roy, & Wilson, 2014)
	• Hebrew (Boser, La Roy, & Wilson, 2014)
	• Finnish (Boser, La Roy, & Wilson, 2014)
	• Georgian (Boser, La Roy, & Wilson, 2014)
	• Spanish (Boser, La Roy, & Wilson, 2014)
	• Korean (Malloy, La Rooy, & Lamb, 2011)
	• Japanese (Malloy, La Rooy, & Lamb, 2011)
	• Swedish (Malloy, La Rooy, & Lamb, 2011)
	• Low verbal abilities (Dion & Cyr, 2008)
APSAC	• English (American Professional Society on the Abuse of Children, 1995; 1997; 2002; 2011)
	• Russian (American Professional Society on the Abuse of Children, 1997)
NCAC	• Spanish (Fontes, 2005; Goodyear, Brown, 2011)
Stepwise protocol	English (Yuille, Hunter, Joffe, & Zaparniuk, 1993)
Oregon interviewing guidelines	• English (Bohannan, S., Chianello, T., Flagor, R., Gallagher, J., Kettner, D., Sieg, C., Sparks, C. & Van Ness, P., 2004)
Center for Child Protection (San Diego) protocol	• English (Davies, D., Cole, J., Albertella, G., McCulloch, L., Allen, K., & Kekevian, H., 1996)
Cognitive interview (CI; Fisher & Geiselman, 1992)	• English (Kohnken, Schimossek, Aschermann & Hofer, 1995)
	• Erman (Kohnken, Schimossek, Aschermann & Hofer, 1995)
	• Portuguese, (Stein & Memon, 2006)
	• Spanish (Hernandez-Fernaud & Alonso-Quecuty, 1997)

the language in which the interview is administered and the child's proficiency level is of utmost importance. Thus, the most salient recommendation that we can offer is that language proficiency be assessed and for children who are not proficient in English, the interview must be conducted in their native language. It is important to note that it may not be sufficient to simply ask the child or parent what language the child speaks most fluently. Indeed even children who have been asked language they would like to speak might answer with "English" due to the pressure to comply.

Children (and/or guardians) should be asked what language they speak at home and what language they would prefer to speak in during the interview (Lau & Treacy, 2009), but this should be in addition to monitoring the linguistic ability of the child during the interview to see if indeed he/she is proficient in English.

Moreover, collateral contacts may be able to provide insight as to the child's level of proficiency. Specifically the parent or caregiver can be asked what the child's native language is as well as what language is most commonly spoken in the home. If the child is school aged, the teacher may be able to shed some light on the child's proficiency level and reviewing school records may also be useful. It is recommended that the child's language proficiency be evaluated/determined prior to beginning the interview to avoid the need to repeat questions because the child did not understand or comprehend the questions asked. This will help to minimize suggestibility and the use of repeated questions. It is important to note that inevitably situations will arise where a competent interviewer who is fluent/proficient in the language in which the child is most proficient will not be available. Where this is the case, using a translator may be the only option (recommendations for using a translator are provided below).

Selecting an interview protocol. Above we made it clear that language proficiency should be evaluated and used to help determine in what language the interview should be conducted. Because so many subgroups exist under the major ethnic categories and subgroups can speak different languages or even different variations of the same language, it can be difficult to find, translate, or validate measures for all subpopulations. Fortunately as can be seen in Table 20.2, several of the existing protocols have been translated into various languages. While it may seem logical to simply use an existing protocol and to have a bilingual interview (or translator) administer it, it has been noted that a direct translation does not ensure equivalence between the original and translated version (Fontes & Faller, 2006). Experts have noted that when culturally adapting an interview protocol, denotation, connotation, specificity of terms, culturally taboo topics, and equivalence of words and items should be considered so as to maximize the quality of the interview (Mestre et al., 2013). The World Health Organization (WHO, 2003) recommends that the following six-step adaptation protocol be used. The steps recommended by the WHO are:

- Forward Translation
- Expert Panel Review
- Independent Back Translation
- Harmonization of Vocabulary
- Pretesting and Cognitive Interviewing
- Final Version of Translated Questionnaire

Because a substantial number of interviews are available in various languages (see Table 20.2) and given the complexities of translating protocols, interviewers may wish to use existing protocols that have already been translated. In the event that a translated protocol is not available, interviewers are encouraged to utilize an adaptation protocol (such as the one described above) to translate the interview.

Using a translator. Interviewers are strongly discouraged from using an on-the-spot translator (particularly a translator who has not been trained to translate in assessment or eventuation contexts) and most certainly discouraged from using a family member or friend as a translator given the high potential for suggestibility and the associated consequences that can occur when suggestibility is introduced in a forensic interview. Indeed, experts agree, for mental health-related interventions (including assessment), using a friend or family member can have deleterious consequences and only in the rarest and most desperate of cases should a family member or friend be used. Using family or friends as translators may hurt privacy during the interview, the translator may have ulterior motives, and most importantly, they are not highly trained experts, so they may leave out or change key aspects of the conversation during the interview (Kuehnle & Sparta, 2006).

With regard to using a translator, forensic interview protocols are highly structured so as to avoid the introduction of suggestibility and to improve the quality of information given (Lamb, Orbach, Hershkowitz, Esplin, & Horowitz, 2007). When this structure is disrupted and questions are rephrased, the assurances of nonsuggestibility can be compromised. For example, the forensic interviewer may ask for additional details by stating: "Can you tell me more about that?" A translator who is not explicitly trained in forensic interviewing could easily slightly change the verbiage and increase the chance of suggestibility.

Above, illustrated above, there are a myriad of complications that can ensue if a translator (particularly one who has not training in forensic interviewing) is used. In addition to the concerns raised above, it is important to consider the issue of rapport as a key component of the forensic interview (Lamb et al., 2009). Thus, if an interpreter is used rapport should be established between the interpreter and the child. Indeed, according to Powell, Fisher, and Wright (2005) an important step in obtaining a detailed quality account of an incident is building a relationship and an environment where the interviewee feels accepted and heard and trust and nonjudgment are essential. Within the health literature it is well established that the rapport between patients and clinicians can be compromised by the interpreter. Interpreters, even with extensive training, can miss important nonverbal and verbal aspects and are often not trained to develop rapport with clients (Fernández, 2010). In fact how interviewees perceive the interpreter (Green et al., 2005) is key to the rapport between the clinician/interviewer and the child (Vallano & Compo, 2011). Thus, when an interpreter is used, care should be taken to ensure that rapport exists between the interpreter and the child.

Ethnic Matching and Racial/Ethnic Concordance

Most typically there is a discrepancy between the evaluator (i.e., in this case the interviewer) and interviewee (Weiss & Rosenfeld, 2012). In terms of the administration of the interview, it is important to note that certain ethnic groups may be less likely to engage when ethnic matching between the interviewee and the interviewer is absent (Kirmayer, Rousseau, Jarvis, & Guzder, 2003; Tseng, Matthews, & Elwyn,

2004). Benuto and Leany (2015) discussed the implications of ethnic and racial concordance between the clinician (in this case this would be the interviewer) and the client or interviewee. Racial and ethnic concordance describes the relationship between a client or patient and a healthcare provider. Typically, research on concordance is on the perception of the quality of care and how that corresponds to the client's utilization (an exemplar of this research can be seen in Saha et al., 1999). Saha et al. reported better utilization of health services and better perceived reports of care when concordance was evident. There is evidence that implicit behaviors can result in less-than-satisfactory doctor–patient relationships, and in the context of forensic interviewing, the interviewer should be cognizant of this in order to reduce this potential (e.g., checking for child's understanding of the questions, ensuring that the child feels comfortable, etc.). Fontes (2008) described the importance of rapport building and suggested that there are culturally appropriate ways to overcome language barriers, use interpreters, and to convey respect. Specifically, Fontes suggested that interviewers should not only be sensitive to issues-related language, but also having "cultural brokerage competency," or the awareness of cultural nuances during the interviewing process. For example, Fontes suggested that interviewers should ask questions in a manner that acknowledge family structure. Similar to our discussion above regarding ensuring that adequate rapport be built between a translator (when used) and the child, here our recommendation is similar. When ethnic matching between the interviewee and the interviewer is absent, the interviewee should be cognizant of this and ensure that rapport is sufficiently established before proceeding with the interview.

Immigration Status

In addition to the cultural considerations that are discussed above, there are factors that have relevance despite that they may not directly impact the interview process. Because when child abuse is disclosed, legal entities become involved, the legal status of the person or family that is impacted is worth discussing. The United States' entire basis is immigration. Indeed, this country was founded by immigrants and since its inception, immigration continues (Walker, 2014). Currently, 13 % (or 39 million foreign-born residents) of the United States' population is composed of immigrants. Of this large number, 11 million are thought to be undocumented or in the country illegally (Martin & Midgley, 2010). The perception of an individual who is here illegally/undocumented is unique. Legal status (or rather lack thereof) can impact a person's decision to either seek out health services (De Jesus & Xiao, 2013; Martinez et al., 2013) or to become involved with the law (Apfelbaum & Sommers, 2013; Reina, Lohman, & Maldonado, 2014). These individuals may believe that interacting with the health system or becoming involved with law enforcement could result in deportation (Falconier et al., 2013; Reina et al., 2014) or other repercussions. With regard to forensic interviewing of children, individuals who have a child who has alleged abuse but do not have legal status may be reluctant to report the alleged abuse to authorities. Thus, the forensic interviewer should be mindful of this and how it might impact the disclosure (and therefore the interview) process. If the child is aware of his/her parents' legal circumstance, the child may be concerned with how his/her answers might impact the family (e.g., will the family be deported, etc.). If the child is apprehensive, it may be necessary to spend extra time establishing rapport with the child and providing reassurance where possible.

Summary and Recommendations

The United States is a diverse country both in terms of the ethnic distribution and languages spoken. Because forensic interviews are such an integral part of the investigation of alleged child abuse, ensuring the interviews be conducted in manner that minimizes suggestibility and maximizes the chance that true and accurate information is obtained from the child is of utmost importance. While research on forensic interviews and cultural sensitivity is essentially absent our review of the existing literature led us to the following conclusions/recommendations:

1. Rapport remains a critical element to the forensic interview and therefore should be carefully established with the child. Rapport can be best established in a language the child is most proficiency in and when ethnic matching has occurred.
2. The child should be interviewed in the language in which s/he is proficient.
3. When possible and/or necessary existing, translated versions of forensic interviewing protocols should be used.
4. If a translator is necessary, the translator should be trained in forensic interviewing.
5. Family or friends should not be used as a translator.
6. There may be cultural factors (e.g., shame, guilt, immigration status) that require consideration in the context of forensic interviewing. These considerations can be addressed by ensuring that adequate rapport has been established with the family and the child.

While the above are best practices that ideally should be followed, there will be situations where the above practices cannot be implemented. For example, given the broad array of languages that are spoken in the United States inevitably there will situations where there is not a forensic interviewer or even trained translator who can speak the language of the child. In these cases, a family member or friend may need to act as the translator. When this is the case, the interviewer should ensure that the family member or friend understands the implications that the forensic interview can have and that s/he understands how to avoid biasing interview practices.

As illustrated throughout this chapter, conducting a forensic interview with an ethnic minority is not without its complications. Published literature on this topic is almost nonexistent and while several protocols have been translated into foreign languages, per our literature search there is no empirical data on these translated interview protocols. Thus, researchers should focus on ensuring that there are adequate psychometrics for these translated interview protocols.

References

Alexander, K. W., Goodman, G. S., Schaaf, J. M., Edelstein, R. S., Quas, J. A., & Shaver, P. R. (2002). The role of attachment and cognitive inhibition in children's memory and suggestibility for a stressful event. *Journal of Experimental Child Psychology, 83*, 262–290.

Apfelbaum, E. P., & Sommers, S. R. (2013). Law and diversity: The legal—behavioral. In Q. M. Roberson (Ed.), *The oxford handbook of diversity and work* (p. 442). New York, NY: Oxford University Press.

Baddeley, A. D. (2003). Working memory and language: An overview. *Journal of Communication Disorders, 36*, 189–208.

Benuto, L. T. (2013). Guide to psychological assessment with Hispanics: An introduction. In L. T. Benuto (Ed.), *Guide to psychological assessment with Hispanics* (pp. 1–13). New York, NY: Springer.

Benuto, L., & Leany, B. (2015). Psychological assessment & evaluations with African American clients. In L. Benuto & B. Leany (Eds.), *Guide to psychological assessment with African Americans*. New York, NY: Springer.

Benuto, L. T., Thaler, N. S., & Leany, B. D. (Eds.). (2014). *Guide to psychological assessment with Asians*. New York, NY: Springer.

Bernal, G., & Scharró-del-Río, M. R. (2001). Are empirically supported treatments valid for ethnic minorities? Toward an alternative approach for treatment research. *Cultural Diversity and Ethnic Minority Psychology, 7*(4), 328.

Bruck, M., & Melnyk, L. (2004). Individual differences in children's suggestibility: A review and synthesis. *Applied Cognitive Psychology, 18*(8), 947–996. doi:10.1002/acp.1070.

Carter, R. T., & Forsyth, J. M. (2007). Examining race and culture in psychology journals: The case of forensic psychology. *Professional Psychology: Research and Practice, 38*(2), 133–142.

Center for Disease Control and Prevention, US Department of Health and Human Services. *Quick facts 2013*. CDC.gov.

Clarke-Stewart, K. A., Malloy, L. C., & Allhusen, V. D. (2004). Verbal ability, self-control, and close relationships with parents protect children against misleading suggestions. *Applied Cognitive Psychology, 18*, 1037–1058.

Coley, R. J., & Barton, P. E. (2004). The chronic under-492 representation of African Americans in medicine. *ETS 493 Policy Notes, 12*, 1–8.

Craig, R. (2005). Clinical and diagnostic interviewing. *Psychology*.

Crossman, A. M. (2001). *Predicting suggestibility: The role of individual differences and socialization* (Unpublished doctoral dissertation). Cornell University, Ithaca, NY.

de Abreu, P. M. J. E., Baldassi, M., Puglisi, M. L., & Befi-Lopes, D. M. (2013). Cross-linguistic and cross-cultural effects on verbal working memory and vocabulary: Testing language-minority children with an immigrant background. *Journal of Speech, Language, and Hearing Research, 56*, 630–642.

De Jesus, M., & Xiao, C. (2013). Cross-border health care utilization among the Hispanic population in the United States: Implications for closing the health care access gap. *Ethnicity & Health, 18*(3), 297–314.

Falconier, M. K., McCollum, E., Austin, J., Wainbarg, M., Hasburn, G., & Mora, S. (2013). Interpartner violence among Latinos: Community perceptions on help seeking and needed programs. *Partner abuse, 4*(3), 356–379.

Fernández, E. I. (2010). Verbal and nonverbal concomitants of rapport in health care encounters: Implications for interpreters. *Journal of Specialized Translation, 14*, 216–228.

Finkelhor, D. (2011). Prevalence of child victimization, abuse, crime, and violence exposure. In J. W. White, M. P. Koss, A. E. Kazdin, J. W. White, M. P. Koss, & A. E. Kazdin (Eds.), *Violence against women and children: Mapping the terrain* (Vol. 1, pp. 9–29). Washington, DC: American Psychological Association. doi:10.1037/12307-001.

Fontes, L. A. (2008). *Interviewing clients across cultures: A practitioner's guides*. New York, NY: Guilford Press.

Fontes, L. A., & Faller, K. C. (2006). Conducting culturally competent sexual abuse interviews with children from diverse racial, cultural, and socioeconomic backgrounds. In K. C. Faller (Ed.), *Interviewing children about sexual abuse: Controversies and best practice* (p. 164). New York, NY: Oxford University Press.

Foynes, M., Platt, M., Hall, G. N., & Freyd, J. J. (2014). The impact of Asian values and victim—perpetrator closeness on the disclosure of emotional, physical, and sexual abuse. *Psychological Trauma: Theory, Research, Practice, and Policy, 6*(2), 134–141.

Geddie, L., Fradin, S., & Beer, J. (2000). Child characteristics, which impact accuracy of recall and suggestibility in preschoolers: Is age the best predictor? *Child Abuse and Neglect, 24*, 223–235.

Glover, D. A., Loeb, T., Carmona, J., Sciolla, A., Zhang, M., Myers, H. F., & Wyatt, G. E. (2010). Childhood sexual abuse severity and disclosure predict posttraumatic stress symptoms and biomarkers in ethnic minority women. *Journal of Trauma & Dissociation, 11*(2), 152–173.

Green, A. R., Ngo-Metzger, Q., Legedza, A. R., Massagli, M. P., Phillips, R. S., & Lezzoni, L. I. (2005). Interpreter services, language concordance, and health care quality: Experiences of Asian Americans with limited English proficiency. *Journal of General Internal Medicine, 20*(11), 1050–1056. doi:10.1111/j.1525-1497.2005.0223.x.

Grisso, T. (2003). *Evaluating competencies: Forensic assessments and instruments*. New York, NY: Springer.

Haboush, K. L., & Alyan, H. (2013). "Who can you tell?" Features of Arab culture that influence conceptualization and treatment of childhood sexual abuse. *Journal of Child Sexual Abuse: Research, Treatment, & Program Innovations for Victims, Survivors, & Offenders, 22*(5), 499–518. doi:10.1080/10538712.2013.800935.

Huss, M. T. (2009). *Forensic psychology: Research, clinical practice, and applications*. Malden, MA: Wiley-Blackwell.

Kirmayer, L. J., Rousseau, C., Jarvis, G. E., & Guzder, J. (2003). The cultural context of clinical assessment. In N. Burton (Ed.), *Psychiatry* (2nd ed.). Chichester, England: Wiley.

Kuehnle, K., & Sparta, S. N. (2006). Assessing child sexual abuse allegations in a legal context. In S. N. Sparta & G. P. Koocher (Eds.), *Forensic mental health assessment of children and adolescents*. New York, NY: Oxford University Press.

Lamb, M. E., Orbach, Y., Hershkowitz, I., Esplin, P. W., & Horowitz, D. (2007). A structured forensic interview protocol improves the quality and informativeness of investigative interviews with children: A review of research using the NICHD investigative interview protocol. *Child Abuse & Neglect, 31*(11), 1201–1231.

Lamb, M. E., Orbach, Y., Sternberg, K. J., Aldridge, J., Pearson, S., Stewart, H. L., & Bowler, L. (2009). Use of a structured investigative protocol enhances the quality of investigative interviews with alleged victims of child sexual abuse in Britain. *Applied Cognitive Psychology, 23*(4), 449–467.

Lau, K., & Treacy, E. (2009). Review of Literature on Forensic Interviewing. In T. Maschi, C. Bradley, & K. Ward (Eds.), *Forensic Social Work: Psychosocial and Legal Issues in Diverse Practice Settings* (p. 167). New York: Springer.

London, K., & Bruck, M. (2004). *The effects of age and gender on children's misinformation effects*. Unpublished raw data.

Lovett, B. B. (2004). Child sexual abuse disclosure: Maternal response and other variables impacting the victim. *Child and Adolescent Social Work Journal, 21*(4), 355–371.

Martin, P., & Midgley, E. (2010). *Population bulletin update: Immigration in America 2010*. Population Reference Bureau. Retrieved May, 2014, from http://www.prb.org/Publications/Reports/2010/immigrationupdate1.aspx
Martinez, O., Wu, E., Sandfort, T., Dodge, B., Carballo-Dieguez, A., Pinto, R., ... & Chavez-Baray, S. (2013). Evaluating the impact of immigration policies on health status among undocumented immigrants: a systematic review. *Journal of Immigrant and Minority Health, 17*(3), 947–970.
McFarlane, F., Powell, M., & Dudgeon, P. (2002). An examination of the degree to which IQ, memory performance, socio-economic status and gender predict young children's suggestibility. *Legal & Criminological Psychology, 7*, 227–239.
McFarlane et al. (2004). As cited in: Individual differences in children's suggestibility: A review and synthesis by M. Bruck & L. Melnyk (2004). *Applied Cognitive Psychology, 18*, 947–996 (with commentary).
Mestre, J. I., Rossi, P. C., & Torrens, M. (2013). The assessment interview: A review of structured and semi-structured clinical interviews available for use among Hispanic clients. In L. T. Benuto (Ed.), *Guide to psychological assessment with Hispanics* (pp. 33–48). New York, NY: Springer.
Ollendick, T. H., & King, N. J. (2012). Evidence-based treatments for children and adolescents: Issues and commentary. In P. C. Kendall & P. C. Kendall (Eds.), *Child and adolescent therapy: Cognitive-behavioral procedures* (4th ed., pp. 499–519). New York, NY: Guilford Press.
Pew Hispanic Center. (2012). *Pew Hispanic Center online database*. Retrieved from http://www.pewhispanic.org/2009/03/05/statistical-portrait-of-hispanics-in-the-united-states-2007/2007-portrait-ofhispanics-22/.
Powell, M. B., Fisher, R. P., & Wright, R. (2005). Investigative interviewing. In N. Brewer & K. D. William (Eds.), *Psychology and law: An empirical perspective* (pp. 11–42). New York, NY: The Guilford Press.
Putnam, F. W. (2003). Ten year research update review: Child sexual abuse. *Journal of the American Academy of Child and Adolescent Psychiatry, 42*(3), 269–278.
Quas, J. A., & Schaaf, J. M. (2002). Children's memories of experienced and nonexperienced events following repeated interviews. *Journal of Experimental Child Psychology, 83*, 304–338.
Reina, A. S., Lohman, B. J., & Maldonado, M. M. (2014). "He said they'd deport me" factors influencing domestic violence help-seeking practices among Latina immigrants. *Journal of Interpersonal Violence, 29*(4), 593–615.
Saha, S., Komaromy, M., Koepsell, T. D., & Bindman, A. B. (1999). Patient-physician racial concordance and the perceived quality and use of health care. *Archives of Internal Medicine, 159*(9), 997–1004.
Shavers-Hornaday, V., Lynch, C., Burmeister, L., & Torner, J. (1997). Why are African Americans underrepresented in medical research studies? Impediments to participation. *Ethnicity and Health, 2*, 31–34.
Stoltenborgh, M., Van Ijzendoorn, M. H., Euser, F. M., & Bakermans-Kranenburg, M. J. (2011). A global perspective on child abuse: Meta-analysis of prevalence around the world. *Child Maltreatment, 16*, 79–101.
Tseng, W. S., Matthews, D., & Elwyn, T. S. (2004). *Cultural competence in forensic mental health: A guide for psychiatrists, psychologists, and attorneys*. New York, NY: Routledge.
U.S. Census Bureau. (2010). *The Hispanic population: 2010*. Retrieved from U.S. Census Bureau online database http://www.census.gov/prod/cen2010/briefs/c2010br04.pdf.
U.S. Census Bureau. (2011). *Language mapper*. Retrieved from https://www.census.gov/hhes/socdemo/language/data/language_map.html.
U.S. Census Bureau. (2013). *State and County QuickFacts*. Retrieved from http://www.census-gov.com/.
Vallano, J. P., & Compo, N. S. (2011). A comfortable witness is a good witness: Rapport-building and susceptibility to misinformation in an investigative mock-crime interview. *Applied Cognitive Psychology, 25*(6), 960–970.

van Toledo, A., & Seymour, F. (2013). Interventions for caregivers of children who disclose sexual abuse: A review. *Clinical Psychology Review, 33*(6), 772–781.

Vrij, A., & Bush, N. (2000). Differences in suggestibility between 5–6 and 10–11 year olds: The relationship with self confidence. *Psychology, Crime & Law, 6*, 127–138.

Walker, K. E. (2014). Immigration, local policy, and national identity in the suburban United States. *Urban Geography, 35*(4), 1–22.

Weil, M. (2010). *A cultural competency program for psychologists: Clinical and supervisory practices with Latino culture and language.* Psychology Dissertations, Paper 175.

Weiss, R. A., & Rosenfeld, B. (2012). Navigating cross-cultural issues in forensic assessment: Recommendations for practice. *Professional Psychology: Research & Practice, 43*(3), 234–240.

WHO. (2003). *Process of translation and adaptation of instruments*. Retrieved from http://www.who.int/substance_abuse/research_tools/translation/en/.

Young, K., Powell, M., & Dudgeon, P. (2003). Individual differences in children's suggestibility: A comparison between intellectually disabled and mainstream samples. *Personality & Individual Differences, 35*, 31–49.

Zink, D., Lee, B., & Allen, D. (2015). Structured and semistructured clinical interviews available for use among African American clients: Cultural considerations in the diagnostic interview process. In L. T. Benuto, B. D. Leany, L. T. Benuto, & B. D. Leany (Eds.), *Guide to psychological assessment with African Americans* (pp. 19–42). New York, NY: Springer Science+Business Media. doi:10.1007/978-1-4939-1004-5_3.

Index

W.T. O'Donohue, M. Fanetti (eds.), *Forensic Interviews Regarding Child Sexual Abuse*, DOI 10.1007/978-3-319-21097-1

GPSR Compliance
The European Union's (EU) General Product Safety Regulation (GPSR) is a set of rules that requires consumer products to be safe and our obligations to ensure this.

If you have any concerns about our products, you can contact us on

ProductSafety@springernature.com

In case Publisher is established outside the EU, the EU authorized representative is:

Springer Nature Customer Service Center GmbH
Europaplatz 3
69115 Heidelberg, Germany

www.ingramcontent.com/pod-product-compliance
Lightning Source LLC
Chambersburg PA
CBHW060747150926
51501CB00003B/117
9783319210964